THE OXFORD

Patricia Craig was born and educated in Belfast before moving to London where she now lives. She is a freelance critic and reviewer and has edited several anthologies including Oxford Books of *English Detective Stories, Travel Stories, and Modern Women's Stories.*

THE OXFORD BOOK OF

Ireland

Edited by
Patricia Craig

OXFORD
UNIVERSITY PRESS

OXFORD
UNIVERSITY PRESS

Oxford University Press, Great Clarendon Street, Oxford OX2 6DP

Oxford New York

Auckland Bangkok Buenos Aires Cape Town Chennai
Dar es Salaam Delhi Hong Kong Istanbul Karachi Kolkata
Kuala Lumpur Madrid Melbourne Mexico City Mumbai Nairobi
São Paulo Shanghai Taipei Tokyo Toronto

Oxford is a trade mark of Oxford University Press

Published in the United States
by Oxford University Press Inc., New York

First published 1998
First published as an Oxford University Press paperback 1999

Reissued 2003

Introduction and selection © Patricia Craig 1998
For additional copyright information see pages 503–11

British Library Cataloguing in Publication Data
Data available

Library of Congress Cataloging in Publication Data
The Oxford book of Ireland / edited by Patricia Craig.
p. cm.
Includes index.
1. English literature—Irish authors. 2. Ireland—Literary
collections. I. Craig, Patricia.
PR8835.O95 1998 820.9'9415—dc21 97-30252

ISBN 0-19-280488-X

1 3 5 7 9 10 8 6 4 2

Typeset by SNP Best-set Typesetter Ltd., Hong Kong
Printed in Great Britain by
Clays Ltd., St Ives plc

Contents

Introduction

This anthology opens with a section entitled 'The Character of Ireland'. The phrase is appropriated from an ill-fated project conceived by Dan Davin in the 1940s, and involving Louis MacNeice and W. R. Rodgers as editors—a project scuppered, as it happened, by Irish conviviality and procrastination. The thing dragged on and on—it was kept going, indeed, until the deaths of both editors and many putative contributors had occurred—without ever taking actual shape. Promises, delays, endless talk, pub meetings, blether, flashes of inspiration . . . you could say it was these accoutrements of the Irish character that short-circuited *The Character of Ireland*. Still, it was a great idea. The book, if it had appeared, would doubtless have got to the bottom of Ireland—or, at any rate, put its finger on a good many of the qualities associated with the state of being Irish. MacNeice had already posed the question (in Section XVI of *Autumn Journal*), 'Why do we like being Irish?', and lumped together a few possible reasons under the heading of 'self-deception'. It is self-deception, indeed, that allows the Irish to take credit for being an other-worldly, spiritual, deeply rooted people—not to mention glorying in the wit, recklessness, charm, locquacity, and so forth, persistently attributed to them by others. But even figments of nationality, whether embraced or repudiated, have their value. They let us see, in the clearest way, what simplifications, facile inferences, or misbeliefs arose at particular times, and why.

One thing is certain, that no nation has gone in to a greater extent for self-scrutiny, or fostered more abundant analysis and evaluation. Everyone has had their say on Ireland, and the resulting reams of comment and definition are often riveting, stimulating, illuminating, or exasperating—or even all of these simultaneously. Ireland has always aroused, and goes on arousing, interest. Its wretched history—does a wretched history, Honor Tracy wonders, have the same effect on a country as a wretched childhood on an individual?—its wretched history, all its romantic disaffection, the beauty of the landscape, the wildness of the west, the drive towards insurgency, the egregious emblems, the alcoholic animation, the frenetic urbanity of Dublin, the disregarded architectural glories, the poignancy of the provinces, the obduracy of the Catholic religion . . . all these betoken full-blooded effects. 'We Irish', in Yeats's grand phrase, adapted from Berkeley—we Irish are surely entitled to revel, if we're so inclined, in the sense of national distinctiveness.

However— the phrase itself immediately raises a question: who exactly are 'we Irish'? We know what the poet had in mind when he used the term, those inheritors of an eighteenth-century aloofness and enlightenment of outlook, uncontaminated by any taint of the huckster mentality. It's not what most people associate with Ireland. Yeats, when he singled out the eighteenth century as 'the one Irish century that escaped from darkness and confusion' was placing his emphasis on figures such as Swift, Berkeley, Burke, and Goldsmith. These stood for cogency and civic responsibility; while Dublin gaiety, Belfast liberalism, and the sense of national consequence acquired in the wake of Grattan's parliament, all contributed something to the Yeatsian image of a mellow era. What this image omits, indeed, is the darkness and confusion engendered by the Penal Laws in Ireland; and for those undergoing persecution, denigration, deprivation and so on, the phrase 'we Irish' would have had to be uttered in a less lofty tone—and probably in a language not available to Yeats, or indeed to many among their own descendants. The loss of the Gaelic language, and consequent sense of a broken tradition, is of the utmost importance in arriving at any adequate assessment of the country.

An anthology such as this can do no more than skim the surface of Ireland, and this Introduction is definitely not the place to point up historical complications, which are endless, or to dwell on unresolvable issues, which refuse to go away. On the topic of what constitutes an Irishman, for present purposes, it is probably sufficient to say, with Robert Lynd, that an Irishman (or woman; I think he means to include women under the heading) is merely a person 'who has had the good or bad fortune to be born in Ireland, or of Irish parents, and who is interested in Ireland more than in any other country in the world'. That should be enough for anyone—and never mind if you subsequently get Patrick Kavanagh (albeit light-heartedly) insisting that 'you cannot be Irish if you are not Catholic'; and the essayist Hubert Butler counter-attacking with the proposition that to be Irish and Catholic debars you from possessing any insight at all into the mentality of Anglo-Ireland. Anglo-Ireland, rural Ireland, Irish-speaking Ireland . . . You will always find a tendency within any particular group to claim exclusive access to certain tracts of the national consciousness.

Revisionist historians have had something of a field day in Ireland over the last fifty-odd years, and achieved considerable adjustment of the ways in which past events are perceived. In their conscientious hands, many myths are deprived of their force, truisms tampered with, and scrupulousness reasserted, all to the great benefit of scholarship and awareness in the country. But the phases and episodes of Irish history remain, even if their implications are expanded. Conquest took place and injustices were enacted, setting up a multiplicity of reverberations. The story of Ireland, though, in its most basic form, can be usefully reduced to a series of potent antitheses, stretching back to the notion of 'civilians and barbarians' (to borrow the title of a Field Day pamphlet of 1983, by Seamus Deane) which characterized relations between England and Ireland in the sixteenth and seventeenth centuries. 'So barbarous a country [i.e. Ireland] must first be broken by war before it will be capable of good government': so wrote John Davies in 1612, echoing the views of Edmund Spenser. Jonathan Swift, over a century later, makes a point of dissociating himself from 'the savage Irish, whom our ancestors conquered several hundred years ago'. The savage Irish: it wasn't how they saw themselves. It's left to Thomas Kinsella, in *The Dual Tradition* (1995), to point out that Swift and Ó Rathaille, Irishmen, contemporaries, and major poets, would have lived their lives in total ignorance of one another's existences.

'Pain, destruction, downfall, sorrow and loss.' Aoghan Ó Rathaille's is among those mordant voices—others belong to Daibhi Ó Bruadair and Seathrun Ceitinn—whose purpose was to deplore the destruction of Gaelic Ireland even while it was taking place. The Battle of Kinsale (1601) makes a kind of watershed; from this point on, anglicization was assured. But Gaelic Ireland was not obliterated overnight. It coexisted with the encroaching regime, and in a sense it flaunted its inaccessibility to ascendant incomer and renegade Irish alike. This 'hidden Ireland'—Daniel Corkery's term—was inhabited by people who took a very poor view indeed of the new English-speaking aristocracy that had ousted the old Irish-speaking one. They never conceded cultural superiority to the conquerors—far from it. The boot was on the other foot, and rearing to kick. Fun is poked (in a bitter spirit) at the kind of ludicrous name, such as Valentine Brown, by which an *arriviste* landowner might call himself—someone inappropriately installed in a demesne of the great MacCarthy family, now dead or dispersed.

> That my old bitter heart was pierced in this black doom,
> That foreign devils have made our land a tomb,
> That the sun that was Munster's glory has gone down
> Has made me a beggar before you, Valentine Brown.

> (Ó Rathaille, trans. Frank O'Connor)

In this world, a speaker of 'cunning English' quickly got himself condemned for opportunism, everything English being associated with the kind of baseness Yeats (for one) decried, when he identified it elsewhere. Ó Rathaille, in fact—in one of those instances of cross-fertilization which indicate strong interconnections in the whole field of Irish writing—turns up in person in Anglo-Irish literature: he's the arrogant old beggar in the Yeats poem 'The Curse of Cromwell', which ends with a line—'His fathers served their fathers before Christ was crucified'—appropriated from Ó Rathaille's 'Cabhair ni Ghairfead' ('I Shall Not Call for Help'), via the translation by Frank O'Connor.

Ascendancy Irish and bog Irish, Catholic and Protestant, Planter and Gaedhal, North and South, landowner and peasant, loyalist and rebel, constitutionalist and seditionist, townsman and countryman, Seoinin and Irish-Irelander . . . the proliferating polarizations point to a fatal dichotomy at the centre of Irish life, a people endlessly at odds with one another. 'Not men and women in an Irish street,' William Allingham lamented, 'But Catholics and Protestants you meet.' Think of virtually any aspect of the country, and immediately its opposite rises up to hit you in the face. Them and us. Always lacking the conditions that make for stability and civility, Ireland instead is characterized by a romantic unrest. Wandering beggarmen aren't the half of it. Atrocities of all kinds, oppression, injustice, neglect, dispossession, misgovernment, rebellion . . . it is easy enough for anyone to dredge up bitter memories at the drop of an evocative phrase: the massacres of 1641, the Flight of the Earls, the Treaty of Limerick. Ireland is not, and never has been, in the business of jettisoning the past. I would wish, said Elizabeth Bowen, that England would hold history in mind more, and Ireland hold it in mind less (or words to that effect). Others, though, have argued that the Irish in fact pay too little attention to history—in the sense of not examining it closely enough, appreciating its ambiguities, or applying its lessons to current exigencies. History, in other words—at its most labour-saving—merely functions as a means of asserting ancestral affiliations.

The Oxford Book of Ireland, indeed, is an anthology, not a history; it is arranged according to theme, not chronology; and the emphasis, if anything, falls on geography, social history, custom, personal observation, recollection, and so on, rather than on history proper. It is, as well, more a literary enterprise than anything else. You can't, however, begin to get to grips with the country without keeping constantly in mind the background of conquest and resistance, along with successive, and overlapping, phases of Irish nationalism (particularly those of the nineteenth and twentieth centuries, with which this anthology is most concerned). The great scourges of Victorian Ireland, famine and emigration, are still embedded in the national psyche. During the last century, too, arose the determination to retrieve insupportable losses— nationhood, the national language, the land itself. The earlier part of the century saw the formulation of Daniel O'Connell's twin objectives, Catholic Emancipation and Repeal of the Union (one achieved, the other not); while the latter half was dominated by the land wars. A good many facets of modern Ireland have their origins around this period: the yoking together of Irishness and Catholicism, the establishment of a Catholic bourgeoisie, the repudiation of cultural importations, particularly those from Britain. Sinn fein: keeping ourselves to ourselves. Douglas Hyde's call, in 1892, for the de-anglicization of Ireland (and subsequent founding of the Gaelic League) was a major step psychologically, even if in practice it couldn't be carried through.

The language was too far gone to be extensively resuscitated. 'The Irish tongue is in a manner banished from among the common People, and what little of it is spoken can be heard only among the inferior Rank of Irish Papists': thus Walter Harris, *c.*1741. One of the last of the Gaelic poets, Art Mac Cubhthaigh, or McCooey (1738–73), wrings his hands over a state of affairs in which a garbled English is increasingly resorted to—'Caismirt Bhearla i mbeol gach aoin'—as back after back is turned on the native tongue. English is the language of survival, of getting ahead. Irish continues to have its uses, however, supplying (in translation) many images and slogans to bolster the sense of national worth and singularity. And, in the end, it proves quite possible to consider oneself deeply Irish, yet express this conviction through the medium of English.

The last outstanding literary work in Irish (before the Revival), Brian Merriman's 'Cuirt a' Mheadhan Oidhche' ('The Midnight Court') was written about 1780 and circulated orally and in manuscript form; it did not appear in print for another seventy-odd years. This extraordinarily inventive and rumbustious 1026-line poem, which is basically a satire on the peculiarly Irish customs of celibacy and late marriage, has been ably translated, in the present century, by Frank O'Connor (among others). The tradition which it rounds off didn't just dwindle to nothing, but went out, in the hands of Merriman, with a considerable flourish. ('The Lament for Art O'Leary', by Eibhlin Dubh ni Chonaill, is another example of this late flowering.) Not that the language has ever faded completely, but the line of continuity in literature became pretty exiguous. The progress of English could not be stemmed; only the remotest, poorest districts in the country remained inviolable. Elsewhere, the Gaelic language was in the keeping of scholars and antiquarians—safe enough, as far as it went, but not very vividly alive. And, because of the interest taken in the rediscovered storehouse of ancient Irish literature—the Sagas and so forth—you found a situation in which a kind of cultural nationalism, not incompatible with unionism, developed alongside a separatist ideology which didn't have any time for Gaeldom. So the wheel of nationalist dogma goes round and round. By the time the Gaelic League came into being, a good many Irish people were primed to revolt against the persistent caricaturing of the whole nation in the pages of *Punch* and elsewhere, a procedure not eschewed by some among the Irish themselves, as the woeful shenanigans of a few popular novelists show. The de-anglicization programme was part of a campaign to add dignity to Ireland, a campaign spearheaded in a slightly different area by Yeats and Lady Gregory. For those fed up with being portrayed as assassins or buffoons, there was consolation to be gained from contemplating Ireland's integrity along with England's iniquity. Turn-of-the-century Irish Irelanders, though, didn't evade ridicule on their own account. The thoroughly Celtic get-up sported by Mary Colum and a friend, for example, only provokes jeers from a row of Dublin fishwives: 'Will yez look at the Irishers trying to look like stained-glass windows . . . Them Irishers are going daft!' And of course the whole impulse to render oneself as Gaelic as possible is splendidly mocked in Flann O'Brien's novel of 1941, *An Beal Bocht* (*The Poor Mouth*; not translated into English until 1973).

The Poor Mouth also includes among its targets the island autobiographers, beginning with Tomas Ó Criomhthain, or Crohan, who emerged in force once their colourful, primitive way of life had been exposed to outside scrutiny; since this way of life was clearly on its last legs, it seemed vital to record its particulars before they became extinct. (A good deal of Irish literature can be read as a lament for one vanishing social group after another—

the old Gaelic nobility, the inhabitants of townlands depopulated by the
Famine, the pre-Union aristocracy of Dublin, the Blasket fishing community,
the Big House people.) And who, the argument must have gone, was better
suited to the task than one of themselves? A certain irony had already been
evident in the attitude of native Irish-speakers of the western seaboard
towards their discoverers—not to be wondered at, when proselytizing outsiders took it upon themselves to teach 'a power of Irish for five weeks and a
half'. But in the event, the native accounts of growing up hardy and aboriginal are framed unironically, and tend (in translation) to be full of phrases
like, 'Wisha, long life to you'. The best-known phrase of all, 'Our like will
never be seen again', is the one appropriated by Flann O'Brien who applies it
to everything that comes within his sights: 'Ambrose was an odd pig and I do
not think that his like will be there again.'

Part of Flann O'Brien's brief is to show up bogusness and play-acting, and
the works of Synge don't escape his ferocious attention; Synge, who could
write as plainly and robustly as anyone when he chose, has gone down in
literary history as the inventor of an exorbitant syntax, along with highly
narcotic—though factitious—swatches of Irish-English. The plushness of
Synge's dramatic manner, indeed, had already proved too much for his earliest Gaelic audiences who suspected him of mockery when he intended only
admiration. But it was his use of the word 'shift' that really got up their noses
and provoked the famous Playboy riots of 1907. Irish Ireland, having seen off
the Paddy-and-Shillelagh defamation purveyed from abroad, wasn't about to
take kindly to any impugning of indigenous chastity, as suggested by Synge's
image of Connemara women in their underwear: 'It's Pegeen I'm seeking
only, and what'd I care if you brought me a drift of chosen females, standing
in their shifts itself, maybe, from this place to the Eastern world?' (Actually,
the whole furore proved pretty fleeting; by 1910—when he was dead—Synge
had gained the approval of the Gaelic League who went so far as to number
his *Playboy*, along with *The Cattle Raid of Cooley* and the anonymous
ballad, 'Farewell to Patrick Sarsfield', among the *tours de force* of the Gaelic
tradition.)

As far as the patriotic drive was concerned—there were many more pro-
ductive outlets than losing one's head in the face of Synge's shifts. Nothing
less than revolution was being fomented, as the architects of the Easter Rising
got their manœuvres under way. But the concomitant refurbishing of the
national image entailed claiming moral superiority over the English in every
area of life, not least that of sexual *mores*. To be Irish was, almost by definition, to be committed to chastity—hence the outcry over the notional
women in their petticoats. And once the new Free State had come into being,
part of its programme was to consolidate every aspect of social usage that
suggested an unassailable (and unimpeachable) national identity. The fusing
together of nationalism and Catholicism, in the present century, has
been well documented: in Conor Cruise O'Brien's *Ancestral Voices*, for

example, or (in outline) in Terence Brown's *Ireland: A Social and Cultural History*. One result of this coalescence was the overlay of puritanism which settled on the country like a wet blanket—a blanket which only began to wear thin in the 1960s. Its manifestations ranged from the oppressive or grim to the purely potty (as readers of this anthology will be reminded). It filtered down from the censorship of literature to the organization formed to promote modesty in dress.

Such absurdities were part and parcel of de Valera's Celtic cloud cuckoo land which saw itself as high-minded, true-hearted, and opposed to materialism, in defiance of the social realities of the mid-century. To meet the requirements of reactionary Irish readers who subscribed to the myth (a large social group) it was necessary to express poetic and other truths in ways not inconsistent with the blandest of moral and political assumptions—*not* a recipe for vigour or flexibility. Still, there were always writers who resisted the lure of such restrictions, who bore in mind the limitless possibilities indicated by Joyce and Beckett, and the immense achievement of Yeats, and activated their literary impulses accordingly. I am thinking of Flann O'Brien, for example; of poets such as Austin Clarke and Patrick Kavanagh, of the novelist Mervyn Wall, of the staff and contributors to Ireland's most adventurous periodical of the 1940s, *The Bell*: a group we might label the O'Faolain dissentients. All these, by engaging energetically (and sometimes enigmatically) in social criticism, place themselves in a line of incomparable Irish writing which stretches back through Joyce and George Moore to the Co. Tyrone novelist William Carleton, who met on every side, in the mid-nineteenth century, with a spur to his outrage—Ribbonism, the Orange Order, famine, distress, intemperance, exploitation.

With those last allusions, a wheel comes full circle—the other notable enterprise in modern Irish writing (along with social criticism) is the retrieval or re-examination of some vivid aspect of the past, generally with reference to the light it casts on the present. History remains crucial, however much it's recharged or revised.

Anyone entrusted with the task of putting together an anthology of Ireland is likely, I think, to find the business both invigorating and daunting. There are, to be sure, a number of problems, the first one being where to start and where to draw the line, given that *any* ingathering of Irish material is bound to look limited and flawed, from one perspective or another. The most you can hope to achieve is the amassing of a personal selection that doesn't diverge too wildly from accepted ideas of what constitutes Irishness, or what fits into an Irish framework—and even possibly extends the definitions a little. My particular aim has been simply to assemble as many striking and exemplary extracts as I can lay my hands on, and to sort them out into various sections, some obvious ('Dublin', 'The Character of Ireland'), others less so ('The Amazing Power of Emblems', 'The Fields Beyond the House').

Not everything in this anthology is of the highest literary quality (though a good deal *is*). Some excerpts are chosen to reinforce a point, provide an essential piece of information, show the other side of an argument, or exemplify some posture or mannerism provoked by an idea of Irishness—Ethel Mannin describing Galway as 'a darlin' town, a darlin' town', for example, has succumbed for a moment to fakery; this—along with one or two other pieces—is included in a spirit of irony, of which readers may or may not approve. I would stress that this book of Ireland has to stand or fall as a personal selection; and add that, although the book as a whole may reflect goodness knows how many subconscious biases, quirks, or *idées fixes* on my part, I have shaped it in accordance with no overt ideological end. It's meant, through an accumulation of detail, to provide in a single volume a good general impression of the country, full of familiar and enlightening images of Ireland and the Irish—and not to promote any political, sociological, literary, feminist, or, for that matter, any other credo. My credentials for the task are basically as follows: an Irish upbringing (born in Belfast), a lifelong familiarity with the country and its literature, and a continuing interest (to put it mildly) in Irish affairs. My concern, here, is to garner passages illustrating attitudes to Ireland, furnishing insights into Ireland, descriptions of Irish goings-on, Irish environments, Irish realities, Irish idiosyncrasies; and to ensure that all these are as lively, pointed, instructive, provoking, or diverting as can be. Most of the passages are fairly short, and arranged—I hope—to interact effectively with one another. The approach, you might say, is at the opposite extreme from that adopted by the editors of the formidable *Field Day Anthology of Irish Writing* of a few years ago (to take that example); with them, the writers came first, and the idea was to include a substantial selection from the work of each. *The Oxford Book of Ireland*, a much more modest undertaking, goes about things differently: the theme, or heading, comes first, and authors are marshalled accordingly. I have also tried to ensure that one thing will lead naturally on to another—for example, 'A Nation of Lunaticks!' ends with a reference to the Land War; agrarian agitation is a central aspect of the next section, 'The Irish Question'; and that in its turn is followed by 'The Fields Beyond the House', which provides a different angle on the land (environment and landscape rather than politics). And so on.

With a subject as wide as this one, the hazards facing any anthologist are intensified—the fear, for example, that you may have overlooked exciting material through ignorance or ill luck, and omitted more because it's too familiar to *you* (though not necessarily to potential readers). As always, though, it boils down to a question of compromise and balance—making sure that essential pieces are in, however well known, along with much that is striking and unexpected. You have to hope that some of the exhilaration experienced in searching out and devouring your source material will be transmitted to readers—and indeed it's hard to think that anyone with an interest in Ireland will fail to be intrigued by such inclusions as Robert Lloyd Praeger's account of a party of botanists attending a symposium on Irish bogs and slowly sinking into one while engaged in intellectual discussion; the intrepid American Asenath Nicholson trudging through the countryside in the 1840s, in her polka coat and velvet bonnet, distributing biblical tracts and never bothering about being an object of wonder to the natives; or the splendid working-class, Co. Armagh hyperbole transcribed by the novelist John O' Connor.

The titles of most sections are self-explanatory, for example 'Western Landscape' and 'Ancestral Houses'. I don't propose to account for deliberate exclusions, except to say that fiction is probably less well represented than non-fiction—the one thing an anthology cannot do is appease the appetite for narrative momentum; and so, with novels and stories, it is necessary to separate moments of description or reflection from episodes requiring knowledge of the plot to make an impact. Some novels, in fact, don't lend themselves at all to this kind of treatment: I am thinking of works like M. J. Farrell's (Molly Keane's) novels of manners, or James Stephens's engagingly eccentric *The Crock of Gold*. It is hard to find a passage of this without a god or a leprechaun in it, and this creates a wrong—a whimsical—impression.

As far as particular topics are concerned—the final section, 'The War Against the Past', indicates a few—just a few—of the ways in which Ireland has come into line with the modern world. 'The Stereophonic Nightmare', which precedes it, tentatively tackles the state of affairs prevailing in the North since 1968—with complete awareness that no anthologist can hope to cover that fraught subject adequately. This is placed towards the end, naturally enough since it's a facet of contemporary life, but also to enable a rough (very rough) clarification of its causes to emerge throughout the course of the anthology. One section—'Brown Rain Falling Heavily'—may be read as a piece of sheer editorial indulgence. I can justify its inclusion by claiming that one of the first things everyone thinks of in connection with the country is its weather; but the truth is that rain has a strong appeal for *me*, I never get enough of it, living mainly in London, as I do—and so I've seized this opportunity to experience drizzles and downpours vicariously. 'Brown Rain', however, shouldn't lower anyone's spirits, since its main effect is to engender a pungent atmosphere: as pungent in its own way as the aroma of turf smoke, combined with a lone curlew's cry, which Lord Dunsany has singled out to encapsulate the country.

I should like to thank the Author's Foundation, whose award of a grant in 1995 enabled me to work extensively on one or two projects, including this one. I am also indebted to the Arts Council of Northern Ireland, to the Librarian and staff of the Linen Hall Library, Belfast, to Patrick Close and the Librarian of St McNissi's College, Garron Tower, to the Librarian and staff of the Berkeley Library, Trinity College, Dublin; and to the following, for advice or help of various kinds: Jeffrey Morgan, Gerry Keenan, Nora T. Craig, Derek Mahon, Maureen Murphy, Gerald Dawe, Michael and Edna Longley, Douglas and Marie Carson, Patricia Mallon and Brice Dickson, Rosalind Shaw, Judith Luna and Nigel May.

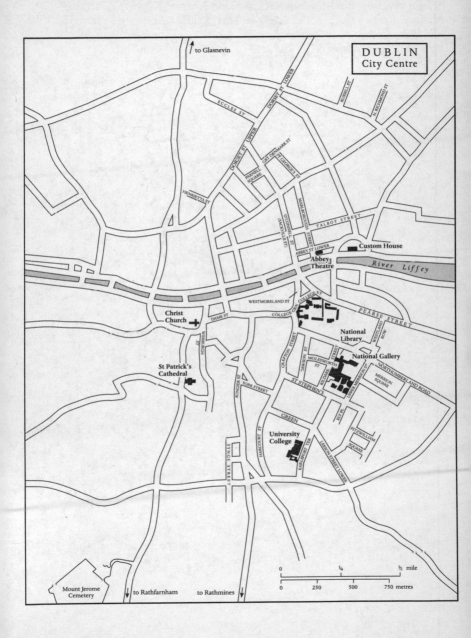

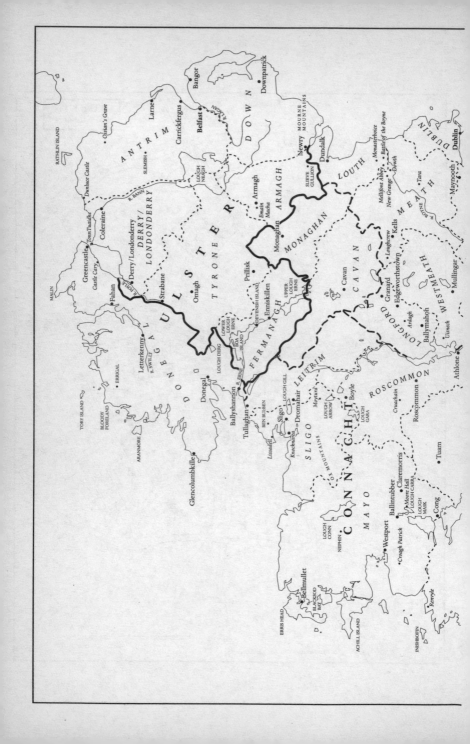

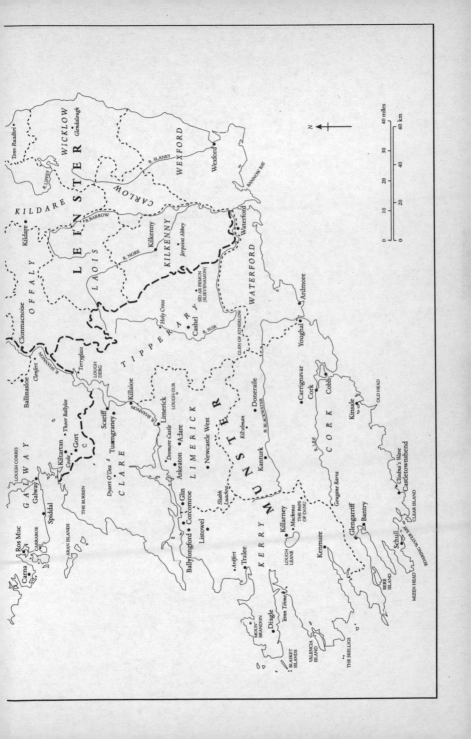

The Oxford Book of Ireland

The Character of Ireland

Pray for me, publicans of Belfast, Dublin, Galway, Bunraw,
Pray for me presbyters and priests and piddlers
of Armagh, Augher, Clogher, Five-Mile-Town,
Pray for me, Shopkeepers, gombeen men of Abbeyfeale,
Rosegreen, How-are-you,
And may God save Ireland from her heroes
For what we need is not heroism,
But normal courage.

W. R. RODGERS, from the Epilogue to
'The Character of Ireland'

Of this I am convinced: what is called 'Irishness' can be understood
only in relation to the homeland. There is a saying that you can take a
boy out of Ireland but you cannot take Ireland out of the boy. In the
long run, I believe geography counts for more than genes.

E. ESTYN EVANS, 'The Irishness of the Irish'

There is no need to begin with any general description of Ireland; that has
been done over and over again, and by hands more skilled than mine. But it
may be desirable to recall a few topographical features which have affected
and still affect much that is within the country. There is, first of all, its unique
position—an island out in the North Atlantic, doubly cut off from direct continental influences by intervening seas. At the same time, it lies, along with
the adjoining and larger island of Great Britain, on a shallow platform, projecting into the ocean between Spain and Norway, so that a slightly higher
level of the land, by spilling the water off this shelf, would allow, and has
allowed at certain periods in the past, free immigration from the Continent.
These times were too long ago to have affected human affairs as we know
them, but they had a considerable influence as regards the peopling of the
land with the animals and plants which still occupy it, and possibly as regards
movements of the earlier races of man.

Next, there is the unusual nature of the surface. Ancient crumplings of the
Earth's crust have resulted in the formation of mountain ranges in the coastal

regions, leaving a broad low plain in the centre. Easy access to the interior has consequently been limited to gaps in the high rim, thus fixing trade routes and the position of coastal towns; but free dispersal over the central parts has been possible once the coastal barrier was passed or evaded. This has profoundly influenced the effect of the various human invasions which Ireland has endured, tending to push pre-existing cultures not into an inaccessible centre, as in most islands, but into the mountain-fringe: witness the present and recent distribution of the native Irish tongue. Again, geological vicissitudes have produced an astonishing variety of rocks, as compared with most areas of similar size: this has given us delightfully varied scenery, and also different kinds of soils, with obvious repercussions on human life. The wholesale mixing-up of superficial deposits caused by the moving ice of the Glacial Period has tended to more uniform and also better soil conditions than would otherwise have been the case. Climate also intrudes itself strikingly in Ireland. The proximity of the island to the warm Atlantic results in high rainfall, cool summers, mild winters, and much wind; these factors influence all life within the island, from man down to mosses. This peculiar position is also at the root of that most delightful of Irish climatic phenomena, its everchanging cloud-effects, so different from the monotonous and more settled skies—whether cloudy or cloudless—that characterize continental areas. The western hills and the clouds which are their legitimate accompaniment are inseparable; the eye is carried upward from the hill-tops for thousands of feet into the infinite blue. The cloudland is indeed so wonderful a creation that Ireland would be a dull place without it: here it is almost always with us, as vital to our enjoyment as is the landscape itself.

Robert Lloyd Praeger, *The Way That I Went*, 1937

from *Autumn Journal*

Why do we like being Irish? Partly because
It gives us a hold on the sentimental English
As members of a world that never was,
    Baptised with fairy water;
And partly because Ireland is small enough
    To be still thought of with a family feeling,
And because the waves are rough
    That split her from a more commercial culture;
And because one feels that here at least one can
    Do local work which is not at the world's mercy
And that on this tiny stage with luck a man
    Might see the end of one particular action.
It is self-deception of course;
    There is no immunity in this island either;

A cart that is drawn by somebody else's horse
   And carrying goods to somebody else's market.
The bombs in the turnip sack, the sniper from the roof,
   Griffith, Connolly, Collins, where have they brought us?
Ourselves alone! Let the round tower stand aloof
   In a world of bursting mortar!
Let the school-children fumble their sums
   In a half-dead language;
Let the censor be busy on the books; pull down the Georgian slums;
   Let the games be played in Gaelic.
Let them grow beet-sugar; let them build
   A factory in every hamlet;
Let them pigeon-hole the souls of the killed
   Into sheep and goats, patriots and traitors.

Louis MacNeice, 1938

Ireland, particularly Celtic southern Ireland, has always had a fascination for most of us. The cities, particularly Dublin, the last stronghold of the art of conversation, are as charming as the countryside. But it is the country districts which occupy us here.

Most of us probably know at least four countrysides in Ireland. Like Caesar we divide our Gaul. But the divisions we make are not geographical. Our four Irelands are lands of the spirit.

Perhaps our first Ireland is the mystic land of the past. This is the land of the 'Celtic twilight', the country of Synge and Yeats and Stephens. It is the seat of an age-old tradition, of the remains of a once brilliant Celtic civilization. Literature has taught us to look for this land in the barren moors and rugged mountains of the west, among the tiny white cabins of Connemara and along the misty headlands of Kerry and West Cork. It is the Ireland of Aran and the Blaskets. There a remnant of the sagas and hero-tales can still be heard, a wandering poet sang but yesterday in the lilt of Blind Rafterty. There old men and old women sitting by turf fires still spin tales of banshees and the good people; and just the other day in Daniel Corkery's hidden Munster the hedge school-master and the wandering scholar had Ovid and Horace at his tongue's tip. And there too the riders to the sea go down to their deaths amid the keening women, whose language rings to us of simple, old-world poetry long ago passed from our own tongues.

A second Ireland is a gay, full-blooded picture, though some among the nationalists dislike it. It is the Ireland of the merry and happy-go-lucky present. Handled badly, it becomes the land of the 'stage-Irishman', that buffoonish figure which the nation's pride so justly resents. But handled well, by a Lady Gregory, a George Birmingham, and on the stage by the Abbey Players, it is a world of its own. In it, innocent boasting, the excitement of a race-meeting, the hurly-burly of a fair, the flashing wit of a court-room, and the staccato thunder of a political campaign, reveal a talkative, mercurial, witty people, amusing and intelligent, romantic and gallant.

The third Ireland most of us know is a more serious scene. One might even call it a grimmer land. It is a sober, hard-working land of minute towns and small farms upon a soil not always grateful. It is a land of hard realities. This Ireland is subject to hot flashes of anger and dispute which throw into relief deep-lying hatreds and fierce loyalties. We all know something of the Land War and Sinn Fein and the bitter internecine strife of the Trouble. If we know anything of Ireland's history we see these rough upheavals of a tranquil scene as great punctuation marks upon a red page of struggle lasting seven hundred years. This is the Ireland of bitter economic fate and political unrest. Much of this can be laid at England's door, but not all. The Ireland of the Irish is no more free of internal strife than any other land.

Most of us recognize a fourth Ireland as well, especially those who are Catholics. It is the Ireland of the Faith, the Island of Saints and Scholars. It is the land of the devout, where word and deed breathe a religious fervour which most of us have forgotten. This is the land of holy wells and pilgrimages and roadside shrines. Well-filled churches rise above every hamlet now and the black-frocked priest is a familiar friendly figure. To many of us, perhaps a paradox lies here. Fierce love of political liberty goes hand in hand with a deep devotion to the most authoritarian of Christian creeds.

CONRAD ARENSBERG, *The Irish Countryman*, 1937

The Irishman is one of the world's puzzles. People seem to be quite unable to agree as to who he is, or as to what constitutes his Irishness. Some people say that he is a Celt. Some say he is a Catholic. Some say he is a comic person. Some say he is a melancholy person. Others say he is both. According to some, he is of a gay, generous nature. According to others, he is a shrivelled piece of miserliness and superstition. 'The least criminally-inclined of all the inhabitants of Europe,' declare those who stand up for him, and they have official statistics on their side. A murderer, a maimer of cattle, a carder of women's hides, squeal the Kiplingesque school of critics, and they, too, have official statistics—very official statistics—on their side. A missionary among the nations, affirm some religious enthusiasts. The buffoon of the world, cry those who are less likely to be found in a church than in a music-hall.

The truth is, there is a great deal of nonsense talked about the 'real Irishman' and the 'typical Irishman'—to mention two phrases common among thoughtless people. The 'real Irishman' is neither essentially a Celt nor essentially a Catholic. He is merely a man who has had the good or bad fortune to be born in Ireland or of Irish parents, and who is interested in Ireland more than in any other country in the world.

ROBERT LYND, *Home Life in Ireland*, 1908

In delivering a lecture on Irish Idiosyncrasies I labour under this disadvantage, that never having been out of Ireland I have never been far enough away to get a proper look at it, and, consequently, although I have lived all my life in this country, I have never once seen it.

Of course we have, and in bewildering plenty, the impressions of Englishmen who have visited Ireland, and, equally, of course, we all as good Irishmen are firm in the determination that we will not believe a word the man says—we have known that visitor too long. We know that his eye is obscured by prejudice or sentimentality or silliness or some other affliction which prevents him getting us in focus.

Some of these impressions have been manufactured by political touts with very definite and detestable ends. Others are written by well meaning simpletons who mistake Rathmines for the Ireland of today, Donnybrook for the cradle of the race, and a peaceful English shire as our objective. Well, Rathmines is Ireland and Donnybrook is Ireland, and Connemara and Belfast are Ireland. There are, indeed, a great many Irelands in Ireland, but the casual tourist is seldom sufficiently Argus-eyed to detect the basic unity which underlies diversity.

JAMES STEPHENS (1910), in Patricia McFate (ed.), *Uncollected Prose*, 1983

You are Irish you say lightly, and allocated to you are the tendencies to be wild, wanton, drunk, superstitious, unreliable, backward, toadying and prone to fits, whereas you know that in fact a whole entourage of ghosts resides in you, ghosts with whom the inner rapport is as frequent, as perplexing, as defiant as with any of the living.

EDNA O'BRIEN, *Mother Ireland*, 1976

I looked with a fresh eye at the shabby street that had once been fashionable and prosperous. It was timidly walked in now. Double rows of troops, dressed in 'feldgrün', set back to back in great lorries, gave it an appearance of unhealthy robustness as they rolled by. They were looked at indifferently by the passers-by. But some, the shabbiest, glared at them furtively after they had passed.

It takes some courage to put up with this and to sustain the weight of despondency it engenders. Have I to carry the town's and country's melancholy on my back? 'By the Light of God,' I swore, 'I'll not let the bagmen or the bogmen drag me down.' Melancholy, indeed! All because a few thousand men have not the guts to protest and agitate against third-rate tyranny! The town and country seem to be in a state of melancholy unrelieved. Only I refuse to be *atrabilious*. Am I an Irishman at all?

Suddenly the thought struck me. Irishmen like to be melancholy. It is the national pastime to brood full of black bile. I remembered the dark figures in the Connemara pub. Even their drink is black! They chew on melancholy as a cow on the cud. Shane Leslie attributes it to 'hushed hate'. It is more than that. It is independent of external circumstances. They take pleasure in darkening with melancholia God's sweet air. They sin against the light. 'Accidia!' Of course, the obsolete deadly sin. There were once eight deadly sins. They are now only seven. Why? Probably the whole country were sinning, and what everyone does cannot (or can it?) be a sin. Something wrong somewhere with my reasoning, I think. It may have been found that there was no remedy for accidia in Ireland and so they let it slide. But what an escape I had! I might have been living in the eighth deadly sin and taking it for a form of patriotism. What an escape! It's a pity it is not a better known sin so that I would have more merit in exemption from it—Accidia!

OLIVER ST JOHN GOGARTY, *As I Was Going Down Sackville Street*, 1937

There arrived while I was out a load of turf, as we always call peat in Ireland. We live on that fringe of green grazed by fat cattle, which lies beyond the red bogs, and we are about ten miles from the nearest. It is from the red bogs that they quarry with spear-like spades the turf for the Irish hearths. The scent of turf from a cottage round here is a thing that one notices: further west they would all be burning it. That scent in the air is, of all odours, the most essentially Irish. Would that this book could give to any reader the atmosphere of Ireland, as the smoke of turf can call it up for me. In this smoke the spirit of Ireland seems to lurk and hide. And here is an idea that I will present to the manager of any theatre who desires to get an Irish atmosphere for some Irish play: let him, if he can imitate it, have the sound of a curlew calling occasionally in the distance and let him send into the auditorium a whiff from a smouldering sod of Irish turf; and he will get the Irish atmosphere by those means, certainly more cheaply, and perhaps more surely, than he has ever got it before. Feeling that way about it, I sent for a load of turf, though it is not the natural fuel of this end of the island. And it arrived today. It came from a bog whose name is an example of the beauty there is so often in Irish names. The name of the bog is Coolronan: through it runs the boundary between Meath and Westmeath, and the view over it in at least one direction has that quality that is so valuable in a view, which is that it is illimitable. In one direction it shares with desert and ocean the splendour of being unbounded by anything but the sky. And now the turf is glowing at me, with that glow of its own that never turns to flame, or only to faintest flame. But, mix the turf with wood, and you have all the merriment of flame combined with the turf's deep glow.

LORD DUNSANY, *My Ireland*, 1937

Ireland! Ireland! Ireland! the word falls on the ear with the gentle persistence of rain on the shores of Kerry. Any book on the burning subject then, even by an ignorant alien, is sure of eager perusers who will read it from cover to cover in an ecstasy of contradiction and pass an enjoyable hour or so in listing the errors of fact, faults of grammar, misprints, foolish opinions, and other evidences of incapacity on the part of writer, printer, and publisher.

More surprising is the amount of interest taken by Ireland's neighbour over the water. This interest is often rooted in misconception, for no one has so completely and loyally accepted Ireland's idea of herself as some of the English have. Their notions verge almost upon the extravagant: they see the Irish as witty, poetic, reckless, mystical, passionately devoted to forlorn hopes and impossible causes, the possessors of a wonderful sense of humour and, of course, charming: there'll always be an Ireland, if England has anything to say in the matter. It is delightful to see people who are better placed historically and geographically than any others to know the truth so cheerfully content with the legend. And yet our Irishman is still far from pleased. A shadow falls across his face and he sets up an angry mutter in which we perhaps may catch the words 'stage Irishmen' and 'colourful natives'. In his eyes, to have swallowed so much of Ireland's own make-believe is merely another and a signal example of English effrontery.

Now that brings me to something else: 'stage Irishry.' The writer on Ireland is certain to be accused of indulging in it. He need only note down an amusing remark or describe an engaging character to be indignantly told he has embroidered, if not invented, the whole affair. Once I asked a Dublin policeman to tell me the exact time, having a reason for wanting the exact time and no other, and he replied at once without the ghost of a smile that the exact time was between two and three. I was enchanted by this, reflecting that a city where time was of that timeless order was the only good place to live nowadays. So pleased was I with that answer, so grateful to the man who made it, that I gave the story in a broadcast; and sure enough by the next post came an angry letter from an Irish listener with a scathing reference to 'that apocryphal cop who never existed except on the boards of the Abbey Theatre'.

On another occasion I printed a story which I overheard one Irishman telling to another. It was a nice little story and one that breathed out the very soul of Ireland. In the days of petrol-rationing some men were asking the landlord of a pub where they could get petrol on the black market. A Sergeant of police heard them at it and advised them to go up the road to a certain garage; and they thanked him profusely and set off. In no time at all they were back, crestfallen, to report a failure. Hardly able to believe his ears, the Sergeant asked if they had revealed who sent them; and they answered that they had.

'There's Ireland for you!' said the policeman, bitterly. 'No respect for the law at all.'

Both the man who told the story and the man who listened to it were chuckling together with the greatest delight. And I myself on one occasion, being in dire need of black-market petrol, had consulted the local police as the source and fountain of it and had not been disappointed. The story not only illustrated in a charming way the humanity of Irish officials but gave an accurate picture of Irish methods of distribution. No sooner was it down in black and white, however, than the usual furious letter arrived accusing me of lies and distortion and inquiring sardonically why I hadn't thrown in a 'Begorrah!' while I was about it. I hadn't done so because I knew better. The Irish may sometimes say Bejabbers and Bejasus and Begob but they do not say Begorrah and, for some reason, they are very insistent on this point. But what was there in the story to make this correspondent boil over? And why was he so sure that I had made it up? That is a thing which no one in Ireland need ever do when it comes to racy dialogue or piquant episode; the most fertile imagination could not hope to compete with real life. It is only when the writer yields to the entreaties of Irish patriots and attempts to write of Ireland 'as she really is'—that is, as of an orderly modern state, making giant strides forward in science, art, education, and social welfare—that he may have to fall back on the inventive faculty.

HONOR TRACY, *Mind You, I've Said Nothing*, 1953

It has always been supposed that some countries have, so to speak, a peculiar magnetic attraction for the souls of their children, and I found plenty of reason, in the conduct of my neighbours as well as my own consciousness, to count Ireland as one of these well-beloved mother-lands. This home-love is strongest in the dwellers in her wild and barren places, rock-strewn mountain glens and windy sea-shores, notwithstanding the chronic poverty in which so many of them live. In these remote and wild parts Erin is the most characteristically herself, and the most unlike to Saxon England. Her strange antiquities, visible in gray mouldering fragments; her ancient language, still spoken by some, and everywhere present in place-names, as well as phrases and turns of speech; her native genius for music; her character—reckless, variable, pertinacious, enthusiastic; her manners—reconciling delicate respect with easy familiarity; her mental movements—quick, humorous, imaginative, impassioned; her habits of thought as to property, social inter-course, happiness; her religious awe and reverence; all these, surviving to the present day, under whatever difficulties, have come down from times long before any England existed, and cling to their refuge on the extreme verge of the Old World, among lonely green hills, purple mountains, and rocky bays, bemurmured day and night by the Western Ocean.

I never came back to the Ballyshannon country after an absence, without thinking that it looked to be the oldest place I ever saw.

WILLIAM ALLINGHAM, '*Autobiography*', in *The Diary of Wm. Allingham*, 1907

Talk runs free in Ulster, as elsewhere in Ireland; but it has a rougher cast, and less grace and fancy; whether among Catholic or Protestant, you find every-where an outspoken independence. In all countries, the North renders a service to the South, and the South tempers the North; but in Ireland there was more than the common interchange of qualities. In Ulster, and in Ulster only, there existed a large working class which was free from the helot's brand, and which was in a position to fight more successfully for its own status. In the eighteenth century it was still part of the policy of State to maintain if not to increase the Protestant interest in Ireland; and Protestant farmers in that era won the Ulster tenant right—which meant simply that the value created by a man's work on a farm could not be confiscated at will by the landowner. It was won by much the same means as were used in the nineteenth century throughout the South and West of Ireland. Men were shot and were boy-cotted; there were rough times before justice could be had. But the Protestant community of the plantation helped to preserve some standard of what was due to labour, and though the example was lost on landlords in the rest of Ireland, still it existed; and Derry is the town created by the men who kept that example alive. It was like a ray of rational order in a dark chaos of mis-government; and, for the sake of it, Ireland owes, perhaps, more than she thinks to the spirit of the plantation.

STEPHEN GWYNN, *The Famous Cities of Ireland*, 1915

The priest is gone on his embassy. The rain, which batters against the case-ment of my little hotel, prevents my enjoying a ramble. I have nothing to read, and I must write, or yawn myself to death.

Yesterday, as we passed the imaginary line which divides the province of Connaught from that of Ulster, the priest said, 'As we now advance northwards, we shall gradually lose sight of the genuine Irish character, and those ancient manners, modes, customs, and language, with which it is inseparably connected. Not longer after the chiefs of Ireland had declared James the First universal monarch of their country, a sham plot was pretended, consonant to the usual ingratitude of the House of Stuart, by which six entire counties became forfeited, which James with a liberal hand bestowed on his favourites; so that this part of Ireland may in some respects be considered as a Scottish colony, and in fact, Scotch dialect, Scotch manners, Scotch modes, and the Scotch character, almost universally prevail. Here the ardour of the Irish constitution seems abated, if not chilled. Here the *cead-mile failta* of Irish cordiality seldom sends its welcome home to the stranger's heart. The bright beams which illumine the gay images of Milesian fancy are extinguished; the convivial pleasures, dear to the Milesian heart, scared at the prudential maxims of calculating interest, take flight to the warmer regions of the south; and the endearing socialities of the soul, lost and neglected amidst the cold concerns of the counting-house and the *bleach green*, droop and expire in the deficiency of that nutritive warmth on which their tender existence depends. So much for the shades of the picture, which however possesses its lights, and those of no dim lustre. The north of Ireland may be justly esteemed the palladium of Irish industry and Irish trade, where the staple commodity of the kingdom is reared and manufactured; and while the rest of Ireland is devoted to that species of agriculture, which, in lessening the necessity of human labour, deprives man of subsistence; while the wretched native of the southern provinces (where little labour is required, and consequently little hire given) either famishes in the midst of a helpless family, or begs his way to England, and offers those services *there* in harvest time, which his own country rejects or wants not; here, both the labourer and his hire rise in the scale of political consideration: here more hands are called for than can be procured; and the peasant, stimulated to exertion by the rewards it reaps for him, enjoys the fruit of his industry, and acquires a relish for the comforts and conveniences of life. Industry, and this taste for comparative luxury, mutually react; and the former, while it bestows the *means*, enables them to gratify the suggestions of the latter; while their wants, nurtured by enjoyment, afford fresh allurement to continued exertion. In short, a mind not too deeply fascinated by the florid virtues, the warm overflowings of generous and ardent qualities, will find in the Northerns of this island much to admire and esteem; but on the heart they make little claim, and from its affections they receive but little tribute.'

'Then in the name of all that is warm and cordial,' said I, 'let us hasten back to the province of Connaught.'

LADY MORGAN, *The Wild Irish Girl*, 1806

The crocuses and the larch turning green every year a week before the others and the pastures red with uneaten sheep's placentas and the long summer days and the new-mown hay and the wood-pigeon in the morning and the cuckoo in the afternoon and the corncrake in the evening and the wasps in the jam and the smell of the gorse and the look of the gorse and the apples falling and the children walking in the dead leaves and the larch turning brown a week before the others and the chestnuts falling and the howling winds and the sea breaking over the pier and the first fires and the hooves on the road and the consumptive postman whistling *The Roses Are Blooming in Picardy* and the standard oil-lamp and of course the snow and to be sure the sleet and bless your heart the slush and every fourth year the February débâcle and the endless April showers and the crocuses and then the whole bloody business starting all over again.

Samuel Beckett, Watt, 1953

It is all very well for the Archpoet [i.e. Yeats] to say 'Go!' but what about the loss of the amenities of this playing field of ours? What town has a beach like Portmarnock, which one can reach in fifteen minutes of a morning and run along in the shallow waves that look like little rainbows if the sun is coming over from Wales and that, if it is not, look as pure as liquid air. Up comes the spray on your chest and if you have the patience to wade out far enough to get your depth, you can go for a swim. Then the Wicklow hills smooth-rolling, streamy, and granite-clean, and just about the right size in proportion to a man; they do not overwhelm mankind like the Rockies or the Alps. And what about the land to the west, the Many Coloured Land, as the old poets called Connemara, where the water-lilies neighbour near to the golden seaweed and the next parish is New York? Truth to tell, there are two Irelands; one is a geographical land of beauty; the other is a state of mind. And what is so annoying is that they are for the native inextricably blent. The visitor may enjoy going to Ireland but no native enjoys being in it all the time. Ireland is the last place for an Irishman to thrive. It comes to this then, that I have to get out of a state of mind. I have to remove myself from the vacuous, the dreamy, the perpetually inept life, and go amongst the strivers and the builders who are building up a civilisation out of a realisable dream which is manifesting itself more materially day by day. It will be a new experience for me to do something pat or, to change the letters, something apt. The English for centuries have been in the habit of coming over here and becoming more Irish than the Irish themselves. It is high time that one of us returned the compliment. I will be modest in my ambition. I will not endeavour nor attempt to become more English than the English themselves I can leave that to the Scots or Welsh. To be one of the mere English shall be enough for me. It will fulfil my ambition.

When Decency returns or de Valera disappears, it will be time to revisit the visionary hills.

Oliver St John Gogarty, Going Native, 1941

'If it had even been a good concert,' Judith remarked, gobbling tea and cake with a heartiness that, taken in connection with an admirable complexion and very clear blue eyes, was in itself attractive to a hungry young man, 'I could have borne it better. But it was absolutely deadly—all but just our own people's turns, of course—a sort of lyrical geography—the map of Ireland set to music! Bantry Bay, Killarney, the Mountains of Somewhere, the Waters of Somewhere else, all Irish, of course! I get so sick of Ireland and her endearing young charms—and all the entreaties to Erin to remember! As if she ever forgot!'

'She remembers her enemies all right,' rejoined Bill Kirby, gloomily, 'but she forgets her friends!'

EDITH Œ. SOMERVILLE and MARTIN ROSS, *Mount Music*, 1919

DOYLE. My dear Tom, you only need a touch of the Irish climate to be as big a fool as I am myself. If all my Irish blood were poured into your veins, you wouldnt turn a hair of your constitution and character. Go and marry the most English Englishwoman you can find, and then bring up your son in Rosscullen; and that son's character will be so like mine and so unlike yours that everybody will accuse me of being his father. (*With sudden anguish.*) Rosscullen! oh, good Lord, Rosscullen! The dullness! the hopelessness! the ignorance! the bigotry!

BROADBENT (*matter-of-factly*). The usual thing in the country, Larry. Just the same here.

DOYLE (*hastily*). No, no: the climate is different. Here, if the life is dull, you can be dull too, and no great harm done. (*Going off into a passionate dream.*) But your wits cant thicken in that soft moist air, on those white springy roads, in those misty rushes and brown bogs, on those hillsides of granite rocks and magenta heather. Youve no such colors in the sky, no such lure in the distance, no such sadness in the evenings. Oh, the dreaming! the dreaming! the torturing, heartscalding, never satisfying dreaming, dreaming, dreaming, dreaming! (*Savagely.*) No debauchery that ever coarsened and brutalized an Englishman can take the worth and usefulness out of him like that dreaming. An Irishman's imagination never lets him alone, never convinces him, never satisfies him; but it makes him that he cant face reality nor deal with it nor handle it nor conquer it: he can only sneer at them that do, and (*bitterly, at* BROADBENT) be 'agreeable to strangers', like a good-for-nothing woman on the streets. (*Gabbling at* BROADBENT *across the table.*) Its all dreaming, all imagination. He cant be religious. The inspired Churchman that teaches him the sanctity of life and the importance of conduct is sent away empty; while the poor village priest that gives him a miracle or a sentimental story of a saint, has cathedrals built for him out of the pennies of the poor. He cant be intelligently political: he dreams of what the Shan Van Vocht said in ninetyeight. If you want to interest him in Ireland youve got to call the unfortunate island Kathleen ni Hoolihan and pretend shes a little old woman. It saves thinking. It saves working. It saves everything except imagination, imagination, imagination; and imagination's such a torture that you cant bear it without whisky. (*With fierce shivering self-contempt.*) At last you get that you can bear nothing real at all: youd rather starve than cook a meal; youd rather go shabby and dirty than set your mind to take care of your clothes and wash yourself; you nag and squabble at home because your wife isnt an angel, and she despises you because youre not a hero; and you hate the whole lot round you because theyre only poor slovenly useless devils like yourself. (*Dropping his voice like a man making some shameful confidence.*) And all the while there goes on a horrible, senseless, mischievous laughter. When youre young, you exchange drinks with other young men; and you exchange vile stories with them; and as youre too futile to be able to help or cheer them, you chaff and sneer and taunt them for not doing the things you darent do yourself. And all the time you laugh, laugh, laugh! eternal derision, eternal envy, eternal folly, eternal fouling and staining and degrading, until, when you come at last to a country where men take a question seriously and give a serious answer to it, you deride them for having no sense of humor, and plume yourself on your own worthlessness as if it made you better than them.

BROADBENT (*roused to intense earnestness by* DOYLE's *eloquence*). Never despair, Larry. There are great possibilities for Ireland. Home Rule will work wonders under English guidance.

GEORGE BERNARD SHAW, *John Bull's Other Island*, 1904

That Ireland which we dreamed of would be the home of a people who valued material wealth only as a basis of right living, of a people who were satisfied with frugal comfort and devoted their leisure to the things of the spirit; a land whose countryside would be bright with cosy homesteads, whose fields and villages would be joyous with sounds of industry, the romping of sturdy children, the contests of athletic youths, the laughter of comely maidens; whose firesides would be the forums of the wisdom of serene old age.

EAMON DE VALERA, St Patrick's Day Broadcast, 1943

In Ireland the development of nationalism, or nationalisms, precipitated a situation of incongruence: 'bad fit' between the state as conceived by Britain, and the historic nation as conceived or reinvented by nationalist Ireland. The further complication of how Unionist Ireland perceived the relationship of state to nation is the part of the border question that endures most obviously today. These questions of incongruence are at the centre of Irish history through the nineteenth and twentieth centuries, but their origins go back very far indeed. In the supposed age of the nation-state, from the end of the sixteenth century, Ireland was undergoing a process of conquest and colonization—which meant being technically subsumed into the theoretical borders of the British state, at a time when that state itself was in the process of formation and definition. This interaction made for a development different from that of other colonies. There was a strong, vital and culturally sophisticated native culture, as well as a native class of notables who were not exterminated; the arrival of the Normans and the pre-Tudor kingship meant that Ireland had claims to joint sovereignty and its own parliament; and finally, Irish identity was, from the sixteenth century, indissolubly linked with the Catholic religion.

All this, after the great conflicts and dispossessions of the seventeenth century, made Ireland's position, as a kind of metropolitan colony, unique; and this is evident when modern nationalism began its formation in the early nineteenth century. The historical frame of reference, and the assertion of continuity with earlier forms of resistance to the British state, complicated the picture; and so did the tradition of colonization in one particular part of the island, the north-east. Here, not only a different religious configuration but a different economic development meant that relationship to the British state would inevitably be viewed differently.

R. F. FOSTER, *Paddy & Mr Punch*, 1993

Ulsterman

Far back the shouting Briton in foray,
the sullen Roman with his tramping host,
the fair beard plaited in the Saxon way,
the horned prow torching terror to the coast:

then the dark chaunting Kelt with cup and cross,
the red Scot flying from a brother slain,
the English trooper plowing whin and moss,
the gaunt Scot praying in the thin grey rain.

These stir and mingle, leaping in my blood,
and what I am is only what they were,
if good in much, in that where they were good—
a truculent and irritable heir.

Kelt, Briton, Roman, Saxon, Dane, and Scot,
time and this island tied a crazy knot.

JOHN HEWITT, *Collected Poems*, 1991

Frequently Joyce and others are shadows that newer Irish writers are trying to avoid being pushed under. It is not just a case that we are presumed to share a city or country with Joyce, but those themes which obsessed him and his generation—Catholicism and Nationalism and the role of the artist—are somehow supposed to be central to our own work, so that at times our work can be judged on how we handle subjects which are, in fact, absent from them. In my early childhood even if *Ulysses* was not actually banned it still had the reputation of being difficult to acquire. A walk through the streets of Dublin today would tell you how Ireland has changed. Any public house which is not currently named after Joyce or one of his characters is likely to be so rechristened should you turn your back. Inside them badly executed pen sketches of Joyce, Yeats, Beckett, Flann O'Brien and Patrick Kavanagh line the walls like photofit portraits of criminals in a police station. Contemporary politicians invoke Joyce and other writers in all kinds of unlikely contexts with a fervour only equalled by that with which clerics once denounced them. If all this lip-service can frequently add up to a sense of claustrophobia for a young Irish writer, it is also the reflection of a society where the printed word is still of prime importance, where writers are still read by a far wider cross-section of the public than elsewhere and—by the nature of the size of the country—where the success of writers can at times be watched, shared or argued about with great intensity.

DERMOT BOLGER, from Introduction to *The Picador Book of Contemporary Irish Fiction*, 1993

The Christmas Mummers
Apology

THIS is the stuff of which I was made,
The crude loud homespun bagging at the knees,
The primitive but not simple barbarities,
The casual labourer with an unskilful spade.
Unsimple ignorance was our only trade;
Our minds untrained to tensions would not seize
The string and stretch it till sincerity's
Tune to the pain-nobled end was played.
We shouted on mountains, but no god gathered
The wise sayings and the extraordinarily pure notes;
All went for nothing, a whole nation blathered
Without art, which is Character's city name.
And that is the story, the reason for the trailing coats;
The unmannerly bravado is the bluff of shame.

THE ROOMER

Room, room my gallant boys and give us room to rhyme,
We'll show you some activity coming on this Christmastime;
We act the rich, we act the poor, the simple and the critical,
We act the scenes that lie behind the public and political
We bring you noble statesmen and poets loused with song
And actors who make stacks of money making fun,
And if you don't believe me and give in to what I say
I'll call in Seamus O'Donavan and he'll soon clear the way.

SEAMUS O'DONAVAN

Here comes I Seamus O'Donavan—against the British menace
I fought when I was younger in the War of Independence;
Encouraged the national language, too old myself to learn it—
And if I got a pension who says I didn't earn it?
In days when 'The Emergency' was no poor cow in labour
But war most awful threatening the world and our neighbour
I took my musket down and joined young men who were no moochers
But soldiering nobly for the land into congenial futures;
My face as you can see is clear-marked old ITA,
An Irish face good-natured, Catholic, liberal and gay
My hair is turning whitish (though in youth severely mauled,
Oddly, no man who ever fought for Ireland goes quite bald).
For the good name of my country I am most insanely zealous
And of comrades who got richer I am not the least bit jealous
And if you don't believe me and give in to what I say
I'll call in a Successful Statesman and he'll soon clear the way.

SUCCESSFUL STATESMAN

Here comes I a Successful Statesman, from the people I am sprung
My father a National Teacher learned in Gaelic rune and song;
My mother was of ancient stock and early taught to me
The fear of God and daily toil and common poverty.
By the worthy Christian Brothers my character was shaped
And we prayed for Mother Erin when by Saxons she was raped;
I played my part in the struggle—played football for my county
And won an All-Ireland medal when I was barely twenty.
And I never deserted poetry—God be good to poor Owen Roe!
And the thousand Kerry poets who were slaughtered by the foe.
And if you don't believe me and give in to what I say
I'll call in Sean Og O'Gum and he'll soon clear the way.

SEAN OG O'GUM

Here comes I Sean Og O'Gum, seven pounds have I
Retainer from the Government for writing poetry:

I write about tinker tribes and porter-drinking men
Who shoulder-shove their minds into the handle of my pen.
The clans are scything song again on rebel-ripened hills
And reason screams for mercy at the scratching of our quills.
We know a hundred thousand ways for saying 'Drink your liquor'
When we toss the coin of language ne'er a ha'penny comes a sticker.
No truck have we with pagans or the foreign-backside licker.
I set my boat's proud prow to sea and hoist my ballad sails
And chant on decks of destiny for the all-too-silent Gaels
And if you don't believe me and give in to what I say
I'll call in a Famous Actor and he'll soon clear the way.

FAMOUS ACTOR

Here comes I, a Famous Actor of films stage and radio,
I was born the son of a peasant in the county of Mayo;
I am the man they call on to speak the verse of Sean
And other Gaelic poets, and lately I have done
A lot of work in English that's well out of the groove—
The popular taste in culture we are aiming to improve;
And last week when adjudicating at a Drama Festival,
I found that Irish audiences liked Eliot best of all.
I've escaped the grind of daily toil and cabins dirty, smelly
And I'm married to the daughter of Senator O'Kelly,
And if you don't believe me and give in to what I say
I'll call in Senator O'Kelly and he'll soon clear the way.

SENATOR O'KELLY

Here comes I Senator O'Kelly a simple businessman,
I make no claims to culture though I do the best I can
To foster our great artists and though business presses so
I go to exhibitions and I spend a lot of dough.
And one thing most I do regret, a thing to me most shocking
And that is certain critics who are far too fond of knocking
The men who make their country known throughout the artistic sphere
Earning dollars with the pictures at which these fellows sneer.
As a common or garden businessman this attitude I deplore
But I thank God for our vigilant Press which shuts on them its door.
And if you don't believe me and give in to what I say
I'll call in a Leading Editor and he'll soon clear the way.

LEADING EDITOR

Here comes I a Leading Editor who knows the Irish dream,
I'm open to every idea that fits in with the regime:
The Liberal Opposition who complain of bishops' mitres
And the rising cost of turnips and the censorship on writers.

The Press is free, the radio gives them a free debate,
New Statesmanism is essential to every well-run state.
These are not Lilliputian cranks as destructive critics scream
They are the Official Liberal Opposition and part of the regime.
And if you don't believe me and give in to what I say
Go to the bogs or Birmingham or Mountjoy right away.

EXPLANATION:

The custom of Mummers or rhymers going around before Christmas performing in rural kitchens still lives on in some parts of Ireland. Each Mummer re-presents some historical or nonsensical character. The formula is exactly as in this piece.

PATRICK KAVANAGH, *Collected Poems*, 1964

Dublin of the Old Statues

I walk of grey noons by the old canal
Where rain-drops patter on the autumn leaves, . . .
THOMAS CAULFIELD IRWIN, from *Sonnets*

The City *Dublyn* called *Diuelin* by the English, and *Balacleigh* (as
seated upon hurdles) by the Irish, is the cheefe City of the Kingdome
and seate of Justice, fairely built, frequently inhabited, and adorned
with a strong Castle, fifteenc Churches, an Episcopall seate, and a faire
Colledge, (an unhappy foundation of an University laid in our Age),
and indowed with many priviledges, but the Haven is barred and made
lesse commodious by those hils of sands.

FYNES MORYSON, *An Itinerary Containing His Ten Yeeres Travell*

Dublin Made Me

Dublin made me and no little town
With the country closing in on its streets
The cattle walking proudly on its pavements
The jobbers the gombeenmen and the cheats

Devouring the fair day between them
A public-house to half a hundred men
And the teacher, the solicitor and the bank-clerk
In the hotel bar drinking for ten.

Dublin made me, not the secret poteen still
The raw and hungry hills of the West
The lean road flung over profitless bog
Where only a snipe could nest.

Where the sea takes its tithe of every boat,
Bawneen and curragh have no allegiance of mine,
Nor the cute self-deceiving talkers of the South
Who look to the East for a sign.

The soft and dreary midlands with their tame canals
Wallow between sea and sea, remote from adventure,
And Northward a far and fortified province
Crouches under the lash of arid censure.

I disclaim all fertile meadows, all tilled land
The evil that grows from it and the good,
But the Dublin of old statutes, this arrogant city,
Stirs proudly and secretly in may blood.

DONAGH MACDONAGH, *The Hungry Grass*, 1947

Dublin with its wide central street, its statues and its time-darkened build-ings, has a dignity such as one associates with some of the southern towns in the United States—a dignity of memories and of manners. Its squares, its railed-in areas, its flights of steps, its tall houses of brick richly-coloured as wine, give it the air of a splendid relic of the eighteenth century. It is unfor-gettably a capital. Soldiers appear and reappear like monotonous red toys, under the shadow of the low classic temple that is now the Bank of Ireland, but that once was the Irish Parliament House. It is as though they were there in temporary occupation: the Parliament House has an air of permanency, of solemn patience, that makes them look like impudent unrealities. Oppo-site to it stands Trinity College with its dingy walls—fortress in chief of the strong masterful colonists, against which wave upon wave of the national desire has beaten and broken, leaving its tide-marks as upon an old rock. Dublin, indeed, is a kind of ambiguous capital, the capital partly of a colony, partly of a nation; it never decided which. It is not without significance that the far-famed Dublin Castle is not much more noticeable in the scheme of the city than a shop in a back street. The Dublin that impresses itself upon the eye and the imagination is the Dublin of the Parliament House and Trinity College, the Dublin of the Anglo-Irish colony and the Irish nation struggling through centuries to its birth.

ROBERT LYND, *Home Life in Ireland*, 1908

Dublin

Grey brick upon brick,
Declamatory bronze
On sombre pedestals—
O'Connell, Grattan, Moore—
And the brewery tugs and the swans
On the balustraded stream

And the bare bones of a fanlight
Over a hungry door
And the air soft on the cheek
And porter running from the taps
With a head of yellow cream
And Nelson on his pillar
Watching his world collapse.

This was never my town,
I was not born nor bred
Nor schooled here and she will not
Have me alive or dead.
But yet she holds my mind
With her seedy elegance,
With her gentle veils of rain
And all her ghosts that walk
And all that hide behind
Her Georgian façades—
The catcalls and the pain,
The glamour of her squalor,
The bravado of her talk.

The lights jig in the river
With a concertina movement
And the sun comes up in the morning
Like barley-sugar on the water
And the mist on the Wicklow hills
Is close, as close
As the peasantry were to the landlord,
As the Irish to the Anglo-Irish,
As the killer is close one moment
To the man he kills,
Or as the moment itself
Is close to the next moment.

She is not an Irish town
And she is not English,
Historic with guns and vermin
And the cold renown
Of a fragment of Church latin,
Of an oratorical phrase.
But oh the days are soft,
Soft enough to forget
The lesson better learnt,
The bullet on the wet

Streets, the crooked deal,
The steel behind the laugh,
The Four Courts burnt.

Fort of the Dane,
Garrison of the Saxon,
Augustan capital
Of a Gaelic nation,
Appropriating all
The alien brought,
You give me time for thought
And by a juggler's trick
You poise the toppling hour—
O greyness run to flower,
Grey stone, grey water,
And brick upon grey brick.

LOUIS MacNEICE, 1939

Dublin, on the east, the Europe-regarding, coast of Ireland, owes her vitality and complexity as a city to a continuous influx of foreign life. The invader, the trader, the opportunist, the social visitor have all added strife or colour. The Norsemen found her a village—called Baile Atha Cliath, or Ford of the Hurdles—on the lowest ford of the Liffey. The river's mouth made a fine harbour, her position was strategic; since their day until lately she was garrisoned by invaders, whose ostentation has always been uneasy. Once her walls went up she became a capital, full of heady passions.

ELIZABETH BOWEN (1936), in *Collected Impressions*, 1950

The quays, with their muddy square-setts, are noisy and dirty as usual, and in the dimming light the waiting buses are dull blobs of blue and yellow and red against the dull buildings. The Liffey is at lowest ebb, and its subaqueous population of forsaken buckets and weedy stones increases as I go rattling and banging up-stream on a wet tram-top. I return to the mud at Grattan Bridge, feeling I am rapidly approaching that stage of dejection which drives the strong-minded to a public-house, when from low down in the western sky there comes a gleam of yellow light, rapidly broadening and brightening. And then suddenly five great swans appear, flying down the centre of the river. In perfect formation, long necks outstretched, broad wings beating in unison, they sweep by majestically, a vision of pure beauty, gleaming plumage all snowy against the old houses opposite. While I still watch their receding forms fading into the smoky mist, a low red sun bursts out from underneath the last bank of cloud. It floods down the river; the long vista of dull houses lights up in a dozen lovely shades through a faint pink haze; the spires and towers behind stand up transfigured; the dirty water turns to gold and silver. One gazes at a dream city, beautiful beyond belief. And while I stand, a breath of softer air, bringing with it hope and a lifting of the spirit, comes from the west; the wind has changed.

ROBERT LLOYD PRAEGER, *A Populous Solitude*, 1941

As a child, I knew Watling Street well, for twice a year, my sisters brought me with them to the store nearby in Thomas Street, where they bought a stone of salt for the large wooden seller at home; and there were many ways by which we could reach that ancient part of the city, with its stalls, its big and little shops. Sometimes we went underneath the last part of the old town-wall, by the fourteenth-century tower of St Audoen's, and by the distillery. We passed Francis Street where our poor relatives lived in rooms, came down Watling Street or under the arch of Winetavern Street to the Quays again.

Many of these old hilly streets are changing and new working-men's flats have been built along them. The Guinness Brewery has long since spread on its monstrous way; vast offices of Victorian ugliness replaced the houses of James's Street, in one of which my mother was born; all day there is the sound of machinery, clanking small trains, and escaping steam. But at evening all is still. Recently I walked through the slums, clearances, tumbledowns of Pimlico, from which I could see, at every turn, the Dublin Mountains, went down shadowy lanes under the walls of the brewery which seemed a mighty stronghold of gain. Suddenly above a queer structure like a ziggurat I saw a wisp of hot vapour rising with religious persistency, and thought how the prophets of the Chosen Race had railed against the worship of the Gentiles.

AUSTIN CLARKE, *Twice Round the Black Church*, 1963

During the eighteenth century the Hall was used not only by the Tailors, its owners, but also by the Barbers, the Sadlers, the Tanners, the Hosiers and the Curriers. In the early part of the century, as the largest public room in Dublin, it was in demand for assemblies and fashionable parties. In 1792 the general Catholic Committee met here, and was nick-named the 'Back-Lane Parlia ment'. Almost simultaneously it was the resort of the Grand Lodge of Dublin Freemasons, and of the United Irishmen until in 1794 their meetings were broken up by the Sheriff and his posse. When the Tailors were threatened with dissolution by the Municipal Corporations Act of 1841, they prudently realised their movable chattels, including portraits of King Charles II, Dean

Swift and St Homohon, a Tailor of Cremona, before the act was passed. The Hall became the 'Tailors' Endowed School' for Protestant boys. In 1873, after a narrow escape from being secured by a distiller as a warehouse, it was leased to a Protestant undenominational organisation who used it for temperance meetings, Sunday-schools, workmen's reading- and coffee-rooms. This organisation vacated it in 1948, and its present future is uncertain.[1] Few buildings in Dublin have seen more varied activities, and few have suffered less alteration in the process.

The derelictions of modern Dublin have opened up a fine view of the rere of the building from Cornmarket. It would not be Dublin if the foreground were not composed of crumbling ruins, hoardings, concrete revetments and great baulks of timber, with ghostly chimney-breasts on the neighbouring gables, high in the open air.

MAURICE JAMES CRAIG, *Dublin 1660–1860*, 1952

He, I know not why, shewed upon all occasions an aversion to go to Ireland, where I proposed to him that we should make a tour. JOHNSON: 'It is the last place where I should wish to travel.' BOSWELL: 'Should you not like to see Dublin, sir?' JOHNSON: 'No, sir; Dublin is only a worse capital.'

JAMES BOSWELL, *Life of Johnson*, 1791

The rainladen trees of the avenue evoked in him, as always, memories of the girls and women in the plays of Gerhart Hauptmann; and the memory of their pale sorrows and the fragrance falling from the wet branches mingled in a mood of quiet joy. His morning walk across the city had begun, and he foreknew that as he passed the sloblands of Fairview he would think of the cloistral silverveined prose of Newman; that as he walked along the North Strand Road, glancing idly at the windows of the provision shops, he would recall the dark humour of Guido Cavalcanti and smile; that as he went by Baird's stonecutting works in Talbot Place the spirit of Ibsen would blow through him like a keen wind, a spirit of wayward boyish beauty; and that passing a grimy marine dealer's shop beyond the Liffey he would repeat the song by Ben Jonson which begins:

I was not wearier where I lay.

JAMES JOYCE, *Portrait of the Artist as a Young Man*, 1915

[1] It is now the headquarters of An Taisce, the National Trust for Ireland.

Those 'eighties and 'nineties and nineteen-hundreds have now become momentous, 'the good old days'—the Castle days, with litanies of names of pubs, and publicans (And never a pharisee?), talkers and jokers, Davy Byrne's, Corless's oyster-bar, the Bailey smoke-room, the Café Cairo, the DBC, Griffith, and Orpen, and Yeats, and A.E., and Casimir Markievicz, and The Bird Flanagan, and Toucher Doyle, and George Moore, and Maud Gonne, and Jim Larkin, and Edward Martyn, and Sinn Fein, and Seumas O'Sullivan and Padraic Colum, and a host of wags and wits of whom only Gogarty and O'Sullivan remain to link these times with that glory. For the glorious and gorious immortal memory of 1916, and after, and Time, and the apparently too-weighty responsibility of self-government have polished off that period. Now instead of telling us all that we may at last have a good time, we are told we must be good boys, and boyos and play-boyos are at the bottom of the market. Well . . . whether the saints or the sinners, the wags or the tail-waggers, have possession of the town, it is plain that it has passed through the guts of the King of the Beggars, been digested slowly in the rumbling belly of the nineteenth century, and has become part of the bloodstream of Ireland. And there it is.

SEAN O'FAOLAIN, *An Irish Journey*, 1940

At the first glance, Dublin nearly always delights the visitor by its grand perspectives and large light squares, its at once airy and mysterious look. Then there is a less happy phase in getting to know the city—when it appears shut-up, faded and meaningless, full of false starts and dead ends, the store plan of something that never realized itself. The implacable flatness of the houses begins to communicate a sort of apathy to the visitor: after her first smile and her first grand effect, Dublin threatens to offer disappointingly little. This stale phase in the stranger's relations with the city can only be cut short by imagination and vigorous curiosity. Dublin is so much more than purely spectacular; she is impregnated with a past that never evaporates. Even the recent past, the nineteenth century, leaves on some outlying quarters of the city a peculiar time-colour. Every quarter—from where the two cathedrals stand in the maze of side-streets, to the latest ring of growth, where red villas straggle into the fields—has, in fact, got a character you could cut with a knife. The more you know, the more you can savour this.

ELIZABETH BOWEN (1936), in *Collected Impressions*, 1950

In the central part of the town, several streets are really fine with their rows of large houses, their gorgeous shops and numberless statues. The women are generally good-looking; well built, well gloved, well shod. They move gracefully; and with a vivacity which is quite southern. They look gentle and modest, and dress almost as well as Frenchwomen, of whom they have the quiet grace. The youngest ones wear their brown hair floating behind, and that hair, fine in the extreme, made more supple by the moistness of an insular climate, is crossed now and then by a most lovely glimmer of golden light.

Most of the men have acquired the significant habit of carrying large knotty cudgels in place of walking sticks.

PHILIPPE DARYL, *Ireland's Disease*, 1888

I got on the Dublin train attired in my new blue ankle-length dress, my dead mother's watch fastened to a long chain and stuck in my belt. Attached to the chain was a silver Child of Mary medal and a little silver cross, and nobody, not even a native of central Africa, could have failed to recognize in me the typical product of a convent school, for my tendency to three of the seven deadly sins was not visible in my outward appearance, certainly not the one that included criticizing the Church. A lot of young people must have got off trains in Dublin that autumn day to pass four years as students. One of them, a boy of about my own age, travelling in the same railway carriage, was armed with a large book about Dublin which had pictures of the eighteenth-century squares and the Georgian houses and Dublin Castle and St Patrick's Cathedral. He was to study what, for me then, was a mysterious branch of learning—architecture—and he pointed out to me in a knowledgeable and superior way the points of interest in the picture of St Patrick's and the part of Christ's Church that had been built at the time Sitric the Dane was king of Dublin. My interest in St Patrick's was that it was Swift's church, where he was buried with the '*saeva indignatio*' epitaph written on his stone, where fierce indignation could tear his heart no more. The boy had his own dream; I had mine, and as for him, a few minutes after he stepped off the train, the Georgian houses he longed to see presented themselves to his gaze, so for me also something of a dream became alive. The drive on an outside car to the university residence house where I was going to live led all over the city from the north to the south side, so I passed through all the well-known streets. But it was not the stately eighteenth-century houses or the statues or Parnell's monument that held my attention. I just noticed them as I went by, but what awoke me to excitement was the figure of a down-at-heel, trampish-looking man walking slowly across O'Connell Bridge with a billboard attached to him back and front—a sandwich man.

On the billboard was printed in large letters on a sort of orange ground a notice that thrilled me so that I nearly fell off the swaying jaunting car: Irish Plays for One Week. *Riders to the Sea*, by J. M. Synge, *Kathleen ni Houlihan*, by W. B. Yeats, *Spreading the News*, by Lady Gregory. My companion on the train was stepping into his beloved squares and streets, but I was stepping right into the Irish Revival. I asked the jarvey to walk his horse slowly so that I could read again the magic names, the magic titles, from the back of the sandwich man. Yeats. Synge. . . . They might be walking the street that very minute.

MARY COLUM, *Life and the Dream*, 1928

It was a bright sunny day with small fleecy clouds scudding over the sky. Having left my things at the hotel I went for a walk. The first hours in Dublin are always delightful, for the city throws all it has at the newcomer, discreetly flattering, gently soothing, feeding at once the eye and the imagination. The airs of grace and of leisure have not departed even if the society which gave them birth is past and gone. It is a city of ghosts, but ghosts of the so newly dead that something of their earthly presence still lingers in the wide streets, the pleasant squares, that were their home; as you walk through them, you feel that Dublin still must be a bed of poetry and wit, almost you expect to see Yeats and A.E. passing each other in Merrion Square as in the famous cartoon, George Moore must at that moment be in Ely Place devoting one more scintillating page to the dissection of a friend or happily ruminating how best to enrage a neighbour. But the truth is you are looking at a lovely shell; the old glory has departed, a new one is not yet in sight. The Georgian houses of rosy brick on the good side of the river are full of Government people, commercial firms, and business-like doctors; and many of those on the other have turned into slums.

HONOR TRACY, *Mind You, I've Said Nothing!*, 1953

Whither next? To what licensed premises? To where the porter was well up, first; and the solitary shawly like a cloud of latter rain in a waste of poets and politicians, second; and he neither knew nor was known, third. A lowly house dear to shawlies where the porter was up and he could keep himself to himself on a high stool with a high round and feign to be immersed in the Moscow notes of the Twilight Herald. These were very piquant.

Of the two houses that appealed spontaneously to these exigencies the one, situate in Merrion Row, was a home from home for jarveys. As some folk from hens, so Belacqua shrank from jarveys. Rough, gritty, almost verminous men. From Moore to Merrion Row, moreover, was a perilous way, beset at this hour with poets and peasants and politicians. The other lay in Lincoln Place, he might go gently by Pearse Street, there was nothing to stop him. Long straight Pearse Street, it permitted of a simple cantilena in his mind, its footway peopled with the tranquil and detached in fatigue, its highway dehumanised in a tumult of buses. Trams were monsters, moaning along beneath the wild gesture of the trolley. But buses were pleasant, tyres and glass and clash and no more. Then to pass by the Queens, home of tragedy, was charming at that hour, to pass between the old theatre and the long line of the poor and lowly queued up for thruppence worth of pictures.

SAMUEL BECKETT, 'A Wet Night', 1934

Grafton street gay with housed awnings lured his senses. Muslin prints, silk, dames and dowagers, jingle of harnesses, hoofthuds lowringing in the baking causeway. Thick feet that woman has in the white stockings. Hope the rain mucks them up on her. Country bred chawbacon. All the beef to the heels were in. Always gives a woman clumsy feet. Molly looks out of plumb.

He passed, dallying, the windows of Brown Thomas, silk mercers. Cascades of ribbons. Flimsy China silks. A tilted urn poured from its mouth a flood of bloodhued poplin: lustrous blood. The huguenots brought that here. *La causa è santa!* Tara tara. Great chorus that. Tara. Must be washed in rainwater. Meyerbeer. Tara: bom bom bom.

JAMES JOYCE, *Ulysses*, 1918

from *The Beckett at the Gate*

When the curtain came down
And the applause had drained away
I turned around to gaze
In rapture at Michelle
But she had slipped away.
Mother of God
Chosen by the Eternal Council!
I walked back down along O'Connell Street,
Muttering to myself, repetitiously,
'Have you not seen Barry McGovern's Beckett?
Have you not been to the Beckett at the Gate?'
Every few steps, covertly,
I gave a kick in the air:
'Have you not seen Barry McGovern's Beckett?
Have you not been to the Beckett at the Gate?'
It was dusk—lucid,
Warm, limpid,
On O'Connell Street Bridge.
Spilling over with self-pity

And lasciviously gazing down
At the bicycle-filled waters
Of the River Liffey running on, on,
I elected to walk on
Back to my bed-sit in Ringsend
(Instead of taking the bus)
Through the east European parts of Dublin city,
Past the gasometer and Grand Canal Dock,
Misery Hill, The Gut, The Drain,
The Three Locks—Camden, Buckingham, Westmoreland.
At Ringsend there was a full moon over
The Sugar Loaf and the Wicklow Hills,
And the crimson lights of the telecommunications aerial
On the Three Rock Mountain were trembling
And on the television transmitter in Donnybrook;
And the hand-painted signs of the local public houses,
FitzHarris's and The Oarsman,
Looked childmade in the lamplight, homely
By the River Dodder
As I balanced in a trance on the humpbacked bridge,
On a fulcrum of poignancy.
And I felt like a stranger in a new city,
An urchin in a New Jerusalem,
A bareheaded protagonist
In a vision of reality,
All caught up in a huge romance,
In a hot erotic cold tumult.
On the street corner in Ringsend village
Not at, but close to, a bus-stop,
A tiny young woman was standing,
Hovering, twirling, stamping,
And when I saw that it was Michelle—
As I passed her by
She scrutinised me serenely
As if she had never seen me before
As if she had never seen me before.
I keep on walking;
I'll go on, I think, I'll go on.
Next year in Carrickmines
I'll play tennis with whatever
Woman will play tennis with me
And I'll never be never again.
Next year in Carrickmines.
On grass. Love all.

Fifteen Love. Thirty Love. Forty Love.
Deuce. Advantage Miss Always.
Game, Set and Match.
Why you, Michelle, why you
Will you join me? Join me?
If you're the joining kind, please join me.
Next year in Carrickmines,
Greystones, Delgany, Killiney, Bray, Dalkey, Shankill, Kilmacud,
Galloping Green, Stillorgan—perhaps even Dublin.

There's a beckett at the gate, there's a beckett
  at the gate, Michelle;
There's a Beckett at the gate, there's a Beckett
  at the gate, Michelle;
There's a beckett at the Gate, there's a beckett
  at the Gate, Michelle;
There's a Beckett at the Gate, there's a Beckett
  at the Gate, Michelle.

PAUL DURCAN, *Going Home to Russia*, 1987

At its centre it is a Georgian city in every line. But it is Georgian with a difference. It is certainly not, never was, a part of Georgian England: not even on the face of it. It is about as Hanoverian as the heel of my boot. Look at it, or even look at a map of it in its own time, and ask yourself if you could imagine it in England or Scotland.

The hub of the city was (and is) a great University with all its playing-fields about it, a thing not to be found in any capital in the world. Its squares were not localized. They measured the city from Fitzwilliam Square in the south to Mountjoy Square in the north. In brief with Arran Quay as centre and the Circular Road as radius, Georgian Dublin was fashionable and residential. Clearly this city had no past worth talking about. Danish and Norman and Elizabethan Dublin would fit into Stephens Green. It rose and was completed within a hundred years, from the end of the Jacobite Wars to the end of the eighteenth century. It was not there in 1700 and it was finished by 1799. Its commercial centre was wholly disproportionate—tiny. Only among the lanes and alleys of the Liberties, where the poor swarmed in indescribable filth, could one have imagined Dublin a typical, gradual, urban development from some antique origin. Then you would have observed that it took in no little villages, as growing London did, and you would have had to realize that the city was, in fact, a lovely artificial, sophisticated, deliberate creation.

SEAN O'FAOLAIN, *An Irish Journey*, 1940

Ten o'clock. Wives, maids and widows washing, wiping, scrubbing, picking, prinking, pinning, parching, painting, hooping, lacing and scolding—Physicians poring over books in their chariots, like malefactors going to the gallows, to give the town a sense of their religion, or rather, deep study—Kept mistresses as lazy in their beds as lifeguardsmen in their quarters—Informers plaguing poor alehousemen, barbers and nosegay-women—Hackney writers, Connaught fortune-hunters, and English solicitors carefully cogging the heels of their stockings, and darning their shirt-collars in order to issue forth from the noisy instances of their landladies to borrow half-a-crown or beg a dinner—Rakes of quality and young students fencing, rehearsing of plays, or humming over opera tunes in their chambers—Churchwardens, select vestrymen, and other tun-bellied parochial officers moving towards church to mock God Almighty—Bakers and pastrycooks robbing their customers' pies and puddings—Vintners and victuallers looking out their worst wines and liquors for the accommodation of such as are to dine with them gratis.

Eleven o'clock. Fine fans, rich brilliants, white hands, envious eyes and gay snuff-boxes displaying in most parish churches—Many excellent stolen sermons preaching by some clergymen who won't take pains to make worse of their own—Folks of fashion humbling themselves in rich lace and tissue and enduring the fatigue of Divine Service with wonderful seeming patience—Drunken beggars battling and breaking one another's heads in the public streets about dividing the charity of ostentatious fools and old women—Hackney coachmen and chairmen lifting up their eyes to Heaven for wet weather—Dabs and portions of beef, pork, and mutton roasting in pack-thread strings in the apartments of married cobblers, porters, penny-postmen and poor harlots. . . .

One o'clock. Politicians dropping their two-pences upon the coffee-house bars and returning home to dinner—Hackney coaches flying about the streets with whole families, new-married couples, uncles, aunts and cousins to dine with their friends and relations—Innocent people of more merit than fortune sitting down to homely, wholesome food, with calm consciences—All the common people's jaws in and around this great metropolis in full employment.

Two o'clock. The sexes ogling and stealing glances at one another as they sit at dinner together—Church bells and tavern bells keep time with one another—Some politicians upon the Catholic bench at the end of Stephen's Green bring the Spanish arms to Gibraltar and Great Britain and do wonders for the Pretender—Those on the Court Bench at the other end led loose a powerful army of Moors upon them and drive them out of their late conquests in Barbary—Poor unbeneficed clergymen brushing their beavers and cassocks, to do journey work for such dignified drones whose ample meals have rendered them incapable of performing the afternoon's drudgery—Pickpockets taking their stands at the avenues into public walks.

Three o'clock. Pawn Brokers' wives dressing themselves with their customers' wearing apparel, rings and watches—Prebendaries, petty canons and choristers, with much reluctancy, quit their couches, wives and bottles for cathedral exercises—Young, handsome wenches demanding adoration instead of paying it in church—The fortunate and great sitting down to meals of pomp and ceremony, attended by sumptuous sideboards, sycophants and little sincerity—City cheesemongers and grocers snoring in churches and meeting-houses—The paths of Rathfarnham, Finglass and Donnybrook found much more pleasant than those of the Gospel—Citizens marching in threes, fours and fives thro' the town, in quest of sour wine and cider—Waiters at taverns and coffee-houses making vast preparations to cut a figure in the Beau Monde—Looking-glasses and——in great favour with the ladies—Women servants, half naked, at their broken bits of looking-glasses, vainly attempting, by the power of soap and labour, to alter the colour of their skins. . . .

Six o'clock. People of quality and distinction drove out of the Green by milliners, manteau-makers, tire-women, sempstresses, clearstarchers, poulterers, staymakers, French peruke makers, dancing-masters, drapers, gentlemen's gentlemen, tailors' wives, starch old maids, and butchers' daughters—Assignations and malicious whisperings at the Ring in the Park—Night-walkers washing their smocks against the close of the day—Vintners' wives and daughters dressed up behind their bars, to decoy young fellows into large reckonings—Match-makers and fortune-hunters in full employment—Beggars converting their coppers into true sterling.

Seven o'clock. Fools and powdered fops admiring themselves in coffee-houses—City apprentices complaining to fond mothers of their masters—Foot-soldiers drunk at their posts with brandy—The Ministry severely censured in ale-houses—Few lawyers at evening lectures—Men, women and children returning from the fields drunk and hungry—Dusty chaises with shores in high-crown hats limping thro' the streets of Dublin—People of quality beginning to pay spiteful visits to one another.

Eight o'clock. Cold beef and pudding most vigorously attacked in taverns and other public-houses—Servants in gentlemen's and tradesmen's kitchens carousing with liquors stolen from their masters—Young shopkeepers, beau journeymen and lawyers' clerks sneaking into town upon broken-kneed horses—Weekly newspapers the subject of much low conversation—Black eyes and broken heads exhibited in the public streets about precedency—People of moderate allowances examining the remaining pence and shillings after the debauch of the day—Hired infants, who have been lent out to beggars, restored to their real parents—Men of quality visiting their wives' chamber maids in the absence of their wives from home.

Nine o'clock. Young rakes conversing with their mothers' maids in taverns—City dames vouching for one another, for the good company they have passed the afternoon in—Sponsors at low christenings pretty far advanced in beer and brandy—Journeymen shoemakers taking off their wearing apparel, as holding it by no longer tenure than the opening of the pawnbrokers' shops the next morning—Children, servants, old women, and others of the same size of understanding, pleasing and terrifying themselves with stories of witches, devils and apparitions.—

D—— S—— (Dean Swift?), *Description of Sunday in Dublin*, 1725

The post-Union exodus of the bright-plumaged people had not (as I saw) been followed by real decay. The Irish Bar and the eminent Dublin doctors kept South Dublin witty and sociable. Judges and specialists now lived round Merrion Square. The front doors were painted, the fanlights and windows polished, the great staircases possibly better swept and the high-ceilinged double drawing-rooms heated and lit for *conversazioni*. In the winters of my childhood this second society was still in full, if not at its fullest, force. The twentieth century governed only in name; the nineteenth was still a powerful dowager. Between England and Anglo-Ireland a time-lag is, I think, always perceptible. Any transition into Edwardian dashingness would have been seen in the Castle set. But the Castle seasons left my father and mother cold. The world my parents inhabited, and the subworld of its children, was still late-Victorian. Their friends were drawn from the Bar, from Trinity College, from among the prelates of the Church of Ireland or landed people quietly living in town.

In fact, the climatic moodiness of South Dublin (a bold Italianate town-plan in tricky Celtic light) must have existed only in my eye. All here stood for stability. The front doors were, as I say, fresh painted—crimson, chocolate, chestnut, ink-blue or olive-green. One barrister friend of my father's had a chalk-white front door I found beautiful. And each door—to this my memory finds no single exception—bore its polished brass plate. Daughter of a professional neighbourhood, I took this brass plate announcing its owner's name to be the *sine qua non* of any gentleman's house. Just as the tombstone says '*Here Lies*' the plate on the front door (in my view) said '*Here Lives*'. Failure to write one's name on one's door seemed to me the admission of nonentity. The householder with the anonymous door must resign himself to being overlooked by by the world—to being passed by the postman, unfed by tradesmen, guestless, unsought by friends—and his family dwelt in the shadow of this disgrace.

ELIZABETH BOWEN, *Seven Winters*, 1943

When O'Grady wrote 'the divine Dodder,' he must have been thinking of long ago, when the Dodder roared down from the hills, a great and terrible river, sweeping the cattle out of the fields, killing even its otters, wearing through the land a great chasm, now often dry save for a peevish trickle which, after many weeks of rain, swells into a harmless flood and falls over the great weir at Tallaght, but only to run away quickly or collect into pools among great boulders, reaching Rathfarnham a quiet and demure little river. At Dartry it flows through mud, but the wood above it is beautiful; not great and noble as the wood at Pangbourne; Dartry is a small place, no doubt, but the trees that crowd the banks are tall and shapely, and along one bank there is a rich growth of cow-parsley and hemlock, and there are sedges and flags and beds of wild forget-me-nots in the stream itself. The trees reach over the stream, and there are pleasant spots under the hawthorns in the meadows where the lovers may sit hand in hand, and nooks under the high banks where they can lie conscious of each other and of the soft summer evening. A man should go there with a girl, for the intrusion of the mere wayfarer is resented. There is a beautiful bend in the stream near the dye-works, and the trees grow straight and tall, and out of them the wood-pigeon clatters. Green, slimy, stenchy at Donnybrook, at Ballsbridge the Dodder reminds one of a steep, ill-paven street into which many wash-tubs have been emptied; and after Ballsbridge, it reaches the sea; as has been said, black and inert as a crocodile.

If O'Grady had called the Dodder 'the Union river,' he would have described it better, for the Dodder must have been entirely disassociated from Dublin till about a hundred years ago. The aristocracy that inhabited the great squares and streets in the north side of Dublin could have known very little about this river; but as soon as the Union became an established fact, Dublin showed a tendency to move towards the south-east, towards the Dodder. Every other city in the world moves westward, but we are an odd people, and Dublin is as odd as ourselves. . . . The building of Merrion Square must have been undertaken a little before, or very soon after the Union; Stephen's Green is late eighteenth century; Fitzwilliam Square looks like 1850. The houses in the Pembroke Road seem a little older, but we cannot date them earlier than 1820. Within the memory of man, Donnybrook was a little village lying outside Dublin; to-day it is only connected with Dublin by a long, straggling street; and beyond Donnybrook is a beautifully wooded district through which the Stillorgan Road rises in gentle ascents, sycamores, beeches, and chestnuts of great height and size shadowing it mile after mile. On either side of the roadway there are cut-stone gateways; the smooth drives curve and disappear behind hollies and cedars, and we often catch sight of the blue hills between the trees.

GEORGE MOORE, Salve, 1912

Oliver St John Gogarty joined the Tyrrell–Mahaffy circle while still an undergraduate and has preserved many of their *bons mots* in his autobiographies and his rambling essay on wit and humour, *Start from Somewhere*

Else. The latter book also records some witticisms by Dubliners of a slightly later generation, such as Thomas Kettle and James Montgomery; I miss the latter's best remark, however, about a river whose banks are a favourite Dublin lovers' lane: 'The trees along the Dodder are more sinned against than sinning.'

VIVIAN MERCIER, *The Irish Comic Tradition*, 1962

The 1946 year of my arrival in Ireland coincided with one of the harshest winters on record. Past Christmas the snows were piled high and even the odd days above freezing point were chillingly damp and cold. The largest municipal park which had so first caught my imagination had massive long high ricks of turf upon which it rained and snowed. These sodden chunks of fuel with which to heat our chambers could rarely be lit due to their wet condition, and if ever lit would only coldly smoulder. In the tall ceilinged and large windowed college rooms, lying long abed mornings, one's frozen feet of the night before not ever thawing before dawn. The dry warmth of Bewley's Oriental Café in Grafton Street becoming the day's first destination. So, too, for the survival of chilled limbs, did I have the early, middle and the latter part of one's evening planned.

In the inner core of Dublin city and within a half mile radius of the centre of O'Connell Street Bridge, you never at any point were more than one hundred and thirty nine and one half paces from a pint of porter or ball of whiskey. Or your trusty bottle of stout standing in their hundreds on shelves ready for their corks to be levered out with a hand puller and a suitable pop. In the better bars were clarets and burgundies, pickled onions, sausages, boiled eggs and sandwiches of ham, cheese and roast beef. But always on the very edges of these blessings lurked the cold desperate reality of the city and its stark gloomy poverty only a stone's throw away. Begging for a penny or selling a newspaper, shoeless urchins, faces streaming phlegm, scattering across the grey glisteningly wet streets.

J. P. DONLEAVY, *J. P. Donleavy's Ireland*, 1986

The darker side . . . was blurred and muddied and stinking; the dramatic character of the misery. In Dublin, the tenements were shocking; the women still wore the long black shawl, the children were often bare-footed. You picked up lice and fleas in the warm weather in the Dublin trams as you went to the North side to the wrecked mansions of the eighteenth century. The poor looked not simply poor, but savagely poor, though they were rich in speech and temperament. There were always ragged processions of protesters, on the general Irish ground that one must keep on screaming against life itself. There were nasty sights: a man led down a mountain road with his wrists tied behind his back, by a couple of soldiers.

V. S. Pritchett, *Midnight Oil*, 1971

We were nearer to poetic drama than we shall ever be again. Intellectual life was astir. Joyce and I used to go to see how the actors were getting on with John Elwood, a medical student, who enjoyed the licence allowed to medical students by the tolerant goodwill of a people to whom Medicine with its traffic in Life and Death had something of the mysterious and magical about it. To be a medical student's pal by virtue of the glamour that surrounded a student of medicine was almost a profession in itself. Joyce was the best example of a medical student's pal Dublin produced, or rather the best example of the type, extinct since the Middle Ages, of a Goliard, a wandering scholar. The theatre off Camden Street was approached through a narrow passage. John Elwood got so drunk one night that he lamented that he could not even see the ladies stepping over him as they came out.

'Synge looks like a fellow who would sip a pint.'

'John,' I said, 'if you had done more sipping and less swallowing you would not have got us all kicked out.'

Joyce knew far better than I what was in the air, and what was likely to be the future of the theatre in Ireland.

Who can measure how great was its loss when Lady Gregory gave him the cold shoulder? Maybe her much-announced search for talent did not contemplate the talent latent in medical students' pals or wandering minstrels. After an unsuccessful interview he met us in a 'snug,' where, very solemnly, with his high, well-stocked forehead bulging over his nose, he recited solemnly, waving his finger slowly:

> 'There was a kind Lady called Gregory,
> Said, "Come to me poets in beggary."
>   But found her imprudence
>   When thousands of students
> Cried, "All we are in that catégory"!'

The elision of 'who' before the 'Said' in the second line is a parody on the synthetic folk speech in Synge's 'Playboy.' And the strained 'catégory' the beginning of his experiment with words. She had no room for playboys except on the stage ... So Ulysses had to strike out for himself. Dublin's Dante had to find a way out of his own Inferno. But he had lost the key. James Augustine Joyce slipped politely from the snug with an 'Excuse me!'

'Whist! He's gone to put it all down!'

'Put what down?'

'Put *us* down. A chiel's among us takin' notes. And, faith, he'll print it.'

Now, that was a new aspect of James Augustine. I was too unsophisticated to know that even outside Lady Gregory's presence, notes made of those contemporary with the growing 'Movement' would have a sale later on, and even an historical interest.

OLIVER ST JOHN GOGARTY, *As I Was Going Down Sackville Street*, 1937

The atmosphere of the city was greatly changed; it was not now the city Joyce celebrated in *Ulysses*, or the city that had made the Abbey Theatre and the Gaelic League, or the city that once worked itself into a frenzy over the plays of John Synge. And where were the famous Victorian survivals that one used to encounter several days a week strolling between Trinity College and O'Connell Bridge? There used to be Professor Mahaffy, all tied up in black gaiters, with his queer plebeian Irish face that now one sees only in caricatures. Mahaffy could talk of Sophocles and Socrates as if he had met them at dinner the night before, where, like Dublin gentlemen, they drank a little too much. Yeats had taught us to writhe when Greek was translated into the Swinburnian meters that Mahaffy quoted, his body seeming to keep time to them as if they were jig tunes. The Gaelic League had taught us to smile when Mahaffy talked of the kings he had dined with. Once when he had returned from a visit to Greek royalty bearing as a gift a strange-looking little dog, Oliver Gogarty, one of the wits of the town, wrote verses on it in the very sort of meter in which Mahaffy was accustomed to quote translations from the Greek:

> He was given the hound
> By the seed of a king
> For the wisdom profound
> Of his wide wandering—
> But was it the owner, or donor, or dog that was
> led by the string?

and stately Professor Dowden, very genteel and New Englandish, repeating over and over again what he had written in his youth about Shelley and Shakespeare. It was always said of Dowden that something withered in him and died after Matthew Arnold wrote that essay on his Shelley book, for Arnold convicted him with his most terrible urbanity, not of being a sublime fool, but merely of being a foolish fool. And where was the gentleman with the monocle and carrying two swords who used to walk so purposefully every afternoon up O'Connell Street and whom Joyce has in *Ulysses*? Lacking these figures, the eighteenth-century streets seemed less lively. George Moore had been off the scene for years, now living in London. Lady Gregory was now too old to walk around in the rain, her skirts turned up over her flowered silk petticoat to save them from becoming bedraggled. And I missed those young men who, when they approached me in the street, would draw their latest poem from a pocket and read it with appropriate gesticulations. Writing a poem as a day's work was no longer the spectacular thing it once was. Some public figure remarked that the young men were all writing constitutions because it was easier than writing sonnets.

MARY COLUM, *Life and the Dream*, 1928

Living among writers who were still at their good moment added to my desire to emulate them. I had the—to me—incredible sight of the beautiful Mrs W. B. Yeats riding a bicycle at St Stephens Green; and of A.E. (George Russell), also riding a bicycle and carrying a bunch of flowers. I had tea with James Stephens one Sunday at that hotel at Dun Laoghaire where people go to day-dream at the sight of the mail-boat coming in from England, that flashing messenger to and from the modern world. This gnome-like talker sparkled so recklessly that one half-dreaded he might fall into his teacup and drown. One afternoon I took tea with Yeats himself in his house in Merrion Square.

It was a Georgian house, as unlike a hut of wattle in a bee-loud glade as one could imagine. To begin with, the door opened on a chain and the muzzle of a rifle stuck through the gap. A pink-faced Free State soldier asked me if I had an 'appointment'. I was shown in to what must have been a dining-room but now it was a guard room with soldiers smoking among the Blake drawings on the wall. Yeats was a Senator and he had already been shot at by gunmen. Upstairs I was to see the bullethole in the drawing-room window. Presently the poet came down the stairs to meet me.

It is a choking and confusing experience to meet one's first great man when one is young. These beings come from another world and Yeats studiously created that effect. Tall, with grey hair finely rumpled, a dandy with negligence in collar and tie and with the black ribbon dangling from the glasses on a short, pale and prescient nose—not long enough to be Roman yet not sharp enough to be a beak—Yeats came down the stairs towards me, and the nearer he came the further away he seemed. His air was bird-like, suggesting one of the milder swans of Coole and an exalted sort of blindness. I had been warned that he would not shake hands. I have heard it said—but mainly by the snobbish Anglo-Irish—that Yeats was a snob. I would have said that he was a man who was translated into a loftier world the moment his soft voice throbbed. He was the only man I have known whose natural speech sounded like verse.

He sat me in the fine first floor of his house. After the years all that remains with me is a memory of candles, books, woodcuts, the feeling that here was Art. And conversation. But what about? I cannot remember. The exalted voice flowed over me. The tall figure, in uncommonly delicate tweed, walked up and down, the voice becoming more resonant, as if he were on a stage. At the climax of some point about the Gaelic revival, he suddenly remembered he must make tea, in fact a new pot, because he had already been drinking tea. The problem was one of emptying out the old tea pot. It was a beautiful pot and he walked the room with the short steps of the aesthete, carrying it in his hand. He came towards me. He receded to the bookcase. He swung round the sofa. Suddenly with Irish practicality he went straight to one of the two splendid Georgian windows of the room, opened it, and out went those barren leaves with a swoosh, into Merrion Square—for all I know on to the heads of Lady Gregory, Oliver St John Gogarty and A.E. They were leaves of Lapsang tea.

V. S. PRITCHETT, Midnight Oil, 1971

Turning down Bachelor's Walk at the Liffey by O'Connell Bridge where British troops fired on the people of Dublin in 1914, you come to the Metal Bridge or, as it is sometimes called, the Ha'penny Bridge. It's known as the Metal Bridge for the very obvious and unIrish reason that it's made of metal, but in my father's day it was better known as the Ha'penny Bridge because you had to pay a halfpenny toll to cross it. Further along there is the Four Courts where the Anti-Treaty forces dug in in 1922. I remember the man that was more or less second-in-command there told me that during the attack on the building, a young IRA man from the country—a boy of seventeen or eighteen—was going up the stairs carrying the Chancellor's large wig. 'Hey, where are you going with that?' he called and the boy answered: 'I'm only going to take the kettle off the fire.'

Near by is O'Meara's pub—the 'Irish House', though why it should be called that in Ireland, I don't know. I used to know the man that owned it—it has changed hands since; and I remember him principally for a few lines of poetry that he recited to me:

> 'Then Hoolihan hit Hannaghan and Hannaghan hit McGilligan
> And everyone hit anyone of whom he had a spite,
> And Larry Dwyer, the cripple, who was sitting doing nothing
> Got a kick that broke his jawbone for not indulging in the fight.'

A friend of mine painted that pub one time—Dinny Bowles, a very famous man—a signwriter he was and a very good one at that.

Pubs are dull enough places at any time though not so dull in Ireland as they are in England. I suppose I know most of them in Dublin and I'd rather have them than the pubs in London. I remember being in the 'Blue Lion' in Parnell Street one day and the owner said to me: 'You owe me ten shillings,' he said, 'you broke a glass the last time you were here.' 'God bless us and save us,' I said, 'it must have been a very dear glass if it cost ten shillings. Tell us, was it a Waterford glass or something?' I discovered in double-quick time that it wasn't a glass that you'd drink out of he meant—it was a pane of glass and I'd stuck somebody's head through it.

It was about the Blue Lion also that I remember my grandmother, Christina, getting into a bit of embarrassment. It's more or less at the back of what was Joyce's Night-town, near Montgomery Street, which was one of the streets in the red light district. My grandmother had me by the hand and as we were walking down the street, we met a friend of hers who said: 'Come on, Christina, and have one', meaning come in for a glass of porter. So my grandmother said all right but she didn't want to go into the 'Blue Lion' because, she says: 'All those characters go in there'—meaning whores; but her friend says: 'Ah, they won't take any notice of us.' So in they went. 'We'll go in the private part,' she says and: 'All right,' says my grandmother. So when they went into the private part all the 'characters' roll up and say: 'Ah, hello, Christina, come on in, we didn't see you these years.'

BRENDAN BEHAN, *Brendan Behan's Island*, 1962

Spring became summer. The tulips and the girls flowered in Stephen's Green; the sunlight reached into the furthest corners of the pubs, revealing figures that had slumbered there unnoticed through the long winter. Twilight would come gently to Grafton Street; the summer darkness arrived with closing time and afterwards the bona fides blazed on the mountains; the noise of strong men swearing eternal fealty and eternal enmity being heard in the deserted city like the rumour of a hostile army, the back-slapping like small-arms fire in the larger noise. At ten o'clock the cars swept out along the mountain roads as if all those who could muster transport were fleeing before a plague; at half-past twelve they swept back, awash with song and Guinness, as if the defences of Dublin had suddenly crumbled before a mechanised, drunken horde; and from then until dawn the noise of breaking glass, of splintering wood and cracking skulls would float out over the warm and star-dappled waters of the bay.

ANTHONY CRONIN, *The Life of Riley*, 1964

from *The Week-End of Dermot and Grace*

There are crowds in Moore Street haggling for cauliflowers,
Crowds in Haffners elbowing for sausages,
Crowds in the Pro-Cathedral queueing for forgiveness;
The pillars of St Audoen's stand up pale
As hyacinths in the sunmote mornings,
And cars hoot their way out to country places,

Floodtide bringing slinky magazines to the beaches,
Nylon and muscular middle-age to the golf links,
Literary flotsam to elizabethan loungebars
And blonde girls to the ruins of the bronze age.

But the barrow-girl keeps her daily station
At the butt of the built stonework,
Sends her cry into the chaos of the traffic
Urging the pippins, the pippins, and the wheel's disclose—
Red were her lips as the ruddy rose. . . .

EUGENE WATTERS, *The Week-End of Dermot and Grace*, 1964

The lower classes of the inhabitants of this city [i.e. Dublin] have afforded abundant materials to the dramatist, as well as to the tourist. They are represented as a wrong-headed and a warm-hearted, a whimsical and eccentric kind of people who get drunk and make bulls, and who cannot open their mouths that something funny and witty does not come tumbling out, like pearls, every time she spoke, from the lips of the fair princess Parizade, in the Arabian Nights' Entertainments. I do not deny that there may be some foundation for this character; but if I am to judge from what I have seen myself, it is greatly exaggerated.

JOHN GAMBLE, *Sketches of Dublin: The North of Ireland*, 1811

Byrne's was beginning to fill up. The cattlemen were coming in. They came in in their heavy boots and long rain-coats, the skin of their faces roughened by the early morning wind and rain at country fairs. They wore their hair rather long and there were gold rings on their thick fingers, hard on the inside from gripping sticks. Leaning back with both hands on a stick, sizing up a heifer at the fairs.

FRANCIS STUART, *The Coloured Dome*, 1932

My first college invitation was to go and have a cup of coffee. Thus one embarked upon this sacred rite in Dublin. To be indulged either by morning, noon, afternoon or all three. Each café with its adherents. In my case it became Bewley's Oriental Café in Grafton Street which involved turning left out the front gates, past the Provost's House and traversing the city's cultural spine of Grafton Street. Paved with its wooden blocks aswarm with bicycles and off which variously extended Suffolk, Duke, Ann, Harry and Lemon

Streets. Although there were cafés in these side street nooks and crannies, the
élite coffee-scented emporiums were all on the socially desired thoroughfare
of Grafton Street. Where early morning gossip could be meteorically spread
between the cheerful chattering of briefly pausing pedestrians. And where the
wives of bank managers with light-hearted things to think and do could
flaunt their better than thou high-heeled utter respectability.

Starting at the bottom of Grafton Street on the left, in a grey stone neo
Georgian building, was Mitchell's. Definitely for the lady of society who'd
been at a play the evening before, and carrying a catalogue from an exhibition of paintings, had just been to a fitting for a frock. Then further up, the
glass table tops of Bewley's, its butter balls piled on plates, its stacks of fragrant fresh buns, its creamy glasses of Jersey milk and its roasted coffee smells
perfuming the street.

J. P. Donleavy, *J. P. Donleavy's Ireland*, 1986

I remember Dublin as dark and dramatic then, at the end of the 1950s, the
streets drifting with smoke and rain. I see it in my mind's eye in black and
white. Pubs and cafés were thrilling, because light and warmth spilled from
them. The students moved like guerrillas around the centre of the city, hardly
visible. They walked everywhere. They borrowed each other's coats. They lent
each other books, and ate egg-and-onion sandwiches and chips with mince
sauce and if they had money, at three o-clock potato cakes came on the menu
in Bewley's. You ate them slowly, a whole pat of butter on each one, sometimes accompanied by the snuffles of Myles na Gopaleen, toying with a white
pudding on toast at the next table.

Middle-aged or young, city people lived alone in cold bed-sitters that smelt
of gas, with stained curtains, and dripping bathrooms down lino-covered
halls. There were hundreds of these lairs, and young men and women walking
and getting busses from one to another. Even Trinity students, supposedly
patrolled by proctors, could disappear into a network of rooms in Kenilworth
Square and Waterloo Road and under pavement level in Leeson Street and
up in the attics of Nassau Street and over the shops in Baggot Street. Couples
went into the musty beds in the afternoons, by silent agreement—she in her
jumper and skirt and suspender belt, he pushing down his trousers under the
blankets. The fumbles led to this and—ugh! ouch!—that. Buddy Holly ser-
enading Peggy Sue on the Dansette so that the fellows playing cards next door
wouldn't hear.

Everything I was learning was new to me. Caring about issues—de Valera's
attempt to remove proportional representation, for example—was new. Politics was new. Nationalism was new. I had a boy friend, that is to say, from a
Tipperary Republican family who used to walk me up and down Molesworth

Street while he plotted to blow up the Grand Lodge of the Freemasons: that was nationalism. Standing on O'Connell Bridge watching the unemployed men march, and wondering whether anything could be done—that was politics. There was no party politics. It wasn't even that Fianna Fáil ran the country: de Valera, personally, ran the country.

Nuala O'Faolain, *Are You Somebody?*, 1996

Trinity College, Dublin. At a party held in the rooms of an undergraduate acquaintance, an American actor, whom I last saw playing the Ghost in *Hamlet* at the Gate Theatre, relates how, returning home about two o'clock in the morning along O'Connell Street, he met an apparition playing on some kind of a rustic pipe and every now and again leaping ecstatically into the air as it rushed along. It had a battered bowler hat, a beard, and it wore boots on only one foot, the other being bare. At first the American was under the impression that he had been reading too much James Stephens, but on questioning an enormous Metropolitan policeman discovered that it was only another of the curiosities of Dublin. 'He does be astray in the head,' said the policeman, 'but he does be doin' no harm'—whereupon the American, in relating the incident, went into ecstasies of appreciation of the innate sense of justice and individual liberty in a city and a country where such eccentricities were not only tolerated but were regarded as a break in the monotony of everyday living.

Denis Ireland, *From the Irish Shore*, 1936

F. R. Higgins told me how one Sunday night, on his way to A.E.'s house, he was puzzled by a small bundle moving along past the lamp-posts. As he came near, he realized, much to his embarrassment, that the bundle was James Stephens, wrapped in a large French Cavalry Officer's cloak, which he had brought back with him from Paris.

Austin Clarke, *A Penny in the Clouds*, 1968

I find by consulting my diary that it was on the 30th of June that I went to Dublin. I am not often in Dublin, though I do not share the contempt for that city which is felt by most Ulstermen. Cahoon, for instance, will not recognize it as the capital of the country in which he lives, and always speaks of Dublin people as impractical, given over to barren political discussion and utterly unable to make useful things such as ships and linen. He also says that Dublin is dirty, that the rates are exorbitantly high, and that the houses have not got bath-rooms in them. I put it to him that there are two first-rate libraries in Dublin.

'If I want a book,' he said, 'I buy it. We pay for what we use in Belfast. We are business men.'

'But,' I explained, 'there are some books, old ones, which you cannot buy. You can only consult them in libraries.'

'Why don't you go to London, then?' said Cahoon.

The conversation took place in the club. I lunched there on my way through Belfast, going on to Dublin by an afternoon train. I was, in fact, going to Dublin to consult some books in the College Library. Marion and I had been brought up short in our labours on my history for want of some quotations from the diary of a seventeenth-century divine, and even if I had been willing to buy the book I should have had to wait months while a second-hand bookseller advertised for it.

Trinity College, when I entered the quadrangle next day, seemed singularly deserted. The long vacation had begun a week before. Fellows, professors and students had fled from the scene of their labours. Halfway across the square, however, I met McNeice. He seemed quite glad to see me and invited me to luncheon in his rooms. I accepted the invitation and was fed on cold ham, stale bread and bottled stout.

Thackeray once hinted that fellows of Trinity College gave their guests beer to drink. Many hard words have been said of him ever since by members of Dublin University. I have no wish to have hard things said about me; so I explain myself carefully. McNeice's luncheon was an eccentricity. It is not on cold ham solely, it is not on stale bread ever, that guests in the Common Room are fed. If, like Prince Hal, they remember amid their feasting 'that good creature, small beer,' they do not drink it without being offered nobler beverages.

GEORGE A. BIRMINGHAM, *The Red Hand of Ulster*, 1912

Perhaps there was never known a wiser Institution than that of allowing certain Persons of both Sexes, in large and populous Cities, to cry through the Streets many Necessaries of Life; it would be endless to recount the Conveniences which our City enjoys by this useful Invention, and particularly Strangers, forced hither by Business, who reside here but a short time; for, these having usually but little Money, and being wholly ignorant of the Town, might at an easy Price purchase a tolerable Dinner, if the several Criers would pronounce the Names of the Goods they have to sell, in any tolerable Language. And therefore till our Law-makers shall think it proper to interpose so far as to make these Traders pronounce their Words in such Terms, that a plain Christian Hearer may comprehend what is cryed, I would advise all new Comers to look out at their Garret Windows, and there see whether the Thing that is cryed be *Tripes* or *Flummery*, *Buttermilk* or *Cowheels*. For, as things are now managed, how is it possible for an honest Country-man, just arrived, to find out what is meant; for Instance, by the following Words, with which his Ears are constantly stunned twice a Day, *Muggs*, *Juggs and Porringers*, *up in the Garret, and down in the Cellar*. I say, how is it possible for any Stranger to understand that this Jargon is meant as an invitation to buy a Farthing's worth of Milk for his Breakfast or Supper, unless his Curiosity draws him to the Window, or till his Landlady shall inform him? I produce this only as one Instance, among a Hundred much worse, I mean where the Words make a Sound wholly inarticulate, which give so much Disturbance, and so little Information.

The Affirmation solemnly made in the cry of *Herrings*, is directly against all Truth and Probability, *Herrings alive, alive here*; the very Proverb will convince us of this; for what is more frequent in ordinary Speech, than to say of some Neighbour for whom the Passing-Bell rings, that *he is dead as a Herring*. And, pray how is it possible, that a Herring, which as Philosophers observe, cannot live longer than one Minute, three Seconds and a half out of Water, should bear a Voyage in open Boats from *Howth* to *Dublin*, be tossed into twenty Hands, and preserve its Life in Sieves for several Hours? Nay, we have Witnesses ready to produce, that many Thousands of these Herrings, so impudently asserted to be alive, have been a Day and a Night upon dry Land. But this is not the worst. What can we think of those impious Wretches, who dare in the Face of the Sun, vouch the very same affirmative of their *Salmon*, and cry, *Salmon alive, alive*; whereas, if you call the Woman who cryes it, she is not asham'd to turn back her Mantle, and show you this individual Salmon cut into a dozen Pieces.

> DEAN SWIFT, from 'An Examination of Abuses, etc. . . . in the City of Dublin', 1732

The Phœnix Park, . . . is a wide timbered expanse of some two thousand acres, full of tame deer, where all that is young in the place may be seen flirting, cricketing, playing all sorts of games, but above all, bicycling. Bicycles seem to be the ruling passion of the Dublin youth. I have seen more than a hundred at a time in a single lane near the Wellington Obelisk. By the way, this was the very avenue where Lord Frederick Cavendish and Mr Burke were murdered five years ago by the *Invincibles*. A cross marks the place where the two corpses were discovered.

The Castle, which the two English officials had the imprudence to leave that day, is the Lord-Lieutenant's official residence. It has not the picturesque majesty of the castles of Edinburgh or Stirling. Instead of rising proudly on some cloud-ascending rock and lording over the town, it seems to hide 'its diminished head' under a little hillock in the central quarters. You must literally stumble over its walls to become aware of their existence; and you understand then why the name of *Dublin Castle* is for the Irish synonymous with despotism and oppression.

This is no Government office of the ordinary type, the dwelling of the Lord-Lieutenant of Ireland is a regular stronghold, encircled with ramparts, bristling with towers, shut up with portcullis, draw-bridge and iron bars. In the inner Castle yard are situated the apartments of the pro-consul, the lodgings of his dependants of all degrees, the offices where decrees are engrossed, the pigeon-holes where they are heaped, all forming a sort of separate city entrenched within its fortifications.

PHILIPPE DARYL, *Ireland's Disease*, 1888

To get the flavour of Dublin's elegant shabbiness, one should go to the King's Inn. It is situated in one of the last of the slums, Henrietta Street, with its fanlights, wrought-iron, grand doors, bygone gentility, squalor, Sean O'Casey— the transition is easy. I am not sure that shabbiness is the correct term for that dusty, gauzy look which begot the ancient epithet 'dirty Dublin'; the look, at any rate, is really much more an attraction than a demerit. Henrietta Street, the Squares and scores of other parts of Dublin have the same indefinable air of having been heavily sand-sprinkled and in dire need of energetic sweeping. If you fail to note this peculiarity, it is because the place has grown on you. You should immediately travel to Belfast and refresh your eyes with a city free from veiling shrouds.

STEPHEN RYNNE, *All Ireland*, 1956

If the stranger be forcibly struck by the number and magnificence of the public buildings, and the general beauty of some of the streets, he is sure to be no less forcibly moved by the very different character of those parts which are termed 'the Liberties.' Here, narrow streets, houses without windows or doors, and several families crowded together beneath the same roof, present a picture of ruin, disease, poverty, filth, and wretchedness, of which they who have not witnessed it are unable to form a competent idea.

JONATHAN BINNS, *The Miseries and Beauties of Ireland*, 1837

The arrangements for continuing his education were made rather suddenly. His mother took lodgings in a Dublin suburb for H and herself from where he went by tram daily to be prepared for the university entrance exam by a young tutor called Grimble.

H hadn't been in Dublin since the County Meath days when, sniffing up its impact through the smells of fresh horse dung from the waiting sidecars, the tang from the river or the brewery, he had stepped across the deep but narrow steamy chasm on to the Amiens Street station platform with a tight grip on his nurse's gloved hand.

Now it was the big yellow tramcars passing the windows of the lodging house that flashed and screeched the message that this was Dublin. Yet when he first made the trip in one of them, getting out at the corner of Grafton Street, he did no more than stand on the crowded pavement watching the tram disappear under a series of violet sparks around a big stone building and then, crossing the street, took the next one back in time for high tea served in their small sitting room.

FRANCIS STUART, *Black List, Section H*, 1975

Dublin was a new and complex sensation. Uncle Charles had grown so witless that he could no longer be sent out on errands and the disorder in settling in the new house left Stephen freer than he had been in Blackrock. In the beginning he contented himself with circling timidly round the neighbouring square or, at most, going half way down one of the side streets: but when he had made a skeleton map of the city in his mind he followed boldly one of its central lines until he reached the customhouse. He passed unchallenged among the docks and along the quays wondering at the multitude of corks that lay bobbing on the surface of the water in a thick yellow scum, at the crowds of quay porters and the rumbling carts and the illdressed bearded policeman. The vastness and strangeness of the life suggested to him by the bales of merchandise stocked along the walls or swung aloft out of the holds of steamers wakened again in him the unrest which had sent him wandering in the evening from garden to garden in search of Mercedes. And amid this new bustling life he might have fancied himself in another Marseilles but that he missed the bright sky and the sunwarmed trellises of the wineshops. A vague dissatisfaction grew up within him as he looked on the quays and on the river and on the lowering skies and yet he continued to wander up and down day after day as if he really sought someone that eluded him.

JAMES JOYCE, *Portrait of the Artist as a Young Man*, 1915

It was beyond O'Connell Bridge that the ruins began, the destruction wrought by British cannon during the insurrection or by opposing factions in the Irish civil war. Sad for the disappearance of historic buildings as well as for the missing faces, I walked off the quays and into the side streets where were the old churches, Christ Church and Swift's St Patrick's, old streets where

in another century had walked men who, too, in their day had made literature and passionate thought seem the most glorious thing in life. Their ghosts
were in the air around me—Swift, the most beloved of them all, so beloved
in his day that an old history of Dublin tells us weeping crowds surrounded
the Deanery where he lay dead and begged for a hair of his head to hand
down to their children. Goldsmith, also beloved, slipping in among the
crowd to listen to a ballad singer trolling out something that Oliver himself
had written. Burke and Sheridan appeared amongst the ghosts, they, too,
lords of language, as well as Sterne and Farquahar, and Thomas Moore, be-
littled by my generation, and also the ghosts of those Yeats had ordered us
to admire—Davis, Mangan, and Ferguson. Yet, considering them all, I was
mindful that the greatest of Dublin's literary figures, Yeats, was still treading
its streets, now actually a greater poet than he had been in my admiring
youth.

MARY COLUM, *Life and the Dream*, 1928

From my temporary lodging in Monkstown I stepped out in a moist mild
breeze on this my first official day as a student at Trinity. And walked past the
small front gardens in a moment of morning sunshine, the smell of the sea
in the air blowing in over Dublin Bay. Near the church at the fork in the road,
I boarded the wood panelled and green upholstered tram. Climbing up its
narrow stairs to the top of its two tiers. Able to look from the windows down
into the passing walled green suburban gardens. Their monkey puzzle trees,
laurels, rhododendrons and subtropical greenery verdantly proclaiming the
respectability of the inhabitants. This utterly beautiful vehicle's bell clanging
as it roared and swayed on its iron wheels along its shiny tracks, destined to
come to a final halt at a tall pillar of granite on which stood a statue of Nelson
on that widest of European boulevards in the city of Dublin.

J. P. DONLEAVY, *J. P. Donleavy's Ireland*, 1986

IT is bleak December noon,
    Winter-wild and rainy grey:
By the old road thinly strewn
    Drifts of dead leaves skirts the way:
        Oh! the long canals are drear,
        And the floods o'erflow the weir,
        And the old deserted Year
Seems dying with the day.

THOMAS CAULFIELD IRWIN, 1889

The hotel [the Shelbourne] stands in the heart of a city now long at peace. For years past, only the sleepy quacking of water-fowl round the Green lake has broken the late-night silence after the traffic stops—or in the distance one hears a horn on the river. Gales roar from winter to winter as of old; but mankind in Dublin is violent no more. First to know terror in our century, this European capital, not unfairly, was among the first to regain calm, and has been foremost in guarding it. Few, indeed, have reason to rate calm higher. Since the stabilization of Ireland as a Free State, succeeding changes of government, ever-advancing steps in the direction of a complete autonomy have accomplished themselves without bloodshed. Constitutionalism— whose apparent defeat killed John Redmond in 1918—now holds firm in Ireland. With those who died for this country, on the gallows, in battle, or by the bullets of execution squads, must be counted those who died of broken hearts—O'Connell, Parnell, Redmond. Let us hope that our living may reward them. We are on our own, which is at once grave and good: new consequence attends every step we take. From the Second World War Ireland remained apart, the only one of the Dominions (for such she then was) to declare neutrality. Her decision, with all that it might involve for herself or others, was as such scrupulously respected. The same held good when, in 1948, she gave notice to terminate her Dominion status. The birth of the Irish Republic was celebrated on Easter Monday, thirty-three years after the day of the Easter rising.

ELIZABETH BOWEN, *The Shelbourne*, 1951

Dubliners regard their city as being divided principally into a northside and a southside, with the river Liffey as the rough dividing line. The southside, particularly when taken to include the borough of Dún Laoghaire which extends from it southwards, is on the whole much more affluent than the northside. Moreover, it contains many important institutions: the Dáil and Senate, government buildings, the Republic's two biggest universities, the national television and radio service (RTE), most of the newspapers and big hotels, and the headquarters of many important companies and banks. The southside jokes about the northside: 'Why did the southside woman marry the northside man? To get her handbag back.' 'What is a northsider in a suit? A bus conductor.'

Since the early to mid-eighties, the name of a postal district in the heart of the southside, Dublin 4, has come to signify a powerful force in Irish politics. This symbolic usage was invented by the Mayo journalist John Healy, in his column in the *Irish Times* during the FitzGerald government of 1982–87. The literal Dublin 4 is characterised by old, leafy suburban roads and contains, besides a number of embassies, the Royal Dublin Society showgrounds,

RTE, University College Dublin, some research institutes and the Chester Beatty Library. But Dublin 4, in the political sense, is understood to include a much wider area of southside life. It is perceived as a powerful social group with a characteristic mentality and agenda, which is located in South Dublin, exists largely outside parliament and the government of the day, but includes varying proportions of both.

DESMOND FENNELL, *Heresy*, 1993

Dublin Airport in late July. Davy Byrne's half empty, as if I had never left. The casually intense manner of conversation resumed by habitually heavy smokers, students of human foibles; button-holers.

Missing: Theatre Royal, Regal Rooms Cinema, Capital and Metropole, Grafton Picture House, Mr Shakespear with golf umbrella. Shell of Moira Hotel. Cambridge's subsumed into Brown Thomas. The hand-cut HB ice-cream replaced by chilled dog-biscuit covered in chocolate.

Constants: Jack Cruise at the Olympia. The International Bar in Wicklow Street (less its cat) and a chance encounter of two long-lost friends after twenty years, neither changed a whit, they swear: beads of sweat on nostrils induced by balls of malt. The heavy woodwork, elements of chance, old-style grey bags and tweed jackets from time of rationing, demob suits.

Toner's. Searson's snug on Portobello Bridge. The quest. Long-nosed paperseller from the past who had a pitch outside Cambridge's corner, covering the Bailey and Davy Byrne's, walking as in a dream by Toner's in heavy overcoat, eyes blasted not by dreams but by the onrushing by-and-by.

Novelty: female bare backs and plunging *décolletage*.

Constants: in the sudden heat of July, with temperatures risen into the eighties, a man dies in the Meath Hospital. Pus coming from neck sore, the heavy smoker consoles the dumpy woman in heavy green overcoat. Smell of the Coombe, wail of the bereaved. Who will tell the widow? The Dublin poor. Set face on the stretcher. The short-tempered nurse, clang of the Emergency door.

Newness: Mansion House with new coat of white paint. Painted doors, no longer all green, and façades of a city in process of transforming itself.

Stephen's Green. The head park keeper breaking in assistant in brown uniform, armband. A face I remember. Much given to whistle-blowing, cane-brandishing, poses of rigid disapproval. (Whose grass is it anyway?) Manner of German gallery guards. Dating from days of Gardai with truncheons, Christian Brothers with sticks.

Oddity: well-designed rustic wooden tables and chairs near the play-ground. Replicas seen later in lay-by near Wicklow pine wood. Bavarian.

The last pawnbroker: Gorman of Cuffe Street.

Cut grass verges of Grand Canal cleared of weeds. Two houses side by side on Appian Way painted orange and shellac white. Ely House seen from Hume Street, in rose and terracotta, white woodwork. Georgian windows, the geometric flux, offset against the clouds.

'A glass of Jameson for the gentleman who just came in.'

As newspapers die elsewhere, bedevilled by unions, rising production costs, new ones start up in Ireland like the proverbial mushroom: the *Western Journal, What's On in Dublin, Hibernia Fortnightly Review* goes weekly.

AIDAN HIGGINS (1976), *Ronda Gorge and Other Precipices*, 1989

Nobody except a Dubliner should write about Dublin; somebody like Jimmy Montgomery, the Film Censor, or Gogarty, or Seumas O'Sullivan, or Alderman Tom Kelly—Dublin gamins. The other day I was at an exhibition of paintings of Dublin streets by Norah McGuinness, and in opening it Michael MacLiammoir praised her exciting pictures by saying that she had made the bricks stir, as if the houses were part of nature, and in that movement the people were part of the streets and the streets were part of the people. That is how Dublin must seem to a Dubliner. In that 'mood of nature', as A.E. might have called it, the hills walk down through the streets and the sea flows into them. Sean O'Casey has that pantheistic feeling for the city, and when he writes about it it seems to lean down and kiss him or kick him.

In that magical evening hour when the view up-river from O'Connell Bridge clothes itself yet once again, as it does every sunfall, in a beauty that halts or at least turns the head of every passer-by, Dublin has this vibrancy. The claret glow at the end of O'Connell Street, the *pays lointain* across Baggot Street Bridge, the suggestion of exciting and interesting life behind every yellow blind, the mountains rolling past the end of the streets going southwest, the colours that come out in rain, especially when the evening lights go up, the great expanses of sky—always *mouvementé*—over the wide streets, the extraordinary, almost painful, brilliance of the sunlight on the houses, are all the phenomena of a collaboration between living and dead matter. The city, built in one tradition, and adorned by another tradition, palpitates, is alive, like a wood in wind, or a ship.

SEAN O'FAOLAIN, *An Irish Journey*, 1940

A Brighter Life

To see what the fun is, that all fun surpasses—
ANON., 'Donnybrook Fair'

———

The name or title of the pome I am about to recite, gentlemen, said Shana-han with leisure priest-like in character, is a pome by the name of the 'Workman's Friend'. By God you can't beat it. I've heard it praised by the highest. It's a pome about a thing that's known to all of us. It's about a drink of porter.

Porter!

Porter.

Up on your legs man, said Furriskey. Mr Lamont and myself are waiting and listening. Up you get now.

Come on, off you go, said Lamont.

Now listen, said Shanahan clearing the way with small coughs. Listen now.

He arose holding out his hand and bending his knee beneath him on the chair.

> When things go wrong and will not come right,
> Though you do the best you can,
> When life looks black as the hour of night—
> A PINT OF PLAIN IS YOUR ONLY MAN.

By God there's a lilt in that, said Lamont.

Very good indeed, said Furriskey. Very nice.

I'm telling you it's the business, said Shanahan. Listen now.

> When money's tight and is hard to get
> And your horse has also ran,
> When all you have is a heap of debt—
> A PINT OF PLAIN IS YOUR ONLY MAN.

> When health is bad and your heart feels strange,
> And your face is pale and wan,
> When doctors say that you need a change,
> A PINT OF PLAIN IS YOUR ONLY MAN.

There are things in that pome that make for what you call *permanence*. Do you know what I mean, Mr Furriskey?

There's no doubt about it, it's a grand thing, said Furriskey. Come on, Mr Shanahan, give us another verse. Don't tell me that is the end of it.

Can't you listen? said Shanahan.

> When food is scarce and your larder bare
> And no rashers grease your pan,
> When hunger grows as your meals are rare—
> A PINT OF PLAIN IS YOUR ONLY MAN.

What do you think of that now?

It's a pome that'll live, called Lamont, a pome that'll be heard and clapped when plenty more. . . .

But wait till you hear the last verse, man, the last polish-off, said Shanahan. He frowned and waved his hand.

Oh it's good, it's good, said Furriskey.

> In time of trouble and lousy strife,
> You have still got a darlint plan,
> You still can turn to a brighter life—
> A PINT OF PLAIN IS YOUR ONLY MAN!

Did you ever hear anything like it in your life, said Furriskey. A pint of plain, by God, what! Oh I'm telling you, Casey was a man in twenty thousand, there's no doubt about that. He knew what he was at, too true he did. If he knew nothing else, he knew how to write a pome. A pint of plain is your only man.

Didn't I tell you he was good? said Shanahan. Oh by Gorrah you can't cod me.

There's one thing in that pome, *permanence*, if you know what I mean. That pome, I mean to say, is a pome that'll be heard wherever the Irish race is wont to gather, it'll live as long as there's a hard root of an Irishman left by the Almighty on this planet, mark my words. What do you think, Mr Shanahan?

It'll live, Mr Lamont, it'll live.

I'm bloody sure it will, said Lamont.

A pint of plain, by God, eh? said Furriskey.

FLANN O'BRIEN, *At Swim Two Birds*, 1939

There were half-a-dozen carriages and a score of led horses outside the fairgreen, a precious lot of ragamuffins, and a good resort to the public-house opposite; and the gate being open, the artillery band, rousing all the echoes round with harmonious and exhilarating thunder, within—an occasional crack of a 'Brown Bess', with a puff of white smoke over the hedge, being heard, and the cheers of the spectators, and sometimes a jolly chorus of many-toned laughter, all mixed together, and carried on with a pleasant

running hum of voices—Mervyn, the stranger, reckoning on being unob-
served in the crowd, and weary of the very solitude he courted, turned to his
right, and so found himself upon the renowned fair-green of Palmerstown.

It was really a gay rural sight. The circular target stood, with its bright concentric rings, in conspicuous isolation, about a hundred yards away, against
the green slope of the hill. The competitors, in their best Sunday suits, some
armed with muskets and some with fowling-pieces—for they were not particular—and with bunches of ribbons fluttering in their three-cornered hats,
and sprigs of gay flowers in their breasts, stood, in the foreground, in an
irregular cluster, while the spectators, in pleasant disorder, formed two broad,
and many-coloured parterres, broken into little groups, and separated by a
wide, clear sweep of green sward, running up from the marksmen to the
target.

In that luminous atmosphere the men of those days showed bright and gay.
Such fine scarlet and gold waistcoats—such sky-blue and silver—such pea-
green lutestrings—and pink silk linings—and flashing buckles—and courtly
wigs—or becoming powder—went pleasantly with the brilliant costume of
the stately dames and smiling lasses. There was a pretty sprinkling of uniforms, too—the whole picture in gentle motion, and the bugles and drums
of the Royal Irish Artillery filling the air with inspiring music.

J. Sheridan Le Fanu, *The House by the Churchyard*, 1863

from *The Lammas Fair (Belfast)*

On this side sits a ging'-bread Joe,
  The tither a grozet barrow;
The plumbs are here—ilk black's a sloe,
  Melts in yeir mouth like marrow.
This way sit barley-sugar Jones,
  Across there apple factors;
The cutler wi' his wheel an' hone's,
  Beside the man an' pictures;
    At wark that day.

Here's yellow-man, an' tuffy sweet,
  Girls will ye taste or pree it;
An aul' wife crys gaun through the street,
  'Boys treat yeir sweethearts tae it.'
'Och, here's the better stuff for them,
  Teetotal sure's the cordial'—
Na, na, quo' Frank, a glass o' rum
  'Fore soda water's preferable
    On onnie day.

Robert Huddleston, *A Collection of Poems and Songs*, 1844

One curious Gaelic story, *The Romance of Mis and Dubh Ruis*, has clearly undergone some erotic rehandling in the earliest manuscript now known, dated 1769.

Mis, who gave her name to the mountain of Slieve Mish in County Kerry, must originally have been a goddess and belongs to the Mythological Cycle. In this story, however, she is the daughter of a human king; she goes mad with grief when she sees her father's dead body, and drinks his blood. Fleeing to Slieve Mish, she terrorizes the countryside round about. Fur and hair grow all over her body, her nails become claws, and she gains superhuman strength—reminding one both of Swift's Yahoos and of Mad Sweeny.

Eventually, the harper Dubh Ruis wins her back to sanity, primarily by having sexual intercourse with her, though he first attracts her by the sound of his harp. Brian Ó Cuív, editor of the text, regards the intercourse as 'presumably part of the early tradition' and the humanization of Mis would be much less convincing without it, but the original motif has doubtless been gleefully elaborated.

Mis first recognized the harp as something her father had owned; then she recognized the silver and gold which Dubh Ruis had spread around him. He had also 'opened his trousers or his breeches and bared himself, for he thought that if he could lie with her and know her, it would be a good means and device for bringing her to her sense or her natural reason'. The story continues as follows:

As she looked at him, she caught sight of his nakedness and his members of pleasure. 'What are those?' she said, pointing to his bag or his eggs—and he told her. 'What is this?' said she about the other thing which she saw. 'That is the wand of the feat,' said he. 'I do not remember that,' said she, 'my father hadn't anything like that. The wand of the feat; what is the feat?' 'Sit beside me,' said he, 'and I will do the feat of the wand for you.' 'I will,' said she, 'and stay you with me.' 'I will,' said he, and lay with her and knew her, and she said, 'Ha, ba, ba, that was a good feat; do it again.' 'I will,' said he; 'however, I will play the harp for you first.' 'Don't mind the harp,' said she, 'but do the feat.'

VIVIAN MERCIER, *The Irish Comic Tradition*, 1962, Irish trans. David Greene

from *The Midnight Court*

'Now was it too much to expect as right
A little attention once a night?
From all I know she was never accounted
A woman too modest to be mounted.
Gentle, good-humoured and Godfearing
Why should we think she'd deny her rearing?
Whatever the lengths his fancy ran
She wouldn't take fright from a mettlesome man,
And would sooner a boy would be aged a score

Than himself on the job for a week or more;
And an allnight dance or Mass at morning,
Fiddle or flute or choir or organ,
She'd sooner the tune that boy would play
As midnight struck or at break of day.
Damn it, you know we're all the same,
A woman nine months in terror and pain,
The minute that Death has lost the game—
Good morrow my love, and she's off again!
And how could one who longed to please
Feel with a fellow who'd sooner freeze
Than warm himself in a natural way
From All Souls Night to St Brigid's day?
You'd all agree 'twas a terrible fate—
Sixty winters on his pate,
A starved old gelding, blind and lamed
And a twenty year old with her parts untamed.
It wasn't her fault if things went wrong,
She closed her eyes and held her tongue;
She was no ignorant girl from school
To whine for her mother and play the fool
But a competent bedmate smooth and warm
Who cushioned him like a sheaf of corn.
Line by line she bade him linger
With gummy lips and groping finger,
Gripping his thighs in a wild embrace
Rubbing her brush from knee to waist
Stripping him bare to the cold night air,
Everything done with love and care.
But she'd nothing to show for all her labour;
There wasn't a jump in the old deceiver,
And all I could say would give no notion
Of that poor distracted girl's emotion,
Her knees cocked up and the bedposts shaking,
Chattering teeth and sinews aching,
While she sobbed and tossed through a joyless night
And gave it up with the morning light.

BRIAN MERRIMAN, *The Midnight Court* (*c.*1780),
trans. Frank O'Connor, 1945

The absence of moral restraint which led to extremes of lawlessness at Donnybrook and elsewhere was a normal and characteristic accompaniment of

these periodic folk-gatherings. Such moral holidays are a feature of many societies which have not been greatly influenced by urban ways and values. Their
purpose appears to be cathartic, but that there is a lingering fertility magic
underlying the excitement is suggested by such strange rituals as those which
mark the 'Puck Fair and Pattern' of Kilorglin at the head of Dingle Bay in Co.
Kerry. The fair is unfortunately not mentioned in the *Parliamentary Gazetteer*,
though the village of Kilorglin is described as 'an unprosperous, sequestered,
and almost squalid seat of population; and appears to have acquired marvel-
lously little profit from the advantageousness of its position for both inland
and seaward trade'. Puck Fair, held every August, is the great event of the year
in West Kerry, and lasts three days. 10th August is 'Gathering Day', the 11th is
'Fair Day', and the 12th 'Scattering Day', terms which have no doubt been
handed down from days when 'the order of the fair' was prescribed and the
business lasted several days. On the evening of Gathering Day a procession
assembles at the bridge and makes its way to the central square carrying
(nowadays in a large cage mounted on a lorry) a billy-goat bedecked with
ribbons. He is chained by the horns on a high platform erected for the purpose
and, supplied with a liberal stock of cabbages, he presides over the fair. Tradition says that the goat used to stand, 'garlanded by greenery' on the old castle
which was erected here by the Geraldines in the thirteenth century. The business of the fair is the sale of livestock, and as with many another larger fair it
is a traditional gathering place for the tinkers who in Ireland take the place of
the gypsies. On the evening of Scattering Day the Puck is borne triumphantly
back to the bridge. The popular explanation of the custom is that it commemorates an occasion when the noise of goats warned the Irish of advancing English forces, but it is more reasonable to see Puck as a symbol of fertility
and good luck. 12th August is Old Lammas, and Lammas Day, the 1st August,
was known to the Irish as 'Lewy's Fair', in memory of a pre-Christian deity.
This season of high summer has many associations with the pastoral freedom
of the hills, with young people and with dancing and courting. There are traditions of other Puck Fairs in the south of Ireland, and there were certain fairs
at which a white horse was paraded through the assembled crowds and then
tied up to preside over the proceedings.

E. ESTYN EVANS, *Irish Folk Ways*, 1957

The Humours of Donnybrook Fair

D'Alton in *History of the County of Dublin* (1838), writing of
Donnybrook, says, 'This place was long celebrated for its annual August
fair—the "Bartholomew" of Dublin; but which, in consequence of
several riotous and disgraceful results, it has been found necessary
to suppress.'

To DONNYBROOK steer, all you sons of Parnassus—
    Poor painters, poor poets, poor newsmen, and knaves,
To see what the fun is, that all fun surpasses—
    The sorrow and sadness of green Erin's slaves.
Oh, Donnybrook, jewel! full of mirth is your quiver,
    Where all flock from Dublin to gape and to stare
At two elegant bridges, without e'er a river:
    So, success to the humours of Donnybrook Fair!

O you lads that are witty, from famed Dublin city,
    And you that in pastime take any delight,
To Donnybrook fly, for the time's drawing nigh
    When fat pigs are hunted, and lean cobblers fight;
When maidens, so swift, run for a new shift;
    Men, muffled in sacks, for a shirt they race there;
There jockeys well booted, and horses sure-footed,
    All keep up the humours of Donnybrook Fair.

The mason does come, with his line and his plumb;
    The sawyer and carpenter, brothers in chips;
There are carvers and gilders, and all sort of builders,
    With soldiers from barracks and sailors from ships.
There confectioners, cooks, and printers of books,
    There stampers of linen, and weavers, repair;
There widows and maids, and all sort of trades,
    Go join in the humours of Donnybrook Fair.

There tinkers and nailers, and beggars and tailors,
    And singers of ballads, and girls of the sieve;
With Barrack Street rangers, the known ones and strangers,
    And many that no one can tell how they live:
There horsemen and walkers, and likewise fruit-hawkers,
    And swindlers, the devil himself that would dare,
With pipers and fiddlers, and dandies and diddlers,—
    All meet in the humours of Donnybrook Fair.

'Tis there are dogs dancing, and wild beasts a-prancing,
    With neat bits of painting in red, yellow, and gold;
Toss-players and scramblers, and showmen and gamblers,
    Pickpockets in plenty, both of young and of old.
There are brewers, and bakers, and jolly shoemakers,
    With butchers, and porters, and men that cut hair;
There are mountebanks grinning, while others are sinning,
    To keep up the humours of Donnybrook Fair.

Brisk lads and young lasses can there fill their glasses
    With whisky, and send a full bumper around;

Jig it off in a tent till their money's all spent,
    And spin like a top till they rest on the ground.
Oh, Donnybrook capers, to sweet catgut-scrapers,
    They bother the vapours, and drive away care;
And what is more glorious—there's naught more uproarious—
    Huzza for the humours of Donnybrook Fair!

ANON., 18th century

The little hamlet, previously quiet and peaceable, was now occupied by upwards of one thousand persons, principally men, dressed in the most grotesque manner. A row of tents, which had been pitched with extraordinary despatch, lined the road for about two hundred yards near the church; and the numerous barrels and fires in their vicinity gave pretty sure evidence that feasting on a liberal scale was to form part of the entertainment. Fiddlers and pipers were also already in attendance to enable the boys and girls to enjoy dancing. In short, had Ballinacourty been a scene in a pantomime, Harlequin could scarcely have effected a more complete change than was now exhibited.

The 'Whiteboys', who formed the majority of the assemblage, were decorated with ribbons, the prevailing colour being green, though other hues were not rejected. Their officers, for they professed obedience to certain chiefs, greatly eclipsed their men in the gaudiness of their costume. Nearly all carried huge swords. Many 'white boys,' in accordance with their name, wore their shirts over their clothes, and some dozen made themselves even more conspicuous and ridiculous by wearing hideous masks, and carrying bags or bladders filled with sand affixed to a long pole, with which they belaboured the surging crowd; and when their hints to make way were inefficacious, two or three acted the parts of hobby-horses, the heads of which were armed with spikes. These, freely used, had a powerful effect in keeping off those who trespassed too closely on their ranks.

The wild crew acknowledged the leadership of a captain, who collected subscriptions for the nominal purpose of keeping up the society, but in reality to purchase whiskey, of which there appeared to be already a large supply. Parading up and down to music was the order of the afternoon, which was succeeded by dances of various descriptions, among which the jig and country dance appeared to be special favourites.

About five o'clock the motley company sat down in the tents to a substantial repast of bacon, mutton, and potatoes, washed down by brimming cups of whiskey punch, concocted with due regard to the Irish recipe. First, put in the sugar, then the whiskey, and be sure not to forget that every drop of water added spoils the punch.

CHARLES RICHARD WELD, Vacations in Ireland, 1857

Last Monday we dined at Mr Forde's, three miles from hence, a very pleasant place and capable of being made a very fine one; there is more wood than is common in this country, and a fine lake of water with very pretty meadows. The house is situated on the side of a hill, and looks down on his woods and water. The house is not a very good one, but very well fill'd; for he has *ten children*, the youngest about 10 years old,—but that's a *moderate family* to some in *this country*. In the afternoon came in two ladies who had been to see me at Dr Mathews's and missing me followed. One is a Mrs Annesly . . . she is daughter to my Lord Tyrone, such another slatternly ignorant hoyden I never saw, and the worst of it is she is very good-humoured, but *will be familiar*: her husband is very like the Duke of Bedford, and well enough. The other lady is a Mrs Baylis, a handsome sprightly woman, well behaved, with a little dash of a fine lady. Her husband, a genteel agreeable man, brother to Sir Nicholas Baylis, that married the Paget, a clergyman very well esteemed in the neighbourhood. On Tuesday the Fordes dined here; and on Wednesday Mr and Mrs Mathews of Newcastle, about six miles from hence. The whole family of the Fordes are religious, worthy people. On Friday we dined at Newcastle at Mr Mathews's: it is situated at the foot of a range of mountains so high that they are at top seldom free from clouds, and the water has made a winding channel and falls down in a cascade; the main ocean bounds them on one side and is so near them that the spray of the sea wets them as they stand at the hall-door. On the other hand of them are hills, fine meadows, winding rivers, and a variety of pretty objects for so bare a country of trees, though on the side of the mountains there are scattering shrubby woods which make the view pleasant. This country is famous for the goat's whey; and at the season for drinking it, which is summer, a great deal of company meet for that purpose, and there are little huts built up for their reception, and they have music and balls and cards, and happy are the family at Newcastle when that season comes, for there are thirteen sons and daughters, most of them never out of that part of the country. Mr Mathews is an attorney, has a very good fortune, is a good sort of man; his wife a sensible agreeable woman, and has brought up all her children extremely well—they are as decent and as healthy a family as ever I saw; and to make up the company, at the head of them are placed both Mr and Mrs Mathews's mothers; old Mrs Mathews is eighty-seven years of age, and the most venerable fine figure I ever saw, and as apprehensive as a woman of five-and-twenty. A lady that went to see her this summer found her darning fine cambrick; her hearing is a little impaired.

Mrs DELANEY, *Life and Correspondence of Mrs Delaney*, 1758

I must tell you of the Irish Play to which I went on Friday night . . . I thought Diarmud and Grania a strange mixture of saga and modern French situations, George Moore and Yeats were palpable throughout. Biblical terms were not shrunk from to describe the progress of the emotions of Grania who was excessively French in her loves. In the first act she is on the verge of an enforced marriage to Finn . . . she states her reasons for objecting to this and finally deludes Finn's friend Diarmud into falling in love with her and taking her away from the marriage feast à la Young Lochinvar. The next act is some time afterwards and the really novel position is that she has become tired of Diarmud—I give George Moore some credit for that—Never was anything like her ecstasies of love for him in the first act—she then falls in love with Finn which she might have done in the beginning and saved the writing of the play—and the curtain is Diarmud's discovery of them in howlts and his resolve to go and hunt an enchanted boar which a family witch (a stout lady in a grey tea gown and a conversational English accent) has prophesied is to be the death of him. Diarmud is carried in to make dying speeches to Finn and Grania and to be carried off to a funeral march with Grania striking attitudes all over the place . . . if this is the lofty purity of the Irish drama I am mystified . . . I saw Maud Gonne at the Play and thought her looks terrific . . . Yeats was with her in a box all the time except when he was with Augusta . . . I never looked his way and I daresay the Irish Literary Revival was quite disastrously unaware of my presence in the shades at the back.

'Martin Ross' to Edith Somerville, 1904; quoted in Gifford Lewis, *The World of the Irish R.M.*, 1985

What was happening in Dublin did not really affect the social life of the Ascendancy as a whole, which continued to be based on local events such as Tramore Races, Lough Derg Regatta or the Annual Cork Industrial Exhibition which in 1912 was opened by Lady Bandon in the presence of a large gathering of county ladies. During that same summer, there was an even more fashionable gathering at the Annual Flower Show and Fête at Knocklofty near Clonmel, the home of Lord and Lady Donoughmore, who had a house party for the occasion as did their neighbours the Duchess of St Albans and the Bagwells of Marlfield. In North Cork, there was Mallow Lawn Tennis Tournament, at which the General Commanding the Forces and Lord and Lady Listowel were present; the tennis-playing girls, who were partnered by young officers from the local garrison, included the daughters of Sir Timothy O'Brien.

Tennis in the summer months provided the daughters of the Ascendancy with as good an opportunity of meeting and attracting young men as hunting did in the winter. 'The girls there were all in short, exceedingly tight white dresses' Lady Talbot de Malahide reported of a County Dublin tennis party in the summer of 1913. 'Nothing of the human form was left to the imagination.' They were as bad as Joan Grubb, the young daughter of a Tipperary

County family, who followed the example of Mrs Sadleir-Jackson and rode astride. As an alternative to tennis, mixed hockey was becoming increasingly popular. At various country houses in County Kilkenny, notably Kilmurry, home of the watercolourist, Miss Mildred Butler, and her sister, it became customary for mixed hockey matches to be followed by dances. The teams would retire upstairs for hot baths and to enable the girls to change into something more alluring; they would then dance to the piano until about eight o'clock, with tea, sandwiches and scones for refreshments.

The chief Ascendancy game was, of course, cricket, in which girls could not participate except by looking decorative among the spectators, having tea with the teams and perhaps dancing with them in the evenings during country house cricket weeks. Cricket in Ireland continued to flourish, the rising stars from the younger generation being Lady Gregory's artist son Robert, Thomas Jameson and two sons of cricketing fathers, George Colthurst and Bob Fowler, son of Captain Robert Fowler of Rahinston in County Meath. As a boy at Eton in 1910, Bob Fowler had been the hero of 'Fowler's Match', the most famous Eton and Harrow match ever played, snatching victory from the Harrow team—which included Thomas Jameson and also Harold Alexander from County Tyrone, a younger brother of the Earl of Caledon—by taking eight wickets for nine runs. Such was his instant fame that a congratulatory telegram addressed to his mother as 'Mrs Fowler, London' was delivered to her that same evening.

Among the patrons of Irish cricket, Lord Bandon and Horace Plunkett's nephew Lord Dunsany—who was now making a name for himself as a poet and playwright—had been joined in 1907 by the wealthy bachelor Stanley Cochrane, son of a baronet whose family fortunes were founded on the manufacture of mineral waters. At Woodbrook, his country house a few miles outside Dublin in County Wicklow, he had made a ground regardless of expense; he would bring over the best English, Australian and South African teams to play here against his own eleven.

MARK BENCE-JONES, *The Twilight of the Ascendancy*, 1987

In late summer, when there were visitors, we used to sit out on the steps in the sun, walk in the demesne or in the country round, drive to Bridgetown to bathe in the Blackwater, drive to Youghal to bathe in the sea. In wet weather we played deck tennis or french cricket up in the Long Room. In the evenings we played *vingt-et-un* at Henry IV's card-tables in the library, or paper games in the half-ring of chairs round the fire. Lamps and candles continued to light our evenings up to two years ago, when I put electricity in.

ELIZABETH BOWEN, *Bowen's Court*, 1942

The green space runs parallel to the whole length of Nassau Street; trees are planted along the low wall, considerably surmounted by a railing, so that passers-by in the tram-cars have the view. About a third of the length is reserved as the Fellows' Garden, pleasantly planted and gardened. The rest, during daylight, is open to the public and, as *Murray's Guide* says, 'devoted to athletic purposes'. I should think it was. Here is a cricket ground, on to which gentlemen of the College can step out straight from their rooms—not, as at Oxford, needing to travel a mile or more. And it is not only the College that profits: Dublin has been able to see there, off and on during all my life, all the most famous performers from W. G. Grace down. More than once some lusty man has lifted a ball to leg and broken a window in Nassau Street: indeed it sticks in my memory that in one of the first Australian teams, when Spofforth was dreaded as the demon bowler, a handsome giant, Bonner, hit a ball off some Irish bowler to a measured distance of 175 yards. But cricket is only one of the games: Rugby football is to be seen there at its very best. Only on rare occasions has a Dublin team been able to match the English universities on the cricket field, but at football they have always held their own.

In the summer term come what used to be one of Dublin's great events— the College Races; though perhaps in the new Dublin, where Trinity counts for less than it did, these athletic sports are not so well attended. One old feature of them has dropped almost out of memory—the walking races of seven miles, which champions used to cover, fair heel and toe, within the hour—pursuing their laborious way round and round the green space, while other events were being decided within it.

But any day in summer I know few things so agreeable in any great town as to enter Trinity by the Lincoln Place Gate, near Westland Row, and stroll along one of the shaded walks through the park, stopping to watch whatever game happens to be in progress; and so out past the long colonnaded front of the Library and through the quadrangles to where close by the main gate women students in their rather becoming caps buzz like bees before a hive: for here is their common-room.—They have all to be outside gates by six o'clock, though.

STEPHEN GWYNN, Dublin Old and New, 1938

Peasant Quality

for Trevor Peters

At last they've started to sing
in this hideous Bloody Foreland pub.
All the gaelic speakers are swaying,
drunk as earls . . . 'Give us the . . . (Gaelic hub bub . . .)'

More alcoholics in Ireland than anywhere.
The greatest view in the world. It's a sin
the windows are misted. I know I'm drunk, but I swear
I can see nothing but the sun blazing in.

The Man with the hat falls on the floor.
Their fields are full of stones
when they want bread and a job and so much more
than TVs and cinemas and telephones . . .

but they're laughing now, every man a star.
Possessed by three unities they will never escape—
ignorance, poverty, hate—they definitely are
stylish, passionate and in great shape.

JAMES SIMMONS, *West Strand Visions*, 1974

We have gone to the movies to see Ann Blyth, not to meditate, although meditation comes surprisingly easily and is pleasant enough in this fairground of lighthearted gaiety, where bog farmers, peat cutters, and fishermen offer cigarettes to and accept chocolates from seductively smiling ladies who drive around during the day in great cars, where the retired colonel chats with the postman about the merits and demerits of East Indians. Here classless society has become reality. It is a pity, though, that the air gets so stale: perfume, lipstick, cigarettes, the bitter smell of peat from clothes, even the music from the phonograph records seems to smell: it exudes the raw eroticism of the thirties, and the seats, splendidly upholstered in red velvet—if you are lucky you get one where the springs are not yet broken—these seats, probably deemed elegant in 1880 in Dublin (they must have seen Sullivan's operas, perhaps also Yeats, Synge, and O'Casey, and early Shaw), these seats smell the way old velvet smells that resists the harshness of the vacuum cleaner, the savagery of the brush—and the theatre is an unfinished new building, still without proper ventilation.

HEINRICH BÖLL, *Irish Journal*, 1957, trans. Leila Vennewitz

I always thought the Luxor the most exotic name ever. It suggested luxury, warmth, sex, Eastern promise. It was an occasion of sin and the priests looked on it that way. Men sat one side, women sat the other. But up on the screen were the false gods of Hollywood and we worshipped them faithfully. But now the place is a ruin. The roof leaks, the seats rot, the damp cuts your nostrils. Old cans for rolls of film lie rooted to the ground with rust. The rust has eaten through the tin. In the box-office, inches of rot and water lie on the floor. The ticket machine is still in position. Tickets, 2/6, 3/6 and 4/-. The cinema staff who were the last to work the place scrawled their names on the box-office wall. One person wrote: '11/1/'78. I hope you feel proud for closing down the last place of entertainment in the town.'

SHANE CONNAUGHTON, *A Border Diary*, 1995

Newry had two cinemas, the Frontier and the Imperial, with admission prices of 4d., 6d. and 9d. In each of them there was a Saturday matinee to which we were admitted for 2d. Those were the days of the great silent epics, of Tom Mix and Buck Jones, Eddie Polo, Charlie Chaplin, Clive Brook, Harold Lloyd, Buster Keaton and many other pioneers of universal popular entertainment. In the newsreels we watched the closing stages of the Civil War in the Free State; the new Irish Army trundling its small cannons behind lorries, moving from town to town in armoured vehicles not unlike those in which the Black and Tans had travelled, spreading its hold on the country and ultimately forcing the Irregulars to give up the struggle.

PATRICK SHEA, *Voices and the Sound of Drums*, 1981

Cycling to Dublin

PULLING the dead sun's weight through County Meath,
We cycled through the knotted glass of afternoon,
Aware of the bright fog in the narrow slot of breath,
And the cycles' rhyming, coughing croon.

'O hurry to Dublin, to Dublin's fair city,
Where colleens, fair colleens are ever so pretty,
O linger no longer in lumbering languor,
Gallop the miles, the straight-backed miles without number.'

We were the Northmen, hard with hoarded words on tongue,
Driven down by home disgust to the broad lands and rich talk,
To the country of poets and pubs and cow-dung
Spouting and sprouting from every stalk. . . .

'O hurry to Dublin, to Dublin's fair city,
Where colleens, fair colleens are ever so pretty,
O linger no longer in lumbering languor,
Gallop the miles, the straight-backed miles without number.'

ROBERT GREACEN, *One Recent Evening*, 1944

I have said that women were in short supply, and so indeed they were; not, of course, in the city of Dublin and its hinterland, for, as has been often enough remarked, nature has blessed the island of the Gael with a plentiful rainfall and a plenitude of personable females. The shortage lay rather in the circles in which most of those present spent their leisured, in fact their waking hours. To the number of those Gaels whose women would no more have ventured into such circles than they would into an orgy of a more overtly sexual order must be added the number who had no wish to bring them; and to them again must be added the army of beggars who could under no circumstances have maintained a fancy woman of their own, independent of the general supply, and who quite properly refused to give up their leisure in the probably futile hope of obtaining one. Some of these beggars were respectably married and supported large broods of children on the proceeds of their craft, but among them, as among the rest of the native stock in general, the Celto-Iberian order of things prevailed: the woman closeted in an atmosphere of domestic fecundity, while the man went abroad in search of converse, social and otherwise.

In short, on this part of the sea-coast of bohemia, if bohemia it was, a heterogenous collection of males had been washed up with an insufficient supply of women. That there was difficulty in recruitment from the outside may be attributed not only to the innate respectability or chastity of the females of the race, but to their fastidiousness as well. The general atmosphere was one of gurrierdom. If the general atmosphere had been one of unrestrained art, girls might have been attracted in greater numbers, but the atmosphere was rather one of thievery and chicanery, modified by art and frequently masquerading as it, not the sort of atmosphere for which a well-brought up girl who had any sense at all would abandon her bourgeois prejudices.

ANTHONY CRONIN, The Life of Riley, 1964

She went out, and in a few moments was part of the crowd which passes and repasses nightly from the Rotunda up the broad pathways of Sackville Street, across O'Connell Bridge, up Westmoreland Street, past Trinity College, and on through the brilliant lights of Grafton Street to the Fusiliers' Arch at the entrance to St Stephen's Green Park. Here from half-past seven o'clock in the evening youthful Dublin marches in joyous procession. Sometimes bevies of young girls dance by, each a giggle incarnate. A little distance behind these a troop of young men follow stealthily and critically. They will be acquainted and more or less happily paired before the Bridge is reached. But generally the movement is in couples. Appointments, dating from the previous night, have filled the streets with happy and careless boys and girls—they are not exactly courting, they are enjoying the excitement of fresh acquaintance; old conversation is here poured into new bottles, old jokes have the freshness of infancy, every one is animated, and polite to no one but his partner; the people they meet and pass and those who overtake and pass them are all subjects for their wit and scorn, while they, in turn, furnish a moment's amusement and conversation to each succeeding couple. Constantly there are stoppages when very high-bred introductions result in a re-distribution of the youngsters. As they move apart the words 'To-morrow night', or 'Thursday', or 'Friday' are called laughingly back, showing that the late partner is not to be lost sight of utterly; and then the procession begins anew.

JAMES STEPHENS, *The Charwoman's Daughter*, 1912

from *The Northern Athens: A Satirical Poem*

XLI

In EASTER times, and all the town let loose,
What prancing, rattling, driving it along!
When tailors' prentices deny their goose,
To cut a dash, and thread the mazy throng—
Cars, tandems, noddies, curricles, in use—
NORTH-STREET and ANN-STREET wedg'd with old and young;
Best bibs and tuckers flaunting in the sun—
Men full of whiskey, maidens full of fun.

XLII

The Long Bridge rattles, and the LAGAN quivers
Beneath the car-borne multitudes that pass,
Threatening to dash each vehicle to shivers,
And drown the unsuspecting souls *en masse*—
A bridge the vilest o'er the first of rivers—
Unworthy cities of *Athenian* class:
But folks will brave it; as of old, the ocean,
And Egypt's plagues, some sought the land of Goshen.

XLIII

To HOLYWOOD th' elated wanderers bend,
The *el dorado* of each bounding hope,
The too short day's too fleeting hours to spend,
And give to pleasure, pleasure's liveliest scope:
To PEGGY BARCLAY'S, troops of travellers wend,
Or straight to CARRICK for the day elope,
The lithe of limb the CAVE HILL's steep ascending,
And brains of such as have them sent a-mending.

XLIV

Bang up the rattling cars and tandems fly,
Through rut or dust, in sunshine or in showers,
Hearts taking hue and colour from the sky—
Gloom'd with the cloud, or sunn'd with all the flowers;
Smart girls, with love and laughter in each eye,
Like Houri peeping forth from GIEL's bowers,
Whose air, fine forms, and elegance outvie
Venus de Medici, although, to-morrow,
Unseen, without all MILL-FIELD's houffs ye harrow.

ANON., 1826

Every true Dubliner will agree that pubs have counted for more than clubs in the social life of many who left the deepest mark on the life of Dublin—from Clarence Mangan, whose bust stands in Stephen's Green, down to Tom Kettle, whose bust now makes a pendant to face Mangan's. Kettle, wit, orator, essayist and poet, was the delight of all companies—in the House of Commons, or the mess of the Dublin Fusiliers, with whom he met his death on the Somme, but most of all in the little Dublin hotels or bar-rooms which journalists and their congeners frequent. They might lie as far towards Stephen's Green as one of the side issues off Grafton Street; they might be on the line of O'Connell Street, or of Dame Street. I associate Kettle most with the Dolphin's smoking-room; but he might as readily have been met in the Moira, in Trinity Street, a favourite haunt of James Winder Good, the best journalist I ever knew in Ireland and the friendliest human being. Or at 'The Bailey' in Duke Street, where Arthur Griffith was a constant diner—the most powerful political writer that Dublin has known since the days of Swift, and the one whose writing produced most consequences. Griffith has the best right to be regarded as the father of Sinn Féin.

STEPHEN GWYNN, *Dublin Old and New*, 1938

We drank wine with our supper and then as usual The Body took too much and got obstreperous and started to shout. He rolled the menu up and bellowed through it:

'Up the Republic, Up Noel Browne, Up Castro, Up me.'

Eamonn was frightened and left the table. He never returned. Being a Pioneer, he did not understand the happy madness which drink could induce in others.

At two o'clock, just when everybody was getting very merry and the band players had begun to toss paper hats around, Baba and I brought The Body home. He was too drunk to drive so we left his blue van there and hired a taxi. We had no idea where he lived. It's funny that we should have known him for a year but did not know where he lived. Dublin is like that. We knew his local pub but not his house. We brought him home and put him on the horsehair sofa in Joanna's drawing-room.

'Baba, Caithleen, I wan't'tell you something, you're two noble women, two noble women, and Parnell was a proud man as proud as trod the ground, and a proud man's a lovely man, so pass the bottle round. What about a little drink, waiter, waiter . . .' He waved a pound note in the air, still thinking he was at the dance.

'Have a sleep,' Baba said, and she put out the light. His voice faded with it and within a minute he was breathing heavily.

We knew that we would have to be up at half six to get The Body out of the house before Joanna's alarm went off at seven.

'We've just three hours' sleep,' Baba said, as she unhooked my dress and helped me out of it. A new boned brassière had made red welts on my skin.

'We'll sue,' she said when she saw the welts. We went to bed without washing our faces, and when I wakened, the pancake make-up felt like mud on my face.

'Oh God,' I said to Baba, as I heard The Body shouting downstairs: 'Girls, les girls, there's no "Gents", there's no bloody service here—where do I *go*?'

We both ran out to the landing to shut him up but Joanna had got there before us.

'Jesus meets his afflicted mother,' The Body said as Joanna came down the stairs towards him in her big red nightdress, with her grey hair in a plait down her back.

'Thief, thief,' she shouted, and before we even knew it she had pressed the button of the small fire-extinguisher that was fixed to the wall at the end of the stairs and trained the liquid on him.

'I want police,' she yelled, and he was struggling to explain things to her but he couldn't make himself heard.

'Stop that bloody thing, he's our friend,' Baba said, running downstairs.

The Body was covered with white, sticky liquid which looked like hair shampoo, and his dress-shirt was drenched. His wet hair fell over his face in oily curls.

'He's our friend,' Baba said, sadly. 'God protect us from our friends.'

'You call him a friend, hah?' Joanna said. He put his hand on the banister and proceeded to go upstairs. Joanna blocked the way.

'I want to see a man about a dog,' he said, wiping the wet off his face with a handkerchief.

'What dog? I have no dog, I say,' she shouted, but he pushed past her.

'Gustav, Gustav,' she called, but I knew that cowardly Gustav would not come out.

'Jesus falls the first time,' The Body chanted as he tripped on a tear in the brown linoleum.

EDNA O'BRIEN, *The Lonely Girl*, 1962

A mile or thereabouts out of Omeath on the Carlingford Road there was an open-air shrine popularly known as Calvary: its official name was Mount St Carmel. There was an altar, and the field was laid out as the Stations of the Cross. At every station there was an image of the Agony, culminating in the Crucifixion. It was a standard trip to make. You could walk, if you had a mind to, or go by horse and jaunting car, a jollier method and pleasant on a sunny day. The jaunting car held four people, not counting the driver, two on either side. While the men were drinking in the public houses up from the jetty, the women and children made the little pilgrimage to Calvary. The Stations of the Cross are a rare devotion now but were common in my day: women, especially, did the stations in the few minutes before Mass. At each of the fourteen stations you recited the appropriate phrase: the first station, Jesus is condemned to death; the second station, Jesus is stripped of his garments. The first time I heard the word 'afflicted' was at the stations: Jesus meets his afflicted mother. Jesus falls the first time. If a priest were conducting the service, he called out the title of the station—Veronica wipes our Lord's face—and asked the congregation to 'consider' some aspect of the event. At the end of the consideration he said: 'I love Thee, Jesus, my love above all things. I repent of my whole heart for having offended Thee. Never permit me to separate myself from Thee again. Grant that I may love Thee always, and then do with me what Thou wilt.' Was it the Our Father or the Hail Mary that followed, when priest and congregation knelt down? Isn't it odd that I can't remember that detail while I recall easily the ritual that preceded it? Catholic churches still have the fourteen stations on the walls, but I haven't seen anyone doing the stations for years now.

DENIS DONOGHUE, *Warrenpoint*, 1991

One is small and dark and round as a pudding, a very tasty pudding. The other tall and redheaded and you'd see her if you closed your eyes and for a long time after, and that evening on the bridge she says to me: Why don't you dance? I'd like to dance with you. I fancy you.

Admittedly, that's flattering. But somewhat to the amazement of Peter, who has never heard the story before, I tell her about the broken ankle that has never properly set; limp a little to prove it too as we climb the stairs and the beat of the music grows louder. It's a lie, not the music but the spiel about the ankle. Because even from Peter I have to conceal that I know as much about the theory of dancing as he does, and as for the practice . . . Well in that as in other things I may be a disgrace to my family, for while they are all elegant dancers I'm no better at it than the renowned Clarence McFadden who, in a song my mother used to sing, went to a dancing-academy to study the waltz: One, two, three, come balance like me, you're a fairy but you have your faults. When your right-foot is lazy your left one is crazy, but don't be unaisy I'll larn you to waltz.

And in the summer Gaelic College in the Rosses of Donegal the whirls and thuds of the dusty stampedes of the Irish dances, the Walls of Limerick, the Siege of Ennis, the High Caul Cap, have simply made me dizzy, when I had the nerve to join them at all: so that my talks with the good man who never tells me why he doesn't sleep with his wife are for me a refuge and a haven. They keep me from being out on that there waxy floor making a bloody fool of myself. On which dangerous floor the daughters and the boy friends go round and round like seraphim on the wing and sway backward and forward like the saplings bent double by the gale when the wood is in trouble on Wenlock Edge.

BENEDICT KIELY, 'Your Left Foot is Crazy', in A Letter to Peachtree, 1987

Although her father still called her a girl, Bridie was thirty-six. She was tall and strong: the skin of her fingers and her palms were stained, and harsh to touch. The labour they'd experienced had found its way into them, as though juices had come out of vegetation and pigment out of soil: since childhood she'd torn away the rough scotch grass that grew each spring among her father's mangolds and sugar beet; since childhood she'd harvested potatoes in August, her hands daily rooting in the ground she loosened and turned. Wind had toughened the flesh of her face, sun had browned it; her neck and nose were lean, her lips touched with early wrinkles.

But on Saturday nights Bridie forgot the scotch grass and the soil. In different dresses she cycled to the dance-hall, encouraged to make the journey by her father. 'Doesn't it do you good, girl?' he'd say, as though he imagined she begrudged herself the pleasure. 'Why wouldn't you enjoy yourself?' She'd cook him his tea and then he'd settle down with the wireless, or maybe a Wild West novel. In time, while still she danced, he'd stoke the fire up and hobble his way upstairs to bed.

The dance-hall, owned by Mr Justin Dwyer, was miles from anywhere, a lone building by the roadside with treeless boglands all around and a gravel expanse in front of it. On pink pebbled cement its title was painted in an azure blue that matched the depth of the background shade yet stood out well, unfussily proclaiming *The Ballroom of Romance*. Above these letters four coloured bulbs—in red, green, orange and mauve—were lit at appropriate times, an indication that the evening rendezvous was open for business. Only the façade of the building was pink, the other walls being a more ordinary grey. And inside, except for pink swing-doors, everything was blue.

WILLIAM TREVOR, 'The Ballroom of Romance', in *The Ballroom of Romance and Other Stories*, 1972

Portumna, Co. Galway. This morning in Portleix we were to have begun a trip to the Comeragh Mountains in Co. Waterford, but since snow could be seen lying on the distant peaks of the mountains in Co. Wicklow we decided to visit the annual point-to-point meeting of the East Galways near Portumna instead. Our route lies due west, through the northern end of Co. Tipperary, pleasant rolling wooded country, with here and there a glimpse of fine estates. Then as Lough Derg and the Shannon come in sight the country becomes even more pleasantly wooded. Here in the west there is no snow, and the weather is typical Irish April, heavy rain-clouds interspersed with bursts of brilliant sunshine. The meeting too is a typical Irish point-to-point; there seems to be very little to distinguish these events, in Co. Down or Galway—except that here the crowd contains perhaps a slightly higher percentage of oddities and 'characters' than would a similar crowd in the North. A gentleman in a top-hat sings like a bird before inviting the crowd to invest in his sweepstake lottery. Then there is the inevitable philanthropist dressed as a jockey who apparently tours the country giving out winners, to a perpetual refrain of 'What did I tell you?' Delightful occupation. Here he is again, as much at home in Galway as he was last year in Co. Antrim, and still moving at his priest-like task. The crowds sway and push; servant-girls from the big houses in the neighbourhood giggle as they lose their sixpences at roulette or spotting the lady. The 'quality' here is to be distinguished by a certain air of genteel shabbiness; ancient riding breeches, dilapidated tweed coats patched at the elbows with leather, almost historical mackintoshes—nobody here seems to have more than ten shillings to bet with, and everybody seems to be happy, all rubbing elbows in a crowd that contains indifferently the most ancient names in Debrett and dilapidated tinkers with no seats to their pants.

DENIS IRELAND, *From the Irish Shore*, 1936

The following afternoon we went riding. I had never been on a horse before. To me the animal smelt of the leather trade. I was surprised to find that horses are warm. I gripped the reins as if they were a life line; I was jellied and bumped by its extraordinary movement. The party began to canter and I was tossed in the air and I got a fixed smile on my face. We arrived in a field to try some jumps. A wicked old trainer shouted bits of advice. I went over one or two gaps and arrived, surprised and askew, but still up. So they tried some more difficult jumps. The party hung about waiting for the slaughter. The animal rose, I fell on its neck, but I did not come off. The stakes were raised; at the next jump the horse and I went to different parts of the sky. I was in the mud. I got up and apologized to the horse, which turned its head away. Afterwards we walked and trotted home; it seemed to take hours. Back in the house, I felt someone had put planks on my legs and turned my buttocks into wooden boxes. So my life as an Irish sportsman and country gentleman came to an end. Still, I had stayed with a baronet. I was snobbish enough to be pleased by that.

I like curious clothes. Back in Dublin I stayed in my riding breeches, bought at a cheap shop in Dublin, and wore them for weeks after, as an enjoyable symbol of the Irish habit of life, until someone tactfully suggested I looked like a stable boy.

V. S. PRITCHETT, *Midnight Oil*, 1971

And, yet, it is a lovely, lovely place. Its slums, that have a hot verminous smell, indescribable and unique—walk down Millard Street of a hot summer day and you get the pure bouquet of it—come back to the memory before everything else with a geyser-gush of nostalgia. Cork's poor are its kings. In these ambition has not sharpened the claw, and passion lives at blood-heat. The shawled women and girls (are they passing away into what they used to call, derisively, 'hatty wans'?) are magnificent. Observe the coal-quay kids—often dressed in a costume, especially a Sunday costume, that I have seen nowhere else—purple stockings, fawny boots, halfway-up the calf, sometimes a bright velvet cap, golden tasselled, reflecting the half-barbaric love of colour that one used to see in the brilliance of the petticoats and shawls, and in the many half-inch-thick finger-rings and dangling earrings of the mothers roaring over the fish-crates. Note the men, in my youth, straightened by bouts in the North Cork Militia or the Munster Fusiliers, swaggering like sergeant-majors. In all of these there is the principle of life at its full.

SEAN O'FAOLAIN, *An Irish Journey*, 1940

The doorman in black evening dress tore our tickets in two and we went out of the day into the artificial light of the dancefloor. The band was playing as I entered. The men and women faced each other across an empty floor, where three or four couples, dancers who had gone to dancing schools, were displaying their steps. As the floor gradually filled, those with less confidence took courage. When the floor was filled all dancing was reduced to one happy universal shuffle. As each dance was called there was a charge of men across the floor towards the prettier girls, who'd turn to the plainer sisters of their group with the formal, 'Excuse me, please.' The girls who hadn't been asked to dance then took step after step of humiliation back to the wall as the ranks about them thinned, before finally sitting down on the long bench to watch out the dance.

'Will you dance, please?' I asked a girl and she nodded and turned to the girls standing with her to say, 'Excuse me, please.'

'Do you like these dances?' I remember the inane awkwardness of all dancehall conversations.

'Not very much. I hardly ever come.'

'Where do you like to dance then?'

'In the holidays. Bundoran.'

'You must be near there then?'

She named where she was from. It was in the heart of the mountains from where my mother had come. I could see past the ballroom to the girl with the emery stone in the hayfields on the side of those iron mountains as we jostled our way round the floor. I learned she'd come out of those mountains the same way as she had come by a county scholarship instead of the old King's to the Marist convent in Carrick and on to the girls' Training College in Carysfort.

She started to ask me about my path to the College, which was hardly different from her own.

The quickstep entered its last interval. I grew nervous. I didn't want her to disappear back into the band of girls. I mightn't get to dance with her again.

JOHN McGAHERN, *The Leavetaking*, 1974

from *The Midnight Court*

'Not to detain you here all day
I married the girl without more delay,
And took my share in the fun that followed.
There was plenty for all and nothing borrowed.
Be fair to me now! There was no one slighted;
The beggarmen took the road delighted;
The clerk and mummers were elated;
The priest went home with his pocket weighted.
The lamps were lit, the guests arrived;
The supper was ready, the drink was plied;
The fiddles were flayed, and, the night advancing,
The neighbours joined in the sport and dancing.

'A pity to God I didn't smother
When first I took the milk from my mother,
Or any day I ever broke bread

Before I brought that woman to bed!
For though everyone talked of her carouses
As a scratching post of the publichouses
That as sure as ever the glasses would jingle
Flattened herself to married and single,
Admitting no modesty to mention,
I never believed but 'twas all invention.
They added, in view of the life she led,
I might take to the roads and beg my bread,
But I took it for talk and hardly minded—
Sure, a man like me could never be blinded!—
And I smiled and nodded and off I tripped
Till my wedding night when I saw her stripped,
And knew too late that this was no libel
Spread in the pub by some jealous rival—
By God, 'twas a fact, and well-supported:
I was a father before I started!

'So there I was in the cold daylight,
A family man after one short night!
The women around me, scolding, preaching,
The wife in bed and the baby screeching.
I stirred the milk as the kettle boiled
Making a bottle to give the child;
All the old hags at the hob were cooing
As if they believed it was all my doing—
Flattery worse than ever you heard:
"Glory and praise to our blessed Lord,
Though he came in a hurry, the poor little creature,
He's the spit of his da in every feature." '

BRIAN MERRIMAN, *The Midnight Court* (c.1780),
trans. Frank O'Connor, 1945

Hoary with History

The whole landscape a manuscript
We had lost the skill to read . . .

JOHN MONTAGUE,
'The Rough Field'

Much blood has been shed round Mallow bridge. This was Desmond
territory: just inside the present Castle demesne gates stands the magnificent shell of the castle built by the Earl of Desmond, lost in the Earl's
rebellion, fortified by the English, granted by Queen Elizabeth, with the
manor of Mallow, to a Sir Thomas Norris, burnt by Lord Castlehaven
and the Confederates. Sir Thomas Norris's heiress married a Sir John
Jephson; the Jephson Norris family put up the present Castle, Jacobean
in manner, on a lawn commanding the Desmond shell. The demesne,
looking at Nagles Mountains, runs down the river below the bridge.

ELIZABETH BOWEN, *Bowen's Court*

Kinsale is, as we say sometimes in the south, 'crawling' with history. It must
go back to Norman times at least. There is high up on the hills to the west,
over the old town, a field, and in that field a protuberance which is the
remains of a far earlier religious settlement. But for every Irishman the word
means only one phrase—1601—the Spanish landing under Don Juan del
Aquila—the hosting of O'Neill and O'Donnell from the north of Ireland—
the all-but-last stand of the old medieval Gaelic Ireland against the new
power of the Renaissance—the ten weeks siege of Mountjoy and Carew—the
fatal and fateful battle on Christmas morning, and then the 'flight of the
earls'—that phrase which rings in the mind of Ireland the knell of its ancient
order.

There is hardly a field about this old town which does not, for that siege
and battle, still the mind with memories. Here in this dyke, overrun by brambles, the Irish dead were piled. There a farm carries the word of 'slaughter' in
its Gaelic name: *Cnocanair*. If you go for a walk here with a local inhabitant,
he will, as casually as inevitably interrupt the conversation, as you pass from

vantage point to vantage point over the rolling hills, to indicate where O'Donnell approached the town, where the English trenches lay, where Carew encamped. One picks (even still) musket bullets out of the ground. The impress of that siege and battle is as fresh in Kinsale as if it were only yesterday that the Irish burst on the English camp at dawn and found to their dismay the troops ready and waiting. I spent a whole day walking the hills with a friend who has served in several campaigns; a soldier to his marrowbones. His expert elucidation made me feel the thing come to life in field after field: especially so when he said, 'But it is in winter one should walk here. The battle was fought in winter. Then the trees would be bare and we would see the terrain just as they saw it, when the morning broke.'

It all reminded me of Egdon Heath in its suffusion of association with times past. This is rare in Ireland. Our history has seemed to fade from the land like old writing from parchment. Traditional memory is broken. Our monuments are finest when oldest, but then so old that their echoes have died away. The *pietas* which is so cherished and nourished in other countries, has here an inadequate number of actual moulds to hold it. National emotion is a wild sea-spray that evaporates like a religion without a ritual. We are moved by ghosts. Something powerful and precious hangs in the air that holds us like a succubus; but what it is we can hardly define because we have so few concrete things that express it. Only in the most rare and most precious places throughout the entire land is there this urn-burial of Kinsale, where the ashes may still be revered in the very vessel which still holds them before our eyes. Aughrim is another such place. The fields of Wexford. Some corners of Limerick city. Derry, Killala, Ballina, Sligo. None of these has the monumental significance of Kinsale, the sense of the die cast, the doom of the decisive hour. Kinsale was one of the decisive battles of these islands. To this day it carries the import which fell on it that bitter winter morning over three hundred years ago.

SEAN O'FAOLAIN, *An Irish Journey*, 1940

History Walks were rarer than Geography, perhaps because they feared to disturb our local nest of pismires. History lay about us in our infancy, with many levels, but only one stratum open. They did not have to explain to us why our new Cathedral had been built on a higher hill. We explored our ancient rival when we ran footloose through town. We marvelled at its echoing emptiness, the rotting flags of Imperial wars. The roll call in the side chapel of the Royal Irish Fuseliers might have taught us something; O's and Macs mingled in death with good Proddy names, Hamilton, Hewitt, Taylor, Acheson.

Instead we ran down the curling, cobbled hill, giggling with guilt. Doomed as any Armada, the lost city of Ard Macha coiled in upon itself, whorl upon whorl, a broken aconite. Layer upon layer had gone to its making, from Cuchulain to St Patrick, from fleet-footed Macha to Primate Robinson's gaggle of Georgian architects. But the elegance of the Mall was of no avail against simple-minded sectarianism; Armagh, a maimed capital, a damaged pearl.

We sensed this as we sifted through the shards in the little County Museum. Bustled around the glass cases by Curly Top, we halted before a Yeoman's coat, alerted by our party song, 'The Croppy Boy'. And we read about the battle of Diamond Hill between 'Peep-o'-Day Boys' and Catholic Defenders which led to the founding of the Orange Order at Loughgall, a canker among the apple blossoms.

We did not discuss this in our History Class, which now dealt with the origins of the First World War, from the shot in Sarajevo. It did crop up in RK, Religious Knowledge, where the Dean warned us against the dangers of Freemasonry. A Catholic could never become King of England or President of the United States; everywhere the black face of Protestantism barred the way to good Catholic boys. Amongst the cannon on the Mall the Protestant boys played cricket, or kicked a queer shaped ball like a pear. According to my Falls pal Protestant balls bounced crooked as the Protestants themselves. One day that banter would stop when a shot rang out on the Cathedral Road.

JOHN MONTAGUE, *Time in Armagh*, 1993

You get all the confusion of Irish history in a few acres. First St Fiachra, then the Norman Forrestals, then, overshadowing them, the Shees, English you would suppose. But no, they are Irish Uí Seaghdha from Kerry, who anglicized their name and their habits with immense rapidity and success in Tudor times. Robert Shee had allied himself with Piers Butler, eighth Earl of Ormond, and had been killed in 1493 in Tipperary fighting against the O'Briens of Munster at the head of a hundred Kilkennymen. The Shees were one of the ten great merchant families of Kilkenny, the other nine all being English. Robert Shee's son, Richard, had become Sovereign of Kilkenny; his grandson, Sir Richard, had been educated at Gray's Inn, became legal adviser to Queen Elizabeth's friend Black Tom Butler, the tenth Earl of Ormond, and when Ormond became Lord Treasurer of Ireland, was made Deputy Treasurer. He and his family acquired great wealth and many houses in Kilkenny town and county and had built the Alms House in which Standish O'Grady had established his knitting industry and permanent craft exhibition. Sir Richard's son, Lucas, married the daughter of Lord Mountgarret, whose other daughter married the eleventh Earl of Ormond. Lucas's son, Robert, when the Civil War broke out, persuaded his uncle Mountgarret to accept the presidency of the Confederation. The royalist parliament was held in the Shee mansion in Parliament Street which till 1865 stood where the gates of the Market now are.

The Shees were an urbane and cultivated family who wrote for each other long epitaphs in elegiacs and hexameters, which are more pagan than Christian. '*Homo bulla* ... (Man is a bubble) ...':

> *Nec genus antiquum nec honesta opulentia rerum*
> *Nec necis imperium lingua diserta fugit*
> *Nec fidei fervor nec religionis avitae*
> *Cultus ab extremo liberat ense nihil.*

> (Neither ancient lineage, nor honourably
> amassed wealth nor eloquence can evade the
> stern summons of death, nor can fervent faith
> and the practice of the religion of our fathers
> reprieve us from the sword of doom.)

Then a prayer is asked for a speedy passage to Heaven, supposing, that is to say, heaven exists:

> *Si tamen haec mors est transitus ad superos ...*

Elias Shee, from whose tomb in St Mary's, Kilkenny, I have taken these five lines, is described by Richard Stanyhurst as 'born in Kilkenny, sometime scholar of Oxford, a gentleman of passing good wit, a pleasing conceited companion, full of mirth without gall. He wrote in English divers sonnets.' I do not think the Shees or the nine other Kilkenny merchant families, all Catholics, all dispossessed by Cromwell, could be considered 'priest-ridden'. Had fate treated them more kindly, would they, like the wealthy Flemish burghers, have become patrons of the arts and sciences; would they have produced their own Erasmus and formed eventually the nucleus of a proud and independent Anglo-Irish civilization? Elias Shee was described by his sorrowing relatives as '*orbi Britannico lumen*', a light to the British world, because of his wit, his learning, his breeding, but his family remained conscious of their Irish descent, calling themselves after Cromwellian times O'Shee, when more prudent families were dropping their Os and Macs.

Yet I cannot feel very confident of any such Anglo-Irish development in the seventeenth century. Is there, perhaps, as AE (George Russell) suggested, 'some sorcery in the Irish mind' rebelling against any peaceful and prosperous fusion, some intense pride of race?

HUBERT BUTLER, 'The Auction', 1952, in *Grandmother and Wolfe Tone*, 1990

This is a country of ruins. Lordly or humble, military or domestic, standing up with furious gauntness, like Kilcolman, or shelving weakly into the soil, ruins feature the landscape—uplands or river valleys—and make a ghostly extra quarter to towns. They give clearings in woods, reaches of mountain or sudden turns of a road a meaning and pre-inhabited air. Ivy grapples them; trees grow inside their doors; enduring ruins, where they emerge from ivy, are the limestone white-grey and look like rocks. Fallen-in farms and cabins take only some years to vanish. Only major or recent ruins keep their human stories; from others the story quickly evaporates. Some ruins show gashes of violence, others simply the dull slant of decline. In this Munster county so often fought over there has been cruelty even to the stones; military fury or welling-up human bitterness has vented itself on unknowing walls. Campaigns and 'troubles', taking their tolls, subsiding, each leave a new generation of ruins to be reabsorbed slowly into the natural scene.

ELIZABETH BOWEN, *Bowen's Court*, 1942

A flat unaccented accent suits the men of the Kildare plains. Here they cannot allow their hopes to rise too much. History has branded them as malcontents. Patriotism in this walled-in and hedged-off enclave has always been a melancholy matter; but then Irish nationalistic fervour has always been tinged with an ancestral sadness. Betrayers and informers hide behind every corner.

AIDAN HIGGINS, *Ronda Gorge and Other Precipices*, 1978

A Disused Shed in Co. Wexford

Let them not forget us, the weak souls among the asphodels.
Seferis, *Mythistorema*, trans. Keeley and Sherrard
for J. G. Farrell

Even now there are places where a thought might grow—
Peruvian mines, worked out and abandoned
To a slow clock of condensation,
An echo trapped for ever, and a flutter
Of wild-flowers in the lift-shaft,
Indian compounds where the wind dances
And a door bangs with diminished confidence,
Lime crevices behind rippling rain-barrels,
Dog corners for bone burials;
And in a disused shed in Co. Wexford,

Deep in the grounds of a burnt-out hotel,
Among the bathtubs and the washbasins
A thousand mushrooms crowd to a keyhole.
This is the one star in their firmament
Or frames a star within a star.
What should they do there but desire?

So many days beyond the rhododendrons
With the world waltzing in its bowl of cloud,
They have learnt patience and silence
Listening to the rooks querulous in the high wood.

They have been waiting for us in a foetor
Of vegetable sweat since civil war days,
Since the gravel-crunching, interminable departure
Of the expropriated mycologist.
He never came back, and light since then
Is a keyhole rusting gently after rain.
Spiders have spun, flies dusted to mildew
And once a day, perhaps, they have heard something—
A trickle of masonry, a shout from the blue
Or a lorry changing gear at the end of the lane.

There have been deaths, the pale flesh flaking
Into the earth that nourished it;
And nightmares, born of these and the grim
Dominion of stale air and rank moisture.
Those nearest the door grow strong—
'Elbow room! Elbow room!'
The rest, dim in a twilight of crumbling
Utensils and broken pitchers, groaning
For their deliverance, have been so long
Expectant that there is left only the posture.

A half century, without visitors, in the dark—
Poor preparation for the cracking lock
And creak of hinges. Magi, moonmen,
Powdery prisoners of the old regime,
Web-throated, stalked like triffids, racked by drought
And insomnia, only the ghost of a scream
At the flash-bulb firing-squad we wake them with
Shows there is life yet in their feverish forms.
Grown beyond nature now, soft food for worms,
They lift frail heads in gravity and good faith.

They are begging us, you see, in their wordless way,
To do something, to speak on their behalf
Or at least not to close the door again.
Lost people of Treblinka and Pompeii!
'Save us, save us,' they seem to say,
'Let the god not abandon us
Who have come so far in darkness and in pain.
We too had our lives to live.

You with your light meter and relaxed itinerary,
Let not our naive labours have been in vain!'

DEREK MAHON, *Poems 1962–78*, 1979

The past crops up everywhere along this shore. At Carrowniskey there are pine stumps like smooth black molars sticking out of the sand below high water. These must also be rooted in Bronze Age peat and perhaps, below that again, there is a sandy beach of the Stone Age. Even the strand we have now feels prehistoric at the worn end of winter, when the sun finds the rough edges of a world being made and unmade.

MICHAEL VINEY, *A Year's Turning*, 1996

Among the Burke castles Clonbeg was one of the most dilapidated. It had once been a spacious building, but being long since deserted it had continued to slip and fall until the roof went altogether and the jagged sidewalls were unstable. The violent thunderstorm of some years back had done for the greater part of it. It had knocked the east gable to the ground, the sidewalls unsupported had followed soon after and lay in shattered masses scattered about. It was a wonder to all that the fierce lightningflash which had struck the castle had left even a stone standing, for it had cut a crevice seven yards long out from the castle, making an abysmal hole in a waterlogged hollow towards the south corner of the greensward. But the west gable remained intact—the gable which had its back to the bleakness of the irrational West, and faced the fertile cultivated Plain—that gable still stood, last of its warlike phalanx, loath to relinquish its immemorial watch on the Galway Plain. It was commonly said in the villages round that it too was cracked and daily splitting apart, yet it was erect still, an immense stone symbol to be seen for miles.

It had been gapped and bitten into many times. A large mass had been gashed from its northern edge and more fell every day. Seen from a distance that gable-edge looked like nothing more than a gapped scythe-blade or a sawtooth sickle. The other edge had lasted well, apart from a few slight dints it was almost untouched. The gable itself was tightly laced with ivy interspersed with patches of moss that in this dry weather became dust to the touch. Both ivy and moss had spread and established themselves with the years and now hid the entire face of the gable apart from an odd stony streak still bare. At its base lay a rubble of stones, powdered lime and mortar, stray chips of oyster-shell, there a solitary boulder, there a window-lintel which had been thrown far out on the greensward when the walls fell. But the gable itself was the most remarkable sight. It looked like a tough old warrior, hacked and solitary, still guarding the gap in the teeth of the attack while his kinsmen lay mown down all sides of him.

People seldom made free with this solitary relic. They agreed to a peaceful co-existence, kept away from it, were careful to keep their stock from going near it. The castle precincts had always had a bad name before ever the gable touched by the thunder had become untrustworthy.

MÁIRTÍN Ó CADHAIN, *The Road to Bright City*, 1939, trans. Eoghan Ó Tuairisc

Shoreline

Turning a corner, taking a hill
In County Down, there's the sea
Sidling and settling to
The back of a hedge. Or else

A grey bottom with puddles
Dead-eyed as fish.
Haphazard tidal craters march
The corn and the grazing.

All round Antrim and westward
Two hundred miles at Moher
Basalt stands to.
Both ocean and channel

Froth at the black locks
On Ireland. And strands
Take hissing submissions
Off Wicklow and Mayo.

Take any minute. A tide
Is rummaging in
At the foot of all fields,
All cliffs and shingles.

Listen. Is it the Danes,
A black hawk bent on the sail?
Or the chinking Normans?
Or currachs hopping high

On to the sand?
Strangford, Arklow, Carrickfergus,
Belmullet and Ventry
Stay, forgotten like sentries.

SEAMUS HEANEY, *Door into the Dark*, 1969

Few in their right minds could doubt that reality is two-thirds illusion in Iar-Connacht, the The-Bays-of-the-Ocean called Connemara. The Maamturks loom and recede, appear only to vanish, an optical illusion. The nights are still as the grave. Terrain so marine in nature, so embattled in history (defeat for the Irish), is entitled to its grave silence. But foxes are returning over the causeways built in Penal days, into Bealadangan, Annaghvaughan, Gorumna, Lettermore. The ghost of Sir Roger Casement coughs at night in the Hotel of the Isles, as the Atlantic wind rushes through the palm tree outside, and a miserable coal fire dies in the grate.

AIDAN HIGGINS (1982), in *Ronda Gorge & Other Precipices*, 1989

from *A Farewell to English*

Half afraid to break a promise
made to Dinny Halpin Friday night
I sat down from my walk to Camas
Sunday evening, Doody's Cross,
and took off my burning boots
on a gentle bench of grass.
The cows had crushed the evening
green with mint:
springwater from the roots
of a hawkfaced firtree on my right
swamped pismires bringing home
their sweet supplies
and strawberries looked out
with ferrets' eyes.
These old men walked on the summer road
súgán belts and long black coats
with big ashplants and half-sacks
of rags and bacon on their backs.
They stopped before me with a knowing look
hungry, snotnosed, half-drunk.
I said 'grand evening'
and they looked at me awhile
then took their roads
to Croom, Meentogues and Cahirmoyle.
They look back once,
black moons of misery
sickling their eye-sockets,
a thousand years of history
in their pockets.

MICHAEL HARTNETT, *A Farewell to English*, 1975

Kilkenny county might be described as the parlour in our Irish habitation of thirty-two counties. It is comfortable, draughtless and elegant. The typical landscape is mellow. The towns and villages have that kind of patina peculiar to ancient objects. The whole territory has a lived-in look, as though used to people. There is only one other county in Ireland to compare with Kilkenny: Armagh. Both are dominated by beautiful cities and both have that sort of cornucopia landscape where gardens, wheat-fields, groves and orchards look as if spilled out over gentle slopes.

Kilkenny city is in a sense the true capital of Leinster. It is hoary with history, the kind that might be described as best-selling. It has seen parliaments, confederations, pageants, plagues, sieges and wars; the actors on its stage have been saints, heroes, rogues, poets, great overlords and a Papal Legate. Not being obliged to give you its history coherently, I am free to indulge my fancy. The Statute of Kilkenny (1366) called the Anglo-Irish to order and forbade them either to marry the natives, or to speak Irish, to wear the native dress, or to play hurling ('the plays which men calls hurlings with great sticks and a ball upon the ground'). This peevish legislation had of course the opposite effect to that intended. The veto on hurling is amusing in the light of Kilkenny's fanatical attachment to that game right down to the present day. In 1645 the Papal Legate, Cardinal Rinuccini, arrived in Kilkenny for the Catholic Confederation. He was conducted into the city with full liturgical ceremonial, but the rain fell in torrents and the canopy carried over his head by four men came in useful for the humdrum office of umbrella. Four years later there was a devastating plague. Bishop Rothe, who was himself ailing, was carried in a litter from door to door so that he might administer to the stricken. Lastly, Kilkenny was the scene of the poet Thomas Moore's courtship of the tenth-rate actress, Bessie Dyke. On summer evenings, they rambled by the river Nore near the Castle. It was only a fairly successful marriage. Poor Bessie and poor Tom: their 'love's young dream' deserved a better sequel.

I remember once having been brought on a tour of Kilkenny city. It was almost an official proceeding and, if I did not actually meet the Mayor, I was at any rate brought into that ungainly eighteenth-century building, the Tholsel, and shown the city treasures. I recall only lovely chandeliers; a venerable map of the city engraved by Rocque; a bust of Gladstone. The position of honour this occupied was at that time under the fire of debate and press correspondence. Was the old English gentleman to stay or to go? I never heard the end of the controversy. For the rest, I retain of that tour a general impression of ruins, tombs, bridges and laneways where wallflowers, valerian and snapdragon brightened the mouldy walls.

STEPHEN RYNNE, *All Ireland*, 1956

Most people, if asked to define the chief symptoms of the Northern Ireland troubles, would say it is that the two communities cannot live together. The very essence of the Ulster question, however, is that they *do* live together, and have done for centuries. They share the same homeland, and, like it or not, the two diametrically opposed political wills must coexist on the same narrow ground. . . .

The unavoidable fact of coexistence dictates the most important aspect of the enduring conflict, which is that it must always be conducted in terms of topography. The exact cause of the quarrel, or more accurately of its survival, is often obscure to the onlooker. In many countries it is assumed that it is a holy war, *al jihad, Konfessionskrieg*, and as such an abnormality in modernized societies, a sickening survival of a mediaeval religious rancour. The fact is, however, that the quarrel is not about theology as such and remains, in its modern form, stubbornly a constitutional problem, though religion is the shibboleth of the contending parties. Essentially the conflict in Ulster is not different from other conflicts in the modern world: it is about political power and who should wield it. People simply assume the political attitudes of the faith into which they were born. They rarely choose their political outlook after mature deliberation, and yet the entire debate on the question is conducted on the assumption that they do. Each side wastes its breath in trying to persuade the other to adopt its view of the situation, as if all men were reasonable creatures, and none the product of his environment and education.

Each community identifies itself with the myth it takes from Irish history. Each believes, mistakenly, that it still consists entirely of descendants of the Gaels or of the planters. In fact many of the IRA have planter surnames, and are probably of planter descent, while an Orangeman may be descended from Gaelic kings. Many who would defend Ulster's 'Protestant heritage' are sons or grandsons of Scots and English businessmen who settled in the province since 1900, while a foreign Catholic who settles in Ulster immediately identifies himself with Irish nationalism.

The segregation of the two religious communities, with the relative rarity of intermarriage, has preserved to a considerable extent the original mosaic of plantation, and population densities, except in Belfast, have remained surprisingly stable since the seventeenth century. The two communities are not intermingled—that is patently what has not happened—but they are interlocked, and in ways which it is probably impossible for anyone except the native of Ulster to understand. This gives rise to a situation in which the 'territorial imperative' is extremely insistent. The quarrel is therefore very much concerned with the relationship of people to land, and that relationship has indeed been considered the central theme of Irish history.

Of its very nature it consists in particulars, the location of a road, a stretch of wall, a church or a cluster of houses, and the pattern has less relevance to abstract concepts of reconciliation, political reform, constitutional innovations, and this or that form of doctrinaire nationalism or unionism than is commonly supposed. Yet the problem is invariably discussed in abstract terms. The war in Ulster is being fought out on a narrower ground than even the most impatient observer might imagine, a ground every inch of which has its own associations and special meaning.

The Ulsterman carries the map of this religious geography in his mind almost from birth. He knows which villages, which roads and streets, are Catholic, or Protestant, or 'mixed'. It not only tells him where he can, or cannot, wave an Irish tricolour or wear his Orange sash, but imposes on him a complex behaviour pattern and a special way of looking at political problems. The nuance is all-important. If you cannot spell Donegall Place or Shankill Road correctly, if you do not know the vital difference between the Shankill district of Belfast and the Shankill district of Lurgan, you can scarcely hope to know what goes on in the minds of the people who live there.

A. T. Q. Stewart, *The Narrow Ground*, 1977

Under Creon

Rhododendrons growing wild below a mountain
and no long high wall or trees either;
a humped road, bone-dry, with no one—
passing one lough and then another
where water-lilies glazed, primed like traps.

A neapish hour, I searched out gaps
in that imperial shrub: a free voice sang
dissenting green, and syllables spoke
holm oaks by a salt shore, their dark tangs
glistening like Nisus in a night attack.

The daylight gods were never in this place
and I had pressed beyond my usual dusk
to find a cadence for the dead: McCracken,
Hope, the northern starlight, a death mask
and the levelled grave that Biggar traced;

like an epic arming in an olive grove
this was a stringent grief and a form of love.
Maybe one day I'll get the hang of it
and find joy, not justice, in a snapped connection,
that Jacobin oath on the black mountain.

Tom Paulin, *Liberty Tree*, 1983

Observe the history of Ireland in the lay-out of Limerick. Irishtown is down at the end of the main street, where the old walls of Limerick may be found embedded in commerce and penury. Compare these cabins of Irishtown at one end, and the graceful Georgian houses at the other. Modern times have added their equally appropriate mark. The hydro-electric scheme behind Irishtown. Suburbia beyond that gracious Crescent. How right, too, that the monument to Dan O'Connell should stand in the Crescent, at the top of George's Street, with the red-brick Georgian houses to his right and left. How right that we find to his west the Dominican Church, and to his east the church of St Joseph—the power that made him and broke him, freed the Irishtowns and then sat on them, took over from Anglo-Ireland, and blessed the villas out to Mungret. Up here it is all planned and regular, pleasant and reasonable, as befitted the age of reason: Cecil Street, Glentworth Street, Harstongue Street, Perry Square, Military Road. The sun warms the ruby faces of the houses, ruddy as the port no longer in the cellars, or where there is a patch of the yellow brick, gold as the vanished madeira and the biscuits. Lovely houses, from whose backs one looks down on the Shannon and can peep at the hills of Clare. Down there, behind the market, it is a network of streets and lanes, and because the Longstone quarries make excellent paving-setts (which have superseded those once imported from Wales and Arklow, once exclusively used in Limerick), the carts rumble, and there always seems to be a drove of pigs going to the bacon-factory, and there is a general smell of corn-stores, hay, hucksters' shops, dairies, and petrol from the garages. The names accord—Pennywell, Whitewine, Gerald Griffin, Ellen, Michael, Garryowen, and the Spital. And then comes the canal, and on a half-island is Englishtown about the castle that you find in all the old prints of Limerick. This is the oldest Limerick, this and Irishtown, which between them were once the fortified city. Here you find what is left of the old walls, including the Ramparts which the women of Limerick defended with bricks and bottles—a buttress twelve yards thick.

SEAN O'FAOLAIN, *An Irish Journey*, 1940

After a hungry cyclist's supper at one of the hotels—and Limerick has some good hotels—I strolled through the city by lamplight. Next morning I was astir early and had made a tour of the principal streets before breakfast. I made several other tours during the day, and found much that was interesting at every other turn and crossing. It would have been the same if I had stayed for a week. Limerick is packed with great memories. It breathes history. Even its very stone-heaps are eloquent. I crossed the river over and over again, strolled through Garryowen, and through the streets where the great Munster fair is held, out to the reservoir. I prowled around the old parts of the city, and through the more modern streets, visited all that is left of the walls, saw where the fighting was hottest, sat on the wharves of the river, rested beside the Treaty Stone, lounged on the bridges, stood at shop doors and at street corners looking at the faces of the passers-by, and when the time came for me to leave I was sorry. I arrived there prejudiced in its favour. Consequently I liked it to some extent before I saw it. I liked the imperfect view I got of it as I entered it in the gloaming. I liked it ten times better when I saw it in the light of day. I liked it better than ever when I was leaving it, not because I was parting from it, for I have told you I was sorry to go, but just because it had grown upon me.

WILLIAM BULFIN, *Rambles in Eirinn*, 1907

Perhaps there is no provincial town in either of the three kingdoms with which there is so much of historical interest associated as the city of Limerick. During the many centuries that Ireland had its provincial kings, and that Munster, of which Limerick was at that time the metropolis, was under their dynasty, Limerick was almost constantly the scene of sieges, and its neighbourhood the seat of war. But the last and most important assault which the city of Limerick had to encounter, was the one made on it in the year 1690, by the army of King William. The siege was laid immediately after the battle of the Boyne, and his soldiers, 20,000 in number, were headed in person by the king himself. The resistance of the garrison, under General Sarsfield, was desperate. The besieging party were twice repulsed. The citizens, and even the women, joined the soldiers in opposing the invading army. The women, with no other weapons than stones, which they carried in their laps, fought with the most determined bravery, and conjointly with the soldiers and male citizens, almost exterminated one of the two divisions of William's army. The loss of the besiegers was, on this occasion, estimated at 1,700 men. A large part of the other division was destroyed by the explosion of a mine. The result was, that the remainder of William's army was obliged to raise the siege, after having continued it for four hours. In August of the following year, the soldiers of William, under the command of General Ginkle, again invested the city of Limerick, and on the twenty-third of September, the garrison, being short of provisions, and disappointed in the succour they expected from France, proposed an armistice. This was agreed to, and it ended on the third of the following month by the signing of the celebrated treaty known in history as the Treaty of Limerick.

The stone on which this treaty was signed is still to be seen. It lies on the north-west side of the river Shannon, which runs through a part of the city, near Thomond Bridge. I was surprised to find that among the lower classes in the immediate neighbourhood, there prevailed an entire ignorance of the historical interest which attaches to this celebrated stone. When I went to see it, two women were sitting on it, and yet they were not aware that any greater interest attached to it than to any other stone.

ANON. (J. Grant), *Impressions of Ireland and the Irish*, 1844

From the moment we left Mallow we were into Geraldine country. In a way it is a reflection of the Butler country about Kilkenny; the same rich, flat, pastoral landscape which every Norman baron sought out; it is the landscape which Spenser described in *The Faerie Queen* but in a curious way its image is blurred—by the rain-clouds coming up the Shannon from the south or the blue hills of Kerry behind; most of all perhaps by the fact that it was beaten flat during the Desmond rebellions. It is mediaeval landscape which has been fused with prehistoric traditions, as the Norman blood of the Fitzgeralds was fused with the older blood of the little kingdoms. That gives it a poetic charm and a certain aimlessness. It can be magical at evening and at early morning; at noonday suffocating with its feeling of wealth and decay. A little river winding through flat country; an old bridge casually blown up in 'The Throubles'; the stump of a castle rooted like an old oak in some heap of rock by the river, blown up by Cromwell; the tapering tower of a ruined Franciscan monastery rising above a tall, slender chancel arch with an aisle and transept added to the nave in the clumsy style of the fifteenth century: that might be the picture of any Desmond township in Cork or Limerick.

FRANK O'CONNOR, *Irish Miles*, 1947

To them [i.e. Irishmen] Irish history is their consolation; their greatest hope; it is always before their eyes, always upon their lips. They live in the past. Everything around them speaks of other days. Round towers, ruins, fallen abbeys, ancient castles, nay, the very desolation of the country itself, bring memories of times gone by. England sees in the faults and vices of Irishmen the true explanation of their misfortunes; Ireland deems the cruelty and tyranny of the English to be the real and only cause of her unhappiness. As Englishmen brazenly shut their eyes to their national misdeeds, so Irishmen complacently shut their eyes to their own shortcomings, and never weary of looking back upon that golden age of Erin, when, whilst England was yet steeped in pagan barbarism, the Irish were the protectors and the pioneers of western civilisation.

L. PAUL-DUBOIS, *Contemporary Ireland*, 1908

Memory of Brother Michael

It would never be morning, always evening,
Golden sunset, golden age—
When Shakespeare, Marlowe and Jonson were writing
The future of England page by page
A nettle-wild grave was Ireland's stage.

It would never be spring, always autumn
After a harvest always lost,
When Drake was winning seas for England
We sailed in puddles of the past
Chasing the ghost of Brendan's mast.

The seeds among the dust were less than dust,
Dust we sought, decay,
The young sprout rising smothered in it,
Cursed for being in the way—
And the same is true to-day.

Culture is always something that was,
Something pedants can measure,
Skull of bard, thigh of chief,
Depth of dried-up river.
Shall we be thus for ever?
Shall we be thus for ever?

PATRICK KAVANAGH, *A Soul for Sale*, 1947

I have always liked Wexford town, . . . with its air of repose and easy good
fellowship, its decent burgess life. The past is there fused and blended with
the present; not, as at Kilkenny, maintained in something of pristine splendour by the continued existence of a great house—still less, as at Galway,
staring bleakly at you, a skeleton broke loose from its cupboard—but comfortably asserting itself in and through the homely existing life. Memories are
many, but they are not raw. The bridge across the Slaney is still where stood
a wooden bridge in 1798, on which a brutal massacre of prisoners was perpetrated by the worse element among the rebels. Here, Father Curran, the
Franciscan, flung himself into danger to rescue the unhappy victims; and he
was not alone. Esmonde Kyan, who had commanded a rebel corps with great
valour at Arklow, was in bed, grievously wounded, when the news reached
him, and he, says Cloney, 'ran, or rather, tottered, to the bridge and saved
several from the fangs of the rabble'. His reputation availed to secure him a
guarantee of protection from General Dundas when he surrendered with the
last of the fighters in Kildare; yet the soldier's honour was disregarded by a
jury which tried Kyan in Wexford and sent him to the gallows. The court-
house in which this and so many dark scenes passed in those days is there
still, unaltered; and I saw a case for poultry stealing being tried in it, as the
chief issue of that sessions.

STEPHEN GWYNN, *The Famous Cities of Ireland*, 1915

Belfast is a village. Strangers meeting always have mutual friends or acquaintances. Sometimes its history can be like that. I rarely walk through Cornmarket without thinking of Henry Joy McCracken, who was hanged at the
Market House there in 1798. The ground on which his 'handsome, manly
figure' was strung up had been given to the town by his great-great-
grandfather. Looking at Gerry Fitt's door, I think of the well-meaning,
doomed revolutionaries, the noble optimism that turned to ashes, their
dream of a nonsectarian Ireland, and the unspeakable bitterness that threw
black paint at the door of a politician who was not sectarian enough. Belfast
has more than its share of dreams and ideals, but sometimes, or time and
again, it looks as if the dreamers and idealists want too much and end up with
nothing.

ROBERT JOHNSTONE, *Images of Belfast*, 1983

I have always believed that local history is more important than national
history. There should be an archive in every village, where stories . . . are
recorded. Where life is fully and consciously lived in our own neighbourhood, we are cushioned a little from the impact of great far-off events which
should be of only marginal concern to us.

HUBERT BUTLER, 'Beside the Nore', in *Escape from the Anthill*, 1985; first
published in *Ireland of the Welcomes*, May–June 1970

Dirty Streets and Proud People

O my small town of Ireland, the raindrops caress you,
  The sun sparkles bright on your field and your Square
As here on your bridge I salute you and bless you,
  Your murmuring waters and turf-scented air.

JOHN BETJEMAN, from 'The Small Towns of Ireland'

All Irish towns have a sufficient number of features in common. The outside cars in the streets, the women going about in their shawls, the number of merry barefoot children, the corner-boys leaning against the walls till the season for the militia-training comes round, the gloom and strength of the policemen's figures going up and down, the proprietorial names above the public-houses, and twenty other things, unite to give a composite picture which will serve for any town.

ROBERT LYND, *Home Life in Ireland*

――――――――

I was making some notes one day while travelling in a train through a boggy country in Ireland when a melodeon player opposite me asked me if I wouldn't stop writing and 'give out a tune' and he handed the melodeon towards me. 'I have no ear,' I said. 'Ah, to hell with ears,' he said, 'I play it with my body. Are you writing a book?' he said. 'Well I am making notes for one,' I said. 'What are you going to call it?' he said. 'I don't know yet,' I said. 'Call it Sligo. It's the name of a town,' he said, 'the only town in Ireland I never was in. I was near it once but I stopped on the brink and took the long car with a unicorn yoked to it for a town called Ballina. Call it Sligo, it ought to be a lucky name.' So Sligo it is. When he asked me to play a tune he pronounced it Chune, a very good way too. If they give me music to my grave I will sooner they will call it a Chune than a Toon: there is a want of dignity about the word 'Toon' and I would not look forward to it. Every town in Ireland has its cry. Of Sligo, they used to sing 'Sligo where all the rogues come from': I am sure 'the rogues' meant were the amusing kind, those 'wild pigs of the world' after which mothers used to call their children. There is 'All on one side' like the town of Athlone, 'Nothing for nothing at Borrisokane.' But Carrick. Ah! 'Carrick I dread you.' That is Carrick-on-Suir. I was not in it yet, but I was often in Cork's own town among 'God's own people'.

JACK YEATS, *Sligo*, 1930

The town itself was small and ordinary. Part of it was on a hill, the part where the slum cottages were, where three or four shops had nothing in their windows except pasteboard advertisements for tea and Bisto. The rest of the town was flat, a single street with one or two narrow streets running off it. Where they met there was a square of a kind, with a statue of Daniel O'Connell. The Munster and Leinster Bank was here, and the Bank of Ireland, and Lacy and Sons, and Bolger's Medical Hall, and the Home and Colonial. Our garage was at one end of the main street, opposite Corrigan's Hotel. The Electric Cinema was at the other, a stark white façade, not far from the Christian Brothers, the convent and the Church of the Holy Assumption. The Protestant church was at the top of the hill, beyond the slums.

When I think of the town now I can see it very clearly: cattle and pigs on a fair day, always a Monday; Mrs Driscoll's vegetable shop. Vickery's hardware, Phelan's the barber's, Kilmartin's the turf accountant's, the convent and the Christian Brothers, twenty-nine public houses. The streets are empty on a sunny afternoon, there's a smell of bread. Brass plates gleam on the way home from school: Dr Thos. Garvey MD, RCS, Regan and O'Brien Commissioners for Oaths, W. Tracy Dental Surgeon

WILLIAM TREVOR, 'The Raising of Elvira Tremlett', 1977

Newry was very different from Clones or Rathfriland or Athlone. It was bigger than any of them, it had a ship canal along which small steam-driven vessels brought grain to the local mills, timber from Scandinavia and coal, for which Newry was a major distributing point, from the mines of Britain. Along the quay there were redbrick grain stores, coal yards, timber stacks, depots from which potatoes were exported to England and hardware and ironmongery warehouses owned by builders' suppliers and the importers of agricultural machinery and implements. The quay was a busy, noisy place, a place of fluttering pigeons and dark dust and many smells. The shops in the main street seemed always to be full and the Thursday market brought Belfast 'cheap-jacks' with their stalls and farmers with a variety of horse-drawn vehicles into the town.

PATRICK SHEA, *Voices and the Sound of Drums*, 1981

Armagh

There is a through-otherness about Armagh
Of tower and steeple,
Up on the hill are the arguing graves of the kings,
And below are the people.

Through-other as the rooks that swoop and swop
Over the sober hill
Go the people gallivanting from shop to shop
Guffawing their fill.
And the little houses run through the market-town
Slap up against the great,
Like the farmers all clabber and muck walking arm by arm
With the men of estate.

Raised at a time when Reason was all the rage,
Of grey and equal stone,
This bland face of Armagh covers an age
Of clay and feather and bone.

Through-other is its history, of Celt and Dane,
Norman and Saxon,
Who ruled the place and sounded the gamut of fame
From cow-horn to klaxon.

There is a through-otherness about Armagh
Delightful to me,
Up on the hill are the graves of the garrulous kings
Who at last can agree.

W. R. RODGERS, *Europa and the Bull*, 1952

As Neilly, Shemie and their granny picked their steps as hastily as possible across the street, the Row was like a place of the dead. The only sound was that of the rustling of the rain, and the harsh vomiting of the spouts. Not another sinner was to be seen. Every door was shut tight; the blistered paint and the rough, grey walls dark with the whippings of the rain.

The Row in which the Coyles' house stood was on a higher level than the other, which thus flooded more quickly, a regrettable fact acknowledged by the Mill owners, and accounting for the reduction in rent of the lower houses, which was only one and ninepence, sixpence less than that of those in the opposite side.

Already, as the Callan was rising, the dark flood-water was slowly swelling all along the gutter beneath the high cribben. They had to help their granny across the channel onto the footpath, and she burst into the house lamenting. Tommy, a dark-haired fellow of twenty-eight, was sitting on the stool at the fire, smoking a cigarette. He was wearing only his trousers; the upper part of his body was smooth, hairless, and glowing softly from the heat. Through the half-closed door of the small room came the crying of a child and the soft 'there now, there now,' of a woman's voice.

An expression of annoyance flickered across the old woman's face.

'Tsk! Tsk! Has she the child up already!' She made to swing the old jacket from her shoulders, and took a quick step towards the room. Then, abruptly, she turned around and hoisted up the old coat again. 'My God the night!' she ejaculated. 'Do I have to go right back again?'

'What's wrong now?' Tommy asked. But the old woman swung the door open again and dashed out without answering. Through the window they peered out at her huddling once more across the fearsome street.

'A shocking woman that, altogether,' Tommy sighed. 'What!'

'She has forgot the washing, I bet you, so she has,' Neilly said.

Though well over sixty, his granny was always on the go, a woman of tireless energy who, having wrought hard all her life, fretted now if she had not enough to keep her busy. She was always on the look out for an extra job, and every Sunday morning she came over to her son's house to gather up any dirty washing that might be lying around, often wrestling with Kitty, if she happened to be there, for an extra shirt or sheet.

'What's wrong with the child, Tommy?' Shemie asked, moving towards the door. 'Will I go in?'

'No, don't go in, Shemie son,' Tommy said. 'Teasie will be lifting it in a minute.'

Neilly sat down at the table facing the window; Shemie crossed over to the fire, holding out his hands and screwing his face away from the heat. On each side of the fire the hob was piled up with damp turf and big, dark-yellow chips of fir.

'Is Eugene up yet?' Tommy inquired.

Shemie shook his head and backed away a few paces.

'My God! How do you stick that heat?'

Tommy hunched his shoulders over, rubbing his hands together.

'Ah, it's great, man dear. You don't know what you're missing. There! Here comes trouble, and we haven't a brick.'

The room door opened, and Teasie came out with the child.

JOHN O'CONNOR, *Come Day—Go Day*, 1948

The people of Belfast in the present generation are principally strangers. Living examples of successful merchants who came into Belfast from the neighbouring districts are to be found in every street; even our late fellow-townsman, James Hart, the advocate of home trade and reciprocal duties, told us that he himself had ridden from the County Armagh into Belfast, and put up his horse in Kilpatrick's yard in Arthur Street when he came to be apprenticed to the manufacture of the staple fabric for which the town has since became so famous. Long may good and enterprising men be attracted here for commercial and scientific purposes, and may our native town prosper and flourish, and extend on every side until it clambers the slopes of the beautiful green hills that encircle it.

THOMAS GAFFIKEN, *Belfast Fifty Years Ago*, 1894

Grey ruins; land and farmsteads subject to disastrous flooding; by contrast the town of Athlone seems a splendid place. But one should approach it with a mind tempered by the surrounding desolation, because to arrive on the Dublin road is to find it just another country town. The desolate regions of Ireland make a man appreciate the towns. As I myself have lived most of my life in rural isolation, I find country towns full of attractions and 'city' lights. Thus I rejoice in Athlone: the boats bobbing on the river, the bustle, the markets, traffic blocks (at times), soldiers, mills, sketchable ruins and riverside warehouses, two Catholic churches of very different styles and a Protestant church in a high, stiff cravat—all contained within a small compass. Owing to its geographical position in the centre of Ireland, astride the Shannon and a pass between two provinces, Athlone has always been considered an invaluable strategic point. Under the British régime, the garrison seldom numbered less than four thousand and, in times of political excitement, its strength was increased. Athlone is the natural capital of Ireland. There is not much hope that it will ever be officially recognised as such, but the Athlone people like the mere suggestion; after all, to be the defeated candidate in a great election is something to boast of.

STEPHEN RYNNE, *All Ireland*, 1956

Galway is more essentially a city in ruins than any I have ever beheld. It is a grey city, a city of noble walls and narrow streets, with the winds of the sea blowing into its mouth and reminding it ever of the days when it sent forth its merchant ships into deep waters, and Spanish captains brought their wares to its quays. Galway has no main street of fashion and elegance. Its warehouses, its ruinous mills, give it the appearance of a city that has been shelled and sacked by an invader. These warehouses and mills were built on a palatial scale, and even in ruin they are noble: by moonlight they have a marble grandeur. A sleepy horse-tram with its sleepy bell winds along one of the streets, as though apologising for its almost modern intrusiveness. The

Claddagh village by the harbour, with its coloured cottages under their grotesque depths of thatch and its fishing population in their jerseys and shawls, helps to give Galway the appearance of the most distinctively Irish city in Ireland. On fair days, too, the Connemara people pour into the market square in their white woollen jackets and their black tam-o'-shanters, and the air is not fuller of the shrieks of pigs and the protesting roar of cattle than of the rich flow of Gaelic so expressive in gossip and in bargaining. Some of the shops of the city have the names of the proprietors written above the windows in Irish—as the shops have, indeed, in a growing number of towns and villages. In some of them you can buy all you want without any need to resort to the use of English at all.

ROBERT LYND, *Home Life in Ireland*, 1908

The 'bus comes at last with a great blaze of headlights, and figures emerge from the darkness and climb aboard. Here and there a light in a cottage window; there is a pale rift in the sky, but no crimson dawn; the light comes slowly, the blackness melting into grey, the grey becoming paler, and somehow the day is upon us, a grey mean sort of a day. But a little over a month ago when I made this journey we ran into a dawn of unforgettable splendour, with great mass formations of cloud like a range of mountains behind the hills, and long swathes of cloud below the tops of the hills, and swirls of mist rising from the water, and everything, bog and mountain and lake, wild and strange and 'lost' and enchanted, and the sky—but you cannot describe either a sunset or a dawn sky and give any true picture of it; you can paint it, but you cannot capture that blaze of crimson and fiery gold in a net of words. Chekhov knew that; he insisted that the best way to describe a sunset was to say that the sun set. . . . Very well, then, the sun rose. God said, Let there be Light, and the heavens opened.

But on this occasion there was no such dramatic performance; the day crept upon us in a mean sneaking sort of way, without enchantment. The 'bus windows steamed over, and we slept. . . .

And then there is Galway, which is a darlin' town, a darlin' town, with its Spanish archway and its rushing rapids of a river, and its turf-carts and its log-carts and hay-carts, its narrow streets and shawled women, its perpetual air of market-day. Over the harbour there is an incessant wheeling of black wings and white wings, as gulls and rooks thread each other's circuits in an endless noisy reel. A rotting boat lies upon its side, its ribs exposed, like a half-picked carcase. There are swans, and old men who stand about with an air of not waiting for anything in particular, but content to wait. The busy-ness of the little town does not reach to the harbour; once across the bridge and into the Claddah you enter a land where it is always afternoon. Here the old men stand and stare, and the old houses prop each other up and stare at the water. The Claddah is not what it was; it has been invaded by the neat ugly little bungalows of the new housing-scheme, but there are still a few thatched, white-washed cottages remaining. The Claddah is not as paintable as in the days when it was a colony of beehive-like cottages, but it is probably a good deal more sanitary and more comfortable to live in; it is only a pity that the little new houses had to be so much like grey boxes.

ETHEL MANNIN, *Connemara Journal*, 1947

Seven miles:—at length turning suddenly a corner, Derry is there to the south of us, close at hand; rising *red* and beautiful on elevated hill or 'bluff' (it must have been once).—Foyle moderately supplied with ships, running broad and clear past the farther side of it. The prettiest-looking town I have seen in Ireland. The free school; a big old building in fields, to right of us before we enter. Two or three *mill* chimneys (*not* corn-mills all of them, a linen-mill or flax-mill one at least visible); coal-yards, appearance of real shipping trade; suburbs, gate; and steep climb by the back of the old walls; Imperial hotel in fine—'one of the best in Ireland,' says report; one of the dearest, and not the best, says experience. Very indifferent bed there (wretched French bed, which species may the devil fly away with out of this British country!); and for lullaby the common sounds of an inn, augmented by a very powerful *cock* towards morning.

A Dr Mc Knight (editor, pamphleteer &^{c}) warned by Duffy, came to night; led us thro' the city wonders, the old cannon &^{c}; gave us, unconsciously, a glimpse into the raging *animosities* (London companies *versus* Derry town was the chief, but there were many) which reign here as in all parts of Ireland, and alas, of most lands;—invites us to breakfast for monday; an honest kind of man, tho' loud-toned and with wild eyes, this Mc Knight; has tobacco too, and a kind little orderly polite wife (a 'poverty honourable and beautiful.') Surely we will go. Steamer is to sail on monday at 1 p.m. for Glasgow; Scotland ho!

THOMAS CARLYLE, *Reminiscences of My Irish Journey*, 1849

The town [i.e. Derry] lay entranced, embraced by the great sleeping light of the river and the green beyond of the border. It woke now and then, like someone startled and shouting from a dream, in clamour at its abandonment. Once, at the height of a St Patrick's Day riot, when the police had baton charged a march and pursued us into our territory, we enticed them to follow us further downhill from the Lone Moor into the long street called Stanley's Walk that ran parallel with our own. We had splashed half a barrel of oil from a ransacked garage on the road surface at the curve of the slope. The police and B Specials raced down after us, under a hail of stones thrown at the cars and the jeeps they rode in or ran alongside. Advertising hoardings at the side of the street took the first volley of our missiles as the two leading cars hit the oil. A giant paper Coca-Cola bottle was punctured, along with the raised chin of a clean-shaven Gillette model. The cars swung and hurtled into the side walls, shredding stones from them like flakes of straw. The oil glittered in the sudsy swathe of the tyres, and one car lit up in a blue circle of flame as the police ran from it. The whole street seemed to be bent sideways, tilted by the blazing hoardings into the old Gaelic football ground.

SEAMUS DEANE, *Reading in the Dark*, 1996

Street Names

I hear the street names on the radio
and map reported bomb or barricade:
this was my childhood's precinct, and I know
how such streets look, down to the very shade
of brick, of paintwork on each door and sill,
what school or church nearby one might attend,
if there's a chance to glimpse familiar hill
between the chimneys where the grey slates end.

Yet I speak only of appearances,
a stage unpeopled, not the tragic play:
though actual faces of known families
flash back across the gap of fifty years;
can these be theirs, the children that today
rage in the fetters of their fathers' fears?

JOHN HEWITT, *Collected Poems*, 1991

As he drove into the town of Bantry, he passed a high stone wall which ran for more than a mile enclosing a huge estate, once the seat of English earls, now a museum to a vanished way of life. Ahead, as he came around the elbow of Bantry Bay, small fishing boats were moored at stone quays, and behind them the edge of the town spilled down to the water in a cluster of gray, severe buildings: convent, warehouse, church. He drove into the main square, which opened on the quays. A fair was in progress. All around were neighing mares, colts, bellowing calves separated from their mothers, dull heifers lifting their tails to drop gobbets of hot turd on the concrete. Wild-looking, poorly dressed people walked about, raw boys and girls, women in mourning black, red-faced farmers in cloth caps. He parked his little red rented Ford in front of a row of plain public houses, whose dark rooms were loud with talk and heavy with the stench of urine and yeast. Buyers and sellers of animals spilled from pub to pavement and back again in the course of constant barter.

Farther up the town, Mangan saw a maze of streets and shops. He walked three blocks before he came to what he sought, a kiosk marked with the word *Telefōn* in the Irish manner.

BRIAN MOORE, The Mangan Inheritance, 1979

Sarah had declared her intention of buying some material at Finnegan's and they were progressing slowly up the main street in that direction, the Major pushing and Sarah chattering, teasing him by turns about his 'Englishness', his 'respectability', his 'ramrod posture' and anything else that came into her head. The Major was only half listening, absorbed in looking round at the men in cloth caps idling on doorsteps (so few of them appeared to have any work to do), at the women in black shawls with shopping baskets, at the barefoot children playing in the gutter. How very foreign, after all, Ireland was!

Their progress up the street was now considerably impeded by a herd of cows ('How delightful, how typical!' thought the Major) which strayed not only over the road but on to the rudimentary pavement as well. Presently a motor car came up behind them with the driver sounding his horn, which did very little good since cows are inclined to panic; one of them almost charged straight back into the motor's radiator but was diverted at the last moment by a lad in a ragged overcoat who was herding the animals with a stick. Sitting beside the driver the Major recognized the burly figure of old Dr Ryan wrapped in a trench coat and numerous mufflers though the day was mild.

J. G. FARRELL, Troubles, 1970

Armagh of the sagas and of medieval times must have been rather different from its present aspect. The city must have been barbarous to judge by some Latin lines which have survived:

> *Carnes crudae,*
> *Mulieres nudae,*

No raw meat was given to me in Armagh nor were any naked women roving the streets when the Newry chemist set me down in The Mall and went off to his *fleadh* at Sligo. The wonder of that golden, Attic morning had changed now into a sumptuous afternoon. Armagh looked like a Ford Madox Brown painting with every leaf, every blade of grass, every stone in every house, looking more real than real, the detail picked out by the strong light and bathed in the golden atmosphere beloved of the Pre-Raphaelites in their more cheerful moments.

The butchering Red Branch Knights and their swords had been replaced by innocuous young men in white flannels with cricket bats on the wide greensward of The Mall. I took a nap, a pleasant dreamy doze filled with the voices of children playing under the beeches and oaks surrounding the green. As so often in Ireland, I had a sense of calm and serenity and of a way of life still persisting long after it had vanished in a neurotic England.

Nor was this entirely an illusion, though as I saw from a statue standing at one end of the green, the rural calm had been threatened by the same storm clouds that broke over late Victorian England, ending in the deluge which swept the old order away in 1914. The most eloquent sculpture I saw anywhere in Ulster was Kathleen Shaw's bronze figure of a young Irish bugler about to sound the Last Post, Armagh's memorial to its men killed in the South African War of 1899.

ROBIN BRYANS, *A Journey Through the Six Counties*, 1964

If you looked back from Cannonhill the prospect was really something: the whole town, spires and all, you could even see clear down into some of the streets; the winding river or rivers, the red brick of the county hospital on a hill across the valley, and beyond all that the mountains, Glenhordial where the water came from, Gortin Gap and Mullagharn and the high Sperrins. Sometime in the past, nobody knew when, there must have been a gun-emplacement on Cannonhill so as to give the place its name. Some of the local learned men talked vaguely about Oliver Cromwell but he was never next or near the place. There were, though, guns there in 1941 when a visit from the Germans seemed imminent and, indeed, they came near enough to bomb Belfast and Pennyburn in Derry City and were heard in the darkness over our town, and the whole population of Gallowshill, where I came from, took off for refuge up the three titanic steps of the Cannonhill road. It was a lovely June night, through, and everybody enjoyed themselves.

If any of those merry refugees had raced on beyond the ridge of Cannon-hill they would have found themselves, Germans or no Germans, in the heart of quietness. The road goes down in easy curves through good farmland to the Drumragh River and the old graveyard where the gateway was closed with concrete and stone long before my time, and the dead sealed off forever. There's a sort of stile made out of protruding stones in the high wall and within—desolation, a fragment of a church wall that might be medieval, waist-high stagnant grass, table tombstones made anonymous by moss and lichen, a sinister hollow like a huge shellhole in the centre of the place where the dead, also anonymous, of the great famine of the 1840s were thrown coffinless, one on top of the other. A man who went to school with me used to call that hollow the navel of nothing and to explain in gruesome detail why and how the earth that once had been mounded had sunk into a hollow.

BENEDICT KIELY, 'The Night We Rode with Sarsfield', 1963

Their path cut diagonally up the mountain. It was loose and stony, and the heat struck up from it in thick waves. Colm and Jamesy led the way, and Alec stopped often to admire the view. Jamesy hurled a stone down the side and heard it bumping until it fell and broke in pieces at the bottom. Colm lifted a brown caterpillar that was crossing the path and placed it on the palm of his hand, counting the rings on its back whenever it stretched itself.

At the top of the mountain they lay in the heather and gazed at Belfast spread out in the flat hollow below them, its lean mill chimneys stretched above the haze of smoke. Rows of red-bricked houses radiated on all sides and above them rose blocks of factories with many of their windows catching the sunlight.

They saw their own street and could make out the splash of whitewash on the wall that Alec had daubed there as a mark for his pigeons: it was all very far away like a street seen through the wrong end of a telescope.

'I can see my mother standing at the back-door throwing a crust to the fowl and Biddy McAteer hanging out her curtains,' joked Jamesy.

'And look at Mrs O'Brien cleaning her ear with a knitting needle,' answered Colm.

Alec gave a loud sniff: 'Man dear, I can smell the sausages frying for our tea.'

Their eyes ranged over the whole city to the low ridge of the Castlereagh Hills, netted with lovely fields and skimming cloud-shadows, to the blue U-shaped lough covered with yachts as small as paper boats, and steamers moving up towards the docks where the gantries stood like poised aeroplanes.

They shouted out to each other the names of all the churches that they knew: there were the green spires of Ardoyne where the sinners brought their great sins to the Passionists, there was the stumpy spire of the Monastery, and farther along in the heart of the city, sticking high above the smoke, were the sharp spires of St Peter's—the church that was always crowded with shawled factory workers saying their beads. Near their own street was the Dominican Convent, its fields very green and its hockey posts very white. And when Jamesy asked was it true that the nuns dug a bit of their graves each day and slept in their coffins at night Alec laughed: 'It'd be a queer deep grave some of them ladies would have for they're as ould as the hills.'

The numerous spires of the Protestant churches were everywhere. Then there was the Falls Park and they could see people walking about in it, and below it Celtic Football ground with its oval field and one grand stand, and farther to the right Linfield Ground with its tin advertisements for cigarettes.

'Wouldn't you think now to see all the churches,' smiled Alec, 'and all the factories and playgrounds that it was a Christian town?' and he lay back in the heather, flung his arms wide, and laughed.

MICHAEL McLAVERTY, *Call My Brother Back*, 1939

It [Derry] started life with a hot temper and it has never cooled down. It has been something of a storm centre all through the ages. And it is a storm centre to-day. You cannot look upon it without a quickening of the pulses. Something of its rugged history speaks to you out of its quaint old streets. It sits there squarely astride of the Foyle under wild Inishowen, the weather-beaten citadel of the fighting North.

It slopes sheerly down to the river after climbing several hills, which give some of its causeways the appearance of trying to stand on end. During the frosty weather all vehicle traffic ceases in several precipitous thoroughfares, and the popular sport of sliding begins. You may call it tobogganing or sleighing or anything you please. It consists of sitting on a board or in a basket and flying down the slippery gradient at the rate of several miles per minute. There are certain arrangements made by which the sliders shall not be dashed to pieces, or across the river into Tyrconnel; but this is a matter of detail. With Bowden brakes you can ride a bicycle down one of those Derry streets; but you would require a ten horse-power engine to work your cranks in the upward direction. If you want to see Derry you must go to work on foot. Go over the bridge and climb the hills on the off side of the river when evening comes, and you will appreciate the situation. Tier over tier of lights shine out from the steamers and electric lamps along the water front right up into the sky. Shops, clubs, long lines of factories, depots and private houses—all contribute something to the illumination. They are perched at different altitudes on the slopes of the hills, some of them having their foundations many feet over the level of the tall roofs of others.

Let us now turn to other phases of Derry's lumpiness. Your rambles through the streets reveal them to you. Here is a Catholic seminary; here is a Presbyterian one. Here is the Orange Hall; here is St Columcille's Hall. Here is a street in which live militant Catholics, here alongside, radiating from a common centre, is a street in which live militant Orangemen. Here is a newspaper office from which issue periodical challenges to Croppies; here is another newspaper office from which said challenges are hurled back with interest. Here are the old seventeenth century walls of the city which were manned by Cromwellians in 1648. Here are the historic gates slammed by the 'prentice boys in the face of the Catholic army of James forty years later. Here are the landmarks left by Columcille; here is the trophy statue to the soldier-pastor who made Derry one of the strongholds of Protestantism.

WILLIAM BULFIN, *Rambles in Eirinn*, 1907

Mr Burke told me that the Methodists now number in Ireland about 29,000 members and 100 preachers. Certainly these indefatigable labourers have done no small business to make their way through Popery, Prelacy, Presbyterianism, and Independency. They are instant in season and out of season. Went to Arklow at seven, and found a plain chapel, with a plain man in the pulpit, and heard a plain sermon preached to a plain people.

ASENATH NICHOLSON, *The Bible in Ireland*, 1852

It was market day at Castlebar when I arrived there, and I strolled for a couple of hours among the market people. Great numbers of women, holding a hank or two of yarn of their own spinning, stood in the streets and offered their trifling commodities for sale. Very few of those whom I addressed could speak English; but some of the men about, seeing the disadvantages under which I laboured, very obligingly stepped forward, and offered assistance as interpreters. This sort of politeness is common to the Irish. I ascertained that the women could not earn by spinning more than a penny or twopence a day, and hundreds of them attended the market whose earnings for the whole week did not exceed sixpence or ninepence; yet notwithstanding this inadequate reward of long and hard labour, their honest countenances wore the habitual impress of cheerfulness and perfect good humour. Scarcely any of the women had shoes, and I felt considerable alarm while threading my way through a dense crowd, lest I should step upon their feet.

JONATHAN BINNS, *Miseries and Beauties of Ireland*, 1837

The town of Carrickfergus, at present, has a much better appearance than at any former period, and extends along the northern shore of that bay to which it gives name, nearly a mile. Within the walls the streets are generally narrow, and are called by the following names: High-street, Castle-street, West-street, North-street, Cheston's-street, or Butcher-row, Essex-street, Lancaster-street, Antrim-street, *alias* Gaol-lane, Church-lane, Back-lane, Governor's place, and Joymount-court.

The houses are built either of stone or brick, mostly of the former, and commonly slated; many of the best houses have been built within the last thirty years. A few still present an antique appearance: the greater part of these are built in frames of oak, in that manner formerly called 'Cadge-work'; some of them had originally windows that projected several feet into the adjoining street.

That part of the town lying without the walls is called the Irish and Scotch quarters. The latter is on the east of the town, and its streets and rows are distinguished by the following names:—Joymount-bank, Scotch-quarter, and the Green, *alias* Green-street.

This quarter takes its name from a colony of fishers who arrived from Argyle and Gallowayshire, chiefly during the persecution in Scotland, about 1665; their descendants still retain their original calling. It is believed that the Irish quarter had its origin soon after. In November, 1678, we find the Duke of Ormond, then lord lieutenant of Ireland, and council, by their proclamation, ordering all Roman Catholics to remove without the walls of forts, cities and corporate towns; a few years after which we find the name Irish quarter noticed in our records, instead of that of West Suburb. The streets of this quarter are called Irish quarter south and west; their west ends are joined by a street called Brewery-lane, or Davy's-street. A few houses a short distance from those places are dignified with the names of Pound-lane and Tea-lane.

SAMUEL McSKIMIN, *History of Carrickfergus*, 1829

from *Carrickfergus*

. . . the Scotch quarter was a line of residential houses,
But the Irish quarter was a slum for the blind and halt.

LOUIS MACNEICE, *The Earth Compels*, 1938

Athlone had the usual traffic jam, a poster announcing the drama festival and beside it one for a sheepdog trial. The cathedral was there, the rampart walls, and as in every Irish town toasted sandwiches from the infra grill. You read how there would be a festival and that the main attraction would be a beauty competition, ballads and extended licensing laws. You were in the centre of Ireland not far from the monastery of Clonmacnoise which at school you had read of as being a quiet watered land, a land of roses fair. You drove to the next town—similar streets, pile-up, a four-faced clock telling conflicting times, a drunk man with a mouth organ doing a jig, a lorry delivering calor gas refills and one of the Gardai studying the licence number of a parked car since in this era of terrorism nowhere is safe now from the brown paper parcel or the rag doll bomb.

'They drive like they fuck, any old way,' so the driver himself tells you, ignoring his own inconsistency and the speed that alters with the motion of his thoughts. He tells you another thing and it's this, that priests are mingling with the common people and that a priest had his 'hall door' out at a wedding in Limerick and did everything bar ask the bride to go to bed with him. For this he wants to register your facial expression and gives you the benefit of himself full face. You point to the wheel and quite openly stare down at a newspaper.

Most Reverend Dr Lucey, Bishop of Cork, fears that the country is not in danger of pollution from the oil rigs of Bantry Bay but that there is much more to dirty the minds of the people and to pollute their souls in the books, papers and films circulating through Ireland.

EDNA O'BRIEN, *Mother Ireland*, 1976

I took a car for Westport. Stopped at Newport. Sir Richard O'Donel and his lady have established schools on liberal principles. The lady herself teaches two or three days in a week, and Sir Richard has an admirably well-fitted schoolroom, where he teaches a Sabbath school himself. The effects of a fair on Monday showed that Ireland is not emancipated from the effects of whisky. Rioting and fighting lasted through the night. I walked to Westport with the peasantry, and at six in the morning was on a car for Castlebar. Called a few moments on a Baptist minister there, who presented me with a bundle of tracts, which were quite too sectarian to suit my purposes in visiting Ireland.

I stayed twenty-four hours in Sligo, and talked to many of the poorer people. I find in all Ireland the labouring classes, when I first speak to them, are ever praising their master. Just as in America, although the slaves may be often under the lash or in the stocks, yet to a stranger they durst not speak out, lest some 'bird of the air should tell the matter'; so the peasantry of Ireland are in such suffering, that lest they should lose the sixpence or eight-pence they occasionally get while employed, they will make an imperious landlord an angel to a stranger.

My next day's ride on the top of a coach was eighty-one miles to Dublin, some part of it romantic. The sea-coast was rocky and wild, and presented little that was inviting for the abode of man. The road took us through a part of Leitrim, Westmeath, and Longford. At the latter place, while waiting for a change of horses, the beggars seemed to have rallied all their forces, followed by the rags and tatters of the town. I told them I had nothing but books to give.

ASENATH NICHOLSON, *The Bible in Ireland*, 1852

Trip to Kilkenny. Sean Heuston Station again. 'Poor Shamus is dartin' back.' Train windows (by British Rail) never to open, air-conditioning that doesn't work, a dauntingly restricted bar. Inchicore sidings transformed by lawns.

Kildare, Athy, Carlow, Thomastown. Kilkenny wheatfields. Last beautiful buildings on a small scale: the lovely wayside granite stations. Thomastown. Protestant architecture, Catholic stone-masons. Old advertisements on sheets of tin, the jolly hand-waving Raleigh cyclist. Kincora Plug. Old shop façades: Murphy the butcher, a cobbler.

AIDAN HIGGINS, *Ronda Gorge and Other Precipices*, 1976

North Wind

If I had gone to live elsewhere in the world, I should never have known that this particular morning ... continues, will always continue, to exist.   (Nadine Gordimer, *The Late Bourgeois World*)

I shall never forget the wind
On this God-forsaken coast.
It works itself into the mind
Like the high keen of a lost
Lear-spirit in agony
Condemned for eternity

To wander cliff and cove
Without comfort, without love.
It whistles off the stars
And the existential, black
Face of the cosmic dark;
We crouch to roaring fires.

Yet there are mornings when,
Even in midwinter, sunlight
Flares, and a rare stillness
Lies upon roof and garden,
Each object eldritch-bright,
The sea scarred but at peace.

Then, from the ship we say
Is the lit town where we live
(Our whiskey-and-forecast world)
A smaller ship that sheltered
All night in the restless bay
Will weight anchor and leave.

What did they think of us
During their brief sojourn?
A string of lights on the prom

Dancing mad in the storm—
Who lives in such a place?
And will they ever return?

But the shops open at nine
As they have always done,
The wrapped-up bourgeoisie
Hardened by wind and sea.
The newspapers are late
But the milk shines in its crate.

Everything swept so clean
By tempest, wind and rain!
Elated, you might believe
That this was the first day—
A false sense of reprieve,
For the climate is here to stay.

So best prepare for the worst
That chaos and old night
Can do to us. Were we not
Raised on such expectations,
Our hearts starred with frost
Through countless generations?

Elsewhere the olive grove,
Le déjeuner sur l'herbe,
Poppies and parasols,
Blue skies and mythic love.
Here only the stricken souls
No high wind can disturb.

Prospero and his people never
Came to these stormy parts;
Few do who have the choice.
Yet, blasting the subtler arts,
That weird, plaintive voice
Choirs now and for ever.

DEREK MAHON (1979), *Courtyards in Delft*, 1981

I went to the Diamond and into the Church of Ireland. The church is on top of the Diamond which is on top of the town. At the back of the church is the cemetery. When you look over the wall you can see directly down on to the rooftops. The building itself is locked on all but Sundays. The headstones stick up like pages from an old directory of Ulster families: Cochrane, Averell,

Lee, Bevis, Gray, Pogue, Nicholl, Armstrong, Robinson . . . There are more dead Protestants than living ones in Clones today. A woman told me that in O'Neill Park, a public-housing scheme, there are 181 houses and all but one of them Catholic. 'Mind you,' she added, 'no Prod would live up there.'

Protestants moved because of the Troubles. The closed Border roads maimed the town economically. The merchants didn't hang around. The rectory stands empty. It has a fan light over the front door shaped like a rising sun. At the back of the rectory are stone-built, slated outhouses. They are falling apart, caving in with age and rot and neglect. In one outhouse are old jam jars and a 1940s perambulator. This pram is crumbling to rust on its wheels. Rust and cobwebs . . . The graveyard is the only dilapidated, over-grown Protestant graveyard I've ever seen. Usually they are spick and span. Here, though, nettles, weeds and grass are as tall as the headstones. The shut-off Border has choked the town and everything in it.

SHANE CONNAUGHTON, *A Border Diary*, 1995

An hour later and they were all on the road, Leo between the two, who smoked all the way, spitting every ten yards, and nodding to almost every-one they passed on the road. Then the elder dealer began to sing a bawdy song in Irish:

> 'Is fada an treimhse na rabhas ag snámh
> Le cailin gan eadach bui sugach 's sámh.
> Mar ba chóir di bheith bog bhi earball éisg
> 's in ionad suidhe ara . . . Ridle-um-randy-do shuidh si ar pléasc.
>
> 'Oh! Lately I went for a nate little shwim
> With a lassie, was naked as nature, and thrim
> As a fish, for her legs were all mackerels' mate
> And you came on her scales when you thought 'twas her . . .
> Ridle-um, randy, hi, randy, hi-ro!'

And so on for a score of verses.

At Patrickswell they saw the spears of Limerick rising above the trees and the great castles of the Shannon, like Carrigogunnel, on its rock. Within an hour they were passing the first low cabins of the city, and the churches and factories, and were cantering down George's Street, where long rows of tall, red-brick houses looked down on the wide and windy river. A donkey was rolling himself in the dust of a side-street. A drove of hogs was meandering slowly to the slaughter-house. A troop of red-coated soldiers were marching to the castle. The mail-car turned off into a side-street, and into another side-street and halted at a shop, on the facia board of which was painted the name Proinnsias O'Domhnall, and on one side, *Flour, Meal, and Bran*, and on the other, *Groceries, Wines, and Spirits*.

SEAN O'FAOLAIN, *A Nest of Simple Folk*, 1934

To look over the roofs of Galway is not the way to increase your love for it. Its animation is its sole charm—unless one ventures forth from the strict and legal highways of charms and counts the questionable: shabbiness, fish smells, decay, blistered paintwork and weedy derelict sites. Galway is a city of broken things. It is like a house where the children have got out of hand, in which the old things are kept on for want of an idea what to do with them: crippled chairs, invalided tables, leprous couches and spectral old presses. Spanish Gate, the grassy quays, the skeleton of a lighter lying half-buried in mud; old infirm and cobwebby mills which might conceal tarantula spiders ready to pounce on passers-by. The Corrib races on, a mixture of black ink and diluted pitch, even its crests are dingy and grubby. But the swans are snowy white farther down where the excited river is calmed by the harbour-locked sea. There is nothing any more to say about the Claddagh: it is sucked sweet; the deed has been done, the fishing colony demolished. University College is as austere as a mortuary chapel. The old Catholic cathedral abounds in character: it is a survival of the bad times when Roman Catholics had to lie low. The building, which is the last word in architectural reticence, is to be replaced; whatever distinctions the new cathedral will have, it will have none of the pathos of the old one.

That, then, is *my* Galway. We have come to an end. Let us take tea in Lydon's, upstairs, over the buoyant aroma of newly baked cakes. The place is crammed and everyone is talking in most melodious and (if it is permitted) grey-eyed, long-lashed tones. Country people, suburban and city people, all unredeemed provincials and enjoying that status to the full. Then to Salthill by the gently nosing, apologetic bus.

There were horse trams in Galway when I was a boy. Somehow one does not miss them; the bus is a horse tram without the horse. (When native Irish speakers were compelled to make a term for the telegraph they concocted something which translates as 'the message that comes on sticks'; when wireless came, the term was extended to 'the message that comes on sticks without the sticks'.) The short bus journey to the seaside gives plenty of interesting glimpses and when it comes to its bay-wide end there is a joyful increase of height, breadth and light. Salthill is as Irish a seaside place as Galway is an Irish city, which is to say that it is entirely Irish and racy.

STEPHEN RYNNE, *All Ireland*, 1956

Its [Limerick's] quiet warehouses and its deserted quay-sides give you the sensations you might feel if you had come suddenly upon the forgotten palace of some Sleeping Beauty. Looking over the bridge by the ruined castle in the evening, you see a river of lights as wonderful as the Thames between Westminster Bridge and St Paul's after nightfall, but it is the Thames of a distant enchanted country—the Thames seen in an exquisite revealing mirage. In the day-time O'Connell Street is filled with fine-looking people who know how to dress, going leisurely about in carriages, in motor-cars, and on foot, and jaunting-cars wait idly at the street-corners for their fares. Limerick has its own fashion and its own elegance. It belongs to a civilisation before trams were invented or tea-shops thought of. It is the stateliest city of its size I know, and built upon the stateliest river.

ROBERT LYND, *Home Life in Ireland*, 1908

In the Lost Province

As it comes back, brick by smoky brick,
I say to myself—strange I lived there
And walked those streets. It is the Ormeau Road
On a summer's evening, a haze of absence
Over the caked city, that slumped smell
From the blackened gasworks. Ah, those brick canyons
Where Brookeborough unsheathes a sabre,
Shouting 'No Surrender' from the back of a lorry.

And the sky is a dry purple, and men
Are talking politics in a back room.
Is it too early or too late for change?
Certainly the province is most peaceful.
Who would dream of necessity, the angers
Of Leviathan, or the years of judgement?

TOM PAULIN, *The Strange Museum*, 1980

Belfast, with its industrial clamour, its new red brick that screams at you, and its electric trams that fly faster than the trams anywhere else, represents . . . the rush of the nineteenth century into Ireland. It is the nineteenth-century in youth, however, not in decadence. Belfast has made itself hastily, too hastily, and when it lies silent through the fear of God on the morning of the seventh day, you see that it is as yet an industrial camp and not a city. . . . It will be pulled down one of these days, and built afresh by people who love it too well to leave it like a jumble of jerry-building in a field. It has too many of the elements of beauty both in its situation and in its people to remain per-manently a discord in the side of Ulster. Spread beneath its hills and along the low shores of its windy lough, it has a bustling population of men who are at once militant and emotional, and of women with a high average of determination and good looks. It seems to me indeed to lack only one thing in order to be a great city: it lacks that healthy nationality which is synonymous with taste. Its people have a promising gladness in spite of the gloom of its conflicting churches. They are idealists, for they would drop all their worldly interests any day to fight, some of them for a green flag, some of them for an orange banner. I do not mean that the town is not full of quiet people who would not fight for any cause whatsoever. What gives Belfast its distinction among cities, however, is the strain of almost savage idealism that runs in the veins of the people. I call the idealism savage, because it has never been given a soul by the churches, or an intellect by the schools and colleges. Belfast has grown up like a child whose parents died in its infancy, and the jerry-builders and the catchword orators have taken merciless advantage of it.

ROBERT LYND, *Home Life in Ireland*, 1908

Early on the morrow, I took a Bianconi for Cork; a long ride of fifty miles in a snowy wintry day, on an open car, with the wind blowing full in my face, and my seat the next one to the horses. A spruce Dublinite, fresh from the army, and two dogs, a big and little one, were seated upon the car, the larger dog upon the seat, the small one upon his master's lap. We had proceeded but a few miles, when a huge Goliath, with brandy-blotched face, and beef-eating front, made application for a seat, and the senior dog was transferred to a box over my head. The restless animal, tied to the box, had no certain resting-place but on my shoulders or bonnet, and at every jostle of the car, his talons took a fresh grip of the foundation beneath him. Twenty miles, in this deplorable plight, brought us at nine o'clock to Cork.

In the morning, after an uncomfortable night, and a breakfast of two potatoes, I made my way through snow and sleet to the house of a Baptist minister, where I passed the day; and here, though a table was spread with knives, forks, and plates, potatoes and salt was my hap alone, for there was no bread.

ASENATH NICHOLSON, *The Bible in Ireland*, 1852

Irish towns have always been little more than crossroad centres. They are market-towns and administrative seats. Their economics is that of distribution, not production. The industrial revolution has passed southern Ireland by. The shop, the pub, the fair bring the towns their life-blood and link them to their hinterlands and to the outside world. Many of them still collect market tolls on rural produce, as if they still had a ring of stone-wall fortification about them. Many of them have no fair green but throw open all their streets to shouting, bargaining men and milling cattle, on the day of the fair, surrendering themselves entirely to the countryside upon which they live.

One still approaches many of them today as one approached them in the sixteenth century, although now perhaps an automobile road breaks a new entrance into them or the railroad halts a jaunting car's distance away. The roads that radiate inward toward the heart of the town are still lined with labourers' and artisans' thatched cottages long before one reaches the town itself. As one proceeds along them, the cottages give way to shops and public houses which rise higher and more stately as one nears the centre, in the market-place or in the central square. There, quite often, that emporium of the most valuable commodity of all—the local bank—now dominates the scene.

Between the shop-fronts, back lanes lead off to the recesses in which the labourers live; and, off by themselves in a proud segregation, stand the more pretentious houses of a residential area, and the great grey buildings in which local government and justice are housed. But the centre remains the point at which the shop-lined streets that lead from deep within the countryside converge. The life of the country and that of the town meet and mingle along these converging lines.

That mingling represents the latest stage of an age-old struggle in which the countryside has won out at last. It has been a conquest of assimilation, like the victories of Chinese life over the barbarian invader. The town in Irish history was originally, and often long remained, a foreign growth. In the great age of Celtic civilization, the monastery and the royal seat centred Irish life. Later the Celto-Norman castle scorned an urban fortress wall. The town was first a Danish importation; only Galway, of Irish cities, was not a Norseman's settlement. Throughout the long wars and counter-wars with the English foe and the alien English life, the town was many times alternately absorbed by native life and reconquered for the alien. Even Galway still bore its famous inscription above its city gate not three centuries ago. 'O Lord,' it read, 'deliver us from the fury of the O'Flaherties.' Law, at first, forbade even the entrance of the 'Irishry' into the towns and then later decreed that no Irishman should trade with another. The towns were to remain English, and later, Protestant, and the merchant-burghers who flourished in them must remain of English blood and habit.

All that, of course, has long since vanished. The Irish have occupied the towns of their own land, their blood and habit hold sway and fashion urban commerce in the towns and cities. The change has been a slow and durable growth, flowing on beneath the surface of political and cultural strife. But like all growth it has been a process of incorporation, too. Today, to a casual eye, the shops, the commerce, the social life of the Irish town is much like that of all modern western Europe.

Conrad Arensberg, *The Irish Countryman*, 1937

In My Childhood Trees Were Green

In my childhood trees were green
And there was plenty to be seen.

LOUIS MACNEICE,
'Autobiography'

Sitting on a window-sill, he could watch the women scouring their doorsteps; or, possibly, one with a little more money, painting it a bright red or a fair blue; or, in old skirts and blouses, cleaning their windows with rags and paraffin, sometimes exchanging gossip from opposite sides of the street, both busy at the windows, and never once turning to look at one another.

He loved to see the bakers' carts trotting into the street, Johnston, Mooney, and O'Brien's cart at one end, and Boland's at the other, one coloured green and the other coloured a reddish brown. The carts were big and box-like, filled with double rows of shallow trays on which rested row after row of steaming loaves, tuppence or tuppence-farthing each. Underneath a deep drawer, going the whole length of the cart, filled with lovely white an' brown squares, soda squares, currant squares, and crown loaves, covered with their shining golden crust, ruggedly tapering at the top, like the upper part of a king's crown. He loved, too, to watch the milk-carts come jingling into the street, filled with shining churns, having big brass taps sticking out through holes in the tailboard, all polished up to the nines; though, as Johnny's mother often said, if they were as particular with the insides as they were with the outsides, the milk'd be safer to drink. From these big churns the milkman filled a can with a long snout on which rattled the half-pint and pint measures used to dish out the milk as it was required to the women waiting at the doors with jugs and mugs in their hands, to buy just enough milk that would temper the bitterness of the tea they so often made for themselves, their husbands, and their children. Whenever he was fit, Johnny used to help the milkman, running around with the long-snouted can, filling half-pints and pints of milk into outstretched jugs; the women constantly grumbling that Mr Divene always gave them a betther tilly, so he did; Johnny defending himself be saying that he had to be careful with other people's property, so he had; and then, when the work was done, with the milkman sitting on the seat, he'd stand up in the cart, gather the reins in his hands, sing out a gee-gee-up, suit his balance cutely to the jig-jog of the cart, and drive the jennet back to the dairy.

SEAN O'CASEY, *I Knock at the Door*, 1939

The Way to School

My sister walked me every day to school
till I grew taller than that infant class;
there then were splendid monuments to pass,
the corner butcher's, tiled with ram and bull,
the harness shop its windows bright with brass,
whips, stirrups, saddles, and that leather smell,
and at the next street-crossing corner was
the Farrier's—a fancy name to spell—
scorched horn to sniff, the clanging anvil sound.
Then past some houses, sweet shops, to the door
open and spilling grains upon the ground,
with jerking pigeons flapping, pecking round;
inside, that dark and sweet hay-scented store.
Who, with a little horse, could ask for more?

JOHN HEWITT, *Collected Poems*, 1991

There was a footpath near our house which ran along by the railway and led to the linen mill. We called it the Cinder Path because it was made of cinders, it put your teeth on edge to walk on it. If you went along there the wrong time of day you met the mill-girls—rude bold creatures, Miss Craig said—all with black shawls over their heads and the older ones haggard, dark under the eyes, their voices harsh and embittered and jeering. Or when we went through the town there were always men standing at the corners—standing there at least till the pubs opened—in shiny blue suits and dirty collarless shirts fastened with a collar-stud, and cloth caps pulled down over narrow leering eyes, and sour mouths which did not open when they spoke but which twisted sideways as they spat. The pavement around them was constellated with spittle and on the drab cement walls at their back there was chalked up 'To Hell with the Pope'.

Then there were the rude bold children who had no shoes and the cripples who swung along on crutches with a jaunty kind of insolence through the slum streets called the Irish Quarter. We rarely went into the Irish Quarter and I used to hold my breath till I got through it. There was a dense smell of poverty as of soot mixed with porter mixed with cheap fat frying mixed with festering scabs and rags that had never been washed. Many of the houses were mere cottages and you looked down over the half-door into a room below the level of the street, always dark but the glow of a grate might show up a mangy cat or a quizzical wrinkled face. The thatch on the roofs came down to within five feet of the street, was sometimes mottled with grass or moss, was usually dripping. And in Irish Quarter West there was a place which I knew was bad—a public house with great wide windows of opaque decorated glass out of which came randy voices and clinks and swear-words and a smell that was stronger than cheese and a mellow yellow light at night that fell on the gutter like a benison.

LOUIS MACNEICE, *The Strings Are False*, 1965

The burning of Woodstock House, the home of poetry and learning, in 1922, was one of the saddest of Ireland's tragedies. But the beautiful plantations survived and there is scarcely in all Ireland a more charming walk than that which runs below the ruins along the Nore. On one side the river with its swans and water lilies, on the other the wooded cliffs and mossy glades sprinkled with ferns and frochans and foxgloves.

When I was young there were plenty of river picnics and neighbours visited each other by cot (long flat-bottomed boats which were used for netfishing). It was every boy and girl's dream to take a cot to Inistioge, where the river becomes tidal. My brother and I once got as far as Thomastown and then our patience ran out and we walked to Inistioge and spent the night at a small hotel. There was a large stuffed white rabbit on a chest of drawers and at dawn we awoke scratching and observed two columns of insects advancing on us from the rabbit.

The hotel turned into a pub and small shops have come and gone but Inistioge is still the most beautiful and peaceful of villages. Not long ago I was sitting on a bench beside the bridge waiting for my grandchildren to come down the river by canoe from Maidenhall. I remember the red valerian, a broad bank of colour reflected on the dappled current. In such a place time stands still. The past comes close in disconnected fragments and I was thinking of the days when we were children and had dancing classes with the young Tighes at the Noreview Hotel in Thomastown; their mother, with my Aunt Harriet, used to run a Christian Science Reading Room opposite the Castle in Kilkenny, two spiders into whose web no fly ever came, and I remember when we went to Woodstock a side-car used to meet us at

Thomastown station and the branches of the trees brushed our faces as we drove along.

HUBERT BUTLER, 'Beside the Nore', in *Escape From the Anthill*, 1985; first published in *Ireland of the Welcomes*, May–June 1970

The roofs of sheds below had blobs of moss between their slates, the galvanized iron was rust-eaten, and, beyond the top-heavy creeper on the wall, a few backyards away, was the side of a gaunt Protestant church. The lancets of that church were dark and unlighted, for the sun never seemed to reach them. The greater and lesser spires, the long row of pinnacles, gleamed greyly when a ray touched them, but on wintry days they were black and looming. Because of its grim, forbidding appearance, this edifice was known locally as the Black Church, and the name, with all its theological implications, was apt.

The Black Church stood in a space to itself and there was a railing with spikes all round it. The doors were locked during week-days, and that surprised us as children, for our chapels were always open from seven o'clock in the morning. After school the little boys and girls from Paradise Lane, which was at the back of our street, scampered around the Black Church. But at night the shadowy gas-lit Place was silent and deserted, except for the echoing footsteps of a passer-by or the rumble of a cab. As children, we were told that anyone who ran round the church three times after dark would meet the Devil himself on the third round, but none of us had the courage to test the legend.

AUSTIN CLARKE, *Twice Round the Black Church*, 1963

There were two open spaces near our house. Behind our row of houses, the back field sloped up towards the Lone Moor Road; it ended in a roadway that curved down towards Blucher Street and then straightened towards the police barracks, three hundred yards away. The roadway was flanked by a stone wall, with a flat parapet, only five feet high on our side, twelve feet high on the other. On the other side was Meenan's Park, although the older people still called it Watt's Field, after the owner of the distillery. We could climb the wall and drop down on the other side; but the wall ran past the foot of the streets—Limewood, Tyrconnell, Beechwood and Elmwood—pierced by a rectangular opening at each street that led to a flight of railed steps down to the park. A line of air-raid shelters separated the top section of the park from the open spaces beyond, where we played football. At night, the field and the park were pitch-black. The only street lighting was a single curved lamp, eight feet high, at the end of each street. We were told never to play in the park at night, for Daddy Watt's ghost haunted it, looking for revenge for the distillery

fire that had ruined him. Those who saw him said he was just a black shape
that moved like a shadow around the park, but that the shape had a mouth
that opened and showed a red fire raging within.

SEAMUS DEANE, *Reading in the Dark*, 1996

They stood together for a few moments. Teasie was just about to move away,
when a terrible outburst of crying suddenly sounded from up at the Corner.
As they looked up, a young boy came round in the Row, hurrying through
the crowd of fellows, howling piteously.

'Sacred Heart of Jesus!' Kitty exclaimed. 'It's Shemie. He's fallen into the
river again.'

They heard Malachey call out to him, as his father recovered from his
astonishment, but Shemie came tottering on heedlessly, roaring at the top of
his voice, and the water running out of him.

Malachey, Pachy and Neilly started after him, and here and there along
both sides of the Row, heads popped out over the half-doors. Old women
clicked their tongues and murmured their sympathy as Shemie passed.

'Ah, God help him, he's drownded. Hurry on home, son, quick.'

'Bring him down, Malachey,' Kitty called, 'bring him on down. Jesus, Mary
and St Joseph, that young fellow will be drownded yet. That's the third time
this month. Now you see what I have to put up with, Teasie. What unlucky
prayer was hanging round my head this day, that I didn't send them off to the
pictures when I had the chance. Come on, come on! If I wouldn't be better
off handcuffed to a ghost it's a quare thing to me.'

JOHN O'CONNOR, *Come Day—Go Day*, 1948

When I was a boy horses were so much in all people's lives in the country
places that an ordinary Tailor would give you strap buttons inside the hem
of the ends of your trouser legs, unless he was particularly told not to. You
had a couple of straps in your pocket, and were so supposed to be always
ready when offered a mount on a horse to be able to strap down your trousers
and hop up into the saddle. This did not apply to myself so much: for there
were few people who would insist on throwing me up into a saddle, for I was
never perhaps born to witch the world with my horsemanship. I was generally on the ground looking on, and you didn't require your trousers strapped
down for that. And a light ashplant could always be carried, and switched
against the leg in a knowing way. But I seem to have been constantly standing in stables admiring horses with the clothes thrown off their quarters, and
listening to wise talk about them, and to the history of horses, and looking
at horses trotting on a road or cantering along the grass at the road's edge, or

with people who rattled ashplants in hard felt hats to make horses show themselves off. And seeing running to us people, on a hot dusty May evening, in
a town, clothed in turf smoke, shot through with the bars of setting sun.
These people would be running because they had a sick horse just taken
from a cart and my friend on the car beside me was a knowing one with a
cure for horses' ailments. I know he told them to put as much of something
as would stand on a shilling and give it to the horse in something. Was it in
porter: I forget. But there are plenty to-day who dream of such medicine,
hopelessly, for themselves, and without anything standing on any shilling.
In those days those strapped trousers were fairly tight in cut. It only shows
how little the horse has to do with the average man's life now. For who
could fancy riding in what the Lady Novelists call 'Varsity Bags'. Boots,
ordinary walking boots, also at that time were narrow to fit into a stirrup iron.
As soon as man began to wear shoes, with an inch of sole jutting out all
round like a miniature bicycle track, I knew that he had definitely come down
on the ground and left the saddle. Half the world then seemed to smell of
horses, old harness, hay, oats, bran mashes, old stables and hub grease.
Anyway a great many smells seem to have disappeared altogether. The smell
of old houses and old apple-rooms were good ones. Now of course there is
the strong, insistent, determined smell of petrol. If you are away from the
smell for some time and get it again it cheers you up. But it has mastered all
the others. Though even before it came our noses had lost their cunning. It
will come back again. The Nose to its glory. It will have a great vogue, so difficult, so precious, so apart, so non-impartable. I understand that smells
cannot yet be photographed so as to be recognized. The whole thing is at
present in the hands, no in the noses, of connoisseurs, who cannot explain
themselves.

JACK YEATS, *Sligo*, 1930

The Mixed Marriage

My father was a servant-boy.
When he left school at eight or nine
He took up billhook and loy
To win the ground he would never own.

My mother was the school-mistress,
The world of Castor and Pollux.
There were twins in her own class.
She could never tell which was which.

She had read one volume of Proust,
He knew the cure for farcy.

I flitted between a hole in the hedge
And a room in the Latin Quarter.

When she had cleared the supper-table
She opened *The Acts of the Apostles,*
Aesop's Fables, Gulliver's Travels.
Then my mother went on upstairs.

And my father further dimmed the light
To get back to hunting with ferrets
Or the factions of the faction-fights,
The Ribbon Boys, the Caravats.

PAUL MULDOON, *Mules*, 1977

We walked along the North Strand Road till we came to the Vitriol Works and then turned to the right along the Wharf Road. Mahony began to play the Indian as soon as we were out of public sight. He chased a crowd of ragged girls, brandishing his unloaded catapult and, when two ragged boys began, out of chivalry, to fling stones at us, he proposed that we should charge them. I objected that the boys were too small, and so we walked on, the ragged troop screaming after us '*Swaddlers! Swaddlers!*' thinking that we were Protestants because Mahony, who was dark-complexioned, wore the silver badge of a cricket club in his cap. When we came to the Smoothing Iron we arranged a siege; but it was a failure because you must have at least three. We revenged ourselves on Leo Dillon by saying what a funk he was and guessing how many he would get at three o'clock from Mr Ryan.

We came then near the river. We spent a long time walking about the noisy streets flanked by high stone walls, watching the working of cranes and engines and often being shouted at for our immobility by the drivers of groaning carts. It was noon when we reached the quays and, as all the labourers seemed to be eating their lunches, we bought two big currant buns and sat down to eat them on some metal piping beside the river. We pleased ourselves with the spectacle of Dublin's commerce—the barges signalled from far away by their curls of woolly smoke, the brown fishing fleet beyond Ringsend, the big white sailing vessel which was being discharged on the opposite quay. Mahony said it would be right skit to run away to sea on one of those big ships, and even I, looking at the high masts, saw, or imagined, the geography which had been scantily dosed to me at school gradually taking substance under my eyes. School and home seemed to recede from us and their influences upon us seemed to wane.

We crossed the Liffey in the ferryboat, paying our toll to be transported in the company of two labourers and a little Jew with a bag. We were serious to the point of solemnity, but once during the short voyage our eyes met and we laughed. When we landed we watched the discharging of the graceful three-master which we had observed from the other quay. Some bystander said that she was a Norwegian vessel. I went to the stern and tried to decipher the legend upon it but, failing to do so, I came back and examined the foreign sailors to see had any of them green eyes, for I had some confused notion . . . The sailors' eyes were blue, and grey, and even black. The only sailor whose eyes could have been called green was a tall man who amused the crowd on the quay by calling out cheerfully every time the planks fell:

'All right! All right!'

When we were tired of this sight we wandered slowly into Ringsend. The day had grown sultry, and in the windows of the grocers' shops musty biscuits lay bleaching. We bought some biscuits and chocolate, which we ate sedulously as we wandered through the squalid streets where the families of the fishermen live. We could find no dairy and so we went into a huckster's shop and bought a bottle of raspberry lemonade each. Refreshed by this, Mahony chased a cat down a lane, but the cat escaped into a wide field. We both felt rather tired, and when we reached the field we made at once for a sloping bank, over the ridge of which we could see the Dodder.

JAMES JOYCE, *Dubliners*, 1915

Around our house there stood little hills all tilled and tame. Yellow flame-blossoms of the whin lit bonfires all over the landscape; the whin was as persistent and as fertile as sin and disease. The sunny side of the hills was good soil and boasted some tall thorn trees, but the black side facing the north was crabbed and poverty-stricken and grew only stunted blackthorns and sorrel plants. There were no trees to speak of except the poplar and the sally; here and there a cranky old elm which had survived the crying of a cold kitchen spread about his trunk and tried to look a forest. From the tops of the little hills there spread a view right back to the days of Saint Patrick and the druids. Slieve Gullion to the north fifteen miles distant, to the west the bewitched hills and forths of Donaghmoyne; eastward one could see the distillery chimney of Dundalk sending up its prosperous smoke, or, on a very bright day, one could see the sun-dazzled tide coming in at Annagasson. To the south stood the Hill of Mullacrew where once was held a fair famous as Donnybrook and it had as many cracked skulls to its credit too.

The name of my birthplace was Mucker; some of the natives wanted to change it to Summerhill which would have been worse. All who could do so without risking the loss of their scant mail cut 'Mucker' out of their postal address altogether. The natives of the place were known far and near as Muckers, which in after years was rhymed obscenely by corner-boys. The name was a corrupted Gaelic word signifying a place where pigs were bred in abundance. Long before my arrival there was much aesthetic heart-aching

among the folk who had to put up with, and up in, such a pig-named townland. In spite of all this the townland stuck to its title and it was in Mucker I
was born.

PATRICK KAVANAGH, *The Green Fool*, 1938

This was our first year at Dunamara, my Aunt Hersey's house by the sea lough
of Mannanen, which is the biggest in Ireland. It was an old, long house with
a white face and a dark, slate roof, set against the trees on the steep hill-side.
It had almost no garden, for it stood on a narrow shelf between the hill and
the lough; fifteen yards of rough, weedy lawn divided it from the lough which,
at spring tides, flowed to the very level of the grass. There was nothing
between the water's edge and the long, formal grass plot but a coping of stone,
level with the grass and a foot wide. In winter storms, of course, waves broke
as far as the doorstep and spray rattled on the roof like shrapnel.

The house had no beauty except the fine proportions of door, window,
chimney and roof. I did not value it then for beauty, but it stands before my
eye now with the dignity of a classical order which owes its forms to the shape
of the real. . . .

We lived in our own tribe, among its ideas, its loves and wars; and the tribes
of other children. I remember the fisherman's children about the shores and
wild hordes of mountain children in their father's cut-down trousers, but
not fishermen or farmers. I was always toiling up some hill with a turf in my
hand to join an ambush; or running with a new-laid egg, probably stolen, to
make a feast; or rushing along by some hedge pursued by a dog or a policeman. We stole boats and borrowed the saddler's pony for rides, or, on Dunvil
Green, one of the grazing donkeys; which threw us against walls or into the
whins.

The rides had gone, but I remember a fall, as if by the light of a lantern
slide reflected from the screen. The flash of conception has this power, to
photograph all surrounding memories; to fix a whole region of experience in
the brain. Full of prickles and bruises, I staggered one day howling through
some long lane between enormous walls as high as the Bastille. I must have
been about six, for the walls could have belonged only to a lane in Dunvil,
the seaside fishing village which was our market town. Perhaps they were
eight foot high. The lane was full of rocks, smoothed out like scones, and
there were piles of fish-boxes against the walls.

JOYCE CARY, *A House of Children*, 1941

Breakfast for all was over by 9.30 when we children and Moll set off across
the hills to school. The men had gone to the fields, the women dispersed—

some to feeding numerous turkeys, geese, hens, ducks, others to wash the dairy and scrub and scald pails, pans, strainers and churns; one to do house-work and another to prepare the men's mid-day meal and perhaps set a great batch of dough to rise in the warmth of the hearth while the brick oven was being heated by burning bundles of furze and sticks. Our dinner was at four o'clock. The evening milking was from five to seven. The morning routine of straining and scalding was repeated. Milking was something of a mystery to us children, as our father forbade us to enter the byres, but from the outside we heard the rythmical swish of milk falling into pails and the dairymaids singing or crooning, each to her cow.

MARY CARBERY, *The Farm by Lough Gur*, 1937

'I was coming along the road,' she began, 'when who should I meet but a big wicked-looking man with a baldy head on his shoulders and two round eyes as big as saucers.'

'Go away out of that, Honeybird,' Patsy interrupted.

'Well, I can tell you they looked like that to me,' said Honeybird, 'and just as he was passing me I saw a wee beak keeking out of his pocket, and says I to myself that's Father Ryan's bantam hen, and says I to him, drop it, says I.'

'God preserve you, child! The man might have hurted you,' said Lull.

'He very near did,' said Honeybird; 'he lifted a big stone and clodded it at me.'

'That's the last time you are out stravaging the roads by your lone,' said Lull. 'You ones will not have to leave the wee soul after this,' she cautioned the others.

They were as frightened as Lull. They treated Honeybird as if she had been rescued from some terrible danger. Next morning Andy was told. He questioned Honeybird closely and said he would give a description of the man to Sergeant McGee. Honeybird remembered that the man had red whiskers and carried a big stick. Later she remembered that he had bandy legs and a squint. The more frightened the others grew at the thought of the danger she had been exposed to, the more terrible grew her description of the man.

Once or twice Jane had a suspicion that Honeybird was adding to the truth; but when questioned Honeybird stuck to the same tale and never contra-dicted herself.

'God be thanked no harm came to the child,' said Lull when Honeybird had gone off to play in charge of Fly and Patsy. 'I'll be afraid to let her out of my sight after this.'

'I'll hold you Sergeant McGee will keep a look out for that man,' said Jane. They were up in the loft getting hay for Rufus.

'Wasn't she a brave wee soul to tell the man to drop the priest's hen?' said Mick.

Jane lifted a bundle of hay.

'She's an awfully good wee child anyway,' she answered. 'What's that scraping in the corner?' she added.

'What is it?' said Mick. Jane did not answer. He repeated his question, and Jane raised a bewildered face.

'Come here and see,' she said.

In the corner where a place had been cleared, a bantam hen was tethered by a string to a nail in the floor.

'God help us, why did he hide it here?' said Mick.

'He!' said Jane, 'don't you see for yourself the meaning of it? *She* stole it and told us all those lies on purpose.'

Mick could hardly be brought to believe this.

'Did you ever hear of such badness?' said Jane.

'Maybe she didn't know what she was doing,' said Mick.

'Didn't she just?' said Jane; 'she knew well enough to tell a queer good lie.'

'We'd better go and ask her if she did it,' said Mick.

They found Honeybird playing on the lawn with Fly and Patsy, and led her away to the top of the garden. Jane began the accusation.

'Do you know, Honeybird, we think you are a wee thief.'

'Dear forgive you!' said Honeybird.

'We've seen the bantam,' said Jane. Honeybird looked up quickly.

'Then just you leave it alone and mind your own business,' she said.

'Do you know you are a thief and a liar, Honeybird Darragh?' said Jane slowly.

'Well, what if I am?' Honeybird answered. 'Sure I'm only a wee child and know no better.'

KATHLEEN FITZPATRICK, *The Weans at Rowallan*, 1905

It was his grandfather, Manus O'Donnell, who owned the house in which Finn, his father and mother and grandmother lived. Before it was a garden with gooseberry and currant bushes and with a bee-hive placed in the shelter of a ditch. In the warm days the young calves lay in this garden and the bees hummed round the currant bushes. A high fuchsia hedge divided it from the roadway and a fuchsia bush with scarlet and purple pendants grew before the door. The road that went by the house was nearly always empty, but one could hear the carts creaking on another road that was across the bog. This road went from the country town to the villages in the mountains and one could see, behind the carts, the mountain horses striding along, each carrying a man with a woman seated behind him. Always above that country there were big gray clouds, and across it, marking one field from another, ran little walls

of loose stones. One could see smooth mown fields with cocks of hay beside
dark-green fields of potatoes and little fields of yellowing corn. Houses were
scattered here and there; they were low, whitewashed and thatched with straw
that had become brown in the weather.

PADRAIC COLUM, *A Boy in Eirinn*, 1916

When I was a Little Girl

WHEN I was a little girl,
In a garden playing
A thing was often said
To chide us delaying:

When after sunny hours,
At twilight's falling,
Down through the garden walks
Came our old nurse calling

'Come in! for it's growing late,
And the grass will wet ye!
Come in! or when it's dark
The Fenians will get ye.'

Then, at this dreadful news,
All helter-skelter,
The panic-struck little flock
Ran home for shelter.

And round the nursery fire
Sat still to listen,
Fifty bare toes on the hearth,
Ten eyes a-glisten.

To hear of a night in March,
And loyal folk waiting,
To see a great army of men
Come devastating.

An Army of Papists grim,
With a green flag o'er them,
Red-coats and black police
Flying before them.

But God (Who our nurse declared
Guards British dominions)

Sent down a fall of snow
And scattered the Fenians.

'But somewhere they're lurking yet,
Maybe they're near us,'
Four little hearts pit-a-pat
Thought 'Can they hear us?'

Then the wind-shaken pane
Sounded like drumming;
'Oh!' they cried, 'tuck us in,
The Fenians are coming!'

Four little pairs of hands
In the cots where she led those,
Over their frightened heads
Pulled up the bedclothes.

But one little rebel there,
Watching all with laughter,
Thought 'When the Fenians come
I'll rise and go after.'

Wished she had been a boy
And a good deal older—
Able to walk for miles
With a gun on her shoulder.

Able to lift aloft
The Green Flag o'er them
(Red-coats and black police
Flying before them).

And, as she dropped asleep,
Was wondering whether
God, if they prayed to Him,
Would give fine weather.

ALICE MILLIGAN, *Hero Lays*, 1908

Easter Monday is a day of very general festivity, and on it cock-fights are usually held. In the afternoon, if the weather is fine, young men and women resort to a green south of the town called the Ranbuy, and join in some rustic sport, which concludes by their return into town late in the evening, playing *thread the needle*. Same day, children dye eggs various colours, and repairing to some gentle declivity, trundle them till they break, on which they are eaten.

This appears to be a remnant of an ancient custom in the Christian church, of presenting eggs at this season, as emblems of the resurrection; there being a striking analogy between the matter of an egg, which is capable of being brought into life, and revival from the dead. The custom is referred to in the ritual of Pope Paul V, made for the use of the people of these kingdoms, in the following words:—'Bless, O Lord, we beseech thee, this thy Creature of *Eggs*, that it may become a wholesome sustenance to thy faithful Servants, *eating* it in Thankfulness to thee, *on Account of the Resurrection* of our Lord Jesus Christ.'

SAMUEL McSKIMIN, History of Carrickfergus, 1829

We had seen a good deal of merriment on the roads between Dublin and Limerick: schoolchildren of all ages trotted gaily—many of them barefoot—through the October rain; they came out of lanes, you could see them approaching between hedges along muddy paths; children without number forming like drops into a rivulet, the rivulets forming streams, the streams little rivers—and sometimes the car drove through them as if through a river that parted readily. For a few minutes the road would remain empty, when the car had just passed through a slightly larger village, and then the drops began collecting again: Irish schoolchildren, jostling and chasing each other, often enterprisingly dressed, in variegated bits and pieces, but all of them, even those who were not merry, were at least relaxed; they often traipse for miles like that through the rain, and home again through the rain, carrying their hurling sticks, their books held together by a strap. For over a hundred miles the car drove through Irish schoolchildren, and although it was raining, and many of them were barefoot, most of them poorly dressed, almost all of them seemed cheerful.

HEINRICH BÖLL, Irish Journal, 1957, trans. Leila Vennewitz

Limerick was an exemplary city. Everyone flocked to confraternities. The friars in their brown robes and sandals moved through the city doing the corporal works of mercy. At the side door of the friary there would be a huddle of people, some who had come to beg for bread and soup, others waiting to hand in their offerings to have masses said for their departed. At ten or eleven years, when on a visit, you sat in a chapel with your legs crossed and were asked by an incensed lady to please uncross them at once. 'Did you not know,' she said, 'that Our Lady blushes whenever a woman does such an indecent thing.'

EDNA O'BRIEN, Mother Ireland, 1976

I went to schools run by four orders. One was the Irish Sisters of Charity. I was cast as St Gabriel in a tableau when I was seven or so, posed at the end of the school concert, standing above the Holy Family with my wings spread protectively. But I saw my friend in the audience and waved my wings at her. The nun beat me around the room afterwards with the leg of a chair. Later, I was a pupil at a Sisters of the Holy Faith school. The nuns had a long leather strap as part of their habit—it was attached to their belts. But the head nun had a special, double-thickness strap which was kept in a cupboard. I was strapped with it many times, and it reduced me to a snivelling suppliant, squeezing my red-hot hands between my knees and begging for forgiveness. . . .

People are reluctant to face the truth. But I believe the truth is that what lay behind the cruelty perpetrated on children was Catholicism itself. It developed the concepts of sexual wickedness and maternal sin which were used to facilitate the expression of sadism. And the more general ordinary abuse of children was in part a consequence of more Catholic teaching, this time on contraception. It was known that almost all the children of large families—almost all children—would never have a stake in Irish society, never have children here themselves, never count for anything. Their eventual unimportance in London or Springfield, Massachusetts was visited upon them early. Why would their minders or teachers value them? Their country didn't value them.

NUALA O'FAOLAIN, *Are You Somebody?*, 1996

By the time Joe was let out of school the town was beginning to lose its colour. The rows of houses up the hill behind had the look of cardboard cut-outs against the draining sky. The wind that blew up the valley was cold and the day's dust and several crisp bags played dismally around Joe's feet as he walked along the road. He was in no hurry to get home. Mam never got back from the café much before a quarter to six and it was more than likely that the old fella'd be sending him out on messages here, there and everywhere, and Mam would catch him at it and there would be ructions. More ructions. It was that sort of day. A ructious day. There weren't many people about. Down below him in the distance a couple of shots were fired and then there was silence. The street lamps were flowering and people had not yet drawn their curtains, so the dusk glittered. He stopped by a long low wall and put his school bag down on it. His mother hated him to loiter. He shoved his clenched fists into the pockets of his anorak and huddled it around him, against the wind. A mist of smoke from the thousands of houses below drifted along the valley. The only colour to be seen now was the green grass of the hill across the valley, on top of which rose the grey walls that surrounded the city. A seagull drifted on the wind, out too late for safety. It was being blown away from the river back towards the hills. With an effort it moved its wings and turned steeply, setting off for home again. Joe picked up his school bag and took the hint. He passed a couple of shops, the windows barricaded, with stripes of light between the planks, 'Business as usual' scrawled on the closed doors. He turned off the main road down the hill, past a row of derelict cottages, the windows frightening holes. He began to run. This stretch of the road always put fear in him. Around the corner a couple of men were strolling casually. Joe slowed his feet. He always felt that to run for no good reason made other people nervous. One of the men laughed at some joke. Joe sauntered past them.

JENNIFER JOHNSTON, *Shadows On Our Skin*, 1977

To Denis, unlike his mother, Cork was for ever remembered as a place of endless summer daylight, that cold Irish daylight without shadows or sun-square, faint-falling from a sky that in its whiteness is so like the night-sky before the sun has gone, and the dawn before it has risen, that they seemed to sleep through light into light, and had no memory of the darkness at all. Each picture that remained to them out of Cork was like those Flemish interiors, where one sees everything without knowing by what light it is seen. The smallest pictures and the most trivial were like that—as a childish playball rising and falling fountain-soft on an elastic, with little grains rattling the cardboard inside. When it rolled on the ground over the red tiles of the kitchen it cast no shadow, and when it rose and sank before the open window, the houses, and the river and roofs behind it, glowed through so cold and mild an atmosphere that they were themselves like a picture in a dark frame.

Down on the quays, he remembered as if it all happened on the same day, a huge brewery horse stood patiently by the kerb, two children running back and forth under his distent belly. The waters lapped the limestone quay walls within a few inches of the passing feet on the pavement, gulls floating backward on its flood, and little naked beggar boys plunged their yellow bodies into the water from the ferry steps up the quay. Denis watched them with his big childish eyes, awed by their daring, squeezing between a throng of grown men to look. A tramway-man clouted a little girl on the head with his cap for something she had said, and then somebody else shouted, 'Police!' and all the dripping bodies scrambled for their clothes and ran naked down the quays, their little bellies moving as they ran. Then the quays were empty and the hills were empty, but he always remembered how, above them, a single cloud fell sideways through the blue like a crumbling tower.

SEAN O'FAOLAIN, *A Nest of Simple Folk*, 1934

'There's not much feedin' in tay or lemonade,' said Nan-nan sullenly as she smoothed down her shiny black skirt and straightened her bonnet. As always, she was annoyed at what she regarded as Seamus's sickly appearance. She would not have minded if he took to the porter, even at that age. It would put some life into him when he wouldn't eat stirabout. After all he was her godson, wasn't he? She had a responsibility. Soon the bus came down the street, coughing and sneezing, and the three climbed in, helped by Tommy. There were two cases and a square thing made of straw, which was very heavy and which Nan-nan kept referring to as her band-box.

The road ran along a railway for miles, with no fence between. They met a train, almost head on. AB pointed out to him Lough Scur, where she said that Queen Elizabeth's hangman, John of the Heads, had his castle and his prison. He killed everyone, men, women and children, let alone priests and nuns. And to make it worse, he was an Irishman, doing what that horrible Englishwoman asked him to do.

'He was just as bad as King Herod, in his own way,' she claimed. She seemed very upset about it all, as she closed her eyes and gripped her chin and lapsed into silence, her head jogging about with the movements of the bus.

Nan-nan pointed out Lough Allen to him. She said that it was really the Shannon, the biggest river in Ireland, England or Scotland, and that it rose in the Shannon Pot, just behind the mountain. And she told him the name of every village and town that they passed through.

The bus stopped at a place where there was a small waterfall. A tree-trunk with a path gouged in it carried the water from the fall across a stream to the side of the road. The driver, Tom Crossan, poured water into the radiator, screwed on the lid quickly, and was off again.

'What's that?' asked Seamus, pointing to what looked like heaps of grey dust which seemed to have fallen from the face of the high mountain rocks. AB told him it was scree, caused by the frost and the sun and the wind over the ages. Nan-nan had fallen asleep by then, and she remained so until the bus jerked to a halt in Bundoran, with the sea and the cliffs in full view.

'Is this Bundoran? Are we here already? Oh, for goodness sake!' She was awake and ready for action.

They quickly found lodgings in a house facing the sea, but back from the street. It was at a low elevation, and it looked sheltered. From their bedroom window upstairs they could see right across Donegal Bay, with the breakers crashing against the nearby cliffs and rocks. In the evening they could see the beacon of the Killybegs lighthouse blinking continuously and without fail. AB said that it was blinking like that so that the ships out on the Atlantic Ocean could see it and know where they were going. Ships would be sinking every day, dozens of them, but for the men who kept the light burning in the Killybegs lighthouse. He thought he would like to work in a lighthouse when he grew up. Slaving away night and day to keep all those ships from sinking.

They stayed nearly two weeks in Bundoran. They walked all over the town and along every cove and stretch of strand or cliff; and they got into conversation with so many people. Early in the morning the Mass bell tolled sombrely over the town: long, deep, solemn chimes. AB often went to early Mass. Sometimes, if he was fully awake and asking too many questions, she told Seamus to wash his face quick, dress himself and to come with her.

The tide seemed to be always out then and wide stretches of beach visible, bare and rocky. The fishermen, back from the sea, drove cartloads of fish around the streets, calling 'Fresh mackerel! Fresh mackerel!' in a low voice, almost as if talking to themselves. In the chapel several priests read Mass at the same time at different altars. This seemed very strange, and rather disrespectful, to Seamus. AB was delighted: the more Masses the merrier.

After breakfast they took their usual long, windy walk along the clifftops and in the direction of the strand. The waves thumped against the rocks below. He liked to watch a wave building up, getting darker and darker and then tumbling over with a roar. They passed the Horse Pool where only the most experienced of swimmers ventured; and further on they could see the strand, with the bathing-boxes ranged in rows and many people in multicoloured bathing-suits moving around and going into the sea. Beyond the strand, on the cliff, AB pointed out the Great Southern Hotel that had hundreds of rooms and was owned by the same people who owned the railway that ran past Drumlahan at home. And behind the hotel was a rock called Roguey where the sea was always so angry that a body could be whipped away from the top of the cliff by the waves and drowned. Away beyond that, out towards Ballyshannon, were the Fairy Bridges, where the rocks were covered with banks of delightful carrageen moss.

CHARLIE O'BEIRNE, *The Good People*, 1985

Most of the well-to-do houses of South Dublin entertained for their children round Christmas-time. Quite often, one's cab crossed the canal, for the spreading mansions along the red roads, with their frosty gardens and steamy conservatories, vied with the cliff-like blocks round Merrion Square. Even houses I knew well became, on these occasions, unfamiliar and heatedly large and light. The front door opened upon the roar of coal fires burning in every festive room. One met *portières* looped back, white paint dazzling in gaslight that poured through crimped pink glass shades, flowers banked up out of harm's way, fur rugs expectantly rolled back and big chintz sofas in retreat against the walls. The pent-up silence in which children assemble, a rustle of fidgeting (like the wind in corn) could be heard as one was led past the drawing-room door to lay off one's coat and shawls in a room above.

ELIZABETH BOWEN, *Seven Winters*, 1943

In the hall the children who had stayed latest were putting on their things: the party was over. She had thrown a shawl about her and, as they went together towards the tram, sprays of her fresh warm breath flew gaily above her cowled head and her shoes tapped blithely on the glassy road.

It was the last tram. The lank brown horses knew it and shook their bells to the clear night in admonition. The conductor talked with the driver, both nodding often in the green light of the lamp. On the empty seats of the tram were scattered a few coloured tickets. No sound of footsteps came up or down the road. No sound broke the peace of the night save when the lank brown horses rubbed their noses together and shook their bells.

JAMES JOYCE, *Portrait of the Artist as a Young Man*, 1915

Carrick Revisited

Back to Carrick, the castle as plumb assured
As thirty years ago—Which war was which?
Here are new villas, here is a sizzling grid
But the green banks are as rich and the lough as hazily lazy
And the child's astonishment not yet cured.

Who was—and am—dumbfounded to find myself
In a topographical frame—here, not there—
The channels of my dreams determined largely
By random chemistry of soil and air;
Memories I had shelved peer at me from the shelf.

Fog-horn, mill-horn, corncrake and church bell
Half-heard through boarded time as a child in bed
Glimpses a brangle of talk from the floor below
But cannot catch the words. Our past we know
But not its meaning—whether it meant well.

Time and place—our bridgeheads into reality
But also its concealment! Out of the sea
We land on the Particular and lose
All other possible bird's-eye views, the Truth
That is of Itself for Itself—but not for me.

Torn before birth from where my fathers dwelt,
Schooled from the age of ten to a foreign voice,
Yet neither western Ireland nor southern England
Cancels this interlude; what chance misspelt
May never now be righted by my choice.

Whatever then my inherited or acquired
Affinities, such remains my childhood's frame
Like a belated rock in the red Antrim clay
That cannot at this era change its pitch or name—
And the pre-natal mountain is far away.

LOUIS MACNEICE, *Holes in the Sky*, 1948

During the Christmas holidays it is yet common with young boys to assemble at night, fantastically dressed with paper ornaments, and to proceed
to the different houses, each repeating in turn the words of some character
in the well known *Christmas rhymes*. After those orations, halfpence are
solicited, and usually given, which are spent in liquors or sweetmeats.

Formerly great numbers of men and boys resorted to the fields on this day,
to play at *shinny*, which game was sometimes warmly contested between the
inhabitants of different townlands; the custom has almost entirely ceased, a
few boys only assembling to this diversion.

Small wooden boxes are bought by children at this season, which are called
Christmas boxes; into these they put halfpence, or such other small presents
as are received at this time, which are also called Christmas boxes. Indeed
Christmas is particularly remarkable as a season of presents, hilarity, and
good cheer, and the meanest person may be said to fare sumptuously on this
occasion. Geese, mutton, and pies, are most sought after; and, in short, every
appendage connected with good eating and drinking. Some burn large
candles, called Christmas candles, during the nights of festivity. The general
salutation at this time is, 'a merry Christmas, and a happy new year.'

Until of late years, branches of holly were put up against the seats and walls
of the church at Christmas, where they remained till Shrove Tuesday.

SAMUEL MCSKIMIN, *History of Carrickfergus*, 1829

The English teacher read out a model essay which had been, to our surprise,
written by a country boy. It was an account of his mother setting the table for
the evening meal and then waiting with him until his father came in from the
fields. She put out a blue-and-white jug full of milk and a covered dish of
potatoes in their jackets and a red-rimmed butter dish with a slab of butter,
the shape of a swan dipping its head imprinted on its surface. That was the
meal. Everything was so simple, especially the way they waited. She sat with
her hands in her lap and talked to him about someone up the road who had
had an airmail letter from America. She told him that his father would be
tired, but, tired as he was, he wouldn't be without a smile before he washed
himself and he wouldn't be so without his manners to forget to say grace

before they ate and that he, the boy, should watch the way the father would smile when the books were produced for homework, for learning was a wonder to him, especially the Latin. Then there would be no talking, just the ticking of the clock and the kettle humming and the china dogs on the mantelpiece looking, as ever, across at one another.

'Now that,' said the master, 'that's writing. That's just telling the truth.'

I felt embarrassed because my own essay had been full of long or strange words I had found in the dictionary—'cerulean', 'azure', 'phantasm' and 'implacable'—all of them describing skies and seas I had seen only with the Ann of the novel. I'd never thought such stuff was worth writing about. It was ordinary life—no rebellions or love affairs or dangerous flights across the hills at night. And yet I kept remembering that mother and son waiting in the Dutch interior of that essay, with the jug of milk and the butter on the table, while behind and above them were those wispy, shawly figures from the rebellion, sibilant above the great fire and below the aching, high wind.

SEAMUS DEANE, *Reading in the Dark*, 1996

Violence alone enlivened my girlhood, for I was allowed out only to go to school and mass. But from my bedroom window, under a ceiling black with night and creeping mould I could see the goings-on. The boys and the Brits, and the RUC. The dim, indistinguishable figures crawling damply through the neglected gardens, or running in cautious relays across the roads. And the sky above all of it, clear and brittle with stars, though more often clouded and changeful, fitfully illuminated by a dangerous moon.

MARY COSTELLO, *Titanic Town*, 1992

When did you last see a woman wringing her hands or an old fellow wearing vulcanite bicycle clips or nervous black greyhounds on the leash or the inextinguishable fires of wayside itinerants and their washing draped on hedges and bushes and they themselves (The Great Unwashed) none too clean?

I recall: Aladdin paraffin lamps and anthracite and coke and Bird's Custard and sago and tadpoles (pollywoggles) wriggling in the pond at the edge of the Crooked Meadow and cruel hare-coursing and blooding of hounds and the baying of the pack after foxes and twists of hardboiled sweeties in paper bags, a pennyworth and tuppenceworth, and Findlater's men carrying in a week's supplies and being checked by the cook and Wild Woodbines in open packets of five for tuppence halfpenny old currency with farthings in the change and the mad dog frothing at the mouth running in mad circles in humpy commonage near Oakley Park one lovely summer's day returning from the village with fags and brother Bun and I feeling sick and giddy from the first tobacco and the PP's alarming *Diktat* from the pulpit on Sunday and pea-picking for Mumu in the garden and the Bogey Man lurking in the cellar with the arrowheads and the mouldy masks and looking for mushrooms in Mangan's long field with Mumu and the Dodo early one morning in summer and the stink of ammonia in the convent class and the damp poor clothes in the hanging cupboard and the musty smell of nuns and the rustle of their habits and the small turf fire dying in the narrow grate when Sister Rumold prepared us for First Holy Communion and told us, 'You must prepare yourself to receive Our Lord' and the hot smell of the big girls and the provenance of sin—a writhing serpent impaled on the Patriarch's crozier and St Brigid the patroness blushing scarlet up on her pedestal and St Patrick watching with his curly beard—and the purple-shrouded statues at Passion Week and the whispering in the dim confessional and Crunchies in golden foil wrappings and chocolate whirls with whipped cream centres that the Dote and I called Dev's Snots and then Bull's Eyes and Peggy's Leg and liquorice twists and fizzy sherbets and stirabout with cream and brown sugar in the dark after early Mass and servants churning in the chilly dairy and butter pats in the tub and bluebottles buzzing against the larder screen and a snipe rotting on a hook and the cat-stink behind the mangle and the sheets airing on the stiffened hillocks of the frozen bleach-green and the tracks of the hare in the snow and lowing cows calving and calves on spindle legs suckling their mothers and mares foaling and stallions mounting with flared nostrils and sows farrowing and ewes lambing and the baldy priest in the awful brown wig saying mass below us at Straffan and the polychrome Christ bleeding with one arm missing at the scourging in the Stations of the Cross that stuck out in little polychrome grottos from the nave and the nun with pinched bloodless lips genuflecting and extinguishing candles with a long snuffer and the lovely byroad by the Liffey to Odlums' and the May procession between the cypress trees along the convent avenue and the gravel biting into my bare knees and I thinking only of the cold roast with lots of salt and the ruffled nun walking against the wind and ruddyfaced Sister Rumold nodding her wimple—like the scuffed lining of a shallow Jacob's biscuit tin or glacé fruit packings—and leaning forward from her highbacked chair in the Holy Faith Convent waitingroom and genteely offering Mumu a Zube from a little oval box sprung open in her white speckled hand and my mother in her blandest grandest way (with fur coat thrown open so that the nun could get an eyeful of her expensive Switzer's dress) saying how important education was and the wimple nodding like mad for Sister Rumold couldn't agree more, for the youngest (aged four) and myself (aged six) the middle child were to be taken under her wing the following Monday in the class of Second Infants and Lizzy Bolger had painted her mouth with the reddest lipstick and seemed to be bleeding from the mouth and was coaxing, 'Gizzakiss, ah g'wan!' and the big girls were tittering in the playground and the men were playing Pitch & Toss after Mass above Killadoon front gate and the hay-bogies were grinding along

the Naas-Celbridge road and the steamroller belching smoke and stinking of
tar and twenty Collegiate College girls in slate-gray uniforms were rounding
Brady's corner and two teachers with long forbidding Protestant horse-faces
pacing along in front and their shadows flitting along the wall and myself in
great embarrassment cycling rapidly by and Satan dining at Castletown (nar-
rated dramatically by the Keegans as if they had been present, carrying in
steaming dishes) and the PP sweating and called in after the Vicar couldn't
shift His Nibs who sat there sneering and then the PP showed him the crucifix and told him to go about his business and the PP himself sweated seven
shirts and died but Satan had gone straight through the floor in a puff of
black smoke, leaving a cracked mirror behind as a memento as you can see
to this day; all that I recall of those grand times that can never return.

AIDAN HIGGINS, *Donkey's Years*, 1995

Balloons and Wooden Guns

O it was lovely round that other house
where I was born and lived for thirty years.
Life surged about us. So that time appears,
dull intervals suppressed, in happy shows:
Italian organ-grinders, parrots, bears;
that blind old Happy Jimmy by himself;
the German bands; the Ulster Volunteers
with wooden guns; the women selling delph;
carts with balloons; great horses galloping,
their huge fire engine brass and funnelled flames;
strung chestnuts every autumn; kites in spring;
girls skipping; slides and snowballs in the snow;
all those activities which bore the names
of May Queen, Kick-the-Tin, and Rally-O.

JOHN HEWITT, *Collected Poems*, 1991

An Ulster Twilight

Ulster the fifth part of *Ireland* is a large Province, woody, fenny, in some
parts fertile, in other parts barren, but in al parts greene and pleasant
to behold, and exceedingly stoared with Cattell.

FYNES MORYSON, *An Itinerary Containing the Ten Yeeres Travell*

. . . independent, rattling, non-transcendent
Ulster—old decency

And Old Bushmills,
Soda farls, strong tea,
New rope, rock salt, kale plants,
Potato-bread and Woodbine.

SEAMUS HEANEY, 'A Postcard from
North Antrim'

The name Ulster is an embarrassing and contentious name, not merely
because it was for many years associated in people's minds with something
called 'the Ulster question', but because at different periods of history the
name has meant a rather different extent of country. For many centuries Ulster
has certainly been an area of northern or north-eastern Ireland, and it has
been the dwelling-place of a distinct community of one kind or another; but
the variations in the accepted frontiers of that area have been enormous.

The earliest account that we have of the ancient Uladh is in the old legend
of the *Táin Bó Cualgne* (Cattle Raid of Cooley) which gives us a picture of
Ulster about the beginning of the Christian era. It tells us that Ireland was
divided at that time into five kingdoms, of which the largest was Uladh, a
kingdom which contained all northern Ireland and extended as far south as
the Boyne and as far west as the Shannon. But, about three centuries later, we
find the kingdom of Uladh reduced approximately to the limits of the two
modern counties of Down and Antrim. Then, by the beginning of the fifth
century AD, a new kingdom of Uladh had been built up again during a further
change of forces in the power politics of the Irish kingdoms.

It was at the time of the Scandinavian invasions that the name Uladh
received its Teutonic ending and came to be known as Ulster.

For many centuries Ulster was a recognized area, but it was by no means clear at all times just where Ulster ended and another province began. Finally, in the reign of Queen Elizabeth, a number of English officials decided to settle the matter. Quite arbitrarily, and with a view to convenience, conquest and administration, they laid down a frontier and defined the province of Ulster as consisting of the nine modern counties of Antrim, Down, Londonderry (then called the county of Coleraine), Armagh, Tyrone, Fermanagh, Donegal, Monaghan, and, as an afterthought some years later, Cavan. This definition of Ulster as a separate province never had much real administrative importance in the centuries that followed; and for a long period the provincial boundaries set up in Ireland had really no significance apart from the basis which they provided for the organization of inter-provincial football matches and similar activities. The frontier of Ulster did to some extent represent the boundary of a distinct community, but not very accurately.

The nine-county Ulster has come in the course of time to be falsely identified with the Uladh of ancient times, which had rather different frontiers. Quite often people, referring to those nine counties which were segregated and defined as 'Ulster' by a little group of English administrators, have written and spoken of them as if they were 'the ancient province of Ulster'. This authoritative and almost sacred character that has been spuriously given to that particular definition of the extent of Ulster has been used to prop up each of two completely opposing political arguments. That is why I am drawing special attention to what actually happened. I am not concerned with politics; and, though those old English officials were doubtless honest fellows according to their lights, they were fairly hard cases, they did not care a pin for ancient Uladh, and their decisions about boundaries have no more authority for us who want to discover what Ulster really is than the conclusions or opinions of anybody else.

And now, today, and during the quarter of a century preceding the time of writing, the name Ulster has acquired a further change in its significance. It has come to be practically identified with the six counties of Northern Ireland, the area in Ireland which has remained part of the United Kingdom, while the Irish Free State, or Eire, or the Republic of Ireland, has become a separate State. But for certain inter-provincial sports events and a number of other private purposes, the old provincial boundaries, including that of the nine-county Ulster, are still used.

HUGH SHEARMAN, *Ulster*, 1949

Ulster Names

I take my stand by the Ulster names,
each clean hard name like a weathered stone;
Tyrella, Rostrevor, are flickering flames:

the names I mean are the Moy, Malone,
Strabane, Slieve Gullion and Portglenone.

Even suppose that each name were freed
from legend's ivy and history's moss,
there'd be music still in, say, Carrick-a-rede,
though men forget it's the rock across
the track of the salmon from Islay and Ross.

The names of a land show the heart of the race;
they move on the tongue like the lilt of a song.
You say the name and I see the place—
Drumbo, Dungannon, Annalong.
Barony, townland, we cannot go wrong.

You say Armagh, and I see the hill
with the two tall spires or the square low tower;
the faith of Patrick is with us still;
his blessing falls in a moonlit hour,
when the apple orchards are all in flower.

You whisper Derry. Beyond the walls
and the crashing boom and the coiling smoke,
I follow that freedom which beckons and calls
to Colmcille, tall in his grove of oak,
raising his voice for the rhyming folk.

County by county you number them over;
Tyrone, Fermanagh . . . I stand by a lake,
and the bubbling curlew, the whistling plover
call over the whins in the chill daybreak
as the hills and the waters the first light take.

Let Down be famous for care-tilled earth,
for the little green hills and the harsh grey peaks,
the rocky bed of the Lagan's birth,
the white farm fat in the August weeks.
There's one more county my pride still seeks.

You give it the name and my quick thoughts run
through the narrow towns with their wheels of trade,
to Glenballyemon, Glenaan, Glendun,
from Trostan down to the braes of Layde,
for there is the place where the pact was made.

But you have as good a right as I
to praise the place where your face is known,
for over us all is the selfsame sky;

the limestone's locked in the strength of the bone,
and who shall mock at the steadfast stone?

So it's Ballinamallard, it's Crossmaglen,
it's Aughnacloy, it's Donaghadee,
it's Magherafelt breeds the best of men,
I'll not deny it. But look for me
on the moss between Orra and Slievenanee.

POSTSCRIPT, 1984

Those verses surfaced thirty years ago
when time seemed edging to a better time,
most public voices tamed, those loud untamed
as seasonal as tawdry pantomime,
and over my companionable land
placenames still lilted like a childhood rime.

The years deceived; our unforgiving hearts,
by myth and old antipathies betrayed,
flared into sudden acts of violence
in daily shocking bulletins relayed,
and through our dark dream-clotted consciousness
hosted like banners in some black parade.

Now with compulsive resonance they toll:
Banbridge, Ballykelly, Darkley, Crossmaglen,
summoning pity, anger and despair,
by grief of kin, by hate of murderous men
till the whole tarnished map is stained and torn,
not to be read as pastoral again.

JOHN HEWITT, *Collected Poems*, 1991

From Ardglass we travelled along the coast to Strangford, by Ballyculter and Kilclief, both of them at the entrance of Strangford Lough. The former is a neat village, containing a beautiful School-house and Alms-houses, built and supported at the expense of Lady Bangor. These buildings display good taste, and are very ornamental to the village. Lord Bangor is an excellent landlord, and both he and his lady are very charitable, and take an active part in promoting the education and prosperity of the country.

The most striking object at Kilclief is the ancient Castle, once the See-house of the Bishops of Down. This castle is now used for a storehouse for grain, being conveniently situated for the shipping of it. The land adjoining is very fertile, and capable of bearing many crops in succession. Our route lay along the side of the Lough, which, when the tide is out, appears a muddy stream. Strangford is beautifully situated on the Lough; the shore is rocky, and commands a fine view of Portaferry opposite, at which place the Lough widens into an extensive sheet of water, formerly called Lough Cane, or Cuan. It is seventeen miles long, and five broad in its widest part; is well supplied with fish, and is said by the inhabitants to contain as many islands as there are days in the year; this number, however, may be reduced to about seventy. The ruins of Walsh's, Audley's, Portaferry, Killyleagh, Comber, and other ancient castles, are all within view of each other near the Lough, and signals might and doubtless have been given from one to another. Here, then, is a feast for those who delight to contemplate the relics of days when men buried themselves within dark walls nine feet thick, and found it necessary to be constantly on the lookout for enemies.

JONATHAN BINNS, *Miseries and Beauties of Ireland*, 1837

The Bracken

The forests of the bracken
    Come up thin lipped and white,
Through the deep spoor of the bullocks
    Pushing into light.

Great fronds put out their branches
    And canopy the plain,
Till the hooves of the cattle find them,
    Or the frost has them slain.

In autumn the poor people
    Take scythes and sharpening stones,
And gather the rusted mattress
    To put under their bones.

JOHN LYLE DONAGHY, *Antrim Song: Flute over the Valley*, 1931

Nowhere in Ireland does one see better farming, or a more prosperous country-side, than say in eastern Down. The people here are a hard-headed, thrifty, hearty race, closely akin to the lowland Scotch, with a dialect also akin, while those of Antrim, adjoining on the north, savour more of the Highlands. The language of both counties is characterized by the large element which it contains of Elizabethan English on the one hand, and of translated Gaelic on the other. The dialect and strong northern accent, indeed, are sometimes bewildering to the stranger. If you think you hear 'ace won', the reference is not to any game of cards, but to the fact that the wind is in the east; and 'key of hell' has nothing to do with the infernal regions, but signifies the Cave Hill near

Belfast. And can you translate the following, supplied by my sister: 'Ther a lock o' carryons an' blethers goin' wi' them gorsoons that's hoakin a wheen o' whuns out o' the sheugh down thonder forninst the boor tree'?[1] And here is a contribution sent by Rev. W. R. Megaw: 'Ere yesterday at dayligone he begood to the banterin' and starts jundyin' our Jamie and him on his hunkers at the bing there, walin' a wheen o' clarty pritas'.[2]

The county of Down (*Dún*, from the great fortress of Downpatrick) is the most attractive portion of this Silurian area, for several reasons. It has an extensive coast-line, curving round from Belfast to Newry, and including the large island-studded lough of Strangford, as well as the border of Carlingford Lough and Belfast Lough. It has high mountains, for at two widely separated epochs there have been outbursts of vulcanism, the first giving us the picturesque hills west of Carlingford Lough, just beyond the Down boundary, and Slieve Croob, the second the adjoining fine group of the Mourne Mountains. In the north is the fertile and richly wooded valley of the Lagan, beyond which the high scarp of the basaltic plateau rises abruptly. About one-fourth of the growing city of Belfast lies on the Down side of the river, and the whole southern shore of Belfast Lough, including Bangor, is practically suburban Belfast. The fifteen-mile strip that lies between Strangford Lough and the Irish Sea, known as The Ards, shows Down at its best—all tilled fields and white cottages and little winding roads, and a low flowery coast-line with alternating points of sharp upturned slates and bays of fine grey sand.

ROBERT LLOYD PRAEGER, *The Way That I Went*, 1937

'Tis Pretty Tae Be in Baile-liosan

'Tis pretty tae be in Baile-liosan,
'Tis pretty tae be in green Magh-luan;
'Tis prettier tae be in Newtownbreda,
Beeking under the eaves in June.
The cummers are out wi' their knitting and spinning,
The thrush sings frae his crib on the wa',
And o'er the white road the clachan caddies
Play at their marlies and goaling-ba'.

O, fair are the fields o' Baile-liosan,
And fair are the faes of green Magh-luan;
But fairer the flowers o' Newtownbreda,
Wet wi' dew in the eves o' June,

---

[1] There is a deal of larking and nonsense going on among those boys who are digging gorse-bushes out of the ditch down there opposite the elder-tree.

[2] Day before yesterday at dusk he began bantering, and started pushing our James while he was squatting at the pit there, sorting a lot of muddy potatoes.

'Tis pleasant tae saunter the clachan thro'
When day sinks mellow o'er Dubhais hill,
And feel their fragrance sae softly breathing
Frae croft and causey and window-sill.

O, brave are the haughs o' Baile-liosan,
And brave are the halds o' green Magh-luan;
But braver the hames o' Newtownbreda,
Twined about wi' the pinks o' June.
And just as the face is sae kindly withouten,
The heart within is as guid as gold—
Wi' new fair ballants and merry music,
And cracks cam' down frae the days of old.

'Tis pretty tae be in Baile-liosan,
'Tis pretty tae be in green Magh-luan;
'Tis prettier tae be in Newtownbreda,
Beeking under the eaves in June.
The cummers are out wi' their knitting and spinning,
The thrush sings frae his crib on the wa',
And o'er the white road the clachan caddies
Play at their marlies and goaling-ba'.

JOSEPH CAMPBELL, *The Mountainy Singer*, 1909

Ulster in the time of our great-grandfathers must have been architecturally beautiful. I say 'must have been', for to-day our heritage is much spoiled and in greater danger probably than that of any part of the British Isles. It is threatened now by prosperity and so-called improvement.

DENIS O'D. HANNA, 'Architecture in Ulster', in Sam Hanna Bell (ed.), *The Arts in Ulster*, 1951

Father of History

A state schoolroom and a master talking
in a limber voice, a spiky burr
like a landrail creaking in the bracken.
Ock there he is with hair like furze,
smiling obliquely on the risen town
and building Lisburn like a warm
plain-spoken sermon on the rights of man.
A sunned Antrim face, he maybe prays

to the New Light in a relished dialect,
the eager accent of a free sept,
broken in the north, in resurrection.
Folded like bark, like cinnamon things,
I traced them to the Linen Hall stacks—
Munro, Hope, Porter and McCracken;
like sweet yams buried deep, these rebel minds
endure posterity without a monument,
their names a covered sheugh, remnants, some brackish signs.

TOM PAULIN, *Liberty Tree*, 1983

At a point where four parallel rows of hot pipes entered the wall Colm sat, and yesterday, feeling a draught rubbing round his legs he had stuffed an old cap into the spaces, but someone had removed it. And now as he felt the chilly breeze blow in he tore pages from a scribbler and shoved them into the gap. Satisfied, he lifted the lid of his desk, rested it on his head, allowing his two hands freedom to rummage. He had been only three weeks in the College and already was thinking of Easter. On the underside of the lid a small calendar was fastened with drawing pins, and each date as it passed was totally obliterated by a square of ink. He began to count the days till Easter: there were forty-three, and to make it an even forty he scored out three in advance.

It seemed a long time since the wintry day he left the island: the row at Ballycastle station because his mother couldn't get him a half-ticket: seeing the snow on Knocklayde from the train, frozen fields with ragged bushes and no cattle, black streams with snow on the stones that stuck up through them; villages hushed and cartwheel marks on the roads; thatched houses stiff in the ground and hayricks huddled in the haggards and dusted with snow; and then as the train raced along by the edge of a thin sea into Belfast, seeing at one side trams with tin advertisements, and boys sliding on a pond whose top was littered with stones.

And then the drive up from the station in the side-car with his mother. How frightened he had been of the motor cars, and the frantic rattling of the car wheels on the street. He had held on grimly, listening to the driver clicking his tongue at the horse, his great bulk perched high on the dicky seat, and the hair on his neck fringing his coat collar. As they turned off the tram lines into the avenue that led to the wine-bricked College the wheels had quietened, and within him he had felt an emptiness that crushed all life from him. Thinking of it now he felt again the same gripping loneliness and he gave a long, loud sigh. The boy in front turned round and Colm smiled back at him with his lips closed.

MICHAEL MCLAVERTY, *Call My Brother Back*, 1939

The open hearth with all its associations is truly the heart and centre of house and home. The fire is, with her children, the 'care' of the woman of the house. 'A woman can never go to the fire', runs an Irish saying, 'without tampering with it.' The manifold duties of the housewife keep her moving about the hearth, tethered to it for most of the day. Her last duty at night is to 'smoor' it, burying a live turf in the ashes to retain a spark which can be fanned into a blaze next morning. This custom was fortified by the belief that the good folk, the fairies, would be displeased if there were no fire for them through the night. I have sat at fires which, it was claimed, had not been allowed to go out for over a century, or for as far back as family memory could go. It is to the fireside seat that the visitor is invited, for this is the place of honour, and it is around the fire that tales of old time are told. The magic of the open fire, playing upon the fancies of generations who have gathered round it, has engendered a host of beliefs and portents. The fire can give warning of wind and weather, of lucky and unlucky visitors, of marriage and death. Above all, it is a shrine to which ancestral spirits return, a link with the living past.

E. ESTYN EVANS, *Irish Folk Ways*, 1957

Lull

I've heard it argued in some quarters
That in Armagh they mow the hay
With only a week to go to Christmas,
That no one's in a hurry

To save it, or their own sweet selves.
Tomorrow is another day,
As your man said on the Mount of Olives.
The same is held of County Derry.

Here and there up and down the country
There are still houses where the fire
Hasn't gone out in a century.

I know that eternal interim;
I think I know what they're waiting for
In Tyrone, Fermanagh, Down and Antrim.

PAUL MULDOON, *Why Brownlee Left*, 1980

The County is observed to be populous and flourishing, though it did not become amesnable to the Laws till the Reign of Queen *Elizabeth*, nor fully till that of King *James* the First. The *English* Habit, Manners, and Language may be said almost universally to prevail here; but a *Shiboleth* of the *Scottish* and North Country *English* Dialects appears on many Tongues, and Multitudes of Words are adopted into the Language from *Cumberland* and *Wesmorland*, a few Specimens of which are these;

> *Mor* or *More* for a *Hill* or *Mountain.*
> *Tiny* for *puny* or *little.*
> *Bracken* for *Fern.*
> *Bearn* for a *Child.*
> To *rowt*, for to *low* like a Cow or Ox.
> *Shear Corn*, for to *reap Corn.*
> *Gang*, for to *go* or *walk.*
> *Till* for *to*, as *till* go to such a Place, for *to* go to such a Place.

The *Irish* Tongue is in a manner banished from among the common People, and what little of it is spoken can be heard only among the inferior Rank of *Irish* Papists; and even that little diminishes every Day by the great Desire the poor Natives have that their Children should be taught to read and write the *English* Tongue in the Charter or other *English* Protestant Schools, to which they willingly send them.

The Inhabitants are warm and well clad at Church, Fairs and Markets, their Trade and Commerce are carried on in the *English* Language. Tillage and the Linen Manufacture keep them in constant Imployment, and free from Idleness; and a busy laborious Life prevents many Excesses and Breaches of the Laws, which in no part of the Kingdom are more reverenced.

WALTER HARRIS, *The Antient and Present State of the County of Down*, 1741

The tendency of Protestant and Catholic in Ulster for some time past has been to unite, and if the clergy and the journalists wished for this unity, the atmosphere of Ulster could be cleared in less than a generation. The Press, however, is in the hands, not of idealists, but of heated politicians, and the same thing holds true to a great extent of the pulpit. Protestants are more likely to be warned in their churches against errors of Catholic doctrine than against errors of Protestant conduct towards Catholics in a misbehaving world. Similarly, if any trouble arises between Catholics and Protestants in the streets, the Unionist Press, instead of commenting upon the case on its merits, denounces it at once as a Nationalist or Catholic outrage, while the Nationalist Press, with equal readiness, represents the same incident as an unprovoked Orange assault on unoffending Catholics. Thus innocent and well-meaning people, who only read papers containing their own views, learn to look on their opponents as a kind of savages, lying in wait for the seed of the righteous with stones, rivets, and bad language.

ROBERT LYND, *Home Life in Ireland*, 1908

The drumlin country seems to have been little used and in parts uninhabited until 1660. Then Scottish Presbyterians fleeing from religious persecution under the Stuarts, came and turned it into farm land, cutting down the forest, and in the process of settlement either driving the original inhabitants to the hills or converting them to their own outlook on life.

The northern granitic slopes of the Mournes are very inhospitable. Under the Penal Laws of the eighteenth century, families could be turned off their holdings for non-conformity and non-payment of tithes. These laws operated most harshly against the Roman Catholics, but their application was not equally severe in all parts of the country. From 1744 onwards a Roman Catholic landlord held possession of the valleys draining down to the gap at Hilltown, and during that period he settled many evicted families in these townlands. If folk history is correct, these families came from Co. Armagh and Co. Louth and were given strips on the hillsides which they reclaimed and settled. The chief agent in this plantation, John O'Neill, is now almost a legendary figure. He established bleaching, flax scutching and corn mills in an effort to industrialize the district. Of these enterprises only flax scutching survives to-day. The memory of Hilltown as a refuge area remained strong, and during the 'troubles' of 1922 some families moved here from north Co. Down.

JOHN M. MOGEY, *Rural Life in Northern Ireland*, 1947

from *Station Island*

'I have no mettle for the angry role,'
I said. 'I come from County Derry,
born in earshot of an Hibernian hall

where a band of Ribbonmen played hymns to Mary.
By then the brotherhood was a frail procession
staggering home drunk on Patrick's Day

in collarettes and sashes fringed with green.
Obedient strains like theirs tuned me first
and not that harp of unforgiving iron

the Fenians strung. A lot of what you wrote
I heard and did: this Lough Derg station,
flax-pullings, dances, summer crossroads chat

and the shaky local voice of education.
All that. And always, Orange drums.
And neighbours on the roads at night with guns.'

'I know, I know, I know, I know,' he said,
'but you have to try to make sense of what comes.
Remember everything and keep your head.'

'The alders in the hedge,' I said, 'mushrooms,
dark-clumped grass where cows or horses dunged,
the cluck when pith-lined chestnut shells split open

in your hand, the melt of shells corrupting,
old jampots in drain clogged up with mud—'
But now Carleton was interrupting:

'All this is like a trout kept in a spring
or maggots sown in wounds—
another life that cleans our element.

We are earthworms of the earth, and all that
has gone through us is what will be our trace.'
He turned on his heel when he was saying this

and headed up the road at the same hard pace.

SEAMUS HEANEY, *Station Island*, 1984

The first time Mary ever watched the scutchers, peering round the open mill-door at them with her usual curiosity, she was struck by the rank smell of the flax and the racking coughs of the workers. It was not difficult to see why they coughed. All the air was filled with flying particles of tow, so that mill walls and ceiling and floor, windows and machinery and workers, were enveloped in the cloud. The workers called it 'pouce' (to rhyme with 'mouse') and the women especially referred deprecatingly to their 'poucy' hair. Later such working conditions would not be tolerated, but in the meantime the scutch-ers had a kind of pouce silicosis, which resulted in the racking coughs Mary heard. But she herself was too fascinated by the diaphanous rainbow arching the water-wheel in the sunshine to think about toil and disease.

The gracious pale beauty of the flax in bloom, waving in powder-blue and green swells, held no signification of the back-breaking labour that would be required before the splendour of a damask tablecloth would cover Victorian mahogany. The flax was a greedy, dirty crop that impoverished the soil and left it full of weeds. It was no favourite with the farmers, but the money it brought in was welcome and the supply required was steady, for the great linen spinning and weaving industries need huge quantities of the raw mater-ial, although even in Mary's childhood much was already being imported—from Russia for coarse weaves and from Belgium for the finest 'Irish' linen of all. Indeed, the very flax-seed was imported from those far-off lands, for the Irish farmer did not harvest his lint-seed, but threw the crop, complete with seeds, into the lint-dam for retting.

The flax was harvested by hand. This was an absolute necessity, as the plant was pulled bodily out of the earth, roots and all, to get fibres as long as possible. Mary hated flax-pulling when she had to do it as the labour was non-stop and almost literally back-breaking, while the strong fibrous plants cut deeper and deeper into creased fingers until the blood ran freely.

In the market in Ballyclare, a flax-growing farmer could buy sprit-bands or rush-bands for binding the flax sheaves or beats. Sprits were a kind of rushes growing in land too boggy to grow even grass. It was wasteful of the crop to tie flax beats with flax bands, though by necessity this was occasionally done. Wives of farm labourers or poor farmers eked out a little extra income by plaiting the sprit-bands for market as the flax season was approaching.

The flax beats were retted in a dam to soften the woody covering of the flax fibre, and this retting was one of the most important processes in the whole business of linen manufacture. It was a living bacterial process, and good retting could be achieved only with water of a certain temperature. If a careful flax-grower used water from a spring-well he allowed eighteen inches of water to run into his lint-dam and lie there for several weeks to gather a little solar heat. The best water was considered to come from a sluggish part of a stream, as this was already full of bacteria from decaying vegetable matter. The dam itself was a great rectangular cavity dug in loamy soil with a clay bottom, and into the foot-and-a-half of water the beats were piled neatly in a solid mass from end to end of the dam, weighted with stones on top, covered completely with water, and left to ret. It was a sad day for the farmer if the weather suddenly turned cold after retting had begun, for the natural process stopped and the only hope of saving the crop lay in dragging all the beats out on to the grass and beginning all over again when the milder weather returned.

The estimated time for maturing the flax crop was approximately one hundred days, so that seed sown in March or April was harvested in July or August. August was the retting month, and nothing in this world could compare with the ferocious smell of the retted flax when, at the end of nine or ten days, it was dragged from the noisome dam and laid, beats opened out, on the grass. However, the smell was reckoned to be very healthful. The crop must lie on the grass only a day or two to rough dry. To lie too long was most harmful to it, and it rotted where it lay. One could sometimes see an extra careful farmer leaning the dripping beats against stretched wires, or more commonly against a stone dyke, so that the crop should not lie on the grass at all.

FLORENCE MARY MCDOWELL, *Other Days Around Me*, 1972

If the road from Larne to Glenarm is beautiful, the coast route from the latter place to Cushendall is still more so; and, except peerless Westport, I have seen nothing in Ireland so picturesque as this noble line of coast-scenery. The new road, luckily, is not yet completed, and the lover of natural beauties had better hasten to the spot in time, ere, by flattening and improving the road, and leading it along the seashore, half the magnificent prospects are shut out, now visible from along the mountainous old road, which, according to the good old fashion, gallantly takes all the hills in its course, disdaining to turn them. At three miles' distance, near the village of Cairlough, Glenarm looks more beautiful than when you are close upon it; and, as the car travels on to the stupendous Garron Head, the traveller, looking back, has a view of the whole line of coast southward as far as Isle Magee, with its bays and white villages, and tall precipitous cliffs, green, white, and grey. Eyes left, you may look with wonder at the mountains rising above, or presently at the pretty park and grounds of Drumnasole. Here, near the woods of Nappan, which are dressed in ten thousand colours—ash leaves turned yellow, nut-trees red, birch leaves brown, lime-leaves speckled over with black spots (marks of a disease which they will never get over), stands a schoolhouse that looks like a French château, having probably been a villa in former days, and discharges as we pass a cluster of fair-haired children, that begin running madly down the hill, their fair hair streaming behind them. Down the hill goes the car, madly too, and you wonder and bless your stars that the horse does not fall, or crush the children that are running before, or you that are sitting behind. Every now and then, at a trip of the horse, a disguised lady's maid, with a canary bird in her lap, and a vast anxiety about her best bonnet in the bandbox, begins to scream; at which the car-boy grins, and rattles down the hill only the quicker. The road, which almost always skirts the hill-side, has been torn sheer through the rock here and there; and immense work of levelling, shovelling, picking, blasting, filling, is going on along the whole line. As I was looking up a vast cliff, decorated with patches of green here and there at its summit, and at its base, where the sea had beaten until now, with long, thin, waving grass, that I told a grocer, my neighbour, was like mermaids' hair (though he did not in the least coincide in the simile)—as I was looking up the hill, admiring two goats that were browsing on a little patch of green, and two sheep perched yet higher (I had never seen such agility in mutton)—as, I say once more, I was looking at these phenomena, the grocer nudges me, and says, 'Look on to this side—that's Scotland, yon.'

WILLIAM M. THACKERAY, *The Irish Sketch Book*, 1842

Cushenden

Fuchsia and ragweed and the distant hills
Made as it were out of clouds and sea:

All night the bay is plashing and the moon
   Marks the break of the waves.

Limestone and basalt and a whitewashed house
With passages of great stone flags
And a walled garden with plums on the wall
   And a bird piping in the night.

Forgetfulness: brass lamps and copper jugs
And home-made bread and the smell of turf or flax
And the air a glove and the water lathering easy
   And convolvulus in the hedge.

Only in the dark green room beside the fire
With the curtains drawn against the winds and waves
There is a little box with a well-bred voice:
   What a place to talk of War.

                                         Louis MacNeice, 1939

As I remembered it from having lived there as a child, Dunmartin Hall had always had an aura of impermanence. The house had both the melancholy and the magic of something inherently doomed by the height of its own ancient colonial aspirations. It was like a grey and decaying palace fortress beleaguered by invasions of hostile native forces. Fierce armies of stinging nettles were seizing its once imposing elm-arched driveway; weeds carpeted its tennis court; in its rose garden the roses had reverted to seed and grown wild because no one ever pruned them. All the flower-beds had become blotted out by grass, and only the brilliant blue of hydrangeas gave colour to Dunmartin's non existent gardens, because they liked a lot of rain and needed no attention.

               Caroline Blackwood, *Great Granny Webster*, 1977

Strangers sometimes assume too readily that a damp atmosphere in Ulster must mean mists and obscured views. They imagine Ulster as existing in a sort of perpetual 'Keltic twilight'. Actually a damp atmosphere, as we experi-ence it in Ulster, often gives excellent visibility and gives intense clarity to the view. I have often noticed this when staying on the foothills of Slieve Croob in County Down. All east Down would lie stretched out below me in close, brilliant detail, every tiny house and hedge standing out hard and clear, and Strangford Lough and the Irish Sea beyond; and the Isle of Man would rise, blue and clear, over sixty miles away. It was when I saw the country like that

that I knew that the atmosphere was damp and that there was going to be rain.

HUGH SHEARMAN, *Ulster*, 1949

More by good luck than calculation, they had timed their departure accurately, for the shrill sound of fifes, soaring above the deep roll and pounding of drums, was already audible in the distance when they emerged on to the main road. Mother and Daddy hurried on, in order to reach the field before the procession, while Tom and Pascoe, who wished to watch it passing, climbed on to a bank.

And here it was—the first banners swinging and dipping round the bend of the road, brilliantly purple and orange in the sunlight. At the same moment the leading band, which had been marking time by heavy drum-beats, suddenly burst into its own particular tune, and Tom, carried away on the wings of the infectious rhythm, raised his voice in song:

> *Sit* down, *my pink and* be *content,*
> *For the cows are in the clover.*

They were the words he had learned from James-Arthur, and whether right or wrong they fitted into the tune; but Pascoe, less excited, nudged him violently in the ribs to show him he was attracting attention. All the same, it *was* exciting—each band playing its special tune, which, as the players drew closer, disentangled itself from all the other tunes, till it became for a minute or two the only one, and then, passing on into the distance, was itself lost in the next and the next and the next—a constant succession. The big drums, crowned with bunches of orange lilies, were splotched and stained with blood from the hands of the drummers, whose crimson faces streamed with sweat. . . . It was great! Flags waved; musical instruments gleamed and glittered; the drums pounded; the fifes screamed! Yet in the midst of all this strident Dionysiac din and colour, the men and boys carrying the great square banners, or simply marching in time to the music, looked extraordinarily grave. It was only the accompanying rag tag and bobtail who exhibited signs of levity, bandied humorous remarks, and threw orange-skins—the actual performers were rapt in the parts they were playing in a glorious demonstration, which, if secular, had nevertheless all the bellicose zeal and earnestness of a declaration of faith. The very pictures on the banners were symbols of that faith. 'The Secret of England's Greatness'—in other words, Queen Victoria presenting Bibles to kneeling blackamoors, passionately grateful to receive them—was a subject second in popularity only to King William himself. It told a story, it expressed an ideal—or if not an ideal at any rate an immovable conviction. . . . And there, marching along and helping to carry a banner, was the other, the more familiar William, yet not quite the William of every day. Tom screamed his name at the top of his voice, but William, who must have heard, took no notice.

'Don't!' Pascoe said, glancing uneasily to right and left.

'Don't what?' answered Tom impatiently.

'You're dancing up and down: everybody's staring at you.'

This was purely a figment of imagination, for nobody was paying the least attention to them, but Pascoe seemed to have a morbid dread of publicity.

FORREST REID, *Young Tom*, 1944

It was a city of bonfires. The Protestants had more than we had. They had the twelfth of July, when they celebrated the triumph of Protestant armies at the Battle of the Boyne in 1690; then they had the twelfth of August when they celebrated the liberation of the city from a besieging Catholic army in 1689; then they had the burning of Lundy's effigy on the eighteenth of December. Lundy had been the traitor who had tried to open the gates of the city to the Catholic enemy. We had only the fifteenth of August bonfires; it was a church festival but we made it into a political one as well, to answer the fires of the twelfth. But our celebrations were not official, like the Protestant ones. The police would sometimes make us put out the fires or try to stop us collecting old car tyres or chopping down trees in preparation. Fire was what I loved to hear of and to see. It transformed the grey air and streets, excited and exciting. When, in mid-August, to commemorate the Feast of the Assumption of Our Lady into heaven, the bonfires were lit at the foot of the sloping, parallel streets, against the stone wall above the Park, the night sky reddened around the rising furls of black tyre-smoke that exploded every so often in high soprano bursts of paraffined flame. Their acrid odour would gradually give way to the more fragrant aroma of soft-burning trees that drifted across the little houses in their serried slopes, gravelled streets falling down from the asphalted Lone Moor Road that for us marked the limit between the city proper and the beginning of the countryside that spread out into Donegal four miles away. In the small hours of the morning, people sitting on benches and kitchen chairs around the fire were still singing; sometimes a window in one of the nearby houses cracked in a spasm of heat; the police car, that had been sitting in the outer darkness of two hundred yards away, switched on its lights and glided away; the shadows on the gable wall shrivelled as the fires burnt down to their red intestines. The Feast of the Assumption dwindled into the sixteenth of August, and solo singers began to dominate the sing-along chorusing. It marked the end of summer. The faint bronze tints of the dawn implied autumn, and the stars fainted into the increasing light as people trailed their chairs reluctantly home.

SEAMUS DEANE, *Reading in the Dark*, 1996

'Come on, come on!' Kitty was crying, wrenching the coats off Neilly and Shemie. 'Get those wet things off for the love and honour of God. I told you not to go out. I could look over it if I hadn't warned you. But no! Well, if I'm living and spared, I'll see that's the last bullet match you'll ever set your heels after. You'll sit in the house like other childer.' She ran her hands distractedly over the boys' shoulders. 'Soaking! Soaking! If I haven't the times of it amongst you. I'm cleaning and drying from I get up in the morning till I go to bed at night.' She gave Shemie's shoulder a rattle. 'And you. If it's not one thing it's another. If you're not falling into the River Callan, you're coming home drownded with the rain. Lord God, Malachey, I thought you had more sense. Where am I going to find room to dry all these clothes?'

'Ah, take it easy, woman dear,' Pachy soothed. 'Don't get your be'rd in a blaze. Here! In the name of the wee man sure you wouldn't call that wet now! Stand well up to the fire, you boys ye, while you have the chance, before your mother brings the donkeys in, and you'll be as dry as a bone in a minute.'

'Oh, you're a great fellow,' Kitty answered bitterly. 'You'll do a lot. You're a great fellow indeed! Here you two, strip off you there, every stitch. I'll put the bullets out of your head. Come on, come on, before I lose my patience altogether. Johnny Kelly won't take a bite out of you, I'm sure.'

'Ah, for God's sake, give our heads peace and let them alone,' cried Malachey, trailing his shirt over his head. 'A drop of rain won't kill them.'

Kitty took dry shirt, socks and semmit from the line across the fire and threw them on the sofa beside him.

'Well, I hope so. But you needn't worry. It isn't you who has the bother of looking after them when they're laid up. And I hope we won't hear you barking the morrow or the next day yourself.'

'You never heard me barking in the reign of your puff—'

At that moment the front door latch clicked.

'Here's Eugene now,' cried Kitty, turning round. 'Where in the name of— oh, it's yourself, Mrs Sheridan.'

'Hell's curse,' gasped Malachey, gathering up his shirt and semmit and hopping, half naked, through the room door, with Pachy and Kelly rocking with laughter after him.

'I thought you were Eugene, Mrs Sheridan. My mind's distracted. These ones are only after coming in on the top of me like drownded rats.'

JOHN O'CONNOR, *Come Day—Go Day*, 1948

The other day, in an inland town, I saw through an open window, a branch of fuschia waving stiffly up and down in the breeze; and at once I smelt the breeze salty, and had a picture of a bright curtain flapping inwards and, beyond the curtain, dazzling sunlight on miles of crinkling water. I felt, too, expectancy so keen that it was like a physical tightening of the nerves; the very sense of childhood. I was waiting for a sail, probably my first sail into the Atlantic. Somebody or something must have fixed that moment upon my dreaming senses, so that I still possess it. Small children are thought happy, but for most of the time they do not even live consciously, they exist; they drift through sensations as a pantomime fairy passes through coloured veils and changing lights. That moment was grasped out of the flux; a piece of life, unique and eternal, and the sail also, is still my living delight. The dinghy had a shiny new gaff, and the mainsail was wet half-way up so that the sun behind it made a bright half-moon on the canvas. She rose to the first swell of the Atlantic, beyond Sandy Point, with a three-angled motion, neither roll nor pitch. Then we were leaping from wave to wave, squattering into rollers that had touched Greenland in their last landfall, and the thin planks sprang and trembled under my body, sitting down among the ballast-bags. Tens of thousands of dark blue waves rushed towards me, rising and falling like dolphins and spouting thick triangles of foam. The land was so far off that the mountains and cliffs seemed like a thin lid sliding backwards over the world to unclose its sun-gazing eye. Nobody could see us now, I felt, even the coastguards' telescope couldn't pick us out.

JOYCE CARY, *A House of Children*, 1941

In summer we went to a whitewashed meeting-house on Sundays. The meeting-house stood amongst the rocks on the seashore, so close to high-water mark that at full tide the thud and backwash of the waves mingled with the singing of the Psalms.

> O God, our help in ages past,
> Our hope for years to come,
> Our shelter from the stormy blast,
> And our eternal home

we sang. Sometimes the head of a seal appeared as a black dot in the channel between the big rocks, and from the gallery on particularly fine Sunday mornings you could look out through the small-paned windows clear across the Irish Sea to the tiny white farmhouses and the green squares of the fields on the Mull of Galloway.

The village shop had glass jars of sweets in the windows. At night it was lit by a single oil lamp that hung from the ceiling. Round the lamp clustered a conglomeration of boots, hams, tin cans, and brushes, all hanging together in confusion. The door had a bell that rang with a faint *ping*. You then made out in the background, beyond the zinc-covered counter, a pile of small dark-wood drawers with glass knobs. These drawers contained, as we knew from experience, everything that a normal man could require, from fish-hooks to pills and plug tobacco.

Saturday night was the big night in the village. On Saturday nights the shop was crowded with women, all patiently waiting with their tin cans concealed under their shawls and their pennies clutched in their hands. Then at midnight the bell would go *ping, ping, ping,* and the women would file out into the darkness to wait for their men outside the public-house. . . . Across the street in M'Gimpsey's the barman would fling out the last customer, remove the corks from the automatic bottle-opener, and swab up the bar with a damp cloth.

Then he would come and stand in the doorway in his shirt-sleeves, outlined against the brilliant interior, survey the crowd, spit once, with emphasis, into the street, and shut the door.

Then more and more lights would go out throughout the village, and more and more plainly the sound of the waves would come up the steep, narrow side-street that led down to the sea.

DENIS IRELAND, *From the Irish Shore,* 1936

Elegy in a Presbyterian Burying-Ground
In Memoriam: J. L. D.

I

The meeting-house is not what it used to be
Since the new church was built,
But the white-washed walls still make a pleasant setting
For the ash-trees at the gate,
And the round windows—though the red panes are gone—
Have dignity upon the simple wall,
And the door, level to the grass, without steps or porchway
Might open yet to all.

II

The white pavilions of gateposts, stained with damp
And with rusty iron (where the gate had hung)
Still point the way to the stable, where horse and pony could
    nuzzle,
Till the second sermon was done,
And the elders came out, to draw the shafts of the traps up,
And load their wives and children into the well
With their bibles and their black dresses and farmyard faces.
Farewell, farewell!

III

I could have buried a poet here under these hedges
And left him happy. Son of the manse he was,
And drew his integrity from these white-walled precincts,

His rhetoric from his father's pulpit phrase.
Though he himself had made his Covenant elsewhere,
An older, darker and more troubled one,
With the certainty of a leaf, of a stone, of a dewdrop,
He knew his Election.

IV

He would remember the nooks where the first primroses
Christened the moss, and the freckled thrush would come
Mating its melody with his own grave elegiacs
To turn a Scottish psalm.
And whenever the men stood up, with their backs to the pulpit,
Hiding their faces from Jehovah's glare,
He would be with them, though he prayed another
And more contentious prayer.

V

There are some townlands more in league with heather
And the dark mountain, than with fields where men
Have sowed and planted; and his rebel spirit
Still sought the farthest glen,
Whose Sabbath was a solitude, whose gossip
Was the wind's whisper. There he broke the bread
Of meaning, in a silence, that his verses
So well interpreted.

VI

Yet he would grieve with me for the dereliction
That has overtaken this place,
For he cared for it. And the burying-ground beside it
Held many of his race.
He would not be surprised to find it sadly neglected,
Who was himself so negligent of fame.
And I?
—I would be proud to be the stoneyard mason
Who had incised his name.

R. N. D. WILSON, 1949

Outside on the gravel, white-bearded Finlay holds the pony ready in the trap.
My father, plucking at the reins, says, 'Go on, Simon.' The trap emerges from
the avenue and goes five miles over small hills on a road between thorn
hedges and rusty wire.

Already for ten years my father has worked in this soft damp place, with sunny, but never hot, summers, under bosomy clouds—where bramble, wild parsley, dandelions, celandine, primrose, congregate and flower in their seasons—here, at a corner of the sea. A couple of miles away over the fields, there is the blue North Channel. From this road you can't in fact see the shore; the sea appears, then, to have no sand or rocks skirting it but to be edged by the green country.

'It's going to rain,' my father predicts. 'You can see the coast of Scotland too clearly.' It's bad to see Scotland too clearly. Far off, in the distance, its promontories lie on the water like half-collapsed balloons.

GEORGE BUCHANAN, Morning Papers, 1965

Tommy spent three penurious years in the Black North, but he talked about it nostalgically for all the remaining days of his life. He learned to sing many of the Protestant and Orange Order songs such as 'The Sash My Father Wore', 'Kick the Pope', 'The Orange Lily' and 'Dolly's Brae' and he sang them with irony and with gusto. The songs were very popular in Drumlahan, but only in so far as they gave a look into the Orange mind. People laughed, and shook their heads in wonder at the ignorance and backwardness of the Northern Protestants who could sing songs like that and, worse still, believe in them. Local Protestants around Ballinwing would be too sedate and too good-mannered to sing songs of this sort:

> Up came a man with a shovel
> In his hand,
> And, sez he, 'Boys go no farther'.
> He tightened up his rope,
> And he made them curse the Pope.
> And, sez he, 'Boys go no farther'.

He often talked about the festive arches erected by the Orangemen around every twelfth of July when they celebrated the victory of a Dutch king over his English father-in-law at the Boyne in 1690. Catholics and Nationalists regarded it as a humiliation to have to walk or drive under these arches. He learned to play hurling in Newry. Hurling and Gaelic football were played for enjoyment, of course; but they were also played to show the Protestants and the English that Catholic Ireland had its own national culture and its own national games and that both were older and grander than what the invaders could produce. Tommy Flynn learned that you made sure you attended the matches; that you cycled or marched in formation, with your hurling stick in your free hand. You took special care to see that the team was properly and correctly turned out: jerseys washed and clean, togs ironed. You attended the meetings without fail. You went to early Mass on the Sunday morning and you made the rest of the day active and full and manly and a credit to the youth of your class. Protestants frowned on Sabbath pastimes, and their youth had little to do on a Sunday afternoon. They seemed bored.

'They just lounged around lusting after the girls,' said Tommy.

He learned Irish dancing, something he knew nothing about before, and he began to learn the Irish language from the books edited by the County Meath priest Fr O'Growney. As a consequence he was later on forever telling Seamus that if he had the money to spare he would send him to a place in County Waterford to learn Irish. 'They'd make a fluent Irish speaker out of you in six months.'

CHARLES O'BEIRNE, *The Good People*, 1985

If Reformers' Tree had a tenth of the advantages possessed by the Custom House Steps in Belfast, it would become the centre from which even greater nonsense would radiate than may be heard on a fine Sunday by the loiterers in Hyde Park. 'The Steps' in Belfast have done more to encourage polemical discussion in the town during the half century of their existence than all the preachers that were ever ordained in the Province, and some of them have been very encouraging indeed to disputation. For many years, anyone who had a theory of life, or a new religion, or a longing for a fight—a trait by no means unknown to the most earnest neophytes—could depend upon getting an audience on a Sunday afternoon on 'The Steps'. The breastwork of the quay is only about a hundred yards away, and yet I never heard of more than an occasional orator having to be fished out of the water after even the most challenging delivery of the most insulting doctrine.

The reason of this was not far to seek. The three-sided square—a favourite street configuration in Belfast—in the middle of which the Custom House stands, was loosely paved with the kidney-shaped cobbles to be found in millions all along the coasts of Antrim and Down, and it was quickly found by the intelligent seekers after truth who sought for it in this locality on Sundays, that, as a medium for replying to such points in the preacher's discourse as were not altogether acceptable to their ears, these cobble pavements could scarcely be surpassed. Thus it was that, after a warm interchange of opinion on a basis of basalt on a Sunday afternoon between opposing factions, the whole neighbourhood had a very untidy appearance, and the strain upon the resources of the surgical staff of the hospital almost reached breaking point.

After the first riot which I saw in this quarter, I know that the street around suggested that a few hundred men had been engaged for some time in looking for a sewer and had forgotten to replace the roadway. For High Street, Victoria Street, and Corporation Street which meet about here, were only macadamised roads, having a surface of broken granite or basalt, far more easily disintegrated even than the cobbled quays, so that a mob might argue with their opponents or with the police without putting themselves to any trouble beyond that involved in kicking up a few dozen stones of the handiest possible size, and possessing as many natural facets as the Koh-i-noor does artificial ones.

F. FRANKFORT MOORE, *The Truth About Ulster*, 1914

From the main entrance a long passage, frosted glass on one side, pitch pine on the other, led past the general office to the private office, where my father sat at a large square table strewn with dusty papers. The view from the window of the private office was of a redbrick distillery, an iron water tank on the skyline, and distant factory chimneys.

Outside, in streets that once resounded to the music of the Irish harp and now re-echoed to the rattle of distillery drays, flowed the fierce life of the city, part product of the dark Satanic mills crowded between the mountains and the river, part of the mythical waters of the Boyne. Changes might appear here, decay there, but beneath the surface the fierce tides flowed unchecked. An eighteenth-century print shows a ship lying in the basin of the Farset river in High Street, her masts and yards silhouetted against the sky. Today no more masts or yards are silhouetted in High Street or any other street; instead squat-funnelled motor ships nightly reflect their floodlit upper works in the waters of the Lagan; the area that was once slobland uncovered by the tide resounds to the clatter of automatic riveters in the shipyards; mail planes drone overhead to their aerodrome beside Lough Neagh; traffic lights wink red and green; business men dial one another on automatic telephones; and mill girls, whose mothers tramped through winter dawns to the sound of factory horns, barefooted and wearing shawls, dance at nights in cheap imported frocks and artificial silk stockings to the sound of saxophones and drums. Belfast, in other words, is learning the tricks of the twentieth century. As one mill girl remarked to another during the fashionable Saturday-night parade of North Street:

'You're stinkin' wi' perfume!'

To which the crushing retort was:

'Holy God, sure I'd be stinkin' if I wasn't.'

The Victorian Economic Men, frockcoated in stone, who surround the City Hall, might be excused if they held up their stone hands in horror at this new century with its cinemas, its dance halls, and its reckless consumption of tobacco. If they did, there would be a certain justification in their attitude. They may have ground the faces of the poor, but in their day the unemployed did not hang about the street corners, their hands in their pockets, congregated like shabby swallows on a wire.

DENIS IRELAND, *Statues Round the City Hall*, 1939

The country I grew up in had everything to encourage a romantic bent, had indeed done so ever since I first looked at the unattainable Green Hills through the nursery window. For the reader who knows those parts it will be enough to say that my main haunt was the Holywood Hills—the irregular polygon you would have described if you drew a line from Stormont to Comber, from Comber to Newtownards, from Newtownards to Scrabo, from Scrabo to Craigantlet, from Craigantlet to Holywood, and thence through Knocknagonney back to Stormont. How to suggest it all to a foreigner I hardly know.

First of all, it is by Southern English standards bleak. The woods, for we have a few, are of small trees, rowan and birch and small fir. The fields are small, divided by ditches with ragged sea-nipped hedges on top of them. There is a good deal of gorse and many outcroppings of rock. Small abandoned quarries, filled with cold-looking water, are surprisingly numerous. There is nearly always a wind whistling through the grass. Where you see a man ploughing there will be gulls following him and pecking at the furrow. There are no field-paths or rights of way, but that does not matter for everyone knows you—or if they do not know you, they know your kind and understand that you will shut gates and not walk over crops. Mushrooms are still felt to be common property, like the air. The soil has none of the rich chocolate or ochre you find in parts of England: it is pale—what Dyson calls 'the ancient, bitter earth'. But the grass is soft, rich, and sweet, and the cottages, always whitewashed and single storeyed and roofed with blue slate, light up the whole landscape.

Although these hills are not very high, the expanse seen from them is huge and various. Stand at the north-eastern extremity where the slopes go steeply down to Holywood. Beneath you is the whole expanse of the Lough. The Antrim coast twists sharply to the north and out of sight; green, and humble in comparison, Down curves away southward. Between the two the Lough merges into the sea, and if you look carefully on a good day you can even see Scotland, phantom-like on the horizon.

C. S. Lewis, *Surprised by Joy*, 1955

from *Clearances*

A cobble thrown a hundred years ago
Keeps coming at me, the first stone
Aimed at a great-grandmother's turncoat brow.
The pony jerks and the riot's on.
She's crouched low in the trap
Running the gauntlet that first Sunday
Down the brae to Mass at a panicked gallop.
He whips on through the town to cries of 'Lundy!'

Call her 'The Convert'. 'The Exogamous Bride'.
Anyhow, it is a genre piece
Inherited on my mother's side
And mine to dispose with now she's gone.
Instead of silver and Victorian lace,
The exonerating, exonerated stone.

SEAMUS HEANEY, *The Haw Lantern*, 1987

In no other spot in the North did I feel the surge of pride which an Ulster-man must feel as he thinks back over his own local history. Had I met an Orangeman as I stood on Walker's Bastion I would have wished to take his hand and shake it. If I were an Ulsterman, I felt, I could never forget Derry, any more than, being a Munsterman I can forget Limerick. Its siege was a magnificent example of heroic endurance, from the 18th of December 1689, when the gates were closed against King James's Irish Army, to 12th August when the relief ships that had for seven weeks been blocked on the Foyle by a boom, having burst through at the end of July, relieved the city and ended its torments. (Had it been some other king I might have felt regret that the city had not fallen, but King James was *such* a fool! As well as a coward.) The men who starved in Derry, and the women who fought with broken bottles to defend Limerick the following autumn have left us the two most stirring memories of the last campaign that the old Ireland fought before she was swallowed up in the darkness of the eighteenth century. To go from Derry, five or six miles out off the Buncrana Road, to the great concentric forts of the Grianan of Aileach—appropriately in Eire—the seat of the O'Neills when they were Kings of Ulster, is to run the gamut of that ancient Ireland's story.

SEAN O'FAOLAIN, *An Irish Journey*, 1940

Rathlin Island or Raghery (*Rachra*, genitive *Rachran*; *Rikina* of Ptolemy) lying a few miles off Ballycastle, continues the Chalk and basalt area out to sea. The intervening gap, which now forms a deep and turbulent strait, prob-ably arose from a collapse of the surface during the many and extensive earth-movements resulting from the disturbances which led to the great vol-canic outpourings. The island, shaped like a letter L, is mostly cliff-bound, but low at the part which is nearest to Fair Head; the surface is heathy, with cultivation on shallow soil and lakelets or marshes in the hollows. There is now no fuel, which has to be brought from Ballycastle. At the west end the cliffs, which the White-tailed Sea-Eagle used to haunt, run up to over 400 feet, with high outlying stacks, and here there are vast colonies of breeding sea-birds, which include Manx Shearwaters and Fulmar Petrels. The whole island is a delightful open breezy place, inspiring and invigorating, and one can now stay there in as much comfort as a lover of nature needs. Before the advent of the motorboat the passage was a precarious undertaking, on account of the powerful currents: if you missed the tide you might go joy-riding away round Fair Head or towards Inishowen, and a high wind might make the passage impossible for days at a time; but now, at least in summer, there is seldom difficulty. A ruined tower on the north-eastern cliffs, still known as Bruce's Castle, is the scene, according to tradition, of the famous episode of the persevering spider: but S. A. Stewart, who was an acute observer of animal life, has reported gravely that he could detect no greater intelligence among the spiders of Rathlin than among any other spiders.

Robert Lloyd Praeger, *The Way That I Went*, 1937

Trade Winds

I

Through Molly Ward's and Mickey Taylor's Locks,
Through Edenderry, Aghalee and Cranagh
To Lough Neagh and back again went Perseverence
And Speedwell carrying turf, coal and cinders.

II

Was it an Armagh man who loaded the boat
With the names of apples for his girlfriend:
Strawberry Cheeks, Lily Fingers, Angel Bites,
Winter Glories, Black Annetts, Widows' Whelps?

III

For smoking at wakes and breaking on graves
Carrick men christened clay pipes in Pipe Lane
Keel Baltic, Swinyard Cutty, Punch Quelp,
Plain Home Rule, Dutch Straws, Bent Unique.

IV

Among the Portavogie prawn-fishermen
Which will be the ship of death: Trade Winds,
Guiding Starlight, Halcyon, Easter Morn,
Liberty, Faithful Promise, Sparkling Wave?

Michael Longley, *Gorse Fires*, 1991

Bitter Memories

IRISH HISTORY

Island of bitter memories, thickly sown
From winding Boyne to Limerick's treaty-stone,
Bare Connaught Hills to Dublin Castle wall,
Green Wexford to the glens of Donegal,
Through sad six hundred years of hostile sway,
From Strongbow fierce to cunning Castlereagh!
These will not melt and vanish in a day.
These can yet sting the patriot thoughts which turn
To Erin's past, and bid them weep and burn.

WILLIAM ALLINGHAM, *Laurence Bloomfield in Ireland*

In Ireland the past has often seemed to matter more than the future.
The Irish have summoned up to the sessions of silent thought a crowd
of witnessing memories. The past of Ireland, if we go back to the days
of Plantations and Penal Codes and Clearances, is a past of many
wrongs. But to brood over the wrongs of the past is no way of salva-
tion for the future.

ERNEST BARKER, *Ireland in the Last Fifty Years*

'I remember Ninety-Eight,' said the fiddler, raising his voice. 'I was at the
Races of Castlebar when the French sent the English flying. I've heard the
screech at the triangle, too, and I've seen the pitch cap like a mocking crown
on the patriot's head and the poor priests flying through the bog with a price
on them for any informer to take. Them times are gone, thank God and our
great Liberator Daniel O'Connell for it. What does it matter if a few people
die of hunger? There's no real persecution no more.'

'Hunger'll be nothing new to the natures of the people,' said Gleeson, 'It's
eighteen years since I was on the roads myself, tramping from the hunger in
Sligo to this place in Galway here. It was a woeful journey.'

'God spare your health,' said Thomsy, 'you've been a godsend to the parish
since you came. It's well I remember the day you came with your good woman

and the children on the donkey-cart. Mary there was only a year old at the time.'

Mary flushed and went into her room. She hated any reference to the way her family arrived in Black Valley. Her father, on the other hand, loved talking about it in public and he always put her to shame with his talk. And the people mocked him about it. They liked to get him to talk and make him excited, in order to amuse themselves with him. Being a conceited fellow, he was indifferent to this mockery, as long as he got an opportunity of discoursing about the great event in his past.

Exhausted by the events of the day, Mary threw herself down on her bed. She heard her father say:

'There was nothing else for it but death from hunger. From place to place we went with the loom on the cart with the children. Many a time we were that weak from hunger that I wanted to sell the loom, but I held on to it all the same. Then one day, outside the village below, we met Mr Coburn, God lighten the darkness on his soul, he's a good man for a Protestant minister. He took pity on us.'

LIAM O'FLAHERTY, *Famine*, 1937

13th [May 1827] . . . There is sad news on Suirside. A poor hungry crowd tried to take meal from the boats which were sailing from Clonmel to Carrick-on-Suir, but the peelers fired on them from the boats. Three of the poor Irishmen were killed and six others very badly wounded. This happened on last Thursday, the tenth of this month.

I went with Tomás Ó Ceallaigh and Seán Ó Mathúna, the son of Tadhg an Chúinne, down by the river to Callan Mills in Millstreet and to Poll Sheáin as far as the Iron Mills which was working iron some years ago. There is an iron spa beside the road without cover or shelter from the road-dust. There used to be another iron mill near Tobar na mBráthar which also burnt the country's forests, in order to prevent the rapparees from hiding in them. These rapparees were poor Irishmen who were plundered by James I, King of England, by Oliver Cromwell and by William of Orange. They used to fight with *ropairi* or short spears, and it was from the word *ropaire* that they got their name.

HUMPHREY O'SULLIVAN, *Diary 1827–35*, 1979, trans. Tomás de Bhaldraithe

My Heart is too heavy to continue this Irony longer, for it is manifest that whatever Stranger took such a Journey, would be apt to think himself travelling in *Lapland* or *Ysland*, rather than in a Country so favoured by Nature as Ours, both in Fruitfulness of Soyl, and Temperature of Climate. The miserable Dress, and Dyet, and Dwelling of the People. The general

Desolation in most parts of the Kingdom. The old Seats of the Nobility and Gentry all in Ruins, and no new Ones in their stead. The Families of Farmers who pay great Rents, living in Filth and Nastiness upon Butter-milk and Potatoes, without a Shoe or Stocking to their Feet, or a House so convenient as an *English* Hog-sty to receive them. These indeed may be comfortable sights to an English Spectator, who comes for a short time only *to learn the Language*, and returns back to his own Country, whither he finds all our Wealth transmitted.

DEAN SWIFT, from 'A short view of Ireland', 1727–8

All the world knows the long and melancholy history of the miseries of Ireland. For eight centuries this country has endured every kind of oppression and of persecution. At first there were the evils of the barbarous conquest, the oppression of the Celtic by the Anglo-Norman race. After the conquest came the continual wars and revolts, which renewed at short intervals the disasters of the first invasion. Ireland of the middle age, always conquered, was never completely subdued. Those powerful Norman barons, whose domination had extended over the whole of England, and had banished the very shadow of Saxon nationality, could not succeed in establishing their empire on the same basis on the other side of St George's Channel. The vast marshes of Ireland, its immense thickets stretching towards the west, in Connaught especially, for centuries offered a sure refuge to the indomitable Celts, and allowed them to maintain a savage independence at the cost of poverty and suffering of every kind.

COUNT CAVOUR, *Thoughts on Ireland*, 1868, trans. W. B. Hodgson

Cabhair Ní Ghairfead

I shall not call for help until they coffin me—
　　What good for me to call when hope of help is gone?
Princes of Munster who would have heard my cry
　　Will not rise from the dead because I am alone.

Mind shudders like a wave in this tempestuous mood,
　　My bowels and my heart are pierced and filled with pain
To see our lands, our hills, our gentle neighbourhood,
　　A plot where any English upstart stakes his claim.

The Shannon and the Liffey and the tuneful Lee,
　　The Boyne and the Blackwater a sad music sing,
The waters of the west run red into the sea—
　　No matter what be trumps, their knave will beat our king.

And I can never cease weeping these useless tears;
  I am a man oppressed, afflicted and undone
Who where he wanders mourning no companion hears
  Only some waterfall that has no cause to mourn.

Now I shall cease, death comes, and I must not delay
  By Laune and Laine and Lee, diminished of their pride,
I shall go after the heroes, ay, into the clay—
  My fathers followed theirs before Christ was crucified.

EGAN O'RAHILLY (*c*.1675–1729), 'No Help I'll Call', trans. Frank O'Connor

One day about the middle of November, in the year 18—, Dominick M'Evoy and his son Jemmy were digging potatoes on the side of a hard, barren hill, called Esker Dhu. The day was bitter and wintry, the men were thinly clad, and as the keen blast swept across the hill with considerable violence, the sleet-like rain which it bore along, pelted into their garments with pitiless severity. The father had advanced into more than middle age; and having held, at a rack-rent, the miserable waste of farm which he occupied, he was compelled to exert himself in its cultivation, despite either obduracy of soil, or inclemency of weather. This day, however, was so unusually severe, that the old man began to feel incapable of continuing his toil. The son bore it better; but whenever a cold rush of stormy rain came over them, both were compelled to stand with their sides against it, and their heads turned, so as that the ear almost rested back upon the shoulder, in order to throw the rain off their faces. Of each, however, that cheek which was exposed to the rain and storm was beaten into a red hue; whilst the other part of their faces was both pale and hunger-pinched.

The father paused to take breath, and supported by his spade, looked down upon the sheltered inland which, inhabited chiefly by Protestants and Presbyterians, lay rich and warm-looking under him.

'Why thin,' he exclaimed to the son—a lad about fifteen,—'sure I know well I oughtn't to curse yez, anyway, you black set! an' yit, the Lord forgive me my sins, I'm almost timpted to give yez a volley, an' that from my heart out! Look at thim, Jimmy agra—only look at the black thieves! how warm an' wealthy they sit there in our own ould possessions, an' here we must toil till our fingers are worn to the stumps, upon this thievin' bent. The curse of Cromwell on it!—You might as well ax the divil for a blessin', as expect anything like a dacent crop out of it.—Look at thim two ridges!—such a poor sthring o' praties is in it!—one here an' one there—an' yit we must turn up the whole ridge for that same! Well, God sind the time soon, when the right will take place, Jimmy agrah!'

WILLIAM CARLETON, 'The Poor Scholar', in *Traits and Stories of the Irish Peasantry*, 1842–4

—We'll put force against force, says the citizen. We have our greater Ireland beyond the sea. They were driven out of house and home in the black 47. Their mudcabins and their shielings by the roadside were laid low by the batteringram and the *Times* rubbed its hands and told the whitelivered Saxons there would soon be as few Irish in Ireland as redskins in America. Even the grand Turk sent us his piastres. But the Sassenach tried to starve the nation at home while the land was full of crops that the British hyenas bought and sold in Rio de Janeiro. Ay, they drove out the peasants in hordes. Twenty thousand of them died in the coffinships. But those that came to the land of the free remember the land of bondage. And they will come again and with a vengeance, no cravens, the sons of Granuaile, the champions of Kathleen ni Houlihan.

—Perfectly true, says Bloom. But my point was . . .

—We are a long time waiting for that day, citizen, says Ned. Since the poor old woman told us that the French were on the sea and landed at Killala.

—Ay, says John Wyse. We fought for the royal Stuarts that reneged us against the Williamites and they betrayed us. Remember Limerick and the broken treatystone. We gave our best blood to France and Spain, the wild geese. Fontenoy, eh? And Sarsfield and O'Donnell, duke of Tetuan in Spain, and Ulysses Browne of Camus that was field-marshal to Maria Teresa. But what did we ever get for it?

—The French! says the citizen. Set of dancing masters! Do you know what it is? They were never worth a roasted fart to Ireland. Aren't they trying to make an *Entente cordiale* now at Tay Pay's dinnerparty with perfidious Albion? Firebrands of Europe and they always were?

—*Conspuez les Français*, says Lenehan, nobbling his beer.

—And as for the Prooshians and the Hanoverians, says Joe, haven't we had enough of those sausageeating bastards on the throne from George the elector down to the German lad and the flatulent old bitch that's dead?

Jesus, I had to laugh at the way he came out with that about the old one with the winkers on her blind drunk in her royal palace every night of God, old Vic, with her jorum of mountain dew and her coachman carting her up body and bones to roll into bed and she pulling him by the whiskers and singing him old bits of songs about *Ehren on the Rhine* and come where the boose is cheaper.

—Well! says J.J. We have Edward the peacemaker now.

—Tell that to a fool, says the citizen. There's a bloody sight more pox than pax about that boyo. Edward Guelph-Wettin!

—And what do you think, says Joe, of the holy boys, the priests and bishops of Ireland doing up his room in Maynooth in his Satanic Majesty's racing colours and sticking up pictures of all the horses his jockeys rode. The earl of Dublin, no less.

—They ought to have stuck up all the women he rode himself, says little Alf.

And says J.J.:

—Considerations of space influenced their lordship's decision.
—Will you try another, citizen? says Joe.
—Yes, sir, says he, I will.
—You? says Joe.
—Beholden to you, Joe, says I. May your shadow never grow less.
—Repeat that dose, says Joe.

JAMES JOYCE, *Ulysses*, 1918

The Stare's Nest by My Window

The bees build in the crevices
Of loosening masonry, and there
The mother birds bring grubs and flies.
My wall is loosening; honey-bees,
Come build in the empty house of the stare.

We are closed in, and the key is turned
On our uncertainty; somewhere
A man is killed, or a house burned,
Yet no clear fact to be discerned:
Come build in the empty house of the stare.

A barricade of stone or of wood;
Some fourteen days of civil war;
Last night they trundled down the road
That dead young soldier in his blood:
Come build in the empty house of the stare.

We had fed the heart on fantasies,
The heart's grown brutal from the fare;
More substance in our enmities
Than in our love; O honey-bees,
Come build in the empty house of the stare.

W. B. YEATS, *The Tower*, 1928

Last July, the 'Government' got up a very horrid massacre in the County Down. There was a great Orange procession of armed men: they marched with banners displayed, through a district chiefly inhabited by Catholics; and there, at Dolly's Brae, between Castlewellan and Banbridge, a collision took place, of course: a large force of police and military was present, and they took part, also, of course, with the Orangemen: five or six Catholics were killed, five or six of their houses burned; only one Orangemen or two seriously hurt—and the procession went on its way in triumph. Lord Roden, it appears, had feasted the Orangemen at Bryansford, and excited them with 'loyal' toasts; and afterwards, when informations were sought against the Orange rioters at the hands of the said Lord Roden, presiding at a bench of magistrates, he very properly refused. Very properly, for there is no law in Ireland now. I know no reason why Orangemen should *not* burn Papists' houses now.

JOHN MITCHEL, *Jail Journal*, 1854

National Presage

UNHAPPY Erin, what a lot was thine!
Half-conquered by a greedy robber band;
Ill governed with now lax, now ruthless hand;
Misled by zealots, wresting laws divine
To sanction every dark or mad design;
Lured by false lights of pseudo-patriot league
Through crooked paths of faction and intrigue;
And drugged with selfish flattery's poisoned wine.
Yet, reading all thy mournful history,
Thy children, with a mystic faith sublime,
Turn to the future, confident that Fate,
Become at last thy friend, reserves for thee,
To be thy portion in the coming time,
They know not what—but surely something great.

JOHN KELLS INGRAM, *Sonnets and Other Poems*, 1900

Roundstone stands upon a pleasant bay, and has a strand about two miles distant, of two miles in length, and in some places of nearly half a mile in width, of the finest white sand, and the most beautiful shells in the whole island. An ancient burying-ground is behind the strand, and many of the dead bodies have been washed out, and found among the sand. The poor peasants, men, women, and children, were gathering seaweed, loading their horses, asses, and backs with it, to manure the wretched little patches of potatoes sown among the rocks. 'Three hundred and sixty-five days a year we have the potato,' said a young man to me bitterly. 'The blackguard of a Raleigh who brought 'em here entailed a curse upon the labourer that has broke his heart. Because the landholder sees we can live and work hard on 'em, he grinds us down in our wages, and then despises us because we are ignorant and ragged.'

ASENATH NICHOLSON, *The Bible in Ireland*, 1852

The people that live thus in these Bollies growe theareby the more Barbarous and live more licentiouslye then they Could in townes usinge what means they liste and practicinge what mischiefs and villanies they will . . . againste private men whom they maligne by stealinge theire goodes or murderinge themselves.

Edmund Spenser, *A View of the Present State of Ireland*, 1596

I Gather Three Ears of Corn

I gather three ears of corn,
And the Black Earl from over the sea
Sails across in his silver ships,
And takes two out of the three.

I might build a house on the hill
And a barn of the speckly stone,
And tell my little stocking of gold,
If the Earl would let me alone.

But he has no thought for me—
Only the thought of his share,
And the softness of the linsey shifts
His lazy daughters wear.

There is a God in Heaven,
And angels, score on score,
Who will not see my hearthstone cold
Because I'm crazed and poor.

My childer have my blood,
And when they get their beards
They will not be content to run
As gillies to their herds!

The day will come, maybe,
When we can have our own,
And the Black Earl will come to us
Begging the bacach's bone!

Joseph Campbell, *The Rushlight*, 1906

Near where Finn lived there was a poor village called Cahirdoney. Every family in it was evicted one rainy day. Finn, very frightened, followed his grandfather down to the village. He saw houses being knocked down by beams swung against them. Policemen were there with rifles in their hands and English soldiers were there in their red uniforms.

'Will they pull down granny's house?' Finn heard a little girl say to a young woman who was standing in the rain. 'And Mrs Sullivan's, and she with the baby? And Cahill's where the children used to make the play in? It makes you feel awful lonesome, doesn't it, Bridget?'

His grandfather made a speech to the people, telling them that they must join a League which had just been started, a League which was formed to help the people who were evicted and to protect those who were not able to pay their rents.

The policemen pushed Finn's grandfather away.

Afterwards, a hut was built for policemen who guarded the place. One night guns were fired into this hut. No one was hurt but the government was resolved to deal very severely with the people who were mixed up in the affair, and at last three men were arrested. One of them was Finn's father. The men were put upon their trial and they were sentenced to three years' imprisonment.

PADRAIC COLUM, *A Boy in Eirinn*, 1916

Before I conclude these reminiscences of Irish peasant life in the Forties, I must mention an important feature of it—the Priests. Most of those whom I saw in our villages were disagreeable-looking men with the coarse mouth and jaw of the Irish peasant undisguised by the beards and whiskers worn by their lay brethren; and often the purple and bloated appearance of their cheeks suggested too abundant diet of bacon and whisky-punch. They worried me dreadfully by clearing out all the Catholic children from my school every now and then on the pretence of withdrawing them from heretical instruction, though nothing was further from the thoughts or wishes of any of us than proselytizing; nor was a single charge ever formulated against our teachers of saying a word to the children against their religion. What the priests really wanted was to obstruct education itself and too close and friendly intercourse with Protestants. For several winters I used to walk down to the school on certain evenings in the week and give the older lads and lassies lessons in Geography (with two huge maps of the world which I made myself, 11 ft by 9 ft!) and the first steps in Astronomy and history. Several times, when the class had been well got together and began to be interested, the priest announced that *he* would give them lessons on the same night, and they were to come to him instead of to me. Of course I told them to do so, and that I was very glad he would take the trouble. A fortnight or so later however I always learnt that the priest's lessons had dropped and all was to be recommenced.

FRANCES POWER COBBE, *Autobiography*, 1894

from *Laurence Bloomfield in Ireland*

We drive through Lisnamoy. Who bows so low?
Father Adair: but well does Bloomfield know
Of Bloomfield's favourite School the deepest foe.
There stands the building, comely brick and stone,
A little backward from the causeway thrown,
Flower-beds and paths in orderly array,
And greensward for the noon's half-hour of play;
All empty now, for eldest child and least
Must share at Croghan Hall the Vernal Feast.
The School has prosper'd, and is prospering still,
Though absent every clergyman's good-will,
Who each would make a primer of his creed,
Since now the vulgar must be taught to read,
The bigot duly with the scholar train,
Weed out man's brotherhood from breast and brain,
Twist every thought and feeling as they grow,—
Neighbour baptized to live his neighbour's foe.
Rome's churchmen seized the new scholastic dower,
Secure to swell by just so much their power,
While haughty shepherds of the legal rite
Declared this vulgar partnership a slight,
And loud demanding separate purse and place,
Flung a big Bible in the statesman's face,
Who handed back the volume with a bow.
So wrath was kindled, and is burning now,
In minds too Christian or perhaps too proud
To fill the legal hour for them allow'd,
Since Popish pastors that same right enjoy'd
With their own lambs, nor left it unemploy'd.
But now the people's alphabet in turn
Must from its first supporters feel the spurn.
How, for one day, could we, shrewd Men of Rome,
Forget th' experience, now again brought home,
That Knowledge acts as poison, if 'tis not
Cook'd in the black ecclesiastic pot,
From cardinals' and bishops' high discourse
Down to the *a b c* of babes at nurse?
As Spain puts garlic into every mess,
So must the sacred flavour more or less
Be mix'd in every atom of the food,
To dye the bones and circle with the blood;

Arithmetic the one true Church must own,
And Grammar have its orthodoxy known;
Or else, keep free from learning's dangerous leaven,
Guided, in blessed ignorance, to Heaven.

WILLIAM ALLINGHAM, *Laurence Bloomfield in Ireland*, 1864

The actual course of Irish history from the late sixteenth century to the end of the eighteenth, provides abundant material for history lessons. . . . All you have to do is to leave out the atrocities committed by your own side, and provide copious details of those committed by the enemy. Thus Protestant historians exaggerated the atrocities committed by Catholics against Protestants in the rebellion of 1641, and minimised or justified the massacres of Catholics by Cromwell's forces eight years later. Catholic historians pounced on the Protestant exaggerations of 1641, and ignored, or played down the Catholic atrocities which had actually occurred. Cromwell's atrocities, on the other hand, got from Catholics the kind of attention Protestants devoted to 1641. All political and religious zealots everywhere do this kind of thing instinctively. The Christian Brothers were exceptional only in that, through them the pedagogic resources of a powerful and efficient (and, in some ways exemplary) religious order became committed to this type of historiography, inculcating it into generations of their pupils, with the blessing of the Irish Catholic hierarchy.

CONOR CRUISE O'BRIEN, *Ancestral Voices*, 1994

The Christian Brothers did not feel any loyalty to Northern Ireland as a political entity. Government of the province was based on the propriety of 'a Protestant parliament for a Protestant people', as its most celebrated Prime Minister described his ideal institution. The Christian Brothers did not encourage us to become rebels, but they recognised that a Catholic growing up in the North must live by a certain stratagem, spiritual secrecy. Everything done in the school was legal, but it was accompanied by the conviction that as Catholics we were by definition Nationalists. Our relation to the government at Stormont in Belfast was bound to be a withholding one, maintained by practising a double consideration. The centre of our universe, as Catholics, was Rome, the Church, its visible head His Holiness the Pope. Our aspirations as Irish boys were most fully articulated by the government in Dublin, even though its writ did not run beyond the Custom Post at Carrickarnon. Our sense of Stormont was therefore ironic. We were entitled to the benefits of British citizenship, a boon we had not chosen, but the Brothers took it for granted that we must enjoy these satisfactions with mental reservations. The

Brothers did not expect that we would grow up to kill British soldiers or
bomb public houses in Belfast, but they encouraged us to be spiritually and
silently insurgent.

The teaching of Irish and of Irish history provided the richest occasions of
this practice. Irish was a fully recognised subject in the official curriculum,
though in practice it was taught mainly in Catholic schools. Learning
Irish was therefore a sign that one's kingdom was not of the Protestant, Unionist world; we lived elsewhere. That Irish and English were such different languages was a further token of spiritual secrecy: to speak Irish, it is necessary
to speak differently, as if we were speaking French or Spanish; different pronunciation, intonation, cadence. It also entailed respecting and maintaining
a form of social continuity which the British Empire and the Irish Famine of
the 1840s had nearly ended. Under the Penal Laws in the eighteenth century,
the Irish language was nearly defeated; it sustained itself only in remote communities along the Western seaboard. After the Famine, surviving parents
knew that their children would have to leave the country or starve; and that
if they left, they would have to speak English in their new countries: America,
Canada, Australia. Besides, Irish was now associated with misery and defeat,
the mark of a dejected people. In the middle years of the nineteenth century
the British government did not have to destroy the language; it was already
beaten. In the twentieth century those teachers who wanted to recover the
Irish language taught it as a sacred trust, a difficult language, since its
grammar and spelling were erratic and it existed in three main dialects. In
Newry we learned the Irish of Ulster and spent a month in the summer speaking it and listening to it in Donegal.

DENIS DONOGHUE, *Warrenpoint*, 1991

Solemn, heavy, dull, slow-moving, red-faced men, and scraggy, wasted, grey-
faced light ones, pushed their way here and there without heed how they
jostled the old or young who had come by train. Donal A'Chailleach, who had
a name for a short temper in the Lower Hills, only grinned when a stocky,
middle-aged man in side-whiskers shouldered him roughly out of the way.
Hughie was puzzled; he felt that here even the grown-ups were afraid. A buzz
of hushed talk arose among the young folk, and instinctively it was in Gaelic.
Round about the Gaelic whispers hung the heavy, solemn, Scotch accent of
the stranger.

'Damn on them,' Donal A'Chailleach said to an old crony. 'Damn on them;
an' it's us should be up here in these lands; bloody lot o' thieves. Sowl, only I
have the youngsters—sh—sh—' he concluded quickly, and turned to touch
his cap and smile at the big-bodied stranger who had come forward
pompously. 'Morrow, Mr Craig,' Donal greeted. 'Are ye wantin' a couple of
good youngsters the day?'

Mr Craig ran his eye over the group round Donal. 'I could be doin' wi' a likely lump o' a lassie,' he said. 'Is the big one yourn?'

'She's that. Come over here, Ellen.' Ellen, a girl of sixteen, came slowly forward, her head down. Mr Craig put his hand under her chin, and tilted her face backwards.

'She's a bit well-featured. I'd sooner hae a homelier face. I don't want men wastin' their time.'

'Ellen's all right,' Donal said.

'Humph,' Mr. Craig commented. 'She's a bit heavy-lookin' on her feet,' he added.

'Is it Ellen?' Donal objected. 'Why, man, she's as full o' life as a kitten. It's the long walk an' no sleep makes her look that way.'

'What ye wantin' for her?' Craig asked.

'She's better worth five pounds than anything in this fair the day, but I'll take four.'

Mr Craig shook his head. 'We're not as much dependin' on your country for servants now as we used to be. There's a big number of back country folk settled an' breedin' here now. If I get a handy one here the day, all right; if not, I hae ma eye on a girl in a cottage down-by.'

Bargaining talk this, Donal knew, but talk with some truth in it too, for in Donal's own day folk from the 'back country' had settled down in the Lagan and were living in cottages, and their children were on the market too. Craig and Donal got down to details of the bargain, while all the time the folk from the 'back country' moved forward towards the market-place, where the Gaelic servants and the planter masters meet and bargain year after year, since the native power was broken in Ulster.

PEADAR O'DONNELL, *Adrigoole*, 1929

During one lunch period I walked along North Street, a tumbledown part of old Newry, to the Butter Market and found myself in the midst of a hiring fair; a fair in which the merchandise was human beings. Those doing business were standing about in small groups, talking quietly; a sturdy man holding out for what he thought he was worth as a ploughman, a rosy-cheeked servant girl listening and nodding as the conditions of the offered engagement were explained to her by a farmer and his wife, a mother handing over her fourteen-year-old son on the understanding that in return for his apprentice labour on a farm he would be kept and given three meals a day and after six months she would be paid perhaps five or six pounds.

Hiring fairs were peculiar to the northern part of Ireland.

PATRICK SHEA, *Voices and the Sound of Drums*, 1981

In a land giving so little sustenance the women have to toil. Theirs has always been the task of knitting. Their work is justly famed. With deft, patient fingers they made in the years that are gone knitted articles that were sold in the little town of Glenties. So fair a place—but its very name stinks in the nostrils of men and women who hate oppression. For this was the great centre of the knitting industry, and it was here that young girls and old women were paid prices as shameless as those of the darkest slums of the East End of London. It was reckoned rare good fortune to make as much as one and fourpence for a dozen pairs of socks; one penny per pair was the price of gloves. There are men in Dungloe to-day who will tell you with flaming bitterness how their mothers walked the sixteen miles to Glenties with their small stock of goods, how they were paid not in coin of the realm but in kind, how they returned heart-sick, footsore, and faint across the hills with a few yards of calico or flannel as the price of their months of toil.

MARIE HARRISON, *Dawn in Ireland*, 1917

A face like that of a sheeted corpse peered up into the greyness, and Norah Ryan looked at it, her face full of a fright that was not unmixed with childish curiosity. There in the white snow, some asleep and some staring vacantly into the darkness, lay a score of women, some young, some old, and all curled up like sleeping dogs. Nothing could be seen but the faces, coloured ghastly silver in the dim light of the slow dawn, faces without bodies staring like dead things from the welter of snow. An old woman asleep, the bones of her face showing plainly through the sallow wrinkles of the skin, her only tooth protruding like a fang and her jaw lowered as if hung by a string, suddenly coughed. Her cough was wheezy, weak with age, and she awoke. In the midst of the heap of bodies she stood upright and disturbed the other sleepers. In an instant the hollow was alive, voluble, noisy. Some of the women knelt down and said their prayers, others shook the snow from their shawls, one was humming a love song and making the sign of the cross at the end of every verse.

'I've been travelling all night long,' said an old crone who had just joined the party, 'and I thought that I would not be in time to catch the tide. It is a long way that I have to come for a bundle of yarn—sixteen miles, and maybe it is that I won't get it at the end of my journey.'

The kneeling women rose from their knees and hurried towards the channel in the bay, now a thin string of water barely three yards in width. The wind, piercingly cold, no longer carried its burden of sleet, and the east, icily clear, waited, almost in suspense, for the first tint of the sun. The soil, black on the foreshore, cracked underfoot and pained the women as they walked. None wore their shoes, although three or four carried brogues tied round their necks. Most had mairteens (double thick stockings) on their feet, and these, though they retained a certain amount of body heat, kept out no wet. In front the old woman, all skin and bones and more bones that skin, whom Norah had wakened, led the way, her breath steaming out into the air and her feet sinking almost to the knees at every step. From her dull, lifeless look and the weary eyes that accepted everything with fatalistic calm it was plain that she had passed the greater part of her years in suffering.

All the women had difficulty with the wet and shifty sand, which, when they placed their feet heavily on one particular spot, rose in an instant to their knees. They floundered across, pulling out one foot and then another, and grunting whenever they did so.

PATRICK McGILL, *The Rat Pit*, 1915

This ground is littered with things, cluttered with memories and multiple associations. It turns out to be a long three miles from Gallowshill to the house of Willy and Jinny Norris. With my mother and my elder sisters I walked it so often, and later on with friends and long after Willy and Jinny were gone and the house a blackened ruin, the lawn a wilderness, the gooseberry bushes gone to seed, the Orange lilies extinguished—miniature suns that would never rise again in that place no more than life would ever come back to the empty mansion of Johnny Pet Wilson. That was just to the left before you turned into the Norris laneway, red-sanded, like a tunnel with high hawthorn hedges and sycamores and ash trees shining white and naked. My father had known Johnny Pet and afterwards had woven mythologies about him: a big Presbyterian farmer, the meanest and oddest man that had ever lived in those parts. When his hired men, mostly Gaelic speakers from West Donegal, once asked him for jam or treacle or syrup or, God help us, butter itself, to moisten their dry bread, he said: Do you say your prayers?

—Yes, boss.

They were puzzled.

—Do you say the Lord's prayer?

—Yes, boss.

—Well, in the Lord's prayer it says: Give us this day our daily bread. Damn the word about jam or treacle or syrup or butter.

When he bought provisions in a shop in the town he specified: So much of labouring man's bacon and so much of the good bacon.

For the hired men, the imported long-bottom American bacon. For himself, the Limerick ham.

He rose between four and five in the morning and expected his men to be already out and about. He went around with an old potato sack on his shoulders like a shawl, and followed always by a giant of a gentleman goat, stepping like a king's warhorse. The goat would attack you if you angered Johnny Pet, and when Johnny died the goat lay down and died on the same day. Their ghosts walked, it was well known, in the abandoned orchard where the apples had become half-crabs, through gaps in hedges and broken fences, and in the roofless rooms of the ruined house. Nobody had ever wanted to live there after the goat and Johnny Pet died. There were no relatives even to claim the hoarded fortune.

—If the goat had lived, my father said, he might have had the money and the place.

—The poor Donegals, my mother would say as she walked past Johnny Pet's ghost, and the ghost of the goat, on the way to see Willy and Jinny. Oh, the poor Donegals.

It was a phrase her mother had used when, from the doorstep of the farm-house in which my mother was reared, the old lady would look west on a clear day and see the tip of the white cone of Mount Errigal, the Cock o' the North, sixty or more miles away, standing up and shining with shale over Gweedore and the Rosses of Donegal and by the edge of the open Atlantic. From that hard coast, a treeless place of diminutive fields fenced by drystone walls, of rocks, mountains, small lakes, empty moors and ocean winds the young Donegal people (both sexes) used to walk eastwards, sometimes barefoot, to hire out in the rich farms along the valley of the Strule, the Mourne and the Foyle—three fine names for different stages of the same river.

BENEDICT KIELY, 'The Night We Rode with Sarsfield', 1963

We set out, pushing our bikes into the teeth of a gale, sheltering from squalls behind hedges and barns, on a desolate road which the map-makers said was in Leinster, though any fool could see it was in Connacht, with boglands to right and left of it, black pine-cones of turf against mother-of-pearl skies and the bright blue hills over by the Shannon Gap for which we were making. The cottages were dirty and unkempt, and we followed a tall, indo-lent man in shirt-sleeves, with his hands in his trousers pockets, who dexter-ously guided a frightened cow with well-placed kicks in the throat and belly—an inspiring sight. We hadn't gone far before I had to mend my first puncture.

By the time the Chinese-green screen of flat hillocks that stood between us and the river had opened up and we saw the belfry of Clonmacnois in the distance, I was exhausted. Célimène cycled on to find us a bed for the night. She had the misfortune to make her enquiries of an old gentleman who gave her a lecture on Irish history instead. Of course, with her English accent and appearance, she was God's gift to an oppressed Gael.

'You didn't happen to listen in last night?' he asked.

'No,' she said wearily. 'Why?'

'There was a broadcast about Clonmacnois.'

'Oh,' she asked, 'was it good?' (That was the English blood breaking out in her. Why didn't she say that she had written it?)

'Wonderful!' he said enthusiastically. 'The whole history of Clonmacnois from the earliest times.'

'But what I really want to know is whether we can get lodgings somewhere for the night,' she persisted.

'No, lady,' he said firmly. 'There is no hotel accommodation in Clonmacnois since the English burned the abbey guesthouse in 1552. You should take a good look at the ruins.'

FRANK O'CONNOR, Irish Miles, 1947

The historian was a clever man, watchful and worldly. He would bide his time, picking up bits and pieces from such dinners and social encounters. He had published very little, and Eamon wondered if his work on government policy in relation to terrorism would ever appear.

After dinner they sat at a side table: there was no more to be said about the report, they had exhausted the possibilities. The waiter came with brandies as they began to talk about their backgrounds, Eamon about Enniscorthy and his family's involvement in 1916 and the War of Independence, the historian about his father's memories of the burning of Cork city.

'Was your father in the Civil War?' the historian asked him.

'He must have been. I know one uncle was on hunger strike, but, to be honest, I'm not sure. It was never talked about. Nineteen sixteen was mentioned all the time, and the Tan War as well, but not the Civil War. I know that my father was aware who did some of the killings in Enniscorthy, a man told him once in a pub, but he swore that he would never tell anyone. And he told me years ago about how they took over the Protestant church in Enniscorthy during the Civil War, and they made mock sermons during the night, but when the shooting started one man shouted out, 'Watch the ricoshits, lads!' and they all thought this was funny. He told me the story as though he was there, but I never asked him. If you asked him he would grow silent. It was a very bitter time for them.'

'They were a strange generation,' the historian said.

The two men had a few more drinks as they talked about the past. Eamon remembered the story about Cathal Brugha and his father's going to Dublin to get permission to have the Big Houses burned. But he said nothing about it. He listened to a story about Michael Collins, nodding and encouraging the historian to go on, all the time thinking back to that evening in his grandmother's house when he first heard the story. He kept listening, more and more sure that he should not mention the story about his father and Cathal Brugha, that he should consign it to the past, to silence, as his father had done with the names of the men who did the killings in Enniscorthy. He smiled as the historian came to the end of his story, and stood up, saying it was time to go.

COLM TÓIBÍN, The Heather Blazing, 1992

The time for courtship between Collins and my great-aunt Kitty proved very short. . . . it was not long before he attracted the attention of the Crown authorities. In April 1918, by which time he knew the Kiernan family well, Collins was arrested on a trumped up disaffection charge after a speech he made near Granard. He was charged in Longford, but jumped bail, going immediately to Granard, where he was welcomed by a tumultuous crowd of Volunteers lining the main street. My family, I imagine, was behind this dramatic celebration. From that moment on, however, everything changed. Collins went on the run, taking with him the innocence of the earlier era. In the years that followed, he was to descend now and again from the hills to visit Kitty, my Gran Peg and the rest of the family, before disappearing with equally dramatic suddenness back into the night. The countryside became caught up in a bitter and increasingly vicious war, of which he was the leading orchestrator on the Irish side. On the evening before Guy Fawkes in 1920, 11 lorry-loads of British troops entered Granard, sacking the town and burning the Greville Arms to the ground, in retaliation for the shooting dead of a police inspector in the hotel bar four days before. The hotel was rebuilt, but after the Free State was established in 1922, the town went into decline, like much of the rest of Ireland. By the time I was growing up there in the Sixties, it was dominated by a harsh, unyielding priest who had ruled the place with an iron fist for decades. The hotel stayed in the family until the late Sixties and as children we used to go there, treating its by now often unoccupied upper floors as a lavish warren of playrooms.

I doubt that Kitty first met Collins while tending his wounds in an outhouse borrowed from *Ryan's Daughter*, as Neil Jordan's movie suggests. Nor was her great gun-toting leap into the fray on his behalf exactly in character. There are lots of other historical short-cuts and omissions in *Michael Collins*. None matters much to me nor, it seems, have any mattered to the Irish public. Robert Kee put it well when he wrote that the film's intentions were honest and its central themes 'historically wholly acceptable'. Not for the first time, however, Kee is in a minority position. The film's historical compression has been transformed by some critics into a cavalier disregard of the facts, a deliberately deceitful Republicanism. Jordan has been excoriated for using the wrong kind of gun in one incident and the wrong kind of bomb in another, as though the exposure of such minor details destroyed the movie's central truth, which is that Michael Collins was the revolutionary leader of a popular movement which defeated the British Forces in most of Ireland. There is an analogy here with the way the British authorities reacted to the IRA ceasefire in 1994, ignoring its dramatic historical implications, and asking instead for proof of permanence and for the prior decommissioning of weapons.

There is something about Britain's attitude to Ireland which causes it to deny truths that are accepted commonplaces in its other post-colonial relationships. Of course, Ireland was never strictly speaking a colony. In 1801 it became an integral part of the United Kingdom, a decision taken jointly by the Irish and British Parliaments the previous year. Irish nationalism poses, therefore, a threat, not of liberation but of dismemberment. This is why the authorities fought so hard against Collins and why there are those who continue to be embittered by his success.

Critics of *Michael Collins* might seem to be on stronger ground when they describe the film as a propaganda coup for the contemporary IRA. Certainly it is a violent film, and its main protagonist is a glamorously efficient killer of British soldiers and their Irish surrogates. Opinion in the Republic has been a little overstated in its claim that there is no connection between Collins's revolutionary violence (legitimate) and the IRA's current campaign of 'terrorism' (illegitimate). The point is a fine one.

CONOR GEARTY, Diary, *London Review of Books*, 28 November 1996

The Flight of the Earls

This was a distinguished crew for one ship; for it is indeed certain that the sea had not supported, and the winds had not wafted from Ireland, in modern times, a party of one ship who would have been more illustrious, or noble in point of genealogy, or more renowned for deeds, valour or high achievements. (Annals of the Four Masters)

The fiddler settles in
to his playing so easily;
rosewood box tucked under chin,
saw of rosined bow
& angle of elbow

that the mind elides
for a while what he plays:
hornpipe or reel to warm
us up well, heel or toecap
twitching in tune

till the sound expands
in the slow climb of a lament.
As by some forest campfire
listeners draw near, to honour
a communal loss

& a shattered procession
of anonymous suffering

files through the brain:
burnt houses, pillaged farms,
a province in flames.

We have killed, burnt and despoiled all along the Lough to within four
miles of Dungannon . . . in which journeys we have killed above a
hundred of all sorts, besides such as we have burned, how many I
know not. We spare none, of what quality or sex soever, and it had bred
much terror in the people who heard not a drum nor saw not a fire of long
time. (Chichester to Mountjoy, Spring 1607)

With an intricate
& mournful mastery
the thin bow glides & slides,
assuaging like a bardic poem,
our tribal pain—

Disappearance & death
of a world, as down Lough Swilly
the great ship, encumbered with nobles,
swells its sails for Europe:
The Flight of the Earls.

JOHN MONTAGUE, *The Rough Field*, 1972

To these few odd things especially characteristic of Ireland perhaps the
Orange drum should be added by way of a stirring finale. I do not refer to
'The Drums'—half a dozen of these instruments, of astonishing power,
which, manned by a stalwart crew and supported by one fife, are paraded at
funeral pace through the streets of the northern towns; words fail to convey
any idea of the impression which that amazing rite leaves on the mind of the
innocent stranger who inadvertently encounters it. Rather I refer to the drum
of Ulster and all that it implies, as may be gathered from the impassioned
speeches of orators on the 12th of July. It is, among other things, an emblem
of an ineradicable characteristic of Irish people—that of looking backward
rather than forward. We can never let the dead past bury its dead. Finn
M'Coul and Brian Boru are still with us; and I should not blame the friendly
Saxon who carries away with him the impression that Catholic emancipation
happened yesterday, that the Battle of the Boyne was fought last Thursday
week, and that Cromwell trampled and slaughtered in Ireland towards the
latter end of the preceding month.

ROBERT LLOYD PRAEGER, *The Way That I Went*, 1937

Until the seventies Ireland was feudal, and we looked upon our tenants as animals that lived in hovels round the bogs, whence they came twice a year with their rents; and I can remember that once when my father was his own agent, a great concourse of strange fellows came to Moore Hall in tall hats and knee-breeches, jabbering to each other in Irish. An old man here and there could speak a little English, and I remember one of them saying: 'Sure they're only mountaineymen, yer honour, and have no English; but they have the goicks,' he added with unction. And out of the tall hats came rolls of bank-notes, so dirty that my father grumbled, telling the tenant that he must bring cleaner notes; and afraid lest he should be sent off on a long trudge to the bank, the old fellow thrust the notes into his hand and began jabbering again. 'He's asking for his docket, yer honour,' the interpreter explained. My father's clerk wrote out a receipt, and the old fellow went away, leaving me laughing at him, and the interpreter repeating: 'Sure, he's a mountainey man, yer honour.' And if they failed to pay their rents, the cabins they had built with their own hands were thrown down, for there was no pity for a man who failed to pay his rent. And if we thought that bullocks would pay us better we ridded our lands of them; 'cleaned our lands of tenants,' is an expression I once heard, and I remember how they used to go away by train from Clare-morris in great batches bawling like animals. There is no denying that we looked upon our tenants as animals, and that they looked on us as kings; in all the old stories the landlord is a king. The men took off their hats to us and the women rushed out of their cabins dropping curtsies to us until the seventies. Their cry 'Long life to yer honour,' rings still in my ears; and the seignioral rights flourished in Mayo and Galway in those days, and soon after my father's funeral I saw the last of this custom: a middle-aged woman and her daughter and a small grey ass laden with two creels of young chickens were waiting at my door, the woman curtseying, the girl drawing her shawl about her face shyly.

GEORGE MOORE, *Vale*, 1914

A Visit to Castletown House

(for Nora Graham)

The avenue was green and long, and green
light pooled under the fernheads; a jade screen
could not let such liquid light in, a sea
at its greenest self could not pretend to be
so emerald. Men had made this landscape
from a mere secreting wood: knuckles bled
and bones broke to make this awning drape
a fitting silk upon its owner's head.

The house was lifted by two pillared wings
out of its bulk of solid chisellings
and flashed across the chestnut-marshalled lawn
a few lit windows on a bullock bawn.
The one-way windows of the empty rooms
reflected meadows, now the haunt
of waterbirds: where hawtrees were in bloom,
and belladonna, a poisonous plant.

A newer gentry in their quaint attire
looked at maps depicting alien shire
and city, town and fort: they were his seed,
that native who had taken coloured beads
disguised as chandeliers of vulgar glass
and made a room to suit a tasteless man
—a graceful art come to a sorry pass—
painted like some demented tinker's van.

But the music that was played in there—
that had grace, a nervous grace laid bare,
Tortellier unravelling sonatas
pummelling the instrument that has
the deep luxurious sensual sound,
allowing it no richness, making stars
where moons would be, choosing to expound
music as passionate as guitars.

I went into the calmer, gentler hall
in the wineglassed, chattering interval:
there was the smell of rose and woodsmoke there.
I stepped into the gentler evening air
and saw black figures dancing on the lawn,
Eviction, Droit de Seigneur, Broken Bones:
and heard the crack of ligaments being torn
and smelled the clinging blood upon the stones.

MICHAEL HARTNETT, *A Farewell to English*, 1975

To behold them thus passing by, like a frieze, group following group, figure
figure, each one more tatterdemalion than the last, less erect, less a member
of a proud confraternity, is to behold the whole Gaelic race of their day
passing by, except that the multitude is heightened and intensified into individual expression—is become wild eyes, bitter lips, and flesh that quivers and
shrinks and fails.

The poets becoming poorer and poorer as one succeeded the other, and each becoming poorer and poorer as the years overtook him, this was to be expected, for everything Irish in that stricken land was decaying; the language itself was, of course, decaying, declining everywhere almost into a *patois*, and the learning that it enshrined was shrinking, until, in the end, a true peasant's brain could easily comprehend it. At last we can find no difference between the songs written by the unnamed poets of the folk and those written by the true successors of the old *filí*, no difference either in thought or diction. The Irish people will yet honour the name Ó Longáin as that of one who did inestimable service in transcribing and rescuing verse wherever it was to be had; but his own verse is poor and thin; and the same may be said of, perhaps, all the poets of his time: their patriotic songs are no better than the same sort of songs that in Ó Longáin's time the Irish people were beginning to write in English.

The Bardic Schools have now been closed for almost two centuries, the Courts of Poetry meet no more. The Gaelic literary tradition is slowly making an end. A poet here and there arises, and, stirred by a local catastrophe—as Máire Bhuidhe Ní Laoghaire (Mary O'Leary), by the agrarian troubles of 1822 in West Cork, strikes out a song full of fire and vigour—or emulous of the men of old, writes patiently a few verses in a bardic metre; but the literary tradition is no more, for it has lost the power of creating new forms.

DANIEL CORKERY, *The Hidden Ireland*, 1925

Merciful God! In what a frightful condition was the country at that time. I speak now of the North of Ireland. It was then, indeed, the seat of Orange ascendancy and irresponsible power. To find a justice of the peace *not* an Orangeman would have been an impossibility. The grand jury room was little less than an Orange lodge. There was then no law *against* an Orangeman, and no law *for* a Papist. I am now writing not only that which is well known to be historical truth, but that which I have witnessed with my own eyes.

WILLIAM CARLETON, *Autobiography*, 1869

NB—The newspaper I have seen says the Queen met with nothing but loyalty; and that '*Young Ireland was nowhere to be seen.*' And the *Times* asks triumphantly, 'Where were the vitriol bottles?' as if anybody had proposed to sprinkle the Queen with vitriol.

NB (2)—Her Majesty wore, at Cork, a 'green silk visite'; also, carried a parasol of purple silk (perhaps vitriol proof). Her Majesty first touched Irish soil at the Cove of Cork, which is henceforth Queenstown. Her Majesty did not visit Spike Island.

NB (3)—Her Majesty, on board her yacht in Kingstown harbour, took her children by the hand, and 'introduced them (in dumb show) to the Irish people,' in a very touching manner.

NB (4)—Synod of Ulster had a deputation of their paid preachers to meet her Majesty in Dublin. Oh! where were the Remonstrant Synod? Do they apprehend no danger to their little *donum*?

NB (5)—Her Majesty did not visit Skibbereen, Westport, or Schull; neither did she 'drop in' (as sometimes in Scotland) to dine with any of the peasantry, on their 'homely fare.' After a few years, however, it is understood that Her Majesty will visit the West. The human inhabitants are expected by that time to have been sufficiently thinned, and the deer and other game to have proportionately multiplied. The Prince Albert will then take a hunting lodge in Connemara.

JOHN MITCHEL, *Jail Journal*, 1854

Rathlin

A long time since the last scream cut short—
Then an unnatural silence; and then
A natural silence, slowly broken
By the shearwater, by the sporadic
Conversation of crickets, the bleak
Reminder of a metaphysical wind.
Ages of this, till the report
Of an outboard motor at the pier
Shatters the dream-time, and we land
As if we were the first visitors here.

The whole island a sanctuary where amazed
Oneiric species whistle and chatter,
Evacuating rock-face and cliff-top.
Cerulean distance, an oceanic haze—
Nothing but sea-smoke to the ice-cap
And the odd somnolent freighter.
Bombs doze in the housing estates
But here they are through with history—
Custodians of a lone light which repeats
One simple statement to the turbulent sea.

A long time since the unspeakable violence—
Since Somhairle Buidh, powerless on the mainland,
Heard the screams of the Rathlin women
Borne to him, seconds later, upon the wind.

Only the cry of the shearwater
And the roar of the outboard motor
Disturb the singular peace. Spray-blind,
We leave here the infancy of the race,
Unsure among the pitching surfaces
Whether the future lies before us or behind.

DEREK MAHON, *The Hunt By Night*, 1982

The truth of the matter is . . . that Ulster Protestants and Ulster Catholics are, to use an expressive phrase, very much of a muchness. There are broad-minded Protestants and broad-minded Catholics, bigoted Protestants and bigoted Catholics. There are cruel Protestants and cruel Catholics, gentle Protestants and gentle Catholics. There are Protestants who would like to see all the Catholics swept out of the country, and Catholics who would like to see Protestants swept out of the country; but, to match them, there are Protestants who want to live in peace and friendship with their Catholic neighbours, and Catholics who want to live in peace and friendship with their Protestant neighbours. For every bigot or black sheep you find on one side, you will, as an English commentator on Ireland would say, find two on the other. Protestant and Catholic have been looking at each other more closely and honestly of late, and have each been amazed to discover how human the other is. There may never have been a more bitter sort of bigotry in Ulster than at the present moment, but, on the other hand, never was so fine and general a spirit of broad-mindedness to be found. Middle-aged—or rather century-old—bigotry is uttering its last cry, and it is a loud and strident cry, so loud indeed that many people are unable to hear beyond it the more pleasant and gathering voices of the peace-bringers.

ROBERT LYND, *Home Life in Ireland*, 1908

There are good historical reasons why Irish Nationalism so often reads like bad poetry and Ulster Unionism like bad prose. Cathleen, of course, has been Muse as well as goddess. Eoin MacNeill tried to lower the political tempera-ture before the Rising by sending round a circular which plainly stated: 'What we call our country is not a poetical abstraction . . . There is no such person as Cathleen Ni Houlihan . . . who is calling upon us to serve her'. Ulster Protestantism, which prides itself on plain statement, has tried to discourage a self-critical prose tradition, let alone qualifying clauses. Literature remains the primary place where language changes, where anorexic categories are exposed. Thus from the 1920s most writers had no option but to constitute themselves an *opposition* to the ideological clamps holding both Irish entities together. In my lifetime, these clamps have distorted ethics, politics, social and personal relations, the lives of women, education, what passes here for religion, and our whole understanding of Irish culture.

EDNA LONGLEY, *From Cathleen to Anorexia*, 1990

Parnell's Funeral

I

Under the Great Comedian's tomb the crowd.
A bundle of tempestuous cloud is blown
About the sky; where that is clear of cloud
Brightness remains; a brighter star shoots down;
What shudders run through all that animal blood?
What is this sacrifice? Can someone there
Recall the Cretan barb that pierced a star?

Rich foliage that the starlight glittered through,
A frenzied crowd, and where the branches sprang
A beautiful seated boy; a sacred bow;
A woman, and an arrow on a string;
A pierced boy, image of a star laid low.
That woman, the Great Mother imaging,
Cut out his heart. Some master of design
Stamped boy and tree upon Sicilian coin.

An age is the reversal of an age:
When strangers murdered Emmet, Fitzgerald, Tone,
We lived like men that watch a painted stage.
What matter for the scene, the scene once gone:
It had not touched our lives. But popular rage,
Hysterica passio dragged this quarry down.
None shared our guilt; nor did we play a part
Upon a painted stage when we devoured his heart.

Come, fix upon me that accusing eye.
I thirst for accusation. All that was sung,
All that was said in Ireland is a lie
Bred out of the contagion of the throng,
Saving the rhyme rats hear before they die.
Leave nothing but the nothings that belong
To this bare soul, let all men judge that can
Whether it be an animal or a man.

II

The rest I pass, one sentence I unsay.
Had de Valéra eaten Parnell's heart
No loose-lipped demagogue had won the day,
No civil rancour torn the land apart.

Had Cosgrave eaten Parnell's heart, the land's
Imagination had been satisfied,
Or lacking that, government in such hands,
O'Higgins its sole statesman had not died.

Had even O'Duffy—but I name no more—
Their school a crowd, his master solitude;
Through Jonathan Swift's dark grove he passed, and there
Plucked bitter wisdom that enriched his blood.

W. B. YEATS, *A Full Moon in March*, 1935

A Nation of Lunaticks!

He gave the little Wealth he had,
To build a House for Fools and Mad:
And shew'd by one satyric Touch,
No Nation wanted it so much:

DEAN SWIFT, from
'On the Death of Dr Swift'

Mad Ireland hurt you into poetry.
Now Ireland has her madness and her weather still
For poetry makes nothing happen . . .

W. H. AUDEN, 'In Memory of W. B. Yeats'

———

Legislate for Ireland! a nation of lunaticks! Reason with Irishmen! Everyone of them stark staring mad from the peer to the peasant. At the publick works where the pay is 2/-a day, to men never used at the highest to more than a shilling, they have all turned out for advance of wages. On the railroads, being equally well paid they have collected all the disorderly women and other profligates for company and run headlong into a career of debauchery which will end in the miserable death of hundreds. The Doctor made me shudder over the slight allusions he made to what has already come under his medical experience. The people are not ready for higher wages, higher tastes must first be produced, otherwise their habits are only lowered by encreasing their means before thy are qualified properly to employ them.

ELIZABETH SMITH, *Irish Journals*, 1846

Stoute and obstinate Rebells suche as will never be made dutifull and obediente nor brought to labour or civill Conversacion havinge once tasted that licentious liffe and beinge acquainted with spoile and outrages but will ever after be readye for the like occasions so as theare is no hope of their amendment or recoverye and therefore nedefull to be cutt of.

EDMUND SPENSER, *A View of the Present State of Ireland*, 1596

The strange air engulfed him. The strange land—charming, savage, mythical—lured him on with indulgent ease. He moved, triumphant, through a new peculiar universe of the unimagined and the unreal. Who or what were these people, with their mantles and their nakedness, their long locks of hair hanging over their faces, their wild battle-cries and gruesome wailings, their kerns and their gallowglas, their jesters and their bards? Who were their ancestors? Scythians? Or Spaniards? Or Gauls? What state of society was this, where chiefs jostled with gypsies, where ragged women lay all day long laughing in the hedgerows, where ragged men gambled away among each other their very rags, their very forelocks, the very . . . parts more precious still, where wizards flew on whirlwinds, and rats were rhymed into dissolution? All was vague, contradictory, and unaccountable; and the Lord Deputy, advancing further and further into the green wilderness, began—like so many others before and after him—to catch the surrounding infection, to lose the solid sense of things, and to grow confused over what was fancy and what was fact.

LYTTON STRACHEY, *Elizabeth and Essex*, 1928

He himself knew more about the topography and economy, the racial and political schisms of Southern Africa (he had taken a strong line on the boycott) than he did about England's island neighbour. A sportsman's paradise of river, bog and mountain . . . rain . . . Celtic mist . . . potatoes (famine?) . . . shamrock . . . sweepstake . . . navvies (drunk) . . . Oh, and some dead (martyred?) radical called Connolly who had been in vogue with a set of mad Glaswegians in Ruskin when he was up. But he at least had known that the country had been partitioned sometime in the Twenties, and that it had more to do with religion than with politics. The Shadow Home Secretary, he'd heard since, had been amazed to learn that the six northern counties were self-governing.

That had been on Monday. After leaving the meeting, Sidney had gone straight to the House library and that night had returned to Sevenoaks laden with books. From then until Friday he had put himself through a crash course on the history of Ireland from Pope Adrian's gift of it to Henry II, through the Elizabethan Plantings, Cromwell and the Settlement, the Williamite Wars, Penal times, the 1798 Rebellion, the Famine, the Fenians, the Land League, Parnell, Gladstone's Home Rule Bill, Carson's Army ('Ulster Will Fight!'), the 1916 Rising, the Treaty, Partition and the Civil War, to the Free State and the various IRA outbreaks since. And on Friday he had emerged from it feeling much like Elizabeth I's Earl of Essex, Robert Devereux, must have felt, wandering bemused at the head of his decimated army through the dreeping boondocks west of the Pale, a fever laden swamp enlivened only by the sight of emaciated, toothless hags giggling drunk in the hedgerows, aware of, but never seeing, the woodkernes who skulked from cover to pick off his rear-guard one by one . . . Poor Devereux's dread may have been of the physical unknown, the black pit of his time; the dread that had grown in Sidney throughout the week was similar, but of his time: the dread of that terrain beyond reason.

JOHN MORROW, *The Essex Factor*, 1982

In travelling through Ireland, a stranger is very frequently puzzled by the singular ways, and especially by the idiomatic equivocation, characteristic of every Irish peasant. Some years back, more particularly, these men were certainly originals—quite unlike any other people whatever. Many an hour of curious entertainment has been afforded me by their eccentricities; yet, though always fond of prying into the remote sources of these national peculiarities, I must frankly confess that, with all my pains, I never was able to develop half of them, except by one sweeping observation; namely, that the brains and tongues of the Irish are somehow differently formed or furnished from those of other people.

SIR JONAH BARRINGTON, *Personal Sketches of His Own Time*, 1827

The custom of these natives is to live as the brute beasts among the mountains, which are very rugged in that part of Ireland where we lost ourselves. They live in huts made of straw. The men are all large-bodied and of handsome features and limbs, and as active as the roe-deer. They do not eat oftener than once a day, and this is at night; and that which they usually eat is butter with oaten-bread. They drink sour milk, for they have no other drink; they don't drink water, although it is the best in the world. On feast-days they eat some flesh half-cooked, without bread or salt. They clothe themselves, according to their habit, with tight trousers and short loose coats of very coarse goat's hair. They cover themselves with blankets, and wear their hair down to their eyes. They are great walkers, and inured to toil.

They carry on perpetual war with the English, who keep garrison for the Queen, from whom they defend themselves, and they do not let them enter their territory, which is subject to inundation, and marshy. The chief inclination of these people is to be robbers, and to plunder each other, so that no day passes without a call to arms amongst them. For the people in one village becoming aware that in another there are cattle, or other effects, they immediately come armed in the night, and 'go Santiago', and kill one another; and the English from the garrisons, getting to know who had taken and robbed most cattle, then come down on them and carry away the plunder. They have, therefore, no other remedy but to withdraw themselves to the mountains, with their women and cattle, for they possess no other property, nor other movables or clothing. They sleep upon the ground on rushes, newly cut, and full of water and ice.

Most of the women are very beautiful, but badly dressed. They do not wear more than a chemise and a blanket, with which they cover themselves, and a linen cloth, much doubled, over the head, and tied in front. They are great workers and housekeepers, after their fashion. These people call themselves Christians.

CUELLAR, *Narrative of the Spanish Armada*, 1588

Consider what Ireland was to the English gentleman. It was a country estate, a ranch. It had some kind of a history, but that was all so long ago that there was no point in going into it. If you did go into it, you found a lot of savages fighting among themselves. Even to-day the natives were little better than savages, slovenly and backward, kept in squalor and ignorance by their priests—like the Spaniards and Italians. England had brought law and order, and a certain amount of prosperity. The people talked English, read English, dressed like the English. They were easy enough to get on with, and made quite good servants. They were superstitious, of course, owing to their religion. Every now and then there had been risings in the past, not with any particular object in view, but merely to let off steam. For, in spite of all the benefits conferred on them, they were, deep down, an unhappy, discontented crowd. One day, provided there were no more of these risings, they might be allowed to have a shot at some mild form of self-government. Nothing dangerous, of course. Just a kind of toy to amuse them, and keep them out of mischief, when they had learnt to be grateful and quiet like the Welsh and the Scots.

How could men who talked like that be expected to understand Easter Week?

J. B. MORTON, *The New Ireland*, 1938

'I shall tell you something about Ireland since you clearly know nothing. Have you even heard of the Easter Rebellion in Dublin?'

Of course he had heard of it, he assured her smiling. That was the treacherous attack by Irish hooligans on the British Army so busily engaged in defending Ireland against the Kaiser.

'Did Ireland ask to be defended?'

'Whether they asked for it or not they obviously wanted it, since so many Irishmen were fighting in the army.'

'Obviously? Nothing was less obvious! The Irish people weren't even con-sulted. No one asked them anything. Why should it make any difference to them whether they were invaded by the Germans or by the British? It might even be better to be subject to the Germans; at least it would make a change . . . ' And the Major was quite wrong in saying that the heroes of the Easter Rising were hooligans. On the contrary, there were many gentlemen among these patriots. Did he know nothing at all? How ignorant the English (only politeness, she laughed, prevented her from saying 'the enemy'), how ignorant the English were. Had he even heard of the débutante Countess Markievicz who with a pistol in her belt defended the College of Surgeons and was sentenced to death for shooting at a gentleman looking out of the window of the Unionist Club (even though the shot missed)? Or did he think that Joseph Plunkett, jewels flaring on his fingers like a Renaissance prince and who *was*, in fact, the son of a papal count, did he think that this man was a hooligan? Already doomed with TB, he had got up out of his bed to fight; did that make him sound like a treacherous criminal? Did the Major know that Joseph Plunkett got married to Grace Gifford (a beautiful young aristo-crat whose Protestant family disowned her, naturally, the pigs) by the light of a candle held by a British soldier in the chapel of Kilmainham gaol in the early hours of the morning shortly before he faced a firing-squad? Did *that* sound like the behaviour of a hooligan?

'Indeed, no,' said the Major smiling. 'It sounds more like the last act of an opera composed by a drunken Italian librettist.'

J. G. FARRELL, *Troubles*, 1970

Belfast. See Denis Johnston's *The Moon in the Yellow River* at the local Reper-tory Theatre. Disappointed: this is the usual Anglo-Irish half-truth about Ireland. Nevertheless, London critics have in several instances hailed it as a work of genius, and no wonder, for it fulfils the first law of Anglo-Irish lit-erature: it makes the native Irish appear a race of congenital idiots.

DENIS IRELAND, *From the Irish Shore*, 1936

As the rhetoric of Young Ireland became more frenetic, *Punch* portrayed the movement as congenitally impossible to please, biting the hand that fed it, and vitriolically parodied Smith O'Brien's variety of patriotic rhetoric. Ingratitude rather than starvation became the leading characteristic of the Irish represented in the magazine: 'slander cast back in requital for food'. The Irish emblem should be the hyena, Mark Lemon decided, whom 'kindness cannot conciliate, nor hunger tame'. It may or may not be surprising that the cartoonist whose work drove this message home, John Leech, was Irish on his father's side; at a later date R. J. Hamerton, one of the most brutal traducers of Irish apishness, was Irish too. Many of the most influential *Punch* commentators were marginalized from the mainstream of Englishness, in one way or another, which may have made them define the concept all the more emphatically; it seems that some of the transplanted Irish entered into this process of psychological compensation with an almost unholy gusto.

Thus *Punch's* sympathy for the starving diminished in proportion as Irish public opinion demonstrated support for the extreme line taken by Young Ireland. The climax of this came in another scorching lead cartoon: 'The Height of Impudence.' Here, a beggar approaches John Bull: 'Spare a thrifle, yet Honour, for a poor Irish lad to buy a bit of . . . a Blunderbuss with.' 'Grateful Paddy' apparently preferred to buy guns rather than bread, and therefore forfeited any sympathy that Mr Punch might have left. By early 1848 open scepticism about Irish suffering was expressed in *Punch*. Soyer's soup kitchens were considered a legitimate subject for mirth; and the grand discovery was announced, of Ireland's real disorder: the Irish were all mad, and the obvious cure for their distress was wholesale incarceration in the new lunatic asylums. Other remedies suggested included enforced emigration on a national scale, unconsciously raising echoes of ideas which had actually been played with in all seriousness by Elizabethan colonizers. Meanwhile, *Punch* rather forlornly regretted the simplicities of a decade before, and called for more Irish Bulls and a return to jolly, joking Paddy. 'The only humour which Ireland has evinced of late has been dreadfully sour.'

The climax of these tasteless jokes, in *Punch's* eyes, was the so-called 'cabbage patch rebellion' of 1848, which gave cartoonists and satirists another heaven-sent opportunity for Irish ridicule.

R. F. FOSTER, *Paddy & Mr Punch*, 1993

11th [January 1834] . . . Fine dry weather is badly needed, as the country is flooded and the yellow clay is gushing up through the dirty streets of 'Callan of the Ructions'. If it ever was 'Callan of the Ructions', it certainly is now, for cursed crowds on either side of the King's River are throwing stones at each other, every Sunday and holiday night—the Caravats on the south side, especially around the Fair Green, Sráid na Faiche, Sráid an Mhuilinn and Sráid an Ghoráin, and the Shanavests on Faiche na nGard, Shepherd's Street or Lána na Leac and on the Kilkenny Road. If they are not stopped, someone will be killed . . . 14th . . . The first warm day this winter . . . I think the weather is improving and settling.

HUMPHREY O'SULLIVAN, *Diary 1827–35*, 1979, trans. Tomás de Bhaldraithe

There never was a more unfounded calumny, than that which would impute to the Irish peasantry an indifference to education. I may, on the contrary, fearlessly assert that the lower orders of no country ever manifested such a positive inclination for literary acquirements, and that too, under circumstances strongly calculated to produce carelessness and apathy on this particular subject. Nay, I do maintain, that he who is intimately acquainted with the character of our countrymen, must acknowledge, that their zeal for book learning, not only is strong and ardent, when opportunities of scholastic education occur, but that it increases in proportion as these opportunities are rare and unattainable. The very name and nature of Hedge Schools are proof of this: for what stronger point could be made out, in illustration of my position, than the fact, that, despite of obstacles, the very idea of which would crush ordinary enterprise—when not even a shed could be obtained in which to assemble the children of an Irish village, the worthy pedagogue selected the first green spot on the sunny side of a quickset-thorn hedge, which he conceived adapted for his purpose, and there, under the scorching rays of a summer sun, and in defiance of spies and statutes, carried on the work of instruction. From this circumstance the name of Hedge School originated; and, however it may be associated with the ludicrous, I maintain, that it is highly creditable to the character of the people, and an encouragement to those who wish to see them receive pure and correct educational knowledge. A Hedge School, however, in its original sense, was but a temporary establishment, being only adopted until such a school-house could be erected, as was in those days deemed sufficient to hold such a number of children as were expected, at all hazards, to attend it.

The opinion, I know, which has been long entertained of Hedge Schoolmasters, was, and still is, unfavourable; but the character of these worthy and eccentric persons has been misunderstood, for the stigma attached to their want of knowledge should have rather been applied to their want of morals, because, on this latter point were they principally indefensible. The fact is, that Hedge Schoolmasters were a class of men, from whom morality was not expected by the peasantry; for, strange to say, one of their strongest recommendations to the good opinion of the people, as far as their literary talents and qualifications were concerned, was an inordinate love of whiskey, and if to this could be added a slight touch of derangement, the character was complete.

On once asking an Irish peasant, why he sent his children to a schoolmaster who was notoriously addicted to spirituous liquors, rather than to a man of sober habits who taught in the same neighbourhood,

'Why do I send them to Mat Meegan, is it?' he replied—'and do you think, Sir,' said he, 'that I'd send them to that dry-headed dunce, Mr Frazher, with his black coat upon him, and his caroline hat, and him wouldn't take a glass of poteen wanst in seven years? Mat, Sir, likes it, and teaches the boys ten times betther whin he's dhrunk nor when he's sober; and you'll never find a good tacher, Sir, but's fond of it. As for Mat, when he's *half gone*, I'd turn him agin the country for deepness in larning; for it's then he rhymes it out of him, that it would do one good to hear him.'

> WILLIAM CARLETON; 'The Hedge School', in *Traits and Stories of the Irish Peasantry*, 1842–4

In its classes [the University's] every fourth student is a Catholic—the best hope I know of for Belfast. If young men meet each other in that free associ-ation, they will inevitably discover that they have much more in common as Ulstermen than divides them as Catholic and Protestant; and they can instantly unite in a common, good-humoured contempt for the rest of Ireland and of the world. I was giving directions to a couple of Belfast lads within a few hours of their first arrival in London. 'Ach,' they said, 'onyone from Belfast can make his way ony place.' They were Catholics, enthusiastic Gaels, artists—for there are some artists now in Belfast; but they had the Belfast temperament. Another of the same gang was with me at a meeting in Donegal, for some Gaelic League function, which brought together the whole neighbourhood. 'What kind of a country is this?' he asked; 'you wouldn't know the odds between one and another.' I said we preferred it so in Donegal. 'I don't know but I would rather live in a place where I would get stones clodded at me for my opinions,' was his answer. Well, probably Belfast will always be that kind of a place; but it is to be hoped that some new opinions will appear to take their turn of having stones clodded at them.

> STEPHEN GWYNN, *The Famous Cities of Ireland*, 1915

Miss Mabel Young, the painter, had come to the Shelbourne in 1914 to help her elder sister, who was manageress, with the extra pressure of work war had entailed. Sometimes she was at the reception desk; her other duties, which varied from day to day, were not less interesting—she entered deeply into the human drama of the hotel. This Easter another sister was over from England on a few days' holiday; and Miss Mabel Young, with an hour or two to spare, decided to show her the beauties of Phœnix Park—which, at the edge of Dublin, extending superbly into the countryside, has its most accessible gate at the far end of the quays, across the river from Kingsbridge station. For the two ladies the agreeable morning went by only too fast: they emerged at lunch-time, ready to board a tram. Amazingly, everywhere was depopulated, empty and still as death. The sinister silence of the quays had no sooner struck them than it was rent by gunfire—distant but unmistakable. Round here all trams had stopped. The Miss Youngs therefore began to foot it along the river towards O'Connell's Bridge, their usual link with home. From the doorways of quayside houses white-faced people called out, warning the sisters back. It was dangerous to go farther into the city: fighting had broken out.

This seemed as preposterous to Miss Mabel Young as it did to many others in Dublin, well on into that day. 'Such things do not happen. . . .' At that time, 1916, be it recalled, battles were associated with battlefields, not yet cities. To that extent, in spite of the Great War, the Edwardian concept of civilization still stood unshaken, firm. . . .

Miss Mabel Young felt that, in any event, she should get back to duty as soon as possible. She saw and succeeded in stopping a jaunting-car, which she and her sister mounted without ado. The man at first did not want to drive them: on learning their destination he agreed to try. Whipping his horse to a gallop, he crossed a near-by bridge, to pursue a course through that network of narrow streets on the south bank, between Dame Street and the river. In this quarter, depressed and primitive, illusion had at no time set her well-shod foot: one believed all that one heard, and imagined more. Lamentation sounded and panic reigned. Wild-haired women rushed out, snatched at the bridle, and attempted to turn the horse, wailing of death ahead. The carman, nettled, laid around with his whip. 'Get out, get back!' he yelled. 'Are you crazy mad? These ladies are going to the *Shelbourne*!'

ELIZABETH BOWEN, The Shelbourne, 1951

Sometimes earnest, well-meaning people go to Aran and they try to counsel the layabouts for their own good. They get little response for their endeavours. A Welsh professor spent his vacation lecturing the people like a missioner with *Self-help Smiles* as his text instead of the bible. A very tall man he was, in short pants, a big stick in his hand, stalking through the islands like the Industrial Revolution. He'd get up at dawn. He'd go swimming. He spent twenty minutes performing the Sokol exercises to clear out and refill his lungs, just like you'd clean out the sump oil from a car in the summer. Then he'd head for the hill and its inhabitants, his stick in hand, his boots knocking sparks out of the road. He'd come to an immediate halt as soon as he'd spot the sleepy faces with the look on them that darkness had passed over them just as the tide abandons the rocks.

The 'feck' of them would ignite him immediately.

'Is this a holiday?' he'd ask them.

They'd gaze at him, one after the other. They wouldn't know if he had spoken or if he hadn't. He'd have to repeat the question.

They'd think a while. One of them would shrug a shoulder.

'How would we know?' another one would ask.

'Have you got no shame?' he'd persist.

They didn't understand him. They were unaware of what emotion he was talking about.

'I have always worked hard,' he'd respond, emotionally banging his stick, 'and I've earned my vacation. I've worked hard since I was a young man. And look at me now.'

Bug-eyed, they'd look at him, from top to toe.

'Don't you have any excuse?' he'd ask, with rising anger.

'Why wouldn't we have holidays as well?' a voice would ask peevishly.

'There's no earthly reason why you shouldn't have a vacation,' and he'd be a little on the defensive now, 'if you'd only be satisfied to do a bit of work. But everybody knows you've never done a stroke of work in your whole lives. Lazy, slovenly, shameless the whole raft of you, and that's the reason why you don't have any vacation now.'

'Yes, but,' the complainer would say, 'but what's to stop us having holidays at the same time as yourself?'

This answer would put a sudden halt to his gallop. 'Bah!' he'd respond and he shaking his stick at them with frustration. They'd back away a bit from him.

He'd stare at them and he about to explode. Off with him then, his stick still threatening, his short pants flapping in the wind with the passion of his stride. They wouldn't manifest even the joy of victory. They'd gaze after him for a while.

Then they'd shift the eyes to the horizon once more.

When he was about to go home, however, they paid him a compliment that they wouldn't offer to just anybody. They left the hilltop and went down in a cluster to the quayside. They assembled around him and they shook hands with him, one after the other. As he was boarding, they promised him they'd declare a special holiday the first day he returned.

They get excited when a curragh comes ashore from 'the islands' (as they sarcastically call the smaller landfalls to the south-east). They have no idea what class of barbarous people live in backward places like them, and they clear out of the way in case they'd find out. The same kind of unease that the aristocratic Roman senators must have felt for the coarse hill tribes from Parthia that they'd meet in the Appian Way.

RICHARD POWER, *Apple on the Treetop*, 1958, trans. Victor Power

We lived in a small, lime-white, unhealthy house, situated in a corner of the glen on the right-hand side as you go eastwards along the road. Doubtless, neither my father nor any of his people before him built the house and placed it there; it is not known whether it was god, demon or person who first raised the half-rotten, rough walls. If there were a hundred corners in all that glen, there was a small lime-white cabin nestling in each one and no one knows who built any of them either. It has always been the destiny of the true Gaels (if the books be credible) to live in a small, lime-white house in the corner of the glen as you go eastwards along the road and that must be the explanation that when I reached this life there was no good habitation for me but the reverse in all truth. As well as the poverty of the house in itself, it clung to a lump of rock on the perilous shoulder of the glen (although there was a fine site available lower down) and if you went out the door without due care as to where you stepped, you could be in mortal danger immediately because of the steep gradient.

Our house was undivided, wisps of rushes above us on the roof and rushes also as bedding in the end of the house. At sundown rushes were spread over the whole floor and the household lay to rest on them. Yonder a bed with pigs upon it; here a bed with people; a bed there with an aged slim cow stretched out asleep on her flank and a gale of breath issuing from her capable of raising a tempest in the centre of the house; hens and chickens asleep in the shelter of her belly; another bed near the fire with me on it.

Yes! people were in bad circumstances when I was young and he who had stock and cattle possessed little room at night in his own house. Alas! it was always thus. I often heard the Old-Grey-Fellow speak of the hardship and misery of life in former times.

> FLANN O'BRIEN, *An Beal Bocht* (*The Poor Mouth*), 1941, trans. Patrick C. Power, 1973

I can find in these papers hardly anything relating to Ireland. Ireland, I do fear, is *too* quiet. The 'Government' papers speak of that country now as a piece of absolute property that has fallen into them, and as to which they have only to consider how best it is to be turned to their advantage. If the country were not lying a dead corpse at their feet, would the *Times* venture to express itself thus—the worthy *Times* is commenting on Lord Roden's dismissal, and recounting what painful but needful measures the 'Imperial Government' has been taking for Ireland of late. 'Law,' says the *Times*, 'has ridden rough-shod through Ireland: it has been taught with bayonets, and interpreted with ruin. Townships levelled with the ground, straggling columns of exiles, work-houses multiplied and still crowded, express the full determination of the legislature to rescue Ireland from its slovenly barbarism, and to plant the institutions of this more civilised land.'

Here is the tone in which these most infamous Government scribblers (who do, however, scribble the mind of the Government), presume to speak of Ireland. And the clearance devastations are evidently as determined as ever: and there is no law in the land in these days; and the O'Connell-Duffys are preaching constitutional agitation; and the Orangemen are crying, 'To hell with the Pope,' and the Catholic bishops are testifying their loyalty; and Murder and Famine and Idiocy are dancing an obscene Carmagnole among the corpses. 'Of a surety,' exclaimed Don Juan D'Aguila, 'Christ never died for *this* people.'

JOHN MITCHEL, Jail Journal, 1854

As the stranger proceeds on his journey through Kerry, which is essentially a mountainous county, he is surprised and shocked at the semi-savage state in which he sees so large a proportion of its population. Groups of girls, whose ages vary from twelve to sixteen, come running after the coach bare-footed and ragged, with their long, rough, uncombed hair flying about their faces as if they were so many lunatics just escaped from some asylum. It is evident that they never, or very rarely, wash either their feet or faces, and that such things as a comb or brush never come in contact with their hair. An Eng-lishman, until he sees this, would hardly have believed that such an exhibi-tion could have been witnessed in the United Kingdom.

ANON. (J. GRANT), Impressions of Ireland and the Irish, 1844

In the following phenomenon we have another grave sign of racial deca-dence: I mean the marked increase of mental disease during the last fifty years. In 1851 Ireland had 5,074 lunatics and 4,906 imbeciles making a total of 9,980 persons of unsound mind, or 1.52 per 1,000 of the population. In 1901 she has 19,834 lunatics and 5,216 imbeciles, or a total of no less than 25,050, say 5.61 per 1,000, whereas in England there are only 4.07, and in Scotland 4.53 per 1,000. Attempts have been made to discover local or special causes for the sad prevalance of mental disease. Some have specified alcohol, or the over-use of tea, especially tea that has been left to stew, according to the custom of the Irish peasant. Others denounce the dullness of life in the pas-toral districts, the isolation, the physical inaction and intellectual void amid which the peasants drag out their lives on the cattle-breeding *latifundia*. And here, indeed, we have a fact worth noting, namely, that it is in the district more especially devoted to grazing, namely, Munster, that the percentage of the mentally unsound reaches its highest level (6.57 per 1,000). The counties in Ireland most subject to the scourge are Waterford, Meath, Clare, Kilkenny, King's County, Tipperary, Wexford, all of them cattle-grazing districts. On the other hand, it is the towns, Belfast, Dublin, and Londonderry, in which the smallest proportion of mental disease is to be found. But such subsidiary causes as these cannot overshadow the true fundamental and essential cause, namely, the degeneration of the race caused by extreme poverty and emigration.

L. PAUL-DUBOIS, Contemporary Ireland, 1908

In your flight you fatally fall upon Nicholas Street, where all those dark alleys open. This is the way to the cathedral, and the great commercial artery of this side of the town. If any doubt remained in you after the insight you had of the houses of the poor in Dublin, about the way they live, that street alone would give you sufficient information.

From end to end it is lined with a row of disgusting shops or stalls, where the refuse of the new and the ancient world seems to have come for an exhibition. Imagine the most hideous, ragged, repulsive rubbish in the dust-bins of two capitals, and you will get an idea of that shop-window display; rank bacon, rotten fish, festering bones, potatoes in full germination, wormy fruit, dusty crusts, sheep's hearts, sausages which remind you of the Siege of Paris, and perhaps come from it; all that running in garlands or festoons in front of the stalls, or made into indescribable heaps, is doled out to the customers in diminutive half-pence morsels. At every turning of the street a public-house with its dim glass and sticky glutinous door. Now and then a pawn-broker with the three symbolic brass balls, and every twenty yards a rag and bone shop.

PHILIPPE DARYL, *Ireland's Disease*, 1888, trans. by the author

The Queen's After-Dinner Speech

(As Overheard and Cut into Lengths of Poetry by Jamesy Murphy,
Deputy-Assistant-Waiter at the Viceregal Lodge).

'ME loving subjects,' sez she,
'Here's me best respects,' sez she,
'An' I'm proud this day,' sez she,
'Of the illigant way,' sez she,
'Ye gave me the hand,' sez she,
'Whin I came to land,' sez she.
'There was some people said,' sez she,
'They was greatly in dread,' sez she,
'I'd be murthered or shot,' sez she,
'As like as not,' sez she,
'But 'tis mighty clear,' sez she,
''Tis not over here,' sez she,
'I have cause to fear,' sez she.
''Tis them Belgiums,' sez she,
'That's throwin' bombs,' sez she,
'And scarin' the life,' sez she,
'Out o' me son and the wife,' sez she.
'But in these parts,' sez she,
'They have warrum hearts,' sez she,

'And they like me well,' sez she,
'Barrin' Anna Parnell,' sez she.
'I dunno, Earl,' sez she,
'What's come to the girl,' sez she,
'And that other wan,' sez she,
'That Maud Gonne,' sez she,
'Dhressin' in black,' sez she,
'To welcome me back,' sez she;
'Though I don't care,' sez she,
'What they wear,' sez she,
'An' all that gammon,' sez she,
'About me bringin' famine,' sez she.
'Now Maud 'ill write,' sez she,
'That I brought the blight,' sez she,
'Or altered the saysons,' sez she,
'For some private raysins,' sez she,
'An' I think there's a slate,' sez she,
'Off Willie Yeats,' sez she.
'He should be at home,' sez she,
'French polishin' a pome,' sez she,
'An' not writin' letters,' sez she,
'About his betters,' sez she,
'Paradin' me crimes,' sez she,
'In the Irish Times,' sez she. . . .

PERCY FRENCH, *Prose, Poems and Parodies of
Percy French*, 1925

To the rank and file of Ulster Presbyterians the Revival was, and still is, the most momentous religious event of the last century; but their leaders and guides, if thrilled, were also perplexed. . . .

This perplexity was, I admit, natural enough. Ulster Presbyterianism, as might be expected from its Calvinistic bias, has always been suspicious of emotionalism in religion. . . The origins of the Revival have never been satisfactorily analysed, but contemporary accounts leave little doubt that the impulse came from the pew rather than the pulpit. Converts were the most energetic missionaries; and in districts where the enthusiasm blazed up most fiercely it is clear enough, to my mind, that many of the clergy felt their influence and authority were being gravely impaired. . . .

When one scans the literature of the time in which [the] physical manifestations are described, one ceases to wonder why scenes and incidents of the Revival still haunt the memory of an older generation in Ulster. 'I witnessed' wrote a Scottish clergyman from Portrush, in 1859, 'the smiting down in every phase of its development—from the simple swoon to the prostration accompanied by the most fearful convulsions of the bodily frame, and overwhelming mental anguish, venting itself in piercing cries for mercy or wailing notes of despair.' At one meeting some two hundred men were 'stricken down' in the space of a few hours. . . .

In his *Home Life in Ireland* Mr Robert Lynd tells us, on the authority of a lady who attended many revival services that 'women used to be carried out from the churches into the open air with all and sundry dragging at the hoops of their crinolines'. It was not only in churches that prostration occurred. Children at their desks in school would suddenly be seized with exaltation; in several places mills and factories had to be closed down for days; and on one occasion compositors, a class not ordinarily given to hysteria, were so overcome by religious fervour that the publication of a Coleraine paper was held up for twenty-four hours.

J. W. GOOD, *Ulster and Ireland*, 1919

In decorating themselves in a traditional Irish manner, the female sex were not behindhand, especially the youthful members thereof. It may be doubted, however, if the women's garment which really had been concocted from pictures was especially Irish: it was probably simply the costume of the medieval European lady with a few fancy Celtic fixtures attached. A girl poet, friend of mine, Moirin Fox, never wore any other garb. She would appear in the Abbey in gorgeous purple and gold, a torc on her forehead, a Tara broach fastening her brath, and various other accouterments of the ancient Irish, including the inevitable amber. The rest of us only occasionally appeared in Gaelic costume, which, of course, had to be of Irish manufactured material. For dressy wear I had a white garment with blue and green embroidery, a blue brath, copper broaches, and other archaeological adornments. For more ordinary wear, I had the Irish costume in blue green, a brath of the same color with embroideries out of the *Book of Kells*. These, as I remember, were chiefly of snakes eating one another's tails. With this went a blue stone necklace, a little silver harp fastening the brath, a silver Claddagh ring, and a silver snake bracelet which I'm afraid was early Victorian rather than early Celtic. This getup was all right for the Abbey Theatre or Gaelic League dances, but once when myself and a friend, Siav Trench, in a similar getup and a more striking color scheme, walked together down a street where the fishwomen were selling their fish, we were openly derided. The fishmongers called out, 'Will yez look at the Irishers trying to look like stained-glass windows? What is the country coming to at all, at all? Them Irishers are going daft!' We were not too sensitive to ridicule, but we did not again wear such garments in parts of the city where anything out of the ordinary was mocked at so vociferously.

MARY COLUM, *Life and the Dream*, 1928

MEG. Ah, they're half mad, these high-up ould ones.

PAT. He wasn't half mad the first time I saw him, nor a quarter mad, God bless him. See that? [*He produces a photo.*] Monsewer on the back of his white horse, the Cross of Christ held high in his right hand, like Brian Boru, leading his men to war and glory.

MEG. Will you look at the poor horse.

PAT. That was the day we got captured. We could have got out of it, but Monsewer is terrible strict and honest. You see, he's an Englishman.

MEG. An Englishman, and him going round in a kilt all day playing his big Gaelic pipes.

PAT. He was born an Englishman, remained one for years. His father was a bishop.

MEG. His father was a bishop. [*All good Catholics, they start to leave.*] Well, I'm not sitting here and listening to that class of immoral talk. His father was a bishop, indeed!

PAT. He was a Protestant bishop.

MEG. Ah well, it's different for them. [*They all come back.*]

RIORITA. They get married, too, sometimes.

PAT. He went to all the biggest colleges in England and slept in the one room with the King of England's son.

MEG. Begad, it wouldn't surprise me if he slept in the one bed with him, his father being a bishop.

PAT. Yes, he had every class of comfort, mixed with dukes, marquises, earls and lords.

MEG. All sleeping in the one room, I suppose?

ROPEEN. In the one bed.

PAT. Will you shut up. As I was saying, he had every class of comfort until one day he discovered he was an Irishman.

MEG. Aren't you after telling me he was an Englishman?

PAT. He was an Anglo-Irishman.

MEG. In the name of God, what's that?

PAT. A Protestant with a horse.

ROPEEN. Leadbetter.

PAT. No, no, an ordinary Protestant like Leadbetter, the plumber in the back parlour next door, won't do, nor a Belfast orangeman, not if he was as black as your boot.

MEG. Why not?

PAT. Because they work. An Anglo-Irishman only works at riding horses, drinking whisky and reading double-meaning books in Irish at Trinity College.

MEG. I'm with you he wasn't born an Irishman. He became one.

PAT. He didn't become one—he was born one—on his mother's side, and as he didn't like his father much he went with his mother's people—he became an Irishman.

MEG. How did he do that?

PAT. Well, he took it easy at first, wore a kilt, played Gaelic football on Blackheath.

MEG. Where's that?

PAT. In London. He took a correspondence course in the Irish language. And when the Rising took place he acted like a true Irish hero.

MEG. He came over to live in Ireland.

PAT. He fought for Ireland, with me at his side.

MEG. Aye, we've heard that part of the story before.

PAT. Five years' hard fighting.

COLETTE. Ah, God help us.

ROPEEN. Heavy and many is the good man that was killed.

PAT. We had the victory—till they signed that curse-of-God treaty in London. They sold the six counties to England and Irishmen were forced to swear an oath of allegiance to the British Crown.

MEG. I don't know about the six counties, but the swearing wouldn't come so hard on you.

ROPEEN. Whatever made them do it, Mr Pat?

PAT. Well, I'll tell you, Ropeen. It was Lloyd George and Birkenhead made a fool of Michael Collins and he signed an agreement to have no more fighting with England.

MEG. Then he should have been shot.

PAT. He was.

MEG. Ah, the poor man.

PAT. Still, he was a great fighter and he fought well for the ould cause.

BRENDAN BEHAN, *The Hostage*, 1958

Among the cottages that are scattered through the hills of County Wicklow I have met with many people who show in a singular way the influence of a particular locality. These people live for the most part beside old roads and pathways where hardly one man passes in the day, and look out all the year on unbroken barriers of heath. At every season heavy rains fall for often a week at a time, till the thatch drips with water stained to a dull chestnut, and the floor in the cottages seems to be going back to the condition of the bogs near it. Then the clouds break, and there is a night of terrific storm from the south-west—all the larches that survive in these places are bowed and twisted towards the point where the sun rises in June—when the winds come down through the narrow glens with the congested whirl and roar of a torrent, breaking at times for sudden moments of silence that keep up the tension of the mind. At such times the people crouch all night over a few sods of turf, and the dogs howl in the lanes.

When the sun rises there is a morning of almost supernatural radiance, and even the oldest men and women come out into the air with the joy of children who have recovered from a fever. In the evening it is raining again.

This peculiar climate, acting on a population that is already lonely and dwindling, has caused or increased a tendency to nervous depression among the people, and every degree of sadness, from that of the man who is merely mournful to that of the man who has spent half his life in the madhouse, is common among these hills.

Not long ago in a desolate glen in the south of the county I met two policemen driving an ass-cart with a coffin on it, and a little further on I stopped an old man and asked him what had happened.

'This night three weeks,' he said, 'there was a poor fellow below reaping in the glen, and in the evening he had two glasses of whisky with some other lads. Then some excitement took him, and he threw off his clothes and ran away into the hills. There was great rain that night, and I suppose the poor creature lost his way, and was the whole night perishing in the rain and darkness. In the morning they found his naked footmarks on some mud half a mile above the road, and again where you go up by a big stone. Then there was nothing known of him till last night, when they found his body on the mountain, and it near eaten by the crows.'

Then he went on to tell me how different the country had been when he was a young man.

'We had nothing to eat at that time,' he said, 'but milk and stirabout and potatoes, and there was a fine constitution you wouldn't meet this day at all. I remember when you'd see forty boys and girls below there on a Sunday evening, playing ball and diverting themselves; but now all this country is gone lonesome and bewildered, and there's no man knows what ails it.'

J. M. SYNGE, In Wicklow and West Kerry, 1912

This island of Achill is more like a foreign land than any I have visited; the natives reside in huts, which a good deal resemble those of the Esquimaux Indians; they are without chimneys or windows, and the roof seems continuous with the walls; the interior is generally undivided, and is tenanted by men, women, children, pigs and poultry, and often goats and cows. These little cabins are built in what may be called loose clusters, varying from twenty to eighty in a cluster; these clusters or villages are sixteen in number, some of them are summer residences only, and are entirely deserted in the winter— others winter residences only, and deserted in summer.

EDWARD NEWMAN, 1838

'Behold! A Proof of Irish Sense!'

Behold! a proof of Irish sense!
  Here Irish wit is seen!
When nothing's left, that's worth defence,
  We build a magazine.

JONATHAN SWIFT, Works, ix/2, 1775

Ireland, her dim and endless enchantments withdrawing far into the recesses of her earth like the Tuatha Dé Danann of ancient times, had shrunk distressingly as far as we were concerned, and become, as George Moore so continually discovered, no broader than a pig's back. There were moments of despair when one could see nothing of her but poverty and ignorance and cant, the famished mouth and stubbly chin, the mackintosh limp with rain, the greasy comb and broken rosary among the litter in the pocket, the blue eye sodden with drink, dribbling with laughter.

MICHEAL MAC LIAMMOIR, *All for Hecuba*, 1949

Numerous tramcars, light and quick, cross Dublin in all directions. Five or six railway stations are the heads of so many iron lines radiating fan-wise over Ireland. All bear their national stamp; but what possesses that character in the highest degree is that airy vehicle called a jaunting-car.

Imagine a pleasure car where the seats, instead of being perpendicular to the shafts, are parallel with them, disposed back to back and perched on two very high wheels. You climb to your place under difficulties; then the driver seated sideways like you (unless the number of travellers obliges him to assume the rational position), lashes his horse, which plunges straightway into a mad career.

This style of locomotion rather startles you at first, not only on account of its novelty, but also by reason of the indifferent equilibrium you are able to maintain. Jostled over the pavement, threatened every moment to see yourself projected into space, at a tangent, you involuntarily grasp the nickel handle which is there for that purpose, just as a tyro horseman instinctively clutches the mane of his steed. But one gets used in time to the Irish car, and even comes to like it. First, it goes at breakneck speed, which is not without its charm; then you have no time to be bored, considering that the care of preserving your neck gives you plenty of occupation; lastly, you have the satisfaction of facing constantly the shop windows and foot paths against which you are likely to be tossed at any moment. Those are serious advantages, which other countries' cabs do not offer. To be candid, they are unaccompanied by other merits.

PHILIPPE DARYL, *Ireland's Disease*, 1888, trans. by the author

Dinner, pleasant and lively talk.

T.—'A Russian noble, who spoke English well, said one morning to an English guest, "I've shot two peasants this morning."—"Pardon me, you mean pheasants." "No, indeed, two men—they were insolent and I shot them."'

W. A.—'In Ireland it's the other way.'

T.—'Couldn't they blow up that horrible island with dynamite and carry it off in pieces—a long way off?'

W. A.—'Why did the English go there?'

T.—'Why did the Normans come to England? The Normans came over here and seized the country, and in a hundred years the English had forgotten all about it, and they were all living together on good terms.'

(I demurred: T. went on, raising his voice).—'The same Normans went to Ireland, and the Irish with their damned unreasonableness are raging and foaming to this hour!'

W. A.—'The Norman Duke had a claim on the crown of England.'

T.—'No rightful claim.'

W. A.—'But suppose all these to be bygones. You speak of a century, a short time in history—think what Ireland had to complain of only in the last century—the penal laws, and the deliberate destruction of their growing industry by the English Government: what do you say to that?'

T.—'That was brutal! Our ancestors *were* horrible brutes! And the Kelts are very charming and sweet and poetic. I love their Ossians and their Finns and so forth—but they are most damnably unreasonable!'

W. A.—'They are most unfortunate.'

Hallam.—'What would you do?'

W. A.—'This last phase of discontent is perhaps the worst—flavoured with Americanism and general irreverence; but what I would have done long ago I would try still—encourage peasant proprietorship to the utmost possible.'

Hallam.—'Get rid of all the landlords and give the land to the people?'

W. A.—'Not at all. There are many good Irish landlords, and they usually get on well with their tenants. The peasant proprietors would have to be made gradually, and on business principles.'

T.—'What is the difference between an English landlord and an Irish landlord?'

W. A.—'Is it a conundrum?'

T.—'Not at all.'

(I tried to explain some great differences. T. came back to his old point.)

T.—'The Kelts are so utterly unreasonable! The stupid clumsy Englishman—knock him down, kick him under the tail, kick him under the chin, do anything to him, he gets on his legs again and goes on; the Kelt rages and shrieks and tears everything to pieces!'

WILLIAM ALLINGHAM, *Journals*, 1880

The Irish Question

A rich land and a poor people. I ask you a question. Why is this?

HUMPHREY O'SULLIVAN, *Diary 1827–35*

'Uncle Josc's tenants have paid up £300 and refuse to give more. The amount due is £1,600. Pleasing prospect for Uncle Joscelyn until eviction forces the brutes to pay.'

EDITH SOMERVILLE, Diary

I was brought up on 'The Irish Question'; but what the Irish Question was I have no idea. (I wonder if anybody has!) From my memory of those times I should think there must have been thousands and thousands of 'Irish Questions'.

Even now as I write strange words come back to me. I don't know now what half of them mean—I most likely never did—but I must have heard them so often, long, long ago, that they are firmly planted in my brain. I imagine this planting must have taken place mostly as I sat watching my father and brothers eating their dinner and listening to their talk. Such words as 'The Home Rule Bill', 'The Kilmainham Treaty', 'Moonlighters', 'The Agrarian Crimes', 'Boycott', 'No Rent Movement', 'Land Purchase Bill', 'Congested Districts Board', 'The United Irish League', 'The Town Tenants Act', 'Evicted Tenants Act', 'Irish Reform Association', 'The Irish Church Act', 'The Fixity of Tenure', 'The Dunraven Treaty', 'The Land Commission', 'Cattle Driving', 'Urban' and 'Rural District Councils'.

SIR WILLIAM ORPEN, *Stories of Old Ireland and Myself*, 1925

Mr Nimmo states, in 1823, that the fertile plains of Limerick, Cork, and Kerry, are separated from each other by a deserted country, hitherto nearly an impassable barrier between them. This large district comprehends nearly 600 Irish, or 970 square miles British. In many places it is very populous. As might be expected under such circumstances, the people are turbulent, and their houses being inaccessible for want of roads, it is not surprising that, during the disturbances in 1821 and 1822, this district was the asylum for whiteboys, smugglers, and robbers, and that stolen cattle were drawn into it as to a safe and impenetrable retreat. Notwithstanding its present desolate state, this country contains within itself the seeds of future improvement and industry. Such was the state of things in 1822; subsequently, an engineer of eminence, Mr Griffith, was employed to execute public works in this district, under the authority of the Government. He confirms the former statement of Mr Nimmo. This tract, he observes, is a wild, neglected, and deserted country, without roads, culture, or civilisation; it chiefly belongs to absentee proprietors, and being for the most part inaccessible, has hitherto afforded an asylum for outlaws and culprits of every description. In the year 1829, after the execution of the works, Mr Griffith reports with respect to the same district, a very considerable improvement has already taken place in the vicinity of the roads, both in the industry of the inhabitants and the appearance of the country. At the commencement of the works the people flocked into them, seeking employment at any rate; their looks haggard, their clothing wretched; they rarely possessed any tools or implements beyond a small ill-shaped spade; and nearly the whole face of the country was unimproved; since the completion of the roads, rapid strides have been made; upwards of sixty new lime-kilns have been built; carts, ploughs, harrows, and improved implements have become common; new houses of a better class have been built, new inclosures made, and the country has become perfectly tranquil, and exhibits a scene of industry and exertion at once pleasing and remarkable. A large portion of the money received for labour has been husbanded with care, laid out in building substantial houses, and in the purchase of stock and agricultural implements; and numerous examples might be shown of poor labourers, possessing neither money, houses, nor land when first employed, who in the past year have been enabled to take farms, build houses, and stock their lands. . . .

At Abbeyfeale and Brosna, observes Mr Kelly, above half of the congregation at mass on Sundays were barefoot and ragged, with small straw hats of their own manufacture, felt hats being only worn by a few. Hundreds, or even thousands of men, could be got to work at sixpence a-day, if it had been offered. The farmers were mostly in debt; and many of the families went to beg in Tipperary and other parts. The condition of the people is now very different; the congregations at the chapels are now as well clad as in other parts; the demand for labour is increased, and a spirit of industry is getting forward, since the new roads have become available.

R. M. MARTIN, *Ireland Before and After The Union*, 1832

To Sir William Osborne's [at Newtownanner Ho., Co. Tipperary], three miles the other side Clonmel. This gentleman has made a mountain improvement which demands particular attention, being upon a principle very different from common ones. Twelve years ago he met with a hearty looking fellow of forty, followed by a wife and six children in rags, who begged. Sir William questioned him upon the scandal of a man in full health and vigour, supporting himself in such a manner. The man said he could get no work. *'Come along with me, I will shew you a spot of land upon which I will build a cabin for you, and if you like it you shall fix there.'* The fellow followed Sir William, who was as good as his word. He built him a cabin, gave him 5 acres of a heathy mountain, lent him £4 to stock with, and gave him, when he had prepared his ground, as much lime as he would come for. The fellow flourished; he went on gradually; repaid the £4, and presently became a happy little cottier. He has at present 12 acres under cultivation, and a stock in trade worth at least £80. His name is John Conory. The success which attended this man in two or three years brought others, who applied for land, and Sir William gave them as they applied. The mountain was under lease to a tenant, who valued it so little, that upon being reproached with not cultivating, or doing something with it, he assured Sir William, that it was utterly impracticable to do anything with it, and offered it to him without any deduction of rent. Upon this mountain he fixed them; gave them terms as they came determinable with the lease of the farm, so that every one that came in succession had shorter and shorter tenures, yet are they so desirous of settling, that they come at present, though only two years remain for a term. In this manner Sir William has fixed twenty-two families, who are all upon the improving land, the meanest growing richer, and find themselves so well off, that no consideration will induce them to work for others, not even in harvest. Their industry has no bounds; nor is the day long enough for the revolution of their incessant labour. Some of them bring turf to Clonmel, and Sir William has seen Conory returning loaded with soap ashes.

He found it difficult to persuade them to make a road to their village, but when they had once done it, he found none in getting cross roads to it, they found such benefit in the first. Sir William has continued to give them whatever lime they come for, and they have desired 1000 barrels among them for the year 1776. Their houses have all been built at his expense, they raise what little offices they want for themselves. He has informed them, that upon the expiration of the lease, they will be charged something for the land, and has desired that they will mark out each man what he wishes to have; some of them have taken pieces of 30 or 40 acres; a strong proof that they find their husbandry beneficial and profitable. He has great reason to believe that nine-tenths of them were Whiteboys, but are now of principles exceedingly different from the miscreants that bear that name. Their cattle are feeding on the mountain in the day, but of nights they house them in little miserable stables. All their children are employed regularly in their husbandry, picking stones, weeding, etc. which shows their industry strongly; for in general they are idle about all the country. The women spin.

Too much cannot be said in praise of this undertaking. It shows that a

reflecting penetrating landlord can scarcely move without the power of creating opportunities to do himself and his country service. It shows that the
villainy of the greatest miscreants is all situation and circumstance. *Employ*,
don't *hang* them. Let it not be in the slavery of the cottier system, in which
industry never meets its reward, but by giving property, teach the value of it.
By giving them the fruit of their labour, teach them to be laborious. All this
Sir William Osborne has done, and done it with effect, and there probably is
not an honester set of families in the county than those which he has formed
from the refuse of the Whiteboys.

ARTHUR YOUNG, *A Tour In Ireland*, 1780

from *Laurence Bloomfield in Ireland*

THIS Irish county bears an evil name,
And Bloomfield's district stands the worst in fame,
For agitation, discord, threats, waylayings,
Fears and suspicions, plottings and betrayings;
Beasts kill'd and maim'd, infernal fires at night,
Red murder stalking free in full daylight.
That landlords and their tenants lived as foes
He knew, as one a truth by hearsay knows,
But now it stands around where'er he goes.

WILLIAM ALLINGHAM, *Laurence Bloomfield in Ireland*, 1864

13th [April 1827] . . . A gentle south-west wind. Sultry, cloud periods and
bright patches. Soft clouds like fleeces on top of each other. From Cill Bhrí-
ocáin Mills I saw the Galtees west of Cathair. The eastern mountain looked
flat, and the western peak was like the top of a volcano. A thin mist-like foam
between me and them. The Déise mountains beckoning to me with their
peaks up over Bearna na Gaoithe gap.

A rich land and a poor people. I ask you a question. Why is this?

HUMPHREY O'SULLIVAN, *Diary 1827–35*, 1979, trans. Tomás de Bhaldraithe

Reilly proceeds to talk of Irish affairs, and informs me of the pending election for New Ross wherein Ireland is to be saved, at last, by the return of Mr
Gavan Duffy, or, as my correspondent writes the name, Mr Give-in Duffy. On
these Irish affairs, he expresses himself, I must admit, in a very wild manner.

'About the "priests and holy wells", all I shall say is, pray God to sink the first
to the bottom of the second!'

SENTENCE>   JOHN MITCHEL, *Jail Journal*, 1854

Half-felled woods were to be seen everywhere, even in the farthest places;
there was, for instance, a great clearance made at Coolmountain in West
Cork, a place where even to-day a stranger's face is hardly ever seen. Some
evil genius, it might seem, was labouring to harmonise all things into an equal
slatternliness. The country, moreover, was speckled with ruins—broken
abbeys, roofless churches, battered castles, burnt houses, deserted villages,
from which the inhabitants were being cleared to make room for beasts; and
these ruins were, for the most part, still raw, gaping, sun-bleached, not yet
shrouded in ivy nor weathered to quiet tones.

                              DANIEL CORKERY, *The Hidden Ireland*, 1925

Ireland is . . . an untidy-looking country, a country of untidy houses, of
untidy stone walls and hedges, of untidy fields. In many parts if a gate is
broken down, as likely as not it will be fixed up temporarily with bits of rope,
or with the help of stones or thorn branches, instead of being properly
repaired. Similarly, if a window is broken or a spout injured, some hopelessly
inefficient steps will often be taken to stave off the critical day when a new
window must be put in or the spout properly seen to. People who do not
examine into the causes of things look upon this untidiness of the countryside as a deep-seated Irish characteristic, born of Irish blood rather than of
Irish conditions. There could not be a shallower thought. The Irish farmer
originally became untidy in self-defence. He knew that, if his house looked
beautiful and his hedges trim, the quick eye of the land-agent would soon
size him up as a prosperous man, and raise his rent accordingly. Ever since
the 1881 Land Act enabled him to stand up to the rent-raising landlord with
some prospect of success—certainly since the beginning of the present
century—there has been a slow but sure tendency to improvement in the
appearance of Irish farms and farm-houses. If the tendency has been too
slight and slow for the censorious, it is because the traditions of generations
cannot suddenly be made as though they were not, and because the farmer
continued to suspect, even under the 1881 Land Act, that the landlord still
reaped no small benefit from the tenant's improvements.

Now that the land is coming into his own hands, the Irish farmer is
showing, as I have stated, a wonderful instinct for improving his surroundings. The farms themselves are still shaggy—I say shaggy rather than

shabby—in appearance, but the houses, especially the houses of the small farmers, are beginning to wear a new air of brightness and prosperity.

ROBERT LYND, *Home Life in Ireland*, 1908

There are few who have not heard of the Ribbon Societies of Ireland; those dark and mysterious confederacies, which, springing up from time to time in different localities, have spread terror and dismay into the hearts of both rich and poor, which have done so much to discourage the influx of capital into Ireland, and to promote the absenteeism of hundreds of wealthy proprietors, who would be only too glad to be allowed to reside upon their Irish estates, and in the midst of their Irish tenantry, could they do so in peace and safety.

But the terrible Ribbon Code is too formidable for most men to face, who have the means of living elsewhere, and who are not bound by any peculiar ties to Ireland. It is the fashion to blame absentees; but can they always be justly blamed? It is a fact, the bitter truth of which has been felt and can be attested by many, that those who have been most earnest and anxious for the improvement of their estates, have come most frequently under the ban of the Ribbonmen; whilst the careless, spendthrift, good-for-nothing landlord, who hunts, and shoots, and drinks, and runs in debt, who even exacts the most exorbitant rents from his tenants, provided only he does not interfere with their time-honoured customs of subdividing, squatting, conacre, and reckless marriages, may live in peace and careless indolence on his estate, in high favour with the surrounding peasantry, and with no fear or danger of being ever disturbed by a Ribbonman.

It is not my intention to enter at present upon any dissertation on this curious and strange phenomenon; neither is it my intention to enter into any analysis of the causes which produced this state of things. We must look back into the history of Ireland for these. Would that some abler hand than mine would investigate and lay bare the truth! My *present* purpose is only to deal with facts, and to tell of scenes and occurrences which have from time to time come under my immediate observation.

The effects of the Ribbon Code were more keenly felt in Ireland some fifteen or twenty years ago than they are now; and indeed we might go back even farther than that. Tipperary County might perhaps be named as the headquarters of the confederation; and the King's County and Queen's County, Meath and Westmeath, Louth, and even Monaghan, where, as 'the gap of the north', it adjoined the midland counties, were from time to time the scene of its unhallowed operations.

It is a mistake to suppose that the Ribbon Code was terrible to the landlords only. The tenant, quite as frequently as the landlord, became the victim;

and many a thriving, harmless, well-conditioned man has perished under its terrible laws.

The main object of the Ribbon Society was to prevent any landlord, under any circumstances whatever, from depriving a tenant of his land. 'Fixity of tenure', which has lately been so boldly demanded by the advocates of tenant-right, was then only secretly proclaimed in the lodges of the Ribbon Society; and 'fixity of tenure' it was determined to carry out to the death, which almost necessarily followed.

The second object was to deter, on pain of almost certain death, any tenant from taking land from which any other tenant had been evicted. These main principles of the society were carried out with relentless severity; and numerous indeed were the victims in all ranks of life, from the wealthy peer to the humblest cottier, who fell under the hand of the assassin, sworn to carry out its decrees.

But it may well be supposed that a society, thus constituted in utter lawlessness, was not very likely to adhere long or accurately to the precise objects for which it had originally been formed; and, accordingly, by degrees it assumed the position of the redresser of *all* fancied wrongs connected with the management of land, or with landed property in any form whatever. I have known frequent instances of landlords receiving threatening notices for evicting tenants, although these tenants had refused to pay any rent whatever, and of tenants receiving similar notices for taking the land of the evicted occupiers. I have also seen a notice, announcing certain death to a respectable farmer, because he dismissed a careless ploughman; and a friend who lived near me, was threatened with death, because he refused to hire a shepherd who had been recommended to him and who was approved of by the local Ribbon lodge. I myself received a letter, illustrated with a coffin in flaring bloody red, and adorned with death's head and cross bones, threatening the most frightful consequences to myself and family, if I did not continue to employ a young profligate carpenter, whom I had discharged for idleness and vice!

W. STEWART TRENCH, *Realities of Irish Life*, 1869

A Ribbon Lodge

Not much for reading do the students care,
Except the *Firebrand*, redd aloud by Mat,
A lazy, pompous man, unclean, and fat;
And oft goes round, when learning proves too dry,
A jar that never met the gauger's eye.
Big is the hearth, the fire is mostly small,
Rough desks and benches range along the wall,

The panes are patch'd with inky leaf and clout;
A useful though unsavoury pile without
May help again, as it has help'd before,
Retreat more quick and private than by door,
'Mong filthy narrow yards and tumbling walls.

   To Matthew's house to-night, as twilight falls,
With passwords, from the lane, and grip of hand,
By ones and twos arrive a secret band,—
'Where are you from?' 'South-aist.' 'The night is dark.'
'A star will shortly rise.' 'You know the mark?'
'Milesius must be ready.' 'What's your sign?'
'Lamh dearg an oughter!' *'Tubbermore* is mine:
'Pass, brother.' Past the sow, and up the stair,
They grope through darkness into ruddy glare,
The two old grimy windows, looking back,
Being curtain'd for the nonce with plies of sack.
The Lodge is filling fast; in various groups
Lounge Captain Starlight's famed and dreadful troops;
Two score in count at last, the most of whom
Are young and brainless, fill the stifling room.

   Beside the door, a knot of 'labourin'-boys,'
The farmer these, and those the squire employs,
Yawn wide and mope, till whiskey in their brain
Kindle its foolish fire, with flashes vain
Wrapt in dull smoke, to send them blundering back
O'er field and fence upon their homeward track.
From outhouse loft, at need, or barnfloor bed,
The clumsy body and the stupid head
Escape, with matchbox, or with stick in fist,
To burn or batter as their leaders list,
With knife to maim the cows, or loaded gun
To rake a peaceful window, and to run.

      WILLIAM ALLINGHAM, from *Laurence Bloomfield in Ireland*, 1864

In Ireland, there is much blame justly attached to landlords, for their neglect and severity, in such depressed times, towards their tenants: there is also much that is not only indefensible but atrocious on the part of the tenants. But can the landed proprietors of Ireland plead ignorance or want of education for their neglect and rapacity, whilst the crimes of the tenants, on the contrary, may in general be ascribed to both? He who lives—as, perhaps, his forefathers have done—upon any man's property, and fails from unavoidable calamity, has as just and clear a right to assistance from the landlord as if the amount of that aid were a bonded debt. Common policy, common sense, and common justice, should induce the Irish landlords to lower their rents according to the market for agricultural produce, otherwise poverty, famine, crime, and vague political speculations, founded upon idle hopes of a general transfer of property, will spread over and convulse the kingdom. Any man who looks into our poverty, may see that our landlords ought to reduce their rents to a standard suitable to the times, and to the ability of the tenant.

> WILLIAM CARLETON, 'Tubber Derg', in *Traits and Stories of the Irish Peasantry*, 1844

from *Station Island*

I who learned to read in the reek of flax
and smelled hanged bodies rotting on their gibbets
and saw their looped slime gleaming from the sacks—

hard-mouthed Ribbonmen and Orange bigots
made me into the old fork-tongued turncoat
who mucked the byre of their politics.

> SEAMUS HEANEY, *Station Island*, 1984

The loss of the land is traumatic, even for those who leave of their own volition. All of those who leave do so because, one way or another, the land cannot satisfy or fully sustain. The incapacity of the land for sustaining life in Carleton's fiction is easily explained. Oppressive or negligent authority— an incompetent landlord, an unscrupulous agent, a crooked lawyer— dispossesses a family, wrongly banishes the young hero, or else does nothing to help reverse the land's tendency to barrenness or decay. Or the peasants themselves are neglectful or inadequate. Or the climate is too unsettled, the soil bad—any number of acts (or omissions) of God. Considered together, rural writers after Carleton present more complex and intractable reasons why people become separated from the ancestral land. The acts of God remain, of course, as do the inadequacies of the farmers, but if oppression remains a divisive force, it is no longer oppression by the Ascendancy but by industry and the city drawing off the land's manpower.

> JOHN WILSON FOSTER, *Forces and Themes in Ulster Fiction*, 1974

'There is Mr Lloyd,' continued Father Hannigan, as that gentleman returned to his seat; 'and if he put out a tenant would you shoot him?'

'The divil a hair uv his head would be touched,' replied Phil.'He gives good lases at a fair rent; and the man that does that won't turn out a tenant unless he desarves to be turned out. Answer me this wan question. Did you ever know uv a good landlord to be shot, or a good agent? Answer me that.'

'Well, no,' replied the priest, 'I never did.'

'There it is,' observed Larry Clancy, as if that settled the question, and Father Hannigan had thrown up the sponge.

'Well, now, Mr Lowe,' said Father Hannigan, 'what's your opinion of this matter?'

'I am almost entirely ignorant of it,' he replied. 'But I confess I came over to Ireland under the impression that the people were lawless and revengeful, particularly in your county.'

'You only saw the dark side of the picture,' returned Father Hannigan. 'We are not so black as we are painted.'

CHARLES J. KICKHAM, *Knocknagow; or The Homes of Tipperary*, 1873

The agrarian agitation known as the Land War, which started in Connaught in 1879 and spread to other parts of the country during the following year, took the Ascendancy by surprise. Despite Lord Leitrim's murder and some other less-publicized crimes, the Irish countryside was on the whole peaceful in the late 1870s. It is true that agricultural prosperity was giving place to a depression, caused by bad harvests and falling prices; by the beginning of 1879 some landlords already felt obliged to reduce their rents, among them the husband of Maria La Touche, who consequently had to get rid of his agent and steward and make other economies. Maria's pony-carriage and ponies had to be sold. 'We have altogether come down in the world', she wrote, but added: 'This is not one of the things that make me sulky. Quite the reverse.'

There had, however, been an even worse agricultural depression in the early 1860s and that did not cause a land war. But when hard times came again in 1879, bringing in their wake the inevitable tensions between landlords and tenants over demands for reductions in rent, the tenants were backed by political forces such as had not existed during the previous depression— those same forces of Nationalism that were sweeping the Home Rulers to victory. Under the dynamic leadership of Parnell—himself the brother of a landlord—and of Michael Davitt, the Irish National Land League was formed to organize the tenants in their demands and to conduct a general agitation against landlordism.

The Land League's policy was to prevail upon tenants to pay no rent at all unless the landlords agreed to the reduction which they demanded. If a landlord retaliated by evicting tenants who refused to pay, the League endeavoured to make it impossible for anybody else to take their holdings by the method which came to be known as boycotting after being used in

November 1880 on Captain Charles Boycott, an English farmer and land agent in County Mayo. The activities of the League inevitably led to violence, and there was a sharp increase in agrarian crime, for which the landlords blamed what they regarded as the weakness of Gladstone, who returned to power with the general election of the spring of 1880. Henceforth, the Grand Old Man was to be the Ascendancy's principal bête noire; chamber pots decorated on the inside with his portrait were to find their way into many an Irish country house.

Mark Bence-Jones, *Twilight of the Ascendancy*, 1987

Within a few years the ascendancy was to be threatened by something much more formidable than a reforming Liberal government. In October 1879 the Irish National Land League was established under the effective leadership of the radical Michael Davitt. The League demanded a reduction in rents, state aid for tenants to buy out the land they worked on and an end to evictions. The League's tactics included the 'boycott' of landowners and agents evicting or attempting to evict tenants. It arranged that all evictions were 'witnessed by gatherings of people'. The witnesses in the nature of things were wont to set about the evictors. The success of the League can be gleaned from the fact that in 1881 there were 4,439 'agrarian crimes' committed in Ireland, an increase of 900 per cent over the 1877 figures.

Eamonn McCann, *War and an Irish Town*, 1974

Resting on the window-sash of the new house was a heavy Waltham pocket watch. It was bought by Uncle James when he began to work at the making of the Leitrim and Cavan narrow-gauge railway in 1885. He was a young man then, with two sisters, one of whom was AB. He had a small morsel of poor land, about nine acres in all. The railway job gave him a little financial leverage; and when the work was finished and the trains running, he began doing small contracts for the Board of Guardians. This consisted in making paved culverts, a skill he had picked up on the railway.

He was on good terms with the local landlord, the Hon. James W. Borroughs, whose family came to the Tully district from the Bass in lowland Scotland in 1610. He regarded Burroughs as a decent enough man in himself. Yet he took an active and secret part in whatever anti-landlord activities went on, because he abhorred the landlord system. He believed that the people should own their own land and that it should be in their possession alone. He regarded the landlords in general as robbers and the descendants of robbers. They got what they had by confiscation.

Charles O'Beirne, *The Good People*, 1985

Suddenly [there] appeared a large lough, ending in a lovely glen.

'What is that?' I asked.

'Lough Veagh; Glen Veagh.'

'Mrs Adair's place? Is that the castle at the head of the lough?'

The driver nodded, looking darker and more 'dour' than ever. And this time I could guess why.

Some years ago, in Glen Veagh was enacted a tragedy, which, though it has reached me with many variations, is, I think, allowed by both sides to have its foundation in certain facts, which, as near as I could get at them, were these. A certain Mr Adair, a wealthy Scotsman, bought large tracts of land here, and had many contests with his tenants, with whom he was far from popular: being an absentee landlord, leaving his affairs to be administered by his agents, who probably understood the peculiarities of Irish nature as little as their master. One—no, more than one of them—was murdered. Then Mr Adair declared that, if in three months the murderers were not given up, he would evict all the inhabitants of the Glen. Any person acquainted with Ireland can guess the result. Everybody knew, but nobody told. Much exasperated, Mr Adair kept his word. The innocent suffered with the guilty. Every family, women and children, young and old, was turned out on the moor—for eviction here, in this desolate place, means entire homelessness.

'And what became of them?' I asked, when the driver and I were left alone in the carriage, and I had somehow made him understand that I knew the story, and was sorry for the poor souls—at least, for the old folks, the women and children.

'Some died, ma'am, and some settled in other parts. A good many went to America. Anyhow, there's not one o' them left here. Not one.'

'And Mr Adair?'

'He's dead.'

The man set his teeth together, and hardened his face—a face I should not like to meet in a lonely road. It was the first glimpse I had had, since our coming to Ireland, of that terrible blood-feud now existing between landlord and tenant, in which neither will see the other's rights—and wrongs; nor distinguish between the just and the unjust, the good and the bad.

MRS CRAIK, *An Unknown Country*, 1880

On the 18th of May, a beautiful bright sunny day at noon, I was riding with a friend to the sessions at Borrisokane. I heard a faint report at a little distance in the fields as of a gun or pistol, but took no notice of it, when almost immediately afterwards a man came running up a lane to meet us, saying,

'Oh! Sir, Mr Hall has just been shot.'

'Shot!' cried I, pulling up my horse, 'do you mean murdered?'

'Oh! yes, Sir,' replied the man, 'he is lying there in the field.'

'Is he dead?' I asked.

'Stone dead!' was the man's reply; and as he said so, I never shall forget the strange mixture of horror and of triumph which pervaded his countenance.

We rode on rapidly down the lane, and just where it emerged upon a little grass lawn, was the body of Mr Hall. He was a man apparently about fifty years of age, and his bald head lay uncovered on the ground. He was quite warm but 'stone dead', lying in the open field. Numbers of people were working all around, planting their potatoes; but not a trace of the murderer could be found.

It was a sessions day at Borrisokane, and several other gentlemen who were also going there joined us almost immediately afterwards. There were a few country-people standing by. I shall not easily forget my feelings on this occasion. There lay the body of a murdered gentleman, wich whom I had been on terms of friendly intercourse—dead on his own estate, and in his own field, in the noonday, whilst on the faces of the peasantry could be plainly seen an expression of triumphant satisfaction; and there we stood, several mounted horsemen—many of us armed, burning to avenge his death and to arrest the murderer, and yet we looked like so many fools not knowing what to do, though it was scarcely more than ten minutes since the fatal shot had been fired.

W. STEWART TRENCH, *Realities of Irish Life*, 1869

There were a few small farmers whose land bounded ours who came every Sunday after Mass to hear what was going on in the world from *Freeman's Journal* which my father took in as well as the weekly Limerick paper. Few if any of them could read or write. Father was their link with Ireland outside the county of Limerick, with England, with the nebulous Beyond called Europe whose single familiar point was Rome, and Rome but the dwelling of the Holy Father and the site of the Holy Catholic Church. They set great store by this chance of enlightenment and believed that what father said could be taken as the truth, all the more so because he was no politician.

The first to arrive was James Regan, a tall, thin man who wore a very tall hat and smooth black clothes. Perhaps it was because of his dark clothes and long sad face that some said he was a spoiled priest. He had no apparent reason for looking dejected for he had a good-looking wife and plenty of sons and daughters. The other farmers I can see before my eyes in corduroy knee-breeches, bright waistcoats and sledge-hammer coats: tall John Heffernan, Jack Donovan, bent almost double with rheumatism; Twomey, whose wife was said to beat him on Sunday night in return for the beating he gave her on Saturday; and old Malachy, he who rented our orchard and was too deaf to hear a word of the reading but enjoyed it all the same.

Each one came in with the greeting, in English or in Irish, 'God save all here,' to which those within responded heartily, 'And you too.' Pipes were lighted and my father proceeded to read the newspaper, his audience commenting in low tones until the close, when one and another would give his opinion while my father listened.

They talked the politics of the day and of the neighbourhood, railing against all landlords and agents except their own landlord, Count de Salis, and his agent. They agreed that most agents deserved to be shot. The Count was humane; he understood the difficulties of the tenants. No one wished to hurt or harm him; he gave timber and slate to build or improve the farms or cottages and although the rents were considered to be too high, the best and most friendly feelings existed between the de Salis family and their tenants. Our landlord understood how great was the small farmer's struggle to make two ends meet, to pay the rent and bring up his generally large family decently.

Unfortunately there were other landlords who were overbearing and tyrannical, who mocked at any attempt on the part of farmers and their families to improve their position by education other than that of the national school, or by wearing boots and stockings and aiming at a better standard of living. These landlords were hated and despised. The railing of the farmers and others against them was the measure of the wounds they inflicted on the feelings of a sensitive people.

MARY CARBERY, *The Farm by Lough Gur*, 1937

At the time that Finn O'Donnell was going to school there was great trouble all through Ireland. If you had been in the country at the time, and had spoken to a man like Finn's grandfather, you would have been told that the trouble came because the people who worked on the fields did not own them. The land of Ireland had been conquered from its original owners in various wars and portions of it had been given to men who were on the conqueror's side. Their descendants, and people connected with their descendants, were now the landlords of Ireland.

If a peasant family wanted to raise crops and stock on a certain piece of land, they had to enter into an agreement with some landlord to pay him a share of what they earned out of the land. This share was called rent. In Ireland it was always too high and its payment generally left the family poor. A while before Finn was born the landlord could evict—that is, he could put the family away from the house they had built and the fields they had cleared—if he did not approve of their religion, or of the way they voted at an election, or if he thought he could get another family to pay him a better rent—that is a bigger share of their earnings. But this power had now been taken from the landlord and he could only evict if the family failed to pay him the rent agreed upon.

PADRAIC COLUM, *A Boy in Eirinn*, 1916

Sean Treacy grew up in an Ireland that was darkened by the passions of the Parnell Split, and in a county where the tradition of resistance to foreign and landlord tyranny was strong and proud. The Land War and Fenianism, Ballycohey and Ballyhurst, lived on on the lips of men who had known both; and on his mother's side, the Allis family had always been prominent in the land and national struggles. When Sean Treacy was three years old the Fenian John O'Leary unveiled the Kickham monument in Tipperary Town nearby. And Treacy heard in his childhood how a near relative of his own, William Allis of Gurtnacoola, Donohill, was out in the Ballyhurst rising in the Fenian times, and was a sturdy fighter afterwards in the Land League. There was a local tradition that when William Allis marched through Thurles with the Fenians in March, 1867, he carried a pistol in each hand. He survived to drill with the Irish Volunteers in 1913. While playing as a child on the Allis farm, Sean Treacy once unearthed one of his old Fenian arms dumps. The tale of Ballyhurst first stirred his imagination among all the tales of the Irish wars.

DESMOND RYAN, *Sean Treacy and the Third Tipperary Brigade*, 1945

One hears a good deal about the gay and rollicking Irish gentleman, but I do not think the Irish gentleman is now half so gay or half so rollicking as he was towards the end of the eighteenth century, when it is said he used to mix with the boys of the countryside on the hurling-field. To the older sort of landlord, indeed, Ireland must now be one broad valley of bitterness and humiliation. There is a titled landlord in the south, who in the old days used to keep his tenants standing bare-headed for hours in the rain on days on which they came to pay their rents. He put them even to the indignity of taking off their boots before he would allow them to come into his rent-office. Lately, he entered into negotiations with them with regard to the sale of his land, and made an appointment for a conference with them in a hotel in a neighbouring market-town. On the appointed day, the tenants held a preliminary meeting in the hotel to discuss what terms they should offer, and while the meeting was in progress the landlord arrived, and sent in word that he was ready. The chairman of the meeting sent back a message that if Lord So-and-so would call back in about three-quarters-of-an-hour they would be prepared to receive him. That scene, even if you have not much imagination, will enable you to realise the measure of the revolution that is changing the face and the character of Ireland.

ROBERT LYND, *Home Life in Ireland*, 1908

Charlie Beresford had spent Easter with the Londonderrys at Mount Stewart, where the house party included Carson and Bonar Law, another of Theresa Londonderry's protégés who was now Leader of the Unionist Opposition in Parliament. Bonar Law and Beresford were among the seventy MPs for English, Scottish and Welsh constituencies who showed their solidarity with the Ulster Unionists at a demonstration held at the Balmoral show grounds outside Belfast on Easter Tuesday, when no fewer than a hundred thousand men marched past the platform. There had been another great rally in the previous September at Craigavon, the home of Carson's lieutenant, the wealthy distiller Captain James Craig. A committee was making plans for a provisional government for Ulster so that the Province could secede from the rest of Ireland if a Home Rule parliament were established. Money was pouring into Carson's Unionist Defence Fund.

In the rest of Ireland, opposition to Home Rule was no less determined, though it lacked the popular backing which made it so formidable in Ulster; outside the Ascendancy it was largely confined to Protestants and to the most prosperous of the Catholic urban middle classes. Anti-Home Rule meetings were held up and down the country. Andrew Jameson of the distilling family, one of the leaders of the Southern Unionists, lent the Ladies Howard his motor to take them to a meeting in Wicklow town which was being chaired by their nephew Ralph Wicklow; the hall was crowded, despite bad weather. While the Unionists of the South naturally felt a bond with their fellow-Unionists in Ulster—Violet Martin travelled north to Coleraine in September to watch the Ulstermen signing their 'Solemn League and Covenant' against Home Rule—the Protestant sectarianism which was the Ulster Unionists' chief weapon was causing them increasing disquiet. Lord Ormonde, speaking from a platform draped with Union Jacks to a gathering of more than a thousand in the picture gallery of Kilkenny Castle in October, assured his audience that neither he nor those beside him on the platform—who included the Catholic Lord Kenmare as well as Protestants such as Lord Desart, Lord Midleton and himself—would have been there had the meeting been 'in the slightest degree of a sectarian character', a statement greeted with cries of 'Hear, hear'. At an anti-Home Rule meeting held at Killadoon, the home of the Protestant County Kildare landowner Henry Clements, great annoyance was caused when the local Church of Ireland clergyman made a speech hostile to Catholics; the situation was saved by the principal speaker, Bernard Shaw's kinsman Sir Frederick Shaw of Bushy Park, who stood up and

said that the Catholic and Protestant Churches were like two billiard balls;
you could hit whichever one you liked and get as far with either.

MARK BENCE-JONES, Twilight of the Ascendancy, 1987

As I continued my walk homeward, first through the broad thoroughfares of
the city and then through the broad highway of the southern suburbs, I met
scores of the same class of the population who had left their houses in the
side streets, and especially in the ultra-Protestant Sandy Row, the scene of
many a fierce encounter between the two religious factions, to put to me in
their own idiom and staccato pronunciation the burning question:

'Is them 'uns bate?'

And when I assured them that the unspeakable Nationalists had been
beaten by a good majority, once more cheers were raised. I was slapped famil-
iarly on the back by half-dressed 'Island-men' (the shipwrights) with shouts
of 'Bully wee fella!' as though the defeat of the measure was due to my personal
exertions; and I remember how the blinds of the bedrooms of many of the
best houses on the road were pulled to one side, while the sunshine of the early
morning disclosed white figures beyond thrusting a head forward to see what
was happening. Some way further on, where the villas of the suburb began, I
was surprised to hear myself hailed by name by someone at a window beyond
the shrubbery of a carriage-drive. I found myself responding to the director
of one of the chief banks. He told me he had been unable to sleep during the
night, and he had risen and sat at his open window to await my passing with
news. At two other houses of the same type I found gentlemen awaiting my
arrival, and at one of these it was with difficulty that I managed to get away
without drinking the health of the majority who had caused the Bill to be
thrown out—that was the penalty which the wealthy damask merchant suggested I should pay for having lifted a great weight from his mind. A tumbler
of whiskey at 4.30 on a lovely summer morning! Only the hospitable impulses
of a Belfast man would have been equal to such a suggestion.

The next night, however, the streets were full of an excited people. The
Roman Catholic clergy had issued strict commands to their flocks to remain
within their houses, or within the boundaries of their own localities, so that
they might not be tempted to respond to the insults which they would be
certain to receive from 'the other side'. This advice had been accepted, though
not without grumbling; but it was undoubtedly the best that could have been
offered to the people. The high spirits of 'the other side' might have been displayed through a medium familiar to both. As it was, the music of the Unionist bands of Sandy Row and the Shankill Road began playing as early as six
o'clock, and there were processions and noise and excitement in the principal thoroughfares until long past midnight. In several directions bonfires had
been lighted within half-an-hour after sunset, and some were still burning

when I passed them at three o'clock in the morning, and boys were watching the expiring embers.

It is unnecessary to say that the Police Commissioner and his officers were extremely uneasy during these days. One of them, who afterwards rose to the highest command in the Force, told me that, in his opinion, if that Home Rule Bill had passed, all the Constabulary in the city would not have been able to prevent such a wrecking of the Roman Catholic quarters as would have changed the whole aspect of the municipality—'wrecking and massacre', were his words; and before another fortnight had passed I agreed with him, for by that time fifteen hundred armed men were unable to drag the city out of the hands of the rioters, and for seven weeks there were daily fights, and these not confined, as previous outbreaks had been, to the usual area of disturbance between the Protestant Shankill and the Roman Catholic Falls, but on the Crumlin Road and the Antrim Road, in the very centre of the town, and through the mile length of York Street, excited mobs had passed, breaking windows and looting shops. They were charged by troops of Lancers, and by bayonets of Highlanders, and by fixed swords of the Constabulary; the hospitals were crowded with wounded men, women, and children, and there was not a newspaper in the city that had not on its staff a reporter who was limping in his walk, or with an arm in a sling, or a head bound up.

F. FRANKFORT MOORE, *The Truth About Ulster*, 1914

from *Autumn Journal*

And I remember, when I was little, the fear
    Bandied among the servants
That Casement would land at the pier
    With a sword and a horde of rebels;
And how we used to expect, at a later date,
    When the wind blew from the west, the noise of shooting
Starting in the evening at eight
    In Belfast in the York Street district;
And the voodoo of the Orange bands
    Drawing an iron net through darkest Ulster,
Flailing the limbo lands—
    The linen mills, the long wet grass, the ragged hawthorn.
And one read black where the other read white, his hope
    The other man's damnation:
Up the Rebels, To Hell with the Pope,
    And God Save—as you prefer—the King or Ireland.

LOUIS MACNEICE, *Autumn Journal*, 1938

And now with Home Rule on the doorstep, Middle Class Ireland queued up for the offices that were to be given out. There was just a little confusion in the queue, and awkward entanglements from conflicting promises by those up near the treasure chest. The confusion in the queue might have developed were it not that a note of alarm rang out sharply and smothered the squabble. New men appeared suddenly and called on the people to push forward in arms for separation from the British Empire. The queue roared out lustily against any such teaching, mocking the new teachers, and warning the masses of the frightful results of following them. Pearse, Clarke, Connolly, MacDermott, and the others were bad men; they were likely to spoil the case for Home Rule which rested so much on a guarantee of loyalty to the British crown, so they were traitors. They were endangering the offices of the friends of the great host of clergymen, so they were anti-religious. Pious people would spurn them, zealous ones attack them; it was a great day for Ireland when they were nearly murdered in Limerick. Ireland was loyal to the Empire; Home Rule depended on loyalty.

And then one day a couple of hundred Dublin workmen, a couple of score of students, a handful of intellectuals, came out into the streets of Dublin, and proclaimed an Irish Republic.

PEADAR O'DONNELL, *The Knife*, 1930

Almost every feature of Northern Ireland's situation contains a paradox. The Orange paradox is that Orangemen have acquired a deserved reputation for narrow fanaticism while all the time they are fighting to preserve a liberal and tolerant society such as they erroneously imagine exists in Northern Ireland. We have now got to the intricate kernel of the whole problem. A liberal and tolerant society, comparable to modern Britain's, has never existed in Northern Ireland because Northern Protestants (not only the 100,000 or so Orangemen, but virtually the entire Protestant community) have felt compelled since the 1830s—and even more since 1920—to discriminate against Catholics lest Romish authoritarianism might demolish Protestant freedom.

That of course is an over-simplification, like almost any statement ever made about Northern Ireland. There have been other complicated reinforcing motives for discrimination—economic, racial and political. But without the religious cement, these would most probably have crumbled by now. Many Northern Protestants are spiritually—and some are physically—descended from the Scottish Covenanters; a study of those brave zealots of the seventeenth century throws considerable light on what is happening in Northern Ireland 300 years later. One spiritual descendant was the Rt Hon. J. M. Andrews. Speaking as Grand Master of the Orange Order, he stated in June 1950, 'I observe from reports in the Press that there are a few Orange brethren who feel that we are exclusively a religious Order. While I agree that we are mainly a religious body, the Order has been in the front rank for generations in preserving our constitutional position. The Orange ritual lays it down that it is the duty of Orangemen to support and maintain the laws and constitution. It is fundamentally important that we should continue to do so, for if we lost our constitutional position within the United Kingdom, "civil and religious liberty for all", which we are also pledged as Orangemen to support, would be endangered.' At first sight, when one looks back over generations of total disregard for the civil rights of Catholics, this seems just another example of the celebrated Orange double-think. But—as they say in the playground—'Who started it?'

We Irish are always being accused of looking backwards too much. Sometimes, however, we don't look back far enough—or carefully enough, or honestly enough.

DERVLA MURPHY, *A Place Apart*, 1978

The years from 1918 to 1923 were to be dramatic ones throughout Ireland. They were to see the ousting of the old Home Rule Party (UIL) by Sinn Fein, the establishment of an illegal Irish parliament in Dublin in defiance of Westminster, and the outbreak of a War of Independence against British rule in Ireland. In the North the violent confrontation between Unionist and Nationalist which had been looming for so long was finally to erupt. The outcome would be partial independence for the bulk of the country in the new Irish Free State, and partition leaving the six north-eastern counties under British rule in the United Kingdom—but with local self-government.

MICHAEL FARRELL, *The Orange State*, 1976

The contacts between native and planter, which in earlier times took place along a broad belt running down the centre of the island, have come to be concentrated in the larger urban centres within this contact belt, and it is significant that Cork in the south and Derry in the north have produced more than their share of men of great ability, who have enriched the life of Dublin and Belfast and the wider world. Potentially the men of Derry, for example, are the inheritors of two cultures, and the decay of Londonderry is one of the worst consequences of partition, which deprived it of the Celtic half of its hinterland. To many historians, fascinated by the actions and motives of outstanding individuals, these locational factors appear to have little interest. Geography is for them merely a map and a means of reference. In its own right it is a part of history, and one can be understood only in the light of the other. It is to the land that you Irish are bound: this is the one enduring fact.

Who will pretend to analyse the emotional and spiritual bonds which tie people to the place of their childhood and to its local environment, and which influence them all their lives in ways they hardly suspect? The most genuine bonds are with small regions such as the Kingdom of Mourne or West Cork. Here are the springs of true patriotism. But they are easily polluted and exploited by myth-makers, of one kind or another. The Irish should be proud of the antiquity and the variety of their heritage, but in my view, if Irish culture is to maintain its historic character it needs constant renewal through exposure to the outside world and to fresh cultural forces. The future must be uncertain in a rapidly changing world, but I suggest that the best way to prepare for it is to expose the myths and to try to put the historic record straight.

E. ESTYN EVANS, *The Irish Association for Cultural, Economic and Social Relations*, 1968

The Fields Beyond the House

I remember a small field in Down . . .
W. R. RODGERS, 'Field Day'

———

Irish countrysides are so different from each other that it is not easy to find an interpreting word which will cover them all. Still, there is one thing which gives a unity—a personality, as it were—to Ireland. It is the glory of light which comes towards evening and rests on every field and on every hill and in the street of every town like a strange tide. Everywhere in Ireland, north, south, east, and west, the evening air is, as a fine living poet has perceived, a shimmer as of diamonds. It gives a new wonderfulness to the untidy farms, to the horses out in the fields as they munch the darkening grass with a noise, to the carelessly clad farmer hanging over a gate with invisible lapwings crying above his head, to the stained white little house with its oil-lamp not yet lit, and the glow of the turf-fire growing momently stronger.

ROBERT LYND, *Home Life in Ireland,* 1908

I have lived for most of my life on the Nore and own three fields upon its banks, some miles before it turns to the south-east and forces its way under Brandon Hill to join the Barrow above New Ross. In sixty years it has changed remarkably little. From a top window, looking across the river towards Black-stairs and Mount Leinster, I can still see the same stretch of cornfields, nut groves and mountain slopes. Beside the woods of Summerhill and Kilfane I can spot the round tower of Tullaherin and Kilbline, the sixteenth-century castle of the Shortalls. There is only one new cottage in sight.

This does not mean that we stagnate. The landscape is domestic and life is mainly prosperous but it has edged away from the rivers. The Nore, which traverses the county of Kilkenny, and passes through the city, and the Barrow, which skirts its eastern border, and all their tributaries gave up work and took to an easy life about a century ago. The mill wheels stopped turning and the roofs fell in on the millworkers' cottages, flags and duck-weed and king-cups choked the mill race and there is so much tranquil beauty around that some hope and many fear that the tourist agencies will soon discover us.

A century ago there were twenty-two flour mills, three large distilleries and four breweries on the Nore between Durrow and Inistiogue. But industry had left the rivers long before I was born and as children we were constantly driving donkey carts down little lanes to riverside ruins beside which we bathed and fished and picnicked. And every ruin had its story and the tradition that these stories are worth recording, correcting, analysing has never died out.

Our riverside ruins are mostly not depressing, for many of their founders were original and complex men, whose lives gave evidence that vision and ingenuity can flourish here. Some of their industries did not survive them for long. They subsided gracefully after a generation or two but, like the flowers of summer, were fertile in their decay. Various economic causes can be alleged for their failure but often there is nothing to be said except that men grow old and have bored or stupid sons and that today there are many prosperous industries which would be more admirable as ruins covered with valerian and wild wall flowers.

One of our favourite picnic places was Annamult Woollen Factory, a very stylish and spacious ruin on the King's river just before it joins the Nore. Before the king-cups and the bullocks took over, it was in 1814 one of the most progressive factories in the British Isles. Its owners, Messrs Shaw and Nowlan, rivalled Robert Owen, the Utopian industrialist, in their concern for their 400 work people. The children all had free schooling and lesson books, their fathers and mothers had health insurance cards, and every Sunday they danced to the fiddle in the large courtyard. George Shaw and Timothy Nowlan were stern but just, and rather quizzical. (Shaw was, I believe, a great great uncle to George Bernard.) Employees who misbehaved were punished but not sacked. Sometimes the offender, dressed in a yellow jacket, was obliged to roll a stone round the courtyard in full view of the Sunday merry-makers. The factory, while it lasted, was hugely successful. The Prince Regent and all the employees of the Royal Dublin Society dressed themselves in its woollens and the fields around Annamult were white with a flock of 600 Merino sheep, vast bundles of wool with tiny faces, which the Prims, a famous Kilkenny family with Spanish relations, had imported from Spain.

The Marble Works at Maddoxtown, below Kilkenny, is another beautiful spot with proud memories. Children still hunt about among the loose strife and the willow herb for polished slabs, green Connemara, pink Midleton, and Kilkenny which is black with white flecks. William Colles, who invented special machinery for cutting and polishing by water power, was so clever that his neighbours thought him a necromancer. He almost succeeded in making dogs weave linen by turning wheels, and he invented an instrument, like an Aeolian harp, which played tunes as it floated down the Nore.

Hubert Butler, 'Beside the Nore' in *Escape from the Anthill*, 1985; first published in *Ireland of the Welcomes*, May–June 1970

Up in the north-east corner of County Cork is a stretch of limestone country—open, airy, not quite flat; it is just perceptibly tilted from north to south, and the fields undulate in a smooth flowing way. Dark knolls and screens of trees, the network of hedges, abrupt stony ridges, slate glints from roofs give the landscape a featured look—but the prevailing impression is, emptiness. This is a part of Ireland with no lakes, but the sky's movement of clouds reflects itself everywhere as it might on water, rounding the trees with bloom and giving the grass a sheen. In the airy silence, any sound travels a long way. The streams and rivers, sunk in their valleys, are not seen until you come down to them.

Across the base of this tract of country the river Blackwater flows west to east, into the County Waterford. South of the Blackwater, from which they rise up steeply, Nagles Mountains cut off any further view. Behind Fermoy town these mountains end in a steep bluff: the main road from Cork to Dublin crosses the bridge at Fermoy, then runs due north over the Kilworth hills that close in this tract on the east. North of Kilworth lies Mitchelstown; above Mitchelstown the Galtees rise to powerful coloured peaks. Galtymore, the third highest mountain in Ireland, dominates this north-east corner of Cork. After their climax in Galtymore the Galtees drop into foothills, the Ballyhouras—this range of small shapely mountains borders the County Limerick and slides gently south, in promontories of bogland, into the County Cork fields. The Ballyhouras, forming its northern boundary, face down on Nagles Mountains across the open country of which I speak. The two blue lines, with space and a hidden river between them, run roughly parallel.

To the west extends a long flattish distance, beyond which, though only on very clear days, the Kerry mountains are to be seen. The country in which Bowen's Court stands is, thus, squared in by hills or mountains on three sides, but melts off into the light and clouds of the west.

This limestone country is pitted with kilns and quarries; the hard white bye-roads run over rock. Our two rivers, the Funcheon and the Awbeg, have hollowed out for themselves, on their courses south to the Blackwater, rocky twisting valleys. Here and there down the valleys the limestone makes cliffs or amphitheatres. In places the rivers flow between steep woods; in places their valleys are open, shallow and lush—there are marshy reaches trodden by cattle, fluttered over by poplars from the embanked lanes. Herons cross these in their leisurely flopping flight; water peppermint grows among the rushes; the orchis and yellow wild iris flower here at the beginning of June. Lonely stone bridges are come on round turns of the stream, and old keeps or watch towers, called castles, command the valleys: some are so broken and weathered that they look like rocks, some have been almost blotted out by the ivy; some are intact shells whose stairs you can still climb.

There are mills on both rivers—one great mill is in ruins—and swans on the Funcheon and the Awbeg. Not far from the Awbeg, under Spenser's castle, there is a marsh where seagulls breed in spring.

Elizabeth Bowen, Bowen's Court, 1942

Autumn

A good stay-at-home season is Autumn; then
    there's work to be done by all:
Speckled fawns, where the brackens make
    covert, range away undeterred;
And stags that were seen upon hillocks, now
    give heed to the call,
To the bellowing call of the hinds, and they
    draw back to the herd.

A good stay-at-home season is Autumn; the
    brown world's marked into fields;
The corn is up to its growth; the acorns teem
    in the wood;
By the side of the down-fallen fort even the
    thornbush yields
A crop, and there by the rath the hazel nuts
    drop from a load.

PADRAIC COLUM, *Dramatic Legends*, 1922

When the sun was warming the bricks of the houses a crowd of boys in their bare feet would call for Colm and Jamesy, and with pieces of bread in their hands they would join them and set off for a swim at Toneroy.

They climbed through the cool fields where the buttercups yellowed their bare legs, stopping now and then to pull the grass from between their toes or to look back at the street and the brickyard falling far below them; out on to the country road with the tar bubbling on it under the sun, racing for a drink at the horse-trough, and then as they came in sight of the mountain pool they began to pull off their jerseys. Then they bathed in the black cold water, and ran nakedly up and down the fields, letting the wind and the sun dry them. They followed the river along cool glens and gathered blue bells with the sun caught in the net of leaves above their heads; after trout under stones; chased by the gamekeeper; up the fields again, panting madly, and so out on to the road again for home, their bodies cool from the bathe, stomachs empty from hunger, pockets empty of the few pence that would buy the dry loaf that would satisfy them. Some would break sticks and bite rings in them with their teeth, the sour taste scorching their mouths.

The smallest and most ragged boy amongst them would be sent up to the little farm-houses to beg and a fight would take place over the bread till the 'beggar' got none. They would splash dust over their legs to pretend they had walked for miles and miles, and then burst into song as the cool of the evening

began to fall like dew and the lights of the city come out as slow as summer
stars.

MICHAEL MCLAVERTY, *Call My Brother Back*, 1939

Field Day

The old farmer, nearing death, asked
To be carried outside and set down
Where he could see a certain field
'And then I will cry my heart out,' he said.

It troubles me, thinking about that man;
What shape was the field of his crying
In Donegal?

I remember a small field in Down, a field
Within fields, shaped like a triangle.
I could have stood there and looked at it
All day long.

And I remember crossing the frontier between
France and Spain at a forbidden point, and seeing
A small triangular field in Spain,
And stopping

Or walking in Ireland down any rutted by-road
To where it hit the highway, there was always
At this turning-point and abuttment
A still centre, a V-shape of grass
Untouched by cornering traffic,
Where country lads larked at night.

I think I know what the shape of the field was
That made the old man weep.

W. R. RODGERS, *Collected Poems*, 1971

She lived in a farmhouse in Ballytra on Inishowen, and once a year we visited
her. Our annual holiday was spent under her roof. And had it not been for
the lodging she provided, we could not have afforded to get away at all. But
we did not consider this aspect of the affair.

On the first Saturday of August we always set out, laden with clothes in
cardboard boxes and groceries from the cheap city shops, from the street
markets: enough to see us through the fortnight. The journey north lasted

nearly twelve hours in our ancient battered cars: a Morris Eight, dark green with fragrant leather seats, and a Ford Anglia are two of the models I remember from a long series of fourth-hand crocks. Sometimes they broke down *en route* and caused us long delays in nauseating garages, where I stood around with my father, while the mechanic tinkered, or went, with my sister and mother, for walks down country lanes, or along the wide melancholy street of small market towns.

Apart from such occasional hitches, however, the trips were delightful odysseys through various flavours of Ireland: the dusty rich flatlands outside Dublin, the drumlins of Monaghan with their hint of secrets and better things to come, the luxuriant slopes, rushing rives and expensive villas of Tyrone, and finally, the ultimate reward: the furze and heather, the dog-roses, the fuchsia, of Donegal.

Donegal was different in those days. Different from what it is now, different then from the eastern urban parts of Ireland. It was rural in a thorough, elemental way. People were old-fashioned in their dress and manners, even in their physiques: weather-beaten faces were highlighted by black or grey suits, shiny with age; broad hips stretched the cotton of navy-blue, flower-sprigged overalls, a kind of uniform for country women which their city sisters had long eschewed, if they ever had it. Residences were thatched cottages . . . 'The Irish peasant house' . . . or spare grey farmhouses. There was only a single bungalow in the parish where my aunt lived, an area which is now littered with them.

All these things accentuated the rusticity of the place, its strangeness, its uniqueness.

ÉILÍS NÍ DHUIBHNE, 'Blood and Water', 1988

Portaferry, Co. Down. To-day I rode from Belfast to Portaferry on a push bicycle, a splendid method of progression in that one can dismount, sit by the roadside, and spend hours looking back the way one has come. With a motor-car there is no looking back, whereas half the fun of progressing through life or anything else consists in orienting one's self with what has gone before; to tear blindly ahead is to lead only half a life, to go to the devil with all the other road hogs. And what a view there is to-day to look back at! A full tide has set the lough brimming with deep blue water; the green hummocks of the islands on the farther shore, with white farm-houses gleaming here and there in the sunshine, appear to be floating on the brimming tide; beyond them again, and apparently changing position as the road leads on, rises the dim blue outline of the Mournes. Backwards the road leads towards Belfast, smoking somewhere beyond the hills to the north-west, past Greyabbey and Mount Stewart, following the lough shore, with heavy woods crowding close to the water's edge. An attractive country, full of variety, with water, woods, islands, distant mountains, ploughed land, pasture land, and, close inshore, the surface of the lough white with wild swans. . . . As the road leads on towards the tip of the peninsula, the character of the country begins to change, grows hillier, not quite so *soigné*; loose stone walls appear here and there instead of hedges—a very different country this from the strip of coast fronting the Irish Sea at the upper end of the peninsula where I spent the summers of my childhood. There the farmers spoke broad Scots, as well they might, seeing that from their farm windows they looked across to Galloway; here one might be running into Catholic and Nationalist Ireland. I turn aside from the main road and climb on to the high ground above Portaferry, to see one of the finest views in Co. Down. The town itself nestles below, half hidden amongst woods, at the edge of the water. But it is to the east that the view is stupendous. Eastwards the North Channel of the Irish Sea appears, owing to some peculiar atmospheric effect, to have been narrowed to the width of a handsome river; a collier in mid-channel resembles a toy model stuck upon a narrow sheet of mirror. To the north-east, bordering the sheet of mirror, lies the Mull of Galloway, then comes the long gap of the Solway Firth, then the twin humps of the Isle of Man, with, behind and appearing almost continuous with them, the dark mountain masses of Cumberland. To the south-west the Mournes rear themselves, a tremendous dark blue barrier, tempering down to the lower ranges of Slieve Croob and the Dromara mountains, beyond Ballynahinch. But it is the lough that is the centre of attraction in this landscape, the whole of it outlined below as on a map, from Scrabo to the sea, with its chain of green islands festooning the farther shore. This is the most important of the ancient seaways into Ireland, the landfall of St Patrick, and later of the Norsemen, who harried the monastery of Nendrum on Mahee Island, farther up the lough. On the opposite shore of the narrow inlet through which the tidal waters ebb and flow, round Strangford, the woods of Cuan crowd close again to the water's edge, the woods of which Deirdre cried out:

> Woods of Cuan, O woods of Cuan,
> In which are the cold waters . . .

But not only the cold waters: noisy waters as well, for at certain states of the tide the roaring of Strangford bar can be positively terrifying. And beyond this narrow, mirror-like strip of swiftly moving water, beyond the dark woods of Cuan above which rooks are wheeling, begins one of the most fateful territories in Ireland, the fertile triangle between the Quoile river at Downpatrick, the outfall of Strangford Lough, and the long beaches of Tyrella: the land where St Patrick preached his first sermon at Saul, later to be studded with castles and ravaged with fire and sword by the Normans, and still marked on old maps as the barony of Lecale. Here, upon the wooded shores of this sea lough, the light of Christianity was caught and reflected back again into the darkness of Europe.

DENIS IRELAND, From the Irish Shore, 1936

On we go through mountain roads, with wide-spreading views, gorges and boulders, forming a rare sight for the sore eyes of a midland farmer. We pass through the zenith of Irish landscape beauty. At first the green hedges, their buds closed, the blinds still down, but wait a few weeks and see what a Mammoth White Sale will here commence. Then high hills, blue-shadowed on olive ground, heathered and brackened; fields fluttering their young grass flags; tender-leaved birches, hazels, and oaks. The road seemed to go dancing before us, up and down, looking back to laugh at us. At first it was a grey road, then red, and finally yellow, the hues graduating with the declivity. The clouds above us were swelling and shrinking, curved and creviced, blue-stained, umber-stained, and grey. The merry water of a far-away lake was dimpling. Hill-slopes were gaudy with blazing furze in a scented spate. Glory be to God, what furze! A cavalry charge of it down a whole range of hills.

STEPHEN RYNNE, Green Fields, 1938

What my neighbours mean by 'fern' is bracken, which in spring lifts a host of clenched fists from last year's rusty litter. Its roots are like telephone cables, black-skinned with tough white cores, and they ramify at a ruthless pace, so that one plant can choke a whole field. 'Horses which eat a few mouthfuls,' warned Anthony Huxley in *Plant and Planet*, 'have their Vitamin B destroyed and rapidly die.' When Michele's pony grazed the field next door, this sent me out in a panic, with the scythe, to mow down bracken fiddleheads on the ditch before Báinín could eat any more. In later springs he was left to take his chances.

The archetype of ferny precision and grace is surely the common male fern, unfolding in a crown of fronds, each plant distinct and statuesque. There is one that I watch for beside a little bridge on the road to the post office. The lifting and unwinding of its crozier heads is part of spring's arrival (like the sudden, lemony flash of wagtails under the bridge).

Early last century, the beautiful forms and soft colours of the ferns enchanted the Victorian middle classes, who raided the countryside by train to trowel up ferns for their conservatories. Great cartloads were carried to the cities, for sale. Wales lost much of its royal fern, *Osmunda regalis*, and Ireland a lot of its Killarney fern, which grows in crevices near waterfalls. Remembering this, I have tried to restrain my own thefts from the wild: a single clump of *Osmunda* from a boggy stream to cast reflections on the frogs' pond; one mossy twig with a frilly polypody fern, kept living and growing for years in a damp pot on the dinner table. At the foot of Mweelrea, water gushes off the mountain through a deep ravine, where oak and aspen, birch and holly lean above the spray. Branches crack and fall to make bridges and here, rooting in moss on the bark, polypody ferns weave aerial gardens. They enjoy, in all essentials, the conditions of a temperate rainforest.

MICHAEL VINEY, *A Year's Turning*, 1996

The primary unit of land division—the townland—is still a very real thing; and as the townland retains its Gaelic name even in the districts of Dublin and Belfast, so there survives beyond the city's influence the social fabric of the townland community. Reeves and Joyce have argued that the careful sub-division of Irish land points to the existence of a considerable settled population in remote antiquity, and recent archæological research supports this view. There are no less than 62,205 townlands in the country; their size, which varies from curiosities of less than an acre to large tracts of moorland of 1,000 acres, averages 325 acres.

The townlands in turn group themselves into baronies corresponding to the petty kingdoms of old. Writers tell us that even into the 19th century one barony could be easily distinguished from another by the dresses peculiar to each. Thus there were the dark blue and damson of Cork and Waterford, the grey of Kerry and the blue of Galway. A traveller in 1830 remarked wisely that 'such peculiarities frequently point out the natural divisions of a country in more important matters than dress': they are an index to regional diversity. The distinctive features of particular districts are well illustrated in the case of 'the Irish Flanders', the isolated tract in Co. Wexford comprising the baronies of Bargy and Forth; while nothing could reveal the separateness of some island communities better than the heaviest punishment meted out to offenders in Rathlin or Clear I.: it consisted of 'banishment to Ireland'.

E. ESTYN EVANS, *Irish Heritage*, 1942

Shancoduff

My black hills have never seen the sun rising,
Eternally they look north towards Armagh.
Lot's wife would not be salt if she had been
Incurious as my black hills that are happy
When dawn whitens Glassdrummond chapel.

My hills hoard the bright shillings of March
While the sun searches in every pocket.

They are my Alps and I have climbed the Matterhorn
With a sheaf of hay for three perishing calves
In the field under the Big Forth of Rocksavage.

The sleety winds fondle the rushy beards of Shancoduff
While the cattle-drovers sheltering in the Featherna Bush
Look up and say: 'Who owns them hungry hills
That the water-hen and snipe must have forsaken?
A poet? Then by heavens he must be poor.'
I hear and is my heart not badly shaken?

PATRICK KAVANAGH, *The Great Hunger and Other Poems*, 1942

I was fishing one day in a very wild part of Wicklow, not far from Lugnaquilla—the trout were numerous and rising fast, and I was intent on my sport, when, as I was taking a step in advance on the bank, which just where I stood was covered with large and knee-deep fern, I felt the ground give way, and was precipitated some half-dozen feet in a very summary and, as I thought, extraordinary manner. On looking about me when I recovered my legs, I found myself in a diminutive hut, face to face with an ancient weather-beaten crone, who was fully as alarmed as myself. I at once guessed the manner of place into which I had been so suddenly and strangely introduced. Nor was I wrong; for after many assurances and protestations of my entire approbation of potheen, the old lady imparted the information that a little business was occasionally done in the narrow dwelling in which we stood, which flourished all the better when not under the supervision of excisemen. There was no still to be seen; but it was not very distant, having been buried in a neighbouring bog, a common hiding-place for such little commodities. Sometimes, however, when the season of work is over, the still is cast into a river.

CHARLES RICHARD WELD, *Vacations in Ireland*, 1857

The County is naturally course and full of Hills, the Air sharp and cold in Winter, occasioned by earlier and longer Frosts than they feel in the South; however in general it may be well reckoned temperate and healthy. The Plague that raged in the last Century about *Dublin, Cork*, and other Places, scarce found a Way into the Northern Counties, and the Quartan Ague is a Disorder very uncommon here. The Soil of it inclines to Wood, unless constantly plowed and kept open, and the low Grounds degenerate into Moss or Bogg, when the Drains are neglected; yet, by the constant Labour and Industry of the Inhabitants, the Morass Grounds have of late, by burning and proper Management, produced surprizing large Crops of Rye and Oats. Course Lands manured with Lime, have answered the Farmer's Views in Wheat, and yielded a great Produce; and wherever Marle is found, there is great Store of Barley. The Barony of *Lecale*, where Marle-pits abound, produces as good Grain of that kind as any in the Kingdom, most of which is exported from *Killough* to *Dublin*.

WALTER HARRIS, *The Antient and Present State of the County of Down*, 1741

One line of the railway strikes north-west, following the valley of the Inny river into Monaghan and so to Fermanagh, and finally through Tyrone into the County of Derry—a country of many rivers and little lakes among uneven, marshy ground; poor, inhospitable, and tenanted by a hardy race of men. The other branch, which is the main one, passing Dundalk, carries the traveller up a steep gradient into a wild, narrow gorge, the Moyry pass, which skirts the western end of the Carlingford range, and as it rises brings you on to a bleak moor. Here Slieve Gullion mountain on your left makes a part of County Armagh, and on your right is County Down, with Slieve Donard and all his brethren of Mourne. This is the Gap of the North; it leads into the true Ulster, that north-eastern region of Ireland which has always held somewhat aloof and apart from the rest—which is in many ways more aboriginal than any other part of the country, and which was fiercely and indomitably Irish when all the land up to Dundalk was shire-ground, fully within the English pale.

STEPHEN GWYNN, *The Famous Cities of Ireland*, 1915

from *A May-Day Revel*

Now, mid the slopes of furrowed earth,
  The peasant drives his wearied yoke;
Now from the crackling cottage hearth
  Mounts tranquilly the azure smoke;
Now, past the winding road anigh,
  The drover guides his dusty sheep;
The lazy waggoner plods by,
  Behind his slow horse, half asleep;
Now groups of rustic lad and lass
Beside the shadowy ferry throng;
  Now through the bright mid-stream they pass,
With oars that time some homely song;

And beached at length above the sea,
    Push homeward up each shadowy height,
While glimmers red and distantly
    Their cottage window's welcome light.
The farms are hushed; beside their way
    The dripping wheels of mountain mills
Stream in the leafy trickling ray;
    The bon-fires blaze along the hills:
They hear the distant voices ring
    In festal echoes of acclaim;
They see the wild forms hurrying
    In twilight dances round the flame;
Till one by one each joyous sound
Dies off upon the lonely air;
    The red fires drowse along the ground,
The dances cease, the hills are bare;
And as the sea-wind stirs the heath,
    And silvery spring-tide floods the shores,
Nought save the moon on grey Omeath
    Moves by the quiet cottage doors.

T. C. Irwin, *Versicles*, 1883

[In the evening at Aldworth.] T. read us the 'Bugle Song'. I said 'That's Killarney.'

T.—'Yes, it was Killarney suggested it. The bugle echoes were wonderful—nine times—at last like a chant of angels in the sky. But when I was there afterwards I could only hear two echoes,—from the state of the air. I complained of this and said, "when I was here before I heard nine." "Oh!" says the bugler, "then you're the gintleman that's brought so much money to the place!"' (The 'Bugle Song' increased the number of tourists to Killarney.)

He said an Irish lady asked him how he liked the scenery—'Too much bog,' he thought, 'black and dismal.' 'O then, where,' she retorted in tones of indignation—'where would you have the poor people cut their turf?'

William Allingham, *Journals*, 1880

'Oh hand in hand let us return to the dear land of our birth, the bays, the bogs, the moors, the glens, the lakes, the rivers, the streams, the brooks, the mists, the—er—fens, the—er—glens, by tonight's mail-train.'

Samuel Beckett, *Murphy*, 1938

Mr Dubourdieu mentions a very fine ass imported from Malaga, by Mr M'Neil, of Larne, from which this gentleman has bred a number of mules: the ass, in his form and movement, a superior animal, his height about fourteen hands. At the time Mr Dubourdieu saw him, his coat was smooth, and his whole appearance handsome; his head not of that heavy dull cast, so common in our unfortunate creatures of the same species, (truly unfortunate, from the ill-treatment which they generally receive in Ireland.) When he was mounted by his keeper, he shewed spirit, but no bad temper, and his paces were strikingly light and agile. The mares, from which Mr M'Neil bred his mules, being of a good description, the progeny have turned out valuable, both in performance and in looks. Mr Dubourdieu saw many of them at work, and there was no appearance of stubbornness in any of them. This gentleman speaks highly of their powers, and of the facility with which they are trained and supported. In this commercial country, where, of necessity, there must be so much land carriage, this useful, hardy, and frugal quadruped, would certainly pay well for both its rearing and keeping; for, though its longevity is almost proverbial, it is at an early age fit for work, and is sold at a high price.

A. ATKINSON, Ireland Exhibited to England, 1823

One of those fortuitous straws which show how the religious wind blows, and marks the difference, strange to say, between the Catholic and Protestant counties, is the relative esteem in which asses are held. Antrim, the most Protestant county in Ireland, has the least use for asses. In every other county, these animals are to be found in thousands: Tipperary, for instance, having over 17,000; Cork nearly 20,000; Mayo 25,000, and so forth—but Antrim, with its great area and a population larger than that of any other Irish county, had only 783 asses within its borders in 1901. The county of Londonderry, the population of which is less than quarter of that of Antrim, kept only 582 asses in the same year. Down, which is the best agricultural and, next to Antrim, the most Protestant county in Ireland, having a population double that of Londonderry, only maintained 1389 asses. Armagh, another of the four counties in which the Protestants are in a majority—and, next to Dublin, the most densely-peopled area in Ireland—only keeps 2000 asses. But in all the Roman Catholic counties—except Tyrone, which is a kind of neutral ground—asses are to be reckoned in thousands, especially in Munster and Connaught. If there were only the same number of asses in the Catholic counties in proportion to population as in the Protestant, there should only be 20,000; instead of which there are 234,180.

MICHAEL J. F. McCARTHY, Irish Land and Irish Liberty, 1911

The Drover

To Meath of the pastures,
From wet hills by the sea,
Through Leitrim and Longford,
Go my cattle and me.

I hear in the darkness
Their slipping and breathing—
I name them the by-ways
They're to pass without heeding;

Then the wet, winding roads,
Brown bogs with black water,
And my thoughts on white ships
And the King o' Spain's daughter.

O farmer, strong farmer!
You can spend at the fair,
But your face you must turn
To your crops and your care;

And soldiers, red soldiers!
You've seen many lands,
But you walk two by two
And by captain's commands!

O the smell of the beasts,
The wet wind in the morn,
And the proud and hard earth
Never broken for corn!

And the crowds at the fair,
The herds loosened and blind,
Loud words and dark faces,
And the wild blood behind!

(O strong men with you best
I would strive breast to breast,
I could quiet your herds
With my words, with my words!)

I will bring you, my kine,
Where there's grass to the knee,
But you'll think of scant croppings
Harsh with salt of the sea.

PADRAIC COLUM, *Collected Poems of Ireland*, 1960

On May Day the young crops were visited with torches and the cattle blessed before being driven to the mountain booleys, and hill-top fires played a large part in the rites. These Beltane fires were originally need-fires, that is they were produced by the friction of two pieces of wood. All hearth fires were extinguished on May Eve, and re-lit from the sacred fire. It is still a common superstition that it is unlucky to give away fire, even as light for a pipe, on May Day, for that would be to give away your luck for the year. In Donegal it is considered unlucky to be the first house to show smoke on May morn: the cattle are milked and the byres cleaned before the fire is made up. The Beltane ritual included the eating of oatcakes 'which must not touch iron', and dancing three times clockwise round the fire. Many volumes could be written on the customs and superstitions connected with this festival, touching fire and food, salt and butter, the rowan and the flowers of the field, especially the marsh-marigold or May-flower. The city urchins have turned the celebrations into a prolonged parading of May Queens and collecting of pennies.

E. ESTYN EVANS, *Irish Heritage*, 1942

The Herons

As I was climbing Ardan Mór
From the shore of Sheelin lake,
I met the herons coming down
Before the water's wake.

And they were talking in their flight
Of dreamy ways the herons go
When all the hills are withered up
Nor any waters flow.

FRANCIS LEDWIDGE, *Songs of the Fields*, 1914

Grimness and desolation intensify from here on, as the coast falls more and more into the power of the sea. This storm beach fades out as the cliff carries it inland, but another starts on the lowest level where the tides come flooding in over wide flats and shallow steps of bare rock. At first it is merely a string of big isolated blocks swept along from under the last of the cliffs, but as one follows it eastwards it becomes a great reef up to twenty feet high that snakes along the coast, dividing the flat shore from the little fields in its lee, into which it occasionally spills stone-falls when a wild winter has heaped up its crest beyond stability. The going is harder now. If the tide is full one has to choose between stumbling from boulder to boulder along the knobbly spine of the storm beach, or sacrifice the sight of the sea and climb wall after wall of the fields inside it; but if the tide has withdrawn one can pick one's way along the slippery flags uncovered, the interior of the island hidden by the looming rampart on one's right but with the left open to the lovely distances of Connemara.

TIM ROBINSON, *Stones of Aran: Pilgrimage*, 1986

from *Train to Dublin*

All over the world people are toasting the King,
Red lozenges of light as each one lifts his glass,
But I will not give you any idol or idea, creed or king,
I give you the incidental things which pass
Outward through space exactly as each was.

I give you the disproportion between labour spent
And joy at random; the laughter of the Galway sea
Juggling with spars and bones irresponsibly,
I give you the toy Liffey and the vast gulls,
I give you fuschia hedges and whitewashed walls.

I give you the smell of Norman stone, the squelch
Of bog beneath your boots, the red bog-grass,
The vivid chequer of the Antrim hills, the trough of dark
Golden water for the cart-horses, the brass
Belt of serene sun upon the lough.

And I give you the faces, not the permanent masks,
But the faces balanced in the toppling wave—
His glint of joy in cunning as the farmer asks
Twenty per cent too much, or a girl's, forgetting to be suave,
A tiro choosing stuffs, preferring mauve. . . .

LOUIS MACNEICE, *Poems*, 1934

Remember that every cottage is white. The whole expanse laughs with these little white dots; it is like nothing so much as the assembly of white foam-caps when a fresh breeze is on a summer sea. And the roads are white too; there is no tarmac yet. And because the whole country is a turbulent democracy of little hills, these roads shoot in every direction, disappearing and reappearing. But you must not spread over this landscape your hard English sunlight; make it paler, make it softer, blur the edges of the white cumuli, cover it with watery gleams, deepening it, making all unsubstantial. And beyond all this, so remote that they seem fantastically abrupt, at the very limit of your vision, imagine the mountains. They are no stragglers. They are steep and compact and pointed and toothed and jagged. They seem to have nothing to do with the little hills and cottages that divide you from them. And sometimes they are blue, sometimes violet; but quite often they look transparent—as if huge sheets of gauze had been cut out into mountainous shapes and hung up there, so that you could see through them the light of the invisible sea at their backs.

C. S. LEWIS, *Surprised by Joy*, 1955

Art McCooey

I recover now the time I drove
Cart-loads of dung to an outlying farm—
My foreign possessions in Shancoduff—
With the enthusiasm of a man who sees life simply.

The steam rising from the load is still
Warm enough to thaw my frosty fingers.
In Donnybrook in Dublin ten years later
I see that empire now and the empire builder.

Sometimes meeting a neighbour
In country love-enchantment,
The old mare pulls over to the bank and leaves us
To fiddle folly where November dances.

We wove our disappointments and successes
To patterns of a town-bred logic:
'She might have been sick. . . . No, never before,
A mystery, Pat, and they all appear so modest.'

We exchanged our fool advices back and forth:
'It easily could be their cow was calving,
And sure the rain was desperate that night . . .'
Somewhere in the mists a light was laughing.

We played with the frilly edges of reality
While we puffed our cigarettes;
And sometimes Owncy Martin's splitting yell
Would knife the dreamer that the land begets.

'I'll see you after Second Mass on Sunday.'
'Right-o, right-o.' The mare moves on again.
A wheel rides over a heap of gravel
And the mare goes skew-ways like a blinded hen.

Down the lane-way of the popular banshees
By Paddy Bradley's; mud to the ankles;
A hare is grazing in Mat Rooney's meadow;
Maggie Byrne is prowling for dead branches.

Ten loads before tea-time. Was that the laughter
Of the evening bursting school?
The sun sinks low and large behind the hills of Cavan,
A stormy-looking sunset. 'Brave and cool.'

Wash out the cart with a bucket of water and a wangel
Of wheaten straw. Jupiter looks down.
Unlearnedly and unreasonably poetry is shaped
Awkwardly but alive in the unmeasured womb.

PATRICK KAVANAGH, *A Soul for Sale*, 1947

Brown Rain Falling Heavily

The rain here is absolute, magnificent, and frightening. To call this rain bad weather is as inappropriate as to call scorching sunshine fine weather.

You can call this rain bad weather, but it is not. It is simply weather, and weather means rough weather. It reminds us forcibly that its element is water, falling water. And water is hard.

HEINRICH BÖLL, *Irish Journal*

———

It was raining with a grim, quiet persistence as I left Sligo and took the road through Bundoran into Donegal.

In the wide square a few drovers stood with long sticks while a few cattle stood about and blundered on the pavement. Now and then carts laden with turf or vegetables set off through the drizzle down the road. Ireland is full of towns whose names have gone round the world with a kind of splendour to them, so that the stranger, expecting towers and turrets and great crowds, comes instead with a kind of wonder to a little town like Donegal where men huddle in the drizzle and a few calves low sadly on the pavement.

This is natural; for the fame of these places has been spread abroad by many exiles. Their greatness is founded on homesickness.

Donegal Bay is one of the most magnificent bays in Ireland. But the beauty of this country is the glory of hill and the splendour of cliffs that fall sharply to the sea.

The rain was a mist that hid the hill-tops and hung out at sea like a white cloth. I went to the edges of cliffs and looked through the mists on waves thundering and breaking furiously against the rocks; and all round me were the formless shadows of hills: hills jutting out into the sea; hills piled back against the land; hills sage-green and smooth in the downpour.

Donegal is surely the most enchanting place in Ireland. Connemara is tribal and epic; Donegal is softer. If anything lies buried beneath the stony acres of Connemara it would be a battle-axe lost in some old fight; but in Donegal you might expect to unearth a crock of gold.

It is worth while to endure an Atlantic storm in these hills for the sake of that moment towards evening when it blows itself out and the rain no longer falls. The clouds thin, the blue 'Dutchman's waistcoat' shows in the watery greyness and an unearthly beauty falls over the land. The countryside is suddenly transfigured. There is a stack of turf in a field. A moment ago it was merely a damp pyramid of peat standing on the edge of a seam. Now with this sudden magic light upon it a queer new value comes to it: it stands out importantly and holds the attention.

H. V. MORTON, *In Search of Ireland*, 1931

Rain Raineth

THERE are diamonds hung on the spray,
And sea-fog blown from the bay,
　　The world's as wet as a river,
　　O thrush, sing now, or sing never,
　　　Spring seems far away.

Sing out, O blackbird, my king,
My heart is sick for the Spring,
　　And O, the drenching grey weather
　　With April half through her tether,
　　　And May on the wing!

For I think when the hawthorn blows,
And the lily's in bud, and the rose,
　　Perhaps one would scarcely remember
　　To grieve for a day of November;
　　　——But nobody knows!

KATHARINE TYNAN, *Ballads and Lyrics*, 1891

In the beginning was the Irish rain and, marshalled by a pious woman described as a 'mother's help', I pressed my nose against the streaming nursery window for a glimpse of the funeral procession on its way to the cemetery the other side of the hawthorn hedge. Our life was bounded by this hedge; a granite obelisk would look over it here, and there across the field of corncrakes could be seen a Norman castle, and trains would pass as if to the ends of Ireland (in fact ten miles to Belfast or twelve to Larne), but, by and narrow, our damp cramped acre was our world. The human elements of this world need not be detailed: guilt, hell fire, Good Friday, the doctor's cough, hurried lamps in the night, melancholia, mongolism, violent sectarian voices. All this sadness and conflict and attrition and frustration were set in this one acre near the smoky town within sound not only of the tolling bell, but of the smithy that seemed to defy it. The soil in the kitchen garden was black and littered with flints, but in easy digging distance beneath it lay a stratum of thick red clay sticky as plasticine. At times everything outside seemed clammy and everything inside stuffy (I am not denying the moments of glory—of apple blossom, dew, haymaking, or those April showers which in Ireland persist for twelve months), so that from a very early age I began to long for something different, to construct various dream worlds which I took it were on the map.

LOUIS MACNEICE, *The Strings are False*, 1965

Pullough Bog, Offaly. The dreariest strip of country I have encountered for a long time. Rain falls, and the dejected-looking bog stretches as far as the eye can see. According to rumour, this is a contentious and litigious parish, and after visiting it on a wet, windy day in April I don't wonder. What it must be like in January it is terrible to imagine—nothing but floods, marsh grass, and starved-looking trees. The Grand Canal from Dublin to the West passes through here; its high-peaked bridges are the only things that stand out from the monotony of the landscape. We visit the local store, a concrete building standing amongst a collection of cottages alongside a wharf where the barges take on and discharge their cargoes of turf and coal, and are received by the storekeeper, a handsome young man in shirt-sleeves and wearing no collar. His dark smouldering eyes dream dreams and see visions—not particularly pleasing visions judging by their melancholy expression. Could he get together a cargo of turf for the next barge? He might now, but then you know what people are; the last time they put fozy turf at the bottom of the bags and the half of it was returned on them, with official complaints from Dublin, and so on and so forth. The young man squares his narrow shoulders, as if facing a dreary, rainy, difficult world; the rain drums on the galvanised-iron roof; the concrete interior of the store sweats damp. Why concrete, except perhaps that it is easier and that it is not really worth while taking trouble to build with brick or stone in a world where everything will be taken away from you in the latter end. So say the dark melancholy eyes of the storekeeper. He is perfectly polite; in fact he is charming; but the dreariness of the bog that stretches for miles beyond his store windows seems to have got into his bones.

DENIS IRELAND, *From The Irish Shore*, 1936

Johnny slid off the seat on to his feet, bent his head and clasped his hands together, while the Reverend Mr Hunter closed the morning's work with the blessing of God the Father, God the Son, and God the Holy Ghost, evermore, world without end, amen. Then he came over to Johnny's class and sent a smile soaring around.

—Would you mind bringing little Casside to church, he said to Miss Valentine, for fear he'd meet with any accident on his way there?

—Oh no, I don't mind in the very least, responded Miss Valentine, not in the very least, for he's a dear little boy, sir, and a dimple twinkled in her cheek.

—Hurry along as quick as you can, said Hunter, for it's pouring out of the heavens, and off he went, leaving the sign of a good growl on Miss Valentine's kisser.

—Pouring outa the heavens, she muttered, and I'm left to pull this half-blind kidger after my heels. Look here, she said, gripping Johnny's arm, you'll have to step it out, or I'll be soaked through before we get half-way there, and I've no intention to be laid up on your beautiful account.

She buttoned her ulster tightly round her body, as she looked sourly out at the rain that was pelting down heavens hard, filling Johnny with fright as he thought how wet he'd be before he reached the shelter of the church-porch in Mary Street. Miss Valentine opened her umbrella with a hasty snap, caught the boy's hand in hers, and hurried him out, saying, C'm along, now, and no nonsense.

He was pulled along at a half-gallop, his spine jolting whenever he stepped from pavement to street or from street to pavement, for he couldn't see when he came to the edge of a path, and sometimes nearly fell on his face when he struck his toe against a kerb, usually followed by an angry comment from Miss Valentine to keep, at least, his good eye open, and not pull her down flat on the mucky pavement.

—The ends of my skirt'll be ruined, she grumbled, for I can't hold it up, keep my umbrella straight, and attend to you all at the same time. It's a positive shame that your mother insists on sending you to school and church, and your eyes the way they are!

The wind blew against their backs as they scuttled along, and Johnny, hot and panting with the haste, felt cool trickles of water running down his legs where the beating rain had entered through the arse of his trousers.

They ran in by the gate, trotted over a narrow concrete path between grass beds, dived into the porch where members of the congregation were taking off wet coats, gabardine ulsters, and folding up streaming umbrellas, till the floor of the poor porch was a pool and the mat at the entrance to the nave a sodden mass of fibre; while the sexton in the middle of the porch was pulling a long rope, sinking his body when he pulled and rising when he let the rope go slack, shaking the bell in the belfry into a monotonous ding-dong ding-dong ding-ding-ding-dong, as the men, women, and children passed from the dim porch into the dimmer body of the church.

—Give your feet a good wipe on the mat, warned Miss Valentine, so that you won't soil the carpet in the aisle, as she went off to her place in the choir, to help in singing loud praises to God.

SEAN O'CASEY, *I Knock at the Door*, 1939

The rain still fell heavily, driving down between the gleaming, chimney-shadowed rooftops, but the darkness in the air was beginning to lift, as a white, glowing patch spread slowly in the sky above the Asylum trees. For a while everything was silent, except for the whisper of the rain and a faint, almost inaudible humming from the now empty Mill. Then, down towards the bottom of the Row, a door opened and three young girls, standing on chairs, leaned out over the half-door. Their young, happy voices, jigged sharply through the street, through the warm, grey, evening air:—

> 'Rain, rain go to Spain; never show your face again.
> Rain, rain go to Spain; never show your face again.
> Rain, rain go to Spain; never show your face again.
> Rain, rain go to Spain; never show your face again. . . .'

JOHN O'CONNOR, *Come Day—Go Day*, 1948

Rain

(Donegal)

All day long
The gray rain beating,
On the bare hills
Where the scant grass cannot cover,
The gray rocks peeping
Through the salt herbage.
All day long
The young lambs bleating
Stand for covering
Where the scant grass is
Under the gray wall,
Or seeking softer shelter
Under tattered fleeces
Nuzzle the warm udders.
All day long
The little waves leaping
Round the gray rocks
By the brown tide borders,

Round the black headlands
Streaming with rain.

SEUMAS O'SULLIVAN, The Twilight People, 1905

Very heavy or very long continued rain is not common in Ulster. The rain is usually rather light and intermittent. There are very few days in the year when one cannot go out for a dry walk; but there are also a lot of days when there are light showers or drizzle. There are many days, also, when it is very damp but there is no rain; when there is great condensation on painted or plastic surfaces, on concrete, glass and metal. Drought is not as common or as severe in Ulster as it can be in southern England or even in the area just north of Dublin.

HUGH SHEARMAN, Ulster, 1949

A Soft Day

A SOFT day, thank God!
A wind from the south
With a honeyed mouth;
A scent of drenching leaves,
Briar and beech and lime,
White elder-flower and thyme
And the soaking grass smells sweet,
Crushed by my two bare feet,
While the rain drips,
Drips, drips, drips from the eaves.

WINIFRED M. LETTS, Songs from Leinster, 1913

It was about the middle of winter. The day was gloomy and tempestuous almost beyond any other I remember: dark clouds rolled over the hills about me, and a close sleet-like rain fell in slanting drifts that chased each other rapidly towards the earth on the course of the blast. The outlying cattle sought the closest and calmest corners of the fields for shelter; the trees and young groves were tossed about, for the wind was so unusually high that it swept in hollow gusts through them, with that hoarse murmur which deepens so powerfully on the mind the sense of dreariness and desolation.

WILLIAM CARLETON, 'Wildgoose Lodge', in Traits and Stories of the Irish Peasantry, 1844

My mental pictures of wild Connacht weather would furnish a municipal gallery, each of them hugely framed in gilt and called something like 'Tempest in Mayo'. The storm the other night would have suited Turner to a T: in the fierce headlights of a friend's minibus, it swarmed about us in flourishes of silver, in washes of ochre and umber. Only a minibus, driven with knowledge of every twist and turn of the road in all conceivable conditions (in other words, the school bus) could have brought us home at all. The road seethed with water. It poured from every gap in the ditch, spilled from every hill stream, hummocked out of boreens. Below our own gable, The Hollow echoed to the crash and grind of boulders, the hollow *thock!* so like the collisions of rams. A quick swing of the flashlamp in the run from the gate to the front door lit a dizzying rush of water just inches below the new footbridge.

MICHAEL VINEY, *A Year's Turning*, 1996

Irish rain of the summer and autumn is a kind of damp poem. It is humid fragrance, and it has a way of stealing into your life which disarms anger. It is a soft, apologetic, modest kind of rain, as a rule; and even in its wildest moods, it gives you the impression that it is treating you as well as it can under the circumstances. It does not come heralded by dust and thunder and accompanied by lightning, and roaring tempests, like the rain of the tropics. Nor does it wet you to the bones in five minutes. You scarcely know when it begins. It grows on you by degrees. It comes on the scene veiled in soft shadows and hazes, and maybe a silver mist. You think the day is beginning to look like rain, and you are not wrong. But you also think that it may clear off; no doubt, it often thinks so itself. Nevertheless, it finally decides not to clear off. The shadows deepen. The hazes thicken. And was that a drop you felt? It was—just a drop. Another comes presently, and you feel it on your cheek. Then a few more come. Then the rest of the family encircle you shyly. They are not cold or heavy or splashy. They fall on you as if they were coming from the eyes of many angels weeping for your sins. They caress you rather than pelt you, and they are laden with perfume from the meadow flowers, or the glistening trees, or the sweet, rich earth, or the heathery bogland. But they soak you all the same. In due course you are wet to the skin. They fold you in, do those spells of Irish rain, and make of you a limp, sodden, unsightly thing in their soft embraces. They soak the road and make it slippy, and your bicycle wobbles now and then; and you have to ride it through the mud by the ditch, where the blades of grass and pebbles and leafdrifts give a grip to the tyres.

At first, perhaps, you dread the rain. You regard it as a calamity. The mud on the road is too much for your tyres, and your limited experience, and you have some unpleasant falls. You are spilled into the ditch or over the handle bars, or thrown on your back a helpless case. You would exchange places with the dirtiest tramp you have ever met on a fair day, or with the most extensively married tinker that you have ever met concentrating on Abbeyshrule. But after two or three months you become weather-proof. You get used to the softness of the weather. You acquire such skill in 'riding for a fall', that even if you do come down it is only on your feet.

WILLIAM BULFIN, *Rambles in Eirinn*, 1907

Outside, in the cobbled yard, hens tacked cautiously around his feet. He looked at the crossroads and there, blurring its outlines, was a rainbow's end. The rainbow arched up and away from this place to disappear behind a brow of mountain. Raindrops spat warnings. Hens stalked to cover. Rain came, wetting to a thick flow. As Kinsella retreated into the shelter of the pub doorway, thunder banged above him. Thunderclouds, massing over the far mountain, advanced to take possession of the sky.

BRIAN MOORE, *Catholics*, 1972

The Lost Heifer

When the black herds of the rain were grazing
In the gap of the pure cold wind
And the watery haze of the hazel
Brought her into my mind,
I thought of the last honey by the water
That no hive can find.

Brightness was drenching through the branches
When she wandered again,
Turning the silver out of dark grasses
Where the skylark had lain,
And her voice coming softly over the meadow
Was the mist becoming rain.

AUSTIN CLARKE, *The Cattledrive in Connaught*, 1925

On that first evening, and it seemed to him as if it were always so, a frozen canopy of cloud hung over the plain. Far away, beyond the Shannon, its shaggy edges drooped down in a smoke of rain over the land, and there only could one see any movement in the banked mass, although the wind whistled in the alders that grew out of the walls along the muddy roads. That thawing cloud would gradually sweep all across the coloured plain, depositing its vapour in the already sodden fields and the browned thatch of the cabins, until after a slow journey of fifty miles its pall blackened into a downpour on the Kerry mountains. Until then there was nothing tall enough to scrape even the lowest cloud, and no shelter for the traveller if it burst too soon.

SEAN O'FAOLAIN, A Nest of Simple Folk, 1934

The Irish roof has been the perennial arch-enemy of those who have lived under it. The roof has always had an almost mystical importance in Ireland because of the incessant rain. Throughout the ages a quite inordinate amount of unsuccessful Irish time and energy has been spent trying to do something about the roof. More and more roof specialists have been called in to take a look at it. They potter about among the chimneys for many weeks and almost invariably put their foot through its comparatively sound patches before they declare it hopeless.

Describing Dunmartin Hall in my grandmother's time, Tommy Redcliffe sounded appalled by the way it seemed to have been so generally and passively accepted that the roof was incurable and could only be kept at bay by pieces of dangling string which helped direct the massive flow of uncountable leaks to the various pots and pans and jam jars in which it suited my family that they should land. Then, just as a ship is bailed out, all these motley receptacles were emptied daily before they started to overflow.

Tommy Redcliffe was an orderly and practical Englishman, and the discouraging sight of all those soggy strings hanging down from the lofty, peeling ceilings of winding state-rooms had made an indelible impression on him.

CAROLINE BLACKWOOD, Great Granny Webster, 1977

As far as the weather in itself was concerned, things were becoming worse. It seemed to us that the rainfall was becoming more offensive with each succeeding year and an occasional pauper was drowned on the very mainland from the volume of water and celestial emesis which poured down upon us; a non-swimmer was none too secure in bed in these times. Great rivers flowed by the doorway and, if it be true that the potatoes were all swept from our fields, it is also a fact that fish were often available by the wayside as a nocturnal exchange. Those who reached their beds safely on dry land, by the morning found themselves submerged. At night people often perceived canoes from the Blaskets going by and the boatmen considered it a poor night's fishing which did not yield to them a pig or a piglet from

Corkadoragha in their nets. It has been said that O'Sanassa swam over from the Rock one night to gaze again at his native countryside; but who knows whether the visitor was but a common seal. It need hardly be said that the local people became peevish at that time; hunger and misfortune assailed them and they were not dry for three months. Many of them set out for eternity gladly and those who remained in Corkadoragha lived on little goods and great littleness there. One day I put the matter to the Old-Fellow and I entered into conversation with him.

—Do you think, oh gentle person, said I, that we'll ever again be dry?

—I really don't know, oh mild one, said he, but if this rain goes on like this, 'tis my idea that the fingers and toes of the Gaelic paupers will be closed and have webs on them like the ducks from now on to give them a chance of moving through the water. This is no life for a human being, son!

—Are you certain that the Gaels are people? said I.

—They've that reputation anyway, little noble, said he, but no confirmation of it has ever been received. We're not horses nor hens; seals nor ghosts; and, in spite of all that, it's unbelievable that we're humans—but all that is only an opinion.

—Do you think, oh sublime ancient, said I, that there will ever be good conditions for the Gaels or will we have nothing for ever but hardship, famine, nocturnal rain and Sea-cattishness?

—We'll have it all, said he, and day-rain with it.

> Flann O'Brien, *An Beal Bocht* (*The Poor Mouth*), 1941, trans. Patrick C. Power, 1973

A gentleman in dish-hat whom I had seen first in Mallow (Lawless, Lord Cloncurry's son as I learned afterwards) came now up beside me: civil English dialect, 'had got *spoiled* potatoes to dinner yesterday at Mallow'. Nothing memorable more. A fierce rain, where we changed horses, when he got up; wretched people cowering about to look at us, or beg, nevertheless: and this ended our rain for that evening.

> Thomas Carlyle, *Reminiscences of My Irish Journey*, 1849

AD 1767—in the beginning of the month of May—I mention it because, as I said, I write from memoranda, an awfully dark night came down on Chapelizod and all the country round.

I believe there was no moon, and the stars had been quite put out under the 'wet blanket of the night', which impenetrable muffler overspread the sky with a funereal darkness.

There was a little of that sheet-lightning early in the evening, which be-tokens sultry weather. The clouds, column after column, came up sullenly over the Dublin mountains, rolling themselves from one horizon to the other into one black dome of vapour, their slow but steady motion contrasting with the awful stillness of the air. There was a weight in the atmosphere, and a sort of undefined menace brooding over the little town, as if unseen crime or danger—some mystery of iniquity—was stealing into the heart of it, and the disapproving heavens scowled a melancholy warning. . . .

It was, indeed, a remarkably dark night—a rush and down-pour of rain! The doctor stood just under the porch of the stout brick house—of King William's date, which was then the residence of the worthy rector of Chapel-izod—with his great surtout and cape on—his leggings buttoned up—and his capacious leather 'overalls' pulled up and strapped over these—and his broad-leafed hat tied down over his wig and ears with a mighty silk kerchief. I dare say he looked absurd enough—but it was the women's doing—who always, upon emergencies, took the doctor's wardrobe in hands. Old Sally, with her kind, mild, grave face, and gray locks, stood modestly behind in the hall; and pretty Lilias, his only child, gave him her parting kiss, and her last grand charge about his shoes and other exterior toggery, in the porch; and he patted her cheek with a little fond laugh, taking old John Tracy's, the butler's, arm. John carried a handsome horn-lantern, which flashed now on a roadside bush—now on the discoloured battlements of the bridge—and now on a streaming window. They stept out—there were no umbrellas in those days—splashing among the wide and widening pools; while Sally and Lilias stood in the porch, holding candles for full five minutes after the doctor and his 'Jack-o'-the-lantern', as he called honest John, whose arm and candle always befriended him in his night excursions, had got round the corner.

J. Sheridan Le Fanu, *The House By the Churchyard*, 1863

Now it began to rain again upon the earth beneath and greatly incommoded Christmas traffic of every kind by continuing to do so without remission for a matter of thirty-six hours. A divine creature, native of Leipzig, to whom Belacqua, round about the following Epiphany, had occasion to quote the rainfall for December as cooked in the Dublin University Fellows' Garden ejaculated:

'himmisacrakrüzidirkenjesusmariaundjosefundblutigeskreuz!'

Like that, all in one word. The things people come out with sometimes!

But the wind had dropped, as it so often does in Dublin when all the respectable men and women whom it delights to annoy have gone to bed, and the rain fell in a uniform untroubled manner. It fell upon the bay, the littoral, the mountains and the plains, and notably upon the Central Bog it fell with a rather desolate uniformity.

SAMUEL BECKETT, 'A Wet Night', in *More Pricks Than Kicks*, 1934

That great bogland behind Urrisbeg recalls a quaint scene on a very wet day in August, 1935. A number of botanists had foregathered at Roundstone, and the particular occasion was a kind of symposium on bogs, held in the middle of one of the wettest of them. There were A. G. Tansley from Oxford, H. E. Godwin from Cambridge, Hugo Osvald from Stockholm, Knud Jessen and H. Jonassen from Copenhagen, G. F. Mitchell from Dublin, Margaret Dunlop from Manchester. We stood in a ring in that shelterless expanse while discussion raged on the application of the terms soligenous, topogenous and ombrogenous; the rain and wind, like the discussion, waxed in intensity, and under the unusual super-incumbent weight, whether of mere flesh and bone or of intellect, the floating surface of the bog slowly sank till we were all halfway up to our knees in brown water. The only pause in the flow of argument was when Jessen or Osvald, in an endeavour to solve the question of the origin of the peat, would chew some of the mud brought up by the boring tool from the bottom of the bog, to test the presence or absence of gritty material in the vegetable mass. But out of such occasions does knowledge come, and I think that that aqueous discussion has borne and will bear fruit. For the bogs and what they can teach us of the past history of our country are yet to a great extent a sealed book, though they will not remain so much longer.

ROBERT LLOYD PRAEGER, *The Way That I Went*, 1937

It had been raining steadily in Galway when I had left it, and rain was descending with grim determination when I returned. However, after waiting a day or two I took to the roads again. Sometimes cycling, sometimes travelling by bus with the bike on the roof, I at last came to Sligo. There the rain really came down. After three days in the hotel, listening to arguments between a combative American priest and a retired British major, I went to the station and bought a ticket for Dublin. On the train I got talking with a young farmer, a man about my own age, who had spent all spring and half the summer trying to keep his ditches open while the rain relentlessly flattened his crops in the fields. He was going up to Dublin to see some movies. At Mullingar, as we stared out at the grey rain-soaked square beyond the station, a wide square in which the only sign of life was a grey rain-soaked dog, the farmer sighed and said, 'Ah, well, as the Turks say, "Fatima, it is fate"'.

JOHN V. KELLEHER, 'With Dick in Dublin 1946', in *Omnium Gatherum: Essays for Richard Ellman*, 1989

'In California,' said the young woman, 'it's so warm, there's so much sunshine. Ireland seems quite strange to me. I've been gone fifteen years; I always count in dollars, I can't get used to pounds, shillings, and pence any more, and you know, Father, Ireland has got sadder.'

'It's the rain,' said the priest with a sigh.

'Of course, I've never been this way before,' said the woman, 'but in other places, years ago, before I went away; from Athlone to Galway—I've done that bit often, but it seems to me that fewer people are living there than before. It's so quiet, it makes my heart stand still. I'm afraid.'

The priest said nothing and sighed.

'I'm afraid,' said the woman in a low voice. 'From Ballymote I have to go another twenty miles, by bus, then on foot, across the bog—I'm afraid of the water. Rain and lakes, rivers and streams and more lakes—you know, Father, Ireland seems to me to be full of holes. The washing on these hedges will never dry, the hay will float away—aren't you afraid too, Father?'

'It's just the rain,' said the priest, 'don't let it worry you. I know that feeling. Sometimes I'm afraid too. For two years I had a small parish, between Crossmolina and Newport, and it often used to rain for weeks, the storm would blow—nothing but the high mountains, dark green and black—do you know Nephin Beg?'

'No, I don't.'

'It was not far from there. Rain, water, bog—and when someone took me to Newport or Foxford, always water—past lakes or past the sea.'

The little girl closed the breviary, jumped up on the seat, put her arms round her mother's neck, and whispered: 'Are we going to drown, really?'

'No, no,' said her mother, but she did not seem very convinced herself; outside the rain splashed against the panes, the train plodded wearily into the darkness, crawling as if through clouds of water.

HEINRICH BÖLL, *Irish Journal*, 1957, trans. Leila Vennewitz

It is certainly a matter for regret that the climate of these northern regions makes it so uncomfortable to get wet and so difficult to get dry. The clothes which the prevailing temperature compels us to wear are even in summer of a thickness which renders them capable of absorbing a vast amount of water, and the air is of a humidity which slows up evaporation, and so keeps them wet. Not but that I think Ireland has a worse reputation as regards weather than she deserves. Rain is frequent, especially in the west, but seldom lasts long. A whole wet day is rare. A wet morning mostly means a fine afternoon, and if the early morning has been very bright the reverse is often true. But even in Kerry I have several times had botanical work interfered with by drought: and when that moist greenhouse-like atmosphere remains dry for a spell, it is mere disaster to all the mosses and liverworts and Filmy Ferns which by their abundance and luxuriance lend so special a charm to the south-west. The whole west coast indeed is a country redolent of wind and rain, with an atmosphere that recalls blue eyes with tears in them: the only conditions under which it can look simply unattractive is in dry weather, with an east wind and that peculiar dispiriting grey haze that mostly accompanies it. Better than that, honest rain sweeping in from the Atlantic, and the sea shouting on the rocks.

Robert Lloyd Praeger, *The Way That I Went*, 1937

It's raining in Eyre Square as if it would rain there forever. In the old days the gypsies fought. In O'Flaherty's B & B, where the Aranmen stay, the beds are hard as penance. The pickpockets too have gone home. Glistening blackly two powerful cannons point at the ivy frontage of the Galway branch of the Bank of Ireland, the handsomest in the land.

'Oh dear God, it's spillen out of the heavens!'
'See you next year.'
'Be good now.'

Aidan Higgins, *Ronda Gorge and Other Precipices*, 1982

Rain

Among those bushy spaces
The grey rain drowns the wind,
Flowing from airy places,
Flowing from hills behind
Her threshold, hushed in grasses;
And now her window-pane
Is aged in brambles casing
The half-light of the rain.
As she has left those grasses,
Then why should I look on
An evening gloss of waters
Without the cloud-blown swan,
Knowing in airy places
The grey rain cannot blur
Those shining airs—the graces
Remembered of her.

F. R. Higgins, *The Dark Breed*, 1927

Coming home from school Colm saw, day after day, youths painting on the gables: NO PARTITION—WE WANT OUR COUNTRY. There were to be elections soon, but Colm took no interest in them except to hear Alec talking at tea-time: 'If Ireland is partitioned now it will take a long time before she's made one again. And when unity does come I heard a man say that it would take a hundred years before these people here'd fit into a National life. They hate the real Ireland! And 'tis a pity for they're hard workers and good fighters.'

After the tea Colm would go up to the pigeon-shed to do his home-work. He would stand as usual at the little window looking at the mountain, seeing long scaffolding of rain falling in front of it, dropping like smoke over the fields, and men racing for shelter to the brickyard. He would hear the shouts of women calling in their children and the children giving joyful screams as they raced home. A woman would pluck the clothes off the line at the approach of the shower; hens with trailing wings would race madly from the waste ground; a goat would run round and round on its tether, me-e-e-e-e-eh loudly, and then stand hunched with its back to the mountain and the on-coming rain.

Soon the rain would reach the street, pelt harshly on the slates, and swish against the pigeon-shed. As Colm listened to it his mind would race to his Uncle Robert, remembering how he used to draw great delight and comfort from the lonely sound of rain. Quickly the shower would pass, leaving the clay in the brickyard pit a dark brown: the goat would shake its ears and the blue-shining slates reflect the chimneys.

Colm would get to his work before the dusk would sweep the light from the shed.

MICHAEL MCLAVERTY, *Call My Brother Back*, 1939

Loud, sudden, the rain came down. Loud because it was the only sound. The sky darkened. The rain beat on the slates, wept against the windows, made the ragged hedgerows in the deserted front garden writhe and twist. He felt alone: never so alone as now. Turning from the rain, he went back into the corridor and climbed up the stairs. In the largest bedroom the little heart-shaped lamp burned like a wound. Awkwardly, he put sheets and blankets on the double bed then, stripping off his clothes, lay down on an old, lumpy mat-tress hollowed from the bodies of other sleepers. The rain beat on the roof but he no longer heard it.

BRIAN MOORE, *The Mangan Inheritance*, 1979

Rain in May

O rain in May, and I recall
You and May and the evenfall;

And every garden drenched and sweet,
And the laburnum drowned in it;
The patter of rain is musical.

You and I in the wet May weather,
You and I and the Spring together.
And in the long suburban road
No other creature walked abroad.
Wildly sweet is the wet May weather.

KATHARINE TYNAN, *Ballads and Lyrics*, 1891

In 1915, near Ventry, in West Kerry, I found a windowless, one-roomed cabin which could be described in lines taken from Brian Merriman's poem, *Cúirt an Mheadhon Oidhche (The Midnight Court)*, written in 1780:

Bothán gan áit chun suidhe ann,	A cabin with no place to sit down,
Ach súgh sileáin is fáscadh aníos ann,	But dripping soot from above and oozings from below,
Fiadhaile ag teacht go fras gan choímse	No end of weeds growing riotously,
Is rian na gcearc air treasna scríobtha,	And the scrapings of hens across it,
Lag ina dhrom 's na gabhla ag lúbadh	Its roof-tree sagging, its couples bending
Is clagarnach dhonn go trom ag túirlint.	And brown rain falling heavily.

Brown rain, because it had come through the soot-impregnated thatch.

These cabins were thrown up anyhow and almost in any place. In the time of the Land League, when evictions were frequent, exactly the same kind of huts were often thrown up in a few hours in the shelter of a ditch, to house the suddenly dispossessed family: though not meant for permanent abodes, some of them were still being lived in forty years after—which should teach us how slowly a landscape wins back to comeliness after a period of disturbance, and enable us further to realise something of the slatternliness of that period in which there had been not even the beginning of recovery.

The cabins of the eighteenth century were sometimes built of stone, mortared or unmortared, but far more frequently of sods and mud. They were thatched with bracken, furze, fern or heath; and must have been often indistinguishable from the bogland, perhaps with advantage. Usually there was but one room, sometimes divided by a rough partition; and often a sort of unlighted loft lay beneath the roof. Chimney there was none, but a hole in the roof allowed portion of the smoke to emerge when the interior had become filled with it. The smoke was often seen to rise up like a cloud from almost every inch of the roof, percolating through as the thatch grew old and thin. The soot that in time came to encrust the walls and thatch within was occasionally scraped off and used as manure.

Between the absence of windows and the ever-present clouds of smoke, the people dwelt in darkness: it did not make for health, nor for quick convalescence when sickness broke out; quite commonly it led to blindness; though one must not forget to add the many prevalent fevers and plagues if one would understand why in any list of the poets of these days one comes so frequently on the word 'Dall' (blind)—Tadhg Dall Ua h-Uigín, Liam Dall Ua h-Ifearnáin, Seumas Dall Ua Cuarta, Donnchadh Dall Ua Laoghaire; Carolan might also have been called 'Dall', while Donnchadh Ruadh Mac Conmara (MacNamara) became blind in his old age. Blind poets, blind fiddlers, blind beggars of all kinds were to be seen tapping their way on every road in the country, from fair to fair, from house to house.

DANIEL CORKERY, *The Hidden Ireland*, 1925

The Thick and Bloody Fight

And in the thick and bloody fight
Let not your courage lag . . .

J. K. O'REILLY, 'Wrap the
Green Flag Round Me, Boys'

Hapless Nation! hapless Land!
Heap of uncementing sand!
Crumbled by a foreign weight:
And by worse, domestic hate.

WILLIAM DRENNAN,
'The Wake of William Orr'

———

Farewell to Patrick Sarsfield

Farewell Patrick Sarsfield wherever you may roam,
You crossed the sea to France and left empty camps at home,
To plead our cause before many a foreign throne
Though you left ourselves and poor Ireland overthrown.

Good luck Patrick Sarsfield you were sent to us by God,
And holy forever is the earth that you trod;
May the sun and the white moon light your way,
You trounced King Billy and won the day.

With you Patrick Sarsfield goes the prayer of everyone,
My own prayer too, and the prayer of Mary's Son,
You rode through Birr, the Narrow Ford you passed,
You beat them at Cullen and took Limerick at last.

I'll climb the mountain a lonely man,
And I'll go east again if I can,
'Twas there I saw the Irish ready for the fight,
The lousy crowd that wouldn't unite!

Who's that I see now yonder on Howth Head?
'One of Jamie's soldiers sir, now the king has fled,
Last year with gun and knapsack I marched with joyous tread,
But this year sir I'm begging my bread.'

And God when I think how Diarmuid went under,
His standard broken and his limbs pulled asunder,
And God Himself couldn't fight a way through
When they chopped off his head and held it in our view.

The corn tumbled soon as the scythes went through,
The twelve Kilkenny men were the first that they slew,
My two brothers died and I held my breath,
But the death that broke me was Diarmuid's death.

At the Boyne bridge we took our first beating,
From the bridge at Slane we were soon retreating,
And then we were beaten at Aughrim too—
Ah, fragrant Ireland, that was goodbye to you.

The fumes were choking as the house went alight,
And Black Billy's heroes were warming to the fight,
And every shell that came, wherever it lit,
Colonel Mitchell asked was Lord Lucan hit.

So goodbye Limerick and your homes so fair,
And all the good friends that quartered with us there,
And the cards we played by the watchfires' glare
And the priests that called us all night to prayer.

But on you Londonderry may misfortune come
Like the smoke that lit with every bursting gun
For all the fine soldiers you gathered together
By your walls without shelter from wind or weather.

Many and many a good lad, all proud and gay,
Seven weeks ago they were passing this way,
With guns and swords and pikes on show,
And now in Aughrim they're lying low.

Aughrim has manure that's neither lime nor sand
But sturdy young soldiers to nourish the land,
The men we left behind on the battlefield that day
Torn like horsemeat by the dogs where they lay

And over the seas are Ireland's best,
The Dukes and the Burkes, Prince Charlie and the rest,

And Captain Talbot their ranks adorning,
And Patrick Sarsfield, Ireland's darling.

ANON., 'Slan le Padraic Sairseal' ('Farewell to Patrick Sarsfield'), *c*.1691,
trans. Frank O'Connor

from *The Boyne Water*

Prince Eugene's regiment was the next, on our right hand advanced,
Into a field of standing wheat, where Irish horses pranced—
But the brandy ran so in their heads, their senses all did scatter,
They little thought to leave their bones that day at the Boyne Water.

Both men and horse lay on the ground, and many there lay bleeding:
I saw no sickles there that day—but, sure, there was sharp shearing.

Now, praise God, all true Protestants, and heaven's and earth's Creator,
For the deliverance that He sent our enemies to scatter.
The Church's foes will pine away, like churlish-hearted Nabal,
For our deliverer came this day like the great Zorobabel.

So praise God, all true Protestants, and I will say no further,
But had the Papists gain'd the day there would have been open murder.
Although King James and many more were ne'er that way inclined,
It was not in their power to stop what the rabble they designed.

ANON., 17th century

Before our generation the names of those who had died for Ireland were the
dearest names of all—Sarsfield, Wolfe Tone, Lord Edward Fitzgerald, Robert
Emmet. Many a young man and woman grew up dreaming of dying for
Ireland and leaving behind a name immortal in the country's memory. Dying
for freedom, suffering for freedom, was the great road to fame and renown,
the sure way of having one's name remembered forever. But in our day, under
the new leadership, young people began to think that living for the country
and doing something for it might be as good as dying for it. The hero of one
of the old sagas, Cuchulainn, had uttered that sentence, 'I care not if my life
have but the span of a night and a day if my deeds be spoken of by the men
of Eirinn,' and many of my fellow students, not only the young men but the
girls, wrote the sentence in their notebooks or beneath their names in the old
Irish texts that everybody was beginning to read, most of us, to be sure, in
Lady Gregory's or Standish O'Grady's English versions. Some of my fellow
students, however, were good Gaelic scholars and could read the original texts
or a modernized version of the original texts.

MARY COLUM, *Life and the Dream*, 1928

Meantime the belief grows that the Volunteers may be able to hold out much longer than had been imagined. The idea at first among the people had been that the insurrection would be ended the morning after it had began. But to-day, the insurrection having lasted three days, people are ready to conceive that it may last for ever. There is almost a feeling of gratitude towards the Volunteers because they are holding out for a little while, for had they been beaten the first or second day the City would have been humiliated to the soul.

People say: 'Of course, they will be beaten.' The statement is almost a query, and they continue, 'but they are putting up a decent fight.' For being beaten does not greatly matter in Ireland, but not fighting does matter. 'They went forth always to the battle; and they always fell.' Indeed, the history of the Irish race is in that phrase.

James Stephens, The Insurrection in Dublin, 1916

The Women at Their Doors

The babes were asleep in their cradles,
And the day's drudge was done,
And the women brought their suppers out
To eat them in the sun.

'To-night I will set my needles, Áine,
And Eoghan will have stockings to wear:
I spun the wool of the horny ewe
He bought at the Hiring Fair . . .

'But what is the sound I hear, Nabla?—
It is like the cheering of men.
God keep our kind from the Devil's snare!'
And the women answered, 'Amen!'

Then the moon rose over the valley,
And the cheering died away,
And the women went within their doors
At the heel of the summer day.

And no men came in at midnight,
And no men came in at the dawn,
And the women keened by their ashy fires
Till their faces were haggard and wan.

For they knew they had gone to the trysting,
With pike and musketoon,
To fight for their hearths and altars
At the rising of the moon!

Joseph Campbell, The Rushlight, 1906

A short time after the recapture of Wexford, I traversed that county, to see the ruins which had been occasioned by warfare. Enniscorthy had been twice stormed, and was dilapidated and nearly burned. New Ross showed most melancholy relics of the obstinate and bloody battle of full ten hours' duration, which had been fought in every street of it. The numerous pits crammed with dead bodies, on Vinegar Hill, seemed on some spots actually elastic as we stood upon them; whilst the walls of an old windmill on its summit appeared stained and splashed with the blood and brains of the many victims who had been piked or shot against it by the rebels. The court-house of Enniscorthy, wherein our troops had burned alive above eighty of the wounded rebels; and the barn of Scullabogue, where the rebels had retaliated by burning alive above 120 Protestants—were terrific ruins! The town of Gorey was utterly destroyed,—not a house being left perfect; and the bodies of the killed were lying half-covered in sundry ditches in its vicinity.

SIR JONAH BARRINGTON, *Personal Sketches of His Own Time*, 1827

Requiem for the Croppies

The pockets of our greatcoats full of barley—
No kitchens on the run, no striking camp—
We moved quick and sudden in our own country.
The priest lay behind ditches with the tramp.
A people, hardly marching—on the hike—
We found new tactics happening each day:
We'd cut through reins and rider with the pike
And stampede cattle into infantry,
Then retreat through hedges where cavalry must be thrown.
Until, on Vinegar Hill, the fatal conclave.
Terraced thousands died, shaking scythes at cannon.
The hillside blushed, soaked in our broken wave.
They buried us without shroud or coffin
And in August the barley grew up out of the grave.

SEAMUS HEANEY, *Door Into the Dark*, 1969

Can we wonder that the people of Wexford should rebel against the British misrule—no wonder—no wonder that Irishmen, to-day, should remember '98! But to cap the climax of tyranny and oppression of the ascendancy party, they burnt the church belonging to Father John Murphy. This aroused the indignation of the people, which, like some volcano, was for some time collecting its fury, to break out with such violence as startled the British government and its satellites and hirelings in Dublin castle from their self-complacency. The priest, while in sight of his burning church, proclaimed to his people, that it was better to die, like men, on the battle field, than to submit longer to the slow, lingering torture and tyranny of the hireling and unholy instruments of British despotism. That it was better to die a thousand deaths than submit longer to British outrage! That they should resist even unto death, the blood-stained 'beasts'—the Jacobs, Gowans, and Whites,—some of the most outrageous magistrates of Wexford. He declared his readiness to lead them to victory or death. This speech was made upon the spot, in sight of the smouldering ruins of his church. Two thousand parrtiots sprang to his and their country's call. In a few hours the multitude of honest and industrious people were assembled on the memorable Oulart Hill, which lies about midway between the sea and the town of Enniscorthy, and eleven miles from the city of Wexford, famous in history. On the same day, they encountered the North Cork militia, commanded by Lieutenant Colonel Foote, and the Wexford yeoman cavalry. The patriots fought with that bravery of a people smarting under centuries of wrong; they routed the cavalry, which galloped back to the shire town; they cut up the North Cork militia—only the colonel, one sergeant, and three privates made good their escape. They, the North Cork militia, which was the pass-word of what was wicked and outrageous and infamous, were utterly annihilated, to be remembered in history only to be despised for deeds of wholesale cruelties! So the people had their revenge. Another priest, Father Michael Murphy, finding his church plundered, and the altar desecrated by wretches in human form, joined the patriots at Kilthomas hill, near Carnew. The glare of the bonfires lighted the whole country for miles, like so many fires from the Danish watch-towers of yore. Horns were sounded, which filled the midnight air with that solemn warning that the people, groaning for years under the tyrant's lash, had resolved to be free. Horses galloped with the awful news that war had begun—civil war, the most alarming and terrible of all wars—that neighbour was arrayed against his neighbour.

P. CUDMORE, *Ireland and Her Oppressors*, 1871

The insurrection there [in Co. Wexford] did not take place till Saturday evening, the twenty-sixth of May, and was begun by a noted character, father John Murphy of Boulavogue chapel, in the parish of Kilcormuck, an assistant curate in the catholic church, who collected his followers by lighting up fires on adjacent hills. The standard of rebellion he hoisted that evening at Boulavogue, between Gorey and Wexford, and thence the doctor, for he was a doctor of divinity, set out on his operations. Intelligence of this nocturnal assembly being communicated to lieutenant Bookey of the Camolin yeomen cavalry, he boldly set out with a part of his troop to oppose them, and meeting them, he ordered them to surrender, to which Murphy replied in defiance, 'come on you heretic dog'. In the attack the lieutenant, being unsupported by his men, was slain, with one of his associates. His house was also set on fire that night, and the houses of all the protestants in the parish. In return for which Murphy's own house, and the houses of a few other rebels were burned by the yeomanry, and some rebels put to death, whom they overtook that night in arms. The morning of the next day, being Whitsunday, the twenty-seventh of May, exhibited many houses in flames or consumed, and other dismal appearances of the work in which the rebels were employed the night before.

The house of the reverend doctor Burrowes, rector of Kilmuckridge, was attacked this morning by a party of rebels under father Murphy. For some time it was bravely defended, but the rebels having first set fire to the office-house and then to the glebe-house itself, doctor Burrowes with his defenders were unable to continue in it, and on receiving a positive promise from Murphy that they would not be injured if they surrendered, they then came out of the house, but, in violation of the promise, this clergyman, with seven of his parishioners, was murdered. Different acts of atrocity of a similar kind were committed on the same day by Murphy and his associates.

REVD SAMUEL BURDY, *History of Ireland*, 1817

The Presbyterians of northern Ireland, rose with the Catholics of the south, in the memorable Irish rebellion which took place at the end of the last century; they fought no less zealously against the English troops, and watched with no less triumph the progress of the French revolution. The republican or democratic tendencies of the northern Protestants, are quite as strong as those of the southern Catholics; yet the two parties are no friends, on the contrary, under particular circumstances, they are the bitterest enemies. O'Connell and his party are less popular in Belfast than in any other Irish town; and on all the agitation-tours and triumphal-progresses, which the great man so often makes through the cities, towns, and villages of the Emerald Isle, he takes good care never to come near Belfast. Once indeed it is said that he gladdened with the light of his countenance the few feeble partisans he possessed at Belfast; but he slunk in at night in a small unpretending car, and made haste away again, early the next morning, before the opposite faction could hear of his arrival. I heard an amusing anecdote at Belfast, how the great musician, Liszt, when he visited the city was unluckily mistaken for O'Connell, and was very near suffering in consequence. As Liszt approached in a large postchaise drawn by four horses, some of the over-zealous protestants of Belfast inquired respecting the traveller, and were told that he was some very great man, nobody exactly knew who; they immediately took it into their heads that he was O'Connell. A mob collected, stopped the carriage, cut the traces, and pulled out the astonished great man, in order to cool his supposed patriotism in true Irish fashion, by a good ducking in a neighbouring pond. Luckily, however, they discovered in time that they had got hold of a young foreign artist, instead of the bulky old agitator they were looking for.

J. G. KOHL, *Ireland*, 1843

The Man From God-Knows-Where

A County Down telling of the winter time of 1795 and the autumn of 1803

Into our townlan', on a night of snow,
Rode a man from God-knows-where;
None of us bade him stay or go,
Nor deemed him friend, nor damned him foe,
But we stabled his big roan mare:
For in our townlan' we're a decent folk,
And if he didn't speak, why none of us spoke,
And we sat till the fire burned low.

We're a civil sort in our wee place,
So we made the circle wide
Round Andy Lemon's cheerful blaze,
And wished the man his lenth o' days,
And a good end to his ride.
He smiled in under his slouchy hat—
Says he, 'There's a bit of a joke in that,
For we ride different ways.'

The whiles we smoked we watched him stare,
From his seat fornenst the glow.
I nudged Joe Moore, 'You wouldn't dare
To ask him, who he's for meetin' there,
And how far he has got to go.'
But Joe wouldn't dare, nor Wully Scott,
And he took no drink—neither cold nor hot—
This man from God-knows-where.

It was closin' time, an' late forbye,
When us ones braved the air—
I never saw worse (may I live or die)
Than the sleet that night, an' I says, says I,
'You'll find he's for stoppin' there.'
But at screek o' day, through the gable pane,
I watched him spur in the peltin' rain,
And I juked from his rovin' eye.

Two winters more, then the Trouble Year
When the best that a man could feel
Was the pike he kept in hidlin's near,
Till the blood o' hate an' the blood o' fear
Would be redder nor rust on the steel.
Us ones quet from mindin' the farms,
Let them take what we gave wi' the weight o' our arms,
From Saintfield to Kilkeel.

In the time o' the Hurry we had no lead—
We all of us fought with the rest—
An' if e'er a one shook like a tremblin' reed,
None of us gave neither hint nor heed,
Nor ever even'd we'd guessed.
We, men of the North, had a word to say,
An' we said it then in our own dour way,
An' we spoke as we thought was best.

All Ulster over, the weemen cried
For the stan'in' crops on the lan'—
Many's the sweetheart an' many's the bride
Would liefer ha' gone till where *he* died,
And ha' murned her lone by her man.
But us ones weathered the thick of it,
And we used to dander along, and sit
In Andy's side by side.

What with discoorse goin' to and fro,
The night would be wearin' thin,
Yet never so late when we rose to go
But someone would say: 'Do ye min' thon snow,
An' the man what came wanderin' in?'
And we be to fall to the talk again,
If by any chance he was *one o' them*—
The man who went like the win'.

Well 'twas gettin' on past the heat o' the year
When I rode to Newtown fair:
I sold as I could (the dealers were near—
Only three pound-eight for the Innish steer,
An' nothin' at all for the mare!)
I met M'Kee in the throng o' the street,
Says he, 'The grass has grown under our feet
Since they hanged young Warwick here.'

And he told that Boney had promised help
To a man in Dublin town.
Says he, 'If ye've laid the pike on the shelf,
Ye'd better go home hot-fut by yerself,
An' polish the old girl down.'
So by Comber road I trotted the gray,
And never cut corn until Killyeagh
Stood plain on the risin' groun'.

For a wheen o' days we sat waitin' the word
To rise and go at it like men.
But no French ships sailed into Cloughey Bay,
And we heard the black news on a harvest day
That the cause was lost again;
And Joey and me, and Wully Boy Scott,
We agreed to ourselves we'd as lief as not
Ha' been found in the thick o' the slain.

By Downpatrick gaol I was bound to fare
On a day I'll remember, feth;
For when I came to the prison square
The people were waitin' in hundreds there,
An' you wouldn't hear stir nor breath!
For the sodgers were standing, grim an' tall,
Round a scaffold built there fornent the wall,
An' a man stepped out for death!

I was brave an' near to the edge of the throng,
Yet I knowed the face again,
An' I knowed the set, an' I knowed the walk,
An' the sound of his strange up-country talk,
For he spoke out right an' plain.
Then he bowed his head to the swinging rope,
Whiles I said, 'Please God' to his dying hope,
And 'Amen' to his dying prayer,
That the Wrong would cease, and the Right prevail,
For the man that they hanged at Downpatrick jail
Was the MAN FROM GOD-KNOWS-WHERE!

NOTE. The 'man' of this ballad was Thomas Russell, who organised Co.
Down, but was in prison and unable to lead in '98. He returned in 1803
to try and rally the North simultaneously with Emmet's Dublin rising,
failed in his effort, and died on the scaffold at Downpatrick. At the
opening of the poem, where he visits the inn, in the depth of winter, '95,
we will suppose he does not make his name or mission known in mixed

company, or maybe does not suspect the possibilities underlying the dour reticence of the group of countrymen, though they afterwards gave a good account of themselves. 'Warwick', alluded to by M'Kee, was a young Presbyterian minister hanged at Newtownards as was Rev. James Porter, at Gray Abbey, some miles away.

FLORENCE M. WILSON, *The Coming of the Earls*, 1918

In Wicklow and Wexford there was no insurrection on the 23rd; but troops were not idle. They executed thirty-four men at Dunlavin in Wicklow without trial on the 24th; twenty-eight at Carnew in Wexford on the 25th. On the 26th, Father John Murphy, curate of Boolavogue, to the east of Gorey, called his people together and advised them to defend themselves, offering to lead them. By his advice they ambushed a detachment of yeoman cavalry who were scouring the country, and killed the whole party of eighteen or twenty men with pitchforks. This gave them command of Camolin Park, where the detachment was stationed, and they secured arms here. The news spread, and men flocked in thousands to the standard of successful resistance. Next day, Sunday 27th, Father Murphy marched at the head of his mob—it was as yet no more—to Oulart Hill, ten miles from Wexford and five from Enniscorthy. Here they were attacked by a mixed force of militia and cavalry, very inferior in numbers. Only five of the militia survived the charge of the pikemen; the cavalry fled. Next day the insurgents marched to Enniscorthy, and after sharp fighting captured this important town. Within three days the outbreak had developed to the proportions of a war. Wexford, held by some 1200 soldiers with artillery, fell next, the garrison evacuating it; and Bagenal Harvey, a leading Protestant landlord of liberal sympathies who had been imprisoned, was liberated, and by a strange movement was named commander-in-chief.

Three considerable engagements followed: one at Newtownbarry, where the insurgents were defeated in their purpose to occupy a frontier town which commands the main road through the mountains into Carlow; another at Gorey, in which they forced 1500 men with five pieces of artillery under General Loftus to evacuate Gorey, thus opening the road to Arklow and the Wicklow coast. The third was the attempt to capture New Ross, and it amounted to a pitched battle of twelve hours' duration. The rebels had to dislodge some 1500 soldiers with artillery from behind walled defences, and they did it after fearful carnage; the town was theirs, but General Johnson, calculating on what would happen with undisciplined men, counter-attacked from across the bridge by which he had retreated, and retrieved the day. . . .

The Wexford rebellion has constantly been represented as a war of religion, and for political purposes this aspect of it was instantly exaggerated, to disgust Protestant Ulster; the device had considerable success. But the statement is quite untrue if it means that Catholics in County Wexford made war on all who were not of their own religion. They chose a Protestant to be their leader, and many other Protestants were prominent among them. But much clearer proof is afforded by the fact that in the county there were many Quakers; none of them went away from his house, and none suffered in any way. The Catholics undoubtedly made war and inflicted reprisals on those whom they believed to be their enemies; the more ignorant of them thought that all Protestants were Orangemen, and they knew that Orangemen were their enemies. Yet there was none that did not know that a Quaker was not a Catholic.

In Wexford the governor of the place, Keogh, was a Protestant. His constant exertions to protect prisoners and maintain decent order were supported by the Catholic bishop and Catholic priests. It is true that Catholic priests led in the field; equally true that two of them showed remarkable military gifts, and that no killing of prisoners took place in the camp where Father Roche commanded.

In truth, the war was not of Catholics against Protestants, but of those who had suffered by the pitchcap and the lash against the party of those who had wielded them. Protestantism had been made the badge indicating the qualification to be in power; it was the monopolising of power and the misuse of power that produced the rebellion. In 1798 and the years leading up to it, the offences of Protestants against Catholics were much more heinous than those of Catholics against Protestants. Yet, as from 1641 so from 1798, the ascendant class remember only the savagery of the conquered when they broke loose; the savagery of the conqueror is regarded only as just retribution, whether before or after the offence.

STEPHEN GWYNN, *History of Ireland*, 1923

from *One*

Your family, Thomas, met with and helped many of the Croppies in hiding from the Yeos or on their way home after the defeat in south Wexford. They sheltered the Laceys who were later hanged on the Bridge in Ballinglen between Tinahely and Anacorra. From hearsay, as far as I can tell the Men Folk were either Stone Cutters or masons or probably both. In the 18 and late 1700s even the farmers had some other trade to make a living. They lived in Farnese among a Colony of North of Ireland or Scotch settlers left there in some of the dispersals or migrations which occurred in this Area of Wicklow and Wexford and Carlow. And some years before that time the Family came from somewhere around Tullow.

Beyond that.

*

Littered uplands. Dense grass. Rocks everywhere,
wet underneath, retaining memory of the long cold.

First, a prow of land
chosen, and webbed with tracks;
then boulders chosen
and sloped together, stabilized in menace.

I do not like this place.
I do not think the people who lived here
were ever happy. It feels evil.
Terrible things happened.
I feel afraid here when I am on my own.

THOMAS KINSELLA, *One and Other Poems*, 1979

The suppression of the '98 Rebellion was a near thing. If Wolfe Tone's plans
had not miscarried; if General Humbert's French expedition had arrived on
time; if it had not been a case of pikes, scythes, bill-hooks and rural implements against artillery; if the commanding officers had been trained soldiers
rather than priests and idealists. The insurgents were for a time successful.
They took Wexford and Enniscorthy; they gained and lost New Ross; they
attacked Arklow and the road to Dublin and possible victory lay open to
them for a brief while. General Lake, having received reinforcements after
reinforcements, defeated the rebels at last in their camp on Vinegar Hill. The
defeat was failure on a magnificent scale: Pitt had his excuse to bring in the
plan for the Union. The Dublin Parliament, a poor thing, but useful, extinguished itself. For a hundred and twenty years, Ireland was a glorified English
shire.

STEPHEN RYNNE, *All Ireland*, 1956

from *Laurence Bloomfield in Ireland*

He saw the '98, and damned alike
The yeoman's pitch-cap and the rebel's pike.

WILLIAM ALLINGHAM, *Laurence Bloomfield in Ireland*, 1864

The rebels now made several attempts to ford the river, both above and below
the bridge, but were galled by the fire of the north Cork militia, whose position at the bridge had at that time a useful effect. However, they proceeded

to parts of the river out of the reach of their fire, and succeeded in wading across it, some being up to the middle, and others to the neck in water. They then set some more houses on fire, and the brave yeomen now found it expedient, after a gallant defence of three hours, to retreat to Wexford, having lost about ninety, including three officers, in killed and wounded. Of the North Cork militia, however, only one serjeant and six privates were killed, and not an officer was hurt. The rebels, it is supposed, lost three hundred at least.

In setting out on their retreat the garrison was obliged to pass through the flames of the burning houses, as were also those who accompanied them, being the loyal inhabitants of the town, and some others who had fled thither for protection. The weather being calm, they were enabled to get through the flames with less injury; yet, certainly, they were objects of compassion, a confused multitude flying for their lives, without distinction of age, sex, or rank, almost all on foot, and leaving all their effects in the hands of their enemies. Many ladies of affluent fortune, accustomed to the ease and indulgence enjoyed by persons of that station, were obliged to escape in the manner above stated, with their children on their backs, to the town of Wexford, fourteen English miles from Enniscorthy. Some who were too feeble to walk, would have been left on the road, had not the yeomen cavalry indulged them with the use of their horses. Those who found it impossible to make their escape from the town, took a melancholy farewell of their friends, having a dismal foresight of the fate that awaited them.

The rebels, on entering the town, set fire to every house belonging to a protestant of any distinction, and massacred such as they met with either in the houses or the streets. These generally were old infirm men, and some of these, with women and children, escaped into the adjacent woods, of which the rebels being informed, sent parties in search of them. The men not immediately butchered were confined, and reserved for future massacre. Early next morning the rebels formed a camp on Vinegar-hill, a mountain quite close to the town, which was afterwards a scene of atrocious deeds.

REVD SAMUEL BURDY, *History of Ireland*, 1817

from *Sliabh na mBan*

It is my sorrow that this day's troubles
    Poor Irishmen so sore did strike,
Because our tyrants are laughing at us,
    And say they fear neither fork nor pike;
Our Major never came to lead us,
    We had no orders and drifted on
As you'd send a drover with a cow to the fair
    On the sunny side of Slievenamon.

Ross was the place we were defeated,
   There we left many a pikeman dead,
Little children burned to ashes,
   Women in holes and ditches hid.
But I promise you the men that slew them
   We'll meet them yet with pike and gun,
And we'll drive the yeomen in flight before us
   When we pay them back on Slievenamon.

The sturdy Frenchman with ships in order
   Beneath sharp masts is long at sea;
They're always saying they will come to Ireland,
   And they will set the Irish free.
Light as a blackbird on a green bough swinging
   Would be my heart if the French would come—
O the broken ranks and the trumpets ringing
   On the sunny side of Slievenamon!

Anon., 'Sliabh na mBan' c.1798, trans. Frank O'Connor

The road to Sligo. A spring morning. 1798. Going into battle. Do you remember, James? Two young gallants with pikes across their shoulders and the *Aeneid* in their pockets. Everything seemed to find definition that spring— a congruence, a miraculous matching of hope and past and present and possibility. Striding across the fresh, green land. The rhythms of perception heightened. The whole enterprise of consciousness accelerated. We were gods that morning, James; and I had recently married *my* goddess, Caitlin Dubh Nic Reactainn, may she rest in peace. And to leave her and my infant son in his cradle—that was heroic, too. By God, sir, we were magnificent. We marched as far as—where was it?—Glenties! All of twenty-three miles in one day. And it was there, in Phelan's pub, that we got homesick for Athens, just like Ulysses. The *desiderium nostrorum*—the need for our own. Our *pietas*, James, was for older, quieter things. And that was the longest twenty-three miles back I ever made.'

Brian Friel, Translations, 1981

Donegore Hill

Ephie's base bairntime, trail-pike brood,
Were arm'd as weel as tribes that stood;
Yet on the battle ilka cauf
Turn'd his backside, an' scamper'd aff.

Psalm 78, v. 9.

THE dew-draps wat the fiels o'braird,
That soon the war-horse thortur'd;
An falds were op'd by monie a herd
Wha lang ere night lay tortur'd;
Whan chiels wha grudg'd to be sae tax'd
An tyth'd by rack-rent blauth'ry,
Turn'd out *en masse*, as soon as ax'd—
An unco throuither squath'ry
                              Were we, that day.

While close-leagu'd crappies rais'd the hoards
O' pikes, pike-shafts, forks, firelocks,
Some melted lead—some saw'd deal-boards—
Some hade, like hens in byre-neuks:
Wives baket bonnocks for their men,
Wi' tears instead o' water;
An' lasses made cockades o' green
For chaps wha us'd to flatter
                              Their pride ilk day.

A brave man firmly leain' hame
I ay was proud to think on;
The wife-obeyin' son o' shame
Wi' kindlin e'e I blink on:
'Peace, peace be wi' ye!—ah! return
Ere lang and lea the daft anes'—
'Please guid,' quo he, 'before the morn
In spite o' a' our chieftains,
                              An' guards, this day.'

But when the pokes o' provender
Were slung on ilka shou'der,
Hags, wha to henpeck didna spare,
Loot out the yells the louder.—
Had they, whan blood about their heart
Cauld fear made cake, an' crudle,
Ta'en twa rash gills frae Herdman's quart,
'Twad rous'd the calm, slow puddle
                              I' their veins that day.

Now *Leaders*, laith to lea the rigs
Whase leash they fear'd was broken,
An' *Privates*, cursin' purse-proud prigs,
Wha brought 'em balls to sloken;
Repentant Painites at their pray'rs,
An' dastards crousely craikin',

Move on, heroic, to the wars
They meant na to partake in,
                    By night, or day.

Some fastin' yet, now strave to eat
The piece, that butter yellow'd;
An' some, in flocks, drank out cream crocks,
That wives but little valu'd:
Some lettin' on their burn to mak',
The rear-guard, goadin', hasten'd;
Some hunk'rin' at a lee dyke back,
Boost houghel on, ere fasten'd
                    Their breeks, that day.

The truly brave, as journeyin' on
They pass by *weans* an' *mithers*,
Think on red fiel's, whare soon may groan,
The *husbands*, an' the fathers:
They think how soon thay bonie things
May lose the youths they're true to;
An' see the rabble, strife ay brings,
Ravage their mansions, new to
                    Sic scenes, that day.

When to the tap o' Donegore
Braid-islan' corps cam' postin',
The red-wud, warpin, wild uproar,
Was like a bee scap castin';
For ******* ***** took ragweed farms,
(Fears e'e has ay the jaundice)
For *Nugent's* red-coats, bright in arms,
An' rush! the pale-fac'd randies
                    Took leg, that day.

The *camp's* brak up. Owre braes, an' bogs,
The *patriots* seek teeir *sections*;
Arms, ammunition, bread-bags, brogues,
Lye skail'd in a' directions:
Ane half, alas! wad fear'd to face
Auld Fogies, faps, or women:
Tho' strong, untried, they swore in pride,
'Moilie wad dunch the yeomen,'
                    Some wiss'd-for day.

Come back, ye dastards!—Can ye ought
Expect at your returnin',
But wives an' weans stript, cattle hought,
An' cots, an' claughin's burnin'?

Na, haste ye hame; ye ken ye'll 'scape,
'Cause *martial worth* ye're clear o';
The nine-tail'd cat, or choakin' rape,
Is maistly for some hero,
On sic a day.

Saunt Paul (auld Knacksie!) counsels weel—
Pope, somewhere, does the samen,
That, 'first o' a', folk sud themsel's
Impartially examine;'
Gif that's na done, whate'er ilk loun
May swear to, never swith'rin',
In ev'ry pinch, he'll basely flinch—
'Guidbye to ye, my brethren.'
He'll cry, that day.

The leuks o' wheens wha stay'd behin',
Were mark'd by monie a passion;
By dread to staun, by shame to rin,
By scorn an' consternation:
Wi' spite they curse, wi' grief they pray,
Now move, now pause a bit ay;
' 'Tis mad to gang, 'tis death to stay,'
An unco dolefu' ditty,
On sic a day.

What joy at hame our entrance gave!
'Guid God! is't you? fair fa' ye!—
'Twas wise, tho' fools may ca't no' brave,
To rin or e'er they saw ye.'—
'Aye wife, that's true without dispute,
But lest saunts fail in Zion,
I'll hae to swear *** forc'd me out;
Better he swing than I, on
Some hangin' day.'

My story's done, an' to be free,
Owre sair, I doubt, they smarted,
Wha wad hae bell'd the cat awee,
Had they no been deserted:
Thae warks pat skill, tho' in my min'
That ne'er was in't before, mon,
In tryin' times, maist folk, you'll fin',
Will act like Donegore men
On onie day.

JAMES ORR, *Poems on Various Subjects*, 1804

24th.—What is this I hear? A poor extemporised abortion of a rising in Tipperary, headed by Smith O'Brien. There appears to have been no money or
provisions to keep a band of people together two days. And O'Brien,
Meagher, O'Donoghue (Pat of Dublin), and Terence M'Manus of Liverpool,
all committed for trial to Clonmel gaol for being parties to the wretched business. I cannot well judge of this affair here, but in so far as I can learn anything about it and understand it, O'Brien has been driven into doing the very
thing that ought not to have been done—that Lord Clarendon will thank
him heartily for doing. An insurrection, indeed, has been too long deferred;
yet, in the present condition of the island, no rising must *begin* in the country.
Dublin streets for that. O'Gorman, Reilly, Doheny, have fled; and all prominent members of the Confederation in country towns are arrested on
suspicion.

What glee in Dublin Castle and the blood-thirsty dens of Downing-street,
at this excuse for 'vigour'! And, of course, all the world thinks Irish resistance
is effectually crushed; and that Ireland's capacity for resistance was *tested* at
this cursed Ballingarry.

Reilly, I am delighted to find, is safe for the present, but Duffy, Williams,
and O'Doherty still lie in gaol, awaiting their trial. Now, my Lord Clarendon,
if your jurors but stand by you, 'law' will get developed and vindicated to a
great extent. What is to be the end of all this? Are there men left in Ireland
who will know how to press the enemy hard *now*? And who will dare to do
it? Then the poor people—God comfort them!—have another famine-winter
before them, for the potatoes have generally failed again; and, to be sure, the
corn is not for the likes of them.

As for juries in these cases, the Clonmel juries will consist merely of
Cromwellian Tipperary magistrates and frightened Protestant landed proprietors. The Castle Judge will put it to *them* to say what they think of revo-
lutions, and what revolutionary characters deserve to suffer. It is possible
these four worthy men may be hanged.

JOHN MITCHEL, *Jail Journal*, 1854

Fenianism . . . had no place in our home, yet twice unpleasant things that had
to do with it happened there. One night, when father was out and mother was
saying the Rosary with children, maids and farmboys kneeling round her, the
door opened quietly and a stranger stole into the room, took the gun from
over the fireplace and went away as stealthily as he came. No one appeared
to notice. Mother's voice did not falter and she went on with the prayer. In
the morning the gun was found on the doorstep; we never heard for what
purpose it had been borrowed.

The second trouble was when two young nephews of mother's came to
the farm after dark, imploring her to hide them from the police who were

searching for them round their home. Nothing but father's great love for mother could have made him agree to their staying in the house. The little room off the kitchen was given up to them; the maids were not supposed to know that it was occupied; they looked the other way when mother or Dooley went in with food for the fugitives. After two weeks they left, stealing away without a word to anyone.

MARY CARBERY, *The Farm by Lough Gur*, 1937

If we draw an imaginary line from Londonderry to Warrenpoint, that is to say, from Lough Foyle to Carlingford Lough, east of this line we shall find the Ulster which is mostly Protestant, west that which is mostly Catholic.

The social effects of this quasi-equivalence of Catholic and Protestant may be easily divined. First of all it separates the two classes by a barrier that is morally insuperable. Each class lives to itself; there are no mixed marriages; where there are no hard words there are hard looks, and where there are no stones there are spites. The religious aspect always, at least apparently, dominates the political aspect of social questions, although at bottom I believe it would be found that a hostility of interest underlies the religious hostility. To the same causes we must ascribe that special passion or madness called 'Ulsteria', which keeps the Protestants of Ulster in its hold, and embitters feeling in quite another way than the 'hysteria' with which the Nationalists are reproached—we mean, of course, anti-Catholic fanaticism.

For over a century, with alternatives of storm and calm, it has been ravaging Ulster, laughable in some of its effects and terribly grotesque and odious in others. It is a permanent factor of civil war; it is the first obstacle in the way of material unity; it is at the same time an inexhaustible source of merriment and of mockery. It is the national sport of the Ulsterman, who, being a Celt of Scotch origin, is violent and passionate by nature, has a fault-finding spirit and loves fighting. That he should not love the Papist is intelligible enough, since the Papist has in the nineteenth century not only regained lands in Ulster, as at the end of the eighteenth, but has acquired political rights, has established his place on Irish soil, and is menacing the hegemony of the 'Garrison'. Ulster even, during the last half of the last century, was the object of a slow but sure reconquest by southern Ireland. Thirty years ago the Nationalists did not possess a single parliamentary seat in the province, now they have 15 or 16 out of 34. But why should a jealousy that is, above all, political and social assume this religious form? Why should aversion for Catholics extend to aversion for Catholicism? It must be remembered that we are dealing here with Presbyterians (or Low Church Anglicans) who have inherited from their Scotch ancestors a fierce and individualistic type of religion which is impatient of any yoke or barrier interposed between them and the

Bible. Such people have no understanding whatever of a Catholicism in which they see only Torquemeda and the butchers, the Madonna and the Christ. They consider themselves as the sole defenders, in a 'Papist' isle, of liberty of conscience and the Christian traditions against the obscurantism and despotism of the priest. But are not the Protestants of Ulster in a majority? Precisely. The Protestants of the south, isolated in the midst of the Catholics, are powerless; and only in Ulster can they speak and act in the defence of their so-called 'persecuted brethren' who lie under the tyranny of Catholic intolerance in Munster and Connaught. In short, you cannot reason with the Ulsterman. Popery is the enemy. Every child is brought up with the idea that its duty in life will be to purge Ireland of the Papists. *To Hell with the Pope!* This is the popular curse. An Englishman in Portadown hearing a street boy shout the well-known refrain, asked him did he not know that the Pope was after all a very respectable old gentleman who . . . 'Maybe,' said the boy, 'but he has a bad name in Portadown.' There is no worse insult than the epithet of Papist, and it is applied right and left.

L. PAUL-DUBOIS, Contemporary Ireland, 1908

The colonists of the Plantation instituted by James I wanted their wood to be hewn for them and their water to be drawn for them; therefore they spared a reasonable number of the original Irish who were quarrelling among themselves, and so (according to the statesmanship of the Middle Ages and of a long time afterwards) should have been swept out of existence altogether; and these survivors became as thorns in their flesh, especially when they were hewing wood or drawing water; and so they have remained to the present day. Ulster is still a colony in the midst of the hostile people who, though they have never (generally speaking) recovered more of their old position than allows of their quarrelling among themselves, are still, as hewers of wood and drawers of water, always ready to fling a faggot at the head of their task-master.

That is, in very truth, what the constant fighting in Ulster has meant. It has been the attempt of the subject race to rebel against the ascendancy. In all the other provinces of Ireland some progress has been made by the conquered race during the past hundred years or so toward regaining the ascendancy which they once enjoyed; and the dominant ones have for long thought it prudent to suspend their domineering; but in Ulster there has never been a need for them to do so. They have always looked with indignant eyes at the attempts of the Hivites and the Hittites and the Jebusites to regain their original position, and called such attempts by the name of rebellion. They have been fighting since the days of the siege of Derry against the intermittent rebellions of the native Irish, who had become their servants; and now when it is suggested to them that these servants should become their masters, some newspaper folk inquire with a seriousness that has its comic side to anyone who knows Ulster and the history of Ulster, 'Will Ulster fight?'

. . . the first incident of my life of which I retain a vivid memory was of Ulster fighting, and the *casus belli* of more than fifty years ago has not been removed; on the contrary, it has been intensified during the latter half of this space of time, until Ulster to-day resembles one of those volcanic basins which only need a single stone to be flung into them to produce such an eruption as may change the whole face of the landscape.

F. FRANKFORT MOORE, *The Truth About Ulster*, 1914

Some years ago, after a bad outbreak of rioting, the City Council proposed to take steps which, it was claimed, would go a long way to prevent future troubles. In the fighting quarter, it should be known, the streets are mainly paved with cobble stones or 'kidneys', to give them their local name. At the first sign of hostilities these are prized up with pokers and stacked in heaps by the women to serve as ammunition dumps for the fighters. The Corporation scheme was to substitute macadam for the cobble-stones, but when the motion came up for discussion it was discovered that the plan was to begin with the Nationalist area, whose representatives, not unnaturally, raised a storm of protest against the unfair advantage this method of disarmament would confer on their opponents. I believe there were some negotiations, but they came to nothing, and to this day the cobble-stones remain.

J. W. GOOD, *Ulster and Ireland*, 1919

Head Constable McKechnie was a Peeler of the old school, Irish style, which often meant no school at all, especially in the case of a natural athlete . . .

At the height of the city riots in 1932, the then Head Constable of the district had been directing a baton charge in an attempt to drive a wedge between two mobs of warring youths when, suddenly, he had spotted a winner. At that time the side streets of the city were still cobbled, and in times of strife these cobbles were dug up and used as missiles. Known as 'kidney pavers' because of their slightly oval shape, they moulded comfortably to the hand, and though heavy for accurate long-distance work, with practice the devotee could develop an over- or underarm swinging action which, though random, could wreak havoc amongst massed opposition in much the same way as a fragmentation grenade.

But that day the Head Constable's attention had been drawn to one youth in particular, a burly fellow in a red white and-blue shirt, who had a style all his own. With the paver poised on the flat of his hand, held level with his right jaw-bone, he took three or four running paces forward and, with a final peculiar hopping movement (accompanied by the appropriate sectarian obscenity), flung his paver at the foe with a devastating impetus and accuracy, his arm shooting out from the shoulder like a piston.

The Head Constable, besides his other duties, was also a coach for the police athletics team, so he recognised natural talent when it hit him up the face—which, in this instance, was very nearly the case. It took three men to subdue the lad—without breaking any bones, as per instructions—and get him down to the barracks. There, after ascertaining that he was above the minimum height and summoning his father to give his permission, the Head Constable had guided the lad's signature on the enlistment form and packed him off to the Depot that very night . . . The result is in the record books: within a year Constable McKechnie was the champion shot-putter of all Ireland; in two years champion of the British Isles; and in 1936 he represented his country—unsuccessfully—in the Berlin Olympic Games.

JOHN MORROW, *The Essex Factor*, 1982

I went out to lunch on Easter Monday, and this involved going from my cousin's house in Rathgar into Dublin and walking down Grafton Street. I remember stopping there to admire a party of the Citizen Army who were marching up the street and were later to take over the College of Surgeons. So I went out to Blackrock to the luncheon party and when that was over, at about three or four o'clock, I suppose, I came back into town by Ballsbridge, and there were people there in knots discussing things, talking about the Rising in Dublin. A tram man who had been held up said something about 'Streets up to your knees in blood'. So I plodded on into the city, up Grafton Street, where I saw British soldiers peeping around the corner, and into Stephen's Green. Opposite the Russell Hotel at Harcourt Street I met a young volunteer in the Citizen Army who was on sentry duty and he told me that the cause of Ireland was not lost. I had been led to believe that perhaps it was, and that only things like Home Rule could be depended on now, but here were men in insurrection and what was happening connected immediately with what I had read of Irish history. This young man told me that the Countess Markievicz was inside, which I found intensely interesting, and would I like to come in. I said, 'No, I'll come back tomorrow,' because I hadn't the heart to leave my poor old cousin, who was a cripple.

MARIE COMERFORD, quoted in Kenneth Griffiths and Timothy E. O'Grady, *Curious Journey*, 1982

Fighting is brisk about Ringsend and along the Canal. Dame Street was said to be held in many places by the Volunteers. I went down Dame Street, but saw no Volunteers, and did not observe any sniping from the houses. Further, as Dame Street is entirely commanded by the roofs and windows of Trinity College, it is unlikely that they should be here.

It was curious to observe this, at other times, so animated street, broad and deserted, with at the corners of side streets small knots of people watching. Seen from behind, Grattan's Statue in College Green seemed almost alive, and he had the air of addressing warnings and reproaches to Trinity College.

The Proclamation issued to-day warns all people to remain within doors until five o'clock in the morning, and after seven o'clock at night.

It is still early. There is no news of any kind, and the rumours begin to catch quickly on each other and to cancel one another out. Dublin is entirely cut off from England, and from the outside world. It is, just as entirely cut off from the rest of Ireland; no news of any kind filters in to us. We are land-locked and sea-locked, but, as yet, it does not much matter.

JAMES STEPHENS, *The Insurrection in Dublin*, 1916

Everybody was up all night standing in the street waiting for rumours and the next day the thing went on. There were no trains or communications then at all with Dublin. So that morning, on the Tuesday, my uncle said to me that he'd like to go to Dublin to see what was happening. Now he was a mature man and I would have expected more sense, but the next thing he said to me was, 'Would you like to come?' Well, I said I'd love it. 'Well then go and ask your aunt,' he said, and I did. She said, 'Surely he's not going,' and I said, 'He is, and I'd love to go with him.' 'Oh no, no, no,' she said, 'it would be too dangerous.' And then she came to me after a while and said, 'Maybe you'd be safer if you were with him.' So I had on a little grey costume and the car came down to pick me up and we set off for Dublin. There was my uncle and myself, a Mr Farrell, whose wife was ill in Dublin, and Tom Bannon, a teacher and a *Gaeilgeoir*—a great, you know, supporter of the movement. It was a lovely day, and the loveliest countryside. Birds singing, trees blossoming, everything glorious and peaceful and happy and there was no sign of trouble or blood-shed or anything. But it was then we came to McKee Barracks—it was Marlborough Barracks then I think but it was renamed later—and we were stopped by a tremendous gathering of troops. They were looking over the wall, over sandbags and barbed wire and rifles and bayonets and all sorts of things. We were told to get out then, and the soldiers started whistling at me. It was rather flattering I suppose. Then my uncle was called forward and he produced his warrant of appointment for them—he was a Peace Commissioner, you see—and he told them that he was wanted at the Castle. It was a lie of course, but then what was a lie here and there to the British. So we were told all right, that we could go ahead, but that we were to leave the car there and walk into Dublin.

So we set off over fields, across through Drumcondra around where the Archbishop lives now and then we finally got into Dorset Street. Well one thing that impressed me very sadly was the number of young people sitting along the footpath just relaxing in the sunshine. No work I presume. And we could hear the guns booming and we could see the smoke, the pall of smoke over the city. So then we walked up to Gardiner Street where my uncle Joe MacGuinness lived, and his wife was there with two or three friends, other members of Cumann na mBan, and they were very frightened and very shattered and they said, 'Oh, it's not going to succeed', they didn't think it could, and they were sure that all the men would be shot. They had been to the Four Courts where my uncle Joe MacGuinness was, and then towards evening that day a message came out that he wanted me to go down, that my cousin, who had been sent on dispatches, had fallen and cut her hand on a lemonade bottle. So I was only too delighted to go down, and that evening Tom Bannon and myself set out, and we walked down Upper Dorset Street, Bolton Street, North King Street, then down into Church Street, sheltering in doorways every now and then when the bullets were flying. We went through barricades of barrels and dustbins across the road and you had to give the password 'Antonio' to get through. First we went down to O'Connell Street and looked at one of the horses, a dead horse, and we saw the GPO and all the fires. And then we got down into the Father Matthew Hall and I met a lot of other friends there. It was very dark there, they had only candlelight and you couldn't see much, but what I did see then was a pillow stained with blood and I said to myself, This is the rebellion at last.

> BRIGHID LYONS THORNTON, quoted in Kenneth Griffith and Timothy E. O'Grady, *Curious Journey*, 1982

The machine-gun cleared the rebels out of the Green. Simultaneously, elsewhere in the city, last stand after last stand was being broken down. While it lasted, the Rising was unpopular with almost all the people of Ireland: the insurgents were seen as reckless, destructive, crazy. It was what came after that changed the feelings—retribution was more than too severe. Executions, wholesale arrests, deportations, savoured to Ireland of Cromwellian reprisals: they were to combine to plough 1916 deep in among other race-memories in the country's heart. There was to be more to come of it, much more.

As for the Shelbourne, it woke from a bad dream. Sandbags gone, soldiers out, staff back, it returned to normal in (virtually) the twinkle of an eye.

> ELIZABETH BOWEN, *The Shelbourne*, 1951

My paternal grandparents and their elder daughter were 'out' in 1916: my father and his younger brother tried to run away from Castleknock College to join the Volunteers but were retrieved in time. I grew up to think of the

GPO in Dublin, from the steps of which Pearse read the Proclamation of the Irish Republic, as a sacred spot. The 1916 myth, like malaria, is in my blood-stream. But fortunately the fever it caused in youth is not recurrent. Ireland's modern miseries help one to build up powerful anti-bodies against it. If one believes, as I do, that Ireland's future well-being depends on an increasing closeness to Europe—and particularly on an uninhibited recognition of our special ties with Britain—then clearly Easter Week was a mistake. But it was a noble mistake, the sort one would expect of a mystical poet-leader like Patrick Pearse. It is impossible for me to condemn it though increasingly I regret that it ever happened. Obviously I would not feel thus had Ireland been able to develop a distinctive way of life based on ancient Gaelic traditions—the dream of the 1916 leaders. But, for that, Irish independence came centuries too late and our attempts to revive an extinct culture led only to humbug-gery. We forced the Irish language on generations of reluctant children whose parents could speak only English. Our Gaelic sports clubs would not allow their members to go to a rugger or cricket or soccer match. We hypocrit-ically pretended to sit on the fence during the Second World War while with one foot we kicked the ball for Britain when nobody was looking. We culti-vated a dishonest smugness about the extent of our independence, when in fact we were and remain economically bonded to Britain by sterling and dependent on her for the employment of our emigrants. In 1937 we produced a disastrous constitution which might have been specially designed to alien-ate forever the Northern Protestants. We showed an exaggerated deference (now slightly waning) to the Catholic church as the one feature of our national life which really does set us apart from Britain. And every year we ritually polished myths that would have been better left to get so rusty they fell apart.

DERVLA MURPHY, *A Place Apart*, 1978

The rebellion of 1916 seems to constitute, at first sight, a grave indictment against the whole system of Irish government, not only in the past, but also in the actual and living present. Whatever benefits the last fifty years have brought to Ireland—whatever the value of judicial rents or land purchase or local self-government—all this, it may seem, and whatever else could be done in addition to this, profited nothing. Ireland desired something more—something different in quality—something above and beyond an infinity of Land Acts, and above and beyond recurrent Home Rule Bills which came to nothing: she desired to possess her own soul. In the very middle of an agon-izing war—our enemies might argue—with the whole British Common-wealth engaged, she stood apart; and she not only stood apart—she took the other side. Rebellion failed, it is true; but could anything be more damning than the mere fact of rebellion?

But the fact is that Ireland did not rebel. There was a rebellion in Ireland: there was not a rebellion of Ireland. And what is more, the rebellion in Ireland was as much, or still more, a rebellion of one Irish party against another, as it was a rebellion of Irishmen against the connexion with Great Britain. The Nationalist party in Ireland stood loyally, side by side with Protestant Ulster, in defence of the general British cause. The rebellion was largely a rebellion of those extremists who have, during the last fifty years, found their enemies no less in the Home Rule party of Ireland than in the British Government.

ERNEST BARKER, *Ireland in the Last Fifty Years*, 1916

from *Easter Christening*

THE SEEKER

All day I have searched from street to Dublin street
Seeking a question or an answer—Liberty Hall
Where Connolly disciplined strength; Saint Enda's where
Pearse and MacDonagh learned force in teaching youth;
Tom Clarke's small shop; Plunkett's prison cell
In the pigeon-fouled wreck of bleak Kilmainham;
The great Post Office where they broke out their flag;
The places where they fought—Boland's Mill,
And Stephen's Green, Jacob's Factory; everywhere
I found the life of Dublin pulsing steadily
And no one proud to stand where once they stood.

THE SOLDIER

Here is one more who stands or loiters by,
A young man with a frown. Ask him if youth
Has given him knowledge. Perhaps being close to them
In age he may inherit their secret.

THE SON

My father died. Seven machine-gun bullets
Cut his body. You ask what he died for?
Dimly I know. A country where eyes turn homeward,
Where no foreign master stalks the land,
A pride in liberty, an unbowed knee,
A steady eye, an unchallenged sovereignty,
The free expansion of the growing tree.
I have grown under the shadow of that tree
And cannot know the world in which they lived,
Can only guess the petty slavery of minds

Turned ever towards a foreign capital.
That I have never seen
The fawning seeker after preferment,
The apeing renegade parodying his master,
The venal official falsifying his reports
Proves, if to me alone, they have not failed. . . .

DONAGH MACDONAGH, *The Hungry Grass*, 1947

Rumours came into the Lower Hills that peace might not come to Ireland after all. The English would not allow Ireland to escape from the Empire and were offering a kind of Home Rule within it, and threatened immediate and terrible war if their offer was refused. The Irish Republican army was over-whelmingly against the British offer, but the priests and the newspapers were for it, and several well-known officers deserted from the army and declared for it too. The majority of people turned against the army, and the English supplied weapons for a Dominion force to oppose it, and enforce the peace terms. Two armies grew up in the country and bitter words were said and clashes took place. The Government departments were administered by the Dominion authorities, and the resources of the country passed under its control, so that they could pay their army, and recruits poured in.

Many people were puzzled and disheartened, and remained aloof, shrinking from the thought of civil war. The war came.

Hughie Dalach and Tom Pheggy and Mickey Sheila talked things over often; Mickey was for the new terms. Down in the village Anthon Donal told him that unless the Republicans were put down the old age pensions would be cut off, and they agreed among themselves that with the hard times it would be sore on the old folk to lose the pensions. Neddy Brian spoke out strong against not finishing a thing that people put their minds to, and he said things about Anthon Donal that did not please Mickey Sheila. It brought gloom to Brigid's mind to think that the boys that used to be so happy together on the straw were not all on the one side in the new fight.

Late one night there was a tap on the window and Neddie Brian himself opened the door. A group of Republican soldiers came in. Neddie Brian built a fire and Brigid herself got up and made tea. The visitors slept in their clothes on the hearth. Next morning Betty Sheila came over early; she wanted one of the children to fetch her starch and blue on the way home from school. The Republicans were hurried to the room when Betty was sighted, and the children were warned on their lives not to say a word. It was the first time neighbours had hidden anything like that from one another in the Lower Hills. Grania and Sheila were not allowed to school that day, for fear they might talk about the strange men. About midday a girl came with a warning message, and the group stole out of Neddie Brian's, creeping carefully under the shelter of the byre until they got safely into the gully that led deep into the mountain.

Working in the fields that day Hughie saw ragged boys, without arms, race along the lake making into the hills. After a time an armed party in green uniforms, carrying rifles, came along the same path. Hughie leaned on his spade and watched them go up through his healthy crops. It didn't seem fair, to men like him, working in the fields growing crops, nor to the ground that grew the crops, that men out of the stock that had made the fields should tramp them like this, without feeling for the crops, and full of anger for one another. He stuck his spade and went up the hill. He was afraid that the armed men that had gone from his house and these others would meet. But the men in the uniforms called to him to halt, and they pointed guns at him and made him go back to his work. The man in charge was a relation of Betty Sheila's, and that evening Betty passed Hughie Dalach and never turned her head in his direction.

PEADAR O'DONNELL, *Adrigoole*, 1929

Suddenly the attack broke with fury. A dozing sentinel on guard and the remaining eleven men of the garrison were awakened by the crashing sound of hammers on the roof, and feet trampling; and then again the crash of hammers and a sudden blaze of light from overhead accompanied by loud explosions,—and the stink of petrol. In silence the attack had started as Seamus Robinson and Ernie O'Malley, armed with a brace of revolvers each, and laden with grenades, detonators and hammers, began to climb the ladders towards the roof, forty feet above them in the darkness. On their backs petrol tins were tied and paraffin-soaked sods of turf were slung around their necks. At the foot of each ladder three men clamped their stockinged feet against the rungs to hold the ladders steady, and remained there under the loopholes of the barracks until O'Malley and Robinson reached the roof. O'Malley's ladder rested against the chimney; Robinson's against one side of the gable. Buckets of petrol and paraffin oil were placed in readiness near the base of the ladders. In spite of the menacing loopholes, the men holding the ladders disregarded O'Malley's appeal to them to retire to cover. Not until the crash of hammers on the slate roof and the leap of flame and the explosions came from above would they move.

Even while the men above gripped their revolvers and lay flat on the wrecked and blazing roof, the police beneath exerted themselves to a furious defence. Through the loopholes came prompt volleys of revolver and rifle fire, followed by the bursting of hand grenades. Rockets and Very lights shot up skywards as a summons to the police and military garrisons in the area to speed help and reinforcements. From the smaller lean-to building the police opened a heavy fusillade against the men on the flaming roof.

O'Malley and Robinson had now been joined by Jim Gorman and continued their work of destruction with buckets of petrol. The slates were hot to the touch and the wind blew reeking smoke and flame in their faces. From the roof, and from the chimney, where O'Malley had climbed, came the rattle of revolver fire in reply to the police in the lean-to building. Robinson and Gorman made journeys up and down the ladders with buckets of oil and petrol to feed the blaze.

Sean Treacy, when he had stationed the party in front to his satisfaction just before the attack, went rapidly backwards and forwards to the neighbouring house to bring up more explosives. The party in front, in obedience to Treacy's final orders, held their fire until the first wild volleys roared and flamed from the loopholes, and the grenades burst around them. . . . Above sounded the roar of O'Malley's and Robinson's revolvers: the police were firing on them through the roof of the lean-to building and through the roof of the blazing barracks . . . A hand grenade slipped from O'Malley's hand as Seamus Robinson was coming up the ladder with a bucket of petrol. . . . the grenade was of a make famous among the fighters of the time for its truly terrifying detonation . . . the grenade hurtled past Robinson's head and burst below with a deafening explosion. Robinson held on grimly and continued up the ladder to rejoin O'Malley.

DESMOND RYAN, Sean Treacy and the 3rd Tipperary Brigade, 1945

My clothes were now a composite collection from many counties. I had my coat from Donegal, my waistcoat from Dublin, my trousers, very voluminous, formerly belonged to Michael Murray of Newmarket-on-Fergus, and he was somewhat rotund; my shirts and socks generally belonged to the county I happened to be in at the time. My trousers billowed around my legs in folds, the waist had to be folded and refolded beneath a belt. Michael Murray had girth.

My hat I seldom wore when passing through towns and villages; when I was given it I do not remember; it was a faded green. Sun and rain had each in turn touched it strongly. There was a bullet hole on either side of the crown near the top. Once in Clare, Peader, Maurteen and myself were cycling from Ennis to Kilfenora. At a cross road we saw police with carbines; at the same time came a command 'Halt there!' We drew our revolvers and fired, running for cover. The police used their carbines. It was near sunset. We had carried our bicycles over the ditch. When twilight came Peadar brought our bicycles across the next field whilst we replied slowly to the ragged police firing. Then we crawled away, reached our bicycles and cycled into the welcome friendly darkness. When I arrived at Maurteen's house I found the bullet hole in the hat. The most obvious sign of my light-headedness in the eyes of the old people was my not wearing a cap or hat; the men usually wore their hats, even in the house, and they always thought I would catch cold in my bare head.

ERNIE O'MALLEY, *On Another Man's Wound*, 1936

The burnings and shootings continued, all the more frightful in the glorious weather. . . . three country houses in north County Cork were burnt in retaliation for a reprisal, one being Convamore. The Listowels were away at the time, but Lord Listowel's niece, Miss Wrixon-Becher, was living in the house; neighbours found her next morning without her false teeth, which she had lost in the fire. A fortnight later the Ascendancy world, growing accustomed to the burning of country houses, was shocked by the shooting of a young girl. She was Winifred Barrington, only daughter of the Bandons' friends Sir Charles and Lady Barrington of Glenstal Castle in County Limerick. She had been driving near her home with two other women, a District Inspector of the RIC and an army officer when a party of armed men opened fire on the car, killing her as well as the police inspector. The IRA maintained that they only intended to shoot the latter, and that Winifred Barrington's death was accidental, which was probably true; it was rash to go driving with a police inspector, who was such an obvious target.

On the day after Winifred Barrington's death another woman was killed, the wife of Captain Blake, also a District Inspector of the RIC, who came from one of the ancient Galway families known as the Tribes. Captain and Mrs Blake, together with Robert Gregory's widow Margaret and two young army officers were driving down the avenue of a country house not far from Coole after a tennis party when they saw that the lodge gates were closed. One of the officers got out to open them and was promptly shot down. The car was then surrounded by armed and masked men, who ordered Mrs Blake and Margaret Gregory to leave. Mrs Blake called out that she would not leave her husband but would die by his side; he and she and the other officer were mown down by volleys fired in quick succession.

MARK BENCE-JONES, *Twilight of the Ascendancy*, 1987

At about this time in Dublin a number of statues were blown up at night; eminent British soldiers and statesmen had their feet blown off and their swords buckled. Reading about these 'atrocities' threw Edward into a violent rage. These were acts of cowardice. Let the Shinners fight openly if they must, man to man! This sort of cowardice must not be allowed to prevail . . . skulking in ambush behind hedges, blowing up statues . . . Had there been one, even one, honest-to-God battle during the whole course of the rebellion? Not a single trench had been dug, except perhaps for seed potatoes, in the whole of Ireland! Did the Sinn Feiners deserve the name of men?

'Of course, there *was* Easter 1916,' suggested the Major mildly.

'Stabbed us in the back!' Edward bellowed with a kind of pain, almost as if he had felt the knife enter between his own shoulder-blades. 'We were fighting to protect them and they stabbed us in the back.'

'Well, not if one looks at it from their point of view, of course . . . Mind you,' he added soothingly as Edward's features stiffened, 'one has to consider both sides.'

A dispiriting silence fell on the room. The Major decided that it would be a sign of strength not to press the matter. Edward inspired more pity than anger these days. Privately, though, he retained his conviction that it was rather amiable of the Sinn Feiners to prefer attacking statues to living people—a proof, as it were, that they too belonged, or almost belonged, to the good-natured Irish people.

J. G. FARRELL, *Troubles*, 1970

It was now dark and I went out into the wet streets. Troops were patrolling them and I was soon stopped by a patrol and frisked once more. More friskings followed as I got to the Liffey. It was enjoyable. I didn't realize that my green velour hat from the Boulevard des Italiens with its wide, turned-down brim, was an item of the uniform of the IRA. I went straight to the Abbey Theatre. In the shabby foyer, a small middle-aged woman with grey hair and looking like a cottage loaf, was talking to a very tall man. He was unbelievably thin. He seemed to be more elongated by having a very long nose with a cherry red tip to it. The woman's voice was quiet and decided. His fell from his height as waveringly as a snow-flake. The pair were Lady Gregory and Lennox Robinson. He took me to his office for an hour and then we went into the theatre. To an audience of a dozen or so people (for the Civil War kept people away), the company were going through the last act of *The Countess Cathleen*, in sorrowing voices. They went on to the horse-play of *The Shewing-Up of Blanco Posnet*. Both plays had caused riots years before when they were first put on. Now the little audience was apathetic.

Soot came down the chimney in my room at the hotel when a bomb or two went off that night.

V. S. PRITCHETT, *Midnight Oil*, 1971

With the coming of June, riots broke out once more. A special police force was recruited from the Orange Order, and on his way to school Colm could see them in their cage cars or standing at street corners with their rifles, canvas bandoliers, and rough black-green uniforms.

'Them's our Black-and-Tans,' he heard a shawled woman shout at them. 'It's a poor show and little sleep we'll get on the Falls Road now!'

Not a day passed in peace, and as Colm played on the waste ground he could hear the shots shattering the summer air, and was thankful that his street was sheltered and away from it all. It was strange to be living in a city where night after night shots rang out and to know nothing of what happened until they read the morning's paper. It was strange, too, to be leaving their game of football when it was still bright and to retire to their houses because of curfew.

But the hours of curfew were not peaceful. From early morning the snipers were at their posts and they did not cease with the coming of curfew and the bare streets.

MICHAEL McLAVERTY, *Call My Brother Back*, 1939

The Dilemma

Born in this island, maimed by history
and creed-infected, by my father taught
the stubborn habit of unfettered thought.
I dreamed, like him, all people should be free.
So, while my logic steered me well outside
that ailing church which claims dominion
over the questing spirit, I denied
all credence to the state by rebels won
from a torn nation, rigged to guard their gain,
though they assert their love of liberty,
which craft has narrowed to a fear of Rome.
So, since this ruptured country is my home,
it long has been my bitter luck to be
caught in the crossfire of their false campaign.

Here at a distance, rocked by hopes and fears
with each convulsion of that fevered state,
the chafing thoughts attract, in sudden spate,
neglected shadows from my boyhood years:
the Crossley tenders caged and roofed with wire,
the crouching Black and Tans, the Lewis gun,
the dead lad in the entry: one by one
the Catholic public houses set on fire:
the anxious curfew of the summer night,
the thoroughfares deserted, at a door
three figures standing, till the tender's roar,
approaching closer, drives them out of sight:
and on the broad roof of the County Gaol
the singing prisoners brief freedom take

to keep an angry neighbourhood awake
with rattled plate and pot and metal pail:
below my bedroom window, bullet-spark
along the kerb, the beat of rapid feet
of the lone sniper, clipping up the street,
soon lost, the gas lamps shattered, in the dark;
and on the paved edge of our cinder-field,
intent till dusk upon the game, I ran
against a briskly striding, tall young man,
and glimpsed the rifle he thought well concealed.
At Auschwitz, Dallas, I felt no surprise
when violence, across the world's wide screen,
declared the age imperilled: I had seen
the future in that frightened gunman's eyes.

JOHN HEWITT, *Collected Poems*, 1991

Well a couple or three years after the Easter Rising in Dublin there were troubled times round our country. You never had peace to go any road and they
even had a curfew put on. You see when the trouble sometimes come on there
were a lot of trouble. They were digging trenches across the road and they
were cutting down trees and there was a lot of trouble getting everywhere at
the time. If you went out of the house you were stopped by somebody. If it
wasn't by soldiers or police it was by IRA or Republicans. You were stopped
by some party anyway and there wasn't much comfort. So then it come on to
be that bad that there was a curfew on for a period of time. You know it broke
out in 1916. The riots broke out in Dublin but then it would be on further. It
would be the 'eighteens or 'nineteens when it would be curfew time about,
or 'twenties maybe. When the curfew come on you couldn't be seen out of
the house after eleven or twelve o'clock. I think it was twelve o'clock when it
started. It come back to eleven o'clock. Of course young fellows they would
run to an odd dance and go to an odd ceilidh and if you were too late you
got into trouble. You might get into jail if you were caught being out after
hours when the curfew was on. I remember coming along one night from old
Paddy's house, Paddy McMahon's. I was coming across the fields, me and
another young fellow the name of McCabe, and just as we were crossing the
road this light shone on us. It was a lorry load of what they called *the Black
and Tans*. So they bid to see a shadow of us crossing the road and we lay down
in *the sheough* going across the field, but they come in. We set out across
country home to beat them. They went round the road of course. They were
listening, I suppose, and flashing their lights and we had to run past our own
house to get clear. They tapped at the door and everywhere but they went
away again, done no harm.

They put the curfew on because times went that bad you see. These men, what you call the IRA or Republicans, they were digging trenches and putting bushes across the road, ambushing them and shooting the soldiers from both sides. When they got them to come to this place where they had the bush across they attacked them on both sides and killed a lot of soldiers. That's what caused them to bring on curfew. If you were found out after it you were liable to be shot. There was nobody caught about our side. It kept fairly quiet only just that you wouldn't want to be out. These Crossley Tenders and all was going the roads, at all hours of the night.

Well you see as it is, I suppose maybe there's some of it going on today. The Catholics would maybe go and if they knowed of a prominent man being busy with these English soldiers or anything they went and maybe burned his house. There was retaliation then, they would come and burn a Catholic house. So it never stopped until it went as far as the towns, and you might say that wee village beside us in Rosslea it was burned to the ground. It would be twenty-one or thereabouts. The Protestant people spilt petrol on the houses, on the Catholic houses all, and burned them out nearly every one of them. there was a song about it I think, but I haven't any of it.

> JOHN MAGUIRE, *Come Day, Go Day, God Send Sunday*; the songs and life story of a traditional singer and farmer from Co. Fermanagh, collated by Robin Morton, 1973

The loss of my only suit so close to the day of travelling was upsetting, but a friendly tailor, near Crookstown, working through the night, made a new one which reached me at O'Mahony's, Belrose, on the morning of the 19th. On that evening the O'Mahony girls delivered me safely outside the Cork Railway Station, handed me my first-class return ticket and a number of pro-British newspapers and periodicals. Thanking those fine girls for their many kindnesses, I walked nervously past some enemy soldiers and Black and Tans to the waiting train. Travelling by train was then unpopular and there were several empty first-class compartments, but deciding that I would be far less noticeable with others, I entered one where three men were already seated. Two of these appeared to be middle-aged staid business men, but the third looked like a British military officer in mufti. I sat directly opposite this man. Within a few minutes we were engaged in friendly conversation and soon he told me he was in the Army and as he put it 'going on a spot of leave and not sorry to leave this damned country'. In turn he learned that I was a medical student going to Dublin to be examined by a specialist for suspected lung trouble. At the first military examination of the passengers at Mallow my companion, producing his own identity card immediately informed the Sergeant in charge of the search party that I was all right and travelling with him. He was to repeat this on two further train inspections so that I had not to answer a single question throughout the journey. I parted with this amiable travelling companion outside the Kingsbridge check barrier; he to report at a military barracks, before crossing to Britain in the morning and I to locate Jim Kirwan's public house in Parnell Street, where General Headquarters had arranged to contact me.

Jim Kirwan was a Volunteer of long standing and all his assistants were members of the IRA. When I asked one of them to tell 'George' I had arrived he returned with Jim, who, after looking me over, brought me to a private room to meet Gearoid O'Sullivan, the Adjutant-General. Gearoid and I left immediately for Liam Devlin's home, nearby in the same street, where in the sitting-room upstairs Michael Collins, Diarmuid O'Hegarty and Sean O'Mhuirthille were waiting for me. Soon afterwards Collins, O'Sullivan and O'Mhuirthille and I set out for the suburbs to the house of Mrs O'Donovan, an aunt of Gearoid's. Here, with the other three, I was to stay during my six nights in Dublin. Each morning with one or more of the others, I left for the IRA offices which were in the centre of the City and being conducted under the guise of harmless businesses. Those six busy days were full of interest for me. I was never alone, spending most of the time with Collins and O'Sullivan and I must have met some thirty officers, including those of GHQ, the Squad and the Dublin Brigade, as well as President de Valera and Cathal Brugha, the Minister of Defence. The way of life of those GHQ officers was in great contrast to that of the West Cork IRA. Dressed like business men, carrying brief or attache cases, with their pockets full of false papers to support their disguise, they travelled freely to their 'business' offices and to keep their various appointments.

TOM BARRY, *Guerrilla Days in Ireland*, 1949

While the ladies gossiped cheerfully and playing-cards continued to snow down on the green baize tables the Major was at his most despondent. Above all, he took a gloomy view of the reprisals at Balbriggan and elsewhere. The result of this degeneration of British justice could only be chaotic. Once an impartial and objective justice was abandoned every faction in Ireland, every person in Ireland, was free to invent his own version of it. A man one met in the street in Kilnalough might with equal justification (provided it fitted into his own private view of things) offer you a piece of apple pie or slit your throat. But given the way things were going (the Major could not help feeling) he would be more likely to slit your throat.

If no throats were actually slit in Kilnalough in the first days after the disturbances, there were, nevertheless, some ugly incidents. Miss Archer was rudely barged into the gutter by two mountainous Irishwomen clad in black and wearing men's boots. She then dropped her muff, which was trampled on and kicked around like a football by a group of urchins. Wisely she left it to them and fled before anything worse happened. Not long afterwards a young hooligan in Kilnalough put his stick through the spokes of Charity's bicycle, causing her to fall and graze her knees and palms. Stones were thrown at the people from the Majestic but without causing any great harm. Viola O'Neill, while buying buttons in the haberdashery (Boy O'Neill informed the Major), had had some obscene words spoken into her innocent ears which, naturally, she had failed to comprehend.

But presently the Major's sense of shock and dismay over the degeneration of British justice evaporated, leaving only a sediment of contempt and indifference. After all, if one lot was as bad as the other why should anyone care? 'Let them sort it out for themselves.'

J. G. FARRELL, *Troubles*, 1970

The Last Republicans

Because their fathers had been drilled.
Formed fours among the Dublin hills,
They marched together, countermarched
Along the Liffey valley, by larch-wood,
Spruce, pine road. Now, what living shout
Can halt them? Nothing of their faces
Is left, the breath has been blown out
Of them into far lonely places.
Seán Glynn pined sadly in prison. Seán
McNeela, Tony Darcy, John
McGaughey died on hunger-strike,
Wasting in the ribbed light of dawn.
They'd been on the run, but every dyke
Was spy. We shame them all. George Plant,
Quick fighter and a Protestant,
Patrick McGrath and Richard Goss,
Maurice O'Neill with Thomas Harte
Were executed when Dev's party
Had won the county pitch-and-toss,
Pat Dermody, John Kavanagh
John Griffith, John Casey, black-and-tanned.
At Mountjoy Gaol, young Charlie Kerins
Was roped; we paid five pounds to Pierpont,
The Special Branch castled their plans,
Quicklimed the last Republicans.

AUSTIN CLARKE, *Flight to Africa*, 1963

The Amazing Power of Emblems

... the pervasive emblems of harp, wolfhound and round tower ...

SEAMUS DEANE, *Celtic Revivals*

My father, who was a dyed-in-the-wool, would-have-died-in-the-last-ditch Unionist, when after the outbreak of the First World War he could not get back into his old Irish regiment at his old rank, scorned to propose himself for the English Army, but offered his services to the French—by whom they were accepted. He often abused the British Government as roundly as any Nationalist. But when one day he met my nurse pushing me, aged two and a bit, in my pram clutching two green flags which Nurse had bought in Mrs MacCormack's shop, his face became suddenly dark and he seized the flags from me.

The trouble was, that on the green was a gold harp—and that in itself was no harm—but on the harp should have been and was not a gold crown.

This was my first memorable introduction to the amazing power of emblems.

GEOFFREY TAYLOR, *The Emerald Isle*, 1952

—Here you are, citizen, says Joe. Take that in your right hand and repeat after me the following words.

The muchtreasured and intricately embroidered ancient Irish facecloth attributed to Solomon of Droma and Manus Tomaltach og MacDonogh, authors of the Book of Ballymote, was then carefully produced and called forth prolonged admiration. No need to dwell on the legendary beauty of the cornerpieces, the acme of art, wherein one can distinctly discern each of the four evangelists in turn presenting to each of the four masters his evangelical symbol a bogoak sceptre, a North American puma (a far nobler king of beasts than the British article, be it said in passing), a Kerry calf and a golden eagle from Carrantuohill. The scenes depicted on the emunctory field, showing our ancient duns and raths and cromlechs and grianauns and seats of learning and maledictive stones, are as wonderfully beautiful and the pigments as delicate as when the Sligo illuminators gave free rein to their artistic fantasy long long ago in the time of the Barmecides. Glendalough, the lovely lakes of Killarney, the ruins of Clonmacnois, Cong Abbey, Glen Inagh and the Twelve Pins, Ireland's Eye, the Green Hills of Tallaght, Croagh Patrick, the brewery of Messrs Arthur Guinness, Son and Company (Limited), Lough Neagh's banks, the vale of Ovoca, Isolde's tower, the Mapas obelisk, Sir Patrick Dun's hospital, Cape Clear, the glen of Aherlow, Lynch's castle, the Scotch house, Rathdown Union Workhouse at Loughlinstown, Tullamore jail, Castleconnel rapids, Kilballymacshonakill, the cross at Monasterboice, Jury's Hotel, S. Patrick's Purgatory, the Salmon Leap, Maynooth college refectory, Curley's hole, the three birthplaces of the first duke of Wellington, the rock of Cashel, the bog of Allen, the Henry Street Warehouse, Fingal's Cave—all these moving scenes are still there for us today rendered more beautiful still by the waters of sorrow which have passed over them and by the rich incrustations of time.

—Shove us over the drink, says I. Which is which?

JAMES JOYCE, *Ulysses*, 1918

People fall in love with Ireland. They go there and are smitten, see the white cottages nestling so to speak beneath the hills, the ranges of brooding blue mountain, the haze above them, the fuchsia hedges in Kerry, the barking dogs, the chalky limestone steppes of west Clare, a phenomenon so unyielding it is as if Wuthering Heights were transmitted from paper to landscape. The visitors talk and are talked at, they fish, they fowl, they eat brown bread, dip into holy wells, kiss wishing stones, are bowled over but have no desire to stay. There must be something secretly catastrophic about a country from which so many people go, escape, and that something alongside the economic exigencies that sent over a million people in coffin ships when a blight hit the potato crops in 1847 and has been sending them in considerable numbers ever since.

EDNA O'BRIEN, *Mother Ireland*, 1976

The Abbey Theatre Fire

One of our verse-speakers, driving
His car at dusk to Alexander
Dock, saw a fine ship on fire, loitered
Among the idlers, urchins, at the gateway,
Came back by crane, warehouse, bollard,

The Custom House, corniced with godlings—
Nilus, Euphrates, detected a smell
Of burning again and in alarm,
Jumped out, to poke the bonnet, turned, noticed
Smoke piling up near Liberty Hall,
Smoulder of clothes. Suddenly, ghosts
In homespun, peasants from the West,
Hurrying out of the past, went by unheard,
Pegeen, her playboy, tramps, cloaked women,
Young girls in nothing but their shifts.
Glimmerers stalked, tall, mournful eyed,
In robes, with playing instruments,
By shadowy waters of the Liffey.
He drove around the corner, guessing
That flames were busier than their smoke
In the Abbey Theatre. Civic Guards
Shouldered, broke down the door-glass, carried
Out portraits in their gilded frames,
Yeats, Lady Gregory, Synge, Máire
O'Neill, Fay, F. R. Higgins, blindly
Staring in disapproval. Gong
And clatter. Firemen booting down
From darkness in their warlike helmets,
While flames were taking a first bow
And flickers in the Greenroom unlocked
The bookcase, turned the dusty pages
Of one-act comedies, cindered
Prompt copy. Noisier in the scene-dock,
Flats vanished, palletted with paint,
The rostrums crackled, wooden harp
And flagon, mether, sword of lath,
Round shield, throne, three-legged stool,
All the dear mummocks out of Tara
That turned my head at seventeen.
The hydrants hissed against the mouthers,
Backing them from the stage and pitfall
Where in a gyre of smoke and coughing,
The plays of Yeats were re-enacted.
Our Lyric Company, verse-speakers,
Actors, had put them on without
A doit for eleven years. We hired
The theatre, profaned the Sabbath
With magic, speculation: *The Countess
Cathleen, The Only Jealousy*

Of Emer, Deirdre, even *The Herne's Egg,*
Moon-mad as Boyne. *The Death of Cuchullin:*
We borrowed a big drum, clarionet, from
The Transport Workers' Union. Ann Yeats
Found in the *Peacock* cellar masks
Dulac had moulded.
                            So, I forgot
His enmity.
                    My own plays were seen there,
Ambiguous in the glow of battens,
Abbot, monk, sinner, black-out of Ireland.
Finis.
            Stage, auditorium, escaped
That fire but not from policy,
Planning new theatre, old mirth.
Yeats had not dreamed an unstubbed butt,
Ill match, would bring his curtain down.

AUSTIN CLARKE, *Flight to Africa,* 1963

Another thing I have a quarrel with—that is the peasant. I deplore and repro-
bate the present glorification of the peasant. I am very sick of peasants. The
Abbey Theatre has given us three or four years of undiluted peasant, so has
the Theatre of Ireland, so have many of our journals. We are beginning to
wear our peasantry as consciously as we do our ancient greatness and our
heroes. It is ridiculous every city man of us marching about with a countryman pinned in his hat.

JAMES STEPHENS (1910), in Patricia McFate (ed.), *Uncollected Prose,* 1983

A lifetime of cogitation has convinced me that in this Anglo-Irish literature
of ours (which for the most part is neither Anglo, Irish, nor literature) (as the
man said) nothing in the whole galaxy of fake is comparable with Synge.
That comic ghoul with his wakes and mugs of porter should be destroyed
finally and forever by having a drama festival at which all his plays should
be revived for the benefit of the younger people of to-day. The younger
generation should be shown what their fathers and grand-daddies went
through for Ireland, and at a time when it was neither profitable nor
popular.

   We in this country had a bad time through the centuries when England
did not like us. But words choke in the pen when one comes to describe
what happened to us when the English discovered that we were rawther

interesting peepul ek'tully, that we were nice, witty, brave, fearfully seltic and fiery, lovable, strong, lazy, boozy, impulsive, hospitable, decent, and so on till you weaken. From that day the mouth-corners of our smaller intellectuals (of whom we have more per thousand births than any country in the world) began to betray the pale froth of literary epilepsy. Our writers, fascinated by the snake-like eye of London publishers, have developed exhibitionism to the sphere of acrobatics. Convulsions and contortions foul and masochistic have been passing for literature in this country for too long. Playing up to the foreigner, putting up the witty celtic act, doing the erratic but lovable playboy, pretending to be morose and obsessed and thoughtful—all that is wearing so thin that we must put it aside soon in shame as one puts aside a threadbare suit. Even the customers who have been coming to the shop man and boy for fifty years are fed up. Listen in the next time there is some bought-and-paid-for Paddy broadcasting from the BBC and you will understand me better.

This trouble probably began with Lever and Lover. But I always think that in Synge we have the virus isolated and recognisable. Here is stuff that anybody who knows the Ireland referred to simply will not have. It is not that Synge made people less worthy or nastier, or even better than they are, but he brought forward with the utmost solemnity amusing clowns talking a sub-language of their own and bade us take them very seriously. There was no harm done there, because we have long had the name of having heads on us. But when the counterfeit bauble began to be admired outside Ireland by reason of its oddity and 'charm', it soon became part of the literary credo here that Synge was a poet and a wild celtic god, a bit of a genius, indeed, like the brother. We, who knew the whole inside-outs of it, preferred to accept the ignorant valuations of outsiders on things Irish. And now the curse has come upon us, because I have personally met in the streets of Ireland persons who are clearly out of Synge's plays. They talk and dress like that, and damn the drink they'll swally but the mug of porter in the long nights after Samhain.

The Plain People of Ireland. Any relation between that man and Synge Street in Dublin where Bernard Shaw was born?
Myself. I don't think so, because Bernard Shaw was born before Synge.
The Plain People of Ireland. The Brothers run a very good school there—manys a good Irishman got his learnin there. They do get a very high place in the Intermediate and the Senior Grade every year.
Myself. Faith you're right.
The Plain People of Ireland. But of course your man Shaw digs with the other foot.
Myself. Aye.

MYLES NA GCOPALEEN (Flann O'Brien) from *The Best of Myles*, ed. Kevin O Nolan, 1968

I have no hesitation at all in saying that every Irish-feeling Irishman, who hates the reproach of West-Britonism, should set himself to encourage the efforts which are being made to keep alive our once great national tongue. The losing of it is our greatest blow, and the sorest stroke that the rapid Anglicisation of Ireland has inflicted upon us. In order to de-Anglicise ourselves we must at once arrest the decay of the language. We must bring pressure upon our politicians not to snuff it out by their tacit discouragement merely because they do not happen themselves to understand it. We must arouse some spark of patriotic inspiration among the peasantry who still use the language, and put an end to the shameful state of feeling—a thousand-tongued reproach to our leaders and statesmen—which makes young men and women blush and hang their heads when overheard speaking their own language.

DOUGLAS HYDE, from 'The Necessity for De-Anglicising Ireland', 1892

The appreciation of poetry, any poetry, is rare enough: a minority pleasure. It is sadly true that even in Ireland (or Scotland) the pleasures of Gaelic poetry are still more rarely known. The problem is of course basically one of language: not merely . . . difficulties of detail . . . , or that of mutual comprehension between the now quite divergent Irish and Scottish 'dialects', but the great and overwhelming difficulty that the language itself is dying. It has been dying for over three hundred years, ever since it became de-institutionalized with the final collapse of the old Gaelic social order in the seventeenth century. (I am thinking mainly of Ireland here—the process was delayed a little in parts of Scotland.) However, despite the erosive effects of intense colonization ('plantation') and the growth of small cities and towns as centres of Anglicization, the great majority of the Irish remained Gaelic-speaking right through the eighteenth century. Even in the first half of the nineteenth century, the two languages were not far from being on equal terms as to strength of numbers in a wildly over-populated country. The Great Famine (1847–8) and consequent mass emigrations helped to solve the population problem, and in a new demographic situation the language went into a sharp decline. It might well have died peacefully, but for the uncovenanted mercy that a number of ineffectual attempts to arrest the process were subsumed and transformed into what became a great popular movement—the Gaelic League—founded in 1893, and led by an unlikely prophet, Douglas Hyde, the son of a country clergyman of colonial stock. Hyde's great aim was the 'De-Anglicization of Ireland' and the restoration of the Gaelic vernacular. In this task he and the League patently failed. But it can be said that from this movement most of what has happened in Ireland in the present century, for good or ill, directly or indirectly derives: 'I have said again and again,' said P. H. Pearse, 'that when the Gaelic League was founded the Irish revolution began.'

SEÁN MAC RÉAMOINN, Introduction to *The Pleasures of Gaelic Poetry*, 1982

What is Irish literature? was a simple question which generations of Irishmen for good instinctive reasons fought shy of. They were afraid of the truth. There is manifestly no essential difference between first-class literary work executed by an English-speaking man born in Ireland, and that executed by an English-speaking man born in England. But we had to make a difference, for though we had adopted the English language, it was death to the man who called our writings by their proper name. Another make-believe had to be manufactured.

We put in 'throths' and 'begors' and 'alannas' and 'asthores' by way of Irish seasoning. But though certain classes of ballad and lyric poetry can be written in dialect, as Burns has proved, you cannot rise to dignity or poetry on 'begors' and 'bedads'. There is something essentially mean about the corrupt English of the Irish peasant, particularly when put into cold print; it passes the power of man to write literature in it.

D. P. MORAN, *The Philosophy of Irish Ireland*, 1900

We had a splendid, patriotic taste in song-books, principally because the nearest newsagent's shop, kept by an old spinster in Devlin Street, had a window occupied by a sleeping tomcat, two empty tin boxes, bundles of pamphlets yellowed by exposure to the light, and all members of a series called Irish Fireside Songs. The collective title appealed by its warm cosiness. The little books were classified into Sentimental, Patriot's Treasury, Humorous and Convivial, and Smiles and Tears. Erin, we knew from Tom Moore and from excruciating music lessons at school, went wandering around with a tear and a smile blended in her eye. Because even to ourselves our singing was painful, we read together, sitting in the sunshine on the steps that led up to my father's house, such gems of the Humorous and Convivial as: 'When I lived in Sweet Ballinacrazy, dear, the girls were all bright as a daisy, dear.' Or turning to the emerald-covered Patriot's Treasury we intoned: 'We've men from the Nore, from the Suir and the Shannon, let the tyrant come forth, we'll bring force against force.'

Perhaps, unknown to ourselves, we were affected with the nostalgia that had brought my godmother and her husband back from the comfort of Philadelphia to the bleak side of Dooish Mountain. It was a move that my mother, who was practical and who had never been far enough from Ireland to feel nostalgia, deplored.

'Returned Americans,' she would say, 'are lost people. They live between two worlds. Their heads are in the clouds. Even the scrawny, black-headed sheep—not comparing the human being and the brute beast—know by now that Dooish is no place to live.'

'And if you must go back to the land,' she said, 'let it be the land, not rocks, heather and grey fields no bigger than pocket handkerchiefs. There's Cantwell's fine place beside the town going up for auction. Seventy acres of land, a palace of a dwelling-house, outhouses would do credit to the royal family, every modern convenience and more besides.'

BENEDICT KIELY, *A Journey to the Seven Streams*, 1963

A Poor Scholar of the 'Forties

My eyelids red and heavy are
With bending o'er the smouldering peat.
I know the Aeneid now by heart,
My Virgil read in cold and heat,
In loneliness and hunger smart;
 And I know Homer, too, I ween,
 As Munster poets know Ossian.

And I must walk this road that winds
'Twixt bog and bog, while east there lies
A city with its men and books;
With treasures open to the wise,
Heart-words from equals, comrade-looks;
 Down here they have but tale and song,
 They talk Repeal the whole night long.

'You teach Greek verbs and Latin nouns,'
The dreamer of Young Ireland said,
'You do not hear the muffled call,
The sword being forged, the far-off tread
Of hosts to meet as Gael and Gall—
 What good to us your wisdom-store,
 Your Latin verse, your Grecian lore?'

And what to me is Gael or Gall?
Less than the Latin or the Greek—
I teach these by the dim rush-light
In smoky cabins night and week.
But what avail my teaching slight?
 Years hence, in rustic speech, a phrase,
 As in wild earth a Grecian vase!

PADRAIC COLUM, *Collected Poems of Ireland*, 1960

The astonishingly swift decline of the Irish language in the years after the Famine and the increasing prominence of shopkeepers, publicans and innkeepers in the Land League and Home Rule movements were clear indications that Yeats's view of the peasantry was outmoded by the 1870s. Their language was dying, their social formation had been drastically altered, their nationalism was fed on the Young Ireland diet of Thomas Moore, James Clarence Mangan and the pervasive emblems of harp, wolfhound and round tower. In addition, the literature of the Gaelic civilization was making its way into Yeats's and indeed into the national consciousness in the form of translation, most of it inept. Yeats came at the end of a long line of amateur antiquarians, most of whom regarded the translation of Gaelic poetry into English as a contribution to the enlightenment of an English (or English-speaking) audience on the nature of the Irish Question. Charlotte Brooke's *Reliques of Irish Poetry* (1789), James Hardiman's *Irish Minstrelsy* (1831), Samuel Ferguson's *Lays of the Western Gael* (1867) and even Douglas Hyde's *Love Songs of Connacht* (1894) helped to consign Gaelic poetry to the bookshelf, transforming it into one of the curiosities of English literature. They were little more than obituary notices in which the poetry of a ruined civilization was accorded a sympathy which had been notably absent when it was alive.

SEAMUS DEANE, *Celtic Revivals*, 1985

Until a few years ago no one challenged the accepted view that politics was the begin-all and end-all of Irish Nationality. And as politics in Ireland consisted in booing against the English Government, and as Irish Nationality was politics, the English Government became logically the sole destroyer of nationality. Of course it was an utterly false and an almost fatal position for us to have taken up. All the time that we were doing our share in the killing of our nation, everything was put down to England. An infallible way to distract criticism from domestic affairs—and this can be clearly seen by observing the state of the public temper in England at the present time—is to get entangled in a foreign war. When a great struggle is on hand domestic reformers may sing for an audience. A people who are watching their nation in death-grips with another are in little humour for attending to the parish pumps, least of all for listening to uncomplimentary criticism. But, supposing this condition of things lasted for a hundred years, what would become of the home economy? And this has practically been the condition under which Ireland has spent the century. We have been fighting England as our only enemy, looking to her as the sole source of all our evils, as the only possible source of all our blessings, inasmuch as until we had settled with her we could do nothing for ourselves. All the while, like Pendennis, we ourselves were our greatest enemies. As politics was nationality, every patriotic Irishman who watched his decaying nation felt new drops of hatred for England descend into his heart. Until England could be brought to her senses no progress could be made, and as the life was all the time ebbing out of the Irish nation, then ten thousand curses be upon her oppressor. This attitude flowed reasonably from the first false position that politics was nationality. When Ireland was great she sent men of learning and religion to instruct and enlighten Europe; when she was at her lowest ebb she sent out desperadoes with infernal machines. The commandment, 'Thou shalt be Irish,' was written alike upon the hearts of all.

From the great error that Nationality is politics a sea of corruption has sprung. Ireland was practically left unsubjected to wholesome native criticism, without which any collection of humanity will corrupt. If a lack of industrial energy and initiative were pointed out, the answer naturally was— 'Away, traitor. England robbed us of our industries; we can do nothing until she restores our rights.' If you said that the people drank too much—'Well, what are the poor people to do? They are only human; wait until our rights are restored, and all that will be altered.' And so on. To find fault with your countrymen was to play into the hands of England and act the traitor.

D. P. MORAN, *The Philosophy of Irish Ireland*, 1899

As former Parnellites and former anti-Parnellites buried their hatchets at the turn of the century, the newly-reunited Catholic-nationalist Ireland began to be increasingly responsive to a new slogan, 'Irish-Ireland'. The slogan was the coinage of a brilliant and pugnacious journalist: D. P. Moran. Moran was intensely Catholic and intensely nationalist: a thoroughgoing 'Faith and Fatherland' person, fully in tune with the basic ideology of the Christian Brothers, but recklessly idiosyncratic in his personal formulations of the same.

The characteristics of an Irish Irelander, as these were beginning to emerge in 1900 were as follows:

He (or she) is Catholic, preferably, but if not Catholic, then thoroughly deferential to Catholic-nationalists, on all questions relating to the definition and practices of Irish-Ireland. He or she is more earnestly nationalistic than other Irish nationalists, including the Irish Parliamentary Party, and most of its supporters. He or she may be either constitutional-nationalist or Republican. Most Irish Irelanders were constitutional nationalists, up to 1914, but critical of the parliamentary leadership and its press.

He or she is enthusiastic about the Irish language, not necessarily able to speak or write the language in the here and now, but actively engaged in learning it, or at the very least, deemed to be doing so.

He or she is passionately opposed to all forms of English influence in Ireland, including the playing of foreign games, such as cricket and rugby, and therefore supports the Gaelic Athletic Association. (Founded in 1884 the GAA has been described as 'intensely Anglophobic and an organisation avowedly nationalist, ostensibly Irish and, crucially, church supported'.)

He or she—especially she—is rigidly chaste, in accordance with the norms of chastity laid down by the Catholic Church, and is dedicated to the suppression of all public manifestations of unchastity, especially in the theatre.

CONOR CRUISE O'BRIEN, *Ancestral Voices*, 1994

Dublin, 24 O'Connell Street. A high brick building in the noisy and populous main artery of Dublin. Above the entrance we read *Connradh na Gaedhilge*, Gaelic League; on the ground floor is a bookshop which sells only Irish books, Irish pamphlets, Irish newspapers. We go up to the first landing and find offices, business clerks: at our first word—in English—we are pulled up sharply by a blonde Celt who says something in Irish. We do not understand, but gather from his disdain that they have no need here for those unfortunates who at this time of the day in Ireland are still backward enough to be able to speak only English. All is soon explained, but we can already understand the astonishment, the irritation, of English people when, in the very heart of the British Isles, ten hours from London, in a city like Dublin, of 350,000 inhabitants, they hear a language spoken which they do not understand—a language 2,000 years old—or when in the West of Ireland, asking the way, they get the answer, given, moreover, in English, *No English, Sir*! When such English visitors are of an observant turn of mind and compare the Ireland of to-day with the Ireland of twenty years ago, they perceive that a great change has taken place, and they are not far wrong when they see in the revival of the Irish language the symbol and the agent of this profound transformation.

This transformation began fifteen or twenty years ago. In the time of recollection and retreat which followed on political disintegration, Ireland came to understand that if liberty had always been refused her it was because her nationality had not been forcibly enough affirmed before English eyes. She understood that independence alone does not make a nation; that independence itself may not always indicate nationhood; that the essential mark of nationhood is the intellectual, social and moral patrimony which the past bequeaths to the present, which, amplified, or at least preserved, the present must bequeath to the future; and that it is this which makes the strength and individuality of a people.

L. PAUL-DUBOIS, *Contemporary Ireland*, 1908

It was now twenty years since Dr Douglas Hyde founded the Gaelic League to revive the Irish language, to return to the native culture, to de-Anglicize the country. Many parts of the country were still Irish-speaking, especially in the West, and of course in the islands on the western coast it was the only language. In English-speaking Dublin the passion for learning Irish showed itself among all ages, all classes, and all professions. In the evenings, after the day's work, shopkeepers, artisans, housewives, students would go to the Gaelic League branches to learn to speak and read the language and to write in its strange characters. Some mysterious romance lay behind every sentence they learned. On holidays and during vacations young men and women would make pilgrimages to the Irish-speaking districts and there practice talking what of the language they knew with people whose forebears had clung to the ancestral language. Summer schools under distinguished scholars were started where adults went to learn, not only the language, but the athletic games and the native dances. These dances had romantic names— the Waves of Tory, the Bridge of Athlone, the Walls of Limerick—and there were jigs and reels danced to old tunes that were athletic exercises in themselves. Even the most vigorous of us in our teens would be breathless after romping through a rousing jig or reel.

Like every activity in life that is a success, it was part play, a good time was had by all. The English Government, on the alert for political and rebel movements, paid no attention to the cultural movements. The attempts to destroy the native language and substitute English had succeeded pretty well, and there still remained the remnants of the penal laws against using Irish. Anybody who had his name printed in Irish on a vehicle was summoned to court and had to pay a fine. Thus, if one Irish-speaking James MacCarvill of Newton called himself by his right Irish name of Seumas MacCearbhaill of Baile nua, he was summoned to court and fined. But there was no law in the way of the Gaelic League, the literary or dramatic movements, so they all flourished. In fact, if anything, England encouraged them, probably thinking they would take the people's minds off the struggle for freedom.

MARY COLUM, *Life and the Dream*, 1928

In the days before the War and the 1916 Rising, the more enlightened of the Anglo-Irish were trying desperately to identify themselves with Ireland. Aunt Harriet organized the first local Feis, an ancient festival of song and dance and miscellaneous junketting which centuries before took place at Tara. At the Kilkenny Feis there were competitions for Irish dancing and singing, lace-making, cake, jam, section honey and craft work. When it was all over Aunt Harriet was presented by the committee with a 'Tara' brooch, a richly ornamented safety pin with which the ancient Irish held their clothes together, mass produced from originals in the National Museum.

The Gaelic League was not 'political' in those days and even the British saw nothing against it. When Lady Aberdeen, Ireland's all but last Vice-Reine, came down to open our local concert hall, she defied the ridicule of the Anglo-Irish neighbours by dressing herself and the ladies of the party in emerald green with Tara brooches. She and her husband were very Scottish; he wore the Gordon tartan and they wrote a book called *We Twa*. They bred Aberdeen terriers and were Aberdonianly thrifty, and it was one of their aims to show how very Scottish one could be and yet loyal to the Crown. Why could not the Irish be the same? She entertained very little in the Vice-Regal Lodge, but started a campaign against tuberculosis with no political over-tones, and motored all over Ireland trying with some success to introduce village nurses into every community.

Despite all this they were unpopular with both the more orthodox Gaels and ordinary Unionists; they were suspected of 'liberalism' which in Ireland was anathema to the traditional Unionist and one of our neighbours wrote a poem about them of which I can only remember one line: 'They cut the penny buns in half when Larkin came to tea.' (Larkin was a celebrated labour leader.)

The Cuffes and Aunt Florence and my mother all threw themselves into the crusade against tuberculosis (Aunt Harriet believed it was a delusion of the mind) and I think the Bennettsbridge village nurse was among the first in Ireland.

> HUBERT BUTLER (1987), 'Aunt Harriet', in *Grandmother and Wolfe Tone*, 1990

At that time you had the Gaelic Renaissance and the Gaelic League. I joined the Gaelic League when I was eight years of age. The Gaelic League was pri-marily to re-establish the Irish language, but it also took in other subjects— Irish literature, dancing and history generally. They gave lectures and talks in these subjects and all that helped. There was an upsurge of everything Irish. We unfortunately haven't given credit to the Irish Parliamentary Party. I would have shot John Redmond at the time, but I've learned a lot since. Their policy with England seemed to decrease the bitterness between the two coun-tries. The old slogan 'No Irish need apply' had gone by the board. And of course when a little bit more liberty and education and all that came along, it meant that more people took up the study of Irish, and Irish ideas. I don't like that horrible expression 'Stand up and be counted', but they were stand-ing up anyway and getting more independent in thought and deed.

> MARTIN WALTON, quoted in Kenneth Griffiths and Timothy E. O'Grady, *Curious Journey*, 1982

The President placed a yellow watch on the table before him, stuck his thumbs into the armpits of his waistcoat and delivered this truly Gaelic oration:

—Gaels! he said, it delights my Gaelic heart to be here today speaking Gaelic with you at this Gaelic *feis* in the centre of the Gaeltacht. May I state that I am a Gael. I'm Gaelic from the crown of my head to the soles of my feet—Gaelic front and back, above and below. Likewise, you are all truly

Gaelic. We are all Gaelic Gaels of Gaelic lineage. He who is Gaelic, will be Gaelic evermore. I myself have spoken not a word except Gaelic since the day I was born—just like you—and every sentence I've ever uttered has been on the subject of Gaelic. If we're truly Gaelic, we must constantly discuss the question of the Gaelic revival and the question of Gaelicism. There is no use in having Gaelic, if we converse in it on non-Gaelic topics. He who speaks Gaelic but fails to discuss the language question is not truly Gaelic in his heart; such conduct is of no benefit to Gaelicism because he only jeers at Gaelic and reviles the Gaels. There is nothing in this life so nice and so Gaelic as truly true Gaelic Gaels who speak in true Gaelic Gaelic about the truly Gaelic language. I hereby declare this feis to be Gaelically open! Up the Gaels! Long live the Gaelic tongue!

When this noble Gael sat down on his Gaelic backside, a great tumult and hand-clapping arose throughout the assembly. Many of the native Gaels were becoming feeble from standing because their legs were debilitated from lack of nourishment, but they made no complaint.

> FLANN O'BRIEN, *An Beal Bocht* (*The Poor Mouth*), 1941, trans. Patrick C. Power, 1973

Until recent times Erse was a language little used—a language spoken only by some of the peasants of the West, and only acquired with difficulty by the new enthusiasts for its use; and the difficulties in the way of its revival were not interposed by the Government, but lay in the nature of the case. But though there was no opposition to its use, and though, as a matter of fact, the instruction given in schools to-day is often bilingual, it was perhaps inevitable that enthusiasts for the study of Erse should often tend to become advocates of separation. It is difficult to ascertain the exact facts; but it is at any rate true that some of the leaders of the Irish language movement were on the revolutionary side during the troubles of this year, most notably P. H. Pearse, the head master of the Irish-speaking school at St Enda's, near Dublin. And though it is unfair to judge the policy of any society from the acts of individual members, it would at any rate seem fair to say that there has always been a section of extremists in the body of the Gaelic League.

> ERNEST BARKER, *Ireland in the Last Fifty Years*, 1916

Within the territory of Irish Ireland, the Gaelic language was fairly widely spread. Men read Irish papers, or at least papers that wrote about Irish. As for class distinction, the only class they troubled themselves about were language classes. It was not true, as native speakers believed, that all Irish Irelanders rode bicycles and said *Lá breagh* [fine day] but they had other peculiarities.

They could all dance and dance well. They said they never waltzed, but one sometimes had doubts about the truth of the statement. They could all sing. If some sang strangely, well, perhaps it was a very special kind of *sean-nós*. 'Irish Irelanders' were not all poets or hurlers (or poetesses and experts at *camóguidheacht*) but the proportion of poets and even of hurlers among them was larger than that in the outer world. In reality, cycling was the pastime of the Irish Irelander rather than any more traditional sport. Irish Irelanders were usually temperate, often total abstainers, always earnest, self-sacrificing, of high character. This is the army that, for near a quarter of a century, has held the trenches of Irish Ireland.

ARTHUR CLERY, *Dublin Essays*, 1919

The children in Irish-speaking areas were taught through the medium of Irish from 1923 onwards, but in an Irish which, . . . had a wide diversity of norms. For centuries the people had had the innate superiority of the English language proclaimed to them by the English administration and, for more than a century now, by their own religious and political leaders; those who still spoke Irish did not read books at all, but were accustomed to the use of English so as to follow local and national affairs in the newspapers, and to deal with those in authority. The newspapers, local and national, continued to appear in English, and the bewildering variations of the Irish used by government agencies did little to convince the people of the superiority of Irish as an official language . . .

DAVID GREENE, *Writing in Irish Today*, 1972

On a muggy November day, Trinity College's façade appears to dilate and quiver like a living thing. Statues of Burke and Goldsmith flank the portals; a smile hovers on Goldsmith's homely face—the hover of a smile is somehow the zenith of pleasant expressions. But we are not now really concerned with the externals of Trinity. As a point of departure for viewing the rest of Ireland, it is helpful to visit its library and look at the famous *Book of Kells*. This illuminated manuscript of the eighth century displays an orgy of ornamentation, with human and animal figures growing into and out of arabesque, never finishing logically as they began, the natural always linked with the supernatural. The point to remember is that this book and its companions (there are four or five others of the same kind in the Library) are the fruit of that happy Golden Age when Christianity came to Ireland like a great and all-flooding white light. The *Book of Kells* is the furnishing to all the bleak time-wrecked monastic ruins you will see in your travels through this island. It is the explanatory footnote to the hundreds of roofless ruins which are strewn in every part of the country, the beehive cells, the island sanctuaries, the 'beds' and the 'stations'. It is like a surviving blossom on a leafless, thorny growth. Someone bent devotedly over this vellum for hours and hours, day after day, the curlews crying on the bogs outside, the larks ascending, and Time like a friendly collaborator standing still.

Stephen Rynne, All Ireland, 1956

Bobby McHugh was born in Brooklyn and came home to Ireland with an enthusiasm for everything Irish. He spent a few months with his uncle at the edge of Donegal Town and partook as deeply as he could of the Irish language, Irish music, Irish speech, Irish poetry and the Irish countryside, but above all of the Irish past. Then he and his wife bought a farm high in the hills. There Bobby hoped to find the old Ireland more fully preserved than anywhere else. He hoped to experience some last remaining drops of its essence. But he was also looking for something more universal, a return to nature, I think, and to what he called 'elemental human values'.

The farm had been occupied until a few years before and so needed only minor repairs. A single slate had slipped on the house roof and the byres all badly needed rethatching but otherwise everything was in acceptable condition. Bobby and Mary moved in and made the improvements needed for a minimum of modern convenience. Not modern by Brooklyn standards but modern for the hills of Donegal. They piped water down from a pure limestone spring that rose on the rock out-croppings behind the house and installed a glittering stainless steel sink and fixtures in the kitchen to receive it. A big white-enamelled iron range provided hot water for the taps and central heating for the rest of the house. A windcharger gave them a useable kind of noiselessly generated electric current for their lights and for a few discreet kitchen machines.

Theirs was the only place for miles around that had electricity and on clear nights it stood out like a beacon among the soft glowing fuzz of the oil lamps of their nearest neighbours. It was an odd sensation to walk along through that remote, primitive region of Europe, in those hills where everything seemed scarcely starting to struggle out of the boundaries of the eighteenth century, much as in the annually late spring of the wet hill climate the grass and leaves and buds pushed their way only reluctantly and slowly forth from the cold ground, and to realize that within the still plain and humble exterior of the old, low crofter's house there had been gathered so much modernity as was represented even by Bobby and Mary's simple life.

Purists might have argued—as I was tempted to—that they had gone about their return to nature and to 'elemental human values' in the wrong way, that they had missed the point altogether, that they had imported the city into the country and so had carefully and all too effectively insulated themselves from the true experience waiting for them out there, the discovery of what life had really been like in pre-modern subsistence-farming days, when water was carried in by hand, and the only heat in the house was from the kitchen hearth, when the cooking was done in heavy soot-blackened pots over the smoky turf fire—so smoky that on sultry drizzly days the rooms filled with heavy white smoke and the consolation was heard from the old people that 'when the smoke goes through the house the warmth is going through it too'—when the only transportation apart from foot was by donkey or pony cart, and houses were built with hand-quarried stone, roofed with hand-cut timbers and thatched with hand-mown rushes, when a dozen children in a three-room house was commonplace and candles were a luxury (but no one knew how to read) and poetry did not arrive in books or little magazines but on the lips of auburn-haired raggedy men with slightly crooked eyes, and music was not an electronic sound from amplifiers and loud-speakers but was the singing and the dancing, the high voices and the rhythmic clap of farm boots on the clay floors of dim and smoky kitchens in time to the over-resined rasp of the local fiddle.

Maybe Bobby and Mary were right. It is not easy to experience the past as it really was. You can play at the past, you can act the role, but the past remains what it is: past. It will not revive for feeble modern imitations.

ROBERT BERNEN, from 'The Fence', in Tales From The Blue Stacks, 1978

The Trumpet had been a smart literary and sociological magazine during the war, when it had been edited by a peasant historian . . . and when Ireland itself had been the home of flourishing artistic movements. It had carried a deal of documentary reportage and statistics about fishing, as well as poems like abbatoirs, full of bones and sinews and thighs and hearts, and jerky short-stories about unevenly articulate peasants whose utterances varied from monosyllabic grunts to phrases like, 'when you shook out the bright scarf of your laughter'.

It had not thrived under Prunshios. For one thing, with the end of the war the cattle-boats had been crammed with departing writers, standing knee-deep amid the puke and porter, quietly forgetting about O'Flaherty and O'Faolain and rehearsing their line on Connolly, Kierkegaard, Kafka and Scotty Wilson. For another, he lacked, let's face it, the flair.

ANTHONY CRONIN, The Life of Riley, 1964

Cathleen

You can't take her out for a night on the town
without her either showing you up or badly letting you down:
just because she made the Twenties roar

with her Black and Tan Bottom—O Terpsichore—
and her hair in a permanent wave;
just because she was a lily grave
in nineteen sixteen; just because she once was spotted
quite naked in Cannought, of beauties most beautied,
or tramping the roads of Moonstare, brightest of the bright;
just because she was poor, without blemish or blight,
high-stepping it by the ocean with her famous swan's prow
and a fresh fall of snow on her broadest of broad brows—

because of all that she never stops bending your ear
about the good old days of yore
when she crept through the country in her dewy high heels
of a Sunday morning, say, on the road to Youghal
or that level stretch between Cork and Douglas.
There was your man Power's ridiculous
suggestion when he was the ship's captain, not to speak
of the Erne running red with abundance and mountain-peaks
laid low. She who is now a widowed old woman
was a modest maiden, meek and mild, but with enough
   gumption
at least to keep to her own
side of the ghostly demarcation, the eternal buffer-zone.

For you'd think to listen to her she'd never heard
that discretion is the better part, that our names are writ
in water, that the greenest stick will wizen:
even if every slubberdegullion once had a dream-vision
in which she appeared as his own true lover,
those days are just as truly over.
And I bet Old Gummy Granny
has taken none of this on board because of her uncanny
knack of hearing only what confirms
her own sense of herself, her honey-nubile form
and the red rose, proud rose or canker
tucked behind her ear, in the head-band of her blinkers.

NUALA NÍ DHOMHNAILL, *The Astrakan Cloak*, 1992, trans. Paul Muldoon

Two passive images are the vulnerable virgin and the mourning mother: images that link Cathleen with Mary. They project the self-image of Catholic Nationalism as innocent victim, equally oppressed at all historical periods. (Is there a subconscious admission that Irish men victimise women?) This assigns to England the perpetual role of male bully and rapist. In Seamus

Heaney's 'Ocean's Love to Ireland': 'The ruined maid complains in Irish'. In the mid-1970s Heaney could still symbolise the Northern conflict as 'a struggle between the cults and devotees of a god and a goddess'; between 'an indigenous territorial numen, a tutelar of the whole island, call her Mother Ireland, Kathleen Ni Houlihan . . . the Shan Van Vocht, whatever' and 'a new male cult whose founding fathers were Cromwell, William of Orange and Edward Carson'. To characterise Irish Nationalism (only constructed in the nineteenth century) as archetypally female both gives it a mythic pedigree and exonerates it from aggressive and oppressive intent. Its patriarchal elements also disappear. Here we glimpse the *poetic* (and Marian) unconscious of Northern Nationalism. At the same time, Heaney's mouldering 'Bog Queen' in *North* may indirectly represent the cult of Cathleen as a death-cult. The book contains an unresolved tension between two Muses: a symbolic mummified or mummifying woman . . . and the warmly creative, if domestic, aunt who bakes scones in the poem 'Sunlight'.

EDNA LONGLEY, From Cathleen to Anorexia, 1990

Dublin. The famous top room in Merrion Square where A.E. is engaged in editing the *Irish Statesman*. The walls are covered with landscapes painted by the editor himself, but the atmosphere is so thick with tobacco smoke that in the murk of an Irish winter afternoon it is difficult to make out the nymphs, hamadryads, or other strange creatures inhabiting those unfamiliar-looking woods. A.E., complete with beard and guarded by a table covered with manuscripts, questions me about the North (from which, incidentally, he originally came himself), and the conversation proceeds rather after the manner of the Shorter Catechism. Puff. Question: What is an Irishman's chief end? An Irishman's chief end is to pull the English leg and confound the British Empire for ever. Puff. Question: Why did the Romans never invade Ireland? Interval for relighting pipes. Answer: Because the Romans had more sense. Loud cheers, and, as Joyce might have remarked in *Ulysses*, sounds of a brass band playing *Let Erin Remember the Days of Old*. Alarums and excursions with secretary. Someone late with copy again. And what does one think of Lord Craigavon? Answer: The less thought about Lord Craigavon the better. America now? Yes, one was on the verge of going to America for the first time, a mute inglorious Columbus armed with a letter of credit and a leather trunk full of samples of Irish linen. Ah, that was interesting—Irish exports to those United States must be maintained. All the same, Irish exports or no Irish exports, I perceive that A.E. is fidgeting to get back to next week's leader, a long procession of American women tourists having reduced him to the level of one of the sights of Dublin—something to be gazed at like Nelson's Pillar, as well as a seer to be consulted about Gaelic Culture or (as they understand it!) the Twilight Sleep of the Mind. Unfortunate A.E.!—why doesn't he put a bodyguard armed with blunderbusses on the stairs, with instructions to shoot everyone wearing glass beads, Tara brooches, and wooden bangles on sight? Nevertheless, it is something to have been seen wheeling a bicycle through Nassau Street (and incidentally through all eternity) in the pages of *Ulysses*.

DENIS IRELAND, *From the Irish Shore*, 1936

Ireland deprives me of my very literacy. I've naturally mastered the more elementary [words] like Dun Laoghaire and Cobh, but I can't feel anything other than a foreigner in a land most of whose geography and history I have not the smallest idea how to pronounce.

And yet. The geography and history of Ireland hold my imagination in a melancholy magic spell. Dublin and Limerick are cities beautiful to me not only with some of the most superb and most neglected architecture in Europe but with a compelling litany, a whole folklore, of tragic and heroic associations. At an Abbey Theatre performance when I was in Dublin earlier this year I discovered I cannot sit through *Cathleen ni Houlihan* without crying. Still, I don't believe this is because I am, if I am, Irish. There are some reasons for it in my personal and family history, but I think it is chiefly for the simple reason that the history of Ireland is unbearably sad.

To the voice which urges that I am mainly Irish by blood, I make the round reply that, nonsense, my blood is entirely Group O. I don't believe in 'blood' in that sense any more than I believe in leprechauns. But it is true that my exact sociological situation is too complex to allow me to make the simple assertion that I am English.

BRIGID BROPHY, 'Am I an Irishwoman?', in *Don't Never Forget*, 1966

from *A Farewell to English*

Chef Yeats, that master of the use of herbs
could raise mere stew to a glorious height,
pinch of saga, soupçon of philosophy
carefully stirred in to get the flavour right,
and cook a poem around the basic verbs.
Our commis-chefs attend and learn the trade,
bemoan the scraps of Gaelic that they know:
add to a simple Anglo-Saxon stock
Cuchulainn's marrow-bones to marinate,
a dash of Ó Rathaille simmered slow,

a glass of University hic-haec-hoc:
sniff and stand back and proudly offer you
the celebrated Anglo-Irish stew.

MICHAEL HARTNETT, *A Farewell to English*, 1975

In those days there were many men in Dublin who returned to the wearing of Gaelic kilts, which differed from the familiar Scots kilts by being plain saffron or green in color; sometimes the kilt would be saffron and the brath green, fastened to the shoulder of the jacket with a Tara broach of silver or copper. For a tall, well-built figure the kilts are the most becoming of all forms of dress for a man, making him look both romantic and virile. Several of the writers affected them: Darrell Figgis, who wrote poetry and novels and had a career later as a politician in the new Irish state, Thomas MacDonagh, who wrote poetry and later taught in the National University, and who signed the proclamation of the Irish Republic in 1916; kilts were occasionally worn by the brothers Pearse—Padraic, who founded a bilingual school, and Willie who was a sculptor. The last three were executed in 1916 as leaders of the insurrection and signers of the proclamation of the Irish Republic. Figgis also had a violent end. He committed suicide as part of the outcome of a tragic love affair. But the most picturesque of those who arrayed themselves in kilts was Lord Ashbourne's son, William Gibson, afterwards himself Lord Ashbourne, who, when he succeeded to the title, insisted on addressing the House of Lords in Irish. He was one of the Celtophiles who refused to speak the English language and confined himself in conversation to French and Irish. To meet him striding around the foyer of the Abbey Theatre or up O'Connell Street in his kilts and to be greeted by him in Irish, '*Dia 'gus Mhuire duit*', or '*Bon jour, mes petites dames*', was to have experienced an added excitement to the day.

MARY COLUM, *Life and the Dream*, 1928

At this time, I was about fifteen years of age, an unhealthy, dejected, broken-toothed youth, growing with a rapidity which left me weak and without good health. I think I never remember before or since so many strangers and gentlemen coming together in one place in Ireland. Crowds came from Dublin and Galway city, all with respectable, well-made clothes on them; an occasional fellow without any breeches on him but wearing a lady's under-skirt instead. It was stated that such as he wore Gaelic costume and, if this was correct, what a peculiar change came in your appearance as a result of a few Gaelic words in your head! There were men present wearing a simple unornamented dress—these, I thought, had little Gaelic; others had such nobility, style and elegance in their feminine attire that it was evident that their Gaelic was fluent. I felt quite ashamed that there was not even one true Gael among us in Corkadoragha. They had yet another distinction which we did not have since we lost true Gaelicism—they all lacked names and surnames but received honorary titles, self-granted, which took their style from the sky and the air, the farm and the storm, field and fowl. There was a bulky, fat, slow-moving man whose face was grey and flabby and appeared suspended between deaths from two mortal diseases; he took unto himself the title of *The Gaelic Daisy*. Another poor fellow whose size and energy were that of the mouse, called himself *The Sturdy Bull*.

FLANN O'BRIEN, *An Beal Bocht* (*The Poor Mouth*), 1941, trans. Patrick C. Power, 1973

The Passing of the Shee

After looking at one of A.E.'s pictures

Adieu, sweet Angus, Maeve and Fand,
Ye plumed yet skinny Shee,
That poets played with hand in hand
To learn their ecstasy.

We'll search in Red Dan Sally's ditch,
And drink in Tubber fair,
Or poach with Red Dan Philly's bitch
The badger and the hare.

J. M. SYNGE, *Poems and Translations*, 1909

Gaelic Ireland, self-contained and vital, lay not only beyond the walls of the larger cities, if we except Galway, but beyond the walls of the towns, if we except Dingle, Youghal, and a few others in Connacht and Donegal. For Irish Ireland had, by the eighteenth century, become purely a peasant nation. Indeed not only did it lie beyond the walls of cities and towns, but its strongholds lay far away beyond all the fat lands, beyond the mountain ranges that hemmed them in. History had seen to that: the rich lands had been grabbed from the Gaels centuries before by successive swarms of land pirates who, in a phrase written by one of themselves (an Elizabethan Brown of Killarney) 'measured law by lust, and conscience by commodity'. In the softer valleys those land pirates had built their houses, and Irish Ireland had withered away in the alien spirit that breathed from them. Even to-day we come on the remains of this Gaelic Ireland only in places where there have been no such alien houses for some hundreds of years.

Irish Ireland, then, while in a sense coterminous with Ireland itself, had its strongholds in sterile tracts that were not worth tilling. The hard mountain lands of West Cork and Kerry, the barren Comeraghs in Waterford, hidden glens in the Galtee and other mountains, the wild seaboard of the South and West, the wind-swept uplands of Clare, the back places in Connemara, much of Donegal—in such places only was the Gael at liberty to live in his own way. In them he was not put upon. Big houses were few or none. Travellers were rare; officials stopped short at the very aspect of the landscape; coaches found no fares, the natives being homekeeping to a fault: 'They seem not only tied to the country, but almost to the parish in which their ancestors lived,' Arthur Young wrote of the Catholics, who had not yet learned to emigrate. Among themselves they had a proverb: 'Is maith an t-ancoire an t-iarta' ('The hearth is a good anchor').

The eighteenth century was everywhere a time of violence and hard-drinking for the rich, and for the poor a time of starvation and brutality. If that period was hard on the poor who tilled the plains of France, the rich lands of England, the golden soils of central Ireland, we may conceive how it must have been with the Gaels, whose only portion was rock and bog and wind-swept seashore!

DANIEL CORKERY, *The Hidden Ireland*, 1925

It was a good life in those days. Shilling came on shilling's heels; food was plentiful, and things were cheap. Drink was cheap, too. It wasn't thirst for the drink that made us want to go where it was, but only the need to have a merry night instead of the misery that we knew only too well before. What the drop of drink did to us was to lift up the hearts in us, and we would spend a day and a night ever and again in company together when we got the chance. That's all gone by now, and the high heart and the fun are passing from the world. Then we'd take the homeward way together easy and friendly after all our revelry, like the children of one mother, none doing hurt or harm to his fellow.

I have written minutely of much that we did, for it was my wish that some-where there should be a memorial of it all, and I have done my best to set down the character of the people about me so that some record of us might live after us, for the like of us will never be again.

TOMÁS Ó CRIOMHTHAIN (1926), *The Islandman*, trans. Robin Flower, 1937

—I always heard that St Finbarr was a Protestant, Mrs Crotty snapped. Dug with the other foot. God knows what put it into the head of anybody to put a name the like of that on the poor *bookul*.

—Nonsense, Mrs Crotty. His heart was to Ireland and his soul to the Bishop of Rome. What is sticking out of that bag, Hanafin? Are they brooms or shovels or what?

Mr Hanafin had reappeared with a new load of baggage and followed Mr Collopy's gaze to one item.

—Faith now, Mr Collopy, he replied, and damn the shovels. They are hurling sticks. Best of Irish ash and from the County Kilkenny, I'll go bail.

—I am delighted to hear it. From the winding banks of Nore, ah? Many a good puck I had myself in the quondam days of my nonage. I could draw on a ball in those days and clatter in a goal from midfield, man.

—Well it's no wonder you are never done talking about the rheumatism in your knuckles, Mrs Crotty said bleakly.

—That will do you, Mrs Crotty. It was a fine manly game and I am not ashamed of any wounds I may still carry. In those days you were damn nothing if you weren't a hurler. Cardinal Logue is a hurler and a native Irish speaker, revered by Pope and man. Were *you* a hurler, Hanafin?

—In my part of the country—Tinahely—we went in for the football.

—Michael Cusack's Gaelic code, I hope?

—Oh, certainly, Mr Collopy.

—That's good. The native games for the native people. By dad and I see young thullabawns of fellows got out in baggy drawers playing this new golf out beyond on the Bull Island. For pity's sake sure that isn't a game at all.

—Oh you'll always find the fashionable jackeen in Dublin and that's a certainty, Mr Hanafin said. They'd wear nightshirts if they seen the British military playing polo in nightshirts above in the park. Damn the bit of shame they have.

—And then you have all this talk about Home Rule, Mr Collopy asserted. Well how are you! We're as fit for Home Rule here as the blue men in Africa if we are to judge by those Bull Island looderamawns.

—Sit over here at the table, Mrs Crotty said. Is that tea drawn, Annie?

—Seemingly, Miss Annie said.

We all sat down and Mr Hanafin departed, leaving a shower of blessings on us.

FLANN O'BRIEN, *The Hard Life*, 1961

Since crossing the border I have several times been asked if I feel no patriotic involvement in the Northern conflict, despite my ancestry; and I am able honestly to answer 'None whatever'. Yet occasionally an atavistic sort of patriotism shows through, flashing out like the fire in a diamond when it is caught in a certain light. The day I crossed the border and saw the Union Jack flying in the grounds of a factory near Lisnaskea I felt a spurt of irrational resentment. This reaction had its source far below that thinking level on which I accept that Northern Ireland's Unionists have every right to fly the British flag in their own corner of Ireland. Then again, a few days ago, I felt a surge of exultation when a prominent Unionist declared that he sees a thirty-two county Irish Republic as ultimately inevitable, however undesirable.

DERVLA MURPHY, *A Place Apart*, 1978

Letter To Seamus Heaney

From Carrigskeewaun in Killadoon
I write, although I'll see you soon,
Hoping this fortnight detonates
Your year in the United States,
Offering you by way of welcome
To the sick counties we call home
The mystical point at which I tire
Of Calor gas and a turf fire.

Till we talk again in Belfast
Pleasanter far to leave the past
Across three acres and two brooks
On holiday in a post box
Which dripping fuchsia bells surround,
Its back to the prevailing wind,
And where sanderlings from Iceland
Court the breakers, take my stand,

Disinfecting with a purer air
That small subconscious cottage where
The Irish poet slams his door
On slow-worm, toad and adder:
Beneath these racing skies it is
A tempting stance indeed—*ipsis
Hibernicis hiberniores*—
Except that we know the old stories,

The midden of cracked hurley sticks
Tied to recall the crucifix,
Of broken bones and lost scruples,
The blackened hearth, the blazing gable's
Telltale cinder where we may
Scorch our shins until that day
We sleepwalk through a No Man's Land
Lipreading to an Orange band.

Continually, therefore, we rehearse
Goodbyes to all our characters
And, since both would have it both ways,
On the oily roll of calmer seas
Launch coffin-ship and life-boat,
Body with soul thus kept afloat,
Mind open like a half-door
To the speckled hill, the plovers' shore.

So let it be the lapwing's cry
That lodges in the throat as I
Raise its alarum from the mud,
Seeking for your sake to conclude
Ulster Poet our Union Title
And prolong this sad recital
By leaving careful footprints round
A wind-encircled burial mound.

MICHAEL LONGLEY, *An Exploded View*, 1973

The Famish'd Land

Most of [the] old women seemed to live very contented lives, after their years of heavy toil. Their tea-drinking, gossip, pinch of snuff or cutty-pipe of tobacco provided them with life's social pleasures. If the food was enough they were content, for these were all survivors of the Famine, and knew more than anyone in the world the worth of a potato.

FLORENCE MARY MCDOWELL, *Other Days Around Me*

The famine of 1845–9 is a major dividing-line in the history of modern Ireland. Politically, economically and socially, the period that followed it appears sharply distinct from the period that preceded it. In some ways this appearance is misleading: one effect of the famine was to concentrate in a few brief years changes that would otherwise have been spread over generations, and thus to disguise the real continuity between the two periods. But the very rapidity of these changes affected their character; and the immense burden of human suffering by which they were accompanied left an indelible mark on the popular memory. The historical importance of the Great Famine lies not only in the physical results that followed from it—the decline in population, the transfer of property, the changes in agriculture—but in the attitude to the government and to the ruling class that it engendered in the great majority of the people.

J. C. BECKETT, *The Making of Modern Ireland 1603–1923*, 1966

'Look about you, and say what is it you see that doesn't foretell famine—famine—famine! Doesn't the dark wet day, an' the rain, rain, rain, foretell it? Doesn't the rottin' crops, the unhealthy air, an' the green damp foretell it? Doesn't the sky without a sun, the heavy clouds, an' the angry fire of the West foretell it? Isn't the airth a page of prophecy, an' the sky a page of prophecy, where every man may read of famine, pestilence, an' death? The airth is soft-ened for the grave, an' in the black clouds of heaven you may see the death-

hearse movin' slowly along—funeral afther funeral—funeral afther funeral
—an' nothing to folly them but lamentation an' woe, by the widow an'
orphan—the fatherless, the motherless, an' the childless—woe an' lamentation—lamentation an' woe.'

WILLIAM CARLETON, The Black Prophet, 1847

Hungry Grass

Crossing the shallow holdings high above sea
Where few birds nest, the luckless foot may pass
From the bright safety of experience
Into the terror of the hungry grass.

Here in a year when poison from the air
First withered in despair the growth of spring
Some skull-faced wretch whom nettle could not save
Crept on four bones to his last scattering;

Crept, and the shrivelled heart which drove his thought
Towards platters brought in hospitality
Burst as the wizened eyes measured the miles
Like dizzy walls forbidding him the city.

Little the earth reclaimed from that poor body;
But yet, remembering him, the place has grown
Bewitched, and the thin grass he nourishes
Racks with his famine, sucks marrow from the bone.

DONAGH MACDONAGH, The Hungry Grass, 1947

From 1782 on, and especially during the Napoleonic wars, when Ireland had
become the granary of England, the country had passed through a period of
great prosperity. Taking advantage of this, the landlords had multiplied the
number of small holdings on their estates, as by this subdivision they
increased the number of their voters and raised the total of their rents. As a
result, the population increased rapidly, and continued to increase notwithstanding a gradual change in economic conditions. On the conclusion of the
war the rise in prices was succeeded by a fall. Tillage ceased to pay, and the
landlords were naturally tempted to turn the agricultural lands into pasture.
A campaign of 'Clearances' was inaugurated and continued without inter-
mission. It became especially vigorous when by the Act of 1829 the smaller
peasants were deprived of the right of voting. The tenantry were driven
out, and their houses razed to the ground. Holdings were 'consolidated'.

Parliament looked on complacently, and passed laws to make ejectment an inexpensive process. As there were no industries to relieve the pressure, the people crowded in upon such remnants of the soil as were left to them. They were compelled to pay famine rents, which, as John Stuart Mill put it, scarcely left them enough to stave off death from starvation. They lived on potatoes as the Chinese live on rice. Were a bad harvest to come a catastrophe must inevitably ensue.

There came not one bad harvest, but three in succession. In the autumn of 1845 three-quarters of the potato crop was destroyed in a few days by a form of blight hitherto unknown. In 1846 and 1847 the whole potato crop perished. From 1846 to 1849 famine reigned throughout the land. No sooner did the plague touch them than the people seemed plunged in a sort of stupor.

'It was no uncommon sight to see the cottier and his little family seated on the garden fence gazing all day long in moody silence at the blighted plot that had been their last hope. Nothing would rouse them. You spoke: they answered not; you tried to cheer them: they shook their heads.'

L. PAUL-DUBOIS, Contemporary Ireland, 1908

If the price of corn fell prodigiously—as at the end of the Napoleonic war, or at the passing of the corn laws in England—the cheaper bread was no help to the peasants, most of whom could never afford to eat it; it only doubled their labour to send out greater shiploads of provisions for the charges due in England. On the other hand, if potatoes rotted, famine swept over the country among its fields of corn and cattle. And when rent failed, summary powers of eviction were given at Westminster under English theories for use in Ireland alone; 'and if any one would defend his farm it is here denominated rebellion.' Families were flung on the bogs and mountain sides to live on wild turnips and nettles, to gather chickweed, sorrel, and seaweed, and to sink under the fevers that followed vagrancy, starvation, cold, and above all the broken hearts of men hunted from their homes. In famine time the people to save themselves from death were occasionally compelled to use blood taken from live bullocks, boiled up with a little oatmeal; and the appalling sight was seen of feeble women gliding across the country with their pitchers, actually trampling upon fertility and fatness, to collect in the corner of a grazier's farm for their little portion of blood. Five times between 1822 and 1837 there were famines of lesser degree: but two others, 1817 and 1847, were noted as among the half-dozen most terrible recorded in Europe and Asia during the century. From 1846 to 1848 over a million lay dead of hunger, while in a year food-stuffs for seventeen million pounds were sent to England. English soldiers guarded from the starving the fields of corn and the waggons that carried it to the ports; herds of cattle were shipped, and skins of asses which had served the famishing for food. New evictions on an enormous scale followed the famine, the clearance of what was then called in the phrase of current English economics 'the surplus population', 'the overstock tenantry'. They died, or fled in hosts to America—Ireland pouring out on the one side her great stores of 'surplus food', on the other her 'surplus people', for whom there was nothing to eat. In the twenty years that followed the men and women who had fled to America sent back some thirteen millions to keep a roof over the heads of the old and the children they had left behind. It was a tribute for the landlords' pockets—a rent which could never have been paid from the land they leased. The loans raised for expenditure on the Irish famine were charged by England on the Irish taxes for repayment.

ALICE STOPFORD GREEN, *Irish Nationality*, 1911

from *Famine and Exportation*

Take it from us, every grain,
We were made for you to drain;
Black starvation let us feel,
England must not want a meal!

When our rotting roots shall fail,
When the hunger pangs assail,
Ye'll have of Irish corn your fill—
We'll have grass and nettles still! . . .

JOHN O'HAGAN (*c.*1847), in *Songs and Ballads of
Young Ireland*, 1896

Why do we not see the smoke curling from those lowly chimneys? And surely we ought by this time to scent the well-known aroma of the turf-fires. But what (may Heaven be about us this night)—what reeking breath of hell is this oppressing the air, heavier and more loathsome than the smell of death rising from the fresh carnage of a battlefield. Oh, misery! had we forgotten that this was the *Famine Year*? And we are here in the midst of those thousand Golgothas that border our island with a ring of death from Cork Harbour all round to Lough Foyle. There is no need of inquiries here—no need of words; the history of this little society is plain before us. Yet we go forward, though with sick hearts and swimming eyes, to examine the Place of Skulls nearer. There is a horrible silence; grass grows before the doors; we fear to look into any door, though they are all open or off the hinges; for we fear to see yellow chapless skeletons grinning there; but our footfalls rouse two lean dogs, that run from us with doleful howling, and we know by the felon-gleam in the wolfish eyes how *they* have lived after their masters died. We walk amidst the houses of the dead, and out at the other side of the cluster, and there is not one where we dare to enter. We stop before the threshold of our host of two years ago, put our head, with eyes shut, inside the door-jamb, and say, with shaking voice, 'God save all here!'—No answer—ghastly silence, and a mouldy stench, as from the mouth of burial-vaults. Ah! they are dead! they are dead! the strong man and the fair, dark-eyed woman and the little ones, with their liquid Gaelic accents that melted into music for us two years ago; they shrunk and withered together until their voices dwindled to a rueful gibbering, and they hardly knew one another's faces; but their horrid eyes scowled on each other with a cannibal glare. We know the whole story—the father was on a 'public work', and earned the sixth part of what would have maintained his family, which was not always paid him; but still it kept them half alive for three months, and so instead of dying in December they died in March. And the agonies of those three months who can tell?—the poor wife wasting and weeping over her stricken children; the heavyladen weary man, with black night thickening around him—thickening within him— feeling his own arm shrink and his step totter with the cruel hunger that gnaws away his life, and knowing too surely that all this will soon be over. And he has grown a rogue, too, on those public works; with roguery and lying about him, roguery and lying above him, he has begun to say in his heart that there is no God; from a poor but honest farmer he has sunk down into a swindling, sturdy beggar; for him there is nothing firm or stable; the pillars of the world are rocking around him; 'the sun to him is dark and silent, as the moon when she deserts the night.' Even ferocity or thirst for vengeance he can never feel again; for the very blood of him is starved into a thin, chill *serum*, and if you prick him he will not bleed. Now he can totter forth no longer, and he stays at home to die. But his darling wife is dear to him no longer; alas! and alas! there is a dull, stupid malice in their looks: they forget that they had five children, all dead weeks ago, and flung coffinless into shallow graves—nay, in the frenzy of their despair they would rend one another for the last morsel in that house of doom; and at last, in misty dreams of drivelling idiocy, they die utter strangers.

JOHN MITCHEL, *Jail Journal*, 1854

The effect of the Famine, which varied from region to region, affected most seriously those areas where the structures of chain emigration were already in place: leaving behind in Ireland, according to Sir William Wilde (father of the well-known emigrant Oscar), a population disproportionately 'poor, weak, old, lame, sick, blind, dumb, imbecile and insane'.

R. F. FOSTER, *Paddy & Mr Punch*, 1993

Oct. 26. Provisions continuing to pour into England from Ireland and yet the famine said to be pressing there. I can't believe it, for besides that both food and work seem to be plenty, it could hardly be that if people were really hungry they would refuse task work which from the Lord Lieutenant's proclamations they must in many places have done, claiming for daily wages, in other words leave to idle. They have got it into their heads that being in distress they are to do nothing to get out of it, but are to sit comfortably down and open their mouths to be fed. Like cousin Bartle, I can't but despise a people so meanspirited, so low-minded, so totally without energy, only I attribute it to the want of animal food; there can be no vigour of mind or body without it.

ELIZABETH SMITH, *Irish Journals*, 1846

They picked over and picked out their blackened potatoes, and even ate the decayed ones, till many were made sick, before the real state of the country was known; and when it fell, it fell like an avalanche, sweeping at once the entire land. No parish need be anxious for neighbouring ones—each had enough under his own eye, and at his own door, to drain all resources, and keep alive his sympathy. It was some months before the rich really believed that the poor were not making false pretences; for at such a distance had they ever kept themselves from the 'lower order', who were all 'dirty and lazy'; that many of them had never *realized* that four millions of people were subsisting entirely on the potatoe, and that another million ate them six days out of seven, entirely; they did not *realize* that these 'lazy ones' had worked six or eight months in the year for eight-pence and ten-pence, but more for six-pence, and even three-pence in the southern parts, and the other four months been 'idle' because 'no man had hired them'; they did not *realize* that the disgusting rags with which these 'lazy' ones disgraced their very gates, and shocked all decency, were the *rags* which they had contributed to provide; and such were often heard to say that this judgment was what they might expect, as a reward for their 'religion and idleness'. But the wave rolled on; the slain were multiplied; the dead by the way-side, and the more revolting sights of families found in the darkest corner of a cabin, in one putrid mass, where, in many cases, the cabin was tumbled down upon them to give them a burial, was somewhat convincing, even to those who had doubted much from the beginning.

ASENATH NICHOLSON, *Lights and Shades of Ireland*, 1850

The famine of the year 1846 had left as its legacy a new and tragic Ireland. Three quarters of a million of the population had died of hunger. The famine was followed by two consequences. One was the Clearances; the other was emigration. The Clearances, or evictions, had some economic justification. The small extent of the peasant's holding, inadequate, in a bad year, to supply the minimum needs of subsistence, had been one of the causes of famine; and some consolidation of holdings was an economic necessity. But whatever its economic justification, the grievance of eviction rankled bitterly in the hearts of the peasantry, who, losing their holdings, lost everything, since they had no alternative occupation to which they could turn. The scale on which eviction was practised made the misery which it involved still more bitter. From 1849 to 1856 over 50,000 families were evicted. In 1863 and again in 1864 the number of families evicted was little short of 2,000; in 1865 and 1866 it sank, but it still remained at the rate of nearly 1,000. Meanwhile the flood of emigration flowed high. Between 1846 and 1851 a quarter of a million of the population emigrated in each year. Between 1851 and 1861 over 100,000 were annually leaving Ireland. Famine, eviction, emigration—this was a triple wave of woes before which men's spirits quailed. They have left their mark deep in Irish memory. They have left a legacy of hatred of England to the third and fourth generation. 'It is probable', writes Lecky, in a passage which Sir Horace Plunkett quotes as confirmed by his own experience, 'that the true source of the savage hatred of England that animates great bodies of Irishmen on either side of the Atlantic has very little connexion with the penal laws, or the rebellion (of 1798), or the Union. It is far more due to the great clearances and the vast unaided emigrations that followed the famine.'

ERNEST BARKER, *Ireland in the Last Fifty Years*, 1916

The river had at this point overflowed its banks and the swirling water was half-way up the potato garden. The pit, however, was still beyond the flood. The old man at once dug into its end with the spade and laid bare the covering of ferns. These he hurriedly pulled aside with his hands. Then he slowly raised himself to his full height, some rotting ferns still in his hands. He stared, speechless, at the mass of corruption into which the potatoes had turned.

Then he drew back a pace and looked sideways up at the sky, his face wrinkled into a foolish grin, as if asking God for an explanation of this awful mischief. As he looked, he drew his hands slowly along his thighs until his arms were rigid. Then he opened his fists suddenly, dropped the ferns and rubbed his palms together making an inarticulate noise in his throat like an enraged idiot. He got on his knees beside the hole that he had made in the pit and plunging his arms up to the elbows into the heap, he groped about among the mass of corruption, to find out if the centre also had rotted.

Thomsy arrived while the old man was groping in this way. He gaped and cried out:

'In the name of God, what is it?'

The old man started, drew back, rose slowly to his feet, turned about and held out his arms towards Thomsy.

'That's all that's left of them,' he stammered, holding out his arms, from which the corruption dripped to the ground.

'God have mercy on us,' said Thomsy, taking off his hat and crossing himself.

The old man walked out of the garden, stooping, his arms hanging limply by his sides. He seemed to have got suddenly old and decrepit. At one blow, the spunk had oozed from his body. As he was climbing the fence from the garden into the neighbouring field, he paused and looked up the Valley.

It was a fearful sight. The sky had not cleared after the rain. It was dark and lowering, with a scant drizzle falling here and there from some shreds of cloud, that hung like floating rags across the sky. In this gloom, the mountains that encircled the Valley seemed to have thrust themselves forward, as if swollen by the rain; and the narrow crater in between, now barren of all growth, looked like a desolate shore from which the sea had been sucked by a monstrous moon. All along the mountain-sides, turbulent streams flowed down upon the sodden, blackened earth to cover its nakedness. The only sound was the roar of the falling water.

'It's a curse that has fallen on the land,' muttered the old man as he continued towards the house.

LIAM O'FLAHERTY, *Famine*, 1937

Tháinig blianta an ghorta agus an droch shaoghal agus an t-ocras agus bhris sin neart agus spiorad na ndaoiní. Ní rabh ann ach achan nduine ag iarraidh bheith beo. Chaill siad a' dáimh le chéile. Ba chuma cé a bhí gaolmhar duit, ba do charaid an t-é a bhéarfadh greim duit le chur in do bhéal. D'imthigh an spórt agus a' caitheamh aimsire. Stad an fhilidheacht agus a' ceol agus damhsa. Chaill siad agus rinne siad dearmad den iomlán agus nuair a bhisigh an saoghal ar dhóigheannaí eile ní tháinig na rudaí seo ariamh arais mar a bhí siad. Mharbh an gorta achan rud.

MÁIRE NÍ GRIANNA, recorded 1945

The years of famine, wretched life and hunger came, and this broke the people's strength and spirit. There was nothing to do but to try to stay alive. All fellow feeling was lost. It didn't matter who was related to you, your friend was the person who'd give you a bite to put in your mouth. All sport and merriment disappeared. Poetry and singing and dancing were no more. The whole lot was lost and forgotten, and when things improved in other ways, it never came back as it had been. The famine killed everything.

trans. P.C.

In 1847 Ireland was predominantly Gaelic-speaking outside the cities and the former Pale. Her people were the virile folk, big of body and exuberant in manner, that won the admiration of so many travellers. Their life, with the boisterous fairs, the fireside *seanchas*, the country dance, the flowing wit and ready song, has lingered in the Gaeltacht until to-day; but the Gaeltacht, which covered the whole countryside on the famine's eve, has shrunk rapidly ever since that dreadful year when the potato first blackened. For the lifetime of three generations, Ireland has been a nation drifting towards extinction.

AODH DE BLÁCAM, Gaelic Literature Surveyed, 1929

Whenever, after a prolonged season of rain, famine swooped on them out of a black mist, the poor souls went down like flies. The world rang with the havoc of 1847, but no one hearkened to the periodic famine cries in the eighteenth century. In the famine of 1740—that famine which set Berkeley ruminating on the virtues of tar-water—400,000 are said to have perished. One writer says that the dogs were seen to eat the dead bodies that remained unburied in the fields. Another contemporary wrote: 'Want and misery are in every face, the rich unable to relieve the poor, the roads spread with dead and dying bodies, mankind the colour of the dock and nettles they feed on, two or three sometimes on a car going to the grave for want of bearers to carry them, and many buried only in the fields and ditches where they perished.'

'I have seen,' wrote still another contemporary, 'the labourer endeavouring to work at his spade, but fainting for want of food, and forced to quit it. I have seen the aged father eating grass like a beast, and in the anguish of his soul wishing for dissolution. I have seen the helpless orphan exposed on the dung-hill, and none to take him in for fear of infection; and I have seen the hungry infant sucking at the breast of the already expired parent.'

And if we move either backward or forward from this midmost period of 1740, things are found to be no better. In 1720 Archbishop King writes: 'The cry of the whole people is loud for bread; God knows what will be the consequence; many are starved, and I am afraid many more will.'

DANIEL CORKERY, The Hidden Ireland, 1925

I happen to be able to recall precisely the day, almost the hour, when the blight fell on the potatoes and caused the great calamity. A party of us were driving to a seven o'clock dinner at the house of our neighbour, Mrs Evans, of Port-rane. As we passed a remarkably fine field of potatoes in blossom, the scent came through the open windows of the carriage and we remarked to each other how splendid was the crop. Three or four hours later, as we returned home in the dark, a dreadful smell came from the same field, and we exclaimed, 'Something has happened to those potatoes; they do not smell at all as they did when we passed them on our way out.' Next morning there was a wail from one end of Ireland to the other. Every field was black and every root rendered unfit for human food. And there were nearly eight millions of people depending principally upon these potatoes for existence!

FRANCES POWER COBBE, Autobiography, 1894

In the spring of 1847, some six hundred of the starving peasantry of the West thronged into the town of Louisburgh, seeking food or a ticket for admission to the workhouse from the Relieving Officer. He informed them that he had no power to give them food or a ticket, and that they should apply personally to the two paid guardians, a Colonel Hograve and a Mr Lecky, who would hold a board meeting the next day in Delphi Lodge, Bundorragha. The Lodge was situated in the wildest, uninhabited region in Ireland, eighteen miles distant from the proper boardroom at Westport, and ten miles distant from Louisburgh. This was a deliberate trap set up by the Government of that day in order to decoy the starving Celts out to this wild region in order to slaughter them.

These six hundred people had no homes to return to; they were in rags, almost naked, and they had not tasted any kind of food for days, so severe was the famine. They sat down in front of the houses in Louisburgh during that night, and many of them were found stark dead where they lay next morning. On that day some four hundred of them arose shivering in their rags, all barefooted and still without food; they sighed and looked up to heaven before setting out on a journey from which none of them was to return.

When they reached Glankeen, they had to wade through the river which was swollen by recent rains. Their rags from the hips downward were saturated with water on that cold, damp day. When they reached the southern bank of this rapid mountain torrent, there was nothing even resembling a road between that spot and Doolough, so that they had to negotiate the dreadful goat track along the brow of the precipice which overhangs the house of the late Captain Houstan. They encountered another river far deeper than that of Glankeen, and since there were no bridges in those days they had to battle their way through the stream, with the result that they were wet to the waist.

When the wet and suffering peasantry reached Delphi Lodge, the vice-guardians were at lunch and could not be disturbed, so the people sat down in their damp, miserable rags among the pine trees, and there many of them expired. When the two gentlemen condescended to see the peasantry, they refused to grant them relief or tickets to the workhouse, so the fearful journey had been all in vain.

JAMES BERRY, *Tales of the West of Ireland*, tales recalled from oral narration; published in the *Mayo News*, 1910–13; and edited by Gertrude M. Horgan, 1966

from *Dublin: A Poem*

Here men of feeling, ere they yet grow old,
Die of the very horrors they behold.
'Tis hard to sleep when one has just stood by
And seen a strong man of sheer hunger die;
'Tis hard to draw an easy, healthful breath,
In fields that sicken with the air of death;
Or where relief invites the living throng
To see the withered phantoms flit along,
Hunger impelling, and exhaustion still
Leaving the weak limbs baffled of the will.
Who, without shortened days, could daily pass
The tottering, fluttering, palpitating mass,
Who gaze and gloat around the guarded dole,
That owned a heart of flesh, or human soul?

SIR SAMUEL FERGUSON, *Dublin University Magazine*, July 1849

One day, when I was eight years of age (I seem to remember that I was standing at the corner of the haggard), I saw a woman coming towards me up the hill. She was barefoot, walking very slowly and panting, as if she had been running. She was blowing so much, her mouth was wide open, so that I had a sight of her teeth. But the thing that amazed me altogether was her feet. Each foot was swollen so that, from the knee down, it was as big and as fat as a gallon-can. That sight took such a firm grip on my mind that it is before my eyes now, every bit as clear-cut as it was that day, although it is around three score years and five since I saw it. That woman had been fairly independent and free from adversity until the blackness had come upon the potatoes.

Another day—I can't tell if it was before or after that —I was inside in our house, standing on the hearthstone, when a boy came in the door. I saw the face that was on him and the terror that was in his two eyes, the terror of hunger. That face and those two eyes are before my mind now, as clear and as unclouded as the day I gave them the one and only look. Somebody gave him a lump of bread. He snatched the bread and turned his back to us and his face to the wall and he started right into eating it so ravenously that you would think he would choke himself. At the time I did not realize that I was so amazed by him or by his voracity, but that sight has stayed in my mind, and will stay as long as I live.

PEADAR Ó LAOGHAIRE (Father Peter Ó Leary), *Mo Scéal Fein* (*my own Story*), 1915, trans. Cyril T. Ó Céirin

Drivers seldom went out without seeing dead bodies strewn along the roadside, without passing over them if it were night. Another eye-witness informs us that in his district on opening the front door in the morning it was 'a common occurrence to find the corpse of some victim leaning against it, who in the night-time had rested in its shelter'. All rites, both civil and religious, had to be given up. There were no coffins for the dead. The corpses were hastily carried off in a coffin with a movable bottom, from which they were thrown straight into a common grave. Those who escaped the famine succumbed to the fever. Priests and doctors died by the hundred. Well-to-do families caught the malady and perished with none to aid them. It was a case of each man for himself. All who could, fled the country. The Irish turned their eyes towards America as the Jews of old towards Jerusalem. But emigrants had to endure sufferings almost as bitter as those who remained behind. The State at first exercised no supervision, and the emigrants were crowded into 'coffin ships', in which they died in thousands during the course of the voyage. How many of her citizens, one naturally asks, did Ireland lose during those terrible years? The number of those who perished of hunger has been reckoned at 729,033, 'far more,' as John Bright said, 'than ever fell by the sword in any war England ever waged'.

L. PAUL-DUBOIS, *Contemporary Ireland*, 1908

12th [April 1827] . . . I hope to God the people's hearts will soften. Three hundred families in Callan are starving. . . .

14th . . . The paupers have light hearts as they expect a bite of meat to-morrow. The country people are gathering in for the market. The country cabin-dwellers eat meat on only three days a year, Christmas Day, Shrove Tuesday, and Easter Sunday.

HUMPHREY O'SULLIVAN, *Diary 1827–35*, 1979, trans. Tomás de Bhaldraithe

I must record some features of the potato-rot as it appeared in other districts less favoured than the Queen's County. The population of that county was never very excessive, the farms were moderate in size, and valuable as the potato was as an esculent, and most useful as I had proved it to be in the reclamation of waste lands, yet it rarely formed, as in other districts, the sole food of the people. During the period whilst I was engaged in organising the system of drainage for the Board of Works, fearful scenes were being enacted in other parts, and especially in the south and west of Ireland. There the cottier system prevailed to its fullest extent; and in the mountain districts where but little corn was grown, and where the people lived almost exclusively upon the potato, the most dire distress arose. Dark whisperings and rumours of famine in its most appalling form began to reach us, but still we could scarcely believe that men, women, and children were actually dying of starvation in thousands. *Yet so it was*. They died in their mountain glens, they died along the sea-coast, they died on the roads, and they died in the fields; they wandered into the towns, and died in the streets; they closed their cabin doors, and lay down upon their beds, and died of actual starvation in their houses.

To us, even at the time, it appeared almost incredible that such things should be. But a cry soon arose from the west, and especially from the district of Skibbereen and Schull in the county of Cork, which left no further doubt as to the real position of affairs—hundreds, nay thousands, of people had died and were dying in those districts of absolute direct starvation.

W. STEWART TRENCH, *Realities of Irish Life*, 1869

The ghastly impressions of famine ... were not confined to those who composed the crowds. Even the children were little living skeletons, wan and yellow, with a spirit of pain and suffering legible upon their fleshless but innocent features; whilst the very dogs, as was well observed, were not able to bark, for, indeed, such of them as survived, were nothing but ribs and skin. At all events, they assisted in making up the terrible picture of general misery which the country at large presented. Both day and night, but at night especially, their hungry howlings could be heard over the country, or mingling with the wailings which the people were in the habit of pouring over those whom the terrible typhus was sweeping away with such wide and indiscriminating fatality.

Our readers may now perceive, that the sufferings of these unhappy crowds, before they had been driven to these acts of violence, were almost beyond belief. At an earlier period of the season, when the potatoes could not yet be dug, miserable women might be seen early in the morning, and, in fact, during all hours of the day, gathering weeds of various descriptions, in order to sustain life; and happy were they who could procure a few handfuls of young nettles, chicken-weed, sorrell, *preshagh*, buglass, or sea-weed, to bring home as food, either for themselves or their unfortunate children. Others again, were glad to creep or totter to stock-farms, at great distances across the country, in the hope of being able to procure a portion of blood, which, on such melancholy occasions, is taken from the heifers and bullocks that graze there, in order to prevent the miserable poor from perishing by actual starvation and death.

WILLIAM CARLETON, *The Black Prophet*, 1847

Bad government, poverty and the vicissitudes of the soil and climate combine to produce one of the major thematic motifs in Ulster fiction, that of *the blighted land*. The motif has lost some of its passionate force in modern rural fiction because the extreme social conditions of Carleton's time have mostly disappeared. Carleton could summon up images of widespread dearth and hunger and lived through the Great Famine, that horrific conjunction of all the Irish peasant's disabilities. It would be difficult for a modern writer to match the apocalyptic vision of *The Black Prophet* with its terrifying evocations of the soup-kitchens, cadaverous beggars and endless funeral processions under a brooding sky. Yet so traumatic was the Famine for the Irish people that it lingers yet in the folk memory. The Victorian and post-Victorian workhouses in Shan Bullock, Patrick MacGill and Michael McLaverty have, even when offstage, inherited some of the emotive currency of the soup-kitchens, and MacGill's Donegal mendicants still bear the haunted and ravaged look of Carleton's famine-struck peasants.

JOHN WILSON FOSTER, *Forces and Themes in Ulster Fiction*, 1974

The 1846 potato crop turned black and rotten after it had been harvested and stored. Potato blight devastates a crop after it has come to fruition. But the 1846 blight did not immediately create panic or complete despair. It meant a long and hungry winter, but that was no new thing to Ireland's peasantry. Many serious blights had occurred before, including the years 1836-7 and 1839. It was the repetition of the blight, its recurrence year after year in every part of the country until 1851, which created protracted and disastrous famine.

Five years without an autumn potato harvest entailed five winters and springs of near or complete starvation. Only the provision of relief by local landlords or Westminster's emergency measures stood between millions of country people and a slow death from hunger. Until help came the worst hunger could temporarily be assuaged by whatever livestock, poultry and farm animals could be eaten or sold. After that—and without milk or eggs— came the domestic pets, berries, nettles, roots, weeds. Without potatoes the tiny holdings of large families, the product of sub-division and early marriage, could offer virtually nothing. The few areas with both the skills and the resource could live for a time on fish. But even there the situation became more and more desperate as each year the blight reappeared.

After much resistance, born of dogmatism, cynicism, incredulity and indifference, the English government finally put relief measures into effect. Public works—the construction of roads, railways and canals—were ordered. Behind this order lay an economic theory: employment would lead to money, and money would lead to markets. The forces of supply and demand would guarantee that traders would station themselves in those markets. It followed from this theory that starvation could not occur if the starving had incomes. Perhaps at no time in the history of this theory have its misconceptions been so exposed and the tenacity of its proponents more bitterly paid for than during the great famine.

HUGH BRODY, *Inishkillane*, 1973

Up in the corner of Farahy churchyard the Famine pit was dug and not slowly filled. The bodies had to be tipped in coffinless, earth shovelled loosely over them, to be disturbed again. The names of many dead were not known; they were mountainy people drawn down to Farahy by hopes of reaching the Bowen's Court soup-kitchen. This movement towards help that was not reached created a higher death-rate in Farahy than in many of the other parishes round. At Bowen's Court, the desperate pressure of people against Eliza Wade's door at the end of the kitchen passage made it necessary that the door should be barred: through a trap she gave out what soup there was, then she had to shut the trap and hear groaning movement continuing hopelessly outside.

ELIZABETH BOWEN, *Bowen's Court*, 1942

The Scar

for Padraic Fiacc

There's not a chance now that I might recover
one syllable of what that sick man said,
tapping upon my great-grandmother's shutter,
and begging, I was told, a piece of bread;
for on his tainted breath there hung infection
rank from the cabins of the stricken west,
the spores from black potato-stalks, the spittle
mottled with poison in his rattling chest;
but she who, by her nature, quickly answered,

accepted in return the famine-fever;
and that chance meeting, that brief confrontation,
conscribed me of the Irishry for ever.

Though much I cherish lies outside their vision,
and much they prize I have no claim to share,
yet in that woman's death I found my nation;
the old wound aches and shews its fellow scar.

JOHN HEWITT, *Collected Poems*, 1991

We drove to Ardenode on Friday and found Augustus West sitting with Mrs George, heard plenty of miseries, writs out, defaulters flying, tenants cheating, and paupers dying. These things are so common now they the less affect us, but I was shocked indeed at our own school, no rosy cheeks, no merry laugh, little skeletons in rags with white faces and large staring eyes crouching against one another half dead. How can we remedy it? No way; how feed sixty children? if we were to coin ourselves into halfpence we could not give a meal to one hundredth part of our teeming neighbourhood a day. The poor little Doyles so clean, so thin, so sad, so naked softened my heart to the foolish parents. They are on our own hill, although not our own people, they must not die of hunger. If I could manage to give a bit of bread daily to each pauper child, but we have no money, much more than we can afford is spent on labour, the best kind of charity, leaving little for ought else, people not being quixotick enough to deny themselves the decencies they have been accustomed to for the support of those who have no claim upon them, who little deserve help and who would not be really benefited by it, only a temporary assistance it would be resulting in no good. These philosophick views are right doubtless, yet when I see hungry children I long to give them food. One meal a day I hear is the general rule among this wretched population. While they can get that they will not hear of the poor house. Yet there are 1,300 in it, and crowds are turned away for want of room.

Feb. 10. Lady M. [Milltown] and her girls called here in high good humour. She had seen them really admired at Lady Portarlington's Ball, and when I told her what I had heard said of them 'so fresh, so happy, so natural and so goodlooking', she was quite affected; the tears stood in her eyes. The Ball at Lady Drogheda's can't be managed and they have given it up with utmost good-humour. So have our own dear girls given up Mrs Purcell's Ball in the same amiable way, though they had been looking forward to it with such pleasure. We had not the wherewithal in the first place, secondly, I am not well enough for the fatigue.

ELIZABETH SMITH, *Irish Journals*, 1849

My Dark Fathers

My dark fathers lived the intolerable day
Committed always to the night of wrong,
Stiffened at the hearthstone, the woman lay,
Perished feet nailed to her man's breastbone.
Grim houses beckoned in the swelling gloom
Of Munster fields where the Atlantic night
Fettered the child within the pit of doom,
And everywhere a going down of light.

And yet upon the sandy Kerry shore
The woman once had danced at ebbing tide
Because she loved flute music—and still more
Because a lady wondered at the pride
Of one so humble. That was long before
The green plant withered by an evil chance;
When winds of hunger howled at every door
She heard the music dwindle and forgot the dance.

Such mercy as the wolf receives was hers
Whose dance became a rhythm in a grave,
Achieved beneath the thorny savage furze
That yellowed fiercely in a mountain cave.
Immune to pity, she, whose crime was love,
Crouched, shivered, searched the threatening sky,
Discovered ready signs, compelled to move
Her to her innocent appalling cry.

Skeletoned in darkness, my dark fathers lay
Unknown, and could not understand
The giant grief that trampled night and day,
The awful absence moping through the land.
Upon the headland, the encroaching sea
Left sand that hardened after tides of Spring,
No dancing feet disturbed its symmetry
And those who loved good music ceased to sing.

Since every moment of the clock
Accumulates to form a final name,
Since I am come of Kerry clay and rock,
I celebrate the darkness and the shame
That could compel a man to turn his face
Against the wall, withdrawn from light so strong
And undeceiving, spancelled in a place
Of unapplauding hands and broken song.

BRENDAN KENNELLY, *Collection One*, 1966

'There have been three cruel plagues,' he said, 'out through the country since I was born in the west. First, there was the big wind in 1839, that tore away the grass and green things from the earth. Then there was the blight that came on the 9th of June in the year 1846. Up to then the potatoes were clean and good; but that morning a mist rose up out of the sea, and you could hear a voice talking near a mile off across the stillness of the earth. It was the same the next day, and the day after, and so on for three days or more; and then you could begin to see the tops of the stalks lying over as if the life was gone out of them. And that was the beginning of the great trouble and famine that destroyed Ireland. Then the people went on, I suppose, in their wickedness and their animosity of one against the other; and the Almighty God sent down the third plague, and that was the sickness called the choler. Then all the people left the town of Sligo—it's in Sligo I was reared—and you could walk through the streets at the noon of day and not see a person, and you could knock at one door and another door and find no one to answer you. The people were travelling out north and south and east, with the terror that was on them; and the country people were digging ditches across the roads and driving them back where they could, for they had great dread of the disease.'

J. M. SYNGE, *In Wicklow and West Kerry*, 1912

from *The Poet's Circuits*

Nor right, nor left, nor any road I see a comrade's face,
Nor word to lift the heart in me I hear in any place;
They leave me, who pass by me, to my loneliness and care,
Without a house to draw my step nor a fire that I might share.

Ochone, before our people knew the scatt'ring of the dearth,
Before they saw potatoes rot and melt black in the earth,
I might have stood in Connacht, on the top of Cruckmaelinn,
And all around me I would see the hundreds of my kin.

PADRAIC COLUM, *Collected Poems of Ireland*, 1960

Death and starvation in Ireland at any rate, progressing rapidly. The roads are crowded with wretched beggars from the south and west, famine too truly depicted on their miserable skeletons, hardly concealed by rags. How thankful I am for the fortune that has placed us here.

ELIZABETH SMITH, *Irish Journals*, 1849

Famine Cottage

Soft flute note of absence;
Above MacCrystal's glen
Where shaggy gold of whin
Overhangs a hidden stream
I stumble upon a cabin,
Four crumbling walls and
A door, a shape easily
Rising from the ground,
As easily settling back:
Stones swathed in grass.

JOHN MONTAGUE, *A Slow Dance*, 1975

Farewell to Barn and Stack and Tree

Blinding in Paris, for his party-piece
Joyce named the shops along O'Connell Street
And on Iona Colmcille sought ease
By wearing Irish mould next to his feet.

SEAMUS HEANEY, from 'Gravities'

'It used to seem to me a very sad thing to see all the people going to
America; the poor Celt disappearing in America, leaving his own
country, leaving his language, and very often his religion.'

GEORGE MOORE, 'A Play-House in the Waste'

The Emigrant

The car is yoked before the door,
And time will let us dance no more.
Come, fiddler, now, and play for me
'*Farewell to barn and stack and tree.*'

To-day the fields looked wet and cold,
The mearings gapped, the cattle old.
Things are not what they used to be—
'*Farewell to barn and stack and tree.*'

I go, without the heart to go,
To kindred that I hardly know.
Drink, neighbour, drink a health with me—
'*Farewell to barn and stack and tree.*'

Five hours will see me stowed aboard,
The gang-plank up, the ship unmoored.
Christ grant no tempest shakes the sea—
'*Farewell to barn and stack and tree.*'

JOSEPH CAMPBELL, *Irishry*, 1913

The scale of emigration from Ireland after 1850 is so enormous that it is unequalled anywhere else in Europe. Against this general picture is the pattern of Irish women's emigration, which developed some unusual features over the next period. The bulk of emigration was to America rather than to Britain, and in the mid-1800s Irish women made up 35 per cent of Irish immigrants there. From this time onwards they left primarily as single women, and generally, they left at a younger age than men. Also, as the century progressed and during many periods of the twentieth century, more women than men emigrated. This is untypical amongst emigrant groups.

> MARY LENNON, MARIE McADAM, and JOANNE O'BRIEN, *Across the Water: Irish Women's Lives in Britain*, 1988

I remember still with emotion the emigration of the young people of the neighbourhood to America. In those days the farmer's children were raised for export. There were times of the year—in spring or fall—when there would be a sort of group emigration; that is, a dozen or so would start off together once or twice a week for a few weeks to take the train to the boat at Queenstown or Derry. Generally each group was bound for the same town in America where they had friends or relatives who had paid their passage money beforehand or sent them their tickets. The night before their departure there would be a farewell gathering called an American wake in one of the houses of the emigrating boys or girls. There would be singing and dancing interlarded with tears and lamentations until the early hours of the morning, when, without sleep, the young people started for the train, the mothers sometimes keening as at a funeral or a wake for the dead, for the parting would often be forever and the parents might never again see the boy or girl who was crossing the ocean. There was, I remember, a steep hill on the road near our house, and when the emigrating party reached the bottom of it, it was their habit to descend from the sidecars and carts to ease the horses, and they would climb the height on foot. As they reached the top from which they could see the whole countryside, they would turn and weepingly bid farewell to the green fields, the little white houses, the sea, and the rambling roads they knew so well. The hill was called the Hill of Weeping in Gaelic, because of all those who had wept their farewells from the top of it.

> MARY COLUM, *Life and the Dream*, 1928

Nearly all young Irishmen keep one eye on the possibility of emigrating. Their characters are formed under the shadow of that possibility, and they look upon their life in Ireland as a transitory fact. They give up their country, and they shape all their endeavours with a view to preparing themselves for a foreign environment. If eventually they do not emigrate they help on the more vigorously the Anglicisation of their neighbours. Some time ago I was driving through a remote part of Kerry, and stopped at a village hotel to have something to eat. I invited the driver—a fine sturdy young chap—in, and he ate with his fingers. 'Now, if I go to America,' said he, 'they'll make game o' me for not bein' able to use a knife and fork.' The eye is always on America or somewhere else. The point which I want this story to impress is this: If that man did not contemplate the probability of going to America he would be content during the course of his life, were it the easier way, to eat with his feet. Every incentive comes from abroad, and the Irish nation so deeply despises itself that it has ceased to develop by force of its own vitality. The Irish people who emigrate, never having been really Irish at all, quickly become absorbed into whatever community they fall among, during their own life-time; and in the next generation all signs of their Irish origin are usually lost. I know there may be some people who will feel inclined to throw down this article at this point and say—'Bosh!' They will be those who consider that the Irish-American of the boasting, blaspheming, vulgar type has preserved his Nationality.

D. P. MORAN, *The Philosophy of Irish Ireland,* 1898

Ardglass Town

The sun is hid in Heaven,
    The fog floats thick and brown,
I walk the streets of London
    And think on Ardglass town.

About the point of Fennick
    The snowy breakers roll,
And green they shine in patterned squares,
    The fields above Ardtole.

Oh, there by many a loaning,
    Past farms that I could name.
Thro' Sheeplands to Gun Island,
    The whins are all aflame.

And my heart bleeds within me
    To think of times I had,
Walking with my sweetheart
    The green road to Ringfad.

RICHARD ROWLEY, *Selected Poems,* 1931

Mary and Michael got to their feet. The father sprinkled them with holy water and they crossed themselves. Then, without looking at their mother, who lay in the chair with her hands clasped on her lap, looking at the ground in a silent tearless stupor, they left the room. Each hurriedly kissed little Thomas, who was not going to Kilmurrage, and then, hand in hand, they left the house. As Michael was going out the door he picked a piece of loose whitewash from the wall and put it in his pocket. The people filed our after them, down the yard and on to the road, like a funeral procession. The mother was left in the house with little Thomas and two old peasant women from the village. Nobody spoke in the cabin for a long time.

LIAM O'FLAHERTY, 'Spring Sowing', 1924

'I remember my sisters going to America in the 1920s and crying and all this business. And I remember the money coming . . . once two of them went, the money soon came for the third one when they were old enough to go, and this is how it went on. And you must remember, in those days they never came back. Nobody ever saw their face again.'

ANON., quoted in MARY LENNON, MARIE McADAM, and JOANNE O'BRIEN,
Across the Water, 1988

Emigration was closely related to social class. Few people from large farms or professional backgrounds emigrated as they were more financially secure, and religious life was an option for the single. The majority of those on the boats to England and America were children from small farms or from unskilled and semi-skilled working-class homes. They were the sons who did not inherit, and the daughters for whom there was no place in the countryside. A woman from a middle-class family remembers that 'even to admit you had relatives in America was to go down socially.'

JENNY BEALE, *Women in Ireland*, 1986

The Exile

Hills of heather, fields of stones,
And the hungry sea that moans
Endlessly beyond them: they
Hold my heart till Judgment Day.

Home is heaven, tho' it were
A burrow in the rock of Clare:
And Clare is seventh heaven to me,
Hanging on the hungry sea.

JOSEPH CAMPBELL, *Irishry*, 1913

'Although we were living in Mexico, far from the company of Gaels or Gaelic-speakers, Gaelic was the fireside language my father and mother used to speak to us. Although English was being used in Mexico, Spanish was the common language there. My mother had little knowledge of Spanish so Gaelic was the language she preferred to speak to us.

'She was only nine years of age,' said he, 'when the bailiffs came to the door to them and threw them out on the road and set fire to the little house they had. 'Tis how they were mocking at the mother when she was beating her hands and crying bitterly. What would she do with her young family, or where would she go with them for the night? But little heed had they for the beating of hands.

'The neighbours made up some little shelter for them for the night, but it was the cold place. The woman and the four children had to live there, but the mother lived only twelve days. She died of grief and heartbreak, and that left my mother with a burden because she had to fend for her brothers who were young and weak. But God helps weakness and as she was growing older she was managing better to aid them and keep them at school. Her father had to be working for the neighbours, because he had neither house nor land then. But they were doing well, for when my mother was eighteen years of age her aunt in California sent her her fare. She managed to get to her and she wasn't long with her aunt when she got work in a good house. As soon as she had any small sum of money earned, she was thinking more about her father and her brothers than about herself. When her oldest brother was twenty years of age, she sent him his fare, and across the sea with him. He got good work, too, and often the two of them were on a visit to their aunt's house, and 'twas she was proud of my mother. It was no wonder, because she was a sensible, modest girl who could easily accept good advice from her aunt.

'One evening, walking alone, she saw a lovely young lad before her in the street. A kind of worry came on her because she perceived that she should recognize him. As soon as he stood in front of her she saluted him with God and Mary and he saluted her, mannerly and softly, with God and Mary and Patrick.

'"Thanks to God," said she, "for a man to meet me in a foreign street who can answer me in my own language! Where are you from, good man?"

'"I am a Kerryman and in Kenmare I lived."

'"What family are you from?" said she.

' "Of the Dillon people—James Dillon are my name and surname," said he.
' "And it's from Glenbeigh I am," said she. "Isn't it lucky how we met each other! I'll have a companion now." '

Peig Sayers, An Old Woman's Reflections, 1939, trans. Seamus Ennis

The County of Mayo

On the deck of Patrick Lynch's boat I sat in woeful plight,
Through my sighing all the weary day and weeping all the night.
Were it not that full of sorrow from my people forth I go,
By the blessed sun, 'tis royally I'd sing thy praise, Mayo.

When I dwelt at home in plenty, and my gold did much abound,
In the company of fair young maids the Spanish ale went round.
'Tis a bitter change from those gay days that now I'm forced to go,
And must leave my bones in Santa Cruz, far from my own Mayo.

They are altered girls in Irrul now; 'tis proud they're grown and high,
With their hair-bags and their top-knots—for I pass their buckles by.
But it's little now I heed their airs, for God will have it so,
That I must depart for foreign lands, and leave my sweet Mayo.

'Tis my grief that Patrick Loughlin is not Earl in Irrul still,
And that Brian Duff no longer rules as Lord upon the Hill;
And that Colonel Hugh McGrady should be lying dead and low,
And I sailing, sailing swiftly from the county of Mayo.

Anon., c.1830, trans. George Fox

Shaw, Yeats, Wilde and Carson were all from the reaches of the Protestant Dublin middle class—the first three from its Bohemian fringe. Marginalization and duality at home made translation to England both easy and necessary. Yeats could not have remade his Irishness in the way he did if he had been permanently based in Dublin; nor could he have achieved his vision of an Irish community, worldwide, united by 'imaginative possessions'. His rooms in Bloomsbury were for decades his only fixed home: symbolically, across the road from Euston Station, where the Irish Mail departed every evening and arrived every morning. Sometimes it brought a visitor from Ireland whose first port of call was breakfast with Yeats in Woburn Buildings. Often it was Lady Gregory or Maud Gonne; on one awkward occasion it was the definitive voice of exile-as-opportunity, James Joyce.

Joyce's use of exile is well known; Yeats's careful manipulation of his permanent status as temporary emigrant has been less considered. One of his earliest works, the novel *John Sherman* (1891), deals with a divided man, caught between provincial, rooted Ireland and the metropolitan temptations of England; his first great popular success was a poem about exile, 'The Lake Isle of Innisfree' (1890), which he later came heartily to dislike. His own early conditioning owed much to the London artistic milieu of Bedford Park, before his explorations in the Celtic Twilight; time and again, at crisis points in his life, he determined to live in England rather than in Ireland (though such resolves had to be elided in his autobiographies). He could use Irishness with artistic ruthlessness, but his nationalism, while *sui generis*, remained intense. He was a cultural founding father of the new state, returned to live there at the height of civil war, became a senator and a formidable committee man. But in the last decade of his life he was again living between England and Ireland.

R. F. FOSTER, *Paddy & Mr Punch*, 1993

These farewells at Irish railway stations, at bus stops in the middle of the bog, when tears blend with raindrops and the Atlantic wind is blowing; Grandfather stands there too, he knows the canyons of Manhattan, he knows the New York waterfront, for thirty years he has been through the mill, and he quickly stuffs another pound note into the boy's pocket, the boy with the cropped hair, the runny nose, the boy who is being wept over as Jacob wept over Joseph; the bus driver cautiously sounds his horn, very cautiously—he has driven hundreds, perhaps thousands, of boys whom he has seen grow up to the station, and he knows the train does not wait and that a farewell that is over and done with is easier to bear than one which is still to come. He waves, the journey into the lonely countryside begins, the little white house in the bog, tears mixed with mucus, past the store, past the pub where Father used to drink his pint of an evening; past the school, the church, a sign of the cross, the bus driver makes one too—the bus stops; more tears, more farewells; Michael is leaving too, and Sheila; tears, tears—Irish, Polish, Armenian tears. . . .

The journey by bus and train from here to Dublin takes eight hours, and what is picked up on the way, the ones standing in the corridors of overcrowded trains with cardboard boxes, battered suitcases, or duffel bags, girls with a rosary still wound around their hands, boys with marbles still clinking in their pockets—this freight is only a small part, only a few hundred of the more than forty thousand who leave this country every year: laborers and doctors, nurses, household help, and teachers—Irish tears that will blend with Polish and Italian tears in London, Manhattan, Cleveland, Liverpool, or Sydney.

HEINRICH BÖLL, *Irish Journal*, 1957, trans. Leila Vennewitz

Valediction

Their verdure dare not show . . . their verdure dare not show . . .
Cant and randy—the seals' heads bobbing in the tide-flow
Between the islands, sleek and black and irrelevant
They cannot depose logically what they want:
Died by gunshot under borrowed pennons,
Sniped from the wet gorse and taken by the limp fins
And slung like a dead seal in a boghole, beaten up
By peasants with long lips and the whisky-drinker's cough.
Park your car in the city of Dublin, see Sackville Street
Without the sandbags in the old photos, meet
The statues of the patriots, history never dies,
At any rate in Ireland, arson and murder are legacies
Like old rings hollow-eyed without their stones
Dumb talismans.
See Belfast, devout and profane and hard,
Built on reclaimed mud, hammers playing in the shipyard,
Time punched with holes like a steel sheet, time
Hardening the faces, veneering with a grey and speckled rime
The faces under the shawls and caps:
This was my mother-city, these my paps.
Country of callous lava cooled to stone,
Of minute sodden haycocks, of ship-sirens' moan,
Of falling intonations—I would call you to book
I would say to you, Look;
I would say, This is what you have given me
Indifference and sentimentality
A metallic giggle, a fumbling hand,
A heart that leaps to a fife band:
Set these against your water-shafted air
Of amethyst and moonstone, the horses' feet like bells of hair
Shambling beneath the orange cart, the beer-brown spring
Guzzling between the heather, the green gush of Irish spring.
Cursèd be he that curses his mother. I cannot be
Anyone else than what this land engendered me:
In the back of my mind are snips of white, the sails
Of the Lough's fishing-boats, the bellropes lash their tails
When I would peal my thoughts, the bells pull free—
Memory in apostasy.
I would tot up my factors
But who can stand in the way of his soul's steam-tractors?
I can say Ireland is hooey, Ireland is
A gallery of fake tapestries,

But I cannot deny my past to which my self is wed,
The woven figure cannot undo its thread.
On a cardboard lid I saw when I was four
Was the trade-mark of a hound and a round tower,
And that was Irish glamour, and in the cemetery
Sham Celtic crosses claimed our individuality,
And my father talked about the West where years back
He played hurley on the sands with a stick of wrack.
Park your car in Killarney, buy a souvenir
Of green marble or black bog-oak, run up to Clare,
Climb the cliff in the postcard, visit Galway city,
Romanticise on our Spanish blood, leave ten per cent of pity
Under your plate for the emigrant,
Take credit for our sanctity, our heroism and our sterile want
Columba Kevin and briny Brandan the accepted names,
Wolfe Tone and Grattan and Michael Collins the accepted names.
Admire the suavity with which the architect
Is rebuilding the burnt mansion, recollect
The palmy days of the Horse Show, swank your fill,
But take the Holyhead boat before you pay the bill;
Before you face the consequence
Of inbred soul and climatic maleficence
And pay for the trick beauty of a prism
In drug-dull fatalism.
I will exorcise my blood
And not to have my baby-clothes my shroud
I will acquire an attitude not yours
And become as one of your holiday visitors,
And however often I may come
Farewell, my country, and in perpetuum;
Whatever desire I catch when your wind scours my face
I will take home and put in a glass case
And merely look on
At each new fantasy of badge and gun.
Frost will not touch the hedge of fuchsias,
The land will remain as it was,
But no abiding content can grow out of these minds
Fuddled with blood, always caught by blinds;
The eels go up the Shannon over the great dam;
You cannot change a response by giving it a new name.
Fountain of green and blue curling in the wind
I must go east and stay, not looking behind,
Not knowing on which day the mist is blanket-thick
Nor when sun quilts the valley and quick
Winging shadows of white clouds pass

Over the long hills like a fiddle's phrase.
If I were a dog of sunlight I would bound
From Phoenix Park to Achill Sound,
Picking up the scent of a hundred fugitives
That have broken the mesh of ordinary lives,
But being ordinary too I must in course discuss
What we mean to Ireland or Ireland to us;
I have to observe milestone and curio
The beaten buried gold of an old king's bravado,
Falsetto antiquities, I have to gesture,
Take part in, or renounce, each imposture;
Therefore I resign, good-bye the chequered and the quiet hills
The gaudily-striped Atlantic, the linen-mills
That swallow the shawled file, the black moor where half
A turf-stack stands like a ruined cenotaph;
Good-bye your hens running in and out of the white house
Your absent-minded goats along the road, your black cows
Your greyhounds and your hunters beautifully bred
Your drums and your dolled-up Virgins and your ignorant dead.

Louis MacNeice, *Poems*, 1935

There is a street in Belmullet, Co. Mayo, called America Street. And it's often said that men from Connemara and the Aran Islands, Gaelic-speakers, know more about the layout of cities like Boston and New York than they do about Dublin, their own capital city.

The talk these days is mostly emigration. Who is leaving, or has gone, or is thinking about going. In one week, three friends of my own left: one to the States, one to England and one to Australia. It's a fairly accepted pattern. The romance of emigration is legend in Ireland: songs have been written, stories told and poems recited, all about the old land, and sometimes about the new one.

Underlying most of the legend is the bitter realisation that the country which many fought for does not exist except as a fiction. This Ireland of de Valerian self-sufficiency has been tarnished by generations of families who left because they could not find a place for themselves to live in and prosper. It is a sad story that has become customary.

Gerald Dawe, *False Faces*, 1994

from *Adieu to Ballyshannon*

Farewell to every white cascade from the Harbour to Belleek,
And every pool where fins may rest, and ivy-shaded creek;

The sloping fields, the lofty rocks, where ash and holly grow,
The one split yew-tree gazing on the curving flood below;
The Lough, that winds through islands under Turaw mountain green;
And Castle Caldwell's stretching woods, with tranquil bays between;
And Breesie Hill, and many a pond among the heath and fern,—
For I must say adieu—adieu to the winding banks of Erne!

The thrush will call through Camlin groves the live-long summer day;
The waters run by mossy cliff, and bank with wild flowers gay;
The girls will bring their work and sing beneath a twisted thorn,
Or stray with sweethearts down the path among the growing corn;
Along the river side they go, where I have often been,—
O, never shall I see again the days that I have seen!
A thousand chances are to one I never may return,—
Adieu to Ballyshannon, and the winding banks of Erne!

Adieu to evening dances, when merry neighbours meet,
And the fiddle says to boys and girls, 'Get up and shake your feet!'
To 'shanachus' and wise old talk of Erin's days gone by—
Who trench'd the rath on such a hill, and where the bones may lie
Of saint, or king, or warrior chief; with tales of fairy power,
And tender ditties sweetly sung to pass the twilight hour.
The mournful song of exile is now for me to learn—
Adieu, my dear companions on the winding banks of Erne!

Now measure from the Commons down to each end of the Purt,
Round the Abbey, Moy, and Knather,—I wish no one any hurt;
The Main Street, Back Street, College Lane, the Mall, and Portnasun,
If any foes of mine are there, I pardon every one.
I hope that man and womankind will do the same by me;
For my heart is sore and heavy at voyaging the sea.
My loving friends I'll bear in mind, and often fondly turn
To think of Ballyshannon, and the winding banks of Erne.

WILLIAM ALLINGHAM, *Irish Songs and Poems*, 1887

The population of Castlebar was, if we were correctly informed, 6000 before the famine; and it is now between 3000 and 4000. Many have gone to the grave; but more have removed to other countries. Large sums are arriving by post, to carry away many more. We were yesterday travelling by the public car, when, at the distance of a few miles from Castlebar, on approaching a cluster of houses, we were startled—to say the truth, our blood ran cold—at the loud cry of a young girl who ran across the road, with a petticoat over her head, which did not conceal the tears on her convulsed face. A crowd of poor people came from—we know not where—most of them in tears, some weeping quietly, others with unbearable cries. A man, his wife, and three young children were going to America. They were well dressed, all shod, and the little girls bonneted. There was some delay—much delay—about where to put their great box; and the delay was truly painful. Of all the crowd, no one cast a momentary glance at anybody but the departing emigrants. The inquisitiveness, the vigilance, the begging, characteristic of those who surround cars, were all absent. All eyes were fixed on the neighbours who were going away for ever. The last embraces were terrible to see; but worse were the kissings and the claspings of the hands during the long minutes that remained after the woman and children had taken their seats. When we saw the wringing of hands and heard the wailings, we became aware, for the first time perhaps, of the full dignity of that civilization which induces control over the expression of emotions. All the while that this lamentation was giving a headache to all who looked on, there could not but be a feeling that these people, thus giving a free vent to their instincts, were as children, and would command themselves better when they were wiser. Still, there it was, the pain and the passion: and the shrill united cry, when the car moved on, rings in our ears, and long will ring when we hear of emigration. They threw up their arms and wailed. When a distant turn in the road showed the hamlet again, we could just distinguish the people standing where we left them. As for the family,—we could not see the man, who was on the other side of the car. The woman's face was soon like other people's, and the children were eating oatcake very composedly.

HARRIET MARTINEAU, *Letters from Ireland*, 1852

'EMIGRATION altered the landscape. My uncle who was born in 1896 used to say he remembered eighty families living on our country road, during his childhood. He could name them and point out their houses. But when we were growing up there in the 1950s, there weren't more than a dozen families.'

ANON., quoted in MARY LENNON, MARIE McADAM, and JOANNE O'BRIEN, *Across the Water*, 1988

Emigrants

Sad faced against the rails,
Suitcases clasped in awkward hands,
They throng the landing stage.
No one would think they go to quest
The shining Grail, the Great Good Place:

Incomprehension is heavy on every face.
Poor subjects for prose or verse,
In their grief, as animals, most piteous.

JOHN MONTAGUE, *Forms of Exile*, 1958

Many were drawn into the stream of the Exodus, and have left the country. How helpless they are in their migrations, poor souls! was proved by one sad story. A steady, good young woman, whose sister had settled comfortably in New York, resolved to go out to join her, and for the purpose took her passage at an Emigration Agency office in Dublin. Coming to make her farewell respects at Newbridge, the following conversation ensued between her and myself:

'So, Bessie, you are going to America?'

'Yes, ma'am, to join Biddy at New York. She wrote for me to come, and sent the passage-money.'

'That is very good of her. Of course you have taken your passage direct to New York?'

'Well, no, ma'am. The agent said there was no ship going to New York, but one to some place close by, New-something-else.'

'New-something-else, near New York; I can't think where that could be.'

'Yes, ma'am, New—New—I disremember what it was, but he told me I could get from it to New York immadiently.'

'Oh, Bessie, it wasn't New Orleans?'

'Yes, ma'am, that was it! New Orleans—New Orleans, close to New York, he said.'

'And you have paid your passage-money?'

'Yes, ma'am, I must go there anyhow, now.'

'Oh, Bessie, Bessie, why would you never come to school and learn geography? You are going to a terrible place, far away from your sister. That wicked agent has cheated you horribly.'

The poor girl went to New Orleans, and there died of fever. The birds of passage and fish which pass from sea to sea seem more capable of knowing what they are about than the greater number of the emigrants driven by scarcely less blind an instinct. Out of the three millions who are said to have gone since the famine from Ireland to America, how many must there have been who had no more knowledge than poor Bessie Mahon of the land to which they went!

FRANCES POWER COBBE, *Autobiography*, 1894

Time was passing and the appointed day approaching. A mournful look was coming over the very walls of the house. The hill above the village which sheltered the houses seemed to be changing colour like a big, stately man who would bend his head in sorrow. The talk throughout the village was all of Maura and Kate going away.

On the last night young and old were gathered together in the house, and though music and songs, dancing and mirth, were flying in the air, there was a mournful look on all within. No wonder, for they were like children of the one mother, the people of the Island, no more than twenty yards between any two houses, the boys and girls every moonlight night dancing on the Sand-hills or sitting together and listening to the sound of the waves from Shingle Strand; and when the moon would wane, gathered together talking and con-versing in the house of old Nell.

The dust was flying from the floor under the heels of the sturdy young men and girls. I went out to the grassy bank. The moon was high in the sky and the Milky Way stretched out to the south-east. I heard the lonely murmur of the waves breaking on the White Strand. It made me mournful.

Maura came out to me. 'Oh, Mirrisheen,' she cried, throwing herself into my arms and bursting into tears, 'what shall I do without you?'

'Be easy. Don't you see everyone is going now, and soon you will see me beyond like the rest of them. Hush now, let us go in and dance.'

She let go of me and sat down on the bank.

'Lift up your heart,' said I again. 'Come in with me now and the two of us will dance a set.'

When we went in: 'Musha, my love for ever, Maura,' cried Peg Oweneen, embracing her and bursting into tears, 'my life will not be long after you.'

'Strike up a tune, Shaun,' said I to Shaun Pats, who had the melodium. He began to play. Four of us arose and I called my sister for the dance.

The day was brightening in the east. We washed ourselves and made ready for the road to Dingle to give Maura a last farewell. The sun was rising in splendour and the cocks crowing all over the village. When nine o'clock came all the old men and old women were coming down towards the house. All was confusion.

We moved down to the quay, Maura and Kate Peg in front of us and the whole village following.

The old women were crying aloud. 'Musha, love of my heart, Maura, isn't it a pity for ever for you to be going from us.'

'Oh, musha, Maura, how shall I live after you when the long winter's night will be here and you not coming to the door nor your laughter to be heard!'

We got free of them at last. We were out in Mid-Bay, looking back at the people of the village waving their hands and their shawls.

We spent the night in Dingle. Next morning we went down to the station and gave them farewell and our blessing with sorrow and tears.

The train whistled. In a moment they were out of sight.

Maurice O'Sullivan, *Twenty Years A-Growing*, 1933, trans. Moya Llewelyn Davies and George Thomson

An Irishman in Coventry

A full year since, I took this eager city,
the tolerance that laced its blatant roar,
its famous steeples and its web of girders,
as image of the state hope argued for,
and scarcely flung a bitter thought behind me
on all that flaws the glory and the grace
which ribbons through the sick, guilt-clotted legend
of my creed-haunted, godforsaken race.
My rhetoric swung round from steel's high promise
to the precision of the well-gauged tool,
tracing the logic in the vast glass headlands,
the clockwork horse, the comprehensive school.

Then, sudden, by occasion's chance concerted,
in enclave of my nation, but apart,
the jigging dances and the lilting fiddle
stirred the old rage and pity in my heart.
The faces and the voices blurring round me,
the strong hands long familiar with the spade,
the whiskey-tinctured breath, the pious buttons,
called up a people endlessly betrayed
by our own weakness, by the wrongs we suffered
in that long twilight over bog and glen,
by force, by famine and by glittering fables
which gave us martyrs when we needed men,
by faith which had no charity to offer,
by poisoned memory, and by ready wit,
with poverty corroded into malice,
to hit and run and howl when it is hit.
This is our fate: eight hundred years' disaster,
crazily tangled as the Book of Kells;
the dream's distortion and the land's division,
the midnight raiders and the prison cells.
Yet like Lir's children banished to the waters
our hearts still listen for the landward bells.

JOHN HEWITT, *Collected Poems*, 1991

On the following morning, which was a Sunday, I was surprised to see strolling along the road, past the low stone-walls, companies of young ladies, dressed in fine frocks, all wearing rayon stockings and high-heeled shoes. At a distance, they seemed as unreal as women of the Sidhe. I saw no cars, and wondered, but said nothing. On Monday morning, the languid strollers had all become rough girls in big boots, working in the little fields, or clattering with buckets from the nearby clachan to the well. Fred explained to me that their sisters, cousins, send them their spare dresses and other finery from the United States. They, too, were hoping to emigrate as soon as they had saved up their steerage fare.

AUSTIN CLARKE, *A Penny in the Clouds*, 1968

from *Letter From Ireland*

Sometimes I go to Cobh and stare
   For ages at water where emigrants waved
To families on the crowded pier.
   In Manhattan or Boston, they saved
   Enough to bring another until all were there.
Old drawings depicted a country dying:
Grim men standing, shawled women crying.

The liners they left on are pictured on walls
   Of bars and hotel lounges, generations marred
By misery and the need to pour all
   Into tickets for White Star or Cunard.
   The country wears their going like a scar.
Today their relatives save to support and
Send others in planes for the new diaspora.

SEAN DUNNE, *The Sheltered Nest*, 1992

Looking from Athlone and Athenry at the plain that lies north-west and north and north-east of the Shannon, I realise that I know it only imaginatively, only out of books and histories. The regions of Maria Edgeworth, Oliver Goldsmith, William Carleton—who that is Irish does not know their characters, formed of poverty and woe and farce and isolation, as three distinctive writers re-created them? Cold, lake-strewn fields of Leitrim, Longford and Roscommon—did we get to know them so well in the readings of our youth that half-forgettingly we assume them now as a part of us? Savage associations of land bitterness, of famine and flight—traces indeed that can still rise anywhere in Ireland—were they most mortally of all driven into these upper midlands? Whatever the cause or the fear, these regions are still too empty, too much of life still flows away from them. There are reasons now which are strictly of our time for this unstemmable emigration of the young, reasons which bear slight relation to the tragic necessity of the nineteenth century; but the habit of departure from the land then established comes mightily and ironically to the support of modern restlessness and of a curiosity towards all of life which is the *Zeitgeist* pure and simple, and will not be deflected. Our young emigrants of today are not emigrants in the sense in which their grandfathers were; simply they are young people who intend to live in the pace and idiom of their time. Modern science brings them news of it, and all they have to do is go and find their contemporary world. It is impossible to ask them not to do what is their clear right; and, as I have said, tradition, accidentally, backs them up. But the empty fields, the emptying villages are sad, nevertheless, as the stranger will find—in Connemara, for instance.

KATE O'BRIEN, *My Ireland*, 1962

Kerr's Ass

We borrowed the loan of Kerr's big ass
To go to Dundalk with butter,
Brought him home the evening before the market
An exile that night in Mucker.

We heeled up the cart before the door,
We took the harness inside—
The straw-stuffed straddle, the broken breeching
With bits of bull-wire tied;

The winkers that had no choke-band,
The collar and the reins . . .
In Ealing Broadway, London Town
I name their several names

Until a world comes to life—
Morning, the silent bog,
And the God of imagination waking
In a Mucker fog.

PATRICK KAVANAGH, *Collected Poems*, 1964

Ancestral Houses

A spot whereon the founders lived and died . . .
W. B. YEATS, 'Coole Park and Ballylee'

———

The paradox of these big houses is that often they are not big at all. Those massive detached villas outside cities probably have a greater number of rooms. We have of course in Ireland the *great* houses—houses Renaissance Italy hardly rivals, houses with superb façades, colonnades, pavilions and, inside, chains of plastered, painted saloons. But the houses that I know best, and write of, would be only called 'big' in Ireland—in England they would be 'country houses', no more. They are of adequate size for a family, its dependants, a modest number of guests. They have few annexes, they do not ramble; they are nearly always compactly square. Much of the space inside (and there is not so much space) has been sacrificed to airy halls and lobbies and to the elegant structure of staircases. Their façades (very often in the Italian manner) are not lengthy, though they may be high. Is it height—in this country of otherwise low buildings—that got these Anglo-Irish houses their 'big' name? Or have they been called 'big' with a slight inflection—that of hostility, irony? One may call a man 'big' with just that inflection because he seems to think the hell of himself.

These houses, however, are certainly not little. Let us say that their size, like their loneliness, is an effect rather than a reality. Perhaps the wide, private spaces they occupy throw a distending reflection on to their walls. And, they were planned for spacious living—for hospitality above all. Unlike the low, warm, ruddy French and English manors, they have made no natural growth from the soil—the idea that begot them was a purely social one. The functional parts of them—kitchens and offices, farm-buildings, outbuildings— were sunk underground, concealed by walls or by trees: only the stables (for horses ranked very highly) emerged to view, as suavely planned as the house. Yet, in another sense, the most ornate, spacious parts of these buildings *were* the most functional—the steps, the halls, the living-rooms, the fine staircases—It was these that contributed to society, that raised life above the exigencies of mere living to the plane of art, or at least style. There was a true bigness, a sort of impersonality, in the manner in which the houses were conceived. After an era of greed, roughness and panic, after an era of camping in charred or desolate ruins (as my Cromwellian ancestors did certainly) these new settlers who had been imposed on Ireland began to wish to add something to life. The security that they had, by the eighteenth century, however ignobly gained, they did not use quite ignobly. They began to feel, and exert, the European idea—to seek what was humanistic, classic and disciplined.

ELIZABETH BOWEN, 'The Big House', 1942, in *Collected Impressions*, 1950

West Cork is a poor land, where bogs and mountains predominate, but there are fertile stretches, such as those along the valley of the Bandon and in the vicinity of the towns of Clonakilty and Skibbereen. Those rich areas were in the hands of a small minority, and the large majority of the people had a hard struggle for existence. Families reared in poverty had nothing to look forward to but emigration to the United States, the Colonies, Great Britain, or to join the British Services. Before the European War of 1914–1918, few young men or girls who had reached the age of twenty remained, and so the poor part of the countryside was sparsely populated. The rich lands had been well planted by the conquerors, and an examination of the names of the occupiers is a history in itself. There predominated the descendants of the mercenary invaders who had defeated Red Hugh in the Battle of Kinsale in 1601. When Gaelic Ireland went down at that battle it was a tragedy for the whole Irish nation, but its consequences were more far-reaching to the Irish in West Cork than to those living in other parts. It was there the battle was fought and it was there the conqueror, in his first flush of victory, with fire and sword sought to destroy the natives. Those left alive were driven to the woods, the bogs and the wastelands, while the invaders settled in their homes and on their lands.

In 1919, the 'Big House' near all the towns was a feature of first importance in the lives of the people. In it lived the leading British loyalist, secure and affluent in his many acres, enclosed by high demense walls. Around him lived his many labourers, grooms, gardeners, and household servants, whose mission in life was to serve their lord and master. In the towns, many of the rich shopkeepers bowed before the 'great' family, and to them those in the big house were veritable gods. The sycophants and lickspittles, happy in their master's benevolence, never thought to question how he had acquired his thousand acres, his castle and his wealth, or thought of themselves as the descendants of the rightful owners of those robbed lands.

TOM BARRY, *Guerrilla Days in Ireland*, 1949

A week later he took up his stick one day and walked down the winding, grass-grown avenue. An ancestor was rector here long years ago, he thought, as in the case of William Yeats, the poet, who died in France on the eve of this war and who had an ancestor a rector long years ago in Drumcliffe by the faraway Sligo sea. Mr Broderick's house had been the rectory. When the church authorities judged it a crumbling, decaying property they had given it to Mr Broderick for a token sum—a small gesture of regard for all that in an active manhood he had done for the village. Crumbling and decaying it was, but peace, undisturbed, remained around the boles of the trees, the tall gables and old tottering chimneys, the shadowy bird-rustling walks. Now, as he walked, yews gone wild and reckless made a tangled pattern above his head.

Weeks before, from the garrison town in the valley, war had spilled its gathering troops over into this little village. Three deep, burdened with guns and accoutrements, they slouched past Mr Broderick on the way down the hill to their courthouse billet. Dust rose around them. They sang. They were three to six thousand miles from home, facing an uncertain future, and in reasonably good humour. A dozen or so who knew Mr Broderick from the tottering house as the old guy who made souvenirs out of blackthorn and bog oak, waved casual, friendly hands. Beyond and behind them as they descended was the blue cone of Knocknashee Hill where the castle was commandeered and where a landlord had once stocked a lake with rainbow trout that like these troops has been carried across the wide Atlantic. The soldiers' dust settling around him in wreaths and rings, Mr Broderick went down the road to collect his mail at the post-office. There had been no troops in this village since 1798 when the bellows had been mutilated and the soldiers then, according to the history books, had been anything but friendly.

The long red-tiled roofs and white walls of the co-operative creamery, the sheen of glasshouses from the slopes of the model farm were a reminder to Mr Broderick of the enthusiasms of an active past. People had, in his boyhood, been evicted for poverty in that village. Now every year the co-operative grain store handled one hundred and fifty thousand tons of grain. An energetic young man could take forty tons of tomatoes out of an acre and a quarter of glasshouses, and on a day of strong sunshine the gleam of the glasshouses would blind you. Crops burst over the hedges as nowhere else in that part of the country. It was good, high, dry land that took less harm than most places from wet seasons and flooding, and the cattle were as heavy and content as creamy oxen in French vineyards.

BENEDICT KIELY, *A Journey to the Seven Streams*, 1963

The very morning after they came home, however, I saw how things were, plain enough, between Sir Kit and my lady, though they were walking together arm in arm after breakfast, looking at the new building and the improvements. 'Old Thady,' said my master, just as he used to do, 'how do you do?'—'Very well, I thank your honor's honor,' said I; but I saw he was not well pleased, and my heart was in my mouth as I walked along after him.—'Is the large room damp, Thady?' said his honor—'Oh, damp, your honor! how should it but be as dry as a bone, (says I) after all the fires we have kept in it day and night—It's the barrack-room your honor's talking on.'—'And what is a barrack room, pray, my dear?' were the first words I ever heard out of my lady's lips. 'No matter my dear?' said he, and went on, talking to me, ashamed like I should witness her ignorance—To be sure to hear her talk, one might have taken her for an innocent, for it was 'what's this, Sir Kit? and what's that, Sir Kit?' all the way we went—To be sure, Sir Kit had enough to do to answer her.—'And what do you call that, Sir Kit?' said she, 'that, that looks like a pile of black bricks, pray Sir Kit?' 'My turf stack, my dear,' said my master, and bit his lip.—Where have you lived, my lady, all your life, not to know a turf stack when you see it, thought I, but I said nothing. Then, by-and-by, she takes out her glass, and begins spying over the country—'And what's all that black swamp out yonder, Sir Kit?' says she—'My bog, my dear,' says he, and went on whistling—'It's a very ugly prospect, my dear,' says she—'You don't see it, my dear,' says he, 'for we've planted it out, when the trees grow up, in summer time,' says he—'Where are the trees,' said she, 'my dear?' still looking through her glass—'You are blind, my dear,' says he, 'what are these under your eyes?'—'These shrubs?' said she—'Trees,' said he—'May be they are what you call trees in Ireland, my dear,' says she, 'but they are not a yard high, are they?'—'They were planted out but last year, my lady,' says I, to soften matters between them, for I saw she was going the way to make his honor mad with her—'they are very well grown for their age, and you'll not see the bog of Allyballycarricko'shaughlin at-all-at-all through the skreen, when once the leaves come out.—But, my lady, you must not quarrel with any part or parcel of Allyballycarricko'shaughlin, for you don't know how many hundred years that same bit of bog has been in the family; we would not part with the bog of Allyballycarricko'shaughlin upon no account at all; it cost the late Sir Murtagh two hundred good pounds to defend his title to it, and boundaries, against the O'Learys who cut a road through it.'—Now one would have thought this would have been hint enough for my lady, but she fell to laughing like one out of their right mind, and made me say the name of the bog over for her to get it by heart a dozen times—then she must ask me how to spell it, and what was the meaning of it in English—Sir Kit standing by whistling all the while—I verily believe she laid the corner stone of all her future misfortunes at that very instant—but I said no more, only looked at Sir Kit.

MARIA EDGEWORTH, *Castle Rackrent*, 1800

We returned from Castleconnell along the back road just at sunset. Miles of stone wall which guarded the estate on our right were humped and rent by great clumps of ivy which straddled them and broke their back. We opened a ruined gate and cycled down a shadowy lane which had once been an avenue, and rounded a great mass of buildings which proved to be stables. Suddenly as we reached the stable yard, the sun went out over the wild Clare hills across the river, and we looked up and saw in the yellow light the green, peeling stucco behind a great Ionic front, reflecting like water the last pale gleam of day. It would be impossible to paint that yellow light on the peeling stucco and the dull smouldering of the masses of brick in the gloomy cavern of the house behind, but it was tremendous; as though the sun going down beyond the Clare hills had clenched his fist and shaken it at the porch, and the porch, like some great beast driven to bay, dug its columns deeper into the ground and snarled back at it. 'A man must be stronger than God to build to the west of his house' goes the Irish proverb, but a man must think himself stronger than Ireland to build that insolent classic front to face the wild hills of Clare.

It must have been an enormous house. Outside we could trace the remains of a sunk garden, but of that nothing remained except a clump of wild daisies among the briars. Behind were acres of magnificent walled garden going wild, wilder I think than anything I have seen elsewhere, or perhaps it was the light which made it seem that the earth was rising to swallow up what remained of the house.

FRANK O'CONNOR, *Irish Miles*, 1947

Going in the Rain

An Adam house among tall trees
Whose glaucous shadows make the lawn
A still pool; bracken on the screes
Wedged above a lichened bawn;
A rectory on a broken coast . . .

Our journey notices these things
Which aid the sense of being lost
In a scoured countryside that clings
To idols someone else imagined.

Georgian architects, ironic
Deists, crossed over from the mainland
To build a culture brick by brick,
And graft their reason to a state
The rain is washing out of shape.

TOM PAULIN, *The Strange Museum*, 1980

The ancient Irish conception of building modified the architecture of the Plantation, and to-day we have towns and villages which, though English in origin, could not be found in that country. There is a region round Lough Neagh basin which is the home of the jamb-wall cottage. Hipped gables do not occur north of Lough Erne. The maritime mode architecture of the coast is easily recognizable, and the red English brick of County Armagh, hiding among its apple-blossom, makes one think of Surrey, and if one considers a nine-county Ulster, including Donegal, you have a region where houses add on pieces as the family grows, till they trail like white caterpillars over the hump of hills. It is a land where the corbie-stepped gable can be found, and where the roofs are held down against the gales of the Atlantic by rope pegged into the eaves.

There is a feeling for strong peasant colour in this country—blue, red, or orange doors against whitewashed walls—and the outside steps leading to a door in the gable is a tradition not only in Donegal but in every Ulster county and, for that matter, in many parts of Ireland. The round gate-pillars with conical tops are a feature of the Province, and if a window tax did nothing else for us it at least left us with the ever-open welcome of the half-door, across which the turf-fire flickers so cheerfully.

DENIS O'D. HANNA, 'Architecture in Ulster', in *The Arts in Ulster*, 1951

Tommy Redcliffe had enjoyed the pheasant-shooting at Dunmartin Hall, but otherwise he did not have very enthusiastic memories of the house where I had lived until my father was killed. Whereas I remembered Dunmartin Hall with affection and nostalgia, he had not seen anything especially attractive in the fact that its smells of damp-infested libraries had mingled with those of cow-dung, potato cakes and paraffin.

He had found the house architecturally very displeasing with its vast and sprawling ivy-coated wings, which at certain periods had been added to, at others pulled down at immense cost in the interests of economy and man-ageability. He had been depressed by the way it seemed like a gigantic monument to more prosperous and eternally lost times, dominating the countryside in its stately dilapidation.

Although he could admit that its tall and formal windows had very beau-tiful views—of gorse-dotted mountain, slate-grey lake, and copses of copper beech, he had not felt that they compensated for Dunmartin Hall's many dis-comforts. He hated the way the food at meals was always stone-cold because it had to be carried by the butler from a dungeon kitchen which was in a dif-ferent wing from the dining-room. Dunmartin Hall had something wrong with its plumbing, and he had been astonished that in a house of such pre-tension there was very rarely hot water and it was considered a luxury if anyone managed to get a peat-brown trickle of a bath.

Tommy Redcliffe suffered from rheumatism and he was convinced that the first fatal seeds of it had been sown when he stayed in that Northern Irish house before the war and his sheets were invariably wringing wet. Years later his voice still trembled with astonished complaint as he remembered nights when there had always seemed to be a bat trapped in his bedroom, nights when the cold had been such that he often found it easier to get to sleep lying fully clothed on the floor-boards under a couple of dusty carpets than in his unaired bed.

When he tried to describe my unknown grandmother, his whole description of her was coloured by sympathy for what he felt she must have suffered when her marriage doomed her to spend years and years of her life in the stultifying isolation and relentless biting damp of that ancestral Ulster house.

CAROLINE BLACKWOOD, *Great Granny Webster*, 1977

He only went there to collect rents, and the same unsentimental errand took me to Ashbrook when I returned from Paris in 1880. Tom Ruttledge and I had driven through Mayo, visiting all my estates, trying to come to terms with the tenants, and at Ashbrook a crowd had followed the car up a boreen, babbling of the disastrous year they had been through: the potato crop had been a failure; 'there was no diet in them.'

The phrase caught on my ear, and I remember well the two-storeyed house standing on a bare hillside. The woods had been felled long ago, all except a few ash-trees left standing in the corner of the field to shelter the cattle from the wind, and the house, having been inhabited by peasants for a long time, presented a sad degradation, a sagging roof, and windows so black that I did not dare to think of the staircase leading to the drawing-room, in which my great-grandmother had stitched that pretty piece of tapestry which is now in the Kensington Museum. Dunne, my tenant, a heavy, surly fellow, whose manners were not engaging (we heard afterwards that he was the leader of a notable conspiracy against us), asked us to step inside, but fearing to meet with chickens in the parlour that perhaps still had the ancient paper on its walls, I pleaded that the day was drawing to a close, and asked him if he would be kind enough to take me to my great-grandfather's grave. He turned aside, and the peasants answering for him said:

'Sure we will, your honour.'

'So this is the brook,' I thought to myself, and watched the water trickle through masses of weeds and rushes. We crossed some fields and came to a ruined chapel, and my peasants pointed to an incised stone let into the wall, the loneliest grave it seemed to me in all the world; and drowsing in my arm-chair, unable to read, the sadness that I had experienced returned to me, and I felt and saw as I had done thirty years before. I had thought then of the poor

old man who had built Moore Hall deciding at last that his ashes were to be
carried to Ashbrook.

GEORGE MOORE, *Vale*, 1914

Visitors to Ireland have not failed to comment on the wide gap which separates the splendid if often dilapidated mansions of the landed gentry from the
humble dwellings of the mass of the rural population. This is a characteristic dichotomy which runs through Irish life and goes deep into the Irish past:
it was foreshadowed in the distinction between the Gaelic overlords
and the tributary tribes who were still in an inferior position at the time of
the Anglo-Norman conquest. By English standards the Irish farmer is a
small-holder Substantial farmhouses with some pretensions to architectural
dignity are in general restricted to the planted areas and they are few in
number compared with the traditional single-storied thatched cabins of the
peasantry. These have so frequently been condemned as artless and insani-
tary that it might be supposed nothing could be said in their favour. Their
disadvantages indeed are obvious, and they have given way in many districts
to slated houses of cement-blocks or bricks and are doomed to vanish
entirely under a wave of thin-walled boxes with garish red roofs. But it is not
only sentimentalists who deplore their disappearance. With their passing,
writes Robin Flower, something of the old world passes away, 'for the older
type of house was in a right harmony with its surroundings, while these high
and bare constructions stand in a perpetual contradiction of the whole environment of hill and sea and sky in which they are so violently set down.'

E. ESTYN EVANS, *Irish Folk Ways*, 1957

Irish Ireland had become in the eighteenth century a peasant nation, harried
and poverty-stricken, with the cottier's smoky cabin for stronghold. But this
does not mean that there were no longer any Big Houses, as we may call them,
nor well-to-do families in these Gaelic-speaking countrysides. Both the
stories of the poets' lives and the songs they have left us save us from such an
idea. Froude tells us that nine-tenths of the land was in 1703 held by Protestants of English or Scotch extraction, an estimate that is probably correct;
yet here and there, and especially in Munster, certain big Gaelic Houses had
escaped destruction; and only for they had, the story of Irish literature in that
century would be very different from what it is, as gradually we shall come
to realise.

Through sheer luck, it might be said, these houses had come to survive.
They represented hardly ever the main branch of any of the historic families;
they were rather the minor branches, far-removed, and not too well known

to the authorities in Dublin. Those city-bred, sometimes English-bred, lawyers and statesmen had often only shadowy ideas of the boundaries of the lands they were confiscating. They were not quite sure when their work was done, either in seizing a property or re-parcelling it out among the adventurers. In Cork, in Kerry, and elsewhere, certain old Gaelic families survived not only as landowners but as local magnates right through all the confiscations and penal laws that followed on 1641 and, later, on the Boyne. They had succeeded in holding or getting back small portions of the lands from which their ancestors had been driven; and in many cases they must subsequently have quietly enlarged the property, however they had established themselves in it.

For such houses, in obscurity lay their chance of safety. The less that was known of them, especially in Dublin, the better their chance. Inquiry into the family's history, or into the leases, would often have meant extinction; and how well they knew this, an anecdote told of the O'Connells of Derrynane—a house we shall often have to mention—will fix in our mind. Dr Smith, the eighteenth-century historian of Cork and Kerry, penetrated into the mountains beyond Cahirciveen, and there partook of the O'Connells' hospitality: we can imagine them as only gradually becoming aware of the Doctor's interest in all that concerned their far places. Nothing could be so little to their taste. It is said that the historian, having set his eye on a pony of good shape, hinted that in exchange for the animal he would give the house honourable mention in his forthcoming work. They at once presented him with the pony, but only on the condition that his history was to be barren of their name. On a subsequent visit, they are said to have kicked him down the stairs.

DANIEL CORKERY, The Hidden Ireland, 1925

The Colonel performed his journey by slow stages, until he reached 'the hall of his fathers',—for it was such, although he had not for years resided in it. It presented the wreck of a fine old mansion, situated within a crescent of stately beeches, whose moss-covered and ragged trunks gave symptons of decay and neglect. The lawn had been once beautiful, and the demesne a noble one; but that which blights the industry of the tenant—the curse of absenteeism—had also left the marks of ruin stamped upon every object around him. The lawn was little better than a common; the pond was thick with weeds and sluggish water-plants, that almost covered its surface; and a light elegant bridge, that spanned a river which ran before the house, was also moss-grown and dilapidated. The hedges were mixed up with briers, the gates broken, or altogether removed, the fields were rank with the ruinous luxuriance of weeds, and the grass-grown avenues spoke of solitude and desertion. The still appearance, too, of the house itself, and the absence of smoke from its time-tinged chimneys—all told a tale which constitutes one, perhaps the *greatest*, portion of Ireland's misery! Even then he did not approach it with the intention of residing there during his sojourn in the country. It was not habitable, nor had it been so for years. The road by which he travelled lay near it, and he could not pass without looking upon the place where a long line of gallant ancestors had succeeded each other, lived their span, and disappeared in their turn.

He contemplated it for some time in a kind of reverie. There it stood, sombre and silent;—its gray walls mouldering away—its windows dark and broken;—like a man forsaken by the world, compelled to bear the storms of life without the hand of a friend to support him, though age and decay render him less capable of enduring them. For a moment fancy repeopled it;—again the stir of life, pastime, mirth, and hospitality echoed within its walls; the train of his long-departed relatives returned; the din of rude and boisterous enjoyment peculiar to the times; the cheerful tumult of the hall at dinner; the family feuds and festivities; the vanities and the passions of those who now slept in dust;—all—all came before him once more, and played their part in the vision of the moment!

As he walked on, the flitting wing of a bat struck him lightly in its flight; he awoke from the remembrances which crowded on him, and, resuming his journey, soon arrived at the inn of the nearest town, where he stopped the night.

WILLIAM CARLETON, 'The Poor Scholar', in *Traits and Stories of the Irish Peasantry*, 1844

The Big House and the outlook and attitude—indeed the civilization—that it betokened was not an integral element in the national life. Nor, it must be insisted, was it a foreign element.

The Protestant landed gentry of Ireland were Irishmen. The peculiar potency of the Irish climate saw to that. In this capacity to absorb and trans-mute foreigners I believe Ireland is unique. It is said that a herd of Friesians transported to Egypt will, in three generations, all be humped cattle of the Nile. It sounds unlikely. Of the English—and our later immigrants have been almost entirely English—becoming in three generations more Irish than the Irish themselves there can, however, allowing for some trivial exaggeration, be no doubt whatever. . . .

The Big House . . . stands out egregiously as a sort of Irish bull. It stands out and is outstanding—first in its architecture.

Architecturally the country houses of Ireland present a striking homogeneity. They are almost without exception eighteenth-century in origin—if not by actual date of building, at least in style. Irish domestic Georgian probably has acknowledged points of difference from its English equivalent. I cannot define these differences, but given a mixed bag of photographs I think I could sort out the Irish houses from the English.

However that may be, these houses are in themselves a dignified possession. Owing to the rapidity with which we carried through our particular revolution, there is a real danger that they may almost all have disappeared before anything nearly as civilized has had time to take their place. Our attitude to old buildings is in keeping with our attitude to time itself. We let them go. We make no serious attempt to staunch their wounds or stay the process of disintegration.

GEOFFREY TAYLOR, *The Emerald Isle*, 1952

Inistioge is an altogether charming village, remote from traffic and complete with hills, river and lime trees in its square. Tiny as it may seem to the man from a great city, it was once a royal borough returning two members to the Irish Parliament. I have a fancy that this dreamy place would make a lovely open stage for a play (perhaps necessitating the removal of some hills and other obstructions to form an auditorium). Near it is Woodstock House, or what is left of it after a disastrous fire. Mary Tighe (1772–1810) was the most distinguished of its inhabitants. Her poetry, according to Sir James Mackintosh (who was at any rate a man of culture) was 'the most faultless series of verses ever produced by a woman'. When I visited Woodstock House, my guide to the terraces, gardens and flights of steps was an elderly man whose information was imparted with an air of sadness and punctuated with sighs. He is a type that is rapidly vanishing, the kind of man who says: 'Her ladyship used to feed the birds from those steps. . . . They kept the carriage in there. . . . They made a bonfire on that hill the time of the Queen's Jubilee.' Few in Ireland today have tears to shed for landlords, but everyone can sympathise with the sincere old people whom they left to end their lives in loneliness.

STEPHEN RYNNE, *All Ireland*, 1956

Afternoon

Inistiogue itself is perfectly lovely,
like a typical English village, but a bit sullen.
Our voices echoed in sunny corners
among the old houses; we admired
the stonework and gateways, the interplay
of roofs and angled streets.

The square, with its 'village green', lay empty.
The little shops had hardly anything.
The Protestant church was guarded by a woman

of about forty, a retainer, spastic
and indistinct, who drove us out.

An obelisk to the Brownsfoords and a Victorian
Celto-Gothic drinking fountain, erected
by a Tighe widow for the villagers,
'erected' in the centre. An astronomical-looking
sundial stood sentry on a platform
on the corner where High Street went up out of the square.

We drove up, past a long-handled water pump
placed at the turn, with an eye to the effect,
then out of the town for a quarter of a mile
above the valley, and came to the dead gate
of Woodstock, once home of the Tighes.

*

The great ruin presented its flat front
at us, sunstruck. The children disappeared.
Eleanor picked her way around a big fallen branch
and away along the face toward the outbuildings.
I took the grassy front steps and was gathered up
in a brick-red stillness. A rook clattered out of the dining
    room.

A sapling, hooked thirty feet up
in a cracked corner, held out a ghost-green
cirrus of leaves. Cavities
of collapsed fireplaces connected silently
about the walls. Deserted spaces, complicated
by door-openings everywhere.

There was a path up among bushes and nettles
over the beaten debris, then a drop, where bricks
and plaster and rafters had fallen into the kitchens.
A line of small choked arches . . . The pantries, possibly.

Be still, as though pure.

A brick, and its dust, fell.

Nightfall

The trees we drove under in the dusk
as we threaded back along the river through the woods
were no mere dark growth, but a flitting-place
for ragged feeling, old angers and rumours . . .

Black and Tan ghosts up there, at home
on the Woodstock heights: an iron mouth
scanning the Kilkenny road: the house
gutted by the townspeople and burned to ruins . . .

The little Ford we met, and inched past, full of men
we had noticed along the river bank during the week,
disappeared behind us into a fifty-year-old night.
Even their caps and raincoats . . .

Sons, or grandsons. Poachers.
                         Mud-tasted salmon
slithering in a plastic bag around the boot,
bloodied muscles, disputed since King John.

The ghosts of daughters of the family
waited in the uncut grass as we drove
down to our mock-Austrian lodge and stopped.

> THOMAS KINSELLA, from 'Tao and Unfitness at Inistiogue on
> the River Nore', *Peppercannister Poems 1972–78*, 1978.

Nowadays the gates hung open, pale with weather and age. The avenue, that curved for half a mile under the tunnel of elms, was rutted and overgrown. The tiny, pillared gate lodge had not been lived in since 1922, when it had been the scene of one of the Civil War's minor incidents. Nettles grew up now through the empty windows, and in the height of summer foxgloves peered over the walls. No one any longer bobbed and smiled, or passed the time of day as the Major drove in and out.

> JENNIFER JOHNSTON, *The Gates*, 1973

On every side were signs of fallen fortunes, of neglect and poverty and ruin. The park was evidently a vast rabbit warren and the sward was overrun with whins. The groves were wide tangles of underbrush. The grand avenue was grass-grown and mossy. The 'big house' itself still made a brave show, but the out offices were woefully dilapidated. Under some of the giant elms and beeches to the rere of the mansion the bare gables of a ruined kennel showed where the foxhounds had once fed and yelped and slept. The lodge at the grand gate was untenanted and neglected. The gate itself was rickety, and swung half open on its crazy hinges.

> WILLIAM BULFIN, *Rambles in Eirinn*, 1907

Nothing abandoned about the place we're in today. It's a nineteenth-century mansion owned by Johnny and Rosaleen Clements. They farm 200 acres, with an additional 100 acres in timber. The Clements speak in the plummy, clipped accents of the Home Counties. When I ask Rosaleen how long they've been here she replies, 'Since the Ulster Plantation—1675, I believe.' We're using one of their hay barns for a scene where an IRA man is shot by the SAS. The IRA man is played by the stuntman from London. Apparently he dies wonderfully.

The Clements are getting on in years now and work the place themselves with a minimum of help from locals. This morning they were up at five, milking the herd of Aberdeen Angus.

The house is stylish, grey cut stone, lovely chimneys, big windows facing the rising sun and surrounded by hills, graceful lawns and, flowing sweetly at the rear of the house, the Annaghlee River. On the other side of the river is an old walled garden and orchard. To get to it you have to cross a very rickety bridge consisting of frail planks held together by wire and nails. In grander times there was a grander stone bridge. You can see the remains of it in the water. The garden is one of the oldest in the country. It is full of plum trees, apples, roses, cabbage . . . It is on a number of levels all leading up from or down to the river. This morning the trees are full of pecking blackbirds. Singing birds are everywhere and the air is sweet with the delicious perfumes of various flowers. It is simple, frugal, uncluttered . . . 'People say to me, "Why don't you get a herbaceous border?" Ugh.'

The owners of these big houses work hard. But the children won't stay. They go off and make their own way. Fathers and sons—the old tale maybe and who can blame either of them? 'We keep it up as best we can,' says Rosaleen. 'If we sell, you see, it will look good and we'll get a good price.' The struggle to keep up appearances is too much. The work is too hard. Finally, time has reached into these dark, delightful corners of Ireland and is slowly crushing the brickwork in the orchard, choking the paths with weeds, slowing down human limbs, heaping debts in the bank. They've had a good innings: 300 years not out. But now, suddenly, the pitch is turning, the wicket's getting sticky. I tell Rosaleen to hang on to their Garden of Eden. The EEC are bound to come to their assistance, or the Irish-American Fund. Maybe Disney will turn it into a theme park, paying them a fortune in the process. In the Cease-fire era, tourists will flock to see fairies at the bottom of the garden and Darby O'Gill and little Cavan people cavorting on the front lawn. Sooner or later in our Gardens of Eden a snake appears. Usually ourselves.

SHANE CONNAUGHTON, *A Border Diary*, 1995

The pipe-stem travelled across the palm.

'I met an old man who took me down one of those avenues to see the ruins of a big house burned out during the troubled times. It was a lovely spring evening. The sky was like milk. The rooks were cawing about the roofless chimneys just like the flakes of a soot come to life again. I spotted a queer little building at the end of a cypress avenue. The old man called it "the ofta-phone". He meant octagon. It was a kind of peristyle. He said, "The Lord"— just like that, "The Lord used to have tea-parties and dances there long ago." I went into it and it had a magnificent view, a powerful view, across the valley over at my mountainy parish, yes, and beyond it to the ridges of the moun-tains, and even beyond that again to the very moors behind with their last little flecks and drifts of snow. They could have sat there and drunk their tea and seen my people—the poor Ryders, and Greenes, and O'Tooles, making little brown lines in the far-off fields in the ploughing time.'

'They could! Oh, begobs, father, so they could!'—and a mighty spit.

'Or at night, of summer evenings, they could have sipped their brandy and coffee and seen the little yellow lights of our cabin windows, and said, "How pretty it is!"'

'Begobs, yes! That's true!'

If anyone entered the carriage then he would have taken us for three friends, we were huddled together so eagerly. The priest went on:

'"They must have had good times here, once?" I said to the man who was with me. "The best, father!" says he. "Oh, the best out. The best while they lasted. And there were never any times like the old times. But they're scat-tered now, father," says he, "to the four winds. And they'll never come back." "Who owns the land, now?" I asked him. "They own it always, but who wants it?" says he. "The people here don't want it. They'd rather live in the towns and cities and work for wages."'

'That's right,' said the farmer, as if we were really discussing his own county. 'Begobs, you're talking sense now, father!'

'"The land was kept from them too long," says he. "And now they have lost the knack of it. I have two grown sons of my own," says he, "and they're after joining the British Army."'

'Begobs, yes!' said the farmer, leaning to catch every word; but the priest stopped and leaned back.

The white, cold fields were singing by us. The cabins so still they might be rocks clung to the earth. The priest was looking at them and we were all looking at them, and at the flooded and frozen pools of water divided by the hedgerows. By his talk he had evoked a most powerful sense of comradeship in that carriage, whether he meant to or not: we felt one. Then, as quickly, he proceeded to break it.

'Well!' I asked eagerly. 'Well?'

'Why, that's all!' said the priest. 'I came back from my voyage of explor-ation, much refreshed. Much improved in spirits. You see, I had extended the pattern of life of my own poor parish. I saw how, how—I mean, how the whole thing had worked, hung together, made up a real unity. It was like putting two halves of a broken plate together. As I walked up another one of those hill-roads on my way home I passed more prosperous houses—smaller houses this time, what you would call private houses. They had neat, green curtains with fine, polished brassware inside on the polished mahogany. And through another window three aluminium hot-water bottles shining on a dark hall-table, signs of comfort as you might say . . . Yes! I had completed the pattern. That parish and my parish made up a world, as neither did by itself, rich and poor, culture and . . .'

'But,' I cried angrily, 'where's your moral unity? Your common thought? It's absurd.'

'Oh, yes! I realized that even before I got home. I just tell you the thing as it happened. But they in their octagon and we in our lighted cabins, I mean to say, it was two halves of a world . . .'

The farmer was looking at us both with dull, stupid eyes. He had lost the thread of the talk.

'Yes, I suppose so,' I agreed, just as lightly. 'But now that the gentry are gone, won't the people, the mountainy people, and so on, begin to make a complete world of their own?'

He shook his head. The farmer listened again.

'I refuse to believe they won't,' I said.

He shrugged his shoulders.

Sean O'Faolain, *A Purse of Coppers*, 1937

At the house of the Martins of Ross, in Galway, a sheep was killed every week and a bullock once a month; what was not eaten was salted down in huge stone pickling troughs. The country round about provided the fare in such a house—meat, fowl, game, rabbits; the rivers and the sea furnished salmon, trout and other fish. The wines, laces, tea, tobacco, as well as the fineries of household ware, such as mirrors, carpets, velvets, etc., were all smuggled in. The raw materials, if one may so name them, were prepared for use on the spot. The corn grown on the surrounding hillsides was threshed in the adjoining barns, winnowed by hand on the winnowing crag, and ground by women folk in the quern. The kitchen walls contained huge cavernous ovens in their thickness: in these ovens turf fires were kindled and allowed to burn away to ashes, which in turn were swept out that the batch of loaves might be thrust in to bake in the afterheat. The flax and wool were carded and spun under the mistress's eyes. In autumn there were vast slaughterings and salt-ings of beeves; and every labourer attached to the house received a salted hide to make himself two pairs of brogues. Of the fat and tallow, mould candles were made for the parlour and 'dips' for the kitchen. 'Add to this the ordinary toil of the laundry, the dairy, the kitchen, and you get some idea of the gangs of people an old-fashioned Irish lady had to rule over.'

Daniel Corkery, *The Hidden Ireland*, 1925

Soon we were heading across country for Charlie's place, thickly coated with white dust. After a short spell of fine weather the roads of Ireland become as dusty as those of central Europe at the end of a long and baking summer. It is one of her peculiarities, like the mountains growing wetter and boggier towards the peak, and the water coming out of the taps in a thin wavering trickle while the country around is more or less under water.

Charlie lived in a big Georgian house that was in urgent need of repair. Plaster fell from the outside walls to the ground in flakes and every now and again a tile slid easily off the roof. The stables, however, were always warm and dry and fitted with every convenience. Inside, the furnishings consisted chiefly of guns, spears, fishing-rods, swords, and medals in glass cases, tattered flags and regimental colours and the stuffed heads and feet of large wild animals. There was also a table or so to be seen here and there in a clearing and a few chairs, hastily covered with chintz: and in the hall a huge chandelier, suspended by a frail wire rope from a hook, was grimly biding its time. Unopened letters were heaped on an old oak chest with rusty fastenings. As we came in a number of wolf-hounds rose and advanced, baring their teeth.

'Don't worry about them,' called Charlie, as he came downstairs. 'They're perfectly all right as long as you show no fear. Damn silly woman started flapping the other week: so they pinned her. Husband made no end of fuss, the old fool: need never have happened.'

A curious aboriginal figure shambled forward out of some nook and, collecting our suitcases, made off with them.

'Mind if we have our drinks in the hall?' said Charlie. 'My bitch is just going to pup and I've made a bed up for her in the library. And we don't use the other rooms now, too much gear.'

HONOR TRACY, Mind You, I've Said Nothing!, 1953

One year I stayed on at Bowen's Court through the late autumn: for the first time I saw the last of the leaves hang glistening, here and there, in the transparent woods or flittering on the slopes of the avenues. The rooks subsided after their harvest flights; in the gale season one or two gulls, blown inland, circled over the lawns. I heard the woods roaring, and, like pistol shots, the cracking of boughs. For years the house had been empty at this time.

At Christmas itself—and there have now been many Christmases—I remember no storms. All winds drop then: a miraculous quiet comes up from the land. When one comes in from walking, at an hour when it would be dark in England, the white mid-winter twilight is still reflected in the many windows of Bowen's Court. We had a cycle of mild Christmases—the moss up the trees was emerald, the hollies and laurels sticky with light; lambs had been born already; our pink mountains glowed behind the demesne. On one such Christmas morning we were able to sit out on the steps, waiting for aunts and uncles, remaining children of Robert, to come to dinner. Only for Christmas dinner, eaten at midday, did I re-open my grandfather's dining-room.

More lately, Christmases have been colder: for one we had a thin fall of snow. Or, the lawns have been tufted and crisp with hoar-frost; the sun came tawny, the moon curdled through low-lying, frosty mists. This change of temperature is no more than a return to the rule of the past—when, I am told, Bowen's Court Christmases were always very cold. It was a mistake to think that my own rule was to see a new era of weather in.

At this season, the family house makes felt the authority of its long tradition. It also embraces those of the country round. Every Christmas Eve I light the Christmas candle, gift of a neighbour in Farahy. Very tall and thick, of green, pink or yellow wax, the candle is planned to burn until Twelfth Night. Wreathed at its base with holly, on to whose berries the wax drops, it stands on a folded card-table at the north end of the library—here was once Eliza Wade's room. In the cottages of Farahy and Kildorrery the fellows of this candle are alight. Here, the room is so high that any light fades before it reaches the ceiling. In the silence you hear the sound of the fire; the underneath of Robert's white marble mantelpiece and its two supporting pillars are flushed. When the library shutters have been shut for the night and the dark heavy curtains drawn over them, mist, starlight or a cloud-thickened darkness lie forgotten outside the chilling panes. In the shadow cast up by the mantelpiece stand vases of holly, and Christmas cards. Footsteps of people taking the shortcut through the demesne are heard, now and then, under the windows.

ELIZABETH BOWEN, *Bowen's Court*, 1942

Coole Park, 1929

I meditate upon a swallow's flight,
Upon an aged woman and her house,
A sycamore and lime-tree lost in night
Although that western cloud is luminous,
Great works constructed there in nature's spite
For scholars and for poets after us,
Thoughts long knitted into a single thought,
A dance-like glory that those walls begot.

There Hyde before he had beaten into prose
That noble blade the Muses buckled on,
There one that ruffled in a manly pose
For all his timid heart, there that slow man,
That meditative man, John Synge, and those

Impetuous men, Shawe-Taylor and Hugh Lane,
Found pride established in humility,
A scene well set and excellent company.

They came like swallows and like swallows went,
And yet a woman's powerful character
Could keep a swallow to its first intent;
And half a dozen in formation there,
That seemed to whirl upon a compass-point,
Found certainty upon the dreaming air,
The intellectual sweetness of those lines
That cut through time or cross it withershins.

Here, traveller, scholar, poet, take your stand
When all those rooms and passages are gone,
When nettles wave upon a shapeless mound
And saplings root among the broken stone,
And dedicate—eyes bent upon the ground,
Back turned upon the brightness of the sun
And all the sensuality of the shade—
A moment's memory to that laurelled head.

W. B. YEATS, *The Winding Stair*, 1935

Everyone is used in Ireland to the tragedy that is bound up with the lives of farmers and fishing people; but in this garden one seemed to feel the tragedy of the landlord class also, and of the innumerable old families that are quickly dwindling away. These owners of the land are not much pitied at the present day, or much deserving of pity; and yet one cannot quite forget that they are the descendants of what was at one time, in the eighteenth century, a high-spirited and highly-cultivated aristocracy. The broken greenhouses and mouse-eaten libraries, that were designed and collected by men who voted with Grattan, are perhaps as mournful in the end as the four mud walls that are so often left in Wicklow as the only remnants of a farmhouse. The desolation of this life is often of a peculiarly local kind, and if a playwright chose to go through the Irish country houses he would find material, it is likely, for many gloomy plays that would turn on the dying away of these old families, and on the lives of the one or two delicate girls that are left so often to represent a dozen hearty men who were alive a generation or two ago.

J. M. SYNGE, *In Wicklow and West Kerry*, 1912

Western Landscape

In doggerel and stout let me honour this country
Though the air is so soft that it smudges the words . . .

LOUIS MACNEICE, from 'Western Landscape'

━━━━━━━

Of all places in Ireland I think this is the most lonesome; of all regions in Ireland this region that calls itself Clare-Galway, the most remote and lost. The villages seem to be descending into the bog. Darkness and mist seems to rise up and envelop everything. Even if it is day and there is sunlight the land looks damp. Life must not so much stop here, when it does stop, as fade and decline and imperceptibly vanish. I stand in the empty bar and try to engage the girl in talk. I remember that a friend of mine was born here, and how she used tell me that as a little girl she used run around the copings of the castle in Athenry and leap the corners, dangerously, and see the rooks' nests underneath with the white bones of the little fledglings in the black nests.

SEAN O'FAOLAIN, *An Irish Journey*, 1940

In any light, in any weather, any smallest piece of Ireland, hideous or ordinary or lovely, looks only like Ireland, and like nothing else at all. This may perhaps be said of many other countries—I could not answer for that. But within my experience nowhere in the measure in which it is—for good and ill—true of Ireland. There are families—we must all have known some—wherein it is seemingly impossible for any member to escape some trait or trick that proclaims his blood. And so with Ireland—from Rathlin to the Blaskets, from Inisbofin to Dalkey, she is always the unmistakable one, reflecting herself and no other in her mirrors of flattery, truth and distortion. But as I drive about Clare, for instance, I wonder whether it takes long knowledge to see that—or only natural affection?

It is thought of the stranger travelling round that has me airing this surmise. For in this Clare, for instance, amid all its stones, broken or standing, Christian or pre-Christian, he cannot after all be aware or wish to be aware, as we natives are whether we intellectualise them or not, of the formative deposits, ancient, forgotten or invented, over which we travel in any direction—and so he may find the careless, windswept land inexpressive sometimes? Not as beautiful, maybe, as the Joneses had seemed to find it? In fact, in its odd austerity, a little boring.

That may well be; for the real beauty of Ireland is much more than skin-deep. And it can hide itself. And I truly think that Ireland at its best is still a secret for connoisseurs.

KATE O'BRIEN, *My Ireland*, 1962

After the mediaeval cathedral, and the snug Georgian and the beefsteaks and resiners, going into Clare was like going into a land of skeletons, a cemetery of civilisations. On every road there were ruined cottages, by every ford and gap was a ruined tower, in every village the ruins of a Georgian Big House and a church of any century from the tenth to the nineteenth. Protestant and Catholic, we are as decent a race of people as you are likely to find, but without the black of your nail of any instinct for conserving things.

FRANK O'CONNOR, *Irish Miles*, 1947

I mounted a horse on Thursday morning, and long before the hotel showed signs of life, was many miles away, careering over the brown moorland, and inhaling the fresh Atlantic breezes. The principal object of my ride was to visit the far-famed cliffs of Moher, about fifteen miles to the north of Miltown Malbay, which are considered to present the grandest maritime scenery on the west coast of Ireland, or indeed in the whole of Europe.

A bridle-road, rough for tender-springed vehicles, but charming for riding, leads you along the summit of the cliffs. Occasionally you come to a piece of deceptive moorland, which soon admonishes you to ride carefully; but for the greater part of the distance the ground is firm, and covered by delicious sward, over which you may canter with perfect safety. Vividly, indeed, do I remember this day's delightful ride, magnificent scenery, bracing air, and joyous health, combining to make existence.

> 'A blessed thing, and the whole world a dream
> Of undimm'd joy, without a single care.'

My horse seemed to participate in his rider's exhilaration, for he went bounding on, snuffing the sea air through his distended nostrils, and tossing his head aloft in very sport. About five miles from Miltown Malbay, the road turns slightly inland, and crosses the estuary of the Oyne, near Lahinch. This passed, you incline seaward again, and after riding four miles, come within view of the Hag's Head. When near this, I dismounted, and gave my horse to a gossoon (*Anglice*, boy) who had followed me for some miles, and bade him lead the animal to Innistymon, where he was fed. Then I walked to the verge of the Head, from whence I commanded a grand view of Liscanor Bay and the Moher Cliffs, which are a couple of miles to the north. The entire coast line is one vast rock precipice, from five hundred to eight hundred feet high; for, although the cliffs attain their greatest sublimity at Moher, the range from the Hag's Head to Doolin is majestically grand. Whether you make this excursion on car or horseback, you will do wisely to send your vehicle or horse to Moher, and walk as near the cliff edge as your brains will permit, between the Hag's Head and the Signal Tower, on Moher cliff; and if you are favoured by a strong west wind, which will blow up the great Atlantic waves, and dash them foaming against the cliffs, you will remember that walk as long as memory remains.

CHARLES RICHARD WELD, *Vacations in Ireland*, 1857

Roads in west Clare are simple: one or two come into a town and one or two go out; there are few complications. On the road to Liscannor, one passes the graveyard which Roger Chauviré alludes to in his preface to the briefest and best of modern Irish histories. Is Ireland really a lotus-eaters' land? 'Well, what about it? Are they not to be envied? Can you imagine a better fortune for a human being than to have been born somewhere in County Clare, Ennistymon or Gort, and there to spend his life without asking answerless questions, and to rest among the immemorial graves in the ruined church of Liscannor, to be lulled to eternal sleep by the familiar waves?' Liscannor has a stricken look: ruined castle, burnt-out coast-guard station, tumbled-down hovels. Many of the houses are roofed with flags from a local quarry. If we had national-minded architects, many buildings throughout the land would be roofed with Liscannor flags. There is a strong smell of fish and tar; flocks of geese trail importantly through ragweed groves and plots of stinking mayweed; there are upturned curraghs, rusty anchors, chains, lamp brackets and damaged skibs and lobster-pots. Spend a million and you would not make a model village out of Liscannor—thanks be to God.

For five miles the cliffs of Moher stretch in rugged opposition to the Atlantic, their height varying from four to seven hundred feet. They are one of the *musts* for the tourist in Ireland. But for me they are a *must not*: the horror of seeing great waves breaking down below without so much as a whisper of sound; the awe of watching dumb birds squawking at their loudest and yet not heard; the gloomy conviction that all this terrifying scene will hit back in hundreds of nightmares. No, I would say to the seeker after sensations that the old classic ones of drink and drugs are still the best.

STEPHEN RYNNE, *All Ireland*, 1956

After driving for about fifteen minutes, having passed through a village called Durrus, he again saw the sea; this time a great lough, a long, wild inland reach of ocean, far below on his right. On the perimeter of this lough were small patchwork-quilt fields, poorer than any he had passed to date. Cottages built lonely in the lee of hillocks overlooked these fields, their windows facing away from the cold sea winds. In the next ten minutes of driving he saw no other car or no living thing, except for some gulls circling a bog. Again the road forked inland and he drove alongside the rim of a deserted stone quarry. On a hill above him were the ruins of three old roofless cottages, abandoned perhaps a hundred years ago. He passed a crossroads, with a tiny grocery shop and placards out front advertising *The Irish Times* and *The Irish Press*. At the crossroads, a sign: DRISHANE 5.

BRIAN MOORE, *The Mangan Inheritance*, 1979

According to the *carte du pays* laid out for me by the fisherman, I left the shore and crossed the summit of a mountain, which, after an hour's ascension, I found sloped almost perpendicularly down to a bold and rocky coast, its base terminating in a peninsula, that advanced for near half a mile into the ocean. Towards the extreme western point of this peninsula, which was wildly romantic beyond description, arose a vast and grotesque pile of rocks, at once forming the scite and fortifications of the noblest mass of ruins in which my eye ever rested. Grand even in desolation, and magnificent in decay—it was the Castle of Inismore! The setting sun shone brightly on its mouldering turrets, and the waves, which bathed its rocky basis, reflected on their swelling bosoms the dark outlines of its awful ruins.

LADY MORGAN, *The Wild Irish Girl*, 1806

The strangeness of this grey limestone country must be seen to be realized; it is like nothing else in Ireland or in Britain—though around Ingleborough you get similar landscape on a smaller scale. One stream, by some miracle, contrives to flow on the surface from source almost to mouth—the Caher River (*Cathair*, a stone fort), which debouches at Fanore: being so rare a phenomenon, it is appropriate that it should contain as one of its abundant plants an extremely rare Pondweed—the hybrid *Potamogeton perpygmaeus*. And this brings me to the subject of the flora of Burren, which is so remarkable, and in spring so beautiful, that it is celebrated far outside the ranks of botanists. Throughout the whole region of the bare limestones—from eastern Mayo away down to the Shannon—this flora is found. Some of its leading members the alpine Spring Gentian, for instance, and the Close-flowered Orchis of the Mediterranean—range from Lough Carra southward almost to Ennis. On the low limestones around Ardrahan this flora is well developed; but to see it at its maximum of profusion and beauty one must go to Burren or to Aran, during the second half of May. Its interest lies in the presence and frequent abundance of many plants elsewhere rare; and these plants display a very remarkable variety of type as regards their normal head-quarters. Extremely profuse are several which are usually found on the mountains or in the far north—such as Mountain Avens, Bear-berry, Spring Gentian and several Mossy Saxifrages. With these are others of quite southern range, like the Close-flowered Orchis and the Maidenhair; and all alike grow mixed together right down to sea-level. Some of the former group are here found further south, in view of their lowland habitat, than they are anywhere else, while some of the latter occur nowhere else so far north. We have, indeed, a very remarkable mixture of northern and southern species, most of which, by a happy chance, are also most beautiful plants. With these are others which are very rare in the British area, like the Hoary Rock-rose and Pyramidal Bugle: others again are conspicuous by their immense profusion, like Bloody Crane's-bill and Madder, Hart's-tongue and Scale Fern. The result of the luxuriance and abundance of these is that over miles the grey limestone is converted into a veritable rock-garden in spring, brilliant with blossom. How do these plants attain such profusion on ground that is mostly bare rock? Many live in chinks and in the rain-widened joints of the limestone, where humus has collected; and the damp Atlantic wind, laden with mist and showers, does the rest. Often a skin of peaty soil only an inch thick, lying on a dry flat rock-surface, will maintain a flora of perhaps twenty species. And how is it that so mixed an assemblage of plants—alpine and lowland, northern and southern—is found crowded together on this queer ground? That is not so simple, but let us consider the peculiar conditions which prevail. There is a very damp climate—very mild also, frost being practically unknown. There is great exposure to wind, yet the rock is full of deep chinks where complete shelter prevails. There is exceptionally good drainage, all water sinking far down into the rock. The warm moist air will account for the abundance of the Maidenhair: the light soil and absence of frost help the Close-flowered Orchis to maintain itself. The presence of alpine plants in profusion right down to sea-level appears more puzzling, but alpine plants do not necessarily need cold in order to be happy: indeed most of them do not like frost, and need the warm dry winter covering of snow which they get on the higher mountains: in our own gardens most do best in a frame, where they escape the damp cold of our winters. During spring and summer the alpines like—and on the mountains obtain—plenty of moisture combined with good drainage: this they get in perfection in Burren; and under these circumstances, the higher temperature of the warm Atlantic seaboard does not appear to incommode them in the least. If alpines attempted to descend into the lowlands in most places, the tall vegetation of summer would inevitably destroy them: but on the Burren rocks exposure and grazing and want of depth of soil combine to produce a population of low-growing plants, among which the alpines are at home. Their most obvious enemies would be the gregarious Bracken and Ling, bushes and coarse-growing grasses: these are all restrained by the factors mentioned, and the Ling also by the presence of limestone rock.

ROBERT LLOYD PRAEGER, *The Way That I Went*, 1937

It was a grey afternoon, with a spatter of rain in the air, but the colours were pure Paul Henry—the misty blues of the distant hills, the golden brown of the mountain, the black and brown of the seaweedy strip of shore at low-tide, the ice-green of the water where the wind whipped it, and the whole of it held in a light to be found nowhere else in the world.

ETHEL MANNIN, *Connemara Journal*, 1947

Denis Donohoe walked over to the dim stack of brown turf piled at the back of the stable. It was there since the early fall, the dry earth cut from the bog, the turf that would make bright and pleasant fires in the open grates of Connacht for the winter months. Away from it spread the level bogland, a sweep of country that had, they said, in the infancy of the earth been a great oak forest, across which in later times had roved packs of hungry wolves, and which could at this day claim the most primitive form of industry in Western Europe. Out into this bogland in the summer had come from their cabins the peasantry, men and women, Denis Donohoe among them; they had dug up slices of the spongy, wet sod, cut it into pieces rather larger than bricks, licked it into shape by stamping upon it with their bare feet, stacked it about in little rows to dry in the sun, one sod leaning against the other.

SEAMUS O'KELLY, *Waysiders*, 1917

The rain eased off, the sky brightened, but the wind seemed to grow in fury, surf and spray went up straight and shining into the air beyond the breakwater, leaped it and came down with a flat slap on the sandy slope and the sleeping small craft. Then, like Apache on an Arizona skyline, the people began to appear: a group of three suddenly, from behind a standing rock; a group of seven or eight rising sharply into sight on a hilltop on the switchback riverside road, dropping out of sight into a hollow, surfacing again, followed by other groups that appeared and disappeared in the same disconcerting manner. As the sky cleared, the uniform darkness breaking up into bullocks of black wind goaded clouds, the landscape of rock and heather, patchwork fields divided by grey, high, drystone walls, came out into the light; and from every small farmhouse thus revealed, people came, following footpaths, crossing stiles, calling to each other across patches of light-green oats and dark-green potatoes. It was a sudden miracle of growth, of human life appearing where there had been nothing but wind and rain and mist. Within three-quarters of an hour there were a hundred or more people around the harbour, lean hard-faced fishermen and small farmers, dark-haired laughing girls, old women in coloured shawls, talking Irish, talking English, posing in groups for the cameraman who in his yellow oilskins moved among them like a gigantic canary. They waved and called to Jeremiah where he stood, withdrawn and on the defensive, in the sheltered doorway of a fish-stinking shed.

BENEDICT KIELY, 'God's Own Country', in *A Journey to the Seven Streams*, 1963

Sligo and Mayo

In Sligo the country was soft; there were turkeys
    Gobbling under sycamore trees
And the shadows of clouds on the mountains moving
    Like browsing cattle at ease.

And little distant fields were sprigged with haycocks
    And splashed against a white
Roadside cottage a welter of nasturtium
    Deluging the sight,

And pullets pecking the flies from around the eyes of heifers
    Sitting in farmyard mud
Among hydrangeas and the falling ear-rings
    Of fuchsias red as blood.

But in Mayo the tumbledown walls went leap-frog
    Over the moors,
The sugar and salt in the pubs were damp in the casters
    And the water was brown as beer upon the shores

Of desolate loughs, and stumps of hoary bog-oak
    Stuck up here and there
And as the twilight filtered on the heather
    Water-music filled the air,

And when the night came down upon the bogland
    With all-enveloping wings
The coal-black turfstacks rose against the darkness
    Like the tombs of nameless kings.

LOUIS MACNEICE, *Collected Poems*, 1948

To spell fuchsia without a dictionary, it helps to remember the name Fuchs, pronounced *fooks*, the sixteenth-century German herbalist thus immortalised, if ultimately garbled. The original stock from which most Irish fuchsia hedges came, from Cork to Donegal and right round to Antrim, was originally planted in Kerry in the middle of the last century. It was a new cultivar, hybridised at Riccarton in Scotland in 1830. Hence, the full name for it: *Fuchsia magellanica* 'Riccartonii'. In the breeding of plants, the words 'hybrid' and 'vigour' are always clasped together, but there can have been few hybrids so possessed of explosive energy. At just the right distance from the sea, the right rainfall and humidity, the right range of winter temperature, *F. magellanica* 'Riccartonii' grows with a crimson passion: even a twig, thrown down in a moist place, will root itself and flower within a year. This generous, even feckless, habit made it possible for farmers to grow hedges without being seen to stoop too much or make finicky motions with their fingers: just snap a bit off, and ram it in.

Montbretia is more genuinely 'a garden escape'. It was bred in the 1870s by a French nurseryman who crossed two irises from southern Africa. *Crocosmia* had the size and brilliant colour, *crocosmiiflora* the hardiness and vigour. Together, they made a plant which has wandered like a gypsy, setting up camp in rough places all over the west of these islands, from Cornish cliffs and heathery Scottish roadsides to the rocky river-banks and lake shores of Connacht. Here it is the poor man's gladiolus, brightening small farms where no other flower has ever been sown. On the moorland road to Cregganbawn, one thicket of montbretia grows all alone on a rocky verge just opposite a farmhouse. Early in autumn, as the flowers light up, the farmer's wife goes out with baler twine to tie them against the first big wind; nowhere else in her world is there any colour quite so free and fiery.

MICHAEL VINEY, *A Year's Turning*, 1996

Those who find the air too stale can go out and lean for a few minutes against the wall of the building: a clear, mild evening outside; the light from the lighthouse on Clare Island, twelve miles away, is not yet visible; the eye falls on the quiet sea across thirty, forty miles, beyond the edge of the bay as far as the mountains of Connemara and Galway—and looking to the right, westward, you see high cliffs, the last two miles of Europe lying between you and America. Wild, the perfect setting for a witches' sabbath, covered with bog and heather, rises the most westerly of Europe's mountains, a sheer drop of two thousand feet on the ocean side; facing you on its slope in the dark green of the bog, a paler, cultivated square patch with a large gray house: this is where Captain Boycott lived, the man for whom the inhabitants invented boycotting: this is where the world was given a new word; a few hundred yards above this house, the remains of a crashed airplane—American pilots, a fraction of a second too early, had thought they had reached the open sea, the smooth surface between them and their native land: Europe's last cliff, the last jag of that continent, was their doom.

Azure spreads over the sea, in varying layers, varying shades; wrapped in this azure are green islands, looking like great patches of bog, black ones, jagged, rearing up out of the ocean like stumps of teeth. . . .

HEINRICH BÖLL, Irish Journal, 1957, trans. Leila Vennewitz

The score of miles that will close the circuit of Árainn, leading back from the Bun Gabhla shore by way of the north coast to the eastern tip of the island, begins with a brief reprise of the cliff-theme of the southern coast, and there-after unfolds its own individualities. Individualities in the plural, because the experiences it offers oscillate between two extremes. The grim rock-banks of the more exposed stretches of coast, in grey weather almost intolerably deso-late, alternate with bays in which a degree of shelter has allowed the accu-mulation not only of bright sands and shingles but of history, of a residual human warmth that the fogs and winter storms do not quite dispel. A walk that takes one in and out of these bays dips into various eras of the past— the Age of the Saints, the centuries of Aran's military significance, the birth-pangs of the modern fishing fleet, the brief and dazzling reign of Flaherty the film-maker—each of which has brought lasting life to its elected sites. On the other hand the intervening monotonies were dedicated only to a laborious task, perennial throughout the darkest times but now abandoned, the crop-ping and burning of seaweed; and that whole long Kelp Age has no monu-ment other than a few stones scattered and scarcely identifiable among millions of others on the storm beach.

In general the severity of the coast moderates from west to east, from the cliffs that face the north-western gales, by way of low rocky shores and shin-glebanks, to the sand dunes in the shelter of Cill Éinne bay. The smaller bays that punctuate this modulation (one can distinguish about a dozen of them), and in particular Port Mhuirbhigh which almost makes a separate island out of the western third of Árainn, produce the sort of focusing of the landscape that is one of the ways in which mere location is intensified into *place*. By these hearths even the wandering sea pauses. On the coasts between them, however, even the most soundly situated human can wander into uncentred and uncentering moods.

TIM ROBINSON, Stories of Aran: Pilgrimage, 1986

I am in Aranmor, sitting over a turf fire, listening to a murmur of Gaelic that is rising from a little public house under my room.

The steamer which comes to Aran sails according to the tide, and it was six o'clock this morning when we left the quay of Galway in a dense shroud of mist.

A low line of shore was visible at first on the right between the movement of the waves and fog, but when we came further it was lost sight of, and nothing could be seen but the mist curling in the rigging, and a small circle of foam.

There were few passengers; a couple of men going out with young pigs tied loosely in sacking, three or four young girls who sat in the cabin with their heads completely twisted in their shawls, and a builder, on his way to repair the pier at Kilronan, who walked up and down and talked with me.

In about three hours Aran came in sight. A dreary rock appeared at first sloping up from the sea into the fog; then, as we drew nearer, a coastguard station and the village.

A little later I was wandering out along the one good roadway of the island, looking over low walls on either side into small flat fields of naked rock. I have seen nothing so desolate. Grey floods of water were sweeping everywhere upon the limestone, making at times a wild torrent of the road, which twined continually over low hills and cavities in the rock or passed between a few small fields of potatoes or grass hidden away in corners that had shelter. Whenever the cloud lifted I could see the edge of the sea below me on the right, and the naked ridge of the island above me on the other side. Occasionally I passed a lonely chapel or schoolhouse, or a line of stone pillars with crosses above them and inscriptions asking a prayer for the soul of the person they commemorated.

I met few people; but here and there a band of tall girls passed me on their way to Kilronan, and called out to me with humorous wonder, speaking English with a slight foreign intonation that differed a good deal from the brogue of Galway. The rain and cold seemed to have no influence on their vitality, and as they hurried past me with eager laughter and great talking in Gaelic, they left the wet masses of rock more desolate than before.

J. M. SYNGE, *The Aran Islands*, 1907

The Rosses, into which we had now entered, is a district which for desolation has no parallel in Europe. Bounded by the sea on one hand, the Derry-Veagh Mountains and lesser hills on the other, its extent is equal to an English county—Rutland for instance. A single road crosses it, to a single village— Dungloe; but beyond this, no maps indicate it, no guide-books describe it. I wish I could! I wish instead of driving through in pelting rain, and seeing it by glimpses from under umbrellas, I could have walked it on my own two feet—young feet, alas! they needed to be—the fourteen miles to Dungloe, and the twenty-two more to Glenties! What a treat for an energetic pedestrian! for the road is very good, and on either side of it opens out a world of wonder and beauty; bog, moor, boulder, tiny mountain tarns, where heaps of trout are said to lurk, ignorant of rod or fly, and everywhere a solitude absolutely unbroken; an interminable wavy ocean of land, as empty and pathless as the sea.

He was a bold man who first planted in this wilderness the tiny town of Dungloe. For a town it is, and must have been for a good many years. The hotel we stopped at had large, old-fashioned, well-built, sitting-rooms, and a long gallery of bedrooms, not uncomfortable, apparently. We got a good meal—of excellent fresh eggs, milk, bread and butter—also a piano, which was made to discourse excellent music while we rested; so far as we could rest, with the longest half of our journey yet to come. And then, under the joyful hope that it would be fair—for it really had ceased to rain—we again went out into the wilderness.

What a glorious wilderness it was! What a sky arched over it! Grey still, but brightened with patches of amber and rose, colouring the distant mountains, and reflected in every tiny lake. Our artist longed to stop and paint, but we might as well have left him like Robinson Crusoe on the desert island. And besides, grand as it was to look at, the scenery was too diffused and monotonous for the pencil. Or, indeed, for the pen. No description is possible. I can only say, Go and see.

We sat and gazed, silently almost, for I know not how many miles. In truth, one ceases to count miles here. They seem a variable quantity. One can half believe the story told to our artist, that the milestones are carried along in a cart, and wherever one of them happens to drop out, there it is set up. I can remember no special point in the landscape, no more than I could in the Atlantic Ocean—had I ever crossed it, which I never shall do now—until the carriage stopped at the top of a sharp descent; so sharp that we all voluntarily turned out, and saw below us a pretty little village and a picturesque river, the Gweebarra, rushing over rocks and boulders into Gweebarra Bay.

Here, at last, would be a lovely place to halt at; but halt we dared not, for the light was fading fast. Skirting the village, though not entering it, the road wound up again into another stretch of monotonous moor, except that even the heather gradually ceased, giving place to continuous masses of great boulders and smaller stones, thrown together in the most fantastic way. Never, except on the top of the Alps, have I seen such a total absence of any green thing. 'Desolation of desolation' was written upon all around.

MRS CRAIK, *An Unknown Country*, 1880

Ten miles north of Donegal Town, in the extreme north-west of Ireland, runs a range of low, rounded hills known as the Blue Stacks. Technically, they are classed as mountains, but to the ordinary eye they look like hills. Their name—taken from the Irish name of the highest peak, Croagh Gorm—is fitting, for from a distance they always appear a deep, purple blue, even on the clearest days. Around these hills lives a small group of farmers whose lives continue to be rooted in eighteenth-century patterns, or earlier. Technologically and agriculturally their methods scarcely reveal modern influence. Tools we read about in histories of ancient and medieval technology can still be seen in use on Blue Stack farms, some of them home-made in forms that have long since disappeared elsewhere. Machines are seldom heard.

Though these old traditions are now rapidly fading, as the last generation of Irish-speaking farmers dies out and young, English-speaking literate ones take their place, something still remains, both in the crafts of life and in its thought-patterns. Habits of thrift and personal independence have kept men as far outside a money-based economy as possible, so that even the houses are often still made from materials found within the boundaries of each farm—unshaped stone, rough wooden rafters, green-thatch rooves. Crops of potatoes and corn are still sown and reaped entirely with spade and scythe; hay is mown by hand; fuel is won from the surrounding bog by laborious hand-cutting and sun-drying. As interesting, however, as the ways of life, are the forms of thought that accompany them, especially in an age that is so rapidly sweeping away all living remnants of its own long past.

ROBERT BERNEN, Foreword to *Tales from the Blue Stacks*, 1978

Donegal is strong meat: strong scenery, strong weather, strong bodies, strong spirits. Look at a map of the county: a picture of frenzy, of perpetual war between land and sea, a tattered flag defiantly stuck out from a jutting of this raft that is Ireland. What an amazing coast-line! The map picture illustrates the fretted territory far better than the most impressive list, giving the figure of coast miles and the number of heads, points, loughs, islands and islets. From the geographical map, turn to the geological one: what a battle of rocks is here! How the various varieties of granite struggled with one another; how the weaker limestone was shouldered out of the fray; how the all-in wrestling match moved over Inishowen, the Rosses, Horn Head! Rock interlocking with rock; turbulence everywhere; Donegal's fate was fashioned out of Genesis millions of years ago by the throwing up of intractable rock. The habitable places were limited to the coast and to hollows running north-east and south-west.

STEPHEN RYNNE, *All Ireland*, 1956

Away out to the north-west, across seven miles of open Atlantic, rises Tory (*Toraigh*, towery, abounding in tors), the most remote and most exposed of inhabited Irish islands. It is utterly windswept, with a rocky coast mostly low, but precipitous at the eastern end. It is strange to find that so desolate and tempestuous a place has been long inhabited, and even fortified. At the cliff-bound end formidable ramparts built across a narrow neck show a prehistoric fortress of great strength. According to legend, this was the stronghold of Balor of the Mighty Blows, chief of the Fomorians, who held the island twelve centuries before Christ. Some seventeen hundred years later, St Columba founded a monastery in this remote spot: the remains of two early churches may still be seen, as well as a round tower without a top; also a cross of the curious 'tau' class, which has arms but no head, and some other relics of bygone days. In spite of the fact that every available sod of peat or semi-peat has been cut for fuel or roofing, so that much of the surface is mere desert, there is a population of several hundred, living by fishing and by the product of small fields of barley, rye and potatoes. Fuel (peat) comes from the mainland, a precarious passage even in summer. The tall lighthouse, the chapel and school, and the excellent boats by which the Congested Districts Board replaced the local canvas curraghs, impart a touch of modernity to this primitive place.

ROBERT LLOYD PRAEGER, *The Way That I Went*, 1937

The women [on Tory Island] moved about the house and shore barefoot. The men sat smoking on the door-stone, talking with me of the clouds bearing from the foreland—a sign that the day was fairing—and of the gannets that pass the Island and do not rest until they come to Fanet Head. A few men were out in curraghs on the brighter water, using a paddle as if they were digging for sea-potatoes with a spade. There was a large patchwork quilt stretched out to air in the sun: it was a craze of dazzling colours against rock and ocean.

The Island is full of horses and the dark-haired girls gallop on them fearlessly without saddle or bit, carrying big creels of sods. There are patches of oats and barley, of an intense rich green as though the barren strength of the island had gathered into those few spots. All around, the surface had been picked bare, for the knotted sods are burned with the turf that is brought over by oar and sail from Magheroarty—the plain of the Spring-tide.

AUSTIN CLARKE, *A Penny in the Clouds*, 1968

The vast 'clamps' (stacks) of peat, the acres upon acres covered with little heaps of the drying 'bricks' of turf, the brown and black terraces, just sprinkled with new heather and weeds, may be dreary; but they are not dismal; for they tell of industry, and some harvest of comfort, however small. But there are other sights,—groups of ruins, as at Athenry—staring fragments of old castles, and churches, and monasteries; and worse than these, a very large number of unroofed cottages. For miles together, in some places, there is scarcely a token of human presence but the useless gables and the empty doorways and window-spaces of pairs or rows of deserted cottages. There is something so painful—so even exasperating in this sight, that one wishes that a little more time and labour could be spared to level the walls, as well as take off the roof, when tenants are either ejected, or go away of their own accord. Yet, while substantial stone walls are thus staring in the traveller's face, what cabins—actual dwellings of families—are here and there distinguishable in the midst of the bog! styes of mud, bulging and tottering, grass-grown, half-swamped with bog-water, and the soil around all poached with the tread of bare feet. In comparison with such places, the stony lands near Galway (a vivid green ground, strewn with grey stones) look wholesome, and almost cheerful, but for the wrecks of habitations. From the time that we enter upon the district of the red petticoats—the red flannel and frieze, which form a part of the dress of most of the Galway people—things look better than in the brown and black region of the bog.

HARRIET MARTINEAU, *Letters from Ireland*, 1852

This evening, after a day of teeming rain, it cleared for an hour, and I went out while the sun was setting to a little cove where a high sea was running. As I was coming back the darkness began to close in except in the west, where there was a red light under the clouds. Against this light I could see patches of open wall and little fields of stooks, and a bit of laneway with an old man driving white cows before him. These seemed transfigured beyond any description.

Then I passed two men riding bare-backed towards the west, who spoke to me in Irish, and a little further on I came to the only village on my way. The ground rose towards it, and as I came near there was a grey bar of smoke from every cottage going up to the low clouds overhead, and standing out strangely against the blackness of the mountain behind the village.

Beyond the patch of wet cottages I had another stretch of lonely roadway, and a heron kept flapping in front of me, rising and lighting again with many lonely cries that made me glad to reach the little public-house near Smerwick.

J. M. SYNGE, *In Wicklow and West Kerry*, 1912

from *Western Landscape*

But for us now
The beyond is still out there as on tiptoes here we stand
On promontories that are themselves a-tiptoe

Reluctant to be land. Which is why this land
Is always more than matter—as a ballet
Dancer is more than body. The west of Ireland
Is brute and ghost at once. Therefore in passing
Among these shadows of this permanent show
Flitting evolving dissolving but never quitting
This arbitrary and necessary Nature
Both bountiful and callous, harsh and wheedling—
Let now the visitor, although disfranchised
In the constituencies of quartz and bog-oak
And ousted from the elemental congress,
Let me at least in token that my mother
Earth was a rocky earth with breasts uncovered
To suckle solitary intellects
And limber instincts, let me, if a bastard
Out of the West by urban civilization
(Which unwished father claims me—so I must take
What I can before I go) let me who am neither Brandan
Free of all roots nor yet a rooted peasant
Here add one stone to the indifferent cairn . . .
With a stone on the cairn, with a word on the wind, with a
    prayer in the flesh let me honour this country.

LOUIS MACNEICE, *c.*1945; *Collected Poems*, 1948

Hallowe'en 1982: Teelin, County Donegal

It is the morning after the night before and snatches of the night before—
fiddle tunes, hubbub, the clink of glasses—keep filtering through from the
memory-bank. We are driving out to the coast to clear our heads—or rather,
up to the coast, towards Slieve League, the highest sea-cliff in Western Europe,
following this precipitous erratic mountain road that winds between stone
walls, potato drills, stone-littered patchy fields, one man idling over a spade
who raises his hand in an understated rhetoric of hail or farewell, and the
clouds piled high between mountains, while these fiddle tunes keep coming
back insistently, hectic, passionate and melancholic; half-remembered fragments. The bits and pieces of the landscape sidle into place, accommodated
by the loops and spirals of the road, its meditated salients and inclines: and
now, as at other times, I wonder if the disciplined wildness of Donegal music
has anything to do with this terrain. For nature, here, is never wholly pristine
or untouched: the land is possessed and repossessed, named, forgotten, lost
and rediscovered; it is under constant dispute; even in its dereliction, it
implies a human history. A line of a sentimental song comes back to me: 'Sure
your hearts are like your mountains, in the homes of Donegal'. Presumably,

the writer intended that we read 'big' for 'mountains'; yet mountains are also hard and stony; they are barriers to be circumvented or defeated. In Donegal fiddle music, this unconscious irony is transformed into purposeful energy. It is a music of driving, relentless rhythm that teeters on the edge of falling over itself; it seems to almost overtake itself, yet reins in at the brink. A jagged melodic line is nagging at me as we arrive at a high promontory. The sea appears from nowhere. On the right, the immense absurd precipice of Slieve League falls into a tiny silent line of foam, some rocks. How far away is it? The eye has nothing to scale: a human figure, if you could imagine it against this, would be lost; that seagull hovering over there is either miles away, or just within reach. Turning back to the sea again, you can hear it, if you listen very closely: a vast lonesome whispering that stretches all the way to North America.

CIARAN CARSON, *Last Night's Fun*, 1996

We moved up more into the crowd till we were by the wall so that they could not see us. Then we crept along slowly till we were near the door. As soon as Mass was over we ran out and up through the fields to the Hill of Clasach.

The day was very sultry.

'The devil, Tomás, let us throw off our shoes and we'll be as light as a starling for the road.'

'A great thought,' said he, and we sat down on the roadside. We tied our shoes together and flung them over our shoulders.

Half-way up the Clasach I looked back and saw the crowds ascending the road from the chapel.

'Oh Lord, look at all the people coming to the races!'

'Oh, mo léir, aren't there many people in the world!'

When we came in sight of the parish of Ventry Tomás was lost in astonishment.

'Oh, Maurice, isn't Ireland wide and spacious?'

'Upon my word, Tomás, she is bigger than that. What about Dingle where I was long ago?'

'And where is Dingle?'

'To the south of that hill.'

'Oh Lord, I always thought there was nothing in Ireland, only the Blasket, Dunquin and Iveragh. Look at that big high hill beyond! Wouldn't it be grand for us to have it at home! What sport we would have climbing to the top of it every evening after school! I wonder what is the name of it!'

'Don't you know it and you looking at it every day from the Blasket? That's Mount Eagle.'

'Is that so, indeed? In the Blasket it seemed as if it were in Dunquin.'

We had a brilliant view before our eyes, southwards over the parish of Ventry and the parish of Maurhan and north to the parish of Kill, green fields covered in flowers on either side of us, a lonely house here and there away at the foot of the mountain, Ventry harbour to the south-east, lying still, three or four sailing-boats at anchor, and a curragh or two creeping like beetles across the water, the mountains beyond nodding their heads one above the other.

We were leaping for mirth and delight. 'Your soul to the devil, Tomás, it is a grand day we will have.'

> MAURICE O'SULLIVAN, *Twenty Years A-Growing*, 1933, trans. Moya Llewelyn Davies and George Thomson

Concerning the house where I was born, there was a fine view from it. It had two windows with a door between them. Looking out from the right-hand window, there below was the bare hungry countryside of the Rosses and Gweedore; Bloody Foreland yonder and Tory Island far away out, swimming like a great ship where the sky dips into the sea. Looking out of the door, you could see the West of County Galway with a good portion of the rocks of Connemara, Aranmore in the ocean out from you with the small bright houses of Kilronan, clear and visible, if your eyesight were good and the Summer had come. From the window on the left you could see the Great Blasket, bare and forbidding as a horrible other-worldly eel, lying languidly on the wave-tops; over yonder was Dingle with its houses close together. It has always been said that there is no view from any house in Ireland comparable to this and it must be admitted that this statement is true. I have never heard it said that there was any house as well situated as this on the face of the earth. And so this house was delightful and I do not think that its like will ever be there again.

> FLANN O'BRIEN, *An Beal Bocht* (*The Poor Mouth*), 1941, trans. Patrick C. Power, 1973

Puritan Ireland

The unknown girl, distraught, caught at Fergus' sleeve.

'Why do they say things like that?'

'Because they're Irish,' Fergus said. 'A nation of masturbators under priestly instruction.'

BRIAN MOORE, Fergus

How can I lie in a lukewarm bed
With all the thoughts that come into my head?

BRIAN MERRIMAN, The Midnight Court

———

At last she was entirely there in all her evil comeliness, an enchanting vision, her form elastic and light, with flexible limbs and a juvenile grace in her every movement. As she moved towards the alarmed prelate, her expressive features and eloquent action harmonised blandly with each other. A sound indicative of his anguish burst from Bishop Flanagan's throat, and seizing the bowl of holy water he flung it desperately at the approaching vision. To his horror it passed right through her and was shivered in atoms against the wall. As she continued to approach he sprang out the far side of the bed and, clutching the book of exorcisms, he swamped her in a deluge from the Vulgate. He did not dare raise his eyes from the page until he was out of breath. When he glanced up fearfully she was still there, scarcely three paces from him, evidently experiencing the greatest difficulty in restraining her merriment.

'Begone!' quavered the Bishop. 'I know you to be nought but a vain impression in the air.'

She regarded him for a moment roguishly; and when she spoke, her voice modulated itself with natural and winning ease.

'I'm thousands of years old,' she said in dulcet tones. 'You'll never get rid of me with that modern Christian stuff.'

Bishop Flanagan's mouth fell open, but no sound came forth. He cowered against the wall as she opened her lips again, and sweet, amatory words came out.

'Why are you so difficult?' she asked. 'You will never find a woman so passionate, so loving or so submissive.'

It is likely that the Bishop would have lost his life through sheer horror at these plausible words, only that he was suddenly recalled to the consciousness that the friar was in the neighbouring room by a series of bull-like roars which proceeded therefrom. Bishop Flanagan was immediately galvanised into action, and seizing the rushlight, he tore open the door and dashed into Furiosus' bedroom. Great as was the Bishop's alarm, he stopped petrified at the sight that met his eyes. The friar was tumbling around on the floor fighting madly to escape from the obscene advances and abandoned caresses of three females of the most luscious character imaginable. But Bishop Flanagan did not forget his own peril for long. He ran to the struggling mass on the floor.

'Nice time,' he snarled, 'to be slaking your lusts, when I'm half-slaughtered by the most hideous apparition that was ever seen!'

With a mighty heave Father Furiosus was on his feet, flinging the three sportful damsels against the far wall. He seized Bishop Flanagan by the throat and pressed him back against the bed-post.

'Let me go,' gasped the Bishop, 'or you will incur the penalty of excommunication.'

'What do you mean by that accusation,' howled the friar, 'and I locked in deadly combat with the forces of Hell? Take it back before I tear the skinny throat out of you.'

'I'm sorry,' panted the Bishop, 'I take it back. I didn't know they were demons too. There's one in my room, the most terrible vision that eye has ever seen.'

Father Furiosus released the Bishop and stood looking around the room breathing heavily. The three high-stepping females had disappeared. The friar tiptoed over to the door and looked into the Bishop's room. It was likewise empty. Then he returned to Bishop Flanagan, and the two of them conversed in whispers.

'She had a singularly evil countenance,' said Bishop Flanagan, his voice still trembling with fear. 'There was a hot, unholy fire in her eye. Neither holy water nor exorcism availed ought against her.'

'That's bad,' replied Furiosus, shaking his head gravely. 'It would appear from what you tell me that these painful phenomena are female elementals, probably sylphides—most difficult to get rid of. However, I will sprinkle my stoup of holy water on the walls and ceiling. While I am so engaged, do you turn up your most powerful exorcism, and we will read it aloud together.'

'What will we do if all four renew the assault in unison?' asked the Bishop shakily.

'It will be a triste and ominous affair,' replied the friar gloomily, 'and may well spell damnation for us both.'

MERVYN WALL, *The Unfortunate Fursey*, 1946

At the Head of *Killough Bay* two Roads break off, one NE leading to *Strang-ford*, the other North to *Down-Patrick*. In this latter District lie the Churches of *Dunsford* or *Dunsport*, *Bally Culter*, and *Kilclief*, the latter being seated on the Entrance into the Bay of *Strangford*. The Castle and Lands of *Kilclief* were an antient See House and Manor of the *Bishops* of *Down*; and it was there that *John Celly*, Bishop of that See, publickly cohabited with *Lettice Thomas*, a married Woman; for which Scandal, *Swain*, Arch-bishop of *Armagh*, in 1441, had him served with a Monitory process in his *Castle of Kilclief*, and there was a Chamber in the said Castle, then called the Hawks Chamber, which by Tradition of the old Natives, was the place where the Bishop's Falconer and Hawks were kept. Yet possibly this tradition might have been taken up from the Figure of a Fowl resembling a hawk, carved on a Stone Chimney Piece in a Room on the second Floor, on which also is cut in Bas Relief a Cross Patee. The Castle is yet entire, though it is covered with Thatch; it is a large Build-ing, and the first Floor of it vaulted, has two Front Wings, in one of which is a Stair-case, and in the other a Stack of Closets. The lands surrounding the Castle are a fine Demesne, and some of the best Land in the Barony, which with a Water Mill on them are held from the Bishop by the Revd *Peter Leslie*; and South is a Denomination of a Land called *Bishops Court*, in Lease to Mr Justice *Ward*, near which are *Sheepland* and *Ballyhernan*.

WALTER HARRIS, *The Antient and Present State of the County of Down*, 1741

They [our Irish women] are chaste in a degree that hardly any country this day can boast of. Adultery, or an intrigue even, is unknown among females in the middle class. A married woman may be violent, may be a termagant; an unmarried one may be pert, may be ignorant, may be flippant, but they are

> Chaste as the icicle
> That hangs on Dian's temple.

To an Englishman, as may be easily conceived, the plainness of their accent would at first be unpleasant. But his ear would soon accommodate itself to it, perhaps even find beauty in it; a great beauty in a female, an apparent freedom from affectation and assumption.

JOHN GAMBLE, *Sketches of Dublin and the North of Ireland*, 1811

A young woman from the West is explaining just why a certain novel was banned at her local library. I myself never read novels, but it appears that thousands of people find themselves quite unable to live without them, the local Sisters of Mary, or some such organisation, being no exception to the rule. Here again I am at a loss. Why it is necessary to band oneself along with other selves labelled as Sisters of Mary or Ancient Orders of Buffaloes or what not, has always been beyond me. Why not just be oneself? But that, it appears, is impossible. And so these western Sisters of Mary having, presumably as Sisters of Mary, read a certain novel, decided, again presumably as Sisters of Mary, that the said novel was immoral and objectionable on the grounds that at one point in the narrative a man and his wife (presumably wealthy, there being no point whatever in reading novels about people who are not wealthy) were changing for dinner and actually carried on a conversation between a dressing-room and a bathroom, the woman being in her bath and the door of the bathroom *unlocked*. This, it appears, was the point at which the Sisters of Mary rose up in their wrath: the door of the bathroom was *unlocked*. In order to discover that the door of the bathroom was unlocked one had, it further appeared, to be reading with the concentrated attention of a female Sherlock Holmes; in fact it was evident that the Sisters of Mary had been doing a bit of concentrated sleuthing, since it was necessary to turn back several pages and collate several apparently unconnected passages in order to *prove* that the bathroom door was unlocked—so that the vigilance and sense of public duty of the Sisters of Mary cannot be too highly commended. With such selfless devotion at work in our midst, lengthening night-dresses, reading the writing on the walls of lavatories in order to erase it, removing the words 'privy' and 'water-closet' from the pages of our national literature, and providing locks for all bathroom and lavatory doors, who can doubt that the moral tone of the island of saints and scholars will be raised to unprecedented heights, to the greater honour and glory of God and the delight of the sellers of smutty second-hand novels?

DENIS IRELAND, *From the Irish Shore*, 1936

There is still in England, in certain quarters, a contempt for the 'native Irish', who are thought of as dirty, dishonourable and uncivilized. That a Protestant should cling to such superstitions is no matter for surprise; but that a Catholic should do so is disgusting.

Their influence will increase, because the movement away from religion leads into darkness, and the example of a strongly Catholic nation so near at hand cannot fail to have an arresting effect. Were there no apologetics, no debating, no active propaganda, that example would still remain.

In Catholic action, that apostolate of the laity which is the reply of our Church to the anti-religious influences of the day, Ireland is taking her full part. On the eve of the Feast of Our Lady's Nativity, seventeen years ago, there met in a house in one of the poor streets of Dublin fifteen working girls and a priest. Prayers were said, and they formed themselves into a society, with the primary object of visiting the sick in the Dublin Union Hospital. From that humble beginning in 1921 has grown the movement which is known as the Legion of Mary, and has been described by the Apostolic Delegate to Missionary Africa as the ideal form of Catholic action. It has spread across the world, but its governing body, the Concilium, is still to be found in Dublin. It has carried the missionary spirit of Ireland to remote settlements and forgotten stations, and its prayers are recited in strange tongues by those who have devoted themselves to the disciplined work of the Legion. It is only one of very many manifestations of Catholic action, but it has caught the attention and stimulated the imagination of all who ask, 'What can the layman do?' and genuinely desire a practical, downright answer to their question.

J. B. MORTON, *The New Ireland*, 1938

Ecclesiastes

God, you could grow to love it, God-fearing, God-
 chosen purist little puritan that,
for all your wiles and smiles, you are (the
 dank churches, the empty streets,
the shipyard silence, the tied-up swings) and
 shelter your cold heart from the heat
of the world, from woman-inquisition, from the
 bright eyes of children. Yes you could
wear black, drink water, nourish a fierce zeal
 with locusts and wild honey, and not
feel called upon to understand and forgive
 but only to speak with a bleak
afflatus, and love the January rains when they
 darken the dark doors and sink hard
into the Antrim hills, the bog meadows, the heaped
 graves of your fathers. Bury that red
bandana, stick and guitar; this is your
 country, close one eye and be king.
Your people await you, their heavy washing
 flaps for you in the housing estates—
a credulous people. God, you could do it, God
 help you, stand on a corner stiff
with rhetoric, promising nothing under the sun.

DEREK MAHON, *Lives*, 1972

I slept at Castlecomer. Or, rather, I stayed long awake. Paul, not to be seduced again by my whims, was gone on to Kilkenny, and as I sat in my bedroom I

began to wonder why the devil I *had* come there. It took me a while to realize
that it was for the sake of James Kildare and Leighlin (1786–1834), James
Warren Doyle, Augustinian priest, and Bishop. He was a great man, the
scourge of his clergy, who had been accustomed to an easy life before he came
their way (he cut down their punch to one glass after dinner), the scourge of
England, the scourge of the Established Church, and not infrequently the
scourge of his flock. That was my mental connexion with Castlecomer. For
in this, Ireland's only colliery town—the collieries are back up the hills—the
basalt figures of the miners have always threatened the peace of mind of men
like J.K.L. In the early nineteenth century secret societies flourished among
them—Ribbonmen, Blackfeet, and Whitefeet. J.K.L. fought them like a tiger;
a very lean tiger, for he was a lean man, all lath and plaster: an ascetic who
thought the Jesuits at Clongowes were all too fat, and who dined regularly,
himself, off scrag-end of mutton. He would come here, dressed in his epis-
copal robes, and, clasping his crozier, he would face these dark-eyed, freize-
coated men of Leix, maybe as many as eight thousand of them, and he would
harangue them in the open (no Catholic churches in those days—only mud
hovels) until the sweat poured down off him. His methods were Hildebrand-
ine. He, too, would have made a king crawl on his knees before him. He would
have his great, iron-clasped book held by a monk, and without mercy
commend to the devil the bodies of all public sinners; he did that once at
Staplestown with a whole junta of soupers—poor wretches who, in famine
days, took Protestant soup—afterwards forgiving them only on condition
that they knelt in public with their coats turned inside out for three Sundays
in succession.

SEAN O'FAOLAIN, *An Irish Journey*, 1940

To one source of poverty, wretchedness, and crime, I shall have frequent
occasion to refer in my communications—namely, the drinking habits of the
people. This love of strong drink is the 'unclean spirit' which seems
as if it could not be bound. The 'fetters and chains' which conscience and
judgment would at times impose upon it are 'plucked asunder', and the
degraded demoniac victim is led onwards, as if by a power which he
cannot resist, to utter destruction. It were easy to multiply the examples of its
dread sway which came under observation in our walks. In one 'court', we
ascended to an upper room, where we found a man and his son in full
and regular employment as shoemakers, engaged by one of the chief shoe
marts of the town: according to their own acknowledgment, they make more
than adequate wages to support them in decency and comfort; but, as the
wife and mother complained (they confessing it), their wages are spent in the
public-house. And sufficient proof was visible to us of the results, in the bare
and furnitureless room, without even a bed, except the miserable bundle

which lay upon the floor. This is but a specimen of what we beheld in various quarters.

One thing connected with this will strike the most cursory observer—the flourishing condition of the 'spirit stores'. These meet you at every turn, in this district—some of them most imposing-looking establishments—and all of them driving a brisk and profitable trade in the material of ruin, or, as Robert Hall well called it, 'liquid fire and distilled damnation'. Can nothing be done to prevent the multiplication of these horrible pests? We talk of theatres. If theatres have destroyed their thousands, these have destroyed their tens of thousands. One of them in this very quarter boasts, in its public placards, that it sold, during the first four months of the present year, 9,380 gallons of whiskey alone! Let us think of the fatal effects of such a deluge as this through the households of the poor, and we shall cease to wonder at the social degradation and vice that prevail.

REVD W. M. O'HANLON, *Walks Among the Poor in Belfast*, 1853

The Envy of Poor Lovers

Pity poor lovers who may not do what they please
With their kisses under a hedge, before a raindrop
Unhouses it; and astir from wretched centuries,
Bramble and briar remind them of the saints.

Her envy is the curtain seen at night-time,
Happy position that could change her name.
His envy—clasp of the married whose thoughts can be alike,
Whose nature flows without the blame or shame.

Lying in the grass as if it were a sin
To move, they hold each other's breath, tremble,
Ready to share that ancient dread—kisses begin
Again—of Ireland keeping company with them.

Think, children, of institutions mured above
Your ignorance, where every look is veiled,
State-paid to snatch away the folly of poor lovers
For whom, it seems, the sacraments have failed.

AUSTIN CLARKE, *Ancient Lights*, 1955

There hasn't been a girl the like of her in these parts since. I was only a gossoon at the time, but I've heard tell she was as tall as I'm myself, and as straight as a poplar. She walked with a little swing in her walk, so that all the boys used to be looking after her, and she had fine black eyes, sir, and she was nearly always laughing. Father Madden had just come to the parish; and there was courting in these parts then, for aren't we the same as other people—we'd like to go out with a girl well enough if it was the custom of the country. Father Madden put down the ball alley because he said the boys stayed there instead of going into Mass, and he put down the cross-road dances because he said dancing was the cause of many a bastard, and he wanted none in his parish. Now there was no dancer like Julia; the boys used to gather about to see her dance, and who ever walked with her under the hedges in the summer could never think about another woman. The village was cracked about her. There was fighting, so I suppose the priest was right: he had to get rid of her. But I think he mightn't have been as hard on her as he was.

GEORGE MOORE, 'Julia Cahill's Curse', in *The Untilled Field*, 1903

We had our tea on the river-bank under the cathedral wall. We made peace. We recognised that in all the articles in dispute, what really ailed us was too much scenery. 'Scenery?' said a Belfast man to us in the middle of Connemara. 'Ah'm sick of scenery!' Nature, as I say, is all very well in its own way, but it produces a ravenous appetite for civilisation, and Killaloe, after all, was only thirteen or fourteen miles from Limerick. You could nearly smell it up the Shannon; the Georgian architecture, the lights, the hotels, the pubs, the picture-houses and the resiners in Géronte's. How long was it since we had seen Géronte last?

At O'Briensbridge, with its tiny sandstone tower lost under the airy blue side of Keeper, the big clouds, lit with gold, sailed massively up the river like granite boulders and tossed silver streamers of light into the fields and the canal. Away to our right were the long hills down which Octave and his companions had galloped in the family coach. We sang. We passed Georgian mansions, orchards and nursery gardens, and at last we came in the dusk to the familiar bridge guarded by its grey drum towers, and above it the skinny old cathedral tower stood up against the sky, bleak and blue-grey and all old-maidish in its curling papers of battlements. As we cycled by it Célimène suddenly jumped off her bicycle and shouted to me to stop. She stood before a hoarding with her eyes popping out.

'What is it?' I cried in alarm.

'Don't you see?' she cried in a frenzy of excitement.

'No,' I said.

'The poster!'

'What's wrong with the poster?' I asked.

'Her chest, man,' shouted Célimène. 'Can't you look at her chest!'

And there it was, with another poster beside it that said 'Every Poster Tells Its Story'—the picture of the Icilma lass, with a modesty vest of brown paper pasted across her pretty chest!

'Civilisation?' I thought, going cold all over. 'Did I say civilisation?'

FRANK O'CONNOR, *Irish Miles*, 1947

'Gosh,' said Fergus, reverting to schoolboy diction. 'Comps Kinneally. Father Maurice Kinneally, MA, Doctor of Divinity.'

Father Kinneally nodded as though confirming his degrees, and reaching into the refrigerator, took out a grape. He held the grape between thumb and forefinger, examining it carefully. Fergus looked at Father's large black boots, at his chin, which should be shaved twice a day and was not, and, with a shock, realized that he himself was now the age Father Kinneally had been when Father Kinneally taught him English at St Michan's College. He remembered hearing that, in his old age, Father Kinneally had been pensioned off and sent to be a parish priest in a village in Down, but it was impossible to imagine him acting as a parish priest, impossible to imagine him, say, hearing the confession of a married woman, he, who would blush scarlet if any boy's mother asked him a question on Sports Day. Yet in class and in chapel Father Kinneally had been an expert on women's wiles, a captain in the Church Militant, ever ready to defend the souls of the boys in his care against the devil and all his female hordes.

'You know, Father,' Fergus said, 'there's one thing I always wanted to ask you. Was it really true that you once went into the school dentist's office and cut all the corset and brassiere ads out of the magazines on the dentist's waiting-room table?'

Father Kinneally, still examining the grape, half-nodded in a gesture which could mean yes or no. 'Did the dentist, Mr—ah—Findlater, did *he* tell you that?'

'Yes, Conor Findlater. He married a woman who was a great friend of my mother's. He told me about it, long after I'd left school.'

Father Kinneally put the grape into his mouth, transferring it with his tongue to his right cheek, where it bulged slightly before he decided to bite on it. 'There were young boys looking at those suggestive drawings,' Father Kinneally said. 'I thought it wise. Remember, an occasion of sin is an occasion of sin, even if it is not intended to be.'

BRIAN MOORE, *Fergus*, 1971

In his efforts to start a Campaign for Modesty in Dress, he did not achieve much success.

The psychology of ladies in the matter of fashion is hard to understand. One would imagine that instinct would incline women to dress so as to please men. It seems certain, however, that they do not; they willingly adopt forms of attire which do not please men—are even ridiculous in men's eyes. Moreover, they seem to imagine that dress and religious duty lie in totally different planes, and have no bearing on each other. This mental eccentricity, which was utterly incomprehensible to Father Cullen's direct habit of thought, has been noticed in women, even pious women, of every country in Europe, and has made them very refractory to the denunciations which clergy, bishops and even Sovereign Pontiffs have so constantly directed against immodesty of attire. Consequently, we are not surprised to hear that Father Cullen's bitter abuse, his mordant sarcasm, his plain-spoken statements of the effect of women's immodest dress upon men's passions, had generally the effect of annoying his female audiences, and effected little for their reform. Possibly if, when starting his Modest Dress League, he had had the vigour of his early days, and had worked at its organisation with all the energy and perseverance with which he had combated intemperance, he might have proved that the perversity of women's ideas in the matter of dress was not more difficult to change than the perversity of public opinion had been as regards drink. Be this as it may, though he expended much energy in preaching in various places on the evils of modern fashions, he never got beyond the preliminary stages in the organisation of his Crusade for combating them. On the Feast of the Purification, 1920, in the Sodality attached to Convent of the Sisters of Charity, Seville Place, he inaugurated his League which was to work mostly through the agency of the BVM sodalities. To a number of these he sent the following circular:

When I left your crowded Quarterly Pioneer Meeting last Tuesday evening, the thought occurred to me, that I might invoke your aid to help to check the widespread evil of immodest dress, which is so painfully present on every side, exhibited by women and girls of every age and condition. Everyone seems to acknowledge the evil and to deplore it, but no suggestion has been offered of any practical remedy. Now it strikes me that sodalities of Children of Mary could effect a very important and inoffensive reformation in this matter, and in this way: A few of the leading children of the Sodality would quietly and unobtrusively band themselves together to restore modesty of dress by counsel and example. They would quietly meet and discuss with the Directress the prevalence of the evil and the need of suppressing it. Their personal observation will prove the necessity and importance of such a praiseworthy undertaking, and suggest prudent ways of counteracting it. A President and Secretary might be chosen, and Minutes of the meetings might be recorded. It would be well to have widely known in the district that such a movement was set on foot. The motives which should impel the members of the little Council would be:

1. The wish to imitate our Blessed Mother in modesty of dress.

2. To avoid being the occasion of evil thoughts to others by unbecoming exposure.

3. To maintain the traditional and proverbial purity and modesty of Irish womanhood.

4. To prevent the laxity of morals which corrupts the atmosphere of family life in its very beginnings by putting insufficient clothing on *little* girls. (What innocence and purity can be expected in later years from girls and women, who in childhood have been inadequately or shamefully clothed?)

5. In the past, spotless purity was taught and practised by Irish mothers, wives, sisters and daughters. Now, in many instances, for its preservation in the Irish household, we have to rely on the men and boys. Little girls are often attired as scantily as ballet-dancers.

6. The evil is glaringly apparent in the indecently short clothes and bare legs of children and grown-up girls, and in the bare and unprotected necks of grown-ups. And as it were to put a crown on the unworthiness of such pagan apparel, we sometimes see Children of Mary wearing their Sodality Medals on uncovered necks. Surely it is especially shocking to good sense and taste—not to speak of religious sentiment—when they approach the Altar for Holy Communion in this repulsive attire.

7. To make this undertaking successful for our Blessed Mother's glory, it should, I think, commence with the children in school, where the Sisters and teachers exercise such a holy influence. (We must not blame the children; the fault lies with the parents and guardians.)

8. I fancy costumiers, dressmakers, etc. (numbers of whom are excellent Children of Mary) could exert an enormous power of reformation in this matter.

9. If you can help to start this project, others will soon follow your example. Later on you will be blessed and praised for it. Sodalities of Children of Mary all over Ireland will quickly take it up.

In this matter, as in all others of religious import, Ireland will lead the way, and Irish womanhood will stem the tide of immoral fashions, at least in English-speaking countries.

> REVD LAMBERT McKENNA, SJ, *Life and Work of Rev. James Aloysius Cullen, SJ*, 1924

Few realize nowadays that after the First World War there was an astonishing change in women's fashions: the era of the low neck and the short skirt had come. Every Sunday, in the sermon after the Gospel, the Dublin clergy denounced the immodesty of the new female dress and pointed out the danger to faith and morals, urging parents to assert their rightful authority and protect their young daughters. But the eloquence of Maynooth was in vain because women, having escaped from the flounces, lace petticoats, camisoles, whalebone and steel stays or corsets, long drawers, and woollen combinations of the Victorian age, could not be persuaded to get into them again, however chilled their legs might be. Even those who had thick ankles or stout calves were forced to reveal their drawbacks.

After some years, the newspapers were actually publishing advertisements and drawings of dainty lingerie—and old-fashioned readers did not dare to object. So the Church, with its male opportunism, accepted the inevitable change. Only in Dublin has ecclesiastical influence been successful and but in one instance. On Sundays and holy days of obligation, the Girl Pipers' Band, marching along briskly, with lifting kilts and bare knees, drew crowds of young and old men to the street corners. By the command of the Catholic Archbishop, the hems of the patriotic kilts had to be let down, two inches. . . .

Despite the gloomy silence of the Church, a poet appeared daily in the streets of Dublin as a champion, endeavouring to save men from the immodest sights around them. Having been separated from his wife for many years, he may have endured the torments of the flesh. Portly, middle-aged, with abundant curly hair and black sombrero, he wore outside his waistcoat a sackcloth apron which reached down to his knees. Walking slowly along, Philip Francis Little stopped women, pointed accusingly at their low necks and short skirts, warning them in a loud voice of the flames of Hell. Mothers, shopping with their leggy little girls, dressed in pretty frocks and socks, did not escape his watchful eye and he implored them to think of the next world. He reproved even boys with short breeches and bare knees on their way home from school, and they stood before him, shame-faced and blushing to the ears. Terror spread from the Town Hall in Rathmines to the neighbouring squares and along the Terenure Road, so that whenever he appeared—a wrathful figure more than a hundred yards away—wives and girls fled round the nearest corner. Soon inside the tram, only men were to be seen for the women went on top in order that they might not be accosted by him.

AUSTIN CLARKE, *A Penny in the Clouds*, 1968

We were from the earliest age so steeped in the idea that chastity was the highest virtue and that being in a nunnery was a greater vocation than a worldly or sensual life that it was hard to resolve the ambivalences, or to perceive the denial of our selves that this *modus vivendi* entailed. It was a way of life based on a dark and frightful ambiguity; women were viewed both as powerful creatures, stained with Pauline and liturgical descriptions of them as darkling female stews, potent potential occasions of sin, and as inferior beings, domestic creatures, with no effective life apart from motherhood and wifehood. The fear of sex, the forbiddenness of any pleasure in sex, was deeply interwoven with our teachings. The same priests and nuns who read out, 'There is no fear in love: but perfect love casteth out fear because fear hath torment. He that feareth is not made perfect in love,' presented the whole issue of human love to us as something darkly morbid, so covered in moral pitch that even to think of it was to risk being besmirched.

POLLY DEVLIN, *All of Us There*, 1983

The Unfrocked Priest

He leant at the door
In his priest's clothes—
Greasy black they were:
And he bled at the nose.

He leant at the door,
And the blood trickled down:
A man of the country,
More than the town.

He was of God's anointed,
A priest, no less:
But he had been unfrocked
For drunkenness.

For that, or worse—
And flesh is only human—
For some wrong-doing
With a woman.

And in his father's house
He lived at ease,
Reading his books,
As quiet as the trees.

No one troubled him
As he went in and out,
And he smoked his clay,
And he grew stout.

And he tramped the parish
In the summer days,
Thinking high thoughts
And giving God praise.

None but blessed him
As he walked the hills,
For he gave to the poor
And he cured their ills.

There was no herb
That grew in the grass,
But he saw its virtue
As in a glass.

No rath, no Mass-bush,
No ogham stone,
But he knew its story
As his own.

He had a scholar's knowledge
Of Greek,
And dabbled in Hebrew
And Arabic.

And in his time
(He died in 'Eighty-Seven)
He wrote two epics
And a 'Dream of Heaven'.

I saw him once only
In his priest's clothes,
At his father's door:
And he bled at the nose.

JOSEPH CAMPBELL, *Irishry*, 1913

There is another corner of Cork I love, and late at night, preferably a Sunday night, when everything is heavy with silence, I will be under Shandon in the narrow street (hardly a street—a lane, rather, a gully up to the towering tower), and I will stand where the butcher's shops overhang the pavement with wooden canopies, and the only sound is the deep boom of the bells' toll overhead. In corners like these, or along the darkening quays, in doors and alleys and coigns of battered houses, the shawled girls and their boys make love; the shawl is wrapped tight about them both and under it they lean in tight embrace. Some silly old women have lately started a Society to rout out these poor homeless lovers. There has even been a movement to introduce women-police into Cork—mainly to stop this natural, passionate, innocent, human courtship. How, under Heaven, except under these heavens of the starry dark, these puritans expect love to blossom among the poor is beyond me. I lay it to his eternal credit that the Bishop (with the tough common-sense and humanity of his country birth), has consistently frowned on these Manichæans. He snuffed out the Society of St Jude; and I trust he will prevent Montenotte morality from bringing in police-women to chase the lovers from the lanes. But this is one of the sore subjects of Irish life, half-absurd, comical, ludicrous, half-hateful, nauseating, mean, and impure.

SEAN O'FAOLAIN, *An Irish Journey*, 1940

In Ireland the Victorian notion prevails that writers, and artists in general, are wonderfully wicked people. A newspaper threatened with litigation by one such miscreant was urged by its lawyer to stand firm on the ground, it is said, that no Irish jury would find for a painter. And the whole question of morals is one on which the Irish people are abnormally sensitive. An old Dublin story is of how a certain store was asked to remove the pink plaster forms from its window, lest their vague resemblance to the female body should trouble the thoughts and figure in the dreams of masculine passers-by. Pious women have been advised not to use a particular object of feminine hygiene, lest their sensual instincts be momentarily gratified by its insertion: whose-ever the inspired mind at the back of this counsel, one can only echo the words of Oliver Gogarty's character, the mother of numerous children, who listened for a few moments to a Franciscan preaching on matrimony and left, remarking 'I wish to God I knew as little about it as that one.'

Nothing is too absurd for them, nothing too far-fetched: they hear the Devil padding after them all the clock round. One day a shop in Dublin came out with a placard advertising 'Honey! Fruit of an Intimate Collaboration between Bee and Flower!' and the next time I passed by, hoping to savour this once again, the placard had disappeared. This may have been purely fortuitous: on the other hand it may have been in response to a shocked protest. Think of the silliest thing possible in this direction, and you will find it capped and outclassed and left far behind by reality.

HONOR TRACY, *Mind You, I've Said Nothing!*, 1953

The Irish-English, touched with two nationalities but belonging to none, should know, if anyone does, that the worst thing an oppressor imposes, when it holds down a nation, is nationalism; the ultimate wickedness committed by England was to drive Ireland into a nationalistic act of cutting off its nose to spite its face—whereupon it is not the nose but the now independent national face that withers. Likewise, they, if anyone, should know the bitter folly of religious intolerance. In Ireland, there are three permissible answers, Catholic, Protestant and Jewish, to the eternal question 'What is your religion?' I, who have to answer 'None', am in Ireland neither a foreigner nor an Irishwoman but an invisible woman; and my husband and I, an ex-Catholic and an ex-Protestant united in happy rationalism (which is the dreadful state each side has feared all along the other would lead to), are the invisible married couple with an invisible child whom it would be, I surmise, virtually impossible for us to educate in Ireland. For this or a hundred other reasons, the Promised Land of the Irish-English class is one which most of them can't return to. The last and most ironic tragedy of Irish history is that though Ireland freed itself from the English it did not acquire English freedom. A year or two ago I stood, an invisible woman (and author of banned books) in one of the finest bookshops in Dublin and copied down the notice pinned to one of the bookcases: 'There are over 8,000 books banned in Ireland. If by chance we have one on display, please inform us, and it will be DESTROYED.'

BRIGID BROPHY, 'Am I An Irish Woman?', in *Don't Never Forget*, 1966

The outspokenness with which de Valera espoused a Catholic position . . . was merely a . . . direct expression of his almost instinctual association of Catholicism with the Irish way of life. For the independent Irish life that independence would allow to develop freely would, in de Valera's view, be Catholic as well as Gaelic. His government, when it came to power, was zealous in its efforts to ensure that Catholic morality should be enforced by legislation and that public life, state occasions, the opening of factories, new housing estates, etc., should be blessed by an official clerical presence. In 1933 a tax was imposed on imported newspapers to the satisfaction of moralists who had inveighed for years against the depredations of the English 'gutter press'. And in 1935 the sale and importation of artificial contraceptives were made illegal.

TERENCE BROWN, *Ireland: A Social and Cultural History*, 1981

I don't begrudge anyone a happy sheltered youth. I only wish it had been like that for all of us. But I'd like to put in a word for the truth of how things were for the majority in the bitter, unloving 1950s. The fact is that the sexual security of privileged boys and girls was bought at the expense of the underprivileged. There was sex in Ireland, urgent, mute, ignorant sex. The class who frequented dance-halls, rather than tennis clubs, could tell you. If there wasn't full sexual intercourse, that's because the penalties for it were so terrible.

The casualties of that system of social control are with us, in the form of ageing men who have never held a woman in their arms, and women with memories that burn. To praise the sexual restraint of the 1950s to them is like praising a diet in front of Famine victims.

Girls were punished so terribly for getting pregnant that in courting they tried very hard to get the boys to stop. Stopping was the only widespread form of contraception. If they couldn't control his drive, or their own, or if they didn't know how babies were made, and they became pregnant, they had to leave home. They had to hide. They had to be walled up in remote mother-and-baby homes, or they had to get the train to Belfast or the boat to England. Children themselves, in the utmost loneliness and fear, they had to face pregnancy and birth.

NUALA O'FAOLAIN, *Are You Somebody?*, 1996

The beauty of the Irish landscape lies in the never-ending change of colour. A momentary break of sun transforms the sky from dull yellow to bright, rain-washed blue. It lights a hillside to brilliant green, or mottles it in brown and green and mauve. A moment later it disappears, dashing the sky back again to mournful purples and misty greys. So it is with the Irish character. What is too harshly called the 'superstition' of Irish folklore coexists with Catholic piety; a puritanical morality goes hand in hand with the hilarity of a race-meeting. The loyalty too harshly named 'clannishness' runs side by side with the personal acquisitiveness of a peasant proprietorship. Small wonder then the Irish feel no foreigner will ever fully understand.

CONRAD ARENSBERG, *The Irish Countryman*, 1937

Lough Derb [*sic*] is studded with numerous islands. None of them are of considerable size, and only one is inhabited. For the most part, they are but small mounds, chiefly of barren rock, emerging from the water. The two islands of greatest note are Saint's Island, and Station Island. The latter is now more generally known by the name of St Patrick's Purgatory. Curiously enough, at one time the former island was called St Patrick's Purgatory. Under what circumstances, or at what time the transfer of the name from the one island to the other, was made, are points on which I was unable to obtain any information on which I could rely. On Saint's Island are still to be seen the remains of a priory. Thither religious devotees were in the habit of resorting to expiate their sins by acts of penance. Whether the superstition, that it was more acceptable to the Deity to do penance for sin on that island than in any other part of the country, preceded the application of St Patrick's Purgatory; or whether its being called St Patrick's Purgatory was the cause of the poor, deluded creatures flocking thither in crowds, under the impression that it was the most proper place in which to do penance, are also matters on which I was unable to obtain any trustworthy information. Station Island, as already remarked, is now the place of St Patrick's Purgatory; and thither the poor, ignorant, superstitious peasantry now resort for purposes of penance.

ANON. (J. Grant), *Impressions of Ireland and the Irish*, 1844

The Straying Student

On a holy day when sails were blowing southward,
A bishop sang the Mass at Inishmore,
Men took one side, their wives were on the other
But I heard the woman coming from the shore:
And wild in despair my parents cried aloud
For they saw the vision draw me to the doorway.

Long had she lived in Rome when Popes were bad,
The wealth of every age she makes her own,
Yet smiled on me in eager admiration,
And for a summer taught me all I know,
Banishing shame with her great laugh that rang
As if a pillar caught it back alone.

I learned the prouder counsel of her throat,
My mind was growing bold as light in Greece;
And when in sleep her stirring limbs were shown,
I blessed the noonday rock that knew no tree:
And for an hour the mountain was her throne,
Although her eyes were bright with mockery.

They say I was sent back from Salamanca
And failed in logic, but I wrote her praise
Nine times upon a college wall in France.
She laid her hand at darkfall on my page
That I might read the heavens in a glance
And I knew every star the Moors had named.

Awake or in my sleep, I have no peace now,
Before the ball is struck, my breath has gone,
And yet I tremble lest she may deceive me
And leave me in this land, where every woman's son
Must carry his own coffin and believe,
In dread, all that the clergy teach the young.

AUSTIN CLARKE, *Collected Poems*, 1936

It was the brandy and Irish coffee stage; wreaths of cigar smoke drifted slowly upwards in the dining-room of the Royal Arms Hotel, Carricklone. In the foreground, balloon glasses caught and reflected light: in the background waiters were grouped in stylish impassivity. His Lordship the Bishop of Carricklone was speaking and he was well known to detest interruption. A small man, with bushy eyebrows incongruously grafted on an old woman's face, he was launched onto one of his favourite subjects—the impurity of modern life. It had nothing to do with the problems of local development but, somehow, it always seemed to crop up in His Lordship's speeches. His pectoral cross danced as he thundered into the home stretch of his peroration.

'Gentlemen, we must never betray this pearl! In this modern world of drinks and dance halls, of so-called progress and speed, our country should remain a solitary oasis. On all sides we are wooed by the sirens of lax living, but—remember this—if Ireland holds a special place in God's plan it will be due to the purity of her men and the modesty of her women.'

The bishop blew his nose with a large white handkerchief and sat down abruptly. As polite applause rippled down the table, John O'Shea looked at the faces of his companions for any response to this stirring call to arms. A dozen well fed (Galway Oysters, Roast Kerry Lamb, Carrageen Moss) and well wined (Chateauneuf Saint Patrice) faces reflected nothing but sensuous contentment. At least it was an audience of adults: the last time His Lordship had spoken it was to warn a Confirmation class in a remote Kerry parish against the dangers of Communism.

JOHN MONTAGUE, *Death of a Chieftain*, 1964

Mr Collopy next morning led me at a smart pace up the bank of the canal, penetrated to Synge Street and rang the bell at the residential part of the Christian Brothers' establishment there. When a slatternly young man in black answered, Mr Collopy said he wanted to see the Superior, Brother Gaskett. We were shown into a gaunt little room which had on the wall a steel engraving of the head of Brother Rice, founder of the Order, a few chairs and a table—nothing more.

—They say piety has a smell, Mr Collopy mused, half to himself. It's a perverse notion. What they mean is only the absence of the smell of women.

He looked at me.

—Did you know that no living woman is allowed into this holy house. That is as it should be. Even if a Brother has to see his own mother, he has to meet her in secret below at the Imperial Hotel. What do you think of that?

—I think it is very hard, I said. Couldn't she call to see him here and have another Brother present, like they do in jails when there is a warder present on visiting day?

—Well, that's the queer comparison, I'll warrant. Indeed, this house may be a jail of a kind but the chains are of purest eighteen-carat finest gold which the holy brothers like to kiss on their bended knees.

FLANN O'BRIEN, *The Hard Life*, 1961

Not half the respect is paid to the priests now that was paid in the days of my youth. When I was a boy, I remember well nobody was considered to have welcomed the priest properly who didn't put one knee to the ground after sweeping his cap right off his head. In the world of to-day if there is a gathering to meet the priest, those in front will doff their caps, but maybe not another cap will be doffed from there to the back. No woman was allowed to go in a boat with a priest in it, whatever her haste or need, and never one of them came near the landing-place. But, for some time now, there's none to say them nay if the boat is crammed with them.

TOMÁS Ó CRIOMHTHAIN, *The Islandman*, 1937, trans. Robin Flower

The Mountain Tomb

Pour wine and dance if manhood still have pride,
Bring roses if the rose be yet in bloom;
The cataract smokes upon the mountain side,
Our Father Rosicross is in his tomb.

Pull down the blinds, bring fiddle and clarionet
That there be no foot silent in the room
Nor mouth from kissing, nor from wine unwet
Our Father Rosicross is in his tomb.

In vain, in vain; the cataract still cries;
The everlasting taper lights the gloom;
All wisdom shut into his onyx eyes,
Our Father Rosicross sleeps in his tomb.

W. B. YEATS, *Responsibilities*, 1914

When I was round about twenty years of age and maybe twenty-one, I was going to a dance here and there to halls and country houses. Me and a comrade I had, the name of McCabe, he used to always travel along with me. We'd have girl-friends and we'd see them home no matter what time it was. The parents never minded, but at that time you know some of the clergy, it wasn't just about our place but near by, they would rather that they'd be separated altogether, the women go home themselves and the men go by themselves. They done that in a lot of places. Clergy visited places to see that they'd go home single. It wasn't in our area but it was near by.

JOHN MAGUIRE, *Come Day, Go Day, God Send Sunday*. The songs and life story of a traditional singer and farmer from Co. Fermanagh. Collected by Robin Morton, 1973

The friar seemed sunk in intolerable dolour until the Bishop replenished his tankard.

'God's ways are not our ways,' said Bishop Flanagan, 'perhaps it was for the best. See all the good that you have been enabled to do.'

'Yes,' said Father Furiosus, rousing himself to drink deeply. 'I became a wandering friar, and as God has given me a spirit that fears neither man, dog nor devil, I have perhaps done some little good. I make my way from settlement to settlement wherever I think my services may be needed, and I assure you it is a sturdy demon or necromancer that can stand against me. I have become expert in demonology and in detecting the darker acts of sorcery. On my way from town to town I clear the lovers from the ditches and the doorways, but that's in the nature of a sideline.'

'Nevertheless, even if it be but a sideline, you have done a man's part in preventing the hateful passion of love from spreading throughout this land.'

'I have a strong arm, thank God,' said the friar.

MERVYN WALL, *The Unfortunate Fursey*, 1946

Protestant Courts Catholic

Too tired and too fastidious for lies,
he said, 'Let's make love when you're free.'
'Just like that?' 'Yes, just like that, no ties.'
She said, 'You wouldn't want to marry me.'

Although his devious honesty made him sick,
'Someone will take your beauty. Who?' he said.
'The unknown husband. I'm a Catholic,'
she smiled. 'Why do you smile and shake your head?'

Intrigued, he argued, but she never budged.
She blamed the Church. He said she was a sham.
'You have to judge in order to be judged.'
Her smile was roguish, false: 'That's how I am.'

'Look, I'm the serpent you have read about.
The law says no, I'd like it if you would.
You're free either to stretch your fingers out
or not. Choose, knowledge or servitude.'

Seducer turned to saviour on a whim,
he lavished hours of rhetoric on her.
Her faith protected her from men like him,
useless at home, dynamic in a bar.

Attentiveness, emotion, made her tremble
inside—poets and children play
so seriously—but girls are brought up to dissemble,
to seem to listen, but to get their way.

'In these cases we still have judgement here.
It's you who'll suffer, so it can't be right
to leave choice to the priests!' Swallowing beer,
smoking, he stood and argued half the night.

And when he left it was so solemnly
you might have thought he went to meet his death.
She had hysterics on her wedding day
when she smelt lager on her husband's breath.

JAMES SIMMONS, *Energy to Burn*, 1971

Miss Doheny, who had looked twice at Beatrice and once at her companion, guessed at their wrong-doing. Tail-ends of conversation had drifted across the lounge, no effort being made to lower voices since more often than not the old turn out to be deaf. They were people from Dublin whose relationship was not that recorded in Francis Keegan's register in the hall. Without much comment, modern life permitted their sin; the light-brown motor-car parked in front of the hotel made their indulgence in it a simple matter.

How different it had been, Miss Doheny reflected, in 1933! Correctly she estimated that that would have been the year when she herself was the age the dark-haired girl was now. In 1933 adultery and divorce and light-brown motor-cars had belonged more in America and England, read about and alien to what already was being called the Irish way of life. 'Catholic Ireland,' Father Horan used to say. 'Decent Catholic Ireland.' The term was vague and yet had meaning: the emergent nation, seeking pillars on which to build itself, had plumped for holiness and the Irish language—natural choices in the circumstances. 'A certain class of woman,' old Father Horan used to say, 'constitutes an abhorrence.' The painted women of Clancy's Picture House—sound introduced in 1936—were creatures who carried a terrible warning. Jezebel women, Father Horan called them, adding that the picture house should never have been permitted to exist. In his grave for a quarter of a century, he would hardly have believed his senses if he'd walked into the Paradise Lounge in Keegan's Railway Hotel to discover two adulterers and one of his flock who had failed to heed his castigation of painted women. Yet for thirty-five years Miss Doheny had walked through the town on Saturday evenings to this same lounge, past the statue of the 1798 rebels, down the sharp incline of Castle Street. On Sundays she covered the same ground again, on the way to and from Mass. Neither rain nor cold prevented her from making the journey to the Church of the Immaculate Conception or to the hotel, and illness did not often afflict her. That she had become more painted as the years piled up seemed to Miss Doheny to be most natural in the circumstances.

WILLIAM TREVOR, Beyond the Pale, 1981

One Wet Summer

Another summer, another July
People going on holiday, women in light dresses
How I once jealously feared for them under the
    printed cotton
Limp unresisting to any man's caresses.

I would have one of my own
And then like other men I could make cynical
    remarks
At the dangers they ran and never be worried about
    summer
And what happens in the shelter of parks.

As it is I praise the rain
For washing out the bank holiday with its moral risks
It is not a nice attitude but it is conditioned by
    circumstances
And by a childhood perverted by Christian moralists.

PATRICK KAVANAGH (1960), in Collected Poems, 1964

Sean-nós/*Old Style*

. . . former simplicity . . . is in a great measure lost.

SAMUEL MCSKIMIN, *History of Carrickfergus*

────────

Sean-nós literally means 'old-style'. In the context of traditional performance, it is often applied to the singing, in Irish, of the *Gaeltachtaí* (or Irish-speaking areas) of the west of Ireland. There are difficulties with the term: whether it was invented by the Gaelic League to distinguish the musical expression of 'a language which the stranger does not know', or whether it is an indigenous expression, is open to some question; certainly, it seems unlikely that native Irish speakers would use the term to describe a native form of singing. Again, there are clear differences (and, granted, parallels) between the singing of the Donegal Gaeltacht and that of Coolea in Munster; should *sean-nós* include them both? Ironically, most singing in Irish, as pro-mulgated by members of the Gaelic League and by Feiseanna Cheoil (Music Festivals), is not what is usually understood by *sean-nós*; nor does it accord to any perception of the notion of 'traditional'. Yet the word *sean-nós* has become a shibboleth, and many *Gaeilgeoirí* (Irish language enthusiasts) go so far as to maintain the patently absurd conclusion that no musician can be a traditional musician without an understanding of the *sean-nós*; others take the converse position, that everything is Irish—and therefore traditional—if expressed in the Irish language.

CIARAN CARSON, *Irish Traditional Music,* 1986

The Yellow Bittern

The yellow bittern that never broke out
   In a drinking bout, might as well have drunk;
His bones are thrown on a naked stone
   Where he lived alone like a hermit monk.
O yellow bittern! I pity your lot,

Though they say that a sot like myself is curst—
I was sober a while, but I'll drink and be wise
   For I fear I should die in the end of thirst.

It's not for the common birds that I'd mourn,
   The black-bird, the corn-crake, or the crane,
But for the bittern that's shy and apart
   And drinks in the marsh from the lone bog-drain.
Oh! if I had known you were near your death,
   While my breath held out I'd have run to you,
Till a splash from the Lake of the Son of the Bird
   Your soul would have stirred and waked anew.

My darling told me to drink no more
   Or my life would be o'er in a little short while;
But I told her 'tis drink gives me health and strength
   And will lengthen my road by many a mile.
You see how the bird of the long smooth neck
   Could get his death from the thirst at last—
Come, son of my soul, and drain your cup,
   You'll get no sup when your life is past.

In a wintering island by Constantine's halls
   A bittern calls from a wineless place,
And tells me that hither he cannot come
   Till the summer is here and the sunny days.
When he crosses the stream there and wings o'er the sea
   Then a fear comes to me he may fail in his flight—
Well, the milk and the ale are drunk every drop,
   And a dram won't stop our thirst this night.

CATHAL BUIDHE MAC GIOLLA GUNNA, 17th cent., trans. Thomas MacDonagh

Thomas MacDonagh

He shall not hear the bittern cry
In the wild sky, where he is lain,
Nor voices of the sweeter birds
Above the wailing of the rain.

Nor shall he know when loud March blows
Thro' slanting snows her fanfare shrill,
Blowing to flame the golden cup
Of many an upset daffodil.

But when the Dark Cow leaves the moor,
And pastures poor with greedy weeds,
Perhaps he'll hear her low at morn
Lifting her horn in pleasant meads.

FRANCIS LEDWIDGE, *Last Songs*, 1917

from *Rime, Gentlemen, Please*

'Long ago,' lips Rahilly, 'Death translated me.'
'And Death translated me and my translator'
comes from the bittern's mourner, Cahal Bwee,
'then he bustled the blackbird boy, was the third lamenter,
up onto the Heavenly Plain, by the way 'twas Meath.'

(O yellow bittern, yours was a brilliant ending;
it bound in a ghostly friendship three like these:
your corpse on the ice took the eyes of three good verse-men;
the last is a dust by the side of the Grecian seas.
Whisper! Old Cahal Bwee Mac Gilla Gunna
turns lovely mourning for your drouthy throat;
Ledwidge renames you, keening for Tom MacDonagh
who keyed the mourning to another note.)

Now Cahal Bwee's long dead who made strong music;
Thomas MacDonagh dead, who made it new;
Ledwidge, the blackbird, drowned in the loud bugles . . .
Ghosts of these poets come and go with you—
son to the one and heir to the three dead men—
under your lowest murmur murmuring 'We
bid you end quick-limed song, and song whose ending
drowned in the battle-horns by the Greek sea.'

ROBERT FARREN, *Rime, Gentlemen, Please*, 1944

If the May Day fires are now more in evidence in the back streets of Belfast than on the high hills, the Midsummer fires still burn strongly in some country districts and their pagan flames have not been so easily quenched. I saw dozens of them in Co. Galway on Midsummer Eve in 1956, mostly at country crossroads. Old men in Donegal have told me that they remembered the time when they had counted from their hilltop fire nearly a hundred others. Young men would show their mettle by jumping to and fro through the flames, and girls by doing so hoped to marry early and have many children. We recall that leaping is in folk tradition a widely approved method of making the crops grow high, and the fires, it is conjectured, were meant to encourage the sun, now at its turning point, to shine on through the harvest. Midsummer was a time when evil influences affecting human beings and the animals and crops were usually potent. It is remembered that 'the oldest woman in the town' would go round the fire three times on her knees, reciting prayers. To walk three times sunwise round the fire was to ensure a year without sickness, and as the flames died down the cattle were driven through the embers and their backs were singed with a lighted hazel wand: the sticks were preserved and utilized for driving the cows. By tradition everyone carried home a burning stick from the fire, and whoever was first to take it into the house brought the good luck of the year with him. A glowing turf from the fire was carried three times sunwise round the dwelling house, and others were thrown into the growing crops. Yarrow was hung in the house to ward off illness. Fernseed was gathered for its magic powers and divinations made from the roots of bracken and lilies. We have already noticed the custom of retaining some of the ashes from the Midsummer fires to mix with the following season's seed corn.

E. ESTYN EVANS, *Irish Folk Ways*, 1957

On May eve, young boys and girls resort to the fields and gather May-flowers, which they spread outside of their doors. Sprigs of rowan tree were formerly gathered same eve, and stuck above the inside of the out-door heads, to keep off the witches. The herb yarrow, (*milfolium*) is gathered to cause young girls to dream of their future husbands. Some females who have cows, rise very early on May morning, and proceed to the nearest spring well, and bring home a portion of its water. This is called, 'getting the flower of the well', and those who practise it believe that their cattle are thus secured against charms for that season. Until of late years, straight tall trees were brought from the country by young men, and planted on this evening for a May pole; which appears to be a remnant of the following custom. Anciently a large company of young men assembled each May day, who were called May-boys. They wore above their other dress, white linen shirts, which were covered with a profusion of various coloured ribbons, formed into large and fantastic knots. One of the party was called king, and another queen, each of whom wore a crown composed of the most beautiful flowers of the season, and was attended by pages who held up the train. When met, their first act was dancing to music round the pole planted the preceding evening; after which they went to the houses of the most respectable inhabitants round about, and having taken a short jig in front of each house, received a voluntary offering from those within. The sum given was rarely less than five shillings. In the course of their ramble the king always presented a rich garland of flowers to some handsome young woman, who was hence called 'the queen of May' till the following year. The money collected was mostly sacrificed to the 'jolly god'; the remainder given to the poor persons of the neighbourhood. This custom ceased about eighty years ago.

Samuel McSkimin, *History of Carrickfergus*, 1829

The Dance

On the white wall flickered the sputtering lamp
And lit the shadowy kitchen, the sanded floor,
The girls by the painted dresser, the dripping men
Late from the sea and huddled,
These on the settle, those by the table; the turf
Sent up faint smoke, and faint in the chimney a light
From the frost-fed stars trembled and died,
Trembled and died and trembled again in the smoke.
'Rise up now, Shane', said a voice, and another:
'Kate, stand out on the floor'; the girls to the men
Cried challenge on challenge; a lilt in the corner rose
And climbed and wavered and fell, and springing again
Called to the heavy feet of the men; the girls wild-eyed,
Their bare feet beating the measure, their loose hair flying,
Danced to the shuttle of lilted music weaving
Into a measure the light and the heavy foot.

Robin Flower, *Poems and Translations*, 1931

The kitchen itself, where I will spend most of my time, is full of beauty and distinction. The red dresses of the women who cluster round the fire on their stools give a glow of almost eastern richness, and the walls have been toned by the turf smoke to a soft brown that blends with the grey earth colour of the floor. Many sorts of fishing tackle, and the nets and oilskins of the men, are hung upon the walls or among the open rafters; and right overhead, under the thatch, there is a whole cow-skin from which they make pampooties.

Every article on these islands has an almost personal character, which gives this simple life, where all art is unknown, something of the artistic beauty of medieval life. The curaghs and spinning wheels, the tiny wooden barrels that are still much used in the place of earthenware, the home-made cradles, churns, and baskets, are all full of individuality, and being made from materials that are common here, yet to some extent peculiar to the island, they seem to exist as a natural link between the people and the world that is about them.

The simplicity and unity of the dress increases in another way the local air of beauty. The women wear red petticoats and jackets of the island wool stained with madder, to which they usually add a plaid shawl twisted round their chests and tied at the back. When it rains they throw another petticoat over their heads with the waistband round their faces, or, if they are young, they use a heavy shawl like those worn in Galway. Occasionally other wraps are worn, and during the thunder-storm I arrived in I saw several girls with men's waistcoats buttoned round their bodies. Their skirts do not come much below the knee, and show their powerful legs in the heavy indigo stockings with which they are all provided.

The men wear three colours: the natural wool, indigo, and a grey flannel that is woven of alternate threads of indigo and the natural wool. In Aranmor many of the younger men have adopted the usual fisherman's jersey, but I have only seen one on this island.

J. M. SYNGE, *The Aran Islands*, 1907

Donal Óg

Donal Ogue, when you cross the water,
Take me with you to be your partner,
And at fair and market you'll be well looked after,
And you can sleep with the Greek king's daughter.

You said you'd meet me, but you were lying,
Beside the sheepfold when the day was dying,
I whistled first, then I started hailing,
But all I heard was the young lambs' wailing.

You said you'd give me—an airy giver!—
A golden ship with masts of silver,
Twelve market towns to be my fortune
And a fine white mansion beside the ocean.

You said you'd give me—'tis you talk lightly!—
Fish-skin gloves that would fit me tightly,
Bird-skin shoes when I went out walking,
And a silken dress would set Ireland talking.

Ah, Donal Ogue, you'd not find me lazy,
Like many a high-born expensive lady;
I'd do your milking and I'd nurse your baby,
And If you were set on I'd back you bravely.

To Lonely Well I wander sighing,
'Tis there I do my fill of crying,
When I see the world but not my charmer
And all his locks the shade of amber.

I saw you first on a Sunday evening
Before the Easter, and I was kneeling.
'Twas about Christ's passion that I was reading,
But my eyes were on you and my own heart bleeding.

My mother said we should not be meeting,
That I should pass and not give you greeting;
'Twas a good time surely she chose for cheating
With the stable bare and the horse retreating.

You might as well let him have me, mother,
And every penny you have moreover;
Go beg your bread like any other
But him and me don't seek to bother.

Black as a sloe is the heart inside me,
Black as a coal with the griefs that drive me,
Black as a boot print on shining hallways,
And 'twas you that blackened it ever and always.

For you took what's before me and what's behind me,
You took east and west when you wouldn't mind me,
Sun and moon from my sky you've taken,
And God as well, or I'm much mistaken.

ANON., 18th century, trans. Frank O'Connor

Molly was brought up in Co. Galway in the early years of this century. She was the eldest of fourteen children and remembers the family home:

We lived in a cottage—it was my grandfather's small farm. There were three rooms, one to one side and one to the other. The kitchen was in the middle. There was a place above the two side rooms, and you had to have steps to get up there. Three or four of the boys used to sleep up there. There were three girls in the bed, myself and two of my sisters. Then there would be smaller ones in cots, and beds here and there. It was very crowded. We couldn't all have a meal at the same time. My mother and father would have theirs first, and two of us would sit with them. After dinner my father used to play his flute. He played the loveliest old tunes.

We had oil lamps, and candles for the bedroom. Then you'd have to go out to the pump for a bucket of water. We often had to go three miles to a well to get a can of spring water as they usen't to like the pump water for drinking.

At the back of our garden was a river. On a Monday I used to hate coming home from school, because my mother would be doing the washing. There would be a big bath of clothes and two buckets, one each side. We'd have to take them down to the river to rinse the clothes, then bring them back up again and hang them on lines or hedges to dry.

JENNY BEALE, *Women in Ireland*, 1986

On Sundays you get an idea of the population: everybody appears. The roads converging on chapels teem with people going to mass. Horses and traps turn out of impossibly narrow lanes; cyclists freewheel with a whirring rattle down from the mountainy farms. Dark Sundayfied figures balance on stepping-stones, take tracks through plantations, leg it over the stiles. After midday mass the streets of the villages give out a static hum. On holy days and on fair days the scene also becomes living and dark; race days, big matches or *feishes* bring all the hired cars out, and people out on the banks to watch the cars. At funerals the *cortèges* are very long. Early on weekday mornings the roads rattle with ass carts taking milk cans up to the creameries. And from dusk on young men gather at the crossroads and bridges and stay talking, faceless, well into the dark. Sometimes they light fires. On fine summer nights there is dancing, twice a week, on boards put down at crossroads or outside villages. Lights burn late in cottages near the dancing, and the music gives the darkness a pulse. When the music stops, the country rustles with movement of people going home. . . . No, it is not lack of people that makes the country seem empty. It is an inherent emptiness of its own.

ELIZABETH BOWEN, *Bowen's Court*, 1942

Except perhaps for raths, duns, and lisses—the fairy forts of legend—nothing in Ireland is more closely associated with the fairy folk than are certain types of tree. Wherever one goes in the country one does not have far to look to see some lone thorn bush growing in a field. The thorn bush is locally reputed to be under fairy protection, but there are many popular misconceptions about the tree, and inaccurate generalities have too often crept into those versions of local folklore which are held by people not close enough to the earth and to the earth folk to distinguish between fact and fiction.

It is, for instance, widely thought that only the whitethorn is sacred to the fairies, and that all whitethorns growing alone in the centre of a field are 'fairy trees'. Indeed, many people include in this category all whitethorns, even when growing in a hedge, provided only that they have a sturdy and fairly venerable appearance; but the whitethorn, although it is the most usual and most popular with the earth folk, by no means has a monopoly of fairy patronage, for it shares that honour with several other kinds of tree. In Ireland its greatest rivals are, in order of merit, the hazel, the blackthorn, the bourtree—which is the English elder—the sally, the alder, the ash, the holly, the birch, the oak—especially a twisted mountain oak—the broom, and the Scots fir; also, to my personal knowledge in at least two instances, the rowan or mountain ash, in spite of its being usually associated with white-magic properties. In addition to all these, although it is a plant, the golden-flowered buacalan bui, or ragwort, must be given a place of importance. In Scotland they have also the juniper and ivy, but I have not heard of these in such a way in Ireland.

The hazel, one of the most important of all, goes back in Irish mythology to an honoured place in the dim mists of the past. Then the hazel nut was the repository of all knowledge, as was the apple in Eden. No wonder the ancient gods and the spirits of today are reputed to revere and care for it. Of the other trees, the fairies do well in cherishing the blackthorn, for it is one of the loveliest trees in the Irish countryside, especially in early spring when its masses of bright, white flowers contrast so strongly with its yet-leafless black twigs; and the toughness of its branches is proverbial.

DERMOT MACMANUS, *The Middle Kingdom*, 1959

The Fairy Thresher

for Michael J. Murphy

That winter night round the blazing turf,
the children on the hobs, the talk ran on,
most from the farmer and his sister Kitty,
his wife not holding much with superstitions,
to rhyme and ramble through familiar stories
of ghosts and fairies, witches, blinks and spells.

For instance, when a cub, the man himself
joined with his brother to herd cattle in,
and a stirk turned and would not be compelled,
when it had strayed across the wee stone bridge,
to follow the others, and a neighbour stood
to mock their efforts till they gave it up,
and he said, laughing, she'll come back all right
when that wee man there goes away,
a wee man threatening by the door of the byre,
seen only by the neighbour and the stirk.

The sister told how once between the lights
in the next house up the road a woman answered
a tap on the half-door, and peering over, saw
a wee old woman standing in the street
who begged her please to empty no more pots
across the bru, for she'd come to lodge there,
and all her family were nearly drowned.

The farmer launched into another tale
of how a man, a famous storyteller,
to whom all happened, who was always present
when freets appeared, one midnight in Glenaan,
carrying in his fist a smouldering turf
which, blown to flame, would better any torch
to clear his homeward steps across the fields,
heard a strange creature girning in the sheugh
and blew on his turf and by its light made out
a wee man with his face where his arse should be,
and charged towards him, thrusting the red turf
into the scowling face, whereat the creature
let out a yell and tore into the hedge,
its speed a hare's, its loud howl murderous.

This, told with vigour and economy,
was new to me. I though of Bosch and Breughel,
and wondered by what roads the tale came here
over Europe, out of the Dark Ages;
but thought it something out of character
with the old forts and thorns and fairy rings,
and distant singing heard and fiddle music
and dancing light on hillsides, which I take
as proper to the ambience of the Glens
and the dim twilight of the tweedy poets.

The father faltered, as it seemed abashed
by his bold coarseness in that company
of children and his womenfolk and us.
But suddenly the sister swept the talk
to charms and hedgerow cures dropped out of use,
for chin-cough and for cleaning of the blood,
that kept the people healthy years ago.
Thereat the brother at this hint began
a rambling story of a man he knew
dead twenty years or more, lived birdalone,
who had a charm for erysipelas, sprains—

with well-attested instances of each—
with nobody that he could pass it to.
He'd got it from an aunt, his father's sister,
and had been sworn to hand it to a niece,
for its transmission had to be from male
to female and to male, alternately
by generation, a secret always held
within that family only. But his niece
was out in Boston. It could not be written.
He could not travel. She would not come back.
So ended what was known from Druid times.

His wife, the mother of the listening weans,
recalled a story that they loved to hear,
a mother's story, how a widow left,
her corn unthreshed, her children infants, heard
a flail thump in the night, and peering out
to thank some kindly neighbour, saw a shadow,
a little shadow, flit across the yard.
And in the light when she went out she found
the clean corn heaped in the middle of the floor.
And next night she heard the flail again,
this time a fall of snow that smeared the ground
exposed the track of feet from barn to gate;
the light impression shewed the feet were small
and bare from heel to toe. So she went down
and bought a pair of shoes in the village shop
to match the little feet that she had measured,
smaller feet than any of her brood.
She set them out beside the flailing floor,
and, waiting late, the third night heard a cry,
a cry of utter anguish and despair
would break your heart to hear it, and she saw
the little shadow running from the barn,
giving his grief these pitiable words,
'She's paid me off—she's given me my wages',
repeated as he ran and dying out
into the darkness of the wall of hills.

We nodded, expectation satisfied:
the children chanted together, 'She's paid me off.
She's paid me off. She's given me my wages'—
they'd only held their tongues till their mother finished:
this was a tale their children would remember,
and a boy or a girl might some day understand.

JOHN HEWITT, *Collected Poems*, 1991

Finn's grandfather was a weaver. Inside the house there were two great looms, the wood of which, though hard and massive, was filled with little holes. The floor of the kitchen was covered with flags that were cracked in many places; the walls were brown and the rafters black with smoke. The fire was not on the grate; it was laid on the stones of the hearth, and it was not of coal, but of sods of peat or turf, as they are called in Ireland. Out of the wide, projecting chimney a crook descended, on which a pot or a kettle was always hanging. The house had two doors in a single doorway: the outer one was so low that a child could look across it; it was kept closed against the hens during the day-time, and at night the full inner door was closed behind it. Near the door was a dresser filled with plates and dishes, mugs, jugs and cups, and hung round with shining tins. Between the dresser and the hearth was a sort of wooden sofa that could be opened into a bed; it was called the settle, and strangers who came to the house slept in it. There was also a great press, a big wooden chest, stools, and a wooden chair at the hearth for Finn's grandmother or grandfather. Near the door was a harness-rack that held a saddle and bridle and a horse's collar. There were three cages on the walls—a linnet was in one, a goldfinch in another and a lark in the third.

This was the kitchen. There were two rooms off it and a loft above it. The room in which his grandfather and grandmother slept was full of sacred pictures, and it had a shrine with a little lamp burning before it. In the room that was his father's and mother's there were brass instruments that had been left by his uncle Bartley who was now living in the town, and there was a clock that was called 'Wag o' the Wall'. It was a clock-face only with weights and chains hanging down. This clock had a loud tick and when it came near striking it would stop like a person catching breath.

Outside there was a stack of black peat that was fuel for the year, and near it was the shed for the donkey cart and the horse cart. At the side of the house was the byre or stable in which the two cows, the two calves and the horse were kept and in which the hens roosted at night. The ass and the goats were left to themselves and they had taken shelter in the shed beside the carts; and the geese, when they returned in the evening, would settle themselves under the shelter of the upturned carts.

PADRAIC COLUM, *A Boy in Eirinn*, 1916

The Ulster Fry has a long and solid history. Its popularity was probably due to two things—firstly, the housewife usually had only an open fire, so more sophisticated methods of cooking were not hers to command; and secondly, every man, woman or child who could do so tried to rear a pig on scraps and chat potatoes and whatever the free-rooting pig could find on its own hoking expeditions. Often it was a crowl, the runt of a litter, given away by a farmer to anyone who wanted to take the trouble to rear it. After the local pig-killer had done his gory work, there would be bacon and hams to be salted or hung up inside the chimney to smoke. The pork ribs, liver and offal would make tasty eating in the meantime for the family and neighbours, and there would be plenty of lard for the Ulster Fry. Little of the pig was wasted, even the feet being boiled for succulent eating. Pigs' trotters are possibly not everyone's fancy, but they had their following.

FLORENCE MARY McDOWELL, *Other Days Around Me*, 1972

The anglicisation of Irish place-names is . . . [an] interesting study. Examples may be had all over Ireland of the way in which the new names express the contempt felt by the conquerors for the defeated. Historical association and descriptive exactness meant nothing to the new land-owners, who were content with the nearest English equivalent to the Irish sounds. This is the explanation of many bizarre place-names. The colonisers also showed a preference for a name that was absurd or funny (according to their sense of humour). The classic example is the Phoenix Park monument in Dublin. Unintentionally it is a monument to the colonisers' frame of mind. When Lord Chesterfield was Viceroy, he considered that the prospect of the park would be enhanced by a monument. When discussing the form this should take, he was told that the original name of the park was *Fionn uisge* (meaning 'clear stream', from a rivulet formerly flowing through it). It was enough for him to hear the phrase once. He did not trouble to ask what it meant, or even how it was spelled. He thought it was *Phoenix*, as the pronunciation is remotely similar, so he ordered a monument crowned with the fabulous bird rising out of its own ashes.

STEPHEN RYNNE, *All Ireland*, 1956

A Lost Tradition

All around, shards of a lost tradition:
From the Rough Field I went to school
In the Glen of the Hazels. Close by
Was the bishopric of the Golden Stone;
The cairn of Carleton's homesick poem.

Scattered over the hills, tribal-
And placenames, uncultivated pearls.
No rock or ruin, *dún* or dolmen
But showed memory defying cruelty
Through an image-encrusted name.

The heathery gap where the Rapparee,
Shane Barnagh, saw his brother die—
On a summer's day the dying sun
Stained its colours to crimson:
So breaks the heart, Brish-mo-Cree.

The whole landscape a manuscript
We had lost the skill to read,
A part of our past disinherited;
But fumbled, like a blind man,
Along the fingertips of instinct.

The last Gaelic speaker in the parish
When I stammered my school Irish
One Sunday after mass, crinkled
A rusty litany of praise:
Tá an Ghaeilge againn arís . . .[1]

Tír Eoghain: Land of Owen,
Province of the O'Niall;
The ghostly tread of O'Hagan's
Barefoot gallowglasses marching
To merge forces in Dún Geanainn

Push southward to Kinsale!
Loudly the war-cry is swallowed
In swirls of black rain and fog
As Ulster's pride, Elizabeth's foemen,
Founder in a Munster bog.

JOHN MONTAGUE, *The Rough Field*, 1972

In the counties of Limerick and Tipperary, when I was a boy, many of the old people could speak Irish only; middle-aged men and women knew both English and Irish, but always spoke the latter to each other; boys and girls understood both languages, but almost always spoke in English. Now it is only very old men and women who know Irish there; the young people do not understand it, and cannot tell the meaning of any Irish word. The same process is going on, though not everywhere so rapidly, in every district, where fifty years ago Irish was the language of the people; and I fear that, notwithstanding the endeavours of a society started not long ago to keep it alive, the Irish language will, before another fifty years, be dead.

W. R. LE FANU, *Seventy Years of Irish Life*, 1893

[1] 'We have the Irish again.'

14th [May 1827]... At the Crossroads I drank a good drop of whiskey in pleasant company. I know the Crossroads a long time, because, having come from Killarney in Kerry to Waterford in 1789, and from Waterford to Callan in March 1790, and having spent the summer in Baile Ruairí, beside Cill Mogeanna, in an orchard, I came with my father, Donncha Ó Súilleabháin, schoolmaster, to a sheep fold owned by Séamas Builtéar, between the Crossroads and Baile Uaitéir, where he stayed until a schoolhouse was built for him at the Crossroads in the summer of 1791. It was certainly a small school cabin, for it wasn't more than ten feet wide and about twenty feet long.

The sod walls were built in one day. The rafters and roof-timbers were put up the next day, and the roof was put on the third day. It was many a long year myself and my father spent teaching school in this cabin, and in another slightly bigger sod-walled cabin at the Tree in Cill Dá Lua; and in a good schoolhouse in Baile Uí Chaoimh, near Cnoc na Carraige. But alas! my father has gone, and the school cabins have gone. There is no trace of their sod walls today, nor any mention of them. But what is the use of complaining? The lime-washed castles, the bright mansions, the four elements and the whole world will pass away like the smoke from a wisp of straw.

Will it be long until this Irish language in which I am writing will disappear? Fine big schools are being built daily to teach this new language, the English of England. But alas! Nobody is taking any interest in the fine subtle Irish language, apart from mean Swaddlers who try to lure the Irish to join their new cursed religion.

HUMPHREY O'SULLIVAN, *Diary 1827–35*, 1979, trans. Tomás de Bhaldraithe

Tragedy ... lies in the fate of one romantic human type in rural Ireland. In the last century before the introduction of railroads and the growth of towns, each local community had its local artisans. Tailors, weavers, carpenters, shoemakers, smiths, followed their lifelong trades and supplied local needs. Open any account of rural Ireland before the last quarter of the last century, such as the tales of William Carleton, and you will be rewarded with a full-blooded picture of this lusty crew. Their crafts were very primitive, but their place was sure. Since then, nearly all of them, except the smith, their peer, have been swept away before the skill of townsmen and factory. These men supplied their neighbours, lived among them, were an integral part of rural life. When poverty struck too deep, they became peripatetics, like the wandering singers, scholars, fiddlers, spalpeen labourers, petty hawkers and beggars who swarmed the roads of Ireland. The world of fairy-tale was not remote from the farmers who knew these men. Rumpelstiltskin, in a Gaelic dress, was at one's very doors.

In remote communities some few of these survive. Where they do, the community can still make use of them. Commissioning them follows a traditional pattern of gifts and courtesies little resembling conventional monetary commerce. Their skill descends, like the farmer's farm, from father to son; it is 'in the blood'. Their surplus children must disperse to towns and in emigration. For theirs too is a familistic world.

CONRAD ARENSBERG, *The Irish Countryman*, 1937

There are (thank God!) four hundred thousand Irish children in the National Schools. A few years, and *they* will be the People of Ireland—the farmers of its lands, the conductors of its traffic, the adepts in its arts. How utterly unlike *that* Ireland will be to the Ireland of the Penal Laws, of the Volunteers, of the Union, or of the Emancipation?

Well may Carleton say that we are in a transition state. The knowledge, the customs, the superstitions, the hopes of the People are entirely changing. There is neither use nor reason in lamenting what we must infallibly lose. Our course is an open and a great one, and will try us severely; but, be it well or ill, we cannot resemble our fathers. No conceivable effort will get the people, twenty years hence, to regard the Fairies but as a beautiful fiction to be cherished, not believed in, and not a few real and human characters are perishing as fast as the Fairies.

Let us be content to have the past chronicled wherever it cannot be preserved.

Much may be saved—the Gaelic language and the music of the past may be handed uncorrupted to the future; but whatever may be the substitutes, the Fairies and the Banshees, the Poor Scholar and the Ribbonman, the Orange Lodge, the Illicit Still, and the Faction Fight are vanishing into history, and unless this generation paints them no other will know what they were.

It is chiefly in this way we value the work before us. In it Carleton is the historian of the peasantry rather than a dramatist. The fiddler and piper, the seanachie and seer, the match-maker and dancing-master, and a hundred characters beside are here brought before you, moving, acting, playing, plotting, and gossiping! You are never wearied by an inventory of wardrobes, as in short English descriptive fictions; yet you see how every one is dressed; you hear the honey brogue of the maiden, and the downy voice of the child, the managed accents of flattery or traffic, the shrill tones of woman's fretting, and the troubled gush of man's anger. The moory upland and the corn slopes, the glen where the rocks jut through mantling heather, and bright brooks gurgle amid the scented banks of wild herbs, the shivering cabin and the rudely-lighted farmhouse are as plain in Carleton's pages as if he used canvas and colours with a skill varying from Wilson and Poussin to Teniers and Wilkie.

THOMAS DAVIS, from Review of William Carleton's *Tales and Sketches Illustrating the Irish Peasantry*, 1845

Just where the road that runs by the bay turns northward to run by the Atlantic, a few white houses on either side turn it for a moment into a street. The grey road was not all grey yesterday, in spite of stones, and sea, and clouds, and a mist that blotted out the hills; for July had edged it with yellow ragweed, the horses of the Sidhe, and with purple heather; and besides the tireless turf-laden donkeys, there were men in white and women in crimson flannel going towards the village. One woman sitting in a donkey-cart was chanting a song in Irish about a voyage across the sea; and when someone asked her if she was to try for a prize at the *Feis*, the Irish festival going on in the village, she only answered that she was 'lonesome after the old times'.

At the *Feis*, in the white schoolhouse, some boys and girls from schools and convents at the 'big town' many miles away were singing; and now and then a little bare-footed boy from close by would go up on the platform and sing the *Paistin Fionn*, or *Is truag gan Peata*. People from the scattered houses and villages about had gathered to listen; some had come in turf-boats from Aran, Irish-speakers, proud to show that the language that has been called dead has never died; and glad at the new life that is coming into it. Men in loose flannel-jackets sang old songs, many sad ones, but not all; for one that was addressed to a mother, who had broken off her daughter's marriage with the maker of the song, turned more to anger than to grief; and there was the love song, 'Courteous Bridget', made perhaps a hundred years ago, by wandering Raftery.

A woman with madder-dyed petticoat sang the lament of an emigrant going across the great sea, telling how she got up at daybreak to look at the places she was going to leave, Ballinrobe and the rest; and how she envied the birds that were free of the air, and the beasts that were free of the mountain, and were not forced to go away. Another song that was sung was the Jacobite one, with the refrain that has been put into English—'Seaghan O'Dwyer a Gleanna, we're worsted in the game!'

LADY GREGORY, *Poets & Dreamers*, 1903

When he was a boy [i.e. 1870s/80s] they used to have thirty men and women employed for the harvest; these workers received sevenpence or eightpence a day, and were fed on oaten bread and buttermilk, with the addition of bacon on Thursdays and Sundays. Some of them could not eat meat (by which is meant bacon, of course), never having tasted it in their lives. It was the practice to add pea-flour to the rough wheaten bread made for these workers, so that it would be more sustaining, as whole-wheat bread was considered too light. They slept in out-houses or out-of-doors. They worked from 5 AM until 'it was so dark that they couldn't find their coats, and they did not want them either in those days, when the summers really were summers. There might be one wet day in a fortnight, but that would be all; there were no showers, and no grey days such as we have now'. The harvesters came from west Cork; they used to walk all the way to the midlands and back. They had their own travel routes, taking the shortest and most direct lines from place to place, these tracks being doubtless the traditional highways of ancient Ireland. They had a habit of collecting bits and scraps of their rations and saving them for journey fare, and they never touched a penny of their wages until they were home again. They worked all day, and could dance most of the night.

STEPHEN RYNNE, *Green Fields*, 1938

The traditional Irish cooking fire is on the hearth, and pots are hung over the fire by a swinging crane. This open-hearth type of cooking is common to all the Atlantic sea-board of Europe and is opposed to the stove for heating and the oven for cooking of central and eastern Europe. Southern and eastern England have this oven cooking with its yeast bread and flat-bottomed cooking pots. Wales, northern England, Scotland and Ireland all belong traditionally to the open-hearth province with the associated thin soda bread and round-bottomed cooking pots. The open hearth fire is particularly adapted to the burning of peat or turf, the local fuel, which needs no draught of air at the bottom of the fire. However, the hearth fire has many disadvantages; it involves a lot of stooping, heavy pots have to be lifted on and off in the full heat of the fire, and flat-bottomed utensils can only with difficulty be used. Such pots and vessels as the teapot or the saucepan have to be set up on a small heap of 'coals' (embers) drawn out from the main fire.

JOHN M. MOGEY, *Rural Life in Northern Ireland*, 1947

For constructional reasons, and also because window glass was long a luxury, the windows of the traditional cabin were few and small and placed for preference on the side away from the prevailing winds. Many of the surviving houses, moreover, were built in the early nineteenth century, when tax was levied on the number of windows. The ever-open door, its lower part closed with the additional half-door, admitted most of the light. The half-door is often regarded as peculiarly Irish, but in fact it is an old-fashioned feature which has lived on longer in the western isle than in Great Britain. It is found in parts of the north of England, for example in miners' cottages in Co. Durham, and it is said to be characteristic of Chinese houses. In Ireland the half-door serves to let in the light while keeping out unwanted animals, and it makes a convenient arm-rest for purposes of conversation or contemplation. This is how a countryman justified it to me: 'A man standing at the open door would be wasting time, but leaning on the half-door he is just passing time.' To give maximum efficiency, the window openings widen internally, an arrangement behind which there may be a lingering tradition of defence against unwelcome strangers. At any rate most of the light came from the doorway, and thus one sees the force of the picturesque phrase referring to the unwanted visitor as one who 'darkens the door'. A wattle frame, a handful of straw or a dried sheepskin served as a substitute for glass, and it is remembered in Co. Fermanagh that a mare's cleanings (the placenta) best served the purpose. My informant added significantly: 'No bayonet would go through it'! In one Donegal parish in 1887, according to a petition sent by the school teacher to the Lord Lieutenant of Ireland, there was 'not more than ten square feet of glass in windows in the whole (some 1,500 houses) with the exception of the chapel, the school house, the priest's house, Mr Dombrain's house and the constabulary barrack'.

E. Estyn Evans, Irish Folk Ways, 1957

The tinkers represented the aristocracy of the men of the roads, but there were varying degrees of the colour which these contributed to the fair. There were the mere tramps, the drovers, the pedlars, the trick-o'-the-loops, but all were essentially related in one aspect; they were emancipated from the land, each it would seem sufficiently to the needs of his own complete expression. They were adventurous aliens in this place, and so the eyes of the men rooted so firmly in the land turned towards them curiously, expectantly, for the diversions they would soon demand of the fair.

'How much d'ye want for the bit of a calf?'

'I'm asking seven pound ten.'

'Seven meaous of me granny's cat.'

'Would ye go be damned, mister, and I'm not asking your pardon.'

Another man crushed in now to bring together the parties to the deal and make them slap hands. The man who wanted to buy the beast was animated only by a sneering indifference. Yet the ash-plant held under his oxter, by a slight flicker, expressed his nervousness with regard to the deal. The seller looked huffed, indignant, and with his face turned away. The man who sought to make an adjustment was vibrant with anxiety to grind his axe as best he could between the two. Yet the eyes of none of them gave token of their minds' endeavour. Their eyes, deep on their business, were the shrewd, peasants' eyes.

Brinsley MacNamara, The Mirror in the Dusk, 1928

The Herb-Leech

I have gathered *luss*
At the wane of the moon,
And supped its sap
With a yewan spoon.

I have sat a spell
By the carn of Medbh,
And smelt the mould
Of the red queen's grave.

I have dreamed a dearth
In the darkened sun,
And felt the hand
Of the Evil One.

I have fathomed war
In the comet's tail,
And heard the crying
Of Gall and Gael.

I have seen the spume
On the dead priest's lips,
And the 'holy fire'
On the spars of ships;

And the shooting stars
On Barthelmy's Night,
Blanching the dark
With ghostly light;

And the corpse-candle
Of the seer's dream,
Bigger in girth
Than a weaver's beam;

And the shy heath-fairies
About the grate,
Blowing the turves
To a whiter heat.

All things on earth
To me are known,
For I have the gift
Of The Murrain Stone!

JOSEPH CAMPBELL, *The Rushlight*, 1906

I went supperless to bed, passed a sleepless night with cows, a horse, men and
boys, and an old woman smoking in the cabin, and walked through mud and
rain till twelve to Tully. Not a loaf of bread was in the town, and the Methodist
lady where we stopped said there had been none for six weeks! Can you
believe, who may read this, that in 1845, when there had been no failure of
crops, an assize town lived six weeks on nothing but potatoes?

At an early hour the next day I set off to visit the island of Omey. Reaching an ancient village, with houses of stone, constructed like a loose stone wall, without gable ends—some with tops like a beehive or inverted basket, some with holes for smoke to ascend, and some with no way for its escape but through the door—I selected one of the largest, knowing that there would be a full turn-out from every cabin and potato-field in sight and hearing. And, as if by magic, in a few moments every neighbouring cabin was vacated, the hillside and bog had not a foot to tread them—every spade was dropped, and the ground of the cabin was literally packed with men, women, and children, in rags and tatters—some with hair erect, and some with caps, and some with hats, but more with none. In one solid mass they all sat down upon their haunches, and began their welcomes to Ireland. My polka coat, my velvet bonnet, and all that outwardly appertained to me passed in review. Taking out a tract, I read a little, while they wondered at my 'plain spache', and thanked God that they had seen such a devotee, going, as they supposed, on penance.

ASENATH NICHOLSON, *The Bible in Ireland*, 1852

The Poor Girl's Meditation

I am sitting here,
Since the moon rose in the night;
Kindling a fire,
And striving to keep it alight:
The folk of the house are lying
In slumber deep;
The cocks will be crowing soon:
The whole of the land is asleep.

May I never leave this world
Until my ill-luck is gone;
Till I have cows and sheep,
And the lad that I love for my own:
I would not think it long,
The night I would lie at his breast,
And the daughters of spite, after that,
Might say the thing they liked best.

Love covers up hate,
If a girl have beauty at all:
On a bed that was narrow and high,
A three-month I lie by the wall:
When I bethought on the lad

That I left on the brow of the hill,
I wept from dark until dark,
And my cheeks have the tear-tracks still.

And, O, young lad that I love,
I am no mark for your scorn:
All you can say of me
Is undowered I was born:
And if I've no fortune in hand,
Nor cattle nor sheep of my own,
This I can say, O lad,
I am fitted to lie my lone!

PADRAIC COLUM, *Dramatic Legends*, 1922, trans.
from the Irish, 'Tá mé 'mo shuidhe'

In the evenings of Sundays and holidays the young men and girls go out to a rocky headland on the north-west, where there is a long, grassy slope, to dance and amuse themselves; and this evening I wandered out there with two men, telling them ghost stories in Irish as we went. When we turned over the edge of the hill we came on a number of young men lying on the short grass playing cards. We sat down near them, and before long a party of girls and young women came up also and sat down, twenty paces off, on the brink of the cliff, some of them wearing the fawn-coloured shawls that are so attractive and so much thought of in the south. It was just after sunset, and Inishtooskert was standing out with a smoky blue outline against the redness of the sky. At the foot of the cliff a wonderful silvery light was shining on the sea, which already, before the beginning of autumn, was eager and wintry and cold. The little group of blue-coated men lying on the grass, and the group of girls further off, had a singular effect in this solitude of rocks and sea; and in spite of their high spirits it gave me a sort of grief to feel the utter loneliness and desolation of the place that has given these people their finest qualities.

One of the young men had been thrown from a car a few days before on his way home from Dingle, and his face was still raw and bleeding and horrible to look at; but the young girls seemed to find romance in his condition, and several of them went over and sat in a group round him, stroking his arms and face. When the card-playing was over I showed the young men a few tricks and feats, which they worked at themselves, to the great amusement of the girls, till they had accomplished them all. On our way back to the village the young girls ran wild in the twilight, flying and shrieking over the grass, or rushing up behind the young men and throwing them over, if they were able, by a sudden jerk or trip. The men in return caught them by one hand, and spun them round and round four or five times, and then let them go, when they whirled down the grassy slope for many yards, spinning like peg-tops, and only keeping their feet by the greatest efforts or good-luck.

J. M. SYNGE, *In Wicklow and West Kerry*, 1912

from *Limerick Town*

HERE I've got you, Philip Desmond, standing in the market-place,
'Mid the farmers and the corn sacks, and the hay in either space,
Near the fruit stalls, and the women knitting socks and selling lace.

There is High Street up the hillside, twenty shops on either side,
Queer, old-fashioned, dusky High Street, here so narrow, there so wide,
Whips and harness, saddles, signboards, hanging out in quiet pride.

Up and down the noisy highway, how the market people go!
Country girls in Turkey kerchiefs—poppies moving to and fro —
Frieze-clad fathers, great in buttons, brass and watch-seals all a-show.

Merry, merry are their voices, Philip Desmond, unto me
Dear the mellow Munster accent, with its intermittent glee;
Dear the blue cloaks, and the grey coats, things I long have longed to
    see.

Even the curses, adjurations, in my senses sound like rhyme,
And the great, rough-throated laughter of that peasant in his prime,
Winking from the grassbound cart-shaft, brings me back the other
    time.

JOHN FRANCIS O'DONNELL, *Poems*, 1891

In the remoter extremities of the county of Limerick, I saw, for the first time, young females and grown-up women carrying large wooden pails full of milk on their heads. This was to me a wonderful as well as novel sight. They walked at as rapid a pace with these wooden pails on their head, without a hand touching them, as if they had been so strapped to their head as to render it impossible for them to fall, or the milk in any way to spill. Neither men nor women in this country, could perform this exploit, though so easy of performance to the female peasantry in the south of Ireland. The further south you go, the more frequently do you see women with pails of milk or of water, and other heavy burthens, on their head. Not only can they walk at full speed with these utensils full of milk or water on their head without the aid of their hands, but some of them can leap over short hedges or small dykes, without the pails being displaced, or even a single drop of their contents being spilt. The female peasantry in the south of Ireland are allowed on all hands to possess finer figures than the women in the rural districts of any other part of that country; and the reason is supposed to be the erect manner in which they are obliged to walk when carrying burthens on their heads which require a certain stateliness as well as steadiness of carriage.

Anon. (J. Grant), *Impressions of Ireland and the Irish*, 1844

In harvest, when the last of the farmer's corn is about to be cut, a small portion of the best is plaited and bound up. The men then stand at a certain distance, and throw their hooks at it till it is cut, on which they give three cheers. This is generally called winning the *churn*, but in some parts of the parish it is called the *hare*. It is carried home and laid above the door: the name of the first young woman who enters afterwards, it is said, will be that of the wife of the young man who has put it there. A like custom is observed in Devonshire, and in all likelihood it came here with the settlers from thence.

On winning the *churn*, the reapers are usually regaled with a special feast, also called the *churn*. Formerly this feast consisted of a profusion of homely fare, such as bread, cheese, butter, cream, &c. and generally concluded with a dance, the master and mistress joining without distinction in the general festivity. Of late years, this rustic feast has been corrupted by the introduction of tea and whiskey, and the former simplicity of the entertainment is in a great measure lost.

Samuel McSkimin, *History of Carrickfergus*, 1829

The art [of storytelling] took a long, long time to wane with our people. In my childhood days, in my Donegal mountains, though the schooled professional shanachie had long disappeared, the homespun storyteller was plentiful—and cherished. There still was not a hill nor a glen but had its noted, sometimes famed and beloved practitioner who had inherited the great wealth of the ancient tales and spent the nights in lavish bestowment of his rare riches on the needy souls surrounding him. By a hundred happy hearths on a thousand golden nights, then I, with my fellows, enthroned me under the chimney brace, or in circle, hunkered on the floor in the fire glow, heartening to the recital, and spellbound by the magic of the loved tales so lovingly told by *fear-a'tighe* (man-of-the-house) or *bean-a-tighe* (woman-of-the-house). Not many women could be termed shanachie, but she was a poor mother who had not at least a dozen or twenty tales on which to bring up her children.

SEUMAS MACMANUS, Preface to *Hibernian Nights*, 1963

In 1932, when I lived in Longford an old woman told my authoress aunt how, when she was a girl of eighteen and worked as a maid at the Big House, on her afternoon off one summer's day, she and some other girls were sitting by a lough not far from the avenue gates when they heard the clatter of horsemen coming along the road. She jumped up at once, saying she must hurry back to the house, as there was 'quality' coming and her help would be needed.

She had not run far when the party of riders came in sight, eight of them, men and young women, in bright clothes and with coloured bridles and saddles, the girls aside, the men astride, and all laughing and talking gaily. They were no more than forty yards from her when they swung to the right over a grassy bank, across a small field, and into the side of a small thorn-ringed fairy fort. Horses and all, they trotted into the earth as coolly and casually as humans would pass through a stable gate. So she shrugged her shoulders and went back to her companions. When asked why she had returned, she replied, 'Ah, 'twas no quality, at all. 'Twas only a pack of fairies going into the fort.' What struck my aunt, who was highly experienced in these matters, and myself was the obviously genuine unaffectedness of her acceptance of fairies as an everyday fact, and no matter at all for wonder or worry.

DERMOT MACMANUS, *The Middle Kingdom*, 1959

Growing up in Sussex, I took for granted a countryside physically rich in the layering of the past: real Tudor beams, clay tiles, flint walls, dew ponds, field paths and stiles. In Ireland so much of what ought to have been history has been disowned; in long stretches of landscape the centuries have passed without leaving any vernacular mark. Say what you like about the fairies, wise women and the rest, they did give meaning to the countryside: particular trees, hill forts, old bridges, gables, bends in the road. Some of this lives on with the shreds of the language, but most of Ireland has broken with folklore, or was uprooted from it in the sharing out of land. So little yet exists to connect people with their landscape, to make it 'part of what they are'.

MICHAEL VINEY, *A Year's Turning*, 1996

Inniskeen Road: July Evening

THE bicycles go by in twos and threes—
There's a dance in Billy Brennan's barn to-night,
And there's the half-talk code of mysteries
And the wink-and-elbow language of delight.
Half-past eight and there is not a spot
Upon a mile of road, no shadow thrown
That might turn out a man or woman, not
A footfall tapping secrecies of stone.

I have what every poet hates in spite
Of all the solemn talk of contemplation.
Oh, Alexander Selkirk knew the plight
Of being king and government and nation.
A road, a mile of kingdom, I am king
Of banks and stones and every blooming thing.

PATRICK KAVANAGH, *Ploughman and Other Poems*, 1936

The book . . . *An tOileánach* 'The islandman' (1929), is a triumph of Irish prose; here, at last, is the speech of the people producing results far beyond the power of O'Leary, and it will live as long as the Irish language is read. And yet it could not, in the nature of things, be a pattern for other writers, for Tomás Crithin was not writing for his own people (who found the praise accorded to the book entirely incomprehensible) but for the new Irish reading public of the towns; indeed, in his most quoted sentence he makes it clear that he, like Geoffrey Keating three hundred years before, is seeking to preserve the memory of a way of life which is doomed. The success of the book inspired other islanders, notably a young man, Muiris Ó Súilleabháin, who published *Fiche Blian ag Fás* (1933) and an old woman, Peig Sayers, with *Peig* (1939). All these writers were translated into English, and *Twenty years a-growing*, the version by Moya Llewelyn Davies and George Thomson of Ó Súilleabháin's book, was described by E. M. Forster as 'an account of neolithic civilisation from the inside', though George Thomson's description of the Blasket society as 'pre-capitalist' is somewhat nearer the mark. It cannot be doubted that it is the exotic nature of that society to the modern reader which has made this strange flowering the best-known aspect of modern Irish literature; as recently as 1969 J. V. Luce published a scholarly article entitled 'Homeric qualities in the life and literature of the great Blasket island'. Indeed, although the Blasket is now deserted and its former inhabitants have been moved to the mainland, 'Blasket literature' still continues, for the sons of Tomás Crithin and Peig Sayers have both published books which continue the tradition. But the gap between documentary and creative writing was not bridged either by Tomás Crithin or by his successors; much had been hoped for from Muiris Ó Súilleabháin, but he died before his promise could be fulfilled.

DAVID GREENE, *Writing in Irish Today*, 1972

As for the houses that we had in my youth, and for some time after, they differed among themselves, just as in other places. Some of them had a handsomer appearance than the rest, and others were pretty wretched. A number of them were only ten feet by eight. Others were larger—from that size to fifteen or twenty feet long. To divide the house into two a dresser stood out from the wall in the middle of the floor, and a partition met it from the other side. There were two beds in the lower portion, where people slept. Potatoes would be stored under these beds. A great chest was kept between the two beds up against the gable end. On the other side of the partition—the kitchen side—the family used to spend the whole day, or part of the day, ten of them perhaps. There was a coop against the partition with hens in it, and a broody hen just by it in an old cooking pot. At night-time there would be a cow or two, calf or two, the ass, the dog on a chain by the wall or running about the house. In a house with a large family you would find a post-bed, or maybe a bed on the floor. The old people used to spend the night in that beside the fire, with an old stump of a clay pipe going, or two pipes if there were two of them living, and smoking away; they would have a wisp of straw for a pipe-lighter. A good fire of fine turf smouldered away till morning; every time they woke they took a light from the fire and puffed at the pipe. If the old woman was alive, the old man would stretch across to give her a light from the wisp; then the smoke from the two old pipes would drift up the chimney, and you could imagine that the couple's bed was a steamship as they puffed away in full blast.

Two or three dogs would stretch out at the foot of the bed, the cow or the cows below them, head to the wall, and there would be a calf or two with the run of the kitchen, or lying muzzle to the fire. The ass would be tied up on the other side of the house opposite the cows, and a cat with a couple of kittens, maybe, in the chimney niche. The rest of the trumpery in the house was stuffed under the post-bed for the night. This bed was more than a couple of feet from the ground, and it was made of wood or iron. Some of the houses had no division to make a room, but there was a post-bed in one corner and a bed on the floor in the other. The dresser was up against the wall or the gable-end. Every kind of house had two or three barrels of fish. And, besides all the other animals, you would find a pet lamb or two running about the house.

TOMÁS Ó CRIOMHTHAIN, *The Islandman*, 1926, trans. Robin Flower

Our concern is with the old-style house as a shelter for man and beast and as the vehicle of family lore and regional tradition. In the crowded clachans limitations of space and the fact that diarying was mainly practised in the summer booleys go far to explain the absence of separate byres or dairies. Sanitation was of the crudest and closets unknown. It is these aspects of Irish rural life that have most readily aroused the amused indignation of the critics and the defensive wrath of Irish patriots. As we read in an earlier description of the Western Isle:

> At one of th' ends he kept his cows,
> At th' other end he kept his spouse.

The custom of housing man and beast together has been very general among pastoral peoples in regions of difficult climate, whether in Highland Britain or the European mountain zone. Parts of Ireland, however, have long had a different type of house giving more family privacy: in the lowland parts of Leinster, East Munster and South Ulster the house with central chimney and fireside partition did not easily allow of the keeping of livestock in the house, and one is inclined to regard this style as an improvement introduced by English settlers. . . . In any event, although stray hens, a pet lamb or a far-rowing pig may occasionally join the cats and dogs in an Irish kitchen, the keeping of cattle in the house is a thing of the past. Yet it was so recently practised, especially along the Atlantic seaboard, that many existing houses are not far removed from kitchen-byres, a cross partition conveniently converting the byre into a bedroom, store or dairy.

E. Estyn Evans, *Irish Folk Ways*, 1957

In Ulster a type of farm building round a courtyard is sometimes seen. This arrangement was foreign to native Ireland, and is said to have come to us through French influence. Such farmyards usually have their dovecote; and the outside steps leading to the barn-loft are a common feature all through the country, with native Irish, English, Scottish and French alike. Orange carts tipped up in the dark shadows of elliptical arches, on a floor of cobblestones, and beyond that a sky of blue with white cloud is a sight to remember. In the farm kitchen will be a large open grate, unless a modern cooker has recently been installed, but, if you are lucky, a pot and crane may be left. The china dogs on the mantelpiece there nearly certainly will be, while round the door you can count on proud, Hussar-like cockerels swaggering and strutting, and a County Down collie with a wall eye and a sharp, welcoming bark. No matter how far inland you may be, you will probably find seagulls contesting with rooks beside the pigs' trough.

Denis O'D. Hanna, 'Architecture in Ulster', in *The Arts in Ulster*, 1951

from *The Woman of the House*

It was her house where we spent holidays,
With candles to bed, and ghostly stories:
In the lake of her heart we were islands
Where the wild asses galloped in the wind.

Her mind was a vague and log-warmed yarn
Spun between sleep and acts of kindliness:
She fed our feelings as dew feeds the grass
On April nights, and our mornings were green:

And those happy days, when in spite of rain
We'd motor west where the salmon-boats tossed,
She would sketch on the pier among the pots
Waves in a sunset, or the rising moon.

Indian-meal porridge and brown soda-bread,
Boiled eggs and buttermilk, honey from gorse,
Far more than we wanted she always offered
In a heart-surfeit: she ate little herself.

Mistress of mossy acres and unpaid rent,
She crossed the walls on foot to feed the sick:
Though frugal cousins frowned on all she spent
People had faith in her healing talent.

She bandaged the wounds that poverty caused
In the house that famine labourers built,
Gave her hands to cure impossible wrong
In a useless way, and was loved for it. . . .

The bards in their beds once beat out ballads
Under leaky thatch listening to sea-birds,
But she in the long ascendancy of rain
Served biscuits on a tray with ginger wine.

Time can never relax like this again,
She in her phaeton looking for folk-lore,
He writing sermons in the library
Till lunch, then fishing all the afternoon.

On a wet winter evening in Ireland
I let go her hand, and we buried her
In the family earth beside her husband.
Only to think of her, now warms my mind.

RICHARD MURPHY, *Sailing to an Island*, 1963

The Stereophonic Nightmare

I still feel surprised whenever I hear Ulster mentioned in the news. It always used to seem like the archetypal place where nothing would, or could, ever happen.

CAROLINE BLACKWOOD, *For All That I Found There*

Sixty-nine the nightmare started.

JAMES SIMMONS, *West Strand Visions*

The word itself, 'Troubles', vague and ill-defined, was a euphemism, but it suited the vague and ill-defined nature of the war in Ireland. It has many sub-definitions: a thing that causes distress; an occasion of affliction; a misfortune; a calamity; public disturbance, disorder or confusion. The Troubles disturbed life—they did not destroy it. Most of the time, for most of the people, nothing untoward happened. The pursuit of capitalism, the rearing of children, the growing of crops, the manufacture of industry, were unaffected. At other times, usually in certain specific places, there were riots, disturbances, threats, beatings, car hijackings, men in masks, fear, and murder. The Troubles, and this is important to remember, were acts of rebellion rather than revolution. No one had a plan to proclaim a 'liberated' Northern Ireland a Marxist state. . . . The Troubles were spasmodic. Their public history was a roll-call of the high points of atrocity and outrage: fifteen killed by a Loyalist bomb in McGurk's Bar in Belfast in 1971; thirteen civil rights marchers killed by British soldiers on Bloody Sunday in Derry in 1972; nine civilians dismembered by IRA car bombs on Bloody Friday in Belfast in 1972; twenty-one disco-goers blown up by the IRA in Birmingham in 1974; thirty-three shoppers blown up by Loyalist car bombs in Dublin and Monaghan in 1974; twelve diners burned to death by an IRA fire-bomb in La Mon restaurant in 1977; ten IRA hunger-strikers dead in prison in 1981; eight IRA Volunteers killed by the SAS at Loughgall in 1987; eleven civilians blown up by the IRA at a Remembrance Day ceremony in Enniskillen in 1987; five civilians shot dead in a bookie's shop by Loyalists in Belfast in 1991; and two children killed by an IRA bomb in Warrington in 1992, and on and on and on. The gaps between significant acts of collective murder were filled by a steady drum-beat of individual whackings (murders) or stiffings.

People often tried to explain the Troubles in terms of other conflicts, but this was not Cuba, nor Algeria, nor South Africa nor Vietnam. It was Ireland and the tenacity of the struggle between the rebels and the Crown was older than all the 'isms' of the twentieth century. The Troubles were an endless series of small military skirmishes. The objective was to go on killing the enemy wherever you could find him, and thereby wear out his will to fight on. The ultimate goal was fairly clear. Ireland was and is divided; six of the nine historic counties of the province of Ulster are under British rule, the other twenty-six counties constitute the Republic of Ireland. The IRA were fighting to remove the British Crown from what they regarded as Irish soil and reunite Ireland. The British government were fighting to defend the Northern Irish state and the desire of the 850,000 strong Northern-Irish-born Protestant population to remain separate from the rest of Ireland. It is the longest war the world has ever known.

KEVIN TOOLIS, *Rebel Hearts*, 1995

from *Letter To Derek Mahon*

And did we come into our own
When, minus muse and lexicon,
We traced in August sixty-nine
Our imaginary Peace Line
Around the burnt-out houses of
The Catholics we'd scarcely loved,
Two Sisyphuses come to budge
The sticks and stones of an old grudge,

Two poetic conservatives
In the city of guns and long knives,
Our ears receiving then and there
The stereophonic nightmare
Of the Shankill and the Falls,
Our matches struck on crumbling walls
To light us as we moved at last
Through the back alleys of Belfast?

MICHAEL LONGLEY, *An Exploded View*, 1973

On 14 August [1969] the North was on the brink of war. The opposition boy-cotted the special session of the Stormont parliament which heard Clark denounce the rioting in a bitter speech,

This is not the agitation of a minority seeking by lawful means the assertion of political rights. It is the conspiracy of forces seeking to overthrow a government democratically elected by a large majority.

Menwhile B Specials were replacing the RUC on the edge of the Bogside and preparing for another attack. But if the Bogsiders had resisted the RUC they would fight the B Specials with far greater vigour.

At 5pm British troops moved into the centre of Derry, fully armed. There was an anxious moment as the rioters watched them take up their positions. There were hurried negotiations between the Defence Association and the British commander and then he agreed to pull the RUC and Specials back behind his troops and not to enter the Bogside. The siege was over. The Bogsiders felt that they had won—not only because they had kept the RUC out of their area but because they had forced the British Army to intervene. They sensed vaguely that direct British intervention re-opened the whole constitutional question.

In Belfast the trouble was only beginning. Tension was at fever pitch. On the Falls Road people were barricading the streets. On the Shankill Road crowds of angry Loyalists filled the streets connecting it with the Falls, and mingling with them were hundreds of the mobilised Specials armed with rifles, revolvers and sub-machine guns. Rioting started at Hasting Street barracks on the Falls. As it continued mobs of Loyalists surged down the side streets towards the Falls, attacking and burning Catholic houses, firing into the Catholic area and eventually planting the Union Jack in Divis Street. The B Specials were prominent among the attackers. Some IRA men with a few weapons, including one Thompson sub-machine gun—most of their weapons had been moved out of Belfast as part of the new political emphasis—fired at the attackers and one Protestant, Herbert Roy, was killed. Eventually the mob of Loyalists and Specials was driven back, but not before they'd burnt out most of the Falls Road, or Catholic, ends of Dover Street and Percy Street.

MICHAEL FARRELL, *The Orange State*, 1976

'We walked quickly to the bottom of Castle Street and began to walk hurriedly up the road. At Divis Street I noticed that five or six shops around me had been destroyed by fire. At Divis flats a group of men stood, it was light by this time. When they heard that Jack was a journalist they began telling him about the firing. It had been going on all night, they said, and several people were dead, including a child in the flats. They took him to see the bullet holes in the walls. The child was in a cot at the time. And the walls were thin. I left him there at Divis and hurried up the road to Conway Street. There was a large crowd there as well, my own people. I looked up the street to the top. There was another crowd at the junction of Ashmore Street—this crowd was from the Shankill—they were setting fire to a bar at the corner and looting it. Then some of the men began running down the street and breaking windows of the houses in Conway Street. They used brush handles. At the same time as the bar was burning, a number of the houses at the top of the street also caught fire in Conway Street. The crowd were throwing petrol bombs in after they broke the windows. I began to run up towards the fire. Several of the crowd also started running with me.

'Then I noticed for the first time, because my attention had been fixed on the burning houses, that two turreted police vehicles were moving slowly down the street on either side. Somebody shouted: "The gun turrets are pointed towards us!" And everybody ran back. I didn't. I was left standing in the middle of the street, when a policeman, standing in a doorway, called to me: "Get back! Get out of here before you get hurt."

'The vehicles were moving slowly down Conway Street towards the Falls Road with the crowd behind them, burning houses as they went. I ran into the top of Balaclava Street at the bottom of Conway Street where our crowd were. A man started shouting at the top of his voice: "They're going to fire. They're going to fire on us!"'

ANNE DEVLIN, 'Naming the Names', 1986

Ulster has always had its own geographical and historical identity, but it is also part of Ireland, historically as well as geographically. Its problems can only be understood in the context of Irish history; and the same is true of the diminished Ulster that emerged as the separate political entity of Northern Ireland in 1920.

The passions and the violence that have ravaged Northern Ireland since 1968 have been due in part to problems characteristic of contemporary industrial society elsewhere—chronic unempolyment, inadequate and insufficient housing, a heightened sense of deprivation and frustration in face of expanding education and rising material standards. There is nothing peculiar to Northern Ireland in civil rights marches and sit-downs or in violence as a form of group protest. And there are ample precedents outside Ireland for such phenomena as the 'tartan gangs' and the 'protection' rackets that flourish in the pathological conditions of life in parts of Belfast. Economic pressures aggravate the disorder and the suffering, but the roots of the present troubles lie in centuries of political and cultural division within Ulster whose disastrous legacy to Northern Ireland has been a tradition of ascendancy, discrimination, sectarianism, and disaffection.

T. W. MOODY, *The Ulster Question*, 1974

The march moved on again, on to the main road, about seven miles from Derry, towards the bridge of Burntollet. Some police vehicles preceded the marchers, followed by a small group with a Union Jack, who had smashed the windscreen of a car carrying newsmen from Derry a short while previously. After them came a district inspector leading steel-helmeted police equipped with roit shields, then about five hundred marchers, and finally more police tenders. A screening force of police, without riot equipment, moved into the fields on the right. The marchers were battered with large stones of several pounds weight, with bottles (delivered by lorry in crate-loads during the night to the ambush site) and by nail-studded cudgels. On the left of the road the ground sloped down a short distance to a stream, the Faughan, and many of the marchers were driven down here. Numbers of girls were thrown into the stream by the attackers, into water which was about three feet deep. Stones were thrown at them in the water, and when they attempted to come out they were beaten back again by home-made cudgels. Other girls were thrown off a bridge into the stream; some were beaten while in the water with clubs from which large nails protruded; others were threatened with rape.

A further ambush, conducted largely by the same people who had taken part in the Burntollet ambush, met the battered and bloody marchers who finally made their way into the outskirts of Derry. This happened in Irish Street, where again large numbers of heavy stones, bottles, and petrol bombs were thrown by the attackers from high ground on to the procession. Among those present here, as the Cameron Commission found, was a District Commandant of the Ulster Special Constabulary, Reverend John Brown. The Cameron Commission, however, contrary to the evidence adduced elsewhere, considered that at Burntollet a serious effort was made by the police to protect the marchers. Before the marchers reached Craigavon Bridge and could cross the River Foyle into Derry, they were held for some time in Spencer Street by a police cordon, while missiles rained down on them. At last they crossed the bridge, and came into the Guildhall Square, where the people of Derry waited to welcome them. They had been directed into a last rerouting by the police and kept from passing into the walled city. In there, their attackers gathered, and, in the late afternoon of Saturday, 4 January 1969, the Burntollet attackers gathered in the high central part of the city and on the walls, shouting, drinking, singing, dancing in triumph. They began now to shower bottles and stones down into the Guildhall Square on the dispersing crowd which had greeted the marchers, most of whom now were having their wounds dressed. The police formed a human barrier across the gates, keeping apart the Protestants armed with sticks, stones, and bottles up on the walls, and the crowd in the Guildhall Square below.

LIAM DE PAOR, *Divided Ulster*, 1970

One event had followed another with startling rapidity; in the working-class areas the old familiar life of the street had gone, it seemed, for good. The reek of CS gas and burnt timber hung in the air, the once ideological barrier between Protestant and Catholic had become an ugly actuality, and tension in the tiny streets was electric. Piles of sandbags at corners, tortured coils of barbed wire on the pavement, all became less evident as the Sappers moved in, as sentry-posts acquired, subtly, the trappings of permanence—armoured glass, corrugated roofs. Social life in the community contracted disastrously as, nightly, each street was sealed off from the next; with the inevitable loss of most transport services and entertainments, rioting or 'area defence' became the sole *raison d'être* for adolescent groupings. Rumour was rife and suspicion of strangers almost pathological.

MORRIS FRASER, *Children in Conflict*, 1973

And now there was an additional excitement, for after fifty years of stagnation the North suddenly burst into a dramatic life caused in part by the activities of a Protestant minister regarded with fondness by many Fenians despite or actually because of his outspoken bigotry.

'Have yese heard the latest?' Sammy asked. 'Ees wife went to the dentist and says the dentist, *How's the mouth?* and says she, *Aw he's grand, he's givin' a rally in Ballymena.*'

'Say nothin' about that man,' Danny Deery countered, looking shrewdly round to see if we could grasp the sophistication of the point. 'Sure isn't he the best friend we ever had?'

No one disagreed. The real enemies were the fearful moderates trying to calm things down. With the wisdom of hindsight we might have been less enthusiastic, but then the only thought was to keep it going at all costs. Turn the heat up! Keep it on the boil! On top of the natural imminence of youth there was the intoxication of an apparently permanent hegemony about to crumble to dust. A thrilling first lesson in mutability. It seems that nothing will ever change, then all at once the brazen axioms collapse. Apocalypse was only a news bulletin away and many, including the Herrons, became lifelong news addicts.

As yet there was no death and little suffering.

MICHAEL FOLEY, *The Road to Notown*, 1996

The Coasters

You coasted along
to larger houses, gadgets, more machines,
to golf and weekend bungalows,
caravans when the children were small,
the Mediterranean, later, with the wife.

You did not go to church often,
weddings were special;
but you kept your name on the books
against eventualities;
and the parson called, or the curate.

You showed a sense of responsibility,
with subscriptions to worthwhile causes
and service in voluntary organisations;
and, anyhow, this did the business no harm,
no harm at all.
Relations were improving. A good
useful life. You coasted along.

You even had a friend or two of the other sort,
coasting too: your ways ran parellel.
Their children and yours seldom met, though,
being at different schools.
You visited each other, decent folk with a sense
of humour. Introduced, even, to
one of their clergy. And then you smiled
in the looking-glass, admiring, a
little moved by, your broadmindedness.
Your father would never have known
one of them. Come to think of it,
when you were young, your own home was never
visited by one of the other sort.

Relations were improving. The annual processions
began to look rather like folk-festivals.

When that noisy preacher started,
he seemed old-fashioned, a survival.
Later you remarked on his vehemence,
a bit on the rough side.
But you said, admit it, you said in the club,
'You know, there's something in what he says'.

And you who seldom had time to read a book,
what with reports and the colour-supplements,
denounced censorship.
And you who never had an adventurous thought
were positive that the church of the other sort
vetoes thought.
And you who simply put up with marriage
for the children's sake, deplored

the attitude of the other sort
to divorce.
You coasted along.
And all the time, though you never noticed,
the old lies festered;
the ignorant became more thoroughly infected;
there were gains, of course;
you never saw any go barefoot.

The government permanent, sustained
by the regular plebiscites of loyalty.
You always voted but never
put a sticker on the car;
a card in the window
would not have been seen from the street.
Faces changed on the posters, names too, often,
but the same families, the same class of people.
A Minister once called you by your first name.
You coasted along
and the sores suppurated and spread.

Now the fever is high and raging;
who would have guessed it, coasting along?
The ignorant-sick thresh about in delirium
and tear at the scabs with dirty finger-nails.
The cloud of infection hangs over the city,
a quick change of wind and it
might spill over the leafy suburbs,
You coasted too long.

JOHN HEWITT, *Collected Poems*, 1991

Most accounts of the current trouble in Northern Ireland begin at 5 October 1968, which is as good a date to start from as any other. It was the day of the first civil rights march in Derry. Had all those who now claim to have marched that day actually done so, the carriageway would have collapsed. It was a small demonstration, perhaps four hundred strong—and a hundred of these were students from Belfast. Most of the rest were teenagers from the Bogside and Creggan. The march was trapped between two cordons of police in Duke Street and batoned into disarray.

EAMONN MCCANN, *War and an Irish Town*, 1974

The dawn of 1972 brought Ulster's people, weary after more than three years of marches, riots, and finally shootings and bombings, the precious hope that the corner had been turned, and that peace, so elusive for so long, was at hand. It was a false hope, and 1972 was to prove easily the worst year in Northern Ireland's history for violence and destruction. Instead of a gradual return to normality, the year saw Ulster slither even more swiftly into chaos and anarchy. The rule of law all but ceased to run in the province, and a new and more terrifying phase of the war emerged in full force: the sectarian assassinations.

> MARTIN DILLON and DENIS LEHANE, *Political Murder in Northern Ireland*, 1973

The Ballad of Gerry Kelly: Newsagent
(for Gus Martin)

Here's a song for Gerry Kelly.
Listen carefully and see
what's the moral of the story.
It makes no sense to me.

Worked ten hours six days a week,
Sundays closed at three.
They say he made a decent living.
Rather him than me.

Social centre for the neighbours—
not much cash in that—
buying fags or blades or tissues,
waiting on to chat.

Sixty-nine the nightmare started.
Loyalist anger rose:
sweet shops, butcher shops and pubs
were burned down, forced to close.

Who'd believe who never saw it . . .
the broken glass, the noise,
voices shouting, 'Fenian bastard'
—little Ulster boys?

Down the hill of lies and horror
Belfast city slipped.
Twice the Tartan thugs came for him.
robbed and pistol-whipped.

Standing in his shattered shop
and taking inventory
of loss and damage, Gerry Kelly
longed to get away.

Who would buy the ruined business
that he'd worked to build?
No one, so he waited, hoping
until he was killed.

One dark evening last November—
turn the lights on till we see—
Gerry Kelly still in business,
wife gone back to make the tea.

Sorting out the evening papers
while his son is selling sweets,
in our time, our town, two gunmen
walk in off the streets.

JAMES SIMMONS, *West Strand Visions*, 1974

If Thomas or Brendan were late in coming home from school Mother would ring the Incident Centre to see if they'd been shot or arrested. She knew that I would have more sense. But she suspected, and quite rightly, that I spent many nights sitting up at the window, wrapped in the patchwork quilt that was Granny's wedding present, watching the local battalion on urban manoeuvres—the Belfast Brigade—or the British soldiers on foot patrol, the frequent riots, the women battering the bin-lids to let the 'boys' know that the soldiers were on the estate.

I held nightly vigils, while the news that would be misreported in the media the following day happened under the window, or over the road.

'Annie, are you out of bed?' Mother would yell up the stairs. A quiet, practised scuffle across the room. The creep in the dark.

'No, I'm almost asleep. Why?' Effective use of the simulated drowsy slur.

'There's shooting outside, stay away from the window.'

'OK. Ni-night.'

'Ni-night, love.'

I lie still for a good thirty seconds and then, with elaborate care, slip from under the forty blankets, and in less than four slow steps I'm on the other bed, lowering my weight gently, silently, between the window and Sinead's feet. She never moves, except to grind her teeth. A sound sleeper.

I pull back the curtain and rub the mist off the window. There's a soldier in the garden, a Gordon Highlander—I can see his pom-pom—lying on his stomach behind the shallow concrete wall. Stupid cow. The street-lamp is directly overhead, one of the few in the street not shot out by the boys, for safety's sake. A rifle cracks in the dark. The soldier raises his head and looks around. Someone in Murray's garden next door snaps an order at him. His head goes down. It's starting to rain. The boys will go in now. Let the Brits lie out in it and get saturated. A man's army. It's spoiled the garden, all this running in and out through it with guns and army-issue boots. There's only the young flowering cherry left in the middle, its spindly, bald branches tied down with cords. To make it droop.

Once, just after we'd moved to Bunbeg, Aunt Kay's husband Jack arrived with armfuls of marigolds. He didn't call at the house first. We just looked out of the window when we heard the thuds, and there he was, stamping the marigolds into the soft earth around the cherry tree with his big boots.

'They'll make a magnificent display this spring coming,' he swore. Not one of them came up.

'They say marigolds will only grow where blood has been spilt,' my father, ever anecdotal, mentioned at the time.

Now they would thrive.

MARY COSTELLO, *Titanic Town*, 1992

I was advised to study the religious geography of the city before cycling around it and a friend lent me his detailed British Army Tribal Map of Belfast, which marks the ghetto areas orange and green. Then my host introduced me to the Catholic ghettos. With a prominent DOCTOR notice displayed on his windscreen he was less likely than other motorists to be delayed at security check points, hijacked by bombers or stoned by gangs of bored boys who for the moment could find no more exciting target.

Perhaps because I never see television, and so was quite unprepared, those ghettos really shattered me. Yet I have known far worse slums in Asia. But Belfast is in affluent Europe and why should large areas of it be swarming with undernourished wild children and knee-deep in stinking litter, and strewn with broken glass glinting in hot sun under a blue sky—all on a summer's day. . . . So many bricked-up houses, reminding me of dead people with their eyes shut—some of them fine substantial buildings from which Protestants had had to flee in terror taking only their resentment with them. So many high brick, or corrugated iron, barricades between identical streets of little working-class homes, to prevent neighbours seeing and hearing each other, and so being provoked to hurt and kill each other. Sometimes, over the barricades, I could glimpse Union Jacks flying from upstairs windows. And I remembered a friend of mine in another part of the North—a retired naval officer—saying how much he resented the British flag being abused as a provocative sectarian symbol.

A filthy four- or five-year-old boy was playing all alone on a broken pavement with a length of stick; it was his gun and he was aiming at us. One would't even notice him in London or Dublin but in Belfast I wondered, 'How soon will he have the real thing?' Already, in his little mind, possession of a gun is equated with bravery and safety, with having the will and ability to defend his own territory against 'the Oranges'. Around the next corner two slightly older children were carefully placing cardboard cartons in the middle of the narrow street. 'Are these pretend bombs?' I asked, appalled. 'They might not be pretend,' replied Jim, driving onto the pavement to avoid one. Even more appalled, I said nothing. Jim looked at me and laughed. 'You'll get used to it!' he said. 'Almost certainly they are pretend. But hereabouts sensible people don't take chances.'

DERVLA MURPHY, *A Place Apart*, 1978

William wears a chunky sweater with red, white and blue stripes. He told me he was ten. I estimated nine and later found from the records that he was eight and a half. He told me that when he grew up he was going to join the Army, and hoped for a posting back to Belfast.

'The Army are needed here to keep the Catholics down. It was Bernadette's fault starting all this; she's a Fenian and should be burned to bits. All the Catholics should be killed or burned. They shoot peelers [policemen] and Protestants, but I'm in the Junior Orange Lodge and we know what to do with them.'

His friend, who was thirteen and looked eleven, was more specific.

'We have steel spars that we get from Metalwork in school; we sharpen them. We are keeping the ends sharp for Fenians. We are working on an idea so they can be fired out of a bow, and we practise on dummies.'

I asked whether he knew any Catholics.

'Some used to live at the end of our street. We never bothered one because she was only an old woman. They've left now. They go whining to the Corporation and pretend they've been threatened.'

Brendan, a stocky youngster, preferred to draw rather than talk. He had selected three chalks from the box—a white, a yellow and an orange. He drew three parallel bands of colour with bold strokes, enclosed them in white, and added a flagpole. Underneath he printed the letters 'The Flag of Ireland'.

'That's why we hate the soldiers,' he said proudly. 'They're British, but we Catholics are Irish, that's why. We wave an Irish flag at them. I've thrown stones at them often.'

'Who started all this?'

'The Protestants. They threw stones at the Civil Rights and started it. It was Paisley shouting at them. We need the Army to protect us from the

Protestants or they would burn us out. But we hate them. We burned a Union Jack once; that was great.

MORRIS FRASER, Children in Conflict, 1973

AMBROSE. I'm not having my photograph taken. Under the terms of the Emergency Provisions Act 1973, you need a certificate signed by a police officer no lower in rank than a Chief Inspector, before you can take a prisoner's photograph.

JACKIE. Is that right? Well, let me tell you something, mate. You're not sitting at no Civil Rights meeting now. Nor standing at a street corner. You're in a police station, arrested as a suspect terrorist, and as such you have no rights. Now keep your hands down by your side and look into this camera.

AMBROSE. I'm not doing it. (*As* JACKIE *positions the camera,* AMBROSE *covers his face with his hand.*)

JACKIE. Right! (*Puts the camera down.*) We'll see about that later on. Stand over by that desk. (AMBROSE *obeys.*) I'm going to take your fingerprints. (*Organises some items on the table.*) Give me your right hand. (AMBROSE *remains silent and motionless.*) I said, give me your right hand. (AMBROSE *shakes his head determinedly.* JACKIE *grabs his arm.* AMBROSE *pulls it back.*) Look, don't make this difficult for yourself. You can co-operate with me now, or I can call in half-a-dozen soldiers to physically take your prints. Which way do you want it done?

AMBROSE. I don't want to have my fingerprints taken. It's against the law.

JACKIE. You know quite a lot about the law.

AMBROSE. Enough to know that to have my photograph or fingerprints taken you need a Chief Inspector's certificate.

JACKIE. Is that so? Right. If that's the way you want to play it, fair enough. If you're going to act the smart Alec, just remember you have three long days and nights ahead of you. If you want to mess us about, just think what we can do to you over three days. (AMBROSE *remains silent.*) But then you seem to be a cocky character. Reckon you'll daddle through this, eh? Do you, Ambrose? (AMBROSE *shrugs his shoulders.*) Well, let me let you into a wee secret. We allowed you to run about too long. Now, we have you by the goolies. All our evidence collected. Signed, sealed and delivered. You'll not walk out of here this time. Now c'mon till I bring you to your cell. You'll have to get used to life in an eight-by-four box. We'll get your photo and prints later on. No hurry. In fact, Fogarty, there's no need to hurry anything anymore, where you're concerned. Let's go. (JACKIE *and* AMBROSE *go out into the main reception area.* KNOX, *by the radio, is discussing a point with* DAVY.) Sergeant, put this man in a cell, please.

MARTIN LYNCH, The Interrogation of Ambrose Fogarty, 1982

from *Letter from Ireland*

for Vincent Buckley

Black sacks flapping on street corners, stiff
  Drummers walk to the Republican plot.
Behind them women in black parade with
  Flags dipped slightly. At the sacred spot
  A sheltered man proclaims a speech— *We will not
Stop struggling until the British leave.
There will be no ceasefire. We give no relief.*

Black sacks on hedges, black sacks on doors.
  Black plastic rustling as black hearses pass.
Fertiliser bags tied to electricity poles
  Signal an anger at the ultimate impasse.
  Refuse sacks, strung and stuffed, have heads to match
Thatcher or Paisley, and across a bridge some hand
Has painted in white: *Remember Bobby Sands.*

Black sacks in the doorway, black sacks in the field,
  Black rifles uncovered on a Donegal strand.
Black border on photographs, black dresses for grief,
  Black berets on coffins, black bowlers and bands,
  Black bullet holes in hallways, black words of command.
Black taxis, black jackets, black bruise and contusion.
Black crepe on a letter box, the Royal Black Institution.

Death stalks the farms of south Tyrone,
  Ruffles its cold clothes and changes
Direction for Armagh, stopping to take home
  A soldier ambushed at greeting's range.
  Nobody seems to think it strange
When Death makes some mistake and takes
As well a girl near a farmyard gate.

SEÁN DUNNE, *The Sheltered Nest*, 1992

The unthinkable had happened. In just sixteen days, four hunger strikers had died. Many in the North had thought there would be concessions from the British after Sands, and most certainly after Hughes. McCreesh had told his family that the strike would be settled before his number was up. Now the men in the Maze could have no doubt that the fast meant death, not brinksmanship. I would have thought, therefore, that there would be just one or two men still willing to sign on, to challenge Mrs Thatcher to a duel. But there weren't one or two—there were eighty. After O'Hara's death, it became apparent that with two-week intervals between fasters, Mrs Thatcher's common criminals could be dying in the Maze for the rest of 1981 and well into 1982. Within days of the deaths of Hughes, McCreesh, and O'Hara, three Republicans had joined the fast to replace them, and once again, there were four prisoners refusing food.

JOHN CONROY, *War as a Way of Life*, 1988

Northern Ireland became world famous during the 1970s as a battle front. For most commentators, the events preceding the outbreak of the Provisional Irish Republican Army's military campaign in 1970 have been relevant mainly as an explanation for the violence of the last two decades. The civil rights movement, therefore, has been seen as a prelude to the violence. But during most of its history Northern Ireland was at peace; even now, for most of the time, the vast majority of Northern Ireland people live together in amity and with a warmth of neighbourliness not to be found in many other places. Northern Ireland is gripped by an unresolved conflict which has its origins further back in history than the creation of the state; but it is wrong to ignore everything in that history except the conflict. The civil rights movement marked the transition from a period of peace to a renewal of the conflict and it has to be seen in the light of the events of the 1970s and 1980s. But it also has to be seen as a consequence of the 1960s and as a product of events that took place during a time of rapid, but peaceful, change. To revisit Northern Ireland in the 1960s is to enter a lost world in which most of the political landmarks are different and different assumptions and aspirations underpin politics. In the 1990s we can see why the society was liable to be torn apart in the 1970s, but the 1960s lacked that foreknowledge and peace seemed secure enough for new departures and new experiments. The civil rights movement was one of these new departures.

BOB PURDIE, *Politics in the Streets*, 1990

from *Whatever You Say, Say Nothing*

This morning from a dewy motorway
I saw the new camp for the internees:
A bomb had left a crater of fresh clay
In the roadside, and over in the trees

Machine-gun posts defined a real stockade.
There was that white mist you get on a low ground
And it was déjà-vu, some film made
Of Stalag 17, a bad dream with no sound.

Is there a life before death? That's chalked up
In Ballymurphy. Competence with pain,
Coherent miseries, a bite and sup,
We hug our little destiny again.

SEAMUS HEANEY, *North*, 1975

The nagging question remains: to what extent does Collins's campaign of
subversion set a moral precedent for the contemporary IRA? The goal—a
united republican Ireland—remains the same, and the political and legal
ethos of Northern Ireland in the Sixties was in many ways as repressive and
even more sectarian than that of Dublin Castle fifty years before. The Special
Powers Act 1922, from which the anti-Nationalist authoritarianism of the civil
authorities in Northern Ireland drew its legitimacy, was a direct descendant
of the Defence of the Realm Regulations, via the Restoration of Order in
Ireland Regulations that had briefly superseded them. The beginning of the
campaign of violence in 1969, as in 1919, lacked explicit political legitimacy;
it was essentially a reaction to state violence and in turn provoked extreme
police and army responses.

Even in those early days of the Troubles, however, the differences were
more marked than the similarities. Repression emanated from the Unionist
sub-state, not from the Westminster establishment. Indeed, the political
classes in London were initially not unsympathetic to the need for reform.
Even in the terrible years of 1969–71, the Army's conduct in Northern
Ireland, though stupid and sometimes brutal, never approached the barbar-
ity of the auxiliaries and the Black and Tans. Nor did officers enjoy such
powers of civilian courts-martial as were assiduously deployed between 1916
and 1921.

Collins's methods were never as savage as those of the contemporary IRA,
and he was supported across the whole of Catholic nationalist Ireland rather
than in a few working-class communities. After the campaign of violence had
got under way, Collins's party was able to secure widespread electoral support
in the local government elections of early 1920, gaining control of 72 out of
127 town councils in the municipal elections in January and also doing well
in the rural plebiscite that followed. The elections held in 1921 under the Government of Ireland Act confirmed this trend. In contrast, the modern Provisional Sinn Fein has always had to grub for support, picking up little outside
its own working-class bastions unless the British Government played into its
hands, as with the mishandling of the hunger strikes in 1981. Collins's Sinn
Fein obliterated Redmond's brand of constitutional Nationalism, but it has
been John Hume's commitment to peaceful change that has made him the
hero of Ireland's latest war.

Above all, and unlike the contemporary IRA, Collins knew when to stop.

Three years into the present conflict, the IRA rejected Edward Heath's power-sharing initiative. One can easily guess what Collins would have had to say about such reckless, bloody nonsense. Criticism of Jordan's film as an apologia for the IRA is particularly foolish when its final, riveting scenes are taken into account, with Collins in the uniform of his new state army seeking to impose an impeccably democratic compromise on De Valera's ideological purists, who are prepared to kill fellow Irish men and women in the pursuit of an already rejected and always unattainable goal. The movie is a celebration of political flexibility. True compromise requires more courage than unyielding certainty and it is this rarely celebrated truth that Jordan's movie has captured.

Collins's early death in a trap sprung by anti-Treaty forces deprived Ireland of its leader, and paved the way for eventual domination by Eamon De Valera. Quite soon after Collins's death, this wily careerist found himself able to accept just those Treaty constraints which he had earlier allowed to precipitate the country into civil war. We remained in thrall to this man's arid, scholastic nationalism for over fifty years, until his death in 1975, just two years after Ireland's entry into the European Community. It was only at this point that Collins's legacy of a politically and culturally confident Ireland could be remembered and realised, though even then it remained qualified and undermined by the conflict in the North. The Republic of Ireland is at last close to the kind of country for which Collins might have hoped: the nation now ready to help Britain to solve its Irish problem, created in its present form when it imposed Partition on Collins as the price of what turned out to be a temporary peace.

CONOR GEARTY, Diary, *London Review of Books*, 28 November 1996

For many citizens it is easy to forget how strange life is in the streets of Belfast. It sometimes needs an unusual event or the reactions of an outsider to remind them. An English friend was staying with me one summer. She went out to a bakery to buy something and came back in a state of excitement. What had happened? While she was in the shop an Army Land-Rover pulled up outside and the soldiers deployed themselves around the shop, taking cover where they could. My friend imagined that she had just got herself into a gun battle, but must have been relieved when one of the soldiers entered the shop and ordered a selection of buns for the squad's lunch.

Later we drove up the Antrim Coast Road so that I could show her the beauties and wonders of Northern Ireland. We stopped for a while in Bally-castle, which she found, I think, a charming but fairly ordinary little town. Now it was my turn to be shocked. I had not left Belfast for a couple of years, and found the ambience of Ballycastle very alien indeed: empty cars were parked all down the main streets, soldiers and security guards were nowhere to be seen. The feeling was of that sense of freedom you get when something you had not realised was there is suddenly removed.

Even dramatic incidents do not produce the expected response. A friend of a friend was walking in the centre of Belfast one day when there was a burst of gunfire close by. Everyone in the street scattered. He dived into a pub and threw himself on the floor. The other patrons were also on the floor, but he was somewhat alarmed to see them all staring intently in the same direction. They were watching a video film of *Superman* and had not taken their eyes off it even as they were taking evasive action.

ROBERT JOHNSTONE, Images of Belfast, 1983

The North's towns and villages seem unnaturally subdued. There are so few cars, so many lines of concrete-filled barrels down the main streets to prevent parking near shops, so few people about and such grim police barracks—fortified, inside giant wire cages, against bombs and machine-guns. These jolt one, in prim-looking little towns, after cycling for hours through tranquil countryside. We are used to thinking of the village police-station or gardai-barracks as a place into which anyone can wander at any hour, without even knocking, for advice and sympathy about a lost cat or a stolen bicycle. It is very much part of our way of life that the police should be acceptable and accessible, not driven to defend themselves from the public like an army of occupation. Until the policing problem has been solved, how can normality be restored anywhere in Northern Ireland?

DERVLA MURPHY, A Place Apart, 1978

Belfast, . . . seemed to have gone berserk. On the news we heard that there were gunfights raging in the Falls, the Markets, Ardoyne, Andersonstown and New Lodge Road. There were many dead. Protestant crowds had joined in the fighting, backing the army up. Whole streets were burning and thousands of refugees began to flee to the South. The twenty-four hours after internment were the bloodiest Northern Ireland had known for decades.

EAMONN McCANN, War and an Irish Town, 1974

As I rode up to the fire, I passed a group of soldiers and two Saracens, parked in a dark empty lot next to the Co-op grocery, ready to spring from their position if Protestants invaded Catholic turf from Ainsworth Avenue or Mayo Street. A few hundred yards up the road, a dozen policemen in flak jackets, some with plastic bullet guns, stood on the Catholic side of the

Springfield, opposite the Woodvale fire, keeping their distance and their eyes on the celebrants.

I rode over to the fire from the Catholic side of the road, and I stood on the side nearest the police. On the other side of the flames, firemen were hosing down the roofs of two abandoned houses which had been ignited by sparks that leapt up from the street. Even as they sprayed the roofs, teenagers were throwing more wood on the fire. The firemen made no move to turn their hoses on the cause of their troubles; if they had, they would have been overwhelmed by the mob. The fire service departed not long after I arrived, and just a few minutes later, sparks from the fire flew back to the sprayed houses, and one roof's underside spurted flame all over again.

I took out my camera and began taking pictures. A girl, about sixteen years old, turned and screamed.

'He's a Taig!' she shouted.

I lowered my camera immediately. Given that night, that place, and those passions, it was a killing accusation. I had no idea how the girl reached her conclusion, unless perhaps she assumed I was Catholic because I had come over from that side of the road. She was drunk, bold, and very loud. A small group turned away from the fire to examine me, and others turned when they saw the beginnings of a new commotion. My accuser stepped forward, clutching a can of beer.

'Are you a Taig?' she asked.

'I'm an American,' I said. The answer had always worked in the past.

'American Catholic or American Protestant?'

'Just American.'

'American what?' she demanded. 'Catholic or Protestant?'

I was raised a Catholic, but by 1980 I hadn't practised for many years. I disagreed with many of the Church's teachings. I had no great fondness for the pope. In short, I didn't think I qualified as Catholic. I was being offered an opportunity many believers would have envied, a chance to stand up for the faith in the face of persecution. I was not enthusiastic. I was scared by the crowd and by the mean spirit I had seen on the Shankill, embarrassed by my uncertainty, and angry that a mob of drunken arsonists, led by a teenage girl, threatened to get the best of me.

I have since decided that I should have claimed Catholicism and solidarity in one breath, admitting that I had been raised a Catholic, but hastily adding that I worked for a living just as the people stoking the fire did, that I ate the same food, that I lived in the same sort of house, that in fact the only difference between us was that I didn't go to a different church than the one that they didn't go to. Belfast Protestants and Catholics would do well to receive strong doses of reality to dispel their myths about each other, and my claims of practicing non-Catholicism would have been a small contribution.

Instead, I lied. I claimed I was a Jew. It was probably one of the few times in the recent history of Europe that someone has claimed to be a Jew in order to avoid religious persecution.

JOHN CONROY, *War as a Way of Life*, 1988

Wounds

Here are two pictures from my father's head—
I have kept them like secrets until now:
First, the Ulster Division at the Somme
Going over the top with 'Fuck the Pope!'
'No Surrender!': a boy about to die,
Screaming 'Give 'em one for the Shankill!'
'Wilder than Gurkhas' were my father's words
Of admiration and bewilderment.
Next comes the London-Scottish padre
Resettling kilts with his swagger-stick,
With a stylish backhand and a prayer.
Over a landscape of dead buttocks
My father followed him for fifty years.
At last, a belated casualty,
He said—lead traces flaring till they hurt—
'I am dying for King and Country, slowly.'
I touched his hand, his thin head I touched.

Now, with military honours of a kind,
With his badges, his medals like rainbows,
His spinning compass, I bury beside him
Three teenage soldiers, bellies full of
Bullets and Irish beer, their flies undone.
A packet of Woodbines I throw in,
A lucifer, the Sacred Heart of Jesus
Paralysed as heavy guns put out
the night-light in a nursery for ever;
Also a bus-conductor's uniform—
He collapsed beside his carpet-slippers
Without a murmur, shot through the head
By a shivering boy who wandered in
Before they could turn the television down
Or tidy away the supper dishes.
To the children, to a bewildered wife,
I think 'Sorry Missus' was what he said.

MICHAEL LONGLEY, *An Exploded View*, 1973

Doyle was a servant and officer of the British Crown, the British Government, in Ireland. He sat in judgement on IRA suspects. He had power and wielded authority. He was a living symbol of the Crown and therefore an enemy of the rebels, the IRA, and they killed him for it. For in Northern Ireland power, authority and legitimacy were in murderous dispute.

Judge Doyle was also the enemy within. He was a Catholic on a Protestant/Unionist judicial bench which asserted the authority of the British Government. He blurred the lines of an ancient struggle but made himself an easy 'stiff' (murder victim) by his regular attendance at Mass at St Brigid's. During the week the Judge was escorted everywhere by armed RUC body-guards and was invulnerable. But at weekends, perhaps tired of the oppres-sive security, he shed his judge's robes, dismissed his guards and reverted to domestic routine amidst the Victorian mansions of the Malone Road. He must have thought he was safe; he must have thought the Malone Road with neat gardens, Mercedes cars and money was immune from the Troubles. He was wrong. Someone in the congregation at St Brigid's had recognized him and told the IRA, and they came on the right Sunday to kill him.

There was an awful Irish intimacy about his death, murdered at Mass in front of the congregation, fingered by someone who was part of that Catholic congregation. The IRA did not need to travel to kill Doyle. Their supporters were already there in St Brigid's, also dressed in suits and Sunday best on the Malone Road, hidden amongst the smiling schoolgirl choir or walking back down the aisle slyly staring after Holy Communion. I wondered what were the passions that allowed, perhaps compelled, someone to kill in that way in that place.

KEVIN TOOLIS, *Rebel Hearts*, 1995

My mother worked in a garments factory and she was very active in union activities there. I won't say that religion took second place to politics for her, but certainly politics were a practical affirmation and extension of her religious belief. She influenced me towards Republicanism in teaching me the need for social change and social development. She wasn't exactly a crusader, but she had a great pride and dignity about her which she instilled in her family. Like many Catholics when the troubles began, she saw how the police and then later the Army always seemed to be on the side of the Protestants.

I myself witnessed a lot of the street riots and fights when I was only a child: and another great influence was television. We saw civil rights marches in the USA, we saw and heard men like Martin Luther King, and we saw that ordinary people if they banded together had a great strength. The State learned the same lesson too: and so they attacked many of the marches, which they genuinely believed were threatening the stability of the State. One of the slogans of the protestors when they marched was 'One Man, One Vote'. I can't help thinking that if the authorities had had the sense to address that demand and promise to satisfy it, a great part of the problem would have gone away. But instead of trying to defuse the situation by doing that, they preferred to try and suppress the people who were making the reasonable demand. The Loyalist ethos was in that well-known phrase used by Lord Craigavon: he said Ulster was a Protestant state for a Protestant people.

Besides being provocative and inflammatory, the remark wasn't true. Ulster was only a section of the island of Ireland which belonged to all the Irish people, Protestant and Catholic. So the Catholics weren't simply trouble-makers: they were only trouble-makers to the Protestants who were oppressing them, who then said they wouldn't do anything to make conditions better until the violence ceased. It's always puzzling that those who want to retain power and privilege aren't more subtle in the way they go about it, isn't it?

Joe Austin, quoted in Tony Parker, *May The Lord in His Mercy Be Kind to Belfast*, 1993

It makes me angry when I see slogans painted on the walls in streets saying 'Brits out'. It's the unthinkingness of it that annoys me so much. Two-thirds of the population of Northern Ireland are British, so what on earth does some idiot with a spraycan mean by 'Brits out'? That's the sort of trivialisation Nationalists and Republicans indulge in that upsets me. It's not a matter for slogans, it's how people live together: they should do it and they could do it, in peace and with respect for each other. I honestly don't believe the troubles in the north of Ireland are the responsibility of anyone except the Nationalists and the Republicans. They simply won't accept the historical inevitability of the situation, the situation of the north of Ireland being British and staying British, and its people preferring to die rather than be taken over by the Republic. Surely they can see that, surely it can be accepted as fact, and a way be found for us all to live together as civilised people? Instead of talk of 'Brits out', it's the Nationalists and Republicans who should go out. If they don't like living here under the British Government, if they won't accept it and don't want it, then they should go peaceably down to the south, and leave the north to us.

Margaret Anderson, quoted in Tony Parker, *May The Lord in His Mercy Be Kind to Belfast*, 1993

In the early Seventies I felt Belfast was rather like the Wild West. My father was making a delivery to the Autolite factory, between Finaghy and Andersonstown, when someone warned him to wait before he left. On the factory's long drive to Finaghy Road North lads were hijacking the cars of workers going home. When supplies were needed for Andersonstown, a local would come down to accompany the driver of the van to make sure he got through. Like riding shotgun. My father told how he had been able to drive from the centre of Belfast to Finaghy in record time by following an Army personnel carrier all the way, speeding through red lights and up the wrong side of the road.

But the incidents that remain most vivid are big horror stories that stand out from all the little horror stories. There was McGurk's Bar on 4 December 1971. A loyalist bomb destroyed the Catholic pub on North Queen Street, killing fifteen men, women and children. Jonathan Bardon, in *Belfast: an illustrated history*, describes the aftermath:

... by the light of arc-lamps surgeons treated the injured in the open; gas escaping from fractured pipes flamed in the rubble as all through the night the dead and mutilated were uncovered brick by brick; and rescue operations were hampered as nearby the army came under fire and rival crowds fought in the darkness.

I was in Derry during Bloody Sunday, 30 January 1972, when British paratroopers shot thirteen people after a march in the Bogside, and I was back in Belfast to see on television what looked like a reprisal, the bombing of the Abercorn restaurant on 4 March. Four people were killed and around 150 injured. It was a story one could not forget: a big restaurant, crowded with Saturday shoppers, the two girls sitting at a table under which was the bomb, the three people who lost both legs, the girl who lost both legs and an arm. And the television pictures of ambulance men in Cornmarket helping the injured out of the rubble, the woman whose head was streaming with blood.

ROBERT JOHNSTONE, *Images of Belfast*, 1983

He stands where he is, simply looking at his house, at his people, at the sycamores, at the last fifty years. Time stands still. The little boy comes running back from the hayshed. Trotting rather. His head down and sideways as if he were playing ponies. He pulls, pulling a bellrope, at his granda's jacket. He says: Granda, there's a funny man in the hayshed.

Granda already knows. The man has stepped out into the open. He has a shotgun. He wears a felt-brimmed hat and a gasmask. The mask has been slashed at the mouth for the sake of sound but the effect still is as if somebody with laryngitis were trying to talk through tissue paper and a comb. He says: Freeze. Everybody freeze.

As in the best or the worst gangster films except that the hoodlums talk and act cool and this fellow seems to be nervous: All of you freeze.

Granda says: Including the children?

He picks the boy up in his arms. The man advances, pointing the shotgun. The wheezes say, almost as if the creator of the wheezes had a cleft palate: One false step. Into the house. All of you. We're all inside.

BENEDICT KIELY, *Proxopera*, 1977

An Indian swami, swaddled in orange cloth, was walking up the Springfield Road, trailed by eight followers. I stopped one of them, a young man with a beard, and he gave me a flier that identified the orange man as Swami Vishnu Devananda. The swami was a Canadian citizen, the paper said, best known for dropping peace leaflets over the Suez Canal in 1971, the same year that he and Peter Sellers demonstrated for peace in Belfast. The bearded follower told me that the group planned to walk through both Catholic and Protestant neighborhoods that day, and he invited me to come to City Hall at 3:00, where the swami and his disciples were going to stand on their heads for an hour for peace.

JOHN CONROY, *War as a Way of Life*, 1988

Some resolution, if not solution, of the present Troubles of Ulster there must eventually be, but it is not yet in sight. It has been an extraordinary experience to live through a period so eventful, when so many shattering changes have taken place, and yet so little has changed fundamentally. The sequence of events has been bewildering, difficult indeed to remember: I doubt if many Ulstermen could without prompting give an accurate chronological account of even the major happenings. The fall of Terence O'Neill; the fall of James Chichester-Clarke; the fall of Brian Faulkner; the fall of Stormont; Sunningdale; the Assembly; the Convention; William Whitelaw; Merlyn Rees; Roy Mason. The rise of the IRA and the splits between Provisional IRA, Official IRA, and the IRSP; the rise of the UDA and the splits between conflicting paramilitary bodies—UDA, UVF, UFF, and a dozen more. The Battle of the Bogside, and Free Derry corner; the burning of Bombay Street, and Farringdon Gardens; the introduction, and the abandonment, of detention without trial; the introduction, and the abandonment, of special status for 'political' prisoners; Bloody Sunday in Derry, Bloody Friday in Belfast. The loyalist bombing of water and electrical installations; the republican bombing of pubs, shops, offices, homes; the selective assassinations, the random sectarian murders; rent strike; Ulster Workers' Council strike; Action Council strike; squatting, intimidation, knee-capping; torture as revolting as any in history. Constant apprehension, heightened at times to immediate fear, and for some people, to moments of utter terror. Out of the Easter Rising, wrote Yeats, a terrible beauty was born. No terrible beauty has been born, or is likely to be born, out of the Troubles of Ulster.

Yet the great majority of the people of Ulster are decent, kindly, and—in their personal relations as individuals—tolerant. They try, as best they may, to carry on a cheerful social and family life despite the horrors around them, and for the most part they succeed. Traffic accidents still cause more deaths and injuries each year than do the Troubles. Where do the assassins and the bombers come from? They are in our midst, and some of them may well be unsuspected acquaintances. Of those charged and convicted, proved guilty beyond any remote possibility of doubt, who by way of confirmation refuse to recognise the Court or shout 'up the UDA!', many have been modest individuals whose friends and families would have sworn them innocent. It is perhaps true that the resurgence of both republican and loyalist paramilitaries in 1969 arose from fear, and that both were (in those early days) primarily defensive in intention. I say 'perhaps', for there is on each side a thread of fanaticism leading back to the troubles of earlier generations. It is demonstrably untrue, though some Englishmen still believe it, that the recourse to violence in Ulster springs directly from high unemployment, bad housing, and low earnings. Other parts of the British Isles, including Eire, have conditions as bad or worse. So long ago as 1836, a shrewd observer, quoted by Dr A. T. Q. Stewart, pointed out that the worst violence occurred, not as one might expect, in the poorest parts of Ireland, where economic conditions were harsh, but in the fertile and more affluent regions. Of the bigots, fanatics, and gunmen on both sides, many come from middle-class homes and comfortable surroundings. By no means all are ill-educated: the distorted idealism of the young intellectual, sometimes a revolutionary of the left, sometimes a reactionary of the right, provides the paramilitary armies with more, and more dangerous, recruits than the thick-headed vandalism of the back streets. It it also untrue, though some Irishmen (and especially middle-class Dubliners) still believe it, that this is a war of national liberation, heroic freedom fighters for the national cause challenging a régime of brutality and oppression.

C. E. B. BRETT, *Long Shadows Cast Before*, 1978

Hamlet

As usual, the clock in The Clock Bar was a good few minutes fast:
A fiction no one really bothered to maintain, unlike the story
The comrade on my left was telling, which no one knew for
  certain truth:
Back in 1922 a sergeant, I forget his name, was shot outside the
  National Bank . . .
Ah yes, what year was it that they knocked it down? Yet, its
  memory's as fresh
As the inky smell of new pound notes—which interferes with the
  beer-and-whiskey

Tang of now, like two dogs meeting in the revolutionary 69 of a
    long sniff,
Or cattle jostling shit-stained flanks in the Pound. For *pound, as*
    some wag
Interrupted, was an off-shoot of the Falls, from the Irish, *fál*, a
    hedge;
Hence, *any kind of enclosed thing*, its twigs and branches
    commemorated
By the soldiers' drab and olive camouflage, as they try to melt
Into a brick wall; red coats might be better, after all. *At any rate,*
This sergeant's number came up; not a winning one. The bullet had his
    name on it.
Though Sergeant X, as we'll call him, doesn't really feature in
    the story:
The nub of it is, *This tin can which was heard that night, trundling*
    down
From the bank, down Balaklava Street. Which thousands heard, and no
    one ever
Saw. Which was heard for years, any night that trouble might be
Round the corner . . . and when it skittered to a halt, you knew
That someone else had snuffed it: a name drifting like an
    afterthought,
A scribbled wisp of smoke you try and grasp, as it becomes
    diminuendo, then
Vanishes. For *fál* is also *frontier, boundary*, as in *the undiscovered*
    country
From whose bourne no traveller returns, the illegible, thorny hedge of
    time itself—
Heartstopping moments, measured not by the pulse of a wristwatch,
    nor
The archaic anarchists' alarm-clock, but a mercury tilt device
Which 'only connects' on any given bump on the road. So, by
    this wingèd messenger
The promise 'to pay the bearer' is fulfilled:

As someone buys another round, an Allied Irish Banks £10 note
    drowns in
The slops of the counter; a Guinness stain blooms on the artist's
    impression
Of the sinking of the *Girona*; a tiny foam hisses round the
    salamander brooch
Dredged up to show how love and money endure, beyond death
    and the Armada,
Like the bomb-disposal expert in his suit of salamander-cloth.

Shielded against the blast of time by a strangely mediaeval visor,
He's been outmoded by this jerky robot whose various
    attachments include
A large hook for turning over corpses that may be booby-trapped;
But I still have this picture of his hands held up to avert the
    future
In a final act of *No surrender*, as, twisting through the murky
    fathoms
Of what might have been, he is washed ashore as pearl and coral.

This *strange eruption to our state* is seen in other versions of the Falls:
A no-go area, a ghetto, a demolition zone. For the ghost, as it turns
    out—
All this according to your man, and I can well believe it—this tin
    ghost,
Since the streets it haunted were abolished, was never heard again.
The sleeve of Raglan Street has been unravelled; the helmet of
    Balaklava
Is torn away from the mouth. The dim glow of Garnet has gone out,
And with it, all but the memory of where I lived. I, too, heard
    the ghost:
A roulette trickle, or the hesitant annunciation of a downpour,
    ricocheting
Off the window; a goods train shunting distantly into a siding,
Then groaning to a halt; the rainy cries of children after dusk.
For the voice from the grave reverberates in others' mouths, as
    the sails
Of the whitethorn hedge swell up in a little breeze, and tremble
Like the spiral blossom of Andromeda: so suddenly are shrouds
    and branches
Hung with street-lights, celebrating all that's lost, as fields are
    reclaimed
By the Starry Plough. So we name the constellations, to put a shape
On what was there; so, the storyteller picks his way between the
    isolated stars.

But, *Was it really like that?* And, *Is the story true?*
You might as well tear off the iron mask, and find that no one,
    after all,
Is there: nothing but a cry, a summons, clanking out from the smoke
Of demolition. Like some son looking for his father, or the father
    for his son,
We try to piece together the exploded fragments. Let these
    broken spars
Stand for the Armada and its proud full sails, for even if

The clock is put to rights, everyone will still believe it's fast:
The barman's shouts of *time* will be ignored in any case, since
  time
Is conversation; it is the hedge that flits incessantly into the
  present,
As words blossom from the speakers' mouths, and the flotilla
  returns to harbour,
Long after hours.

CIARAN CARSON, *Belfast Confetti*, 1989

The War Against the Past

Where I came from, Edwardian days lasted until 1939.

BENEDICT KIELY, 'Make Straight for the Shore'

It could be truly said that the old order, and the old way of life, finally came to an end in Drumlahan in 1935. For once the loy ceased to be regarded as a credible agricultural implement, life in that district was never the same again.

CHARLES O'BEIRNE, *The Good People*

... there have indeed been many changes, and it almost looks as if during the years 1954 and 1955 we had caught Ireland at that historic moment when it was just beginning to leap over a century and a half and catch up with another five.

HEINRICH BÖLL, *Irish Journal*

The Siege of Mullingar

At the Fleadh Cheoil in Mullingar
There were two sounds, the breaking
Of glass, and the background pulse
Of music. Young girls roamed
The streets with eager faces,
Shoving for men. Bottles in
Hand, they rowed out a song:
Puritan Ireland's dead and gone,
A myth of O'Connor and Ó Faoláin.

In the early morning the lovers
Lay on both sides of the canal
Listening on Sony transistors
To the agony of Pope John.
Yet it didn't seem strange or blasphemous,
This ground bass of death and

Resurrection, as we strolled along:
Puritan Ireland's dead and gone,
A myth of O'Connor and Ó Faoláin.

Further on, breasting the wind
Waves of the deserted grain harbour,
A silent pair, a cob and his pen,
Most nobly linked. Everything then
In our casual morning vision
Seemed to flow in one direction,
Lines simple as a song:
Puritan Ireland's dead and gone,
A myth of O'Connor and Ó Faoláin.

JOHN MONTAGUE, *The Rough Field*, 1972

Most of the new housing estates through the country are really National Modernism, a style which is in full agreement with the modern use of structure, but is a growth of, and not a break with tradition, and is insistent in claiming that architecture is a visual art, and not simply the intellectual working out of a problem, structural, economic, or political. But much of our Ulster National Modernism, as in other countries, finds it hard to hold the right balance between the National and the Modern. When this synthesis has been satisfactorily achieved we should undoubtedly have a very beautiful country, for we start with the advantage of a good native tradition, which still looks at us imploringly across the centuries for recognition, through the defilements of pebbledash, rusting corrugated-iron roofs, and much insensitive use of colour and texture. But more than once Ulstermen have been innovators, and may be so again in a generation which is calling out for noble and homely qualities in its modern architectural movement.

Ulster architecture bears the same relationship to that of England as a homespun tweed bears to serge, or a wholemeal wheaten loaf to white bread. It is a beautiful architecture, nevertheless, and highly suitable to a western windswept outpost of Europe, for when we stand on Ulster cliffs and face the sunset we are on what for centuries was the lip of the world.

DENIS O'D. HANNA, 'Architecture in Ulster', *The Arts in Ulster*, 1951

Captain Olley's Airways are as good as, if not better than, most of the air services of the world. It is not his fault that the little Irish company which took toll of him should have painted a name in Irish on the wing: *Aer Lingus*. Of course there is no word for Airways in Irish, there never was; but that is no reason why the attempt to make a name should make a mistake. The word *lingus* occurs only in Latin as a part of a medical term of which the less said the better. But even the English machine had to suffer from the fatuity of the country and the foolery of the patriots whose patriotism largely consists in an attempt to revive an old language by turning it into an unintelligible new. I was at the inauguration ceremony of the new Airways from Baldonnell to Croydon. The machine had to be named and blessed. I like the idea of blessing a machine. It gives it a kind of soul. This may have caused it to take off late on inauguration morn; but more likely unpunctuality was due to a genial fussy fellow, who never flew in his life, going about in Gaelic League breeches (horsey pattern for riding a bicycle), explaining with a bemused smirk that Olley's Airways were now Gaelic. They were touched down on Irish earth.

OLIVER ST JOHN GOGARTY, *Going Native*, 1941

One of the minor justifications of our successful Revolution is that from 1922 we have minted an Irish coinage of the same denominations as the English, but of a different design.

The new Irish Government set up a Commission to select this new design, which was open to world competition. W. B. Yeats, the poet, was a member of the Commission. He was also a great admirer of the meritricious Balkan sculptor, Maestrovic. The designs came anonymously before the Commissioners, and Yeats at once spotted a 'hen and chickens' in one of the series which reminded him of Maestrovic's pseudo-Byzantine stylization. Yeats therefore persuaded his fellow members to accept the hen and chickens penny. The result was that, by a curious accident, we have what is probably the most beautiful coinage in modern Europe.

The designer of these Irish coins was, of course, not the Balkan sculptor, but a Yorkshireman named Metcalfe. He also designed the Egyptian coins, but there he was too closely restricted by Mahommedan tradition. For the Irish coins he had, so far as I know, an entirely free hand; and he used it to our great advantage. The obverse of all the coins represents Brian Boru's harp. It is the various reverses that are of sculptural interest.

The designs of these reverses are all zoomorphic, as befits what is or ought to be a mainly rural community whose business is agriculture and its recreation sport. The largest silver coin, corresponding in size and value to the English half-crown, bears a realistic representation of an Irish thoroughbred horse. The two-shilling piece has a leaping salmon. The penny, as I have already mentioned, has a decidedly stylized hen and chickens, the halfpenny a pig and bonnhams, the farthing a very prettily contrived woodcock in flight. The threepenny piece has a hare, and the sixpence an Irish wolfhound. The threepence and the sixpence are of white nickel—an unsatisfactory metal compared with silver or bronze.

All these coins are excellent in design and composition; and their various degrees of naturalism and stylization by no means detract from the unity of the series as a whole. But I have not mentioned the high-light of our coinage. This is the shilling.

The reverse of the shilling bears the figure of a bull. It is not quite a naturalistic bull, yet it is not very noticeably stylized. One might say that it is an ideal bull. The design, maintaining its originality, harks back to ancient Greece—to, I think, a silver coin of Thurium in the fifth century BC, and to another bull on a gold stater of Philip of Macedone.

It is appropriate that our best coin should be a bull. Ireland might almost be called bull-ridden. We have already glanced at those beef-bones of contention that were the Red Bull of Ulster. Later came the Papal Bull of English Adrian, the very thought of which is a red rag to an Irishman. And beside these there is the notorious Irish Bull—'A lot of underhand work is afoot,' said one of our ablest Ministers in the Dail the other day. Indeed, temperamentally Ireland may be likened to a china-shop in which red coat-tails are madly waved. And now to triumph over them all comes this noble and lovely silver bull on our shilling pieces.

                                        GEOFFREY TAYLOR, *The Emerald Isle*, 1952

The language revival movement has been well aware of the need to make Gaelic, once again, an adequate instrument for representing the world. It has made it capable of rendering the Treaty of Rome, teaching chemistry, and discussing aesthetics in a contemporary manner. There is probably a Department of Education manual that supplies Gaelic names for all the parts of a car. But virtually none of this has impinged on the Gaeltacht. The language movement has been largely an urban—and principally a Dublin—phenomenon, and it has not concerned itself with supplying the Gaeltacht's needs. Thus, the 'new Gaelic' of the language revival has seemed for Gaeltacht people, by and large, a strangers' language. For this reason, most Gaeltacht schoolteachers shy away from it in the classroom. Just as they would be embarrassed to speak it at home or to their neighbours, they would be embarrassed to teach it to the children with whom they share a common *native* language of impoverished Gaelic mixed with English.

                                        DESMOND FENNELL, *Heresy*, 1993

As with the fields and paths, so with the language; there are ominous signs of disuse and decay. Irish, the irreplaceable distillate of over two thousand years' experience of this country, which has been poured down the drains in the rest of Ireland but which was carried unspilt even through the famine century in those few little cups, the western *Gaeltachtaí* of Aran, Connemara and parts of Donegal and Kerry, is now evaporating even here (as if a word or two disappears every day, the name of a field becomes unintelligible overnight, an old saying decides that its wisdom or foolishness is henceforth inexpressible), while what remains is splashed with the torrents of English. Many in Aran, as elsewhere, stake heavily on the future of Irish (and it is an awesome choice for parents to entrust their children's mental development, or a writer a life's work, to an endangered language), but the cruel twists of history have put the survival of Irish in the hands of English; at least as essential as the dedication of Irish speakers would be a tolerance, indeed a positive welcoming, among English speakers, of cultural diversity, an awakening to the sanity of differences—and such wisdom is contrary to the stupefying mainstreams of our time. However, at present Irish is a vigorous reality in Aran, and is now as it has been for over a century one of the reasons for the outside world's fascination with this bare little place.

TIM ROBINSON, *Stones of Aran: Pilgrimage*, 1986

The Language Issue

I place my hope on the water
in this little boat
of the language, the way a body might put
an infant

in a basket of intertwined
iris leaves,
its underside proofed
with bitumen and pitch

then set the whole thing down amidst
the sedge
and bulrushes by the edge
of a river

only to have it borne hither and thither,
not knowing where it might end up;
in the lap, perhaps,
of some Pharaoh's daughter.

NUALA NÍ DHOMHNAILL, *Pharaoh's Daughter*, 1990,
trans. Paul Muldoon

Suddenly the war was over. Britain had to be rebuilt. The countryside emptied towards London and Luton. The boat trains were full and talk was of never-ending overtime. After weeks in England, once easy gentle manners, set free from the narrow rule of church and custom, grew loud, uncertain, coarse.

At home a vaguely worried church joined a dying language to declare that learning Irish would help to keep much foreign corrupting influence out. Red Algier tractors with long steering columns and the sound of low-flying airplanes—they were said to have the original Messerschmitt engine—started to replace the horse and cart. A secondary school was opened by the Brothers in the town. Race memories of hedge schools and the poor scholar were stirred, as boys, like uncertain flocks of birds on bicycles, came long distances from the villages and outlying farms to grapple with calculus and George Gordon and the delta of the River Plate.

JOHN MCGAHERN, 'Oldfashioned', 1985

New democratic Ireland no longer denounces the big house, but seems to marvel at it. Why fight to maintain life in a draughty barrack, in a demesne shorn of most of its other land, a demesne in which one can hardly keep down the thistles, far from neighbours, golf links, tennis clubs, cinemas, buses, railways, shops? 'What do you *do* all day? Isn't it very lonely? Do servants stay with you? Can you keep warm in winter? Isn't it very ghostly? How do you do your shopping?'

ELIZABETH BOWEN, 'The Big House,' in *Collected Impressions*, 1942

Driving South

Driving South, we pass through Cavan,
lakeside orchards in first bloom,
hawthorn with a surplice whiteness,
binding the small holdings of Monaghan.

A changing rural pattern means clack
of tractor for horse, sentinel shape
of silo, hum of milking machine:
the same from Ulster to the Ukraine.

Only a sentimentalist would wish
to see such degradation again:
heavy tasks from spring to harvest;
the sack-cloth pilgrimages under rain

to repair the slabbery gaps of winter
with the labourer hibernating
in his cottage for half the year
to greet the indignity of the Hiring Fair.

Fewer hands, bigger markets, larger farms.
Yet something mourns. The iron-ribbed
lamp flitting through the yard at dark,
the hissing froth, and fodder-scented warmth

of a wood-stalled byre, or leather thong
of flail curling in a barn, were part
of a world where action had been wrung
through painstaking years to ritual.

Acknowledged when the priest blessed
the green-tipped corn, or Protestant
lugged thick turnip, swollen marrow
to robe the kirk for Thanksgiving.

Palmer's softly lit Vale of Shoreham
commemorates it, or Chagall's lovers
floating above a childhood village
remote but friendly as Goldsmith's Auburn—

Our finally lost dream of man at home
in a rural setting! A giant hand,
as we pass by, reaches down
to grasp the fields we gazed upon.

Harsh landscape that haunts me,
well and stone, in the bleak moors of dream
with all my circling a failure to return
to what is already going
                            going
                    GONE

JOHN MONTAGUE, *The Rough Field*, 1972

Down below us there is supposed to be a village of about fourteen families that is completely deserted. The entire village left during the famine. I haven't looked for the village. It is back off the road that runs by our house and, in a way, it does not really matter if it exists or not.

The Irish countryside is full of such stories. They are rarely far below the surface. Maybe not famine, but certainly a sense of harsh times, work not there, cruel poverty. This is why Irish people still tend to respect money, big cars, flashy houses. They respect the outward trappings of wealth and are not in the least bit ungenerous in congratulating those who have 'got on', often to the chagrin of the sophisticated recipient of such praise. Getting above one's station in life is not an Irish conception. Always in the background, though, even with those who have not lived on the land or in the country for several generations, there is a pervasive, if near-imperceptible, sense of uncertainty.

GERALD DAWE, *False Faces*, 1994

Ireland had been brought to its present pass (in the North), not by Britain's conniving with the Ulster unionist rebellion of 1912 and its ignoring of the will of most of the people of Ireland, particularly of the Northern nationalists; nor by the scandalous fifty years of British rule in the North; nor again by the continuing refusal of Britain to recognise the Irish nation and its rights there. No, Ireland had been brought to its present pass by theories of revolution, of nationality, and of history that we Irish had entertained; the present dire situation had been caused, in other words, by *ourselves*, by our nationalism. The cause of the present evil was not the wrong ideas and action of British imperialist nationalism but the wrong ideas and action of our liberationist nationalism.

DESMOND FENNELL, *Heresy*, 1993

Northern Ireland has been called a 'failed political entity'. I think it's time to admit that both parts of Ireland are failed *conceptual* entities. That is, the ideas which created them and the ideologies which sustained them have withered at the root. If 'Northern Ireland' has visibly broken down, the 'Republic' as once conceived has invisibly broken down. And since 1969 each has helped to expose the inner contradictions of the other.

EDNA LONGLEY, *From Cathleen to Anorexia*, 1990

'The Gold Coast', the southern edge of Belfast Lough is called. You can see the money more clearly than elsewhere in Ireland because the shops in the villages of north Down sell the luxuries—fitted kitchens, patchwork quilts, garden lighting—which the wealthy of Dublin and Cork go into their cities to buy. Otherwise, the bourgeoisie of that coast are the same as the bourgeoisie of Dun Laoghaire or Kinsale: none of them go anywhere near the areas where poverty and crime and alienation might hurt them. None of them take responsibility for their respective west Belfasts.

What makes the privileged people of North Down different, however, is that they see the upholding of their way of life as a duty, as a bulwark raised against anarchy, as a moral imperative. 'We must go on,' a woman says. 'We can't let the terrorists win. We must do what we always did. We must look

after our families and live a normal life and enjoy ourselves, because otherwise they'll think they're getting the upper hand.' When a way of life is represented as heroic, it is above criticism.

NUALA O'FAOLAIN, *Are You Somebody?*, 1996

from *From the Canton of Expectation*

Once a year we gathered in a field
of dance platforms and tents where children sang
songs they had learned by rote in the old language.
An auctioneer who had fought in the brotherhood
enumerated the humiliations
we always took for granted, but not even he
considered this, I think, a call to action.
Iron-mouthed loudspeakers shook the air
yet nobody felt blamed. He had confirmed us.
When our rebel anthem played the meeting shut
we turned for home and the usual harassment
by militiamen on overtime at roadblocks.

II

And next thing, suddenly, this change of mood.
Books open in the newly-wired kitchens.
Young heads that might have dozed a life away
against the flanks of milking cows were busy
paving and pencilling their first causeways
across the prescribed texts. The paving stones
of quadrangles came next and a grammar
of imperatives, the new age of demands.
They would banish the conditional for ever,
this generation born impervious to
the triumph in our cries of *de profundis*.
Our faith in winning by enduring most
they made anathema, intelligences
brightened and unmannerly as crowbars.

SEAMUS HEANEY, *The Haw Lantern*, 1987

The 1947 Education Act made a great difference to places like the Bogside. It
created an educational obstacle-course which, if one could negotiate it,
opened the way to grammar school and even university education—and
Catholics had no handicap. Those who passed went to St Columb's College.

Catholic Derry is steeped in the influence of St Columb's. Almost every Catholic teacher, Catholic doctor, Catholic solicitor, Catholic architect, accountant and businessman in the city was schooled there. The headmaster of a local intermediate school has no one on his staff whom he himself did not teach when he worked at St Columb's. Before the introduction of state scholarships St Columb's was the preserve of the Catholic middle class and, until the school got used to it, Bogsiders who arrived were made aware that they were intruding. Priest in a maths class: 'Where do you come from?' 'Rossville Street.' 'Oh yes, that's where they wash once a month.'

EAMONN McCANN, War and an Irish Town, 1974

The tide that emptied the countryside more than any other since the famine has turned. Hardly anybody now goes to England. Some who went came home to claim inheritances, and stayed, old men waiting at the ends of lanes on Sunday evenings for the minibus to take them to church bingo. Most houses have a car and colour television. The bicycles and horses, carts and traps and sidecars, have gone from the roads. A big yellow bus brings the budding scholars to school in the town, and it is no longer uncommon to go on to university. The mail car is orange. Just one policeman with a squad car lives in the barracks.

JOHN McGAHERN, 'Oldfashioned', 1985

Georgian Tenement

The high court of dry rot, after a long
Unreportable session behind airtight doors,
Has mouthed a verdict. Rafters know what's wrong.
Death and cremation. Up with my soft floors.

I've got to be rebuilt. Some new, banal
Office block is decreed to fill my place.
The whores under the trees by the canal
Increase their turnover while I lose face.

Young lovers of old structures, you who squat
To keep my form intact, when guards arrive
With riot gear and water gun, we cannot
Under such tonnage of cracked slate survive.

Would that your free hands in my spongy wood
Could cure fungosity, make my flaws good.

RICHARD MURPHY, The Price of Stone, 1985

Poor Dublin remains poor, the destitute drunks around Mercer's Hospital, a new spleen in the graffiti, now gone all political. A taxi driver says trade is getting rougher; fishnetting protecting an optician's interior display from its own customers, just off Grafton Street. Few of the public clocks agree. Lawlessness on the rise. People offering cigarettes around in bars as in Spain. Would you prefer to be nearly drowned or nearly saved?

Flocks of magpies, and civic guards, on Palmerston Road, where Garret FitzGerald lives. The burglar-alarm business booming; broken shop windows and car glass everywhere. Fifty per cent of school-leavers jobless, but fivers and tenners flashed more than before in the bars that seem emptier, sadder. The jig-tune of the penny-whistler in the Green Arcade reminding one, in case one needed reminding, that the Irish are both shifty and merry. The venom of one side ('To hell with the Pope!') matched by the venom of the other ('Fuck the Queen!'), an accident-ward aseptic tinge prevails.

AIDAN HIGGINS, *Ronda Gorge and Other Precipices*, 1976

The charm I had felt in Kingstown, I mean Dun Laoghaire, did not endure into the city. My seat at the front on the top deck of the bus—my old seat, my favourite!—showed me scenes I hardly recognised. In the ten years since I had last been here something had happened, something had befallen the place. Whole streets were gone, the houses torn out and replaced by frightening blocks of steel and black glass. An old square where Daphne and I lived for a while had been razed and made into a vast, cindered car-park. I saw a church for sale—a church, for sale! Oh, something dreadful had happened. The very air itself seemed damaged. Despite the late hour a faint glow of daylight lingered, dense, dust-laden, like the haze after an explosion, or a great conflagration. People in the streets had the shocked look of survivors, they seemed not to walk but reel. I got down from the bus and picked my way among them with lowered gaze, afraid I might see horrors. Barefoot urchins ran along beside me, whining for pennies. There were drunks everywhere, staggering and swearing, lost in joyless befuddlement. An amazing couple reared up out of a pulsating cellar, a minatory, pockmarked young man with a crest of orange hair, and a stark-faced girl in gladiator boots and ragged, soot-black clothes. They were draped about with ropes and chains and what looked like cartridge belts, and sported gold studs in their nostrils. I had never seen such creatures, I thought they must be members of some fantastic sect. I fled before them, and dived into Wally's pub. Dived is the word.

JOHN BANVILLE, *The Book of Evidence*, 1989

Blessed cloister calm of Merrion Square West, perfect for ruminating *flâneurs*, elegant, spacious, cool, far from the fevers and vulgarities of

O'Connell Street—the GPO republicans, the slot-machine palaces and the maniac driving up and down with a life-sized Virgin Mary strapped to the roof of his car.

We proceed across Baggot Street and then into Ely Place, where the great town houses of the Anglo-Irish gentry have been taken over by the new forward-looking, professional, business-suited Ireland.

MICHAEL FOLEY, *The Road to Notown*, 1996

Glenageary was full of Dublin working-class people who, like my own parents, had made good in Sean Lemass's Ireland and become middle class. And it was full of country people who had migrated to Dublin to find work, then turned their backs on the land. The only echo of a rural past was in the names they gave their houses. Mountain View, Glenside, River View. These people were living lives which were very far from the ideal which Yeats and de Valera had so incongruously shared. The maidens were not dancing at the crossroads. They were watching The Rolling Stones on the latest colour TV set. And if they were not exactly fumbling in the greasy till, they were certainly fumbling in the latest Zanussi washing machine from time to time. Glenageary was *Gleann na gCaorach* in Irish, the glen of the sheep, but the only sheep around when I was a child were the ones wrapped in clingfilm and deposited in the brand new freezers which hummed their hymns in every double garage.

JOSEPH O'CONNOR, *The Secret World of the Irish Male*, 1995

There is ignorance and wilful ignorance. It is very possible for people in the comfortable suburbs to shut their minds to conditions in the troubled areas. On the other hand, the paramilitaries are often quite mistaken when they estimate the effect of their own actions on the rest of the population.

A friend tells me of his childhood on the Antrim Road, again mentioning the attachment and pride Belfast people have for their own original corner of the city. What he remembers is the beauty of a spring day with the trees in bloom and a view across Fortwilliam Golf Course and the sparkling Lough to County Down. There are still select avenues running down from the Antrim Road to the Shore Road where spring bursts in pink and white above your head as a thousand cherry blossoms flower. But the area has changed in a different way from Finaghy.

I drive up the Limestone Road. Something is wrong, the messages do not connect. There are the trees that civilise a city street, there are the odd walls that the child of a peaceful time would use as landmarks in his personal topography—the high tan escarpment shaped like a railway cutting, the little

low wall of that distinctive white stone. But a solid-looking Victorian terrace
has doors stopped with breezeblocks and scribbles of hate and calf-love on
the cream tiles of its doorways. Past the graffiti announcing 'Tiger Bay YNF'
(how carefully the slogan-writers name their area, like Indians in a Western
plotting out their happy hunting-grounds) there is an image that might stand
for so much of the city: in a wasteland of rubble and rubbish (a bombsite?—
more likely bulldozed down by the Housing Executive) remains a solitary
cube of the original block, a little shop with a flat above, one of those sell-
everything stores. Untidy, with slogans splashed around it, it has an air of
being under siege.

On the corner of the New Lodge Road a huge brown sign announces a
Housing Executive development and, despite the unpromising appearance of
potholes and stones in the road, an abandoned car weathering to pieces, the
street has clusters of new brick houses built on a scale suitable for human
beings (no more mistakes, let us hope, like the noise-barrier flats on the
Shankill). But my Yellow Pages must be out of date, for the place I am looking
for is no longer there.

ROBERT JOHNSTONE, *Images of Belfast*, 1983

Ireland is . . . a society which has changed, in some respects, more rapidly in
the past quarter of a century than many European countries. Independence
for the South was followed by several decades of adjustment that were characterized by an inward-looking stagnation, and this sense of isolation was
reinforced by Ireland's neutrality in the Second World War—far more under-
standable when one remembers that it was just seventeen years since we had
finally and forcibly persuaded a foreign army, whom we would have had to
invite back in, to end a seven-hundred-year occupation. All this, plus a stringent censorship and mass emigration, kept the post-war changes sweeping
through Europe at bay. It was only in the 1960s, . . . that Ireland began to
emerge from this stagnation.

In many instances since then, sections of the country have taken to the
twentieth century like Hollywood Indians to whiskey. From being an essentially drug-free culture some years previously, by the mid-eighties Dublin
had become the heroin capital of Europe. Where many European countries
have a declining population, almost half the Irish population in now under
twenty-five. For the past quarter of a century the most extraordinary violence
has been an everyday reality in Northern Ireland. And the more intense the
Northern violence has become, the greater the distance has grown between
the two states on the island. Although some commentators still speak simply
about two cultures existing in Ireland—a Catholic/Nationalist and Protes-
tant/Unionist one, the response of the largely untouched South to the frequent barbarism of both sides in the North has been such that recent

statistical analysis has shown the citizens of the Irish Republic to feel now
that they have more in common with the Scottish, Welsh and English than
with any section of the population in the North.

DERMOT BOLGER, from Introduction to *The Picador Book of Contemporary
Irish Fiction*, 1993

from *Letter from Ireland*

My Ireland has no tin whistle wailing
   Against creels and mists on open bogs,
And neither has it place for imitation
   Thatch on houses, or for mock
   Blather to camouflage how dog eats dog.
I have no time for the view that Ireland's
The sum of the scenes at a Munster Final.

My Ireland has no dark clichéd hag
   Toothless in turfsmoke as she cackles.
I have seen the face of a woman dragged
   Through bedrooms screaming, battered
   And bruised until her body blackened.
Deirdre of the Sorrows thrives
Mostly in the home for battered wives.

The theme is changing, my rage revives.
   Memory Ireland. They shoot heroin these
Times in streets where Connolly said lives
   Were lost in slumland hunger and disease
   While gentrified suburbs sat in cushioned ease.
Archaeologists point to our early tribes
Where flatlands shelter fifty thousand lives.

SEAN DUNNE, *The Sheltered Nest*, 1992

A key aspect of the 'post-Catholic' Ireland agenda is the insistent blackening
of every element of Catholic Ireland's past. The entire history of our country
is now painted as though darkly governed by a cowled Inquisition of priests
and crozier-bearing bishops who treated politicians like puppets, regarding
the populace as moral serfs and dominating everything they touched by a
form of terror. It will be noticed that De Valera is demonised at every turn—
the portrayal of Dev as a devious hypocrite and probable assassin of Collins

was very deliberately crafted by Neil Jordan, a strong 'post-Catholic Ireland' man—because Dev is now assoicated with that Catholic Irish past in which everything was so grim and 'repressive'.

The true picture of Catholic Ireland in the past—that the Church was most ardently, most passionately, and most fiercely supported and defended by the people: that the politicians curried favour shamelessly with bishops whenever they could for the same cynical reasons that they now curry favour with Brussels—because they reckoned it meant votes, and thus power and revenue, and that such 'repressive' aspects of the past as literary censorship were not led primarily by priests, but by little old ladies on library committees who, in their thousands, submitted books to the Censorship Board demanding that these not be available in the public realm.

In fact, liberal priests such as Fr John Kelly and Fr Peter Connolly, through campaigns carried out in periodicals such as *The Furrow*, and on public platforms elsewhere in the early 1960s, were prime movers in relaxing the Irish censorship. The late Brian Lenihan, who, as Minister for Justice in 1967, dismantled the fiercest elements of the censorship laws, told me that he was greatly influenced by these liberal and cultivated priests who had argued for more personal freedom in the right to read.

One of the commonest calumnies about Catholic Ireland in the past was that the Church was so obsessed with sexual prohibitions that it preached on nothing else. This is utter baloney. An examination of the themes underlined in the Catholic devotional and ecclesiastical magazines in the 1940s and Fifties shows that probably the most common theme for Church guidance was honesty. They preached vehemently against crime and behaving dishonestly, and ever underlined the importance of acting justly in trading and working exchanges. They were dead hot on restitution. Sins of dishonesty (or of calumny) could not be pardoned until restitution was made.

Not coincidentally, I think, one of the most salient aspects of 'post-Catholic Ireland' now is an alarming rise in crime—and murder—and the disappearance, in the countryside, of that trust and openness which used to be characteristic of rural Ireland.

Spirituality among the Irish is always strong, but it is a free-floating spirituality now, settling on everything from Buddhism to Scientology to New Age crystal-gazing and tree-hugging. Whether the Catholic Church in Ireland can compete with these new forms of faith—let alone compete with the consumerism and the political power that has taken its place—must, I suppose, depend upon the Holy Spirit eventually. But sociologically speaking, no system which has lost its confidence can survive, and I think the saddest thing of all is that Catholicism in Ireland has totally lost its confidence, its nerve, its belief in itself and its affirmation of its own values.

Mary Kenny, article in the *Catholic Herald*; reprinted in the *Independent*, 13 March 1997

When women formed the first women's liberation group in Dublin in 1971, there was, from a feminist point of view, a great deal that needed to be changed. Women in Ireland had fewer rights than in most European countries, and many aspects of women's situation in the Republic compared unfavourably with that of their counterparts in Northern Ireland. Contraception was illegal, divorce was banned in the Constitution and abortion was a criminal act. Single mothers and separated women were ineligible for welfare payments, and women were openly discriminated against in education, employment and the tax and welfare systems. A marriage bar was in operation in the Civil Service and other occupations, forcing women to give up their jobs on marriage. Women had few rights under family law, and were in a highly vulnerable position if their marriages broke down. The illegitimacy law stigmatised children born out of wedlock, and their mothers with them.

In 1971, few of these issues were even discussed. Some, like contraception and abortion, were taboo. Others were dismissed as irrelevant or went unrecognised, as many people prefered to hold to a vision of Ireland as a good Catholic society in which people were committed to family life, rather than face the more uncomfortable reality.

JENNY BEALE, *Women in Ireland*, 1986

The Ulster Protestant community, though dragged forward faster by Westminster legislation, is as traditionally patriarchal as Catholic Nationalism. This tribe too has its cult of male chieftains: Carson, Moses, Paisley the 'Big Man' (compare Dev the 'Long Fellow', the Pope, the Boss). And the whole country abounds in Ancient Orders of Hibernian Male-Bonding: lodges, brotherhoods, priesthoods, hierarchies, sodalities, knights, Fitzwilliam Tennis Club, Field Day Theatre Company. But at least Unionism does not appropriate the image of woman or hide its aggressions behind our skirts. Nor does it—as a reactive ideology—seek ideological mergers. A Unionist feminist could be these things separately, though genuine feminism might erode her Unionism. A Nationalist/Republican feminist, less readily regarded as a contradiction in terms, claims that her ideologies coincide. And in so doing she tries to hijack Irish feminism.

Terry Eagleton (in *Nationalism: Irony and Commitment*) develops an analogy between Nationalism and feminism as responses to 'oppression'. He argues that Nationalism must not prematurely sell its soul to revisionism and pluralism, just as feminism—until women have been truly liberated—must not sell its soul to 'a troubling and subverting of all . . . sexual strait-jacketing'. . . . With respect to the history of women and Nationalism, straitjackets tend to remain in place after the revolution unless their removal has been intrinsic to the revolution. Eagleton does not recognise that Catholic

Nationalism has often been as great an oppressor of Irish people, Irish women, as British imperialism or Ulster Unionism. Perhaps the equivalent of advanced feminist 'troubling and subverting' is precisely what our Nationalist and Unionist patriarchal strait-jackets need.

EDNA LONGLEY, *From Cathleen to Anorexia*, 1990

Hand-me-down and imported notions about man, the world, psychology, the consumer society, feminism, socialism and so on passed through the media, but apart from some debate about the nature of feminism these large themes evinced no disputation. The only aspect of human life that was publicly discussed with some interesting insights was its beginnings in the womb! Apart from the topics—contraception, divorce, abortion, Charlie Haughey—the ideas most talked about in the media were old ethnic and religious ideas that had been knocked about in Ireland for centuries with a respite of about fifty years in the present century. There was the cluster *Irishness: awfulness of (in life); excellence of , with reservations (in art); right and wrong kinds of; what is?* dating, respectively, from Giraldus Cambrensis, the Statute of Kilkenny and Shakespeare's *Henry V. Awfulness of (in life)* was thrashed out in all the media in many contexts: Irish mothers, Irish men, Irish lovers, Irish sex, Irish society, Irish nationalism, Irish politicians, Irish Constitution, Irish religion, Irish clergy. The last two overlapped with another cluster dating from the Reformation: *Roman Catholicism: harm it does; wrongness of.* And this, in turn, figured in various contexts: Catholic morality, authoritarianism and bishops, Catholic guilt, intolerance, marriage and so on. Probably the liveliest intellectual discussion, in which Dublin participated with Derry, Belfast and London, was that about writers, texts and critics of English Irish literature and the intersections of all these with politics and ideology.

DESMOND FENNELL, *Heresy*, 1993

Making Love outside Áras an Uachtaráin

When I was a boy, myself and my girl
Used bicycle up to the Phoenix Park;
Outside the gates we used lie in the grass
Making love outside Áras an Uachtaráin.

Often I wondered what de Valera would have thought
Inside in his ivory tower
If he knew that we were in his green, green grass
Making love outside Áras an Uachtaráin.

Because the odd thing was—oh how odd it was—
We both revered Irish patriots
And we dreamed our dreams of a green, green flag
Making love outside Áras an Uachtaráin.

But even had our names been Diarmaid and Gráinne
We doubted de Valera's approval
For a poet's son and a judge's daughter
Marking love outside Áras an Uachtaráin.

I see him now in the heat-haze of the day
Blindly stalking us down;
And, levelling an ancient rifle, he says 'Stop
Marking love outside Áras an Uachtaráin.'

PAUL DURCAN, *Sam's Cross*, 1978

The official pretence—that there was still a sizeable Irish-speaking community in the Gaeltacht—was exploded by Desmond Fennell at the end of the 1970s; and he himself returned to a Dublin where most of the poets were already trying to gear Irish to a post-Gaeltacht, post-industrial, post-Christian, post-everything society. Davitt's jibe at the 'céad míle fáilte' (hundred thousand welcomes), offered to the incoming visitor by the Irish Tourist Board, took the form of a hundred and one farewells offered to the few post-inflationary visitors and departing emigrants; but such nose-thumbing could not conceal the fact that the Irish were virtual tourists in their own country now. The same material greed which priced Irish holidays out of the international market had served also to erase centuries-old traditions. Thatched cottages were abandoned to ruin, as hacienda bungalows rose up in their stead, with names like 'South Fork' and 'High Chapparal'. So rapid were the changes that the native Irish themselves began to take the place of absent foreign visitors, in an attempt to exhume on a fortnight's holiday their all-but-buried past. Tourist slogans which, a generation earlier, might have been beamed at a British or American audience, were now directed at the Irish themselves: 'Discover Ireland; it's part of what you are'. Significantly, the latter phrase had already been used in government promotional campaigns for the Irish language. Some city boys, like Ó Muirthile in Maoinis, or even Behan, in an earlier generation, on the Blaskets, were beguiled for a time by such pastoralism; but a majority endorsed the war against the past.

DECLAN KIBERD, Introduction to *An Crann Faoi Bhláth* (*The Flowering Tree*), 1991

A Runaway Cow

for Liam Ó Muirthile

I'd say he'd had too much
of the desolation that trickles down
through the glens and the hillocks
steadily as a hearse;
of the lifeless villages in the foothills
as bare of young folk as of soil;
of the old codgers, the hummock-blasters
who turned the peat into good red earth
and who deafened him pink year after year
with their talk of the grand sods of the old days;

of the little white bungalows, attractive
as dandruff in the hairy armpit of the Glen;
of the young people trapped in their destinies
like caged animals out of touch with their instinct;
of the Three Sorrows of Storytelling
in the pity of unemployment, of low morale,
and of the remoteness and narrow-mindedness
of both sides of the Glen;
of the fine young things down in Rory's
who woke the man in him
but wouldn't give a curse for his attentions;

of clan boundaries, of old tribal ditches,
of pissing his frustration against the solid walls
race and religion built round him.
He'd had too much of being stuck in the Glen
and with a leap like a runaway cow's one spring morning
he *cleared* the walls and *hightailed* away.

CATHAL Ó SEARCAIGH, *An Bealach 'na Bhaile* (*Homecoming*),
1993, trans. Patrick Crotty

Acknowledgements

The editor and publisher gratefully acknowledge permission to include the following copyright material:

Conrad Arensberg, from *The Irish Countryman* (Harvard University Press, 1937).

W. H. Auden, 'In Memory of W. B. Yeats' from *Collected Poems*, by permission of the publishers, Faber & Faber Ltd.

John Banville, from *The Book of Evidence* (Secker & Warburg, 1981), by permission of Random House UK Ltd.

Ernest Barker, from *Ireland in the Last Fifty Years* (Oxford, 1916), by permission of Oxford University Press.

Tom Barry, from *Guerrilla Days in Ireland* (Irish Press, 1949), copyright holder not traced.

Jenny Beale, from *Women in Ireland* (Macmillan Education, 1986), by permission of Macmillan Press Ltd.

J. C. Beckett, from *The Making of Modern Ireland 1603–1923* (1966), by permission of the publishers, Faber & Faber Ltd.

Samuel Beckett, from *More Pricks Than Kicks* (Chatto, 1934), *Watt* (1953), and *Murphy* (1938), by permission of Calder Publications Ltd. and Grove/Atlantic, Inc.

Brendan Behan, from *Brendan Behan's Island* (Hutchinson, 1962), by permission of Random House UK Ltd.; extract from *The Hostage* (Methuen, 1958) by permission of the Tessa Sayle Agency.

Mark Bence-Jones, from *Twilight in the Ascendancy* (Constable, 1987), copyright © 1987 by permission of Constable Publishers and Sheil Land Associates.

Robert Bernen, from *Tales from the Blue Stacks* (Poolbeg, 1980), reprinted by permission of Poolbeg Press.

John Betjeman, from 'The Small Towns of Ireland' in *High and Low* (1966), by permission of John Murray (Publishers) Ltd.

George A. Birmingham, from *The Red Hand of Ulster* (1912), by permission of A. P. Watt Ltd. on behalf of Althea C. Hannay and Susan Harper.

Aodh de Blácam, from *Gaelic Literature Surveyed* (Talbot Press, 1970), by permission of C. de Blácam.

Caroline Blackwood, from *Great Granny Webster* (Duckworth, 1977), by permission of the Wylie Agency.

Dermot Bolger, from introduction to *The Picador Book of Contemporary Irish Fiction* edited by Dermot Bolger (1993), by permission of Macmillan Publishers.

Heinrich Böll, from *Irish Journal* translated by Leila Vennewitz (Secker & Warburg, 1983) by permission of Random House UK Ltd. and of Tanja Howarth Literary Agency on behalf of Verlag Kiepenheuer & Witsch.

Elizabeth Bowen, from *Seven Winters* (Longmans Green, 1943) © 1943 by Elizabeth Bowen, and *Collected Impressions* (Longmans Green, 1950), © 1950 by Elizabeth Bowen, by permission of Curtis Brown Ltd., London on behalf of The Estate of Elizabeth Bowen; from *Bowen's Court* (Longmans Green, 1942) © 1942, 1964 and renewed 1970 by Elizabeth Bowen, by permission of Curtis Brown Ltd., London on behalf of The Estate of Elizabeth Bowen, and of Alfred A. Knopf, Inc.; from *The Shelbourne* (Harrap, 1951).

C. E. B. Brett, from *Long Shadows Cast Before* (John Bartholomew, 1978), by permission of the author.

Hugh Brody, from *Inishkillane: Change and Decline in the West of Ireland* (Allen Lane, 1973), by permission of the author.

Brigid Brophy, from *Don't Never Forget* (Cape, 1966), by permission of Sheil Land Associates.

Terence Brown, from *Ireland: A Social and Cultural History* (Fontana, 1981), by permission of HarperCollins Publishers Ltd.

Robin Bryans, from *A Journey Through the Six Counties* (Faber, 1964), by permission of the author.

George Buchanan, from *Morning Papers* (Gaberbocchus, 1965), by permission of S. Buchanan, Literary Executor to George Buchanan.

Hubert Butler, from *Escape from the Anthill* (Lilliput, 1985), *Grandmother and Wolfe Tone* (Lilliput, 1985) and *The Children of Drancy* (Lilliput, 1988), by kind permission of The Lilliput Press, Arbour Hill, Dublin 7.

Mary Carbery, from *The Farm by Lough Gur* (Longman Green, 1937; Mercier, 1973), by permission of Mercier Press.

Ciaran Carson, 'Hamlet' from *Belfast Confetti* (Gallery, 1989), by kind permission of the author and The Gallery Press; from *Irish Traditional Music* (Appletree, 1986), by permission of Appletree Press Ltd.; from *Last Night's Fun* (Cape, 1996), copyright © 1996 by Ciaran Carson, by permission of Random House UK Ltd. and North Point Press, a division of Farrar, Straus & Giroux, Inc.

Joyce Cary, from *A House of Children* (Michael Joseph, 1941), by permission of Andrew Lownie.

Austin Clarke, poems by permission of R. Dardis Clarke, 21 Pleasants Street, Dublin 8; prose from *Twice Round the Black Church* (RKP, 1963), and from *A Penny in the Clouds* (RKP, 1968), by permission of Routledge and R. Dardis Clarke.

Mary Colum, from *Life and the Dream* (Macmillan, 1928), by permission of Máire Colum O'Sullivan.

Padraic Colum, 'The Drover', 'Poor Scholar of the 'Forties', and 'A Rann of Exile' from *The Poet's Circuits* (*Collected Poems of Ireland*) (OUP, 1960); 'Autumn' and 'The Poor Girl's Meditation' from *Dramatic Legends* (Macmillan, 1922); all reprinted by permission of Máire Colum O'Sullivan for the Estate of Padraic Colum; extracts from *A Boy in Eirinn* (J. M. Dent, 1916), by permission of the Orion Publishing Group Ltd.

Shane Connaughton, from *A Border Diary* (1995), by permission of the publishers, Faber & Faber Ltd.

John Conroy, from *War as a Way of Life* (Heinemann, 1988) by permission of David Higham Associates.

Daniel Corkery, from *The Hidden Ireland* (1925), by permission of the publishers, Gill & Macmillan.

Mary Costello, from *Titanic Town* (Methuen, 1992), by permission of Random House UK Ltd.

Maurice James Craig, from *Dublin 1660–1860* (Cresset Press, 1952), by permission of the author.

Anthony Cronin, from *The Life of Riley*, reprinted by permission of Brandon Book Publishers Ltd.

Gerald Dawe, from *False Faces* (Lagan, 1994), by permission of the author.

Seamus Deane, from *Celtic Revivals* (1985), by permission of the publishers, Faber & Faber Ltd.; from *Reading in the Dark* (Cape, 1996), by permission of Random House UK Ltd.

Anne Devlin, from *The Way-Paver* (1986), by permission of the publishers, Faber & Faber Ltd.

Polly Devlin, from *All of Us There* (Weidenfeld & Nicolson, 1983), copyright © Polly Devlin 1983, by permission of the author c/o Rogers, Coleridge & White Ltd., 20 Powis Mews, London W11 1JN.

Martin Dillon and Denis Lehane, from *Political Murder in Northern Ireland* (Penguin, 1973).

John Lyle Donaghy, 'The Bracken' from *Antrim Songs: Flute over the Valley* (Inver Press, 1931), copyright holder not traced.

J. P. Donleavy, from *J. P. Donleavy's Ireland* (Michael Joseph, 1986), by permission of the author.

Denis Donoghue, from *Warrenpoint* (Cape, 1991), copyright © 1991 by Denis Donoghue, by permission of Random House UK Ltd. and Alfred A. Knopf, Inc.

Seán Dunne, 'Letter from Ireland' from *The Sheltered Nest* (Gallery, 1992), by kind permission of the author and The Gallery Press.

Lord Dunsany, from *My Ireland*, copyright Lord Dunsany 1937, by permission of Curtis Brown Ltd., London on behalf of Lord Dunsany's Will Trust.

Paul Durcan, 'The Beckett at the Gate' from *Going Home to Russia* (Blackstaff, 1987), by permission of The Blackstaff Press; 'Making Love Outside Aras an Uachtarain' from *Sam's Cross* (Profile, 1978), by permission of the author.

E. Estyn Evans, from *Irish Heritage* (Dundalgan, 1942), by permission of Dundalgan Press (W. Tempest) Ltd.; 'The Irishness of the Irish' from *Ireland and the Atlantic Heritage: Selected Writings* (Lilliput, 1995), and from *Irish Folk Ways* (RKP, 1957, new edition to be published by Lilliput 1998) by kind permission of The Lilliput Press, Arbour Hill, Dublin 7.

J. G. Farrell, from *Troubles* (Cape, 1970), copyright © 1970 J. G. Farrell, by permission of the Estate of J G Farrell c/o Rogers, Coleridge & White Ltd., 20 Powis Mews, London W11 1JN.

Michael Farrell, from *The Orange State* (Pluto, 1976), by permission of Pluto Press.

Robert Farren, from 'Rime, Gentlemen, Please', copyright holder not traced.

Desmond Fennell, from *Heresy* (Blackstaff, 1993), by permission of the author.

Robin Flower, 'The Dance' from *Poems and Translations* (Lilliput, 1995), by kind permission of The Lilliput Press, Arbour Hill, Dublin 7.

Michael Foley, from *The Road to Notown* (Blackstaff, 1996), by permission of The Blackstaff Press.

John Wilson Foster, from *Forces and Themes in Ulster Fiction* (1974), by permission of the publishers, Gill & Macmillan.

R. F. Foster, from *Paddy and Mr Punch: Connections in Irish and English History* (Allen Lane, 1993), copyright © R. F. Foster 1993, by permission of Penguin Books Ltd.

Morris Fraser, from *Children in Conflict* (Secker & Warburg, 1973), by permission of the Peters Fraser & Dunlop Group Ltd.

Brian Friel, from *Translations* (Faber, 1981), by permission of the publishers, Faber & Faber Ltd. and of The Catholic University of America Press.

Conor Gearty, from 'Diary', in *London Review of Books*, 28 November 1996 by permission of the author and *London Review of Books*.

Oliver St John Gogarty, from *As I Was Going Down Sackville Street*, by permission of The O'Brien Press Ltd.; from *Going Native* (Constable, 1941).

Robert Greacen, 'Cycling to Dublin' by permission of the author.

David Greene, from *Writing in Irish Today* (Mercier, 1972), by permission of Mercier Press.

Lady Gregory, from *Poets and Dreamers* (1903), by permission of Colin Smythe Ltd. on behalf of Anne de Winton and Catherine Kennedy.

Kenneth Griffiths and Timothy O'Grady, from *Curious Journey* (Hutchinson, 1982).

Stephen Gwynn, from *Dublin Old and New* (Harrap, 1938); from *The Famous Cities of Ireland* (Macmillan, 1915), and *History of Ireland* (Macmillan, 1923), copyright holder not traced.

Denis O'D. Hanna, 'Architecture in Ulster' from *The Arts in Ulster* ed. Sam Hanna Bell (Harrap, 1951).

Michael Hartnett, 'A Farewell to English' and 'A Visit to Castledown House' from *Selected and New Poems* (Gallery, 1994), by kind permission of the author and The Gallery Press.

Seamus Heaney, 'Shoreline', 'Requiem for Croppies', 'Gravities', and 'Whatever you Say, Say Nothing' from *Poems 1965–1975*, copyright © 1980 by Seamus Heaney; 'A Postcard from North Antrim' from *Field Work* (Faber, 1979), copyright © 1981 by Seamus Heaney; from *Station Island* (Faber, 1984), copyright © 1984 by Seamus Heaney; 'Clearance' and 'From the Canton of Expectation' from *The Haw Lantern* (Faber, 1987), copyright © 1987 by Seamus Heaney; all by permission of the publishers, Faber & Faber Ltd. and Farrar, Straus & Giroux, Inc.

John Hewitt, 'The Dilemma', 'The Coasters', 'The Scar', 'The Fairy Thresher', 'The Way to School', 'Balloons and Wooden Guns', 'Ulster Names', 'Ulsterman', 'Street Names', and 'An Irishman in Coventry', all from *The Collected Poems of John Hewitt* edited by Frank Ormsby (Blackstaff, 1991), by permission of The Blackstaff Press on behalf of the Estate of John Hewitt.

Aidan Higgins, from *Ronda Gorge and Other Precipices* (Secker & Warburg, 1989) and *Donkey's Years* (Secker & Warburg, 1995), by permission of Random House UK Ltd. and the author.

Douglas Hyde, from *The Necessity for De-Anglicising Ireland* (1892), by permission of Douglas Sealy.

Denis Ireland, from *From the Irish Shore* (Rich & Cowan, 1936), and from *Statues Round the City Hall* (Rich & Cowan, 1939), by permission of Mrs H. M. Ireland.

Jennifer Johnston, from *Shadows On Our Skin* (Hamish Hamilton, 1977), copyright © Jennifer Johnston 1977, and *The Gates* (Hamish Hamilton, 1973), copyright © Jennifer Johnston 1973, by permission of Penguin Books Ltd. and Felix de Wolfe.

Robert Johnstone, extracts from *Images of Belfast* (Blackstaff, 1983), by permission of the author.

Patrick Kavanagh, 'One Wet Summer', 'Kerr's Ass', and 'The Christmas Mummers' from *Collected Poems* (McGibbon & Kee, 1964); 'Shancoduff' from *The Great Hunger and Other Poems* (Cuala Press, 1942); 'Memory of Brother Michael' and 'Art McCooey' from *A Soul for Sale* (Macmillan, 1947); 'Inniskeen Road: July Evening' from *Ploughman and Other Poems* (Macmillan, 1936); and from *The Green Fool* (Michael Joseph, 1938), by kind permission of the Trustees of the Estate of Patrick Kavanagh and by permission of Peter Kavanagh.

John V. Kelleher, 'With Dick in Dublin 1946' from *Omnium Gatherum: Essays for Richard Ellmann* (Smythe, 1989), by permission of Colin Smythe Ltd. on behalf of John V. Kelleher.

Brendan Kennelly, 'My Dark Fathers' from *A Time for Voices: Selected Poems 1960–1990* (Bloodaxe Books, 1990), by permission of the author and the publisher.

Mary Kenny, article by permission of *The Catholic Herald*.

Declan Kibberd, from introduction to *The Flowering Tree* (1991), by permission of the publishers, Wolfhound Press.

Benedict Kiely, 'Your Left Foot is Crazy' from *A Letter to Peachtree* (Gollancz, 1987), by permission of Victor Gollancz Ltd.; from *Proxopera*, *A Journey to the Seven Streams*, and 'The Night We Rode with Sarsfield', by permission of A. P. Watt Ltd. on behalf of Benedict Kiely.

Thomas Kinsella, 'Afternoon' and 'Nightfall' from 'Tao and Unfitness at Inistiogue on the River Nore', and lines from 'One', by permission of the author.

Mary Lennon, Marie McAdam, and Joanne O'Brien, from *Across the Water: Irish Women's Lives in Britain* (Virago, 1988), by permission of Little Brown.

C. S. Lewis, from *Surprised by Joy* (Bles, 1955), copyright © 1956 by C. S. Lewis Pte Ltd. and renewed 1984 by Arthur Owen Barfield, by permission of HarperCollins Publishers Ltd. and Harcourt Brace & Co.

Edna Longley, from *From Cathleen to Anorexia* (Attic Press, 1990), by permission of the publisher.

Michael Longley, 'To Seamus Heaney', 'To Derek Mahon', and 'Wounds' from *An Exploded View* (Gollancz, 1973), by permission of the author; 'Trade Winds' from *Gorse Fires* (Secker & Warburg, 1991), by permission of the author, and Random House UK Ltd.

Martin Lynch, from *The Interrogation of Ambrose Fogarty* (Blackstaff, 1982), by permission of the author.

Robert Lynd, from *Home Life in Ireland* (1908).

Eamonn McCann, from *War and an Irish Town* (Penguin, 1974), by permission of the author.

Donagh MacDonagh, 'Dublin Made Me', 'Hungry Grass', and 'Easter Christening' (a radio masque), from *The Hungry Grass* (1947), by permission of the publishers, Faber & Faber Ltd.

Florence Mary McDowell, from *Other Days Around Me* (Blackstaff, 1972), copyright © The Estate of Florence Mary McDowell 1966, 1972, by permission of Campbell Thomson & McLaughlin Ltd. on behalf of the author's estate.

John McGahern, from *The Leavetaking* (Faber, 1974) copyright © 1974 by John McGahern and from 'Oldfashioned' in *High Ground* (Faber, 1985), copyright © 1985 by John McGahern, by permission of Faber & Faber Ltd. and of Russell & Volkening as agents for the author.

Patrick McGill, from *The Rat Pit* (1915), by permission of Caliban Books.

Lambert McKenna, from *The Life and Work of Rev. James Aloysius Cullen SJ* (Longman Green & Co., 1924), by permission of Addison Wesley Longman.

Michael McLaverty, extracts from *Call My Brother Back* (Longman, 1939), by permission of Maura Cregan, Literary Executor of the Estate of Michael McLaverty.

Micheal mac Liammoir, from *All For Hecuba* (Methuen, 1946), by permission of Michael Williams.

Dermot MacManus, from *The Middle Kingdom*, copyright © 1959 Diarmuid MacManus, by permission of Colin Smythe Ltd.

Seumas MacManus, from the preface to *Hibernian Nights* (Macmillan, NY, 1963), by permission of Patricia MacManus.

Brinsley MacNamara, from *The Mirror in the Duck* (Samson & Low, 1928).

Louis MacNeice, poems from *Collected Poems* (Faber, 1966), and prose from *The Strings Are False* (Faber, 1965), by permission of David Higham Associates.

Seán Mac Réamoinn, from introduction to *The Pleasures of Gaelic Poetry* (Allen Lane, 1982), copyright holder not traced.

John Maguire, from *Come Day, Go Day, God Send Sunday*, collected by Robin Morton (RKP, 1973), by permission of Routledge.

Derek Mahon, 'A Disused Shed in Co. Wexford' and 'Ecclesiastes' from *Poems 1962–1978* (OUP, 1979), copyright © Derek Mahon 1979; 'Rathlin' and 'North Wind' from *The Hunt By Night* (OUP, 1982), copyright © Derek Mahon 1982; all by permission of Oxford University Press.

Ethel Mannin, from *Connemara Journal* (Westhouse, 1947).

Vivian Mercier, from *The Irish Comic Tradition* (OUP, 1962).

Alice Milligan, 'When I Was A Little Girl' from *Poems* (1954), by permission of the publishers, Gill & Macmillan.

John M. Mogey, from *Rural Life in Northern Ireland* (OUP, 1947), by permission of Oxford University Press.

John Montague, 'Emigrants', 'The Flight of Earls', 'The Siege of Mullingar', 'A Lost Tradition', 'Driving South ...', 'Famine Cottage', and 'The Rough Field' from *John Montague: Collected Poems* (Gallery, 1995); from *Time in Armagh* (Gallery, 1993); all by kind permission of the author, The Gallery Press, and Wake Forest University Press; from *Death of A Chieftain* (Poolbeg, 1964), by permission of the author.

T. W. Moody, from *The Ulster Question* (Mercier, 1974), by permission of Mercier Press.

Brian Moore, from *The Mangan Inheritance* (Cape/Farrar, Straus & Giroux, 1979), copyright © 1979 by Brian Moore, from *Fergus* (Cape/Holt, Rinehart, 1971), copyright © 1970 by Brian Moore, and from *Catholics* (Cape/E. P. Dutton, 1972), copyright © 1972 by Brian Moore, by permission of Curtis Brown Ltd., New York, and Random House UK Ltd.

George Moore, from *Vale* (1914), *Salve* (1912), and *The Untilled Field* (1903), by permission of Colin Smythe Ltd. on behalf of the Estate of J. C. Medley.

John Morrow, from *The Essex Factor* (Blackstaff, 1982), by permission of the author.

H. V. Morton, from *In Search of Ireland* (1931).

J. B. Morton, from *The New Ireland* (Paladin, 1938), copyright holder not traced.

Paul Muldoon, 'The Mixed Marriage' from *Mules and Early Poems* (1977), and 'Lull' from *Why Brownlee Left* (1980) both by Paul Muldoon, by permission of the publishers, Faber & Faber Ltd. and Wake Forest University Press.

Dervla Murphy, from *A Place Apart* (1978), by permission of John Murray (Publishers) Ltd.

Richard Murphy, 'The Woman of the House' from *Sailing to an Island* (Faber, 1963) and 'Georgian Tenement' from *The Price of Stone* (Faber, 1985), by permission of the author.

Nuala Ní Dhomhnail, translated by Paul Muldoon, 'The Language Issue' from *Pharaoh's Daughter* (Gallery, 1990) and 'Cathleen' from *The Astrakhan Cloak* (Gallery, 1992), by kind permission of the author and The Gallery Press.

Éilís Ní Dhuibhne, 'Blood and Water' in *Blood and Water and Other Stories* (Attic Press, 1988), by permission of the publisher.

Charles O'Beirne, from *The Good People* (Blackstaff, 1985), by permission of the author.

Conor Cruise O'Brien, from *Ancestral Voices* (Poolbeg, 1994), reprinted by permission of Poolbeg Press.

Edna O'Brien, from *Mother Ireland* (Weidenfeld & Nicolson, 1976), by permission of the Orion Publishing Group Ltd. and the Wylie Agency; from *The Lonely Girl* (Cape, 1962), retitled *The Girl With Green Eyes*, by permission of the Wylie Agency.

Flann O'Brien, from *At Swim Two Birds* (Longmans Green, 1938); from *The Poor Mouth*, translated by Patrick C. Power (Dolman, 1941); from *The Hard Life* (McGibbon & Kee, 1961); and from *The Best of Myles* (McGibbon & Kee, 1968); all copyright © The Estate of the Late Brian O'Nolan, by permission of A. M. Heath.

Kate O'Brien, from *My Ireland* (Batsford, 1962), by permission of B. T. Batsford Ltd.

Máirtín Ó Cadhain, translated by Eoghan Ó Tuairisc, from *The Road to Bright City* (Poolbeg, 1981), reprinted by permission of Pooleg Press.

Sean O'Casey, from *I Knock at the Door* (Macmillan, 1939), by permission of Macmillan Publishers.

Frank O'Connor, translations of anonymous poems, 'Farewell to Patrick Sarsfield', 'Sliobh na mBan', and 'Donal Og', of 'The Midnight Court' by Brian Merriman, and 'No Help I'll Call' by Egan Ó Rahilly; and from *Irish Miles* (Macmillan, 1949); all by permission of the Peters Fraser and Dunlop Group Ltd. on behalf of The Estate of Frank O'Connor.

John O'Connor, from *Come Day—Go Day* (Blackstaff, 1984).

Joseph O'Connor, from *The Secret World of the Irish Male* (Minerva, 1995), copyright © Joseph O'Connor 1994, by permission of the Blake Friedman Literary Agency and Random House UK Ltd.

Tomás Ó Criomhthain [O'Crohan], translated by Robin Flower, from *The Islandman* (OUP, 1951), by permission of Oxford University Press.

Peadar O'Donnell, from *Adrigoole* (Cape, 1929) and *The Knife* (Cape, 1930).

Nuala O'Faolain, from *Are You Somebody?* (New Island Books, 1996), copyright © 1996 Nuala O'Faolain, by permission of the publishers New Island Books, Hodder and Stoughton Ltd., and Henry Holt and Company, Inc.

Sean O'Faolain, from *An Irish Journey* (Longman & Green, 1940), copyright © 1940 Sean O'Faolain, from *A Nest of Simple Folk* (Cape, 1934), copyright © 1934 Sean O'Faolain, and from *A Purse of Coppers* (Cape, 1937), copyright © 1937 Sean O'Faolain; all by permission of the author, c/o Rogers, Coleridge & White Ltd., 20 Powis Mews, London W11 1JN.

Liam O'Flaherty, from *Famine* (Cape, 1937), by permission of the Peters Fraser and Dunlop Group Ltd. on behalf of the Estate of Liam O'Flaherty.

Ernie O'Malley, from *On Another Man's Wound* (Anvil Books, 1979), by permission of the publishers.

Cathal Ó Searcaigh, 'Bó Bhradach' from *Homecoming* (1993), translated from the Irish by Patrick Crotty as 'A Runaway Cow' and published by Blackstaff Press in *Modern Irish Poetry: An Anthology* (1995), by permission of Cló Iar-Chonnachta.

Humphrey O'Sullivan, translated by Tomás de Bhaldraithe, from *Diary 1827–35* (Mercier, 1979), by permission of Mercier Press.

Maurice O'Sullivan, translated by Moya Llewelyn Davies and George Thomson, from *Twenty Years A-Growing* (Chatto & Windus, 1933), by permission of Random House UK Ltd. and Maura Kavanagh.

Seumas O'Sullivan, 'Rain' from *The Twilight People*, by permission of Frances Sommerville.

Liam de Paor, from *Divided Ulster* (Penguin, 1970), copyright © Liam de Paor 1970, by permission of Penguin Books Ltd.

Tony Parker, from *May the Lord in His Mercy* (Cape, 1993), by permission of Random House UK Ltd.

Tom Paulin, 'In the Lost Province' and 'Going in the Rain' from *The Strange Museum* (1980), 'Under Creon' and 'Father of History' from *The Liberty Tree* (1983), all by permission of the publishers, Faber & Faber Ltd.

Richard Power, translated by Victor Power, from *Apple on the Treetop* (Poolbeg, 1980), reprinted by permission of Poolbeg Press.

Robert Lloyd Praeger, from *The Way That I Went* (Hodges Figgis, 1937), copyright holder not traced.

V. S. Pritchett, from *Midnight Oil* (Chatto & Windus, 1971), by permission of Random House UK Ltd. and the Peters Fraser and Dunlop Group Ltd.

Bob Purdie, from *Politics in the Streets* (Blackstaff, 1990), by permission of the author.

Forrest Reid, from *Young Tom* (Faber, 1944), by permission of John Johnson Ltd.

Tim Robinson, from *Stones of Aran: Pilgrimage* (Lilliput, 1986), by kind permission of The Lilliput Press, Arbour Hill, Dublin 7.

W. R. Rodgers, 'Field Day' and Epilogue to 'The Character of Ireland' from *Poems* (Gallery, 1993), by kind permission of the author and The Gallery Press; 'Armagh' from *Europa and the Bull* (Secker & Warburg, 1952), by permission of Random House UK Ltd.

Richard Rowley, 'Ardglass Town' from *Selected Poems* (Duckworth, 1931), copyright holder not traced.

Desmond Ryan, from *Sean Treacey and the Third Tipperary Brigade* (Anvil, 1964), copyright holder not traced.

Stephen Rynne, from *Green Fields* (Brandon, 1995), by permission of Brandon Book Publishers Ltd.; from *All Ireland* (Batsford, 1956), by permission of B. T. Batsford Ltd.

Peig Sayers, translated by Seamus Ennis, from *An Old Woman's Reflections* (OUP, 1962), by permission of Oxford University Press.

Bernard Shaw, from *John Bull's Other Island* (1904), by permission of The Society of Authors on behalf of the Bernard Shaw Estate.

Patrick Shea, from *Voices and the Sound of Drums* (Blackstaff, 1981), by permission of E. Shea.

Hugh Shearman, from *Ulster* (Robert Hale, 1949), copyright © Hugh Shearman, by permission of A. M. Heath.

James Simmons, 'The Ballad of Gerry Kelly: Newsagent' and 'Peasant Quality' from *Poems 1956–1986* (Gallery, 1986), by permission of the author and The Gallery Press; 'Protestant Courts Catholic' from *Energy To Burn* (Bodley Head, 1971), by permission of the author.

Edith Somerville and Martin Ross, from *Mount Music* (1919) by permission of Addison Wesley Longman; from Edith Somerville's *Diary* and letter from Martin Ross to Edith Somerville, copyright E. A. O. Somerville and Martin Ross, by permission of Curtis Brown Ltd., London on behalf of the Executors of Sir Patrick Coghill, Bt.

James Stephens, from *The Charwoman's Daughter* (Macmillan, 1912), *Insurrection in Dublin* (1916), and *Uncollected Prose* ed. Patricia McFate (Gill & Macmillan, 1983), by permission of The Society of Authors as the Literary Representatives of the Estate of James Stephens.

A. T. Q. Stewart, from *The Narrow Ground* (Faber, 1977/Blackstaff, 1997), by permission of The Blackstaff Press.

Francis Stuart, from *Black List, Section H* (Martin Brian & O'Keeffe, 1975), by permission of the author.

Geoffrey Taylor, from *The Emerald Isle* (Evans, 1952), copyright holder not traced.

Colm Tóibín, from *The Heather Blazing* (Pan, 1992), by permission of A. P. Watt Ltd. on behalf of Colm Tóibín.

Kevin Toolis, from *Rebel Hearts: Journeys Within the IRA's Soul* (Picador, 1995), copyright © 1995 by Kevin Toolis, by permission of Macmillan Publishers and St Martin's Press, Incorporated.

Honor Tracy, from *Mind You I've Said Nothing* (Penguin, 1961, originally Methuen, 1953).

William Trevor, from *Beyond the Pale and Other Stories*, copyright © 1981 by William Trevor, by permission of Viking Penguin, a division of Penguin Books USA, Inc and the Peters Fraser and Dunlop Group Ltd.; from *The Collected Stories*, by permission of the Peters Fraser and Dunlop Group Ltd.; and from *The Ballroom of Romance and Other Stories* (Bodley Head, 1972), by permission of Random House UK Ltd. and the Peters Fraser and Dunlop Group Ltd.

Michael Viney, from *A Year's Turning* (Blackstaff, 1996), by permission of The Blackstaff Press.

Mervyn Wall, from *The Unfortunate Fursey* (Pilot, 1946).

Eugene Watters, from *The Weekend of Dermot and Grace* (Allen Figgis, 1964), copyright holder not traced.

R. N. D. Wilson, 'Elegy in a Presbyterian Burying-Ground' (1949), copyright holder not traced.

Jack Yeats, from *Sligo* (Wishart, 1930), by permission of Lawrence & Wishart.

W. B. Yeats, from 'Three Songs to the One Burden', copyright 1940 by Georgie Yeats, copyright renewed © 1968 by Bertha Georgie Yeats, Michael Butler Yeats, and Anne Yeats; 'The Stare's Nest By My Window', copyright 1928 by Macmillan Publishing Company, copyright renewed © 1956 by Georgie Yeats; 'Parnell's Funeral', copyright 1934 by Macmillan Publishing Company, copyright renewed © 1962 by Bertha Georgie Yeats; 'Coole Park, 1929', copyright 1933 by Macmillan Publishing Company, copyright renewed © 1961 by Bertha Georgie Yeats; and 'The Mountain Tomb', copyright 1916 by Macmillan Publishing Company, copyright renewed © 1944 by Bertha Georgie Yeats; all poems reprinted from *The Collected Works of W. B. Yeats, Volume 1: The Poems*, revised and edited by Richard J. Finneran, by permission of Simon & Schuster.

Index of Authors